MANHATTAN LSAT

Logical Reasoning

LSAT Strategy Guide

This strategy guide takes you from novice to master on Logical Reasoning. Using a nuanced approach that emphasizes connections between question types, this guide includes ample practice sets to you develop both your intuitive and formal understandings of arguments and logic.

Logical Reasoning LSAT Strategy Guide, 3rd Edition

10-digit International Standard Book Number: 1-935707-85-X
13-digit International Standard Book Number: 978-1-935707-85-1
eISBN: 978-1-937707-27-9

Layout Design: Dan McNaney and Cathy Huang
Cover Design: Evyn Williams and Dan McNaney
Cover Photography: Alli Ugosoli

INSTRUCTIONAL GUIDE SERIES

Logic Games
(ISBN: 978-1-935707-84-4)

Logical Reasoning
(ISBN: 978-1-935707-85-1)

Reading Comprehension
(ISBN: 978-1-935707-86-8)

PRACTICE BOOKS

10 Real LSATs Grouped by Question Type
Practice Book I
(ISBN: 978-1-937707-36-1)

15 Real, Recent LSATs
Practice Book II
(ISBN: 978-1-937707-12-5)

MANHATTAN
LSAT

October 23, 2012

Dear Students,

In your hands is the end result of years of hard work. At the core of this book is the brainpower of the most talented teachers and curriculum developers that I know. Many moons ago, Mike Kim and Dan Gonzalez pored through years of LSATs to figure out what makes the test tick and together they wrote our original Logic Games Strategy Guide. One found mastering the LSAT to be nearly effortless while the other had to work hard to unlock the LSAT's inner logic and tendencies; it is the combination of the two that underlies our curriculum.

We pride ourselves on teaching that goes far beyond lecture-style classes. Not only does this mean our students are actively engaged in the material, but also that our teachers are always rethinking how to unlock complex ideas in ways that make students truly understand. Each new edition of this book incorporates what we've learned from helping our students learn. So, along with thanking our teachers and book team for their invaluable input—especially Brian Birdwell, Dmitry Farber, Cathy Huang, Elizabeth Krisher, Dan McNaney, Matt Sherman and Patrick Tyrrell—I must thank our students for raising their hands to ask and answer interesting questions.

At Manhattan LSAT, we're always looking to improve and to provide you with the best prep available. While we hope that you'll find the book you're holding to be exactly what you need, we appreciate any feedback you may have, whether it's positive or not. Please e-mail me at noah@manhattanlsat.com with any comments, and we'll be sure to consider them for future editions.

Good luck as you prepare for the LSAT!

Sincerely,

Noah Teitelbaum
Executive Director of Academics
Manhattan Prep

HOW TO ACCESS YOUR ONLINE STUDY CENTER

If you...

> ## are a registered Manhattan LSAT student

and have received this book as part of your course materials, you have AUTOMATIC access to ALL of our online resources. To access these resources, follow the instructions in the Welcome Guide provided to you at the start of your program.

Do NOT follow the instructions below.

> ## purchased this book from the Manhattan LSAT online store or at one of our centers

1. Go to: http://www.manhattanlsat.com/studentcenter.cfm.

2. Log in using the username and password used when your account was set up. Your one year of online access begins on the day that you purchase the book from the Manhattan LSAT online store or at one of our centers.

> ## purchased this book at a retail location

1. Create an account with Manhattan LSAT at the website https://www.manhattanlsat.com/createaccount.cfm.

2. Go to: http://www.manhattanlsat.com/access.cfm.

3. Follow the instructions on the screen. Your one year of online access begins on the day that you register your book at the above URL.

You only need to register your product ONCE at the above URL. To use your online resources any time AFTER you have completed the registration process, log in to the following URL: http://www.manhattanlsat.com/studentcenter.cfm.

Please note that online access is nontransferable. This means that only NEW and UNREGISTERED copies of the book will grant you online access. Previously used books will not provide any online resources.

> ## purchased an eBook version of this book

1. Create an account with Manhattan LSAT at the website https://www.manhattanlsat.com/createaccount.cfm.

2. Email a copy of your purchase receipt to books@manhattanlsat.com to activate your resources. Please be sure to use the same email address to create an account that you used to purchase the eBook.

For any technical issues, email books@manhattanlsat.com or call 800-576-4628.

TABLE *of* CONTENTS

TABLE *of* CONTENTS

Chapter *of* 1

Logical Reasoning

Logical Reasoning
Overview

1

Logical Reasoning

The Logical Reasoning section of the LSAT is designed to test your ability to understand and evaluate arguments that are presented in a written form. Each Logical Reasoning question has a short—generally two or three sentences—stimulus, a question stem, and five answer choices. Here is a sample Logical Reasoning question:

> _PT36, S1, Q25_
>
> A 1991 calculation was made to determine what, if any, additional health-care costs beyond the ordinary are borne by society at large for people who live a sedentary life. The figure reached was a lifetime average of $1,650. Thus people's voluntary choice not to exercise places a significant burden on society.
>
> Which one of the following, if true and not taken into account by the calculation, most seriously weakens the argument?[1]
>
> (A) Many people whose employment requires physical exertion do not choose to engage in regular physical exercise when they are not at work.
> (B) Exercise is a topic that is often omitted from discussion between doctor and patient during a patient's visit.
> (C) Physical conditions that eventually require medical or nursing-home care often first predispose a person to adopt a sedentary life-style.
> (D) Individuals vary widely in the amount and kind of exercise they choose, when they do exercise regularly.
> (E) A regular program of moderate exercise tends to increase circulation, induce a feeling of well-being and energy, and decrease excess weight.

In order to perform well on the Logical Reasoning section, you need strong reasoning and reading skills. Previous academic experience with formal logic can be helpful, but it's certainly not necessary. Much of this book is designed to help you develop and sharpen the reasoning skills the LSAT most rewards. Just as important, if not more so, much of this book is designed to strengthen your reading skills. The one characteristic that is common to all 170+ level test-takers is that they are effective and critical readers.

---

1   The correct answer is (C). For a full explanation of this problem, please refer to page 229.

MANHATTAN
LSAT

Where Logical Reasoning Fits in the Big Picture

1

The entire LSAT exam is comprised of the following sections:

Section	Questions	Scored?	Time
Logic Games	22–23	Yes	35 minutes
Reading Comprehension	26–28	Yes	35 minutes
Logical Reasoning (1)	24–26	Yes	35 minutes
Logical Reasoning (2)	24–26	Yes	35 minutes
Experimental	22–28	No	35 minutes
Essay	1 essay	No	35 minutes

The first five sections can come in any order. The essay will always be your final section, and it will not factor into your overall score.

The experimental section is used for the internal purposes of the makers of the LSAT, and will also not count towards your overall score. It will either be an extra Logic Games, Reading Comprehension, or Logical Reasoning section. We do not recommend that you try to identify which section is experimental during the exam.

Of the four sections that do count towards your score, two of them will be Logical Reasoning. Therefore, Logical Reasoning is the question type that will most significantly impact your performance, and it should be a priority in your studies.

As you will see, certain Logical Reasoning questions are designed to take more time to solve, and certain ones less, but based on the typical number of questions in a section, it's helpful to consider that overall your timing for Logical Reasoning should average out to about 1:20 per question.

In all sections, every question is worth exactly one point. There is no guessing penalty—that is, selecting a wrong answer has the same consequence as leaving an answer choice blank—you will get zero points for that problem. Therefore, it is to your advantage to bubble in an answer for every single question.

In total, you should expect to see about 100 or 101 scored questions. Each correct answer adds one point to your raw score. This raw score is then converted to a score that fits on a 120–180 scale, and this converted score will be based on how you performed on your exam relative to how other people performed on that same exam.

Because each pool of test-takers is unique, the conversion scale varies slightly—typically by no more than a point or two—from test to test.

1

Here is a sample conversion scale that is representative of the most recent LSATs:

Raw Score (minimum correct out of 100 total questions)	Scaled Score	Percentile Rank (percentage of test-takers you outperformed)
98	180	99.9%
94	175	99.5%
88	170	97.5%
81	165	92%
75	160	80%
66	155	64%
56	150	44%

Because you'll be seeing about 100 questions, it can be helpful to think of your goal score in terms of the percentage of questions you will need to get correct. For example, if your goal is to score 165, it should be helpful to know that, overall, you'll need to get a little more than 80 percent of the questions correct.

The Logical Reasoning Dichotomy

When it comes to Logical Reasoning, there are some noticeable differences between the common approaches, skills, and attitudes of the average scorer and those of a top scorer:

Most LSAT Test-Takers	170+ Test-Takers
Fail to recognize the tendencies of the different question types	Know these tendencies and exploit them
Don't consider the structure of arguments	Utilize structure to inform understanding
Read passively and without direction	Read with a purpose and from a perspective
Have difficulty prioritizing key details	Recognize which details are most significant
Lack confidence in eliminating incorrect answers	Actively look for wrong answer characteristics and confidently eliminate wrong choices
Struggle to assimilate and apply all the tricks and gimmicks they've been taught	Apply their knowledge and understanding efficiently and intuitively

If you feel like you already have many of the characteristics of a top test-taker, great! If not, don't worry—that's what we're here for. This book is designed to help you develop the skills that are necessary to succeed on the exam at the highest level.

Advice on How to Prepare for the LSAT

1

It is important to begin your study process with a good plan and the right mind-set. Here is some advice meant to help set you off on the right path:

1. Strive for Mastery.

Mastery means something far greater than simply knowing the right answer. We want you to maximize the learning that you get out of every question that you try. Consider carefully how each argument is constructed—how it is organized, how components are meant to link up, and what some of the built-in traps might be. Consider carefully each answer choice—in particular, incorrect answer choices. Don't let yourself off the hook by saying, "Oh, this answer is obviously wrong." Imagine that you have to explain the problem to someone who thinks the answer is right. What would you say? Don't let it go until you have a great response. Get to understand a problem to such a point that you feel a hundred percent certain that you could explain the same problem perfectly weeks later. This may seem like a lot of work to put into just one question, but we know that if you truly understand a single problem completely, this mastery will have a significant and positive impact on numerous other questions that you will encounter.

2. Always Consider Process.

Your process is the strategy you use in order to arrive at an answer. Perhaps a more effective way to think about process is that it is the manner in which you *choose* to apply your understanding and judgment.

Many LSAT problems are like jokes in a certain way: with (good) jokes, punch lines make complete sense after the fact, but leave you feeling like you would be no better at anticipating the punch line the next time you hear a similar joke. Many challenging LSAT questions make complete sense after the fact—when you review the problem and see the clever play on words, or the unexpected link between premises—but leave you feeling like you would have no better chance of getting that type of question correct the next time you see one.

Though problems can seem this way, the reality is that every problem has its tells—the key signs that point you in the right direction in terms of what you ought to think about and how you ought to think about it. The key to being able to see these tells consistently is to have a sound and intuitive process.

A process won't tell you what is right and what is wrong, but if you use it correctly, it will position you to make the right decisions. A process helps you think about the right things at the right time. We cannot overemphasize the significance of this. There is likely no other action that you can take during your studies that will positively impact your score more than developing a sound and consistent process for every type of Logical Reasoning question. This will be a primary focus in each of the chapters.

3. Work from Tendencies to Twists.

Let's imagine that you wake up one morning and suddenly realize that your life's mission is to become a world-class expert on engines. How should you go about becoming one? Does it make sense to start with the most unusual and advanced engines—maybe the engine for some sort of new space shuttle? And does it make sense to focus first on the aspects of that engine that are most unusual or advanced? Perhaps, for a certain type of learner, this might be best, but for most of us, it would make a lot more

1

sense to start with that which is most common, or essential, to an engine. What does an engine actually do? What's the basic mechanism by which it does this? From here, you can imagine, it would be natural to start getting more specific—maybe there are three major types of engines. You start digging in to all three, learning more and more as you go, tying new knowledge to the base of understanding you already have. Soon enough, you have the expertise to TRULY understand what makes, say, an advanced engine advanced, or an unusual engine unusual.

Focus on learning one problem type at a time, and start by trying to understand that which is most consistent, and most essential, to the nature of that type of question. We do not mean to suggest that you should focus only on easier problems (we don't want you to do that) or that you shouldn't study the hardest ones (you need to!). Our suggestion has to do more with mind-set. Make it your goal to first identify that which is most important or essential, then work to relate unusual challenges to that norm. Not only will this help you understand these challenges far better, it will increase the chances that such understanding will match up with relevant situations on test day.

4. Master Each Question Type, Then Focus on Mixed Review.

At the heart of every Logical Reasoning problem are common reading and reasoning issues, but each type of question requires something unique from you. An analogy could be made to learning a variety of musical instruments. There is great commonality in what is required to understand and play each instrument, but each instrument also has its unique characteristics that need to be understood and mastered.

The best way to master a question type, and to develop a process for it that is intuitive and automatic, is to immerse yourself in questions of just that type. Focus your energies on learning and developing strategies for one problem type at a time. Spend a week doing just Assumption questions, breaking them down, seeing what is common to them, and how challenging questions play off of that commonality. We feel this type of problem-specific immersion is the most efficient way to build your mastery. This mastery won't guarantee that you will get every single Assumption question correct on the exam, but it will mean that you will know what you ought to think about—which issues are more important and which ones are less so—every time you face an Assumption question.

Mixed review, which commonly comes in the form of practice exams, has many obvious benefits, but it can also have some negative consequences. For one, mixed review reinforces general habits. If you have a lot of bad habits that you don't want to reinforce, it might be helpful to take a break from mixed review as you do your content-specific work. Mixed review can also cause you to improperly blend together strategies for a variety of problem types. Finally, it can have a net effect of dulling your instincts so that, for example, you have a broad sense of what characterizes incorrect answers in general, instead of what characterizes incorrect answers for specific question types.

Therefore, we recommend that you think of your study time in phases. During the first part of your training, you want to emphasize content-specific, or focused, work, while making sure to add in a little bit of mixed practice. During the second part of your training, you want to emphasize mixed review—mostly in the form of practice exams, so that you can get comfortable implementing all that you have learned and developed into your performance.

MANHATTAN
LSAT

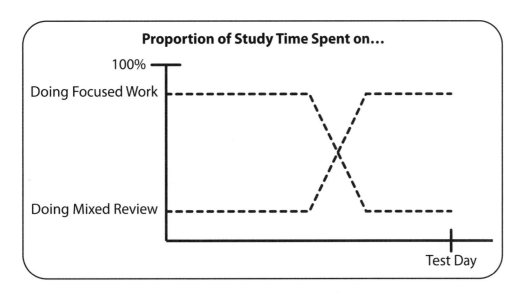

This book is primarily designed to guide you in your content-specific work. Most of the chapters are designed to help you focus on one question type at a time. Make sure to get in some mixed review on your own along the way, and, more importantly, make sure to leave time after you have completed this book to do more mixed review before test day.

Chapter 2

of

Logical Reasoning

Argument Core

Getting Familiar

To start, go ahead and try these five Logical Reasoning questions. Give yourself no more than eight minutes total. We'll revisit these questions later on in the chapter.

PT7, S4, Q5

The government provides insurance for individuals' bank deposits, but requires the banks to pay the premiums for this insurance. Since it is depositors who primarily benefit from the security this insurance provides, the government should take steps to ensure that depositors who want this security bear the cost of it and thus should make depositors pay the premiums for insuring their own accounts.

Which one of the following principles, if established, would do most to justify drawing the conclusion of the argument on the basis of the reasons offered in its support?

(A) The people who stand to benefit from an economic service should always be made to bear the costs of that service.

(B) Any rational system of insurance must base the size of premiums on the degree of risk involved.

(C) Government backed security for investors, such as bank depositors, should be provided only when it does not reduce incentives for investors to make responsible investments.

(D) The choice of not accepting an offered service should always be available, even if there is no charge for the service.

(E) The government should avoid any actions that might alter the behavior of corporations and individuals in the market.

PT7, S1, Q1

Before the printing press, books could be purchased only in expensive manuscript copies. The printing press produced books that were significantly less expensive than the manuscript editions. The public's demand for printed books in the first years after the invention of the printing press was many times greater than demand had been for manuscript copies. This increase demonstrates that there was a dramatic jump in the number of people who learned how to read in the years after publishers first started producing books on the printing press.

Which one of the following statements, if true, casts doubt on the argument?

(A) During the first years after the invention of the printing press, letter writing by people who wrote without the assistance of scribes or clerks exhibited a dramatic increase.

(B) Books produced on the printing press are often found with written comments in the margins in the handwriting of the people who owned the books.

(C) In the first years after the printing press was invented, printed books were purchased primarily by people who had always bought and read expensive manuscripts but could afford a greater number of printed books for the same money.

(D) Books that were printed on the printing press in the first years after its invention often circulated among friends in informal reading clubs or libraries.

(E) The first printed books published after the invention of the printing press would have been useless to illiterate people, since the books had virtually no illustrations.

PT7, S1, Q15

Eight years ago hunting was banned in Greenfield County on the grounds that hunting endangers public safety. Now the deer population in the county is six times what it was before the ban. Deer are invading residential areas, damaging property and causing motor vehicle accidents that result in serious injury to motorists. Since there were never any hunting related injuries in the county, clearly the ban was not only unnecessary but has created a danger to public safety that would not otherwise exist.

Which one of the following, if true, provides the strongest additional support for the conclusion above?

(A) In surrounding counties, where hunting is permitted, the size of the deer population has not increased in the last eight years.

(B) Motor vehicle accidents involving deer often result in damage to the vehicle, injury to the motorist, or both.

(C) When deer populations increase beyond optimal size, disease and malnutrition become more widespread among the deer herds.

(D) In residential areas in the county, many residents provide food and salt for deer.

(E) Deer can cause extensive damage to ornamental shrubs and trees by chewing on twigs and saplings.

PT7, S1, Q14

Marine biologists had hypothesized that lobsters kept together in lobster traps eat one another in response to hunger. Periodic checking of lobster traps, however, has revealed instances of lobsters sharing traps together for weeks. Eight lobsters even shared one trap together for two months without eating one another. The marine biologists' hypothesis, therefore, is clearly wrong.

The argument against the marine biologists' hypothesis is based on which one of the following assumptions?

(A) Lobsters not caught in lobster traps have been observed eating one another.

(B) Two months is the longest known period during which eight or more lobsters have been trapped together.

(C) It is unusual to find as many as eight lobsters caught together in one single trap.

(D) Members of other marine species sometimes eat their own kind when no other food sources are available.

(E) Any food that the eight lobsters in the trap might have obtained was not enough to ward off hunger.

PT10, S1, Q5

Some people have questioned why the Homeowners Association is supporting Cooper's candidacy for mayor. But if the Association wants a mayor who will attract more businesses to the town, Cooper is the only candidate it could support. So, since the Association is supporting Cooper, it must have a goal of attracting more businesses to the town.

The reasoning in the argument is in error because

(A) the reasons the Homeowners Association should want to attract more businesses to the town are not given

(B) the Homeowners Association could be supporting Cooper's candidacy for reasons unrelated to attracting businesses to the town

(C) other groups besides the Homeowners Association could be supporting Cooper's candidacy

(D) the Homeowners Association might discover that attracting more businesses to the town would not be in the best interest of its members

(E) Cooper might not have all of the skills that are needed by a mayor who wants to attract businesses to a town

The Assumption Family of Questions

Each of the five problems on the previous pages seems to be asking a different type of question, right? Yes, it's true that the question stems are a bit different, but our goal in this chapter is to illustrate that these five questions are actually birds of a feather: they require the same thought process and the same skills. Each one of these questions requires that you identify a core argument being made, and furthermore, that you recognize the assumptions within that core. Each of these questions falls into a broader category that we refer to as the Assumption Family.

The following question types, each to be discussed in greater detail in later chapters, are what we categorize as Assumption Family questions. Combined, these questions make up more than half of all Logical Reasoning questions on the exam:

- Assumption questions
- Flaw questions
- Strengthen questions
- Weaken questions
- Principle Support questions

In this chapter, we will outline the keys to understanding and answering Assumption Family questions. We'll finish by revisiting the questions you've just completed.

The first step is to establish a reading perspective.

Reading from a Perspective

Kennedy-Nixon

The first ever nationally televised presidential campaign debate took place in September of 1960. Democratic Senator John F. Kennedy and Republican incumbent Vice President Richard Nixon squared off in what would become one of the most famous debates in history. The idea of relevant experience had become a major issue in the campaign; the Republicans had cited inexperience as the main reason why Senator Kennedy was unqualified to lead from the White House. The first question of the evening was directed to Senator Kennedy (quoted from debate transcripts):

> **MODERATOR:** Senator, the Vice President [Richard Nixon] in his campaign has said that you were naïve and at times immature. He has raised the question of leadership. On this issue, why do you think people should vote for you rather than the Vice President?

> **MR. KENNEDY:** Well, the Vice President and I came to the Congress together in 1946; we both served in the Labor Committee. I've been there [in Congress] now for fourteen years, the same period of time that he has [referring to Nixon's six years in congress and eight years as Vice President], so that our experience in, uh, government is comparable....

MODERATOR: Mr. Nixon, would you like to comment on that statement?

MR. NIXON: I have no comment.

Perhaps it was a calculated move, but Vice President Nixon seemed to have bought into Kennedy's argument. He didn't even respond.

Most of the time, we tend to go along with people's arguments without much thought. If they speak forcefully enough, or with enough passion (as Senator Kennedy most likely did during the debate), we end up *wanting* to go along. Let's face it: we're easily convinced and gullible, especially when politicians are talking!

Kennedy's argument above sounds great. It makes sense: 14 years equals 14 years, right? However, there are some inherent gaps in his logic. We'll get to these momentarily.

Assumption Family questions are all about reading an argument, such as the one given by Kennedy above, deconstructing the argument, and identifying any gaps or weaknesses in the logic used to form the argument. Complacency won't cut it. Giving the benefit of the doubt won't work. In order to be successful in this endeavor, you must be super-critical of everything you read, and in order to properly focus your critical eye, you must read with a purpose.

Perspective and Purpose

Have you ever read a paragraph in a book or a magazine and then realized that you can't remember anything that you've read? That sort of situation is perhaps unavoidable in life, but it is something that you can and should make sure to avoid on the LSAT. On the Logical Reasoning section, you will find yourself confronted with arguments and passages on topics that you're not familiar with and not particularly interested in. If you're not entirely sure what parts of the passage are important and what parts are not, the risk of "spacing out" is particularly high. When this happens, you'll find yourself rereading certain sentences two or three times as you struggle to concentrate. You might even decide to start over from the top and read the whole thing over again! This is obviously not a good use of time. So, how can you avoid this?

Research shows that the best readers, and the most efficient readers, all read with a clearly defined purpose. Having a clear sense of why you are reading something, and what is most important to understand about what you read, will help you avoid losing focus. However, there are often situations in life, such as when you take standardized exams, when it can be very difficult to know what your specific purpose should be as you read.

An effective way to define *purpose* is to consider the *perspective* of a reader. Here are a few examples to illustrate this point:

From the Perspective of…	Purpose
a beach lounger reading a novel	pure entertainment… no real purpose
a mother of two, dinner time, a pound of leftover ground beef in the freezer, reading a cookbook	find recipes that use ground beef (how much time do you think she'll spend trying to absorb the details of a chicken recipe?)

2

a Robert Frost scholar, preparing to give a lecture on Frost's use of "nature's ritual," reading an anthology of poems by Robert Frost	connect different poems using the ritualism of nature as a theme
a sports show host, getting ready to interview Tiger Woods, reading the New York Times the morning after the biggest golf tournament of the year	scan for Tiger's tournament results, look for inexplicable events that Tiger might be able to shed light on in a live interview

In each of these real-life situations, we can see that the reader's perspective is what determines the purpose of his or her read. For each of these situations, we can say that *perspective* drives *purpose*.

Many students read LSAT arguments with a vague or incorrect sense of purpose. Some read LSAT arguments with no purpose at all. This leads to slow reading and low comprehension. To better your chances of success on Logical Reasoning, you need to read quickly, efficiently, and with a high level of comprehension. Having a clearly defined sense of purpose is the key to this, and an effective way to ensure that your purpose is sound is to read from the right perspective.

Reading Like a Debater

Let's revisit the Kennedy-Nixon excerpt in order to define the perspective that will drive your purpose when reading Logical Reasoning arguments. Consider Kennedy's argument one more time:

> **MR. KENNEDY:** Well, the Vice President and I came to the Congress together in 1946; we both served in the Labor Committee. I've been there [in Congress] now for fourteen years, the same period of time that he has [referring to Nixon's six years in congress and eight years as Vice President], so that our experience in, uh, government is comparable….

There are many different perspectives from which Kennedy's argument can be heard or read. Here are some:

1. Reporter. Someone listening or reading from the perspective of a reporter would listen or read with the purpose of accurately transcribing the comments. He or she would listen closely for details (1946, 14 years, etc.) to be sure they were noted accurately.

2. Historian. Someone listening or reading from the perspective of a historian might listen or read with the purpose of connecting the comments to similar arguments made in historical debates, perhaps attempting to draw out comparisons with the famous Lincoln-Douglas debates.

3. Debater. Someone listening or reading from the perspective of a debater (in this case Vice President Nixon) should listen or read with the purpose of analyzing the logic of the argument and attempting to uncover the logical gaps or flaws. You may have guessed it…

This is the best perspective to use for the Logical Reasoning section.

Assumption Family questions will ask you to evaluate the logic of an argument, or to identify flaws in an argument. If you are reading these arguments through the critical eye of a debater, your purpose will be to actively seek out the inherent gaps and flaws. So, as you read, put yourself in the shoes of a

MANHATTAN
LSAT

debater. Prepare yourself for an effective rebuttal, and when your chance comes, don't be caught flat-footed like Richard Nixon was!

Let's take a closer look at specifically what it is that you need to attend to as you read from the perspective of a debater.

The Structure of Arguments

Imagine yourself in Nixon's shoes. In order to effectively rebut Kennedy's argument, you first need to figure out what the main point of his argument is. What exactly is he trying to say? What is his conclusion?

> **CONCLUSION** (main point): "…so that our experience in, uh, government is comparable…."

The conclusion of the argument is the main point, final claim, or main opinion. It is always the most important part of the argument; you must identify the conclusion if you are to have any chance at understanding, evaluating, or attacking the argument. The conclusion is sometimes triggered by words such as *so, thus, therefore,* and *consequently.*

Next, you must consider how the conclusion is drawn. Why is this conclusion made? What support is given for this conclusion? What are the supporting premises?

> **SUPPORTING PREMISE** (supporting fact): "…we both served in the Labor Committee."

> **SUPPORTING PREMISE** (supporting fact): "I've been there [in Congress] now for fourteen years, the same period of time that he has [referring to Nixon's six years in congress and eight years as Vice President]…."

Supporting premises are stated facts or claims that are meant to provide support for the conclusion. Premises are sometimes triggered by words such as "because" or "since" (more on trigger words, or language cues, later).

Once you've identified the conclusion and the supporting premises, you'll be in a good position to be critical of the argument. In this case, the argument is suspect because Kennedy makes a few questionable *assumptions.*

> **ASSUMPTION** (unstated): Two people who serve on the same committee necessarily gain the same experience.

> **ASSUMPTION** (unstated): The amount of time spent in Congress is a good measure of experience.

> **ASSUMPTION** (unstated): The work of a Senator provides the same relevant experience as the work of a Vice President.

Assumptions are the underlying, unstated elements of the argument that need to be true in order for the argument to work. Almost all LSAT arguments have underlying assumptions. Your job is to actively uncover these assumptions as if you were devising your counter response in a debate. We'll discuss the

2

nature of assumptions more carefully in a later chapter, so don't worry if you weren't able to see the ones above initially.

Assuming Nixon had (1) understood Kennedy's conclusion, or main point, (2) attended to the premises that Kennedy used to support his conclusion, and (3) actively used this understanding to uncover the gaps inherent in Kennedy's argument, he could have responded much more forcefully.

Let's rewrite history:

> **MR. KENNEDY:** Well, the Vice President and I came to the Congress together in 1946; we both served in the Labor Committee. I've been there [in Congress] now for fourteen years, the same period of time that he has [referring to Nixon's six years in congress and eight years as Vice President], so that our experience in, uh, government is comparable....
>
> **MODERATOR:** Mr. Nixon, would you like to comment on that statement?
>
> **MR. NIXON:** Yes, I would like to comment. Senator Kennedy assumes that his work as a Senator provides the same relevant experience as my work as Vice President. This assumption is flawed. The executive experience I have gained as Vice President is much more relevant to the executive work that we all know to be the primary work of the President. In fact, our experience is *not* comparable. I am much better prepared to be President.

When you read a Logical Reasoning passage, take on the perspective of a debater. Perspective gives you purpose, and purpose gives you focus, speed, and comprehension. Make it your purpose to be critical of the argument at hand. Actively search for conclusions, the supporting premises, and the underlying assumptions. Challenge the language that's used, including absolute or extreme words or phrases. In the same way that you would be skeptical of an opponent's argument in a debate, be skeptical of the author's argument in an LSAT passage.

The Argument Core

Definition

Thus far, we've discussed the core elements of an argument. An argument is a premise, or set of premises, used to arrive at a claim (conclusion). From this point forward, we will refer to this simple relationship as the argument core, and we will diagram the argument core using a "therefore" arrow:

Argument Core: A premise, or set of premises, used to arrive at a conclusion.

Let's look at a quick example of an argument core:

MANHATTAN
LSAT

The sun rises only on Mondays. ➡️ The sun does not rise on Fridays.

We would read this argument core as follows:

The sun rises only on Mondays. THEREFORE, The sun does not rise on Fridays.

In this argument, the premise that the sun rises only on Mondays is used to support the claim that the sun does not rise on Fridays.

Do you think this is a valid argument? Does it make any assumptions? Take a few seconds to think about it before reading on.

Evaluating the Logic of the Core

On Assumption Family questions, your job will be to evaluate the logic of the argument core. When doing so, it's important that you have the right mind-set. Let's look at the argument core again:

The sun rises only on Mondays. ➡️ The sun does not rise on Fridays.

Here are two ways to think about it:

1. The real-world approach.

"No way! Terrible argument! We all know that the sun rises every day, not just on Mondays."

2. The logical approach.

"Well, if we take the premise as a given truth, that the sun rises ONLY on Mondays, is this enough to substantiate the claim that the sun does NOT rise on Fridays? Yes. Logically speaking, this argument is sound."

Now, most likely you haven't been studying for the LSAT for very long, but you've probably figured out that the LSAT folks aren't very interested in testing your ability to make evaluations of whether real-world facts are true or untrue. They are, however, very much interested in testing your ability to evaluate logic, the manner in which elements of an argument connect to one another.

In evaluating an argument, your job is NOT to evaluate the truth of its parts. Your job is to evaluate the logic: does the evidence given validate the conclusion? In this case, it does.

Let's try another one:

Everyone in the room is wearing a jacket. Jim must be wearing a jacket.

2

Remember, the arrow means "therefore." We would read this argument core as follows:

Everyone in the room is wearing a jacket. THEREFORE, Jim must be wearing a jacket.

As you evaluate the logic of this argument core, you want to ask yourself if the premise allows you to draw the conclusion without any problems. Does the premise substantiate the conclusion? In this case, it doesn't. In fact, the argument makes a pretty big assumption—it assumes that Jim is one of the people in the room! Notice how the assumption, when inserted into the argument, actually strengthens the argument:

Everyone in the room is wearing a jacket. (Jim is in the room). THEREFORE, Jim must be wearing a jacket.

The assumption functions as a connecting bridge between the premise and the conclusion.

So, to this point, we've seen an argument core that was rock solid, and one that needed an assumption. **Almost all LSAT arguments have cores that require an assumption or assumptions in order to be sound.** Sometimes the assumption is easy to spot, but other times it's more difficult. You'll get better and better at recognizing and defining these gaps as you continue your study, but here is some advice to get you started.

Beware of Implicit Connections

Tendency #1: Real-world synonymous

LSAT arguments will often include assumed connections between concepts that we generally see as being synonymous in real life. In real life, it is often helpful to focus on how these concepts are similar. However, for the LSAT, it is critical that you pay attention to the differences. Take this, for example:

Hiroshi always does what is right.   Hiroshi is a moral person.

This seems to make good sense, doesn't it? If you heard this argument at the dinner table, you wouldn't bat an eye. However, on the LSAT, this argument is flawed. It assumes that doing what is right and being a moral person are equivalent concepts. Don't take this for granted. Let's insert the assumption into the core to see how it strengthens the argument:

Hiroshi always does what is right. (Always doing what is right is the same as being a moral person.) Hiroshi is a moral person.

Ah. Now it's airtight. Remember, real-world synonymous is not necessarily the same as LSAT synonymous.

Tendency #2: Subtle wording changes and modifiers

Sometimes the LSAT will make an implicit connection between two things that are subtly different based on just one word. Try this:

Great writers always imbue their writing with their own personal experiences. It's clear, then, that the most popular writers use personal experiences in their stories.

This may seem like a good argument at first, but notice the difference between "great" in the premise and "the most popular" in the conclusion. To be great, and to be the most popular, are not the same. The argument assumes that the "most popular writers" are "great writers." Notice how much stronger the argument becomes when we insert this assumption:

> Great writers always imbue their writing with their own personal experiences. (The most popular writers are great writers.) It's clear, then, that the most popular writers use personal experiences in their stories.

Beware of Other Paths to the Conclusion

Many LSAT arguments will be faulty because the author will assume that one path to a certain outcome is the only path to that outcome.

Have a look at this one:

Bert lost 15 pounds last summer. Bert must have been on a diet last summer.

Sure, that's one possibility, but are we able to conclude for certain that a diet was the reason for the weight loss? Of course not. Maybe he had a health issue that led to a drop in weight, or maybe he exercised each day over the summer. This argument assumes that nothing else, aside from a diet, could have accounted for Bert's weight loss. Let's insert it:

> Bert lost 15 pounds last summer. (Nothing else, aside from a diet, could have contributed to Bert's weight loss.) Bert must have been on a diet last summer.

Much better.

Notice that this assumption helps the argument by eliminating every other possible explanation, but note that some assumptions can help the argument by partially bridging the gap, or by eliminating just one of the alternative possibilities.

> Bert lost 15 pounds last summer. (Exercise did not account for Bert's weight loss.) Bert must have been on a diet last summer.

Is this assumption enough on its own to make the argument valid? No, but it's certainly necessary to make the argument valid.

Don't worry at this point if you feel unsure of your ability to spot gaps in the logic. Later on in the chapter, and for the next four chapters, you'll have a chance to work on identifying assumptions. For now, let's move on to discuss the task of finding the argument core.

Identifying the Argument Core

At this point, you've learned about the argument core, and you've had some practice evaluating the logic of the core. This is a crucial skill that you'll need to answer Assumption Family questions. Unfortunately, evaluating the logic of the core is only one piece of the process. Before you can evaluate the logic, you need to correctly identify the core. Sometimes it'll be easy to spot, as it was in the Kennedy/Nixon example from earlier. Kennedy stated a premise…

> "I've been there [in Congress] now for fourteen years, the same period of time that he has [referring to Nixon's six years in Congress and eight years as Vice President]…"

and then finished with his conclusion…

> "…so that our experience in, uh, government is comparable…."

The LSAT won't always make it this easy on you. Let's discuss some of the challenges that you'll be faced with.

One quick note: we are NOT suggesting you write out argument cores during the LSAT. This mostly will be an internal process.

Organizational Structure

The LSAT will often change the organizational structure (order) of the argument components to make things a bit trickier. Here are two different ways that the same argument can be ordered:

1. PREMISE-CONCLUSION

This is the ordering that Kennedy used in his argument. It's the simplest of the possible orderings:

> I will be out of town more this month than I was last month. Thus, my electricity bill will be less this month than it was last month.
>
> *[By the way, if you're thinking about the inherent assumptions made in this argument, you're reading like a debater!]*

2. CONCLUSION-PREMISE

The LSAT will often construct arguments that place the support after the conclusion:

> My electricity bill will be less this month than it was last month because I will be out of town more this month than I was last month.

These two arguments are identical. The thing to notice here is that *organizational structure* has nothing to do with *logical structure*. Regardless of how we arrange the pieces, we still have the same argument core:

out of town more this month than last ➡ electricity bill will be less this month than it was last month

2

Getting a handle on an argument's organization becomes more challenging as the argument is lengthened and other parts added. Let's continue this discussion after we've looked at these other argument components.

Background Information

Sometimes you'll see argument components that don't seem like supporting premises or conclusions. Often, the LSAT will include neutral background information in an attempt to orient (or disorient) the reader before the real argument starts. Don't let this confuse you, though. We're still looking for the argument core. Take this one:

> Next week, our school board will vote on a proposal to extend the school day by one hour. This proposal will not pass. A very similar proposal was voted down by the school board in a neighboring town.

Here's a breakdown of the argument, point by point:

> **BACKGROUND:** Next week, our school board will vote on a proposal to extend the school day by one hour.
>
> **CONCLUSION:** This proposal will not pass.
>
> **SUPPORTING PREMISE:** A very similar proposal was voted down by the school board in a neighboring town.

Maybe you correctly identified the conclusion, but had trouble figuring out which sentence, the first or the last, was the supporting premise. When this happens, identify the conclusion and then ask "Why?" The proposal will not pass. Okay, why does the author believe this? Is it because the board will vote on the proposal? No. Is it because a similar proposal failed in a nearby town? Ah, yes. This must be the supporting premise.

When looking for the argument core, you want to consider just the premise → conclusion relationship:

similar proposal voted down in nearby town proposal will not pass

The rest of the information is background information to provide context for the argument core. Context is important, but remember that it's only there to help you understand the core.

Intermediate Conclusions and the Therefore Test

A chain of logic will often contain an intermediate conclusion that supports the final conclusion. This adds further complexity. Take a look at the example below. Notice anything different?

2

A new lemonade stand has just opened for business in the town square. The stand will surely fail. A popular juice store already sells lemonade in the town square, so the new lemonade stand will not be able to attract customers.

You can see that as more and more complicating elements are added in, the argument core becomes more difficult to track. In this case, there seem to be two possible conclusions, or opinions: (1) the stand will surely fail, or (2) the new lemonade stand will not be able to attract customers. Remember, before you can answer any question related to such an argument, you MUST know what the main point, or final conclusion, is. There can be only one. Let's use what we call "The Therefore Test" to identify the final conclusion. We'll propose two possible P → C relationships between our two candidates:

Case #1: The new lemonade stand will surely fail. THEREFORE, the new lemonade stand will not be able to attract customers.

Case #2: The new lemonade stand will not be able to attract customers. THEREFORE, the new lemonade stand will surely fail.

The first case doesn't make a whole lot of sense. In the second case, however, the first part of the statement clearly supports, or leads into, the second part of the statement. Because the stand will not be able to attract customers, it will surely fail. (If you're having trouble, try thinking about it in terms of chronology—what happens first? The stand doesn't attract new customers, and this leads to the failure of the stand.) Thus, the final conclusion, the main conclusion, is that "The stand will surely fail." Any conclusion that supports the final conclusion is called an intermediate conclusion. Intermediate conclusions are always supported by a premise.

Let's break this argument down:

> **BACKGROUND:** A new lemonade stand has just opened for business in the town square.
>
> **CONCLUSION (final opinion):** The stand will surely fail.
>
> **SUPPORTING PREMISE (fact):** A popular juice store already sells lemonade in the town square,
>
> **INTERMEDIATE CONCLUSION (opinion):** so the new lemonade stand will not be able to attract customers.

Here it is in argument core form: (P) premise → (IC) intermediate conclusion → (C) conclusion.

popular juice store already there ➡ new store won't be able to attract customers ➡ new store will fail

Notice that we actually have two embedded arguments in this complex core: (1) P → IC, and (2) IC → C. In the context of the real exam, we would need to evaluate both arguments for potential issues. However, the LSAT tends to base questions on the gap between the intermediate conclusion and the final conclusion.

Opposing Points

Think about the arguments that you make on a daily basis (you probably make more than you realize). Sometimes you can add to your argument by conceding a point or two to the other side. In doing so, you show that you've considered alternate viewpoints, and you also steal the thunder of the person who might be arguing against you! The LSAT does this all the time. Let's revisit the lemonade argument with an added twist:

> A new lemonade stand has just opened for business in the town square. The price per cup at the new stand is the lowest in town, but the store will surely fail. A popular juice store already sells lemonade in the town square, so the new lemonade stand will not be able to attract customers.

In this case, the fact that "the price per cup at the new stand is the lowest in town" is an opposing point; it is a counter premise that would seem to support the opposite claim (that the lemonade stand will NOT fail). Notice that the contrast with the main conclusion is set up with the word "but." Here's another, slightly different example:

> A new lemonade stand has just opened for business in the town square. The columnist in the local paper writes that the stand will succeed, but it will surely fail. A popular juice store already sells lemonade in the town square, so the new lemonade stand will not be able to attract customers.

Notice again the contrast word "but." In this case, the opposing point ("the columnist in the local paper writes that the stand will succeed") is actually a counterclaim. It is directly opposed to the claim made by the author (that the stand will surely fail).

Again, the LSAT often uses opposing points to add more texture (and confusion!) to a passage. Some opposing points are counter premises, others are counterclaims. Regardless, it'll be important that you separate the opposing points from the elements of the argument core. Don't confuse the sides! In this case, the argument core is still:

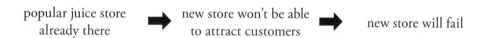

Multiple Premises

The LSAT often presents arguments that seem to contain multiple premises. In these cases, it can be difficult to figure out what the real core of the argument is. There are a few ways that the LSAT structures multiple-premise arguments.

1. Complementary Premises

> Last year, Karina spent 20% of her income on rent. This year, she spent 30% of her income on rent. Thus, Karina spent more money on rent this year than last year.

2

Here's a breakdown of the argument structure:

> **SUPPORTING PREMISE:** Last year, Karina spent 20% of her income on rent.
>
> **SUPPORTING PREMISE:** This year, she spent 30% of her income on rent.
>
> **CONCLUSION:** Thus, Karina spent more money on rent this year than last year.

Notice that the author uses the two premises in a complementary way in order to arrive at the conclusion. One premise is no more important than the other, and both are needed to arrive at the conclusion. One way to tell that both premises are going to be important is to notice that the conclusion makes a relative comparison between two things (money spent on rent last year vs. money spent on rent this year). In a case like this where such a relative comparison is made, supporting information generally comes from two premises (in this case, one stating a fact about last year and one stating a fact about this year). We can think of the argument core as follows: P + P → C:

(By the way, are you seeing the issue with this argument? What assumption is made? Hint: I spend 50% of my income on rent. Donald Trump spends 40% of his income on rent. Therefore, I spend more money on rent than Donald Trump does. Hmmm.)

2. Duplicate Premises

> In recent years, global sales of so-called "smartphones" have skyrocketed. In increasing numbers, people from all over the world are purchasing devices that have the capability to play music, snap photos, surf the internet, and receive incoming phone calls. It must be the case that smartphone manufacturers are making huge profits.

Here's a breakdown of the argument structure:

> **SUPPORTING PREMISE:** In recent years, global sales of so-called "smartphones" have skyrocketed.
>
> **SUPPORTING PREMISE:** In increasing numbers, people from all over the world are purchasing devices that have the capability to play music, snap photos, surf the internet, and receive an incoming phone call.
>
> **CONCLUSION:** It must be the case that smart-phone manufacturers are making huge profits.

Wow. Lots of information! How do we know what the argument core is? Should we use the first premise or the second? Maybe the two premises complement each other as in the example we saw previously? Look closely and note that the two supporting premises actually say the same thing in slightly different words. From a logical perspective, the premises are duplicates, not complements. In essence, the argument core is this:

MANHATTAN
LSAT

increasing sales of smart
phones   manufacturers must be
                                making huge profits

(Again, be sure you're thinking about the assumption that is made in this argument. Are sales figures the only important factor in determining profit levels?)

Here's another, slightly different example:

> Some people claim that a low-carbohydrate diet is essential to maintaining a healthy body weight. This is simply not true. Many Europeans regularly eat foods that are very high in carbohydrates. Italians, for instance, eat lots of breads and pastas.

What's the conclusion? What's the supporting premise? Think about it before reading on.

OPPOSING POINT: Some people claim that a low-carbohydrate diet is essential to maintaining a healthy body weight.

CONCLUSION: This is simply not true.

SUPPORTING PREMISE: Many Europeans regularly eat foods very high in carbohydrates.

SUPPORTING PREMISE: Italians, for instance, eat lots of breads and pastas.

Okay, so we have the conclusion, but what's the premise that supports this conclusion? Both of the premises seem to support the conclusion, but note that the second premise is simply an example of the first! The second premise doesn't really say the same thing (it's more detailed), but it doesn't add any crucial additional information. Our core would simply be:

many Europeans eat lots
of carbs   low-carb diet NOT
                                essential to maintaining
                                healthy body weight

(What is this argument assuming about Europeans? It assumes that they maintain a healthy body weight!)

Borrowed Language

Take another look at the argument core above. Notice that we reworded the conclusion from "this claim is simply not true" to "low-carb diet NOT essential to maintaining healthy body weight." The LSAT will often try to make things difficult on you by using borrowed language to hide or disguise the argument core. It sounds complicated, but it's really not. If you know your English grammar rules, you're already familiar with the concept of borrowing information from other parts of the sentence or from other sentences. Here's an example:

> Jack spends his Saturday afternoons driving his Porsche on the mountain roads. He loves doing that.

This short paragraph has two sentences. The second sentence borrows information from the first. "He" borrows the "Jack" from the first sentence, and "that" borrows the "driving his Porsche on the mountain roads" from the first sentence.

In Logical Reasoning arguments, premises and conclusions sometimes borrow information from other parts of the passage. When this happens, it's easy to get things confused and end up with a misinterpretation of the core. Take this simple example:

> Some doctors recommend taking aspirin to relieve the symptoms of a fever. This is bad advice. A fever is part of the body's natural defense against illness.

Here's a breakdown of the argument structure:

> **OPPOSING POINT:** Some doctors recommend taking aspirin to relieve the symptoms of a fever.

> **CONCLUSION:** This is bad advice.

> **SUPPORTING PREMISE:** A fever is part of the body's natural defense against illness.

The core of the argument is:

fever part of body's natural defense against illness   ➡   this is bad advice

Hmm. Read that again. Taken on its own, this argument core makes no sense because we don't know what "this" is. What is bad advice? Here, the conclusion borrows language from the opposing point! "This" refers to the recommendation to take aspirin to relieve the symptoms of a fever. In order to correctly analyze the logic of the core, we need to know exactly what that advice is. Thus, when we consider the core argument, we need to consider it as follows:

fever part of body's natural defense against illness   ➡   shouldn't take aspirin to relieve symptoms of a fever

Now we're in a position to evaluate the logic of this core. Does the premise validate the conclusion? Are any assumptions made? Yes. For one, the argument assumes that relieving the *symptoms* of a fever hinders the fever's ability to provide defense against illness.

Here's another, more difficult example of language borrowing:

> **Teacher:** Many of our students think that the earth is further from the sun in the winter than in the summer. This erroneous thinking shows that our science curriculum has not been effective.

What's the core of the argument? Go ahead and think about it for a moment before reading on.

It's very difficult to classify the parts of this passage. We always need to start by finding the conclusion, and in this case we can use a word/phrase cue to help us. The phrase "This … shows that…" is the same

2

as saying, "this demonstrates X" or "this supports X." So, the conclusion will likely be the X. This is the main point, or primary opinion of the argument:

CONCLUSION: Our science curriculum has not been effective.

Now we need to ask ourselves "why?" What supports this claim? Well, "This erroneous thinking" shows that the science curriculum has failed. What is "this erroneous thinking?" The word "this" borrows information from the first sentence. The erroneous thinking is believing that the earth is further from the sun in the winter. We have the conclusion, and we now have the supporting premise, so we've got our core:

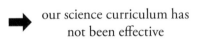

students erroneously believe earth is further from sun in winter ➡ our science curriculum has not been effective

We've covered a host of issues that increase the challenge when it comes to identifying the argument core. Most of the information above is meant to illuminate common patterns and argument structures so that you can more easily identify the pieces of the text that matter most. In this last example, we used a language cue ("this shows that") in order to help us find the core. Let's take a closer look at language cues.

Language Cues

The English language is full of cue words or phrases that are designed to serve as signposts for the listener or reader. Below, we will list the most common of these cues. That said, please note that the LSAT is on to you. They know that when you see the word "thus" you will automatically be thinking "conclusion!" Sometimes, the LSAT will attempt to fool you. All of this is to say that these cues are good helpers, but they are tendencies, NOT absolutes. Below are four language cues:

1. Conclusion Cues. The following words or phrases typically (not always) are indicators of opinions or claims. The LSAT will often use them to introduce a conclusion or an intermediate conclusion:

so	thus	therefore	thereby	consequently
clearly	as a result	for this reason	this demonstrates that	they conclude that

2. Supporting Premise Cues. The LSAT will often use the following words or phrases to introduce a supporting premise:

since	because
the reason is	for (as in, "…for he's a jolly-good fellow")

3. Opposing Point Cues. Opposing points often come at the start of an Logical Reasoning passage, and they are commonly introduced with the following type of language:

Some believe that	Some say that
Most people claim that	Experts have asserted that

4. Transition Cues. Transition, or pivot, words are extremely common on the exam. They are used to indicate a change in direction, or a change in opinion (usually from an opposing point to a supporting premise or the main conclusion). Some common transition words and phrases are:

but	however	nonetheless	even so
despite this	rather	yet	

Here's an example chock-full of language cues:

> Some of my friends say that skiing is the best way to burn calories, but this is ridiculous. Since the act of skiing down a mountain is primarily driven by the pull of gravity, skiing requires very little physical exertion. Thus, skiing doesn't burn many calories.

We start off with an opposing point ("Some of my friends say…"), and then we encounter a big transition word ("but") that indicates a change in direction. Sure enough, we get the author's opinion/conclusion next ("this is ridiculous"). The word "this" serves to borrow language from the opposing point. "This" refers to the claim that skiing is the best way to burn calories. Essentially, the author is saying "skiing is NOT the best way to burn calories." At this point, we should expect some supporting reasoning. We encounter a supporting premise cue ("since"), which leads into the supporting fact: gravity is the primary driver. What does it support? It supports the intermediate conclusion ("skiing requires very little physical exertion"). Then we get a fake-out "thus!" In this case, "skiing requires very little physical exertion" supports the intermediate conclusion that "skiing doesn't burn many calories," which supports the final conclusion that skiing is NOT the best way to burn calories. Watch out for the fake-out "thus!" So, here's the argument core: P → IC → IC → C:

skiing primarily driven by gravity ➡ requires little physical exertion ➡ doesn't burn many calories ➡ not best way to burn calories

DRILL IT: Identifying the Argument Core

Identify the argument core for each of the passages given below. For the purposes of this exercise, take the time to write the core, in arrow form, on your paper. Be sure to check your answers against the solutions we've given (check your answer after each question so that you can learn from your mistakes before attempting the next one). Your paraphrases may not always be identical to ours—that's okay. Just make sure the general P → C relationship is the same.

The first 10 arguments are of average LSAT difficulty. The final 5 arguments come from questions of high difficulty. "PT, S, Q" refers to the LSAT PrepTest from which the question was taken, the section of that PrepTest, and the question number.

1. PT7, S1, Q10

A large group of hyperactive children whose regular diets included food containing large amounts of additives was observed by researchers trained to assess the presence or absence of behavior problems. The children were then placed on a low additive diet for several weeks, after which they were observed again. Originally nearly 60 percent of the children exhibited behavior problems; after the change in diet, only 30 percent did so. On the basis of these data, it can be concluded that food additives can contribute to behavior problems in hyperactive children.

2. PT7, S1, Q20

According to sources who can be expected to know, Dr. Maria Esposito is going to run in the mayoral election. But if Dr. Esposito runs, Jerome Krasman will certainly not run against her. Therefore Dr. Esposito will be the only candidate in the election.

3. PT7, S4, Q1

In 1974 the speed limit on highways in the United States was reduced to 55 miles per hour in order to save fuel. In the first 12 months after the change, the rate of highway fatalities dropped 15 percent, the sharpest one year drop in history. Over the next 10 years, the fatality rate declined by another 25 percent. It follows that the 1974 reduction in the speed limit saved many lives.

4. PT7, S4, Q2

Some legislators refuse to commit public funds for new scientific research if they cannot be assured that the research will contribute to the public welfare. Such a position ignores the lessons of experience. Many important contributions to the public welfare that resulted from scientific research were never predicted as potential outcomes of that research. Suppose that a scientist in the early twentieth century had applied for public funds to study molds: who would have predicted that such research would lead to the discovery of antibiotics—one of the greatest contributions ever made to the public welfare?

5. PT7, S4, Q3

When workers do not find their assignments challenging, they become bored and so achieve less than their abilities would allow. On the other hand, when workers find their assignments too difficult, they give up and so again achieve less than what they are capable of achieving. It is, therefore, clear that no worker's full potential will ever be realized.

6. PT7, S4, Q13

The National Association of Fire Fighters says that 45 percent of homes now have smoke detectors, whereas only 30 percent of homes had them 10 years ago. This makes early detection of house fires no more likely, however, because over half of the domestic smoke detectors are either without batteries or else inoperative for some other reason.

2

7. PT7, S4, Q20

Graphologists claim that it is possible to detect permanent character traits by examining people's handwriting. For example, a strong cross on the "t" is supposed to denote enthusiasm. Obviously, however, with practice and perseverance people can alter their handwriting to include this feature. So it seems that graphologists must hold that permanent character traits can be changed.

8. PT9, S2, Q7

Waste management companies, which collect waste for disposal in landfills and incineration plants, report that disposable plastics make up an ever-increasing percentage of the waste they handle. It is clear that attempts to decrease the amount of plastic that people throw away in the garbage are failing.

9. PT9, S2, Q1

Crimes in which handguns are used are more likely than other crimes to result in fatalities. However, the majority of crimes in which handguns are used do not result in fatalities. Therefore, there is no need to enact laws that address crimes involving handguns as distinct from other crimes.

10. PT9, S2, Q4

Data from satellite photographs of the tropical rain forest in Melonia show that last year the deforestation rate of this environmentally sensitive zone was significantly lower than in previous years. The Melonian government, which spent millions of dollars last year to enforce laws against burning and cutting of the forest, is claiming that the satellite data indicate that its increased efforts to halt the destruction are proving effective.

11. PT7, S1, Q24

Many major scientific discoveries of the past were the product of serendipity, the chance discovery of valuable findings that investigators had not purposely sought. Now, however, scientific research tends to be so costly that investigators are heavily dependent on large grants to fund their research. Because such grants require investigators to provide the grant sponsors with clear projections of the outcome of the proposed research, investigators ignore anything that does not directly bear on the funded research. Therefore, under the prevailing circumstances, serendipity can no longer play a role in scientific discovery.

12. PT7, S1, Q7

Coherent solutions for the problem of reducing health care costs cannot be found within the current piecemeal system of paying these costs. The reason is that this system gives health care providers and insurers every incentive to shift, wherever possible, the costs of treating illness onto each other or any other party, including the patient. That clearly is the lesson of the various reforms of the 1980s: push in on one part of this pliable spending balloon and an equally expensive bulge pops up elsewhere. For example, when the government health care insurance program for the poor cut costs by disallowing payments for some visits to physicians, patients with advanced illness later presented themselves at hospital emergency rooms in increased numbers.

13. PT7, S4, Q8

George: Some scientists say that global warming will occur because people are releasing large amounts of carbon dioxide into the atmosphere by burning trees and fossil fuels. We can see, though, that the predicted warming is occurring already. In the middle of last winter, we had a month of springlike weather in our area, and this fall, because of unusually mild temperatures, the leaves on our town's trees were three weeks late in turning color.

14. PT9, S2, Q19

A university should not be entitled to patent the inventions of its faculty members. Universities, as guarantors of intellectual freedom, should encourage the free flow of ideas and the general dissemination of knowledge. Yet a university that retains the right to patent the inventions of its faculty members has a motive to suppress information about a potentially valuable discovery until the patent for it has been secured. Clearly, suppressing information concerning such discoveries is incompatible with the university's obligation to promote the free flow of ideas.

15. PT9, S2, Q3

Balance is particularly important when reporting the background of civil wars and conflicts.

Facts must not be deliberately manipulated to show one party in a favorable light, and the views of each side should be fairly represented. This concept of balance, however, does not justify concealing or glossing over basic injustices in an effort to be even-handed. If all the media were to adopt such a perverse interpretation of balanced reporting, the public would be given a picture of a world where each party in every conflict had an equal measure of justice on its side, contrary to our experience of life and, indeed, our common sense.

SOLUTIONS: Identifying the Argument Core

The solutions below will demonstrate the real-time thought process for finding the argument core. All comments in italics represent the thoughts of the test-taker.

1. PT7, S1, Q10

A large group of hyperactive children whose regular diets included food containing large amounts of additives was observed by researchers trained to assess the presence or absence of behavior problems.

Definitely background information. This is setting us up to receive research findings of some kind.

The children were then placed on a low additive diet for several weeks, after which they were observed again.

More setup. (By the way, this is very common on arguments that make conclusions from research studies. They generally start by giving background information on the way the study was administered.)

Originally nearly 60 percent of the children exhibited behavior problems;

One of the findings from the study.

after the change in diet, only 30 percent did so.

The other finding from the study. I bet the next part will use both of these findings, or premises, to draw a conclusion.

On the basis of these data, it can be concluded that food additives can contribute to behavior problems in hyperactive children.

"On the basis of these data...." Okay, so these two data points (complementary premises) are being used to support the conclusion.

60% originally had
behavior problems

+

30% had behavior
problems after decreasing
additives in diet

food additives can
contribute to behavior
problems in hyperactive
children

2

According to sources who can be expected to know, Dr. Maria Esposito is going to run in the mayoral election. But if Dr. Esposito runs, Jerome Krasman will certainly not run against her. Therefore Dr. Esposito will be the only candidate in the election.

Pretty straightforward argument with two complementary premises and an easy-to-spot conclusion:

if Esposito runs, Krasman
will not
            +   ➡   Esposito will be only
                                                candidate in race
Esposito will run

In 1974 the speed limit on highways in the United States was reduced to 55 miles per hour in order to save fuel.

This is a historical fact. It's probably just background information.

In the first 12 months after the change, the rate of highway fatalities dropped 15 percent, the sharpest one year drop in history.

This feels like it's going to be support for something. (Statistics will generally be used as supporting evidence.)

Over the next 10 years, the fatality rate declined by another 25 percent.

Another statistic. These two stats will probably complement each other to come up with a final claim.

It follows that the 1974 reduction in the speed limit saved many lives.

And there's the claim. The core of the argument is:

in first year after reduction,
15% drop in deaths
            +   ➡   reduction has
                                                saved many lives
another 25% drop over next
10 years

Some legislators refuse to commit public funds for new scientific research if they cannot be assured that the research will contribute to the public welfare.

MANHATTAN
LSAT

"Some legislators…." This has the tone of an opposing point that is about to be countered.

Such a position ignores the lessons of experience.

This seems to be the main conclusion, a counter to the legislators view above. "Such a position" borrows language from the first sentence. The author is claiming that the legislators' refusal to commit public funds because of a lack of assurance of results is a position that ignores the lessons of experience. You can anticipate that the "lessons of experience" are forthcoming!

Many important contributions to the public welfare that resulted from scientific research were never predicted as potential outcomes of that research.

And here's the support—lessons of experience.

Suppose that a scientist in the early twentieth century had applied for public funds to study molds: who would have predicted that such research would lead to the discovery of antibiotics—one of the greatest contributions ever made to the public welfare?

Lots of information here, but it's duplicate information. It's a specific example of the premise above, an example of a case in which contributions to the public welfare (discovery of antibiotics) were not predicted. The core is:

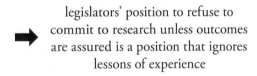

| many important contributions came from research but were never predicted as potential outcomes | ⟶ | legislators' position to refuse to commit to research unless outcomes are assured is a position that ignores lessons of experience |

5. PT7, S4, Q3

When workers do not find their assignments challenging, they become bored and so achieve less than their abilities would allow. On the other hand, when workers find their assignments too difficult, they give up and so again achieve less than what they are capable of achieving. It is, therefore, clear that no worker's full potential will ever be realized.

Straightforward argument that uses two complementary premises to arrive at an easy-to-spot conclusion:

workers underachieve when assignments are not challenging enough

+

workers underachieve when assignments are too challenging

⟶ no worker's full potential will ever be realized

2

6. PT7, S4, Q13

The National Association of Fire Fighters says that 45 percent of homes now have smoke detectors, whereas only 30 percent of homes had them 10 years ago.

"The National Association of Fire Fighters says…." Seems like it'll be opposing information of some sort.

This makes early detection of house fires no more likely, however,

The word "however" indicates a pivot, or transition away from the first sentence. The information given by the fire fighters, that more homes now have detectors, would seem to indicate that detection of home fires WOULD be more likely, but the author is saying that the detection of fires would NOT be any more likely. Is this the author's conclusion, or is it just a fact being used for something else?

because over half of the domestic smoke detectors are either without batteries or else inoperative for some other reason.

"Because" indicates that this is support for the author's claim above. The core is:

over half of domestic detectors are without batteries or are inoperative increase in detectors from 30% to 45% does not make home fires any less likely

7. PT7, S4, Q20

Graphologists claim that it is possible to detect permanent character traits by examining people's handwriting.

This sort of opposing point ("Graphologists claim…") is starting to get easy to recognize!

For example, a strong cross on the "t" is supposed to denote enthusiasm.

Simply an example to help explain the graphologists' claim.

Obviously, however, with practice and perseverance people can alter their handwriting to include this feature.

The word "however" indicates that this statement counters the graphologists' claim. Is this the final claim or just a factual statement that will support something else? Hard to tell for now.

So it seems that graphologists must hold that permanent character traits can be changed.

Ah. The word "so" indicates that this is the main conclusion, and the part before is simply support for this conclusion.

people can change their
handwriting characteristics graphologists must hold that
people can change their permanent
character traits

2

8. PT9, S2, Q7

Waste management companies, which collect waste for
disposal in landfills and incineration plants, report that
disposable plastics make up an ever-increasing percentage of
the waste they handle.

*"Waste management companies report…" This seems to be another example of an opposing point that will be
refuted or countered somehow.*

It is clear that attempts to decrease the amount of plastic that
people throw away in the garbage are failing.

*Oh, wait. We get no counter point. In fact, "it is clear" indicates that this is the conclusion. The waste
management companies' reports are actually meant to serve as support for the conclusion.*

waste management reports
increasing percentage of
disposable plastics for disposal
in landfills and incinerators attempts to decrease amount of
plastic people throw away in garbage
are failing

9. PT9, S2, Q1

Crimes in which handguns are used are more likely than other
crimes to result in fatalities.

Seems like a statement of fact. Hard to say exactly how it will function at this point.

However, the majority of crimes in which handguns are used
do not result in fatalities.

This is tricky. The "however" doesn't seem to refute the first statement. It just introduces a related fact.

Therefore, there is no need to enact laws that address crimes
involving handguns as distinct from other crimes.

*This is obviously the conclusion, and now we can see that the two points made earlier ARE in fact in
opposition to each other. The conclusion is that we don't need laws for handgun crimes in particular. The
first statement (that handgun crimes are more likely to result in deaths) would seem to suggest that we DO
need special laws, but the second statement (the majority of handgun crimes do not result in deaths) would be
evidence to suggest that we DON'T need the special laws. So, the second statement supports the conclusion:*

most crimes in which handguns
are used do not result in deaths no need to enact special laws for
crimes involving handguns

2

Data from satellite photographs of the tropical rain forest in Melonia show that last year the deforestation rate of this environmentally sensitive zone was significantly lower than in previous years.

Factual information. Maybe just background information? Hard to say just yet.

The Melonian government, which spent millions of dollars last year to enforce laws against burning and cutting of the forest,

Another fact. The government spent millions of dollars to stop burning and cutting of forests.

[The Melonian Government] is claiming that the satellite data indicate that its increased efforts to halt the destruction are proving effective.

The conclusion! The word "claiming" gives it away. Notice that the conclusion ties together information about the deforestation rate and the efforts made by the government to curb burning and cutting. This is a case where two complementary premises are used to support the final claim:

deforestation rate decreasing

+

government spent millions to curb cutting and burning

➡️   government efforts are proving effective

Many major scientific discoveries of the past were the product of serendipity, the chance discovery of valuable findings that investigators had not purposely sought.

Statement of fact. Not yet sure how it will be used.

Now, however, scientific research tends to be so costly that investigators are heavily dependent on large grants to fund their research.

Another statement of fact that provides a contrast between then and now.

Because such grants require investigators to provide the grant sponsors with clear projections of the outcome of the proposed research,

"Because" indicates support for something, and that something must be coming up...

investigators ignore anything that does not directly bear on the funded research.

MANHATTAN
LSAT

Could this be the final claim, then?

> Therefore, under the prevailing circumstances, serendipity can
> no longer play a role in scientific discovery.

*Ah. This is the final claim. So we actually have a three-part argument core with an intermediate conclusion
in the middle:*

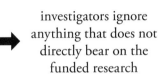 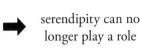

grants require investigators to provide clear outcome projections → investigators ignore anything that does not directly bear on the funded research → serendipity can no longer play a role

12. PT7, S1, Q7

> Coherent solutions for the problem of reducing health care
> costs cannot be found within the current piecemeal system of
> paying these costs.

This sounds like an opinion. Could it be the final conclusion?

> The reason is that this system gives health care providers and
> insurers every incentive to shift, wherever possible, the costs of
> treating illness onto each other or any other party, including
> the patient.

*"The reason is that…" is a big language cue. This must be support for the first sentence! So, it seems we got the
conclusion first, immediately followed by a supporting premise.*

> That clearly is the lesson of the various reforms of the 1980s:
> push in on one part of this pliable spending balloon and an
> equally expensive bulge pops up elsewhere. For example, when
> the government health care insurance program for the poor
> cut costs by disallowing payments for some visits to physicians,
> patients with advanced illness later presented themselves at
> hospital emergency rooms in increased numbers.

*Wow, lots of information, but all of this is simply illustrating, or providing an example of, the shifting costs
described in the premise above it. We can think of all this as duplicate information. Our core is:*

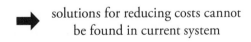

system gives incentive to shift costs to others → solutions for reducing costs cannot be found in current system

13. PT7, S4, Q8

> George: Some scientists say that global warming will occur
> because people are releasing large amounts of carbon dioxide
> into the atmosphere by burning trees and fossil fuels.

"Some scientists say…." Sounds like an opposing point that's about to be refuted!

2

We can see, though, that the predicted warming is occurring already.

Yes, "though" provides a transition into the author's claim: the warming is happening already. You can anticipate that you'll get some support for this next.

In the middle of last winter, we had a month of springlike weather in our area,

One piece of evidence to support the claim that the warming is already happening.

and this fall, because of unusually mild temperatures, the leaves on our town's trees were three weeks late in turning color.

And another piece of complementary evidence. Two premises support the author's claim:

springlike weather in winter

\+

mild fall weather delayed color change on leaves

predicted warming already happening

14. PT9, S2, Q19

A university should not be entitled to patent the inventions of its faculty members.

Strong opinion. Could be the conclusion.

Universities, as guarantors of intellectual freedom, should encourage the free flow of ideas and the general dissemination of knowledge.

Another opinion that seems to support the first!

Yet a university that retains the right to patent the inventions of its faculty members has a motive to suppress information about a potentially valuable discovery until the patent for it has been secured.

Tricky. The word "yet" seems to indicate that a change in direction/opinion is afoot, but this statement actually seems to support the notion that universities shouldn't be allowed to patent inventions. There's not really any transition here at all.

Clearly, suppressing information concerning such discoveries is incompatible with the university's obligation to promote the free flow of ideas.

This seems to be more support for the first statement. The core is complex. It uses three pieces of complementary information to support its final claim:

2

universities should promote free flow
and dissemination of ideas

+

universities with right to patent have
incentive to suppress information

university should not
be entitled to patent
inventions by faculty

+

suppressing information is
incompatible with obligation to
promote free flow of ideas

15. PT9, S2, Q3

Balance is particularly important when reporting the background of civil wars and conflicts.

Seems like an opinion. Could it be the conclusion?

Facts must not be deliberately manipulated to show one party in a favorable light, and the views of each side should be fairly represented.

This seems like a duplicate claim! It's really just saying that balance is important.

This concept of balance, however, does not justify concealing or glossing over basic injustices in an effort to be even-handed.

Oh. This is a transition. Okay, balance is important, but not important enough to conceal injustices. Now this feels like the conclusion. Will it get support?

If all the media were to adopt such a perverse interpretation of balanced reporting, the public would be given a picture of a world where each party in every conflict had an equal measure of justice on its side, contrary to our experience of life and, indeed, our common sense.

Yes, this is a reason why we can't have balance trumping everything else. This is the support.

if all media were to adopt
balanced reporting, public would
be given inaccurate representation
of justice

concept of balance does
not justify concealing
injustices

Putting It All Together

You've learned how to read like a debater. You know that your purpose on Assumption Family questions is to identify the argument core. You know that the core of the argument will require assumptions and that it's your job to uncover these assumptions. Now, let's put it all together by revisiting the five questions you tried at the start of the chapter.

Before reviewing the solution, try each question again, giving yourself 1:30. Then check your work against our solution before moving on to the next question.

PT7, S4, Q5

The government provides insurance for individuals' bank deposits, but requires the banks to pay the premiums for this insurance. Since it is depositors who primarily benefit from the security this insurance provides, the government should take steps to ensure that depositors who want this security bear the cost of it and thus should make depositors pay the premiums for insuring their own accounts.

Which one of the following principles, if established, would do most to justify drawing the conclusion of the argument on the basis of the reasons offered in its support?

(A) The people who stand to benefit from an economic service should always be made to bear the costs of that service.

(B) Any rational system of insurance must base the size of premiums on the degree of risk involved.

(C) Government backed security for investors, such as bank depositors, should be provided only when it does not reduce incentives for investors to make responsible investments.

(D) The choice of not accepting an offered service should always be available, even if there is no charge for the service.

(E) The government should avoid any actions that might alter the behavior of corporations and individuals in the market.

1. The question stem.

Which one of the following principles, if established, would do most to justify drawing the conclusion of the argument on the basis of the reasons offered in its support?

This question asks us to choose a principle that would justify the conclusion. As we'll learn later, this is essentially the same as choosing an assumption to bridge the gap between the premises and the conclusion. This is an Assumption Family question. Thus, we need to find the argument core.

2. The argument.

> The government provides insurance for individuals' bank deposits, but requires the banks to pay the premiums for this insurance.

This is a statement of fact, probably background information or a supporting premise.

> Since it is depositors who primarily benefit from the security this insurance provides,

"Since" indicates supporting premise. So, what is it supporting?

> the government should take steps to ensure that depositors who want this security bear the cost of it

Okay, so this is supported by the "since" statement, but there's still some passage left to be read…

> and thus should make depositors pay the premiums for insuring their own accounts.

This seems like the final claim. The "and thus" seems to indicate that this is being supported by the point made just before it. We have a three-part core with an intermediate conclusion:

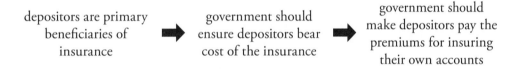

> *(Again, note that this is NOT something we would suggest writing out as you are taking the exam.)*

We can prepare for the answer choices by attempting to spot any obvious assumptions made in the argument core. In this case, because we have a three-part core, we have two relationships to analyze:

Do you see the assumption? Think about it for a second.

This part of the argument assumes that the government should ensure that those who receive the benefits actually pay for the benefits. The second relationship is:

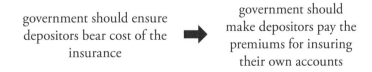

This assumes that if the government needs to ensure that the depositors bear the cost, it should do so by making the depositors pay premiums. What about other ways of ensuring they bear the cost?

2

Okay, maybe there are other assumptions made, but the LSAT is a timed test! At this point we're ready to take a look at the answer choices. We need to keep in mind that the assumptions we've identified may not actually come up in the choices. Regardless, we've narrowed our focus and we understand how the argument core is working, so we'll be ready to spot an answer that addresses the core.

3. The answer choices.
Remember that we're looking for a general principle that will support the argument. Again, this is another way of saying we're looking for an assumption that will support the argument.

> (A) The people who stand to benefit from an economic service should always be made to bear the costs of that service.

This answer is a pretty close match with the assumption we spotted: the government should ensure that those who receive the benefits actually pay for the benefits. Let's keep this for now.

> (B) Any rational system of insurance must base the size of premiums on the degree of risk involved.

The core of this argument has nothing to do with how to assess the size of premiums, but rather whether the investors should be forced to pay the premiums. Eliminate this.

> (C) Government backed security for investors, such as bank depositors, should be provided only when it does not reduce incentives for investors to make responsible investments.

The core of this argument has nothing to do with determining when to provide insurance to investors, but rather whether the government should force the investors to bear the cost. Eliminate this.

> (D) The choice of not accepting an offered service should always be available, even if there is no charge for the service.

The core of this argument has nothing to do with offering a choice for a service, but rather who should pay for that service (in this case, who should pay for the insurance). Get rid of this.

> (E) The government should avoid any actions that might alter the behavior of corporations and individuals in the market.

This may be true, but it doesn't address the argument core. The argument core has nothing to do with whether the government should act based on how the actions might affect market players, but rather whether the government should force beneficiaries of insurance to pay for that insurance. Get rid of this.

(A) is the only answer remaining, so we should choose it and move on. For the sake of this exercise, however, let's examine again how (A) addresses the argument core. We'll insert (A) into the middle of the first part of the core:

Depositors are primary beneficiaries of insurance. (The people who stand to benefit from an economic service should always be made to bear the costs of that service.) Government should ensure depositors bear cost of the insurance.

Notice how the principle in answer (A), in parentheses, bridges the gap between the premise and the conclusion.

PT7, S1, Q1

Before the printing press, books could be purchased only in expensive manuscript copies. The printing press produced books that were significantly less expensive than the manuscript editions. The public's demand for printed books in the first years after the invention of the printing press was many times greater than demand had been for manuscript copies. This increase demonstrates that there was a dramatic jump in the number of people who learned how to read in the years after publishers first started producing books on the printing press.

Which one of the following statements, if true, casts doubt on the argument?

(A) During the first years after the invention of the printing press, letter writing by people who wrote without the assistance of scribes or clerks exhibited a dramatic increase.

(B) Books produced on the printing press are often found with written comments in the margins in the handwriting of the people who owned the books.

(C) In the first years after the printing press was invented, printed books were purchased primarily by people who had always bought and read expensive manuscripts but could afford a greater number of printed books for the same money.

(D) Books that were printed on the printing press in the first years after its invention often circulated among friends in informal reading clubs or libraries.

(E) The first printed books published after the invention of the printing press would have been useless to illiterate people, since the books had virtually no illustrations.

1. The question stem.

Which one of the following statements, if true, casts doubt on the argument?

This is a Weaken question, which is a question type that will be covered in Chapter 6. As you'll learn later, the way to weaken an argument is to attack an assumption. For this reason, Weaken questions are Assumption Family questions. You'll need to find the argument core.

2

2. The argument.

Before the printing press, books could be purchased only in expensive manuscript copies.

Sounds like a fact—probably background information.

The printing press produced books that were significantly less expensive than the manuscript editions.

Another fact.

The public's demand for printed books in the first years after the invention of the printing press was many times greater than demand had been for manuscript copies.

Hmmm. Another fact. This seems like more background. Still no signs of the argument core.

This increase demonstrates that there was a dramatic jump in the number of people who learned how to read in the years after publishers first started producing books on the printing press.

Ah. "This increase demonstrates…" is a big language cue. X demonstrates Y. X is the supporting premise and Y is the conclusion. "This increase…" borrows from the previous point. It refers to the increase in demand for printed books over manuscripts. So, the core is:

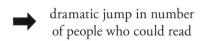

increase in demand for printed books over manuscripts → dramatic jump in number of people who could read

You can prepare for the answer choices by attempting to spot any obvious assumptions made in the argument core. Remember the example with Bert?

Bert lost 15 pounds last summer. → Bert must have been on a diet last summer.

In this example, the argument assumes that nothing else could have led to the weight loss. The flaw in the Bert argument is similar to what's happening in the printing press example. It takes for granted that an increase in demand is indicative of an increase in reading ability. In other words, it assumes that there wasn't another reason, aside from an increase in reading ability, for the increase in demand. It assumes there are no other possibilities. To weaken the argument, look for the answer that would suggest another possibility.

3. The answer choices.

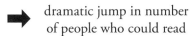

increase in demand for printed books over manuscripts → dramatic jump in number of people who could read

(A) During the first years after the invention of the printing press, letter writing by people who wrote without the assistance of scribes or clerks exhibited a dramatic increase.

This certainly doesn't offer another explanation for the increased demand. If anything, this seems to strengthen the argument! If unassisted letter writing increased, we could make a case that literacy rates (reading ability) were increasing at that time, and that might possibly explain why more people wanted books. Remember, we want to weaken this argument. Eliminate this.

(B) Books produced on the printing press are often found with written comments in the margins in the handwriting of the people who owned the books.

This is completely out of scope and irrelevant. Writing in the margins has nothing to do with an explanation for why demand increased. Get rid of it.

(C) In the first years after the printing press was invented, printed books were purchased primarily by people who had always bought and read expensive manuscripts but could afford a greater number of printed books for the same money.

Ah, yes! More books for the same money! This would give an alternate reason for the increase in demand. Keep it for now.

(D) Books that were printed on the printing press in the first years after its invention often circulated among friends in informal reading clubs or libraries.

Great, but this doesn't give an explanation for why demand increased. The circulation doesn't require that more books are purchased. Eliminate it.

(E) The first printed books published after the invention of the printing press would have been useless to illiterate people, since the books had virtually no illustrations.

Tempting (since it mentions illiteracy), but the fact that books would have been useless to illiterate people doesn't weaken the claim that an increase in reading ability accounted for an increase in demand. Get rid of this.

Again, we've eliminated four answers and (C) is the only remaining choice. Choose it and move on.

PT7, S1, Q15

Eight years ago hunting was banned in Greenfield County on the grounds that hunting endangers public safety. Now the deer population in the county is six times what it was before the ban. Deer are invading residential areas, damaging property and causing motor vehicle accidents that result in serious injury to motorists. Since there were never any hunting related injuries in the county, clearly the ban was not only unnecessary but has created a danger to public safety that would not otherwise exist.

Which one of the following, if true, provides the strongest additional support for the conclusion above?

(A) In surrounding counties, where hunting is permitted, the size of the deer population has not increased in the last eight years.

(B) Motor vehicle accidents involving deer often result in damage to the vehicle, injury to the motorist, or both.

(C) When deer populations increase beyond optimal size, disease and malnutrition become more widespread among the deer herds.

(D) In residential areas in the county, many residents provide food and salt for deer.

(E) Deer can cause extensive damage to ornamental shrubs and trees by chewing on twigs and saplings.

1. The question stem.

Which one of the following, if true, provides the strongest additional support for the conclusion above?

This is a Strengthen question, which is a question type that will be covered in Chapter 6. As you'll learn later, the way to strengthen an argument is to make the assumption explicit (as we did with the principle question earlier). For this reason, Strengthen questions are Assumption Family questions. You'll need to find the argument core.

2. The argument.

Eight years ago hunting was banned in Greenfield County on the grounds that hunting endangers public safety.

This is a fact. Seems like background information.

Now the deer population in the county is six times what it was before the ban.

Another fact. More background, perhaps? Perhaps implying that the ban has led to the increase in the deer population?

Deer are invading residential areas, damaging property and causing motor vehicle accidents that result in serious injury to motorists.

Hmmm. This is more factual information. Could be a supporting premise, but where's the argument?

Since there were never any hunting related injuries in the county,

Ah. The word "since" indicates that this is going to be supporting information for some claim.

clearly the ban was not only unnecessary but has created a danger to public safety that would not otherwise exist.

The word "clearly" indicates a conclusion. So the author makes the claim that the hunting ban has created a danger to public safety. Why does the author believe this? As we look back at the passage, we see a few reasons given: (1) before the hunting ban, there were never any hunting related injuries, and (2) since the hunting ban, the deer population has increased by six times and deer are now causing motor vehicle accidents that result in serious injury to motorists. The author uses these two premises in a complementary fashion to arrive at the conclusion:

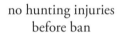

no hunting injuries
before ban

+

after ban, increased deer
pop causing motor vehicle
injuries

➡️

hunting ban unnecessary
and has created public
safety danger that would
not exist otherwise

To prepare for the answer choices, look for any obvious gaps in the logic. If an assumption is made, we could strengthen the argument by making that assumption explicit. In this case, it's important to key in on an important phrase in the conclusion: the hunting ban has *created* a public safety danger. This implies, or assumes, that the hunting ban has caused the deer population to increase. In other words, it assumes that nothing else, aside from the hunting ban, could have caused the increase in the deer population. Remembering back to our basic assumption tendencies, this is an example of an assumption that eliminates other possibilities. Maybe there's another reason for the increase.

3. The answer choices.

no hunting injuries
before ban

+

after ban, increased deer
pop causing motor vehicle
injuries

➡️

hunting ban unnecessary
and has created public
safety danger that would
not exist otherwise

We've uncovered at least one gap in the logic, but the correct answer may focus on a gap that we haven't yet considered. We need to remain open and flexible.

2

(A) In surrounding counties, where hunting is permitted, the
    size of the deer population has not increased in the last
    eight years.

Hmm. Not sure about this one. Let's leave it and move on.

(B) Motor vehicle accidents involving deer often result in
    damage to the vehicle, injury to the motorist, or both.

*We already know this, don't we? The passage says that deer cause motor vehicle accidents that result in serious
injury to the motorist. This is already used as a supporting premise! If we already know it to be true, it can't
further strengthen the argument. Get rid of this answer.*

(C) When deer populations increase beyond optimal size,
    disease and malnutrition become more widespread among
    the deer herds.

This seems related to public safety risks. Let's keep it for now.

(D) In residential areas in the county, many residents provide
    food and salt for deer.

*This has nothing to do with the argument core. The core posits that the hunting ban has created a public
danger that wouldn't otherwise exist. This is irrelevant. Get rid of it.*

(E) Deer can cause extensive damage to ornamental shrubs
    and trees by chewing on twigs and saplings.

Again, irrelevant. What about the public safety risk? Get rid of this.

We've eliminated everything but (A) and (C). How many times in your test-taking life have you gotten
down to two answers and then chosen the wrong one? Do you suffer from the "Down-to-Two Blues?"
The temptation is to bounce back and forth between the two answers. Read (A). Read (C). Read (A)
again. Read (C) again. The thing is, by the time you get down to two answers, you are, at a minimum,
60 seconds removed from the core of the argument. Remember, the core is, well, the core! A more
effective approach is to compare each answer with the core of the argument. Let's get the core back in
our minds:

no hunting injuries
before ban

\+

after ban, increased deer
pop causing motor vehicle
injuries

→

hunting ban unnecessary
and has created public
safety danger that would
not exist otherwise

Let's also remind ourselves of our task: we're looking to strengthen the argument. We want to make the argument more plausible. Which answer makes it more likely that the hunting ban is unnecessary and has created a public safety danger?

(A) In surrounding counties, where hunting is permitted, the size of the deer population has not increased in the last eight years.

This provides evidence, if only a little bit, that hunting does tend to control the deer population. Remember, when we were preparing for the answer choices we spotted an assumption: that the hunting ban was actually responsible for the increase in the deer population. If this answer is true, it strengthens the argument by giving us reason to believe the assumption is true. It's not ideal though—maybe there's something different about those other counties. Let's see about (C).

(C) When deer populations increase beyond optimal size, disease and malnutrition become more widespread among the deer herds.

Hmmm. Disease and malnutrition among the deer herds, but what about among people? Does this create a public safety danger? Besides, this doesn't address the main issue, which is whether the hunting ban *has created the danger.*

Answer (A) it is. Perhaps it's not perfect, but it's the best of the bunch.

PT7, S1, Q14

Marine biologists had hypothesized that lobsters kept together in lobster traps eat one another in response to hunger. Periodic checking of lobster traps, however, has revealed instances of lobsters sharing traps together for weeks. Eight lobsters even shared one trap together for two months without eating one another. The marine biologists' hypothesis, therefore, is clearly wrong.

The argument against the marine biologists' hypothesis is based on which one of the following assumptions?

(A) Lobsters not caught in lobster traps have been observed eating one another.
(B) Two months is the longest known period during which eight or more lobsters have been trapped together.
(C) It is unusual to find as many as eight lobsters caught together in one single trap.
(D) Members of other marine species sometimes eat their own kind when no other food sources are available.
(E) Any food that the eight lobsters in the trap might have obtained was not enough to ward off hunger.

1. The question stem.

> The argument against the marine biologists' hypothesis is based on which one of the following assumptions?

Ah, an Assumption question! This is definitely part of the Assumption Family. Let's find the core.

2. The argument.

> Marine biologists had hypothesized that lobsters kept together in lobster traps eat one another in response to hunger.

This is a common start. Some group of experts hypothesizes, or makes a claim about something. Feels like an opposing point.

> Periodic checking of lobster traps, however, has revealed instances of lobsters sharing traps together for weeks.

Yes, the word "however" is a transition word. It leads to information (lobsters sharing traps for weeks) that seems to counter the marine biologists' hypothesis. So, what's the author's conclusion? Probably coming up...

> Eight lobsters even shared one trap together for two months without eating one another.

Oops. One more piece of countering information, but this is just a duplicate of what we just had: example of lobsters sharing traps without eating each other.

> The marine biologists' hypothesis, therefore, is clearly wrong.

Here's the conclusion. This uses borrowed language: "The marine biologists' hypothesis" is the claim that lobsters kept close together in traps eat each other in response to hunger. The author says this claim is wrong, based on the fact that there have been instances of lobsters sharing traps for weeks. The core is:

lobsters sometimes share traps together for weeks   lobsters kept together in traps do NOT eat each other in response to hunger

Remember the example about "great writers" from before?

Great writers always imbue their writing with their own personal experiences.   It's clear, then, that the most popular writers use their own personal experiences in their stories.

This example made an implicit connection between two things that seem similar but are slightly different based on one subtle modifier: great writers vs. the most popular writers. We have a similar issue here. The conclusion says that the lobsters don't eat each other "in response to hunger." Well, maybe the lobsters that were observed weren't hungry. In this case, the argument makes an implicit connection between two things that seem similar but are slightly different based on one modifier: lobsters (in the premise) vs. hungry lobsters (in the conclusion).

3. The answer choices.

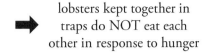

lobsters sometimes share traps together for weeks → lobsters kept together in traps do NOT eat each other in response to hunger

2

    (A) Lobsters not caught in lobster traps have been observed eating one another.

If we know the core, we know this is out of scope. The core argument is about lobsters in *traps. Any other lobsters are irrelevant. Eliminate it.*

    (B) Two months is the longest known period during which eight or more lobsters have been trapped together.

The length of time is irrelevant. Get rid of this.

    (C) It is unusual to find as many as eight lobsters caught together in one single trap.

Whether it's common to find eight lobsters in a trap together doesn't really help us figure out if the lobsters eat each other in response to hunger. Eliminate it.

    (D) Members of other marine species sometimes eat their own kind when no other food sources are available.

Other marine species? Irrelevant! Get rid of it.

    (E) Any food that the eight lobsters in the trap might have obtained was not enough to ward off hunger.

Ah. This mentions hunger. The assumption we had anticipated was that the observed lobsters were actually hungry at some point while they were trapped. This answer eliminates the possibility that the lobsters were NOT hungry. Correct answer!

PT10, S1, Q5

Some people have questioned why the Homeowners Association is supporting Cooper's candidacy for mayor. But if the Association wants a mayor who will attract more businesses to the town, Cooper is the only candidate it could support. So, since the Association is supporting Cooper, it must have a goal of attracting more businesses to the town.

The reasoning in the argument is in error because

(A) the reasons the Homeowners Association should want to attract more businesses to the town are not given

(B) the Homeowners Association could be supporting Cooper's candidacy for reasons unrelated to attracting businesses to the town

(C) other groups besides the Homeowners Association could be supporting Cooper's candidacy

(D) the Homeowners Association might discover that attracting more businesses to the town would not be in the best interest of its members

(E) Cooper might not have all of the skills that are needed by a mayor who wants to attract businesses to a town

1. The question stem.

The reasoning in the argument is in error because

This is an Identify a Flaw question, which means this is an Assumption Family question. Identify a Flaw questions will be covered in detail in Chapter 4. For now, let's find the core:

2. The argument.

Some people have questioned why the Homeowners Association is supporting Cooper's candidacy for mayor.

This has the feel of an opposing point, doesn't it? "Some people…" is a telltale sign. We can anticipate that the author will believe the Homeowners Association SHOULD support Cooper. Let's see what we get.

But if the Association wants a mayor who will attract more businesses to the town, Cooper is the only candidate it could support.

Pivot word "But." We definitely get a change in direction. This seems like the main conclusion: Cooper is the only candidate it could support.

So, since the Association is supporting Cooper, it must have a goal of attracting more businesses to the town.

Wait a second. The language cue "So" indicates that this might be the conclusion. And we also see what looks like a premise introduced by the word "since." So maybe the argument core is:

The Association is
supporting Cooper. Association must have a
goal of attracting more
businesses to town.

But what about the second sentence? That must play into this as well. Maybe the core is:

If the Association wants
a mayor who will attract
businesses, Cooper is only
choice The Association is
supporting Cooper, so
Association must have a
goal of attracting more
businesses to town.

When we see it like this, it becomes clear that this is a conditional logic flaw.

Before we finish discussing this particular question, let's introduce the basic principles of conditional logic. Then we'll come back and wrap this one up.

2

Conditional Logic 101

Introduction

Conditional logic is a logical structure that the LSAT tests in the Logical Reasoning and Logic Games sections of the exam. Over the course of your LSAT preparation with Manhattan LSAT, you will get many "touches on the ball" when it comes to conditional logic. In fact, there will be an entire chapter dedicated to conditional logic principles later on in this book. However, because we will often make reference to conditional logic principles before then, we want to be sure you understand the basics right from the start. To that end, let's dig in.

Conditional Logic in Logical Reasoning

Conditional logic comes up frequently enough in Logical Reasoning questions to warrant preparation. Here's a very simple example to illustrate:

> When Jasmine wakes up early in the morning she is not productive at work that day. Jasmine woke up early in the morning on Wednesday.

If the above statements are true, which one of the following must also be true?

(A) If Jasmine was unproductive at work on any particular day, then she must have woken up early on that day.

(B) Jasmine was not productive at work on Wednesday.

This abbreviated Logical Reasoning question contains a conditional relationship. If condition X (waking up early) is met, then Y (unproductive at work) is guaranteed. Thus, if Jasmine woke up early on Wednesday, then we can infer that she was not productive at work on Wednesday. Answer (B) is correct.

But (A) seems correct too, doesn't it? In fact, it is NOT necessarily correct. Let's explore the ins and outs of conditional logic in order to explain why not.

What Is a Conditional Statement?

Conditional statements have two parts: the trigger and the outcome. The most basic type of conditional statement uses "If … then" phrasing, where the "if" portion is the trigger and the "then" portion is the outcome:

> IF John attends the party, THEN Mary attends as well.

We can express this using an arrow symbol: J → M (trigger → outcome).

[NOTE: We use an arrow symbol to indicate a conditional relationship, and we've also used an arrow symbol to express the "therefore" in an argument core. These aren't the same thing—don't confuse them.]

This essentially means that John attending the party (the trigger) is enough to guarantee that Mary will attend as well (the outcome). John's attendance is sufficient to trigger Mary's attendance. Another way to think of it is that Mary necessarily attends if John attends. You can't have John without Mary. So, we can say that the first part of the statement is the sufficient condition, and the second part is the necessary condition. In fact, this is the formal way to refer to the two parts of a conditional statement.

SUFFICIENT CONDITION: John attends the party. (The trigger is enough, or sufficient, to guarantee the outcome.)

NECESSARY CONDITION: Mary attends the party as well. (The outcome necessarily happens when the trigger occurs.)

Conditional Inferences

When you are presented with a conditional statement on the LSAT, your primary job will be to figure out what inferences you *can* make from the given statement and what inferences you *cannot* make. Take the following example:

If Sally lives in Boston, then Sally lives in Massachusetts. B → M

Given the statement above, consider the following inferences. Which ones do you think are valid? Think about them from a common sense standpoint based on what you know about geography.

1. If Sally does not live in Boston, then Sally does not live in Massachusetts. –B → –M
2. If Sally lives in Massachusetts, then Sally lives in Boston. M → B
3. If Sally does not live in Massachusetts, then Sally does not live in Boston. –M → –B

If you said that the third inference is the only valid inference, you are correct! The first two don't make any sense because Sally could certainly live in a different part of Massachusetts, say Worcester, MA.

Let's summarize all the statements in notation form:

Given	B → M	
Bad inference	–B → –M	Illegal negation
Bad inference	M → B	Illegal reversal
VALID INFERENCE!	–M → –B	Reverse & Negate!

From this example, we can make a general rule. This rule states that whenever we have a conditional statement, we can make one valid inference from that statement. That inference is called the contrapositive:

CONTRAPOSITIVE: The reversed and negated version of a given conditional statement.

All other inferences are invalid! Don't be tempted to make any other inferences aside from the contrapositive. Let's practice this. Take the contrapositive of the following conditional statement:

2

If a passenger has no ticket, she cannot board the plane.

We can diagram this statement as:

$$-\text{ticket} \longrightarrow -\text{board}$$

To get the contrapositive, we'd reverse and negate:

$$\text{board} \longrightarrow \text{ticket}$$

Now, putting that back into English:

If a passenger has boarded the plane, she has a ticket.

Revisiting Jasmine

Here's our example from earlier. Take a second now to think about why (A) is NOT a correct answer:

When Jasmine wakes up early in the morning she is not productive at work that day. Jasmine woke up early in the morning on Wednesday.

If the above statements are true, which one of the following must also be true?

(A) If Jasmine was unproductive at work on any particular day, then she must have woken up early on that day.
(B) Jasmine was not productive at work on Wednesday.

If you said (A) illegally reverses the logic, you would be correct! The original statement says: When Jasmine wakes up early in the morning she is not productive at work that day.

We can symbolize this as: E → –P.

Answer (A) says: If Jasmine was unproductive at work on any particular day, then she must have woken up early on that day.

We can symbolize this as: –P → E.

Notice that this is simply the reverse of the original. Bad inference! Couldn't there be other reasons why she was unproductive at work? Maybe her phone kept ringing. Maybe the fire alarm went off. Maybe she was sick.

Okay. Now you know the very basics when it comes to conditional logic. There's much more to learn later on, but for now let's get back to the last example question. Let's review where we left off....

2

PT10, S1, Q5

Some people have questioned why the Homeowners Association is supporting Cooper's candidacy for mayor. But if the Association wants a mayor who will attract more businesses to the town, Cooper is the only candidate it could support. So, since the Association is supporting Cooper, it must have a goal of attracting more businesses to the town.

The reasoning in the argument is in error because

(A) the reasons the Homeowners Association should want to attract more businesses to the town are not given

(B) the Homeowners Association could be supporting Cooper's candidacy for reasons unrelated to attracting businesses to the town

(C) other groups besides the Homeowners Association could be supporting Cooper's candidacy

(D) the Homeowners Association might discover that attracting more businesses to the town would not be in the best interest of its members

(E) Cooper might not have all of the skills that are needed by a mayor who wants to attract businesses to a town

1. The question stem.
This is a Flaw question, which means this is an Assumption Family question. We'll need to find the core.

2. The argument.

Some people have questioned why the Homeowners Association is supporting Cooper's candidacy for mayor.

This has the feel of an opposing point, doesn't it? "Some people…" is a telltale sign. We can anticipate that the author will believe the Homeowners Association SHOULD support Cooper. Let's see what we get.

But if the Association wants a mayor who will attract more businesses to the town, Cooper is the only candidate it could support.

Pivot word "But." We definitely get a change in direction. This seems like the main conclusion: Cooper is the only candidate it could support.

So, since the Association is supporting Cooper, it must have a goal of attracting more businesses to the town.

Wait a second. The language cue "So" indicates that this might be the conclusion. And we also see what looks like a premise introduced by the word "since." So maybe the argument core is:

2

The Association is
supporting Cooper. Association must have a
goal of attracting more
businesses to town.

But what about the second sentence? That must play into this as well. Maybe the core is:

If the Association
wants a mayor who
will attract businesses,
Cooper is only choice The Association is
supporting Cooper, so
Association must have a
goal of attracting more
businesses to town.

When we see it like this, it becomes clear that this is a conditional logic flaw. The premise says:

If the Association wants a mayor who will attract businesses, Cooper is only choice.
B → C

The conclusion says:

The Association is supporting Cooper, so Association must have a goal of attracting
more businesses to town. C → B

Notice that the conclusion reverses the logic in the premise. This is flawed reasoning. It implies that if the Association supports Cooper, it must be true that the Association wants a mayor who will attract business. Couldn't there be another reason why they support Cooper? Maybe he's a good speaker. Maybe he supports the crime bill.

Okay, we have a good sense for why this argument is flawed. Time for the answers.

3. The answer choices.

    (A)   the reasons the Homeowners Association should want to
              attract more businesses to the town are not given

The issue isn't WHY it wants to attract business, but whether support for Cooper indicates a goal of attracting business.

    (B)   the Homeowners Association could be supporting
              Cooper's candidacy for reasons unrelated to attracting
              businesses to the town

Ah, yes! There could be other reasons why they support Cooper. This looks good. Keep it for now.

    (C)   other groups besides the Homeowners Association could
              be supporting Cooper's candidacy

This is out of scope. We don't care about other groups, only the Homeowners Association. Get rid of this.

(D) the Homeowners Association might discover that attracting more businesses to the town would not be in the best interest of its members

2

Sure, this might be true, but this doesn't have anything to do with the argument core. The issue isn't whether it SHOULD try to attract business, but rather whether support for Cooper indicates a desire to attract business. Stay focused on the core!

(E) Cooper might not have all of the skills that are needed by a mayor who wants to attract businesses to a town

Irrelevant. We already know (from the passage) that Cooper is the only choice. It doesn't matter if he ends up being a bad choice. The issue isn't whether it SHOULD support him, but rather whether its support for him indicates a desire to attract business.

This leaves us with (B), which is the correct answer. Maybe you didn't consider the formal logic underneath this problem. That's fine—and that probably shows you've got a strong, intuitive sense of logic. But, be sure to practice using formal logic as it will come in handy.

Conclusion

In this chapter, we've emphasized the following:

1. Assumption Family Questions. These are the most common questions on the exam. While they appear in various forms, all Assumption Family questions require you to analyze an argument and identify gaps in logic.

2. Read Like a Debater. To read quickly and efficiently, you must read with a purpose. On Assumption Family questions, think about reading through the eyes of a debater. What's the main conclusion? What's the evidence used to support the conclusion? What are the gaps in the logic? Be critical!

3. The Argument Core. We defined the basic concept of the argument core: P → C. We developed skills for identifying the P → C relationship, and we examined common variations on the standard P → C form.

4. Using the Core to Solve Assumption Family Questions. We've shown examples of how to use the core to solve Assumption Family questions.

Now it's time to examine the various Assumption Family question types in greater detail. Let's get to it.

> If you want some extra practice in identifying the parts of arguments, try playing "Name That Role" in the LSAT Arcade: www.manhattanlsat.com/arcade.

Chapter *of* 3
Logical Reasoning

Assumption Questions

Getting Familiar

To start, go ahead and try these four Logical Reasoning questions. Give yourself no more than six minutes total. We'll revisit these questions later on in the chapter.

PT35, S4, Q14

Marian Anderson, the famous contralto, did not take success for granted. We know this because Anderson had to struggle early in life, and anyone who has to struggle early in life is able to keep a good perspective on the world.

The conclusion of the argument follows logically if which one of the following is assumed?

(A) Anyone who succeeds takes success for granted.
(B) Anyone who is able to keep a good perspective on the world does not take success for granted.
(C) Anyone who is able to keep a good perspective on the world has to struggle early in life.
(D) Anyone who does not take success for granted has to struggle early in life.
(E) Anyone who does not take success for granted is able to keep a good perspective on the world.

PT24, S3, Q18

The widespread staff reductions in a certain region's economy are said to be causing people who still have their jobs to cut back on new purchases as though they, too, had become economically distressed. Clearly, however, actual spending by such people is undiminished, because there has been no unusual increase in the amount of money held by those people in savings accounts.

Which one of the following is an assumption on which the argument relies?

(A) If people in the region who continue to be employed have debts, they are not now paying them off at an accelerated rate.
(B) People in the region who continue to be employed and who have relatives who have lost their jobs commonly assist those relatives financially.
(C) If people in the region who have lost jobs get new jobs, the new jobs generally pay less well than the ones they lost.
(D) People in the region who continue to be employed are pessimistic about their prospects for increasing their incomes.
(E) There exist no statistics about sales of goods in the region as a whole.

PT24, S2, Q21

Newspaper editor: Law enforcement experts, as well as most citizens, have finally come to recognize that legal prohibitions against gambling all share a common flaw: no matter how diligent the effort, the laws are impossible to enforce. Ethical qualms notwithstanding, when a law fails to be effective, it should not be a law. That is why there should be no legal prohibition against gambling.

Which one of the following, if assumed, allows the argument's conclusion to be properly drawn?

(A) No effective law is unenforceable.
(B) All enforceable laws are effective.
(C) No legal prohibitions against gambling are enforceable.
(D) Most citizens must agree with a law for the law to be effective.
(E) Most citizens must agree with a law for the law to be enforceable.

PT22, S4, Q22

Dinosaur expert: Some paleontologists have claimed that birds are descendants of a group of dinosaurs called dromeosaurs. They appeal to the fossil record, which indicates that dromeosaurs have characteristics more similar to birds than do most dinosaurs. But there is a fatal flaw in their argument; the earliest bird fossils that have been discovered date back tens of millions of years farther than the oldest known dromeosaur fossils. Thus the paleontologists' claim is false.

The expert's argument depends on assuming which one of the following?

(A) Having similar characteristics is not a sign that types of animals are evolutionarily related.
(B) Dromeosaurs and birds could have common ancestors.
(C) Knowledge of dromeosaur fossils and the earliest bird fossils is complete.
(D) Known fossils indicate the relative dates of origin of birds and dromeosaurs.
(E) Dromeosaurs are dissimilar to birds in many significant ways.

Assumption Questions and the Assumption Family

In the last chapter we discussed the concept of Assumption Family questions. The following question types are Assumption Family questions:

- Assumption questions
- Identify a Flaw questions
- Strengthen questions
- Weaken questions
- Principle Support questions

For each of these question types, we want to (1) identify the argument core, and (2) evaluate the logic of the core to uncover any assumptions or gaps in the reasoning. As we saw in the previous chapter, identifying underlying assumptions is critical on just about all Assumption Family questions.

In this chapter, we will focus on the grandfather of the Assumption Family: Assumption questions. Assumption questions require us to identify an underlying assumption made in an argument. These questions can be quite subtle and difficult, but you already possess the basic skills needed to succeed on Assumption questions. Your approach will be the same: (1) identify the argument core, and (2) evaluate the logic of the core.

By the end of this chapter, you should have a strong sense of how assumptions fit into arguments. This will provide the background you will need to further hone your skills on the remaining Assumption Family question types, which we will break down in future chapters.

Argument Core Review

The argument core is a premise, or set of premises, used to arrive at a conclusion. The argument core in its most basic form is expressed as follows:

$$P \rightarrow C$$

You will remember from the last chapter that the LSAT will often make it difficult for you to identify the argument core. You need to be aware of the challenges that will be presented. If you're having a hard time remembering what these challenges are, take the time now to review the "Identifying the Argument Core" section of Chapter 2. If you feel confident that you've become a master at finding the core, try your hand at this one for review:

> Over the last two years, EBC TV has experienced a steady decline in primetime television ratings. Entertainment industry analysts posit that the decline is partially a result of a huge increase in the amount and variety of cable television programming offered over the past two years. In this case, the analysts' view is mistaken. Over the past two years, EBC TV has slashed its advertising budget, which has had a significant impact on viewership.

3

What's the argument core? Start by finding the conclusion, and then determine what information is used to support that conclusion. Here's a breakdown of the argument, point by point:

> **BACKGROUND:** Over the last two years, EBC TV has experienced a steady decline in primetime television ratings.

> **OPPOSING POINT:** Entertainment industry analysts posit that the decline is partially a result of a huge increase in the amount and variety of cable television programming offered over the past two years.

> **CONCLUSION:** In this case, the analysts' view is mistaken.

> **SUPPORTING PREMISE:** Over the past two years, EBC TV has slashed its advertising budget, which has had a significant impact on viewership.

So the argument core is:

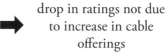

Slash in advertising budget has impacted viewership ➡ drop in ratings not due to increase in cable offerings

In this case, the background information and the opposing point set the context for the argument core. The conclusion borrows language from the opposing point—the "analysts' view" refers back to the view that increased cable offerings have led to a decline in EBC ratings.

Again, if you're feeling unsettled at this point, go back and review Chapter 2. Understanding how to find the core will be crucial to your success on assumption questions.

Evaluating the Logic of the Core

What Assumptions ARE

Once you've got the core, what do you do with it? Your job is to evaluate the logic. Does the premise logically substantiate the conclusion? If not, why not? We touched on this briefly in the last chapter. Here's a reminder:

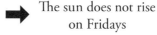

The sun rises only on Mondays ➡ The sun does not rise on Fridays

Remember that the arrow in the argument core represents the word "therefore."

> The sun rises only on Mondays. *THEREFORE,* the sun does not rise on Fridays.

We discussed two ways to think about this argument core:

1. The real-world approach: Evaluate the truth of its parts.
"No way! Terrible argument! We all know that the sun rises every day, not just on Mondays."

2. The logical approach: Evaluate the arrow. Is it justified?
"Well, if we take the premise as a given truth, that the sun rises ONLY on Mondays, is this enough to substantiate the claim that the sun does NOT rise on Fridays? Yes. Logically speaking, this argument is sound."

Remember that the LSAT requires the logical approach. Instead of evaluating the truth of the parts, you want to evaluate the *arrow*. In this case, the arrow is justified and the logic of the argument is sound.

This will not be the case with Assumption Family questions. **For all Assumption Family arguments, the arrow will NOT be justified and the logic of the core will NOT be sound.**

Try this mini-question:

> Janet can bench-press a maximum of 180 pounds. Thus, Janet can bench-press more weight than Steve can.
>
> Which one of the following assumptions is required for the conclusion to be properly drawn?
>
> (A) Janet can actually bench-press 180 pounds.
> (B) Janet can bench-press more than Steve can.
> (C) The maximum weight that Steve can bench-press is more than 180 pounds.
> (D) The maximum weight that Steve can bench-press is less than 180 pounds.
> (E) Janet can do more push-ups than Steve can.

This isn't a terribly difficult question, but it does provide an opportunity to explore the nature of assumptions. Let's look at the argument core first (not so difficult to identify in this case!):

Janet can bench-press a maximum of 180 pounds. Janet can bench-press more weight than Steve can.

When evaluating the logic of this core, we want to evaluate the space *between* the premise and the conclusion. We can see that this argument makes a huge assumption about the amount of weight that Steve can bench-press. Without knowing anything about his capacity, it's impossible to draw the conclusion. Notice, however, when we insert the correct answer (D) *between* the premise and the conclusion, the argument is strengthened. Read the entire argument again, this time with the assumption inserted:

> Janet can bench-press a maximum of 180 pounds. (The maximum weight that Steve can bench-press is less than 180 pounds.) Janet can bench-press more weight than Steve can.

It's important to understand that assumptions, when stated explicitly, bridge the space between the premise and the conclusion. In so doing, they actually help to strengthen the argument.

What Assumptions Are NOT

Let's look at the other four answer choices. Here's the argument core one more time:

Janet can bench-press a maximum of 180 pounds. 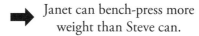 Janet can bench-press more weight than Steve can.

3

(A) Janet can actually bench-press 180 pounds.

This is a tempting answer choice, right? Isn't the argument *assuming* that Janet can bench-press 180? Actually, no. The argument *states as fact* that Janet can bench-press 180. Our job is NOT to evaluate or question the truth of the premise. Rather, we want to evaluate how well the premise substantiates the conclusion. Don't be tempted by answer choices that are simply premise boosters.

(B) Janet can bench-press more than Steve can.

Here's another attractive answer choice. Isn't the argument *assuming* that Janet can bench-press more than Steve can? Actually, no. The argument is *concluding* that Janet can bench-press more. This answer choice is simply a restatement of the conclusion! Our job is to look in the space *between* the premise and the conclusion. We want to spend our energy in the center of the argument core, not on its edges. Don't be tempted by answers that simply restate the conclusion.

(C) The maximum weight that Steve can bench-press is more than 180 pounds.

This may look very good at first glance, but look what happens when we insert it into the argument core. Read carefully:

$$\left(\begin{array}{c} \text{The maximum weight that} \\ \text{Steve can bench-press is more} \\ \text{than 180 pounds} \end{array} \right)$$

Janet can bench-press a maximum of 180 pounds. Janet can bench-press more weight than Steve can.

Wait a second. This is the exact opposite of what we want! This assumption, when made explicit, weakens the argument. It destroys the validity of the conclusion. It may be easy to see here, but often an answer choice that is exactly the opposite of what you want is very attractive. Don't fall for answer choices that hurt the argument.

(E) Janet can do more push-ups than Steve can.

While this might seem to help our conclusion (if she can do more push-ups, maybe she can bench-press more weight than Steve can), this statement is irrelevant to the argument at hand. Our argument is about bench-pressing, not push-ups. Don't be tempted by answer choices that are out of scope or that require you to add further assumptions to make the answer choice work (in this case, you would need to add that the number of push-ups correlates to how much one can bench-press).

MANHATTAN
LSAT

Wrong Answer Characteristics

The analysis of the four wrong answers above provides the basis for understanding incorrect answer patterns on Assumption questions. The common incorrect answer types are:

1. Premise Boosters (answers that try to convince us that the premise is true)
2. Conclusion Redundancy (answers that simply restate the conclusion)
3. Opposites (answers that actually hurt the argument instead of help)
4. Out of Scope (answers that fall outside the scope of the argument core)

Let's apply this to an example that's just a bit more LSAT-like. Take a minute to try the following question:

> Car salesman: Some automobile industry experts claim that the Sport Utility Vehicle (SUV) is falling out of favor with American automobile consumers. This just simply isn't true. National sales figures indicate that sales of larger, less fuel-efficient vehicles are growing at a rate higher than ever before.
>
> Which one of the following assumptions allows the conclusion to be properly drawn?
>
> (A) The national sales figures cited by the salesman are widely accepted as accurate among industry professionals.
> (B) The SUV continues to be a popular vehicle among American car buyers.
> (C) Despite pressures from environmental groups, sales of smaller, more fuel-efficient vehicles are down.
> (D) The popularity of SUVs cannot always be predicted by the popularity of larger vehicles in general.
> (E) Growth trends in the sale of larger, less fuel-efficient vehicles are representative of the popularity of SUVs among American automobile consumers.

This argument begins with an opposing point (SUVs are falling out of favor). The conclusion of the argument is that SUVs are NOT falling out of favor. The supporting premise comes last (national sales figures of larger vehicles are higher than ever before). Here is our argument core:

> National sales figures of larger, less fuel-efficient vehicles growing at rate higher than ever before. → SUV not falling out of favor with American auto consumers.

Were you able to spot any issues with this argument? The change in subject from SUVs to larger vehicles should raise a red flag. Do the growth trends in the sale of larger, less fuel-efficient vehicles *in general* represent the popularity of SUVs *specifically*? The car salesman assumes that they do. Answer choice (E) is thus the correct answer. If we insert the assumption into the argument core, we can see that the argument is strengthened:

National sales figures of larger, less fuel-efficient vehicles growing at rate higher than ever before. (Growth trends in the sale of larger, less fuel-efficient vehicles are representative of the popularity of SUVs among American automobile consumers.) SUV not falling out of favor with American auto consumers.

The correct assumption closes the gap between the premise and the conclusion. What about the wrong answers? Before reading on, go back through the wrong answers and see if you can clearly articulate why each one is incorrect. Hint: use the incorrect answer tendencies we discussed above!

3

Let's take a closer look. Here's our argument core one more time:

National sales figures of larger, less fuel-efficient vehicles growing at rate higher than ever before. 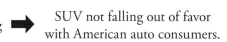 SUV not falling out of favor with American auto consumers.

(A) The national sales figures cited by the salesman are widely accepted as accurate among industry professionals.

This answer choice is attractive to the test-taker who questions the truth of the premise! Remember, our job is not to evaluate the premise, or make the premise more believable. Our job is to choose an answer that connects the premise and the conclusion. Answer (A) is a premise booster.

(B) The SUV continues to be a popular vehicle among American car-buyers.

This is simply a restatement of the conclusion.

(C) Despite pressures from environmental groups, sales of smaller, more fuel-efficient vehicles are down.

This is irrelevant to the argument core, which focuses on larger vehicles and SUVs, not smaller vehicles. This is out of scope.

(D) The popularity of SUVs cannot always be predicted by the popularity of larger vehicles in general.

This looks good. It connects larger vehicles and SUV popularity. Wait! This is exactly the opposite of what we want! Look what happens when we insert (D) into the argument core:

$$\left(\begin{array}{c} \text{The popularity of SUVs cannot} \\ \text{always be predicted by the popularity} \\ \text{of larger vehicles in general} \end{array} \right)$$

National sales figures of larger, less fuel-efficient vehicles growing at rate higher than ever before SUV not falling out of favor with American auto consumers

This destroys the argument.

It's important to note that these wrong answer tendencies are just that—tendencies. Not every wrong answer to an Assumption question can be put into one of these categories. Furthermore, your job

during the exam is NOT to categorize wrong answers. We've introduced them here to give you a sense for how assumptions work and don't work on the LSAT. In your practice, review questions you've done. See if you can give clear reasons why each wrong answer is wrong. The more you practice this, the quicker you'll recognize wrong answers and avoid choosing them on the exam.

Now that we have a general sense for how assumptions work, let's dig into the nuances.

Sufficient Assumptions

Here is a very basic argument:

It's raining outside.   ➡️   It's cold outside.

Remember that the arrow means "therefore." It's raining outside. THEREFORE, it's cold outside. Is the arrow justified in this case? Of course not. There's a huge gap in this argument. We'll represent this visually by expressing the core with an empty arrow between the premise and the conclusion:

It's raining outside.   ⇨   It's cold outside.

Our job is to choose an assumption that helps fill the arrow. The argument assumes that when it rains it's also cold outside. Let's insert the assumption:

(If it's raining outside
then it's cold outside)

It's raining outside.   It's cold outside.

Notice that the assumption completely equates the two sides of the argument, and completely fills the arrow, validating the conclusion. In a sense, the assumption is a perfect bridge between the premise and the conclusion, between rain and cold. The assumption is *enough*, or *sufficient*, to arrive at the conclusion. Here are some more examples:

> The teacher is strict. Therefore, the teacher is mean.
>
> **WITH ASSUMPTION:** The teacher is strict. (If the teacher is strict, then the teacher is mean.) Therefore, the teacher is mean.
>
> Jeremy won the trophy last year. Thus, Jeremy will win the trophy this year.
>
> **WITH ASSUMPTION:** Jeremy won the trophy last year. (If Jeremy won the trophy last year, then he will win the trophy this year.) Thus, Jeremy will win the trophy this year.

3

Sally is a child. Thus, Sally must be afraid of the dark.

WITH ASSUMPTION: Sally is a child. (If Sally is a child, then she must be afraid of the dark.) Thus, Sally must be afraid of the dark.

Again, these assumptions simply and perfectly equate the premise with the conclusion. They perfectly fill the arrow, and in each case the assumption is *sufficient* to validate the conclusion.

The LSAT will sometimes explicitly ask you to choose a sufficient assumption. You can tell by the way the question is asked:

The conclusion follows logically if which one of the following is assumed?

The correct answer to such a question will be an answer that allows the conclusion to "follow logically." In other words, it will be *sufficient*, on its own, to get to the conclusion.

Often, arguments that are associated with Sufficient Assumption questions will involve term shifts.

The Term Shift

In the last chapter, we discussed the idea of "real-world synonymous" concepts that aren't necessarily LSAT synonymous. This is the example we used:

Hiroshi always does what is right. ⟹ Hiroshi is a moral person.

It may seem that doing what is right and being a moral person are equivalent concepts, but you can't take that for granted on the LSAT. This argument contains a subtle shift in term, or concept, from "doing right" to "being moral." It *assumes* that doing what is right and being a moral person are equivalent concepts. Note that you can make the argument whole by inserting an assumption that equates the sides:

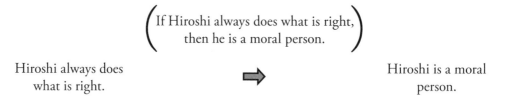

On the LSAT, this kind of "perfect" assumption is often the correct answer when an argument contains a shift in term. Let's revisit one of the questions you did to start the chapter. Take a second to review it.

PT35, S4, Q14

Marian Anderson, the famous contralto, did not take success for granted. We know this because Anderson had to struggle early in life, and anyone who has to struggle early in life is able to keep a good perspective on the world.

The conclusion of the argument follows logically if which one of the following is assumed?

(A) Anyone who succeeds takes success for granted.
(B) Anyone who is able to keep a good perspective on the world does not take success for granted.
(C) Anyone who is able to keep a good perspective on the world has to struggle early in life.
(D) Anyone who does not take success for granted has to struggle early in life.
(E) Anyone who does not take success for granted is able to keep a good perspective on the world.

First, note that this question asks us to choose an assumption that allows the "conclusion of the argument to follow logically." We're looking for a Sufficient Assumption. Before we consider the choices, however, we need to do some work to identify the argument core. We can break this argument down as follows:

CONCLUSION: Marian Anderson did not take success for granted.

BACKGROUND: Marian Anderson is a famous contralto.

SUPPORTING PREMISE: We know this [think… what is "this"?] because Anderson had to struggle early in life.

SUPPORTING PREMISE: Anyone who has to struggle early in life is able to keep a good perspective on the world.

The two premises used in this argument are complementary premises—they work together to support the conclusion. The argument core is:

Anderson had to struggle early in life.

\+

Anyone who struggles early in life is able to keep a good perspective on the world. $\Rightarrow$ Anderson did not take success for granted.

Before reading on, take a second to compare the set of premises with the conclusion. More specifically, look for a term shift.

Did you find it? There is a term shift, or concept shift, between "having a good perspective" and "not taking success for granted." While these may seem equivalent in a real-world context, on the LSAT you can't take this equivalence for granted. This argument *assumes* that "having a good perspective" means that one will "not take success for granted." If you've spotted this shift in terms, you can easily predict the answer choice:

(Those who have a good perspective on the world don't take success for granted.)

Anderson had to struggle early in life.

+

Anyone who struggles early in life is able to keep a good perspective on the world.

⇒

Anderson did not take success for granted.

3

Here's the full question again. Now that you've got a strong sense of the core, and now that you've evaluated the logic, see if you can pick out the right answer:

PT35, S4, Q14

Marian Anderson, the famous contralto, did not take success for granted. We know this because Anderson had to struggle early in life, and anyone who has to struggle early in life is able to keep a good perspective on the world.

The conclusion of the argument follows logically if which one of the following is assumed?

(A) Anyone who succeeds takes success for granted.
(B) Anyone who is able to keep a good perspective on the world does not take success for granted.
(C) Anyone who is able to keep a good perspective on the world has to struggle early in life.
(D) Anyone who does not take success for granted has to struggle early in life.
(E) Anyone who does not take success for granted is able to keep a good perspective on the world.

Answer (B) is the correct answer. Notice that the assumption expressed in answer (B) simply and perfectly equates the concept in the premise with the concept in the conclusion. It's *sufficient* on its own to validate the conclusion.

Let's examine the incorrect answer choices:

(A) Anyone who succeeds takes success for granted.

This answer choice is out of scope. While the argument does have something to do with people who take success for granted, it has nothing to do with people who succeed or don't succeed. Remember, we're looking to connect those who have a good perspective with those who don't take success for granted.

(C) Anyone who is able to keep a good perspective on the world has to struggle early in life.

MANHATTAN
LSAT

This answer choice fails to address the concept in the conclusion: taking success for granted. In fact, answer (C) deals only with the second premise: Anyone who struggles early in life is able to keep a good perspective on the world. Answer (C) tries to boost this premise by strengthening the relationship between struggling and having a good perspective. However, remember that we never need to boost a premise when answering an Assumption question. Besides, even if we did, (C) gives the *reverse* of the premise.

(D) Anyone who does not take success for granted has to struggle early in life.

We need to connect having a good perspective to not taking success for granted. This answer choice fails to make that connection.

(E) Anyone who does not take success for granted is able to keep a good perspective on the world.

This is an attractive choice because it does connect the two concepts that need to be connected. Here's what we're looking for: Anyone who keeps a good perspective does not take success for granted. Answer (E) gives: Anyone who does not take success for granted is able to keep a good perspective. This is exactly the reverse of what we need! Does this remind you of the conditional logic discussion in Chapter 2? A → B is NOT the same as B → A. Be careful of reversed logic!

Earlier in the chapter, we introduced four common incorrect answer characteristics. Let's add this last one to the list. The four we covered earlier were:

1. **Premise Boosters** (answers that try to convince us that the premise is true)
2. **Conclusion Redundancy** (answers that simply restate the conclusion)
3. **Opposites** (answers that actually hurt the argument instead of help)
4. **Out of Scope** (answers that fall outside the scope of the argument core)

Now, we'll add a fifth:

5. **Reversed Logic** (answers that reverse the order of the desired logical statement)

Reversed Logic In Depth

Reversed logic answers tend to be some of the most tempting wrong answers for Assumption questions. For this reason, they deserve some extra attention. Perhaps the explanation to answer (E) above makes good sense, but let's dig a little deeper just to be sure.

Sam is playing outside. Therefore, it must be sunny.

Simple argument, right? It's got a simple core, and hopefully the gap is clear. Which of the following assumptions would make the argument logically sound?

(A) Whenever it is sunny, Sam plays outside.
(B) It is sunny only when Sam plays outside.
(C) Sam plays outside only when it is sunny.
(D) Whenever Sam plays outside, it is sunny.

3

To many test-takers, these four answer choices all look and sound the same. Even for the savvy test-taker, under the pressure of the clock it can be very difficult to differentiate between such answers choices.

All four answers relate the concept in the premise (Sam playing outside) to the concept in the conclusion (sunny). However, not all of these answer choices relate the concepts in a manner that makes the argument logically sound, and two of them relate the concepts in a manner that is the reverse of what this argument requires.

Before we figure out which is which, let's break down the argument:

Sam is playing outside.   ➡   It must be sunny.

What is the author assuming in using this evidence to reach this conclusion? He is assuming that if Sam is playing outside, it must be sunny. We can think of the assumption using conditional logic language:

    IF Sam is playing outside, THEN it must be sunny.

Notice we can tell this assumption is sufficient because, if we insert it into the argument, and if we think of it as something that must be true, it makes the argument sound:

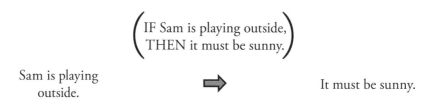

Let's evaluate the answer choices and see which ones match the assumption we've laid out.

    (A) Whenever it is sunny, Sam plays outside.

According to this statement, every time it is sunny, Sam plays outside. Does this mean that if Sam plays outside it must be sunny? No it doesn't. Maybe he plays outside on some cloudy days, too.

We can think of this answer in the following If/Then form:

    IF it is sunny, THEN Sam plays outside.

Notice that this is the reverse of the logic that would make the argument sound.

If that answer choice confused you, consider for a moment what you can determine based on the rule given in (A)—that whenever it is sunny, Sam plays outside—if you were to know each of the following:

    1. It is sunny.
    2. It is not sunny.
    3. Sam is playing outside.
    4. Sam is not playing outside.

In the first situation—if it were sunny—we'd know Sam is playing outside. In the second, we would not know what Sam is doing; perhaps he still went out to play. In the third situation, if we knew that Sam is playing outside, we would not know the weather—perhaps that's one of the days that Sam decides to play in cloudy weather. This is why (A) is incorrect—we cannot know for a fact that it is sunny outside based on the rule that (A) provides. In the final situation, in which Sam is not playing outside, we can infer that it's not sunny outside; if it were sunny, then we know he'd be out there. This is employing the contrapositive (a term we'll study more later on) of the rule in (A).

Running through the possible "triggers" for conditional statements as we just did can help you grasp their meaning if you become confused.

(B) It is sunny only when Sam plays outside.

According to this statement, sunny days coincide only with days that Sam is outside playing. Thus, if Sam didn't play on a certain day, we know it couldn't have been sunny. But it's still possible that he plays outside on some cloudy days as well, right? So if Sam is outside playing, do we know for sure that it's sunny out? No, we don't. Notice that what we know for sure is that if it is sunny, it must be true that Sam is playing outside.

IF it is sunny, THEN Sam is playing outside.

Once again, this is the reverse of the logic that would make the argument sound.

Carefully consider conditional situations involving the word "only." They often can feel counterintuitive. We will revisit "only" conditional statements in greater detail in a later chapter.

(C) Sam plays outside only when it is sunny.

According to this statement, Sam doesn't play on cloudy days. He plays only when it's sunny. So if Sam is outside playing, do we know for sure that it's sunny out? Yes, we do.

IF Sam is playing outside, THEN it is sunny.

This assumption guarantees the conclusion of our argument. This would be a correct answer.

(D) Whenever Sam plays outside it is sunny.

In essence, this answer choice is identical to (C). According to this statement, Sam doesn't play on cloudy days, so if Sam is out playing, we know for certain that it is sunny.

IF Sam is playing outside, THEN it is sunny.

The conclusion is guaranteed. This would be a correct answer as well. (But don't expect two right answers on an LSAT question!)

In short, when you're down to two attractive answers on an assumption question, two answers that both seem to connect the concept in the premise with the concept in the conclusion, be sure to consider the direction of the logic. It's often the case that one answer will present the logic in the reverse direction.

Necessary Assumptions

In order to get into law school, you must take the LSAT, right? You must also fill out an application. Because you must do both, neither one of these actions is *enough*, or *sufficient*, on its own to get you in, but each one is *required*, or *necessary*, to get you in.

Some assumptions work the same way. Take the following argument core as an example:

Johnson is successful. Therefore, Johnson is both smart and funny.

The author is assuming that a successful person is also a smart and funny person. If we state this assumption in explicit terms, it's *enough*, or *sufficient*, to fill the arrow and validate the conclusion:

$$\left(\begin{array}{c} \text{A successful person is also a} \\ \text{smart and funny person.} \end{array} \right)$$

Johnson is successful.   ⇨   Johnson is both
                                                              smart and funny.

But what if we considered just the smart part? What if we left out the funny, like this:

Johnson is successful. (A successful person is also a smart person.) Therefore, Johnson is both smart and funny.

Notice that this assumption is no longer *sufficient* on its own to validate the conclusion. That is, by itself, this assumption is not enough to get us to a completely justified conclusion. However, it is an assumption that is *necessary* for this particular argument to hold. A successful person must be a smart person for this argument to hold any water. We can think of this assumption as getting us partway to the conclusion, bridging part of the gap, or filling in part of the arrow:

$$\left(\begin{array}{c} \text{A successful person is also a} \\ \text{smart person.} \end{array} \right)$$

Johnson is successful.   ⇨   Johnson is both
                                                              smart and funny.

Likewise, if we had just the funny part on its own we'd only get partway to the conclusion (we'd fill the other half of the arrow):

$$\left(\begin{array}{c} \text{A successful person is also a} \\ \text{funny person.} \end{array} \right)$$

Johnson is successful.   ⇨   Johnson is both
                                                              smart and funny.

Both of these assumptions are *necessary* for the argument to hold, but neither one alone is sufficient.

The Negation Test

We can tell if an assumption is necessary by applying the negation test. Let's apply the negation test to each of the three assumptions we looked at above. Here's the argument one more time:

> Johnson is successful. Therefore, Johnson is both smart and funny.

And here are the three assumptions we considered, along with their negated forms:

Assumption	Negated Assumption
A successful person is also a smart person.	A successful person is NOT a smart person.
A successful person is also a funny person.	A successful person is NOT a funny person.
A successful person is also a smart and funny person.	A successful person is NOT both a smart and funny person.

If we insert the first one into the argument core we get:

> Johnson is successful. (A successful person is NOT a smart person.) Therefore, Johnson is both smart and funny.

What do you think? Good argument? Of course not! The negated assumption completely destroys the argument. So, when the original assumption is not true (when it's negated), the argument doesn't work. This means that the original assumption is required, or necessary, for the argument to hold.

You know already that the negated version of the second assumption would destroy the argument as well. Thus, the second assumption is required. Let's try the negation of the third assumption:

> Johnson is successful. (A successful person is NOT both a smart and funny person.) Therefore, Johnson is both smart and funny.

This one destroys the argument as well! So that means the original version of the third assumption is required for the argument to hold. Remember, this assumption was also *sufficient* to bridge the entire distance between the premise and the conclusion. Thus, we can say that this assumption is both *necessary* for the argument to hold, and *sufficient* on its own for the argument to hold. Here's a summary of what we've discovered:

Assumption	Necessary?	Sufficient?
A successful person is also a smart person.	Yes	No
A successful person is also a funny person.	Yes	No
A successful person is also a smart and funny person.	Yes	Yes!

Keep in mind that necessary and sufficient are not mutually exclusive characteristics.

3

The LSAT will often explicitly ask you to choose a necessary assumption. You can tell by the way the question is asked:

Which one of the following is REQUIRED for the argument to hold?

The argument DEPENDS ON which one of the following assumptions?

Which one of the following assumptions is NECESSARY for the argument to hold?

In each of these cases, the correct answer will be an assumption that is required for the argument to work. However, since we are asked to identify a *necessary* assumption rather than a *sufficient* one, the answer does NOT need to bridge the entire distance between the premise and the conclusion (though it could).

Truth be told, the "smart and funny" example above isn't very LSAT-like. It's a simple example meant to illustrate the nature of necessary assumptions. Let's look at something that's slightly tougher and a bit more LSAT-like:

> Fundraiser: Last year, we implemented an initiative to increase the total number of people who donate to our organization. The initiative has worked, as evidenced by the fact that last month we collected more donation dollars than ever before for any given one-month period.

Take a second to consider the fundraiser's argument. Start by finding the conclusion, identifying the support for that conclusion, and then evaluating the logic of the argument core you've identified. Is the argument sound? Does the premise justify the conclusion? If not, what assumptions are made?

The first sentence in this paragraph is background information. This background information helps us to understand the "initiative" that is mentioned in the conclusion. The conclusion is supported by the statistic that is mentioned last. So, our core is:

> Last month, collected more donation dollars than in any previous month. ⟹ Initiative to increase number of donors has been successful.

You may have already identified a number of assumptions made by this argument. Here are some of them:

1. Assumes that the increase was not caused by something other than the iniative that was put in place last year (maybe there was a general upswing in the economy and that is what made more people feel particularly generous last month).

2. Assumes that the same number of people, or fewer people, didn't account for the increase in the total dollar amount by making particularly large donations (maybe one person decided to donate a trillion dollars). Remember, the conclusion is that the initiative to increase the *number of donors* has been successful.

Notice that in each of these two cases the assumption gets us partway across the arrow by *eliminating* an alternate explanation. The first assumption eliminates the possibility that something else caused the

increase in dollars donated. The second assumption eliminates the possibility that the same number of people, or fewer, accounted for the increase by donating more money than usual.

We can prove that these assumptions are necessary assumptions by applying the negation test. Let's try it with the first assumption:

> Last month, we collected more donation dollars than in any previous month. (The increase WAS caused by something other than the initiative.) The initiative to increase the number of donors has been successful.

If it was caused by something other than the initiative, can we conclude that the initiative has been successful? Of course not. This negated assumption destroys the argument, which means the *original* assumption is required for the assumption to hold. Let's try the second assumption in negated form:

> Last month, we collected more donation dollars than in any previous month. (The increase in donation dollars was caused by larger than normal donations from fewer than normal donors.) The initiative to increase the number of donors has been successful.

If fewer people donated more money, then the initiative to increase the total number of donors did not succeed. This negated assumption destroys the argument, which means the *original* assumption is required for the argument to hold.

Now let's take a look back at one of the questions you did to start the chapter. Take a minute to review the following:

PT24, S3, Q18

The widespread staff reductions in a certain region's economy are said to be causing people who still have their jobs to cut back on new purchases as though they, too, had become economically distressed. Clearly, however, actual spending by such people is undiminished, because there has been no unusual increase in the amount of money held by those people in savings accounts.

Which one of the following is an assumption on which the argument relies?

(A) If people in the region who continue to be employed have debts, they are not now paying them off at an accelerated rate.

(B) People in the region who continue to be employed and who have relatives who have lost their jobs commonly assist those relatives financially.

(C) If people in the region who have lost jobs get new jobs, the new jobs generally pay less well than the ones they lost.

(D) People in the region who continue to be employed are pessimistic about their prospects for increasing their incomes.

(E) There exist no statistics about sales of goods in the region as a whole.

Note that the question asks us to identify a necessary assumption—"an assumption on which the argument *relies,*" or *depends.* First things first, though. Let's analyze the argument structure in order to uncover the argument core. The structure of this argument is very standard—you know it well by now. It starts with an opposing point, transitions to the conclusion, and then provides support for the conclusion. Did you notice the language cues? The phrase "...are said to be" indicates an opposing point, "clearly" is a sign that the conclusion is imminent, "however" indicates a pivot, or transition, away from the opposing point, and "because" introduces the support.

3

OPPOSING POINT: The widespread staff reductions in a certain region's economy are *said to be* causing people who still have their jobs to cut back on new purchases as though they, too, had become economically distressed.

CONCLUSION: *Clearly, however*, actual spending by such people is undiminished,

SUPPORTING PREMISE: *because* there has been no unusual increase in the amount of money held by those people in savings accounts.

So the argument core is:

No unusual increase in $
in savings accounts of those   ⇨   Spending by those who've
who've kept jobs.   kept jobs has not gone down.

The argument is essentially this: people with jobs aren't putting more money in their savings accounts, so these people must be spending as much as before. Evaluate the logic of this argument core. What are the assumptions? Let's list a few:

1. Assumes these people aren't saving money in places other than in savings accounts—maybe they're stuffing their mattresses with all the money they're saving from cutting their spending!

2. Assumes these people are not using their excess money for other things aside from purchases—maybe they're gifting their extra trillion in cash to a favorite charity organization instead of making new purchases!

At this point we have a pretty good sense of what's going on in this argument. We have the core and we see a few problems with the logic. It's important to note that we may not see an answer choice that expresses an assumption that we've anticipated. That's okay. As long as we've focused on the right parts of the argument, we'll be prepared for the answer choices. The thinking we've done here has put us in a good position to make a correct selection.

> (A) If people in the region who continue to be employed have
>   debts, they are not now paying them off at an accelerated
>   rate.

This answer may seem wildly out of scope (where did debts come from?), but it's actually relevant. It essentially eliminates the possibility that these people are using their excess money to pay down debts from old purchases rather than to buy new things. This is actually very similar to the second assumption that we had anticipated above: Assumes these people are not using their excess money for other things aside from purchases. Keep it for now.

> (B) People in the region who continue to be employed and
>   who have relatives who have lost their jobs commonly
>   assist those relatives financially.

Oh no! This one seems to do the same thing as (A), right? It says these people are using their money for something *other* than new purchases. But wait a second. This does the exact *opposite* of what we want. It hurts the argument. We want an assumption that says they are NOT using their money on other things. Be careful! Answers that express the opposite are very attractive on Assumption questions.

> (C) If people in the region who have lost jobs get new jobs, the
>   new jobs generally pay less well than the ones they lost.

Out of scope. The subject of the argument core is the group of people who have NOT lost their jobs.

> (D) People in the region who continue to be employed are
>   pessimistic about their prospects for increasing their
>   incomes.

Out of scope. Whether these people are optimistic or pessimistic is irrelevant. We care only about whether their spending has decreased.

> (E) There exist no statistics about sales of goods in the region
>   as a whole.

In a sense, this answer choice can be thought of as a premise booster. Perhaps if we know there are no good stats we'll be more likely to accept the evidence used in the argument—money in savings accounts has not increased—as a proxy. But remember that we don't need to boost the premise. That's not our job.

So, the correct answer is (A). Note that while this answer is *necessary* for the conclusion to hold, it is not *sufficient* to guarantee that those who have kept their jobs are spending just as much as before. The fact that they're not using the money to pay off debts does increase, ever so slightly, the likelihood that they are spending the money on new purchases (the conclusion), but it doesn't guarantee that they're not giving it to charity, or gifting it to their children, or stuffing it in their mattresses, or using it to light the charcoal grill. In other words, there are various other possibilities that this answer choice does *not* eliminate.

So, this answer choice is one that partially fills the arrow:

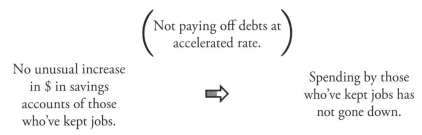

The Subtleties of Sufficient and Necessary Assumptions

You now have the background needed to understand the nuances of difficult Assumption questions. You know that a Sufficient Assumption bridges the entire distance between the premise and the conclusion. A Sufficient Assumption is *enough,* on its own, to validate the conclusion. It fills the entire arrow. You know that a Necessary Assumption is *required* for the argument to hold, but may not be *enough* on its own for the argument to hold. A Necessary Assumption generally fills only part of the arrow.

Here's another example:

> The sweater costs $40. Thus, Ramon has enough money in his wallet to buy the sweater.

In concluding that Ramon has enough money in his wallet to buy the sweater, we are certainly making some assumptions. Take a second and think about this argument. Before reading on, see if you can do the following:

> 1. Write a sufficient assumption for this argument, one that would fill the entire arrow and allow the conclusion to be drawn.

> 2. Write a necessary assumption for this argument, one that is required for the argument to hold but does not necessarily bridge the entire distance.

Okay, now that you've thought about it and come up with your own ideas, let's discuss a sufficient assumption.

If you put more than $40 in Ramon's wallet, then you created a sufficient assumption:

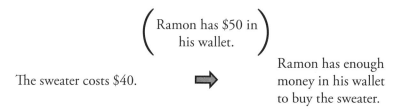

Seems logical, right? This assumption is sufficient to arrive at the conclusion. But is it necessary? No. How do we know? Negate it. Ramon does NOT have $50 in his wallet. The negated assumption does not destroy the argument (maybe he has $45 in his wallet), which means the assumption is not necessary for the conclusion to hold. So, this assumption is sufficient but not necessary. Now let's come up with an assumption that isn't sufficient but is necessary:

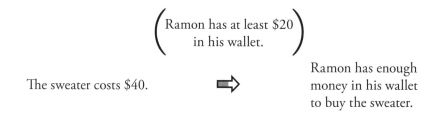

In order to afford the sweater, Ramon *must* have at least $20 in his wallet. How do we know that this must be true? Negate it. Ramon does NOT have at least $20 in his wallet. All of a sudden the argument is destroyed. This assumption is necessary, or required, for the argument to hold. That said, it's certainly not *sufficient* on its own to validate the conclusion. Knowing that he has at least $20 doesn't guarantee that he can buy the $40 sweater.

Now, here comes the really challenging stuff. Let's look at the argument core again. Go ahead and consider the assumption we've written in over the empty arrow below. Is it necessary? Is it sufficient? How would you fill in the arrow to visually represent the effect of this assumption?

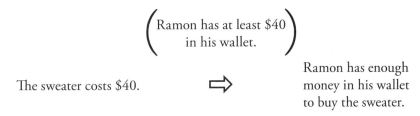

If you said it's sufficient, you're right. Knowing that he has at least $40 is *enough* to guarantee that he has enough in his wallet to buy the $40 sweater. But is this assumption necessary for the conclusion to hold? Yes, it is necessary as well! How do we know? Negate it:

> The sweater costs $40. (Ramon does NOT have at least $40 in his wallet.) Ramon has enough money in his wallet to buy the sweater.

The negated assumption destroys the argument, which means it's necessary. Let's try one last one. Consider this assumption:

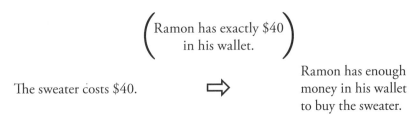

This assumption is clearly sufficient, but is it necessary? You should know what to do at this point—go ahead and negate it. If Ramon does NOT have exactly $40, does this destroy the conclusion that he has enough to buy the sweater? No! He still could have $41, or $49, or $120 in his wallet. He also might have only $27, but since we don't know what he has, we can't say that the negated assumption *destroys* the argument, so this assumption is NOT required. We don't *need* to know that Ramon has *exactly* $40. So, this assumption is sufficient to guarantee the conclusion, but it's not necessary to arrive at the conclusion.

When an LSAT question asks for a Sufficient Assumption, often the answer will provide not just enough information to arrive at the conclusion, but more information than is necessary to arrive at the conclusion. In a sense, the assumption is more than sufficient. We can think of the arrow as being over-filled:

$$\left(\begin{array}{c} \text{Ramon has \$50 in his} \\ \text{wallet.} \end{array} \right)$$

The sweater costs \$40.   Ramon has enough
money in his wallet
to buy the sweater.

Let's look at an example from the start of the chapter. Take a minute to redo this question:

PT24, S2, Q21

Newspaper editor: Law enforcement experts, as well as most
citizens, have finally come to recognize that legal prohibitions
against gambling all share a common flaw: no matter how
diligent the effort, the laws are impossible to enforce. Ethical
qualms notwithstanding, when a law fails to be effective,
it should not be a law. That is why there should be no legal
prohibition against gambling.

Which one of the following, if assumed, allows the argument's
conclusion to be properly drawn?

(A) No effective law is unenforceable.
(B) All enforceable laws are effective.
(C) No legal prohibitions against gambling are enforceable.
(D) Most citizens must agree with a law for the law to be
     effective.
(E) Most citizens must agree with a law for the law to be
     enforceable.

The language in the question stem ("…allows the argument's conclusion to be properly drawn")
indicates that this question is asking for a sufficient assumption. Our answer, on its own, needs
to be enough to validate the conclusion. As an Assumption question, this question is a part of the
Assumption Family, so we need to start by finding the argument core. If you didn't find the core the
first time, go back now and be sure to do so before reading on.

Here is the ideal real-time thought process for finding the core of this argument:

Newspaper editor: Law enforcement experts, as well as most citizens, have finally come
to recognize that legal prohibitions against gambling all share a common flaw: no
matter how diligent the effort, the laws are impossible to enforce.

*This seems like it could be an opposing point that the author will ultimately take issue with. However, the fact
that they've "finally come to recognize" indicates that the author believes this realization is long overdue—
realization of an obvious fact perhaps. Maybe the author agrees that laws against gambling are impossible to
enforce.*

Ethical qualms notwithstanding, when a law fails to be effective, it should not be a law.

This feels like an opinion. Maybe it's the conclusion? If so, the support should be coming next…

That is why there should be no legal prohibition against gambling.

Oh. This is the conclusion. "That is why" is a language cue indicating that the middle sentence actually supports this one. So the author believes there should be no legal prohibition against gambling, and the support used is that laws against gambling can't be enforced, and ineffective laws should not be laws. The argument core is:

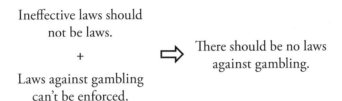

Notice that the two premises work in tandem—they are complementary premises. Together, they are meant to lead to the conclusion. However, this argument makes a huge assumption. Have you spotted it yet? If so, excellent! If not, consider the following analogous argument:

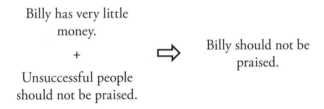

Do you see the problem? This argument assumes that Billy is unsuccessful (because he has very little money).

In the original argument, the author assumes that gambling laws are ineffective laws (because they cannot be enforced). Let's put this assumption into the core and read it again:

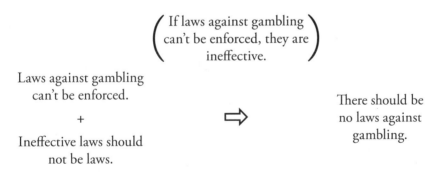

Pretty good, right? This assumption seems to fill the entire gap. It's sufficient to arrive at the conclusion. Interestingly, what it does is join the two premises so that they form a unified premise that the laws are unenforceable and ineffective. Let's see if we can find something similar in our answer choices:

(A) No effective law is unenforceable.

This isn't what we anticipated, but it does seem to link effectiveness with enforceability. Not sure. Keep it for now.

    (B) All enforceable laws are effective.

Same thing here. Keep it for now.

    (C) No legal prohibitions against gambling are enforceable.

3

This just restates the premise! We already know that legal prohibitions against gambling can't be enforced. This is a premise booster. Eliminate it.

    (D) Most citizens must agree with a law for the law to be effective.

The argument core isn't about whether citizen agreement makes laws effective, it's about whether unenforceability makes a law ineffective. Out of scope. Eliminate it.

    (E) Most citizens must agree with a law for the law to be enforceable.

The argument core isn't about whether citizen agreement makes laws enforceable, it's about whether unenforceability makes a law ineffective. Out of scope. Eliminate it.

So we're down to (A) and (B), but neither looks like our anticipated assumption. Remember, our anticipated assumption was:

    If laws against gambling can't be enforced, they are ineffective.

We can think of our assumption in conditional terms:

$$\text{gambling laws unenforceable} \longrightarrow \text{gambling laws ineffective}$$

So, if a law against gambling is unenforceable, then this law against gambling is ineffective. This is our assumption.

Let's look at (A) again:

    (A) No effective law is unenforceable.

We can write this in conditional form as well. It's basically saying that if a law is effective then it must be enforceable.

$$\text{effective law} \longrightarrow \text{enforceable law}$$

You know from Chapter 2 that we can take the contrapositive of this by reversing AND negating the terms:

$$\text{unenforceable law} \longrightarrow \text{ineffective law}$$

This looks pretty good when we compare it to our anticipation, but it mentions nothing about laws against *gambling*, right? It's much too general, right? Well, consider the following. Imagine we have this argument:

> John is not happy. Therefore, John is not healthy.

The assumption here is very simple:

> John is not happy. (If John is not happy, then John is not healthy.) Therefore, John is not healthy.

This assumption is certainly enough to validate the conclusion. But what about this one:

> John is not happy. (Anyone in the world who is not happy is also not healthy.) Therefore, John is not healthy.

This works too, doesn't it? We might say it's very general and very broad, and that it doesn't mention John specifically, but the sweeping nature of this assumption is exactly what makes it *sufficient* to guarantee our conclusion! If *anyone* who is not happy is also not healthy, then certainly *John* not being happy guarantees that he is not healthy. After all, John is included in *anyone*.

The same thing holds for answer (A). If *any* unenforceable law is ineffective, then certainly unenforceable laws *against gambling* are ineffective. So, answer (A) gets us the following:

Note that this assumption is sufficient, and then some. It's certainly enough to guarantee the conclusion, but we don't *need* to know that every single unenforceable law in the universe is ineffective. In fact, simply knowing that unenforceable *gambling* laws in particular are ineffective would have been enough. It's the difference between saying Ramon has at least $40 in his wallet and saying that Ramon has $50 in his wallet. The first is sufficient, the second is certainly sufficient, and then some. Since we're looking for a sufficient assumption, (A) is the correct answer.

Let's look at the other attractive answer choice:

> (B) All enforceable laws are effective.

This can be translated to:

enforceable law   ⟶   effective law

Think back to the previous chapter and our discussion of valid contrapositives (reverse and negate). This is the same as:

ineffective law   ⟶   unenforceable law

But we want the reverse! Remember, we're looking for:

unenforceable law   ⟶   ineffective law

Answer (B) is tempting, but it reverses the logic. Remember, this is one of those common incorrect answer characteristics we discussed earlier in the chapter. Don't fall for it!

Okay. Take a breath. Tough question! Just to review, that was an example of a question for which the correct answer was sufficient, and then some, to validate the conclusion. The correct answer *over*-filled the arrow. This is okay, and quite common, if the question asks us for a sufficient assumption.

What if we had that same argument but with a different question stem? What if instead of…

> *Which one of the following, if assumed, ALLOWS the argument's conclusion to be properly drawn?*

we had…

> *Which one of the following assumptions is REQUIRED for the conclusion to be properly drawn?*

So, instead of looking for an assumption that "allows" (on its own) the conclusion to be drawn, we'd be looking for an assumption that is "required" for the conclusion to be drawn. This slight change in language turns a sufficient assumption question into a necessary assumption question. Here's how the entire question would look:

PT24, S2, Q21

Newspaper editor: Law enforcement experts, as well as most citizens, have finally come to recognize that legal prohibitions against gambling all share a common flaw: no matter how diligent the effort, the laws are impossible to enforce. Ethical qualms notwithstanding, when a law fails to be effective, it should not be a law. That is why there should be no legal prohibition against gambling.

Which one of the following assumptions is REQUIRED for the conclusion to be properly drawn?

(A) No effective law is unenforceable.
(B) All enforceable laws are effective.
(C) No legal prohibitions against gambling are enforceable.
(D) Most citizens must agree with a law for the law to be effective.
(E) Most citizens must agree with a law for the law to be enforceable.

Again, (A) is essentially saying that all unenforceable laws are ineffective. Do you think (A) would still be correct? No, it wouldn't. Remember, we don't *need* to assume that every single unenforceable law in the universe is ineffective. We just need to assume that unenforceable *gambling* laws are ineffective. So, on a question that asks for a Necessary Assumption, "sufficient and then some" answers are too much. Answer (A) would be wrong. In fact, this question no longer has a correct answer! (While the LSAT will never leave you without a correct answer, it might try to trick you by tempting you with a sufficient assumption when you are asked to identify a necessary one—more on that in a bit.)

If you're still having trouble seeing this, think back to our sweater example:

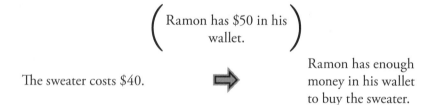

Again, knowing that Ramon has $50 is sufficient to guarantee that he has enough money, but we don't *need* it to be $50. $40 would be good, or $47, or even $107. If a question asked us for a necessary assumption, this one wouldn't be the correct answer.

If this makes sense, you're ready to reexamine the fourth question you did to start the chapter. Try it again, and think about the sweater!

3

Dinosaur expert: Some paleontologists have claimed that birds are descendants of a group of dinosaurs called dromeosaurs. They appeal to the fossil record, which indicates that dromeosaurs have characteristics more similar to birds than do most dinosaurs. But there is a fatal flaw in their argument; the earliest bird fossils that have been discovered date back tens of millions of years farther than the oldest known dromeosaur fossils. Thus the paleontologists' claim is false.

The expert's argument depends on assuming which one of the following?

(A) Having similar characteristics is not a sign that types of animals are evolutionarily related.
(B) Dromeosaurs and birds could have common ancestors.
(C) Knowledge of dromeosaur fossils and the earliest bird fossils is complete.
(D) Known fossils indicate the relative dates of origin of birds and dromeosaurs.
(E) Dromeosaurs are dissimilar to birds in many significant ways.

This is a Necessary Assumption question: "…*depends* on assuming which one of the following." As we do with all Assumption Family questions, we want to start by finding the argument core. We'll model the real-time thought process of an expert test-taker below:

Some paleontologists have claimed that birds are descendants of a group of dinosaurs called dromeosaurs.

Sounds like an opposing point: "Some paleontologists have claimed…." We can anticipate that this will be refuted at some point in the argument.

They appeal to the fossil record, which indicates that dromeosaurs have characteristics more similar to birds than do most dinosaurs.

This is the support for the opposing point, so this is more opposing evidence. Some paleontologists think that birds descended from dromeosaurs BECAUSE dromeosaurs have characteristics similar to birds.

But there is a fatal flaw in their argument.

Ah. Here's the author's claim, opposing the paleontologists. I bet his evidence will come next…

The earliest bird fossils that have been discovered date back tens of millions of years farther than the oldest known dromeosaur fossils.

This is the evidence supporting the author's claim that the paleontologists are wrong.

Thus the paleontologists' claim is false.

And here's the author's conclusion one more time: the paleontologists' claim is false. So, because known bird fossils date back farther than known dromeosaur fossils, birds could not have descended from dromeosaurs. So the argument core is:

Earliest discovered bird fossils date back tens of millions of years before earliest known dromeosaur fossils. 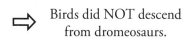 Birds did NOT descend from dromeosaurs.

Do you see any issues with this argument core? What assumptions are made? If you're not certain, take a look at this simpler example:

The oldest records of my family tree that I can find are for my great-grandfather James. Thus, my great-grandfather James was the original progenitor of my family.

This makes no sense at all! Of course we know that James had two parents, and that those parents had parents, and so on. Just because James is the oldest progenitor that we *know* about doesn't mean he actually *is* the original progenitor. We just haven't discovered the people before him yet.

We can use the same logic to uncover the flaw in the dinosaur example. Just because the oldest *known* fossils of dromeosaurs came after the oldest *known* fossils of birds doesn't necessarily mean that dromeosaurs came after birds. Maybe there are earlier dromeosaur fossils that we haven't yet discovered. In reaching the conclusion that dromeosaurs did NOT descend from birds, the author is assuming that the current fossil record is representative of the time periods during which the animals lived. In other words, the author is assuming that the existing fossil record is accurate. Let's look at the answer choices. Remember, we're looking for a necessary assumption.

> (A) Having similar characteristics is not a sign that types of
>   animals are evolutionarily related.

This is tempting. It would certainly help the author's claim and hurt the paleontologists' claim, but keep in mind the evidence used to support the author's claim: the known fossil record for dromeosaurs comes after that for birds. This is the evidence the author uses to make his claim. This is the evidence used in the argument core. The author never questions the paleontologists' point about dromeosaurs and birds having similar characteristics, nor does he question that they might be related in some general way. This answer does not help to bridge the distance between the premise and the conclusion. Eliminate it.

> (B) Dromeosaurs and birds could have common ancestors.

We don't need to assume that they could have common ancestors in order to conclude that birds did not descend from dromeosaurs. Out of scope. Eliminate it.

> (C) Knowledge of dromeosaur fossils and the earliest bird fos-
>   sils is complete.

Ah. This helps! If knowledge of dromeosaur fossils and bird fossils is complete, then we know that the current fossil record is accurate, and that birds could not have descended from dromeosaurs. This is very similar to what we anticipated. Keep it for now.

3

(D) Known fossils indicate the relative dates of origin of birds and dromeosaurs.

Uh oh. This one helps as well. If known fossils indicate the relative dates of origin of birds and dromeosaurs, then we'd know that birds could not have descended from dromeosaurs, and we could conclude that the paleontologists are wrong. Keep it for now.

(E) Dromeosaurs are dissimilar to birds in many significant ways.

This is completely irrelevant. We don't need to assume this in order to conclude that birds did not descend from dromeosaurs. This does not inform the relationship between the fossil record and the order of origin of birds and dromeosaurs. Eliminate it.

So we're left with two answers, (C) and (D). Let's take a closer look, and let's be sure to keep in mind what our task is: find a *necessary* assumption!

(C) Knowledge of dromeosaur fossils and the earliest bird fossils is complete.

$$\left(\begin{array}{c} \text{Known fossil record} \\ \text{is complete.} \end{array} \right)$$

Earliest discovered bird fossils date back tens of millions of years before earliest known dromeosaur fossils.　　　　Birds did NOT descend from dromeosaurs.

Is it *necessary* to know that knowledge of the fossils is *complete?* Knowing that the current record gives us a *complete* fossil record would certainly be *enough* to conclude that dromeosaurs came after birds, but is it *necessary* for the record to be absolutely complete? No, it's not. This would be like saying Ramon needs to have exactly $40 in his wallet to buy the sweater. Yes, that would guarantee he has enough to buy the sweater, but does it have to be exactly $40? No. Likewise, we don't need to assume that there is absolutely nothing left to discover about the fossil record, just that the record is indicative of the relative dates of origin.

If we negate answer (C), we get: Knowledge of the fossil records is NOT complete. Does this destroy the argument? No. Consider the hypothetical possibility that there is one more dromeosaur fossil that we haven't discovered, and it's from the same period as the current dromeosaur fossils. This would mean our knowledge is not complete, but it certainly doesn't damage the conclusion at all. In the end, answer (C) is sufficient, and then some, to guarantee the conclusion, but it is not necessary.

Too much! This brings us to (D).

(D) Known fossils indicate the relative dates of origin of birds and dromeosaurs.

Let's try negating this one: Known fossils do NOT indicate the relative dates of origin of birds and dromeosaurs. In other words, the fact that known dromeosaur fossils came after known bird fossils does NOT mean that dromeosaurs came after birds. This would kill the argument! (D) is therefore a necessary assumption, and (D) is the correct answer.

To review, we've just looked at a question that has two perfectly good answer choices. The thing is, answer (C) would be the correct answer to a *Sufficient* Assumption question, not a Necessary Assumption question. Knowing your task on Assumption questions is crucial.

3

DRILL IT: Necessary and Sufficient Assumptions

For each of the following exercises, you will be presented with an argument, two question prompts (numbered 1 and 2), and a series of answer choices. Next to each answer choice, write a "1" if the answer is a correct answer for question prompt 1, write a "2" if the answer is a correct answer for question prompt 2, write a "1" and a "2" if it's a correct answer for both prompts, and write an "X" if it is not a correct answer for either. This is a tough drill, so check your work after each problem and think carefully!

3

Example:

The sweater costs $40. Thus, Ramon has enough money in his wallet to buy the sweater.

(1) The argument above depends on assuming which one of the following?

(2) Which of the following assumptions allows the conclusion above to be properly drawn?

  X Ramon has enough money in his wallet to buy a pair of jeans.

  1 Ramon has at least $10 in his wallet.

1, 2 Ramon has at least $40 in his wallet.

  2 Ramon has $50 in his wallet.

  X Ramon has less than $35 in his wallet.

  2 Ramon has exactly $40 in his wallet.

1. Studies have shown that private tutoring is an effective approach for learning a second language. Thus, private tutoring is a fun way to learn a second language.

(1) Which of the following is an assumption that is required in order for the argument to hold?
(2) The conclusion follows logically if which of the following is assumed?

_____ Anything that is an effective approach for accomplishing a goal is also a fun approach for accomplishing that goal.

_____ The studies mentioned were conducted by a team of reputable linguists.

_____ Some activities that are effective are also fun.

2. Of the 25 movies released this year, only the three highest rated movies ("first" being the highest rating) of the year will be eligible for the award. Therefore, the movie *Darkness* will not be eligible for the award.

(1) Which of the following is an assumption upon which the argument relies?
(2) The conclusion can be properly drawn if which of the following is assumed?

_____ Of the 25 movies released this year, *Darkness* was the lowest rated movie.

_____ Of the 25 movies released this year, *Darkness* was rated fourth or worse.

_____ Many of the people who saw *Darkness* did not enjoy it.

_____ Of the 25 movies released this year, *Darkness* was not rated second.

3. The monthly revenue for Chad's Burger Shack was higher in July than it was in April. Thus, Chad's Burger Shack must have sold more burgers in July than in April.

(1) Which of the following is an assumption upon which the argument depends?
(2) The conclusion follows logically if which of the following is assumed?

_____ Chad's Burger Shack is gaining popularity.

_____ In the summer months, people tend to dine out more frequently than they do at other times of the year.

_____ The difference in revenue between April and July was not due solely to an increase in beverage sales.

_____ A third-party audit verified that the monthly revenue for Chad's Burger Shack was higher in July than it was in April.

_____ The difference in revenue between April and July was due solely to an increase in the sales price of a Chad's Burger Shack burger.

_____ Total costs for Chad's Burger Shack were not lower in July than they were in April.

_____ For any restaurant, any difference in revenue from month to month can be explained by a difference in the number of burgers sold.

4. Maria must be a person who values faith because she attends church every Sunday.

(1) Which of the following is an assumption upon which the argument relies?
(2) The conclusion can be properly drawn if which of the following is assumed?

_____ Anyone who attends church every Sunday is a person who values faith, family, and community.

_____ There are no Sundays on which Maria is unable to attend church.

_____ Maria never gets bored when she is attending church services.

_____ If Maria attends church every Sunday, then she is a person who values faith.

5. An automatic bell above the front door rings whenever a customer enters the front door of the Town Convenience Store. Therefore, one can accurately determine the number of customers who enter Town Convenience on any given day simply by counting the number of rings from the front door bell.

(1) The argument depends on which of the following assumptions?
(2) The conclusion follows logically if which of the following is assumed?

_____ The bell rings each time a customer leaves the store through the front door.

_____ The bell does not ring when employees enter the store.

_____ The bell never fails to ring when a customer enters the front door of the store.

_____ On any given day, there are customers who visit the Town Convenience Store.

SOLUTIONS: Necessary and Sufficient Assumptions

1. Studies have shown that private tutoring is an effective approach for learning a second language. Thus, private tutoring is a fun way to learn a second language.

(1) Which of the following is an assumption that is required in order for the argument to hold?
(2) The conclusion follows logically if which of the following is assumed?

  2 Anything that is an effective approach for accomplishing a goal is also a fun approach for accomplishing that goal.

This is enough to validate the conclusion, and more. We don't need to assume that *anything* that is effective is also fun. This is sufficient, but not necessary.

  X The studies mentioned were conducted by a team of reputable linguists.

This is a premise booster! We already know that studies have shown that private tutoring is an effective way to learn a second language. We don't need to support the premise, and we certainly don't need to assume that the study was conducted by linguists. Wouldn't it be okay if the study were conducted by social scientists?

  1 Some activities that are effective are also fun.

This answer might seem too weak to be relevant, but try negating it. *No activity that is effective is also fun.* If that were the case, how could one conclude that tutoring is fun?

2. Of the 25 movies released this year, only the three highest rated movies ("first" being the highest rating) of the year will be eligible for the award. Therefore, the movie *Darkness* will not be eligible for the award.

(1) Which of the following is an assumption upon which the argument relies?
(2) The conclusion can be properly drawn if which of the following is assumed?

  2 Of the 25 movies released this year, *Darkness* was the lowest rated movie.

If it's the lowest rated, we know for sure that it's not getting an award. Sufficient. But do we *need* it to be the *lowest* rated? No. Anywhere from 4th to 25th would suffice.

  1, 2 Of the 25 movies released this year, *Darkness* was rated fourth or worse.

This has to be true for the conclusion to hold, so this is necessary. It's also sufficient to know that *Darkness* is not getting an award.

  X Many of the people who saw *Darkness* did not enjoy it.

Who cares if many people didn't enjoy it? This tells us nothing about the rating.

  1 Of the 25 movies released this year, *Darkness* was not rated second.

We need this to be true in order for the conclusion to hold. We can tell by negating it: *Darkness* WAS rated second. This negation would destroy the argument, which means the original assumption is required. Is this assumption sufficient? No. Knowing that it was not rated second doesn't eliminate the possibility that it was rated first or third.

3. The monthly revenue for Chad's Burger Shack was higher in July than it was in April. Thus, Chad's Burger Shack must have sold more burgers in July than in April.

(1) Which of the following is an assumption upon which the argument depends?
(2) The conclusion follows logically if which of the following is assumed?

_X_ Chad's Burger Shack is gaining popularity.

This might help us explain why the shack had higher revenues in July, but it doesn't help us determine if more burgers were sold.

_X_ In the summer months, people tend to dine out more frequently than they do at other times of the year.

Again, this might help us explain why the shack had higher revenues in July, but we're not interested in explaining the premise. We want something that makes it more likely that the increase was due to an increase in burger sales. This doesn't help.

_1_ The difference in revenue between April and July was not due solely to an increase in beverage sales.

This is a necessary assumption. Try negating it: The increase WAS due solely to an increase in beverage sales. If this is the case, then the increase was NOT due to an increase in burger sales! The negated assumption destroys the argument. Note that this assumption on its own is not enough to guarantee the conclusion. Perhaps there's still another explanation for the increased revenue, such as higher prices or an increased number of t-shirt sales, or both.

_X_ A third-party audit verified that the monthly revenue for Chad's Burger Shack was higher in July than it was in April.

We certainly don't need to boost the premise in this way.

_X_ The difference in revenue between April and July was due solely to an increase in the sales price of a Chad's Burger Shack burger.

Careful! This says the increase WAS due solely to an increase in the sales price of the burgers. If this is the case, then we know that the *number* of burgers sold was NOT the cause of the increase in revenue. By providing an alternate explanation for the increase, this assumption does the exact opposite of what we want. It weakens the argument.

_X_ Total costs for Chad's Burger Shack were not lower in July than they were in April.

This is irrelevant. Costs have nothing to do with revenue.

_2_ For any restaurant, any difference in revenue from month to month can be explained by a difference in the number of burgers sold.

This may be far-fetched, but it's certainly enough to guarantee that the increase at Chad's was due to the number of burgers sold. While it's sufficient to guarantee the conclusion, it's certainly not necessary to assume that this is the case for *any* restaurant.

4. Maria must be a person who values faith because she attends church every Sunday.

(1) Which of the following is an assumption upon which the argument relies?
(2) The conclusion can be properly drawn if which of the following is assumed?

_2_ Anyone who attends church every Sunday is a person who values faith, family, and community.

Sufficient! If anyone who attends church every Sunday values faith, family, and community, then Maria attending church every Sunday guarantees that she values faith. We don't *need* to assume that this is the case for *anyone,* or that anyone who attends church every Sunday values family and community in addition to faith, but it's certainly enough.

_X_ There are no Sundays on which Maria is unable to attend church.

We already know this to be true. She attends church every Sunday. No need to boost the premise.

_X_ Maria never gets bored when she is attending church services.

Irrelevant. Don't be tempted into thinking that those who are faithful don't get bored.

_1, 2_ If Maria attends church every Sunday, then she is a person who values faith.

This is both necessary and sufficient. It allows us to draw the conclusion, but if we negate the answer, we cannot.

5. An automatic bell above the front door rings whenever a customer enters the front door of the Town Convenience Store. Therefore, one can accurately determine the number of customers who enter Town Convenience on any given day simply by counting the number of rings from the front door bell.

(1) The argument depends on which of the following assumptions?
(2) The conclusion follows logically if which of the following is assumed?

_X_ The bell rings each time a customer leaves the store through the front door.

This hurts the argument! If the bell rings when customers leave, then our counting would get messed up. We need to assume that the bell does NOT ring when customers leave. This assumption does the exact opposite of what we want.

_1_ The bell does not ring when employees enter the store.

We need this to be true. We can negate it to be sure: The bell DOES ring when employees enter. This would mess up our counting of customers, right? The negation destroys the argument, so the assumption is necessary.

_X_ The bell never fails to ring when a customer enters the front door of the store.

Premise booster! We already know this to be true. The passage tells us "An automatic bell above the front door rings whenever a customer enters the front door of the Town Convenience Store."

_X_ On any given day, there are customers who visit the Town Convenience Store.

We don't need to assume that customers visit the store. All we care about is counting them when they do come.

Negating Assumptions

Negating an assumption is a great way to decide between two tempting answers for a Necessary Assumption question. However, some assumptions are surprisingly tricky to negate. Let's look at some of the twists that we might have to contend with.

Let's start with a basic example:

> Darnell walked to the store.

This is pretty straightforward to negate; simply negate the verb:

> Darnell did not walk to the store.

But how would you negate the following sentence?

> Sasha always walks to the store.

Perhaps you thought, "Sasha never walks to the store." Or perhaps you arrived at, "Sasha does not always walk to the store."

If you're told that Sasha always walks to the store and you want to dispute that claim, do you need to prove that Sasha *never* walks to the store? No. You only need to prove that she does not *always* walk to the store. Do not jump to the most extreme negation of a statement if there's a less extreme version that negates the statement. With statements that establish how many or how often something occurs, negating the statement does not require negating the verb. Instead, you should focus on the modifier.

For example, try negating this statement:

> Some New Yorkers are quite friendly.

Imagine you are hired to defend this statement and debate anyone who disagrees with it. Odd occupation, but you take your job seriously. If someone were to say, "No, some New Yorkers are not friendly." Does he disagree with you? Not necessarily. You do not have to debate this individual. You could respond with, "I agree with you, friend, some of them are not friendly, but I still believe that some *are* quite friendly."

What would be the negation of the statement you've been hired to defend? It would be "No New Yorker is quite friendly." Similar to the previous example, to negate the pro-New Yorker statement, we do not negate the verb, but the modifier "some."

In summary, if there's a modifier in a statement, negate that. If there is no modifier, negate the central verb.

DRILL IT: Negating Statements

Negate each of the following. For many of the statements, there are multiple correct answers. See if you can derive more than one.

1. All of us are with you.

2. Some dogs are vicious.

3. Most of these apples are rotten.

4. Not all of the pots are ready.

5. None of the actors is in the union.

6. John is probably the tallest.

7. It is unlikely that Simone will come.

8. Lisa never apologizes.

9. The prettiest houses are always painted white.

10. Francine sometimes sneaks off to eat candy.

11. Toni lives with neither water nor electricity.

12. People who suffer from migraines sometimes feel better simply by drinking water.

13. There have been many instances in which the team has proven itself to be honorable.

SOLUTIONS: Negating Statements

Note that there are often multiple ways to state a negation.

1. All of us are with you.

> Not all of us are with you.
> Some of us are not with you.

2. Some dogs are vicious.

> No dog is vicious.
> All dogs are not vicious.

3. Most of these apples are rotten.

> At least half of these apples are not rotten.

4. Not all of the pots are ready.

> All of the pots are ready.

5. None of the actors is in the union.

> Some of the actors are in the union.
> Not all of the actors are not in the union.

6. John is probably the tallest.

> It is not likely that John is the tallest.

7. It is unlikely that Simone will come.

> It is not unlikely that Simone will come.

8. Lisa never apologizes.

> Lisa sometimes apologizes.

9. The prettiest houses are always painted white.

> The prettiest houses are not always painted white.
> Some of the prettiest houses are not painted white.

10. Francine sometimes sneaks off to eat candy.

> Francine does not sneak off to eat candy.
> Francine never sneaks off to eat candy.

11. Toni lives with neither water nor electricity.

> Toni lives with water or electricity.

12. People who suffer from migraines sometimes feel better simply by drinking water.

> People who suffer from migraines never feel better simply by drinking water.

13. There have been many instances in which the team has proven itself honorable.

> There have not been many instances in which the team has proven itself to be honorable.

You now have practiced using all the tools you'll need to tackle assumption questions. Let's practice with some real LSAT questions.

DRILL IT: Assumption Questions

Give yourself no more than 20 minutes to complete the following problems.

3

1. PT22, S2, Q1

Braille is a method of producing text by means of raised dots that can be read by touch. A recent development in technology will allow flat computer screens to be made of a material that can be heated in patterns that replicate the patterns used in Braille. Since the thermal device will utilize the same symbol system as Braille, it follows that anyone who is accustomed to reading Braille can easily adapt to the use of this electronic system.

Which one of the following is an assumption on which the conclusion depends?

(A) Braille is the only symbol system that can be readily adapted for use with the new thermal screen.

(B) Only people who currently use Braille as their sole medium for reading text will have the capacity to adapt to the use of the thermal screen.

(C) People with the tactile ability to discriminate symbols in Braille have an ability to discriminate similar patterns on a flat heated surface.

(D) Some symbol systems encode a piece of text by using dots that replicate the shape of letters of the alphabet.

(E) Eventually it will be possible to train people to read Braille by first training them in the use of the thermal screen.

2. PT32, S4, Q4

Psychiatrist: Take any visceral emotion you care to consider. There are always situations in which it is healthy to try to express that emotion. So, there are always situations in which it is healthy to try to express one's anger.

The conclusion of the argument follows logically if which one of the following is assumed?

(A) Anger is always expressible.

(B) Anger is a visceral emotion.

(C) Some kinds of emotions are unhealthy to express.

(D) All emotions that are healthy to express are visceral.

(E) An emotion is visceral only if it is healthy to express.

3. PT30, S2, Q15

During the recent economic downturn, banks contributed to the decline by loaning less money. Prior to the downturn, regulatory standards for loanmaking by banks were tightened. Clearly, therefore, banks will lend more money if those standards are relaxed.

The argument assumes that

(A) the downturn did not cause a significant decrease in the total amount of money on deposit with banks which is the source of funds for banks to lend

(B) the imposition of the tighter regulatory standards was not a cause of the economic downturn

(C) the reason for tightening the regulatory standards was not arbitrary

(D) no economic downturn is accompanied by a significant decrease in the amount of money loaned out by banks to individual borrowers and to businesses

(E) no relaxation of standards for loanmaking by banks would compensate for the effects of the downturn

4. PT33, S1, Q13

Ethicist: Studies have documented the capacity of placebos to reduce pain in patients who believe that they are receiving beneficial drugs. Some doctors say that they administer placebos because medically effective treatment reinforced by the placebo effect sometimes helps patients recover faster than good treatment alone. But administering placebos is nonetheless ethically questionable, for even if a placebo benefits a patient, a doctor might, for example, have prescribed it just to give the patient satisfaction that something was being done.

The ethicist's argument depends on which one of the following assumptions?

(A) A patient's psychological satisfaction is not a consideration in administering medical treatment.

(B) The motivation for administering a placebo can be relevant to the ethical justification for doing so.

(C) Medical treatment that relies on the placebo effect alone is ethically indefensible.

(D) The pain relief produced by the placebo effect justifies the deception involved in administering a placebo.

(E) Administering a placebo is not ethically justified if that treatment is not prescribed by a doctor.

5. PT11, S2, Q22

Oil company representative: We spent more money on cleaning the otters affected by our recent oil spill than has been spent on any previous marine mammal rescue project. This shows our concern for the environment.

Environmentalist: You have no such concern. Your real concern is evident in your admission to the press that news photographs of oil-covered otters would be particularly damaging to your public image, which plays an important role in your level of sales.

The environmentalist's conclusion would be properly drawn if it were true that the

(A) oil company cannot have more than one motive for cleaning the otters affected by the oil spill

(B) otter population in the area of the oil spill could not have survived without the cleaning project

(C) oil company has always shown a high regard for its profits in choosing its courses of action

(D) government would have spent the money to clean the otters if the oil company had not agreed to do it

(E) oil company's efforts toward cleaning the affected otters have been more successful than have such efforts in previous projects to clean up oil spills

3

6. PT22, S2, Q6

Astorga's campaign promises are apparently just an attempt to please voters. What she says she will do if elected mayor is simply what she has learned from opinion polls that voters want the new mayor to do. Therefore, voters are not being told what Astorga actually intends to do if she becomes mayor.

Which one of the following is a questionable assumption on which the argument relies?

(A) If she is elected mayor, Astorga will not be capable of carrying out the campaign promises she has made.

(B) The opinion polls on which Astorga's promises are based do not accurately reflect what voters want the new mayor to do.

(C) Most voters are unlikely to be persuaded by Astorga's campaign promises to vote for her in the mayoral election.

(D) Astorga has no strong opinions of her own about what the new mayor ought to do in office.

(E) Astorga does not actually intend, if elected, to do what she has learned from the public opinion polls that voters want the new mayor to do.

7. PT17, S3, Q14

Many artists claim that art critics find it is easier to write about art that they dislike than to write about art that they like. Whether or not this hypothesis is correct, most art criticism is devoted to art works that fail to satisfy the critic. Hence it follows that most art criticism is devoted to works other than the greatest works of art.

The conclusion above is properly drawn if which one of the following is assumed?

(A) No art critic enjoys writing about art works that he or she dislikes intensely.

(B) All art critics find it difficult to discover art works that truly satisfy them.

(C) A work of art that receives extensive critical attention can thereby become more widely known than it otherwise would have been.

(D) The greatest works of art are never recognized as such until long after the time of their creation.

(E) The greatest works of art are works that inevitably satisfy all critics.

8. PT32, S4, Q7

Figorian Wildlife Commission: The development of wetlands in industrialized nations for residential and commercial uses has endangered many species. To protect wildlife we must regulate such development in Figoria: future wetland development must be offset by the construction of replacement wetland habitats. Thus, development would cause no net reduction of wetlands and pose no threat to the species that inhabit them.

Figorian Development Commission: Other nations have flagrantly developed wetlands at the expense of wildlife. We have conserved. Since Figorian wetland development might not affect wildlife and is necessary for growth, we should allow development. We have as much right to govern our own resources as countries that have already put their natural resources to commercial use.

Which one of the following is an assumption on which the argument advanced by the Figorian Wildlife Commission depends?

(A) More species have been endangered by the development of wetlands than have been endangered by any other type of development.

(B) The species indigenous to natural wetland habitats will survive in specially constructed replacement wetlands.

(C) In nations that are primarily agricultural, wetland development does not need to be regulated.

(D) Figorian regulation of development has in the past protected and preserved wildlife.

(E) The species that inhabit Figorian wetlands are among the most severely threatened of the designated endangered species.

9. PT29, S1, Q20

The price of a full-fare coach ticket from Toronto to Dallas on Breezeway Airlines is the same today as it was a year ago, if inflation is taken into account by calculating prices in constant dollars. However, today 90 percent of the Toronto-to-Dallas coach tickets that Breezeway sells are discount tickets and only 10 percent are full-fare tickets, whereas a year ago half were discount tickets and half were full-fare tickets. Therefore, on average, people pay less today in constant dollars for a Breezeway Toronto-to-Dallas coach ticket than they did a year ago.

Which one of the following, if assumed, would allow the conclusion above to be properly drawn?

(A) A Toronto-to-Dallas full-fare coach ticket on Breezeway Airlines provides ticket-holders with a lower level of service today than such a ticket provided a year ago.

(B) A Toronto-to-Dallas discount coach ticket on Breezeway Airlines costs about the same amount in constant dollars today as it did a year ago.

(C) All full-fare coach tickets on Breezeway Airlines cost the same in constant dollars as they did a year ago.

(D) The average number of coach passengers per flight that Breezeway Airlines carries from Toronto to Dallas today is higher than the average number per flight a year ago.

(E) The criteria that Breezeway Airlines uses for permitting passengers to buy discount coach tickets on the Toronto-to-Dallas route are different today than they were a year ago.

Challenge Questions

10. PT30, S2, Q11

Teacher to a student: You agree that it is bad to break promises. But when we speak to each other we all make an implicit promise to tell the truth, and lying is the breaking of that promise. So even if you promised Jeanne that you would tell me she is home sick, you should not tell me that, if you know that she is well.

Which one of the following is an assumption on which the teacher's argument depends?

(A) Most people always tell the truth.

(B) It is sometimes better to act in a friend's best interests than to keep a promise to that friend.

(C) Breaking a promise leads to worse consequences than does telling a lie.

(D) Some implicit promises are worse to break than some explicit ones.

(E) One should never break a promise.

11. PT28, S3, Q16

Historian: We can learn about the medical history of individuals through chemical analysis of their hair. It is likely, for example, that Isaac Newton's psychological problems were due to mercury poisoning; traces of mercury were found in his hair. Analysis is now being done on a lock of Beethoven's hair. Although no convincing argument has shown that Beethoven ever had a venereal disease, some people hypothesize that venereal disease caused his deafness. Since mercury was commonly ingested in Beethoven's time to treat venereal disease, if researchers find a trace of mercury in his hair, we can conclude that this hypothesis is correct.

Which one of the following is an assumption on which the historian's argument depends?

(A) None of the mercury introduced into the body can be eliminated.

(B) Some people in Beethoven's time did not ingest mercury.

(C) Mercury is an effective treatment for venereal disease.

(D) Mercury poisoning can cause deafness in people with venereal disease.

(E) Beethoven suffered from psychological problems of the same severity as Newton's.

3

Historian: The spread of literacy informs more people of injustices and, in the right circumstances, leads to increased capacity to distinguish true reformers from mere opportunists. However, widespread literacy invariably emerges before any comprehensive system of general education; thus, in the interim, the populace is vulnerable to clever demagogues calling for change. Consequently, some relatively benign regimes may ironically be toppled by their own "enlightened" move to increase literacy.

Which one of the following is an assumption on which the historian's argument depends?

(A) A demagogue can never enlist the public support necessary to topple an existing regime unless a comprehensive system of general education is in place.

(B) Without literacy there can be no general awareness of the injustice in a society.

(C) Any comprehensive system of general education will tend to preserve the authority of benign regimes.

(D) A lack of general education affects the ability to differentiate between legitimate and illegitimate calls for reform.

(E) Any benign regime that fails to provide comprehensive general education will be toppled by a clever demagogue.

Some government economists view their home countries as immune to outside influence. But economies are always open systems; international trade significantly affects prices and wages. Just as physicists learned the shortcomings of a mechanics based on idealizations such as the postulation of perfectly frictionless bodies, government economists must look beyond national borders if their nations' economies are to prosper.

The argument's conclusion follows logically if which one of the following is assumed?

(A) A national economy cannot prosper unless every significant influence on it has been examined by that nation's government economists.

(B) Economics is weakly analogous to the physical sciences.

(C) Economic theories relying on idealizations are generally less accurate than economic theories that do not rely on idealizations.

(D) International trade is the primary significant variable influencing prices and wages.

(E) Some government economists have been ignoring the effects of international trade on prices and wages.

MANHATTAN
LSAT

_14. PT20, S1, Q20_

Some people have been promoting a new herbal mixture as a remedy for the common cold. The mixture contains, among other things, extracts of the plants purple coneflower and goldenseal. A cold sufferer, skeptical of the claim that the mixture is an effective cold remedy, argued, "Suppose that the mixture were an effective cold remedy. Since most people with colds wish to recover quickly, it follows that almost everybody with a cold would be using it. Therefore, since there are many people who have colds but do not use the mixture, it is obviously not effective."

Each of the following is an assumption required by the skeptical cold sufferer's argument EXCEPT:

(A) Enough of the mixture is produced to provide the required doses to almost everybody with a cold.

(B) The mixture does not have side effects severe enough to make many people who have colds avoid using it.

(C) The mixture is powerful enough to prevent almost everybody who uses it from contracting any further colds.

(D) The mixture is widely enough known that almost everybody with a cold is aware of it.

(E) There are no effective cold remedies available that many people who have colds prefer to the mixture.

DRILL IT: Solutions

3

1. PT22, S2, Q1

Braille is a method of producing text by means of raised dots that can be read by touch. A recent development in technology will allow flat computer screens to be made of a material that can be heated in patterns that replicate the patterns used in Braille. Since the thermal device will utilize the same symbol system as Braille, it follows that anyone who is accustomed to reading Braille can easily adapt to the use of this electronic system.

Which one of the following is an assumption on which the conclusion depends?

(A) Braille is the only symbol system that can be readily adapted for use with the new thermal screen.

(B) Only people who currently use Braille as their sole medium for reading text will have the capacity to adapt to the use of the thermal screen.

(C) People with the tactile ability to discriminate symbols in Braille have an ability to discriminate similar patterns on a flat heated surface.

(D) Some symbol systems encode a piece of text by using dots that replicate the shape of letters of the alphabet.

(E) Eventually it will be possible to train people to read Braille by first training them in the use of the thermal screen.

(C) is correct.

The conclusion of this argument is that anyone who is used to reading raised Braille dots can easily adapt to a new system of representing words as a pattern of heated dots on a flat surface. The argument explains that these readers will adapt easily because the new system will employ the same pattern as standard raised Braille. The core of this argument can be represented as:

New heated dots Braille uses the same pattern as raised dot Braille		Those who can read raised Braille dots will easily adapt to reading the new heated dot Braille.

One gap that might have come to your mind is whether these readers can transfer their skill from reading raised dots to reading heated flat dots. Maybe the nerves in our fingers that detect raised dots are different than those that detect heated ones. Or perhaps learning to read in one manner somehow "blocks" our ability to learn in another. As we can see, there are plenty of strange situations that would make this transfer a problem, so we can expect that the answer will eliminate one of these possibilities; indeed, eliminating an alternate solution is often what a necessary assumption does.

(A) is suspect because of the word "only," but let's dig into exactly why this answer is wrong (the word "only" does not mean that an answer is incorrect, but for many questions it is a warning signal). If we negate (A)—there are other symbolic systems that could be represented with heated patterns, (e.g., mathematical symbols)—traditional Braille readers might still find it easy to adapt to *this* heated pattern system. Negating (A) does not destroy the argument.

(B) also has a suspicious "only," but let's look at whether the negation of (B) destroys the argument: people *other than* current Braille readers (to paraphrase) will be able to adapt to the thermal system. Is that a problem for this argument? No! The traditional Braille readers may still find it easier to adapt than these newcomers. Negating (B) does not destroy the argument.

(D) is out of scope. It's unnecessary and irrelevant if there are other symbolic systems that work differently.

(E) is more tempting than (D) but is also out of scope. This argument is not about people who do not already read traditional Braille dots. While you probably were able to eliminate (E) based on it being out of scope, if you negate (E)—it will never be possible to train people to read Braille by using the heated Braille system (instead of training them with the raised dots)—we can still conclude that those who already know how to read traditional Braille would have an easy time of adapting to the heated system.

Bravo if you arrived at (C) without using the negation test and instead just eliminated the four rather sorry answer choices above; you're working wrong-to-right. But it's good to practice the negation test during your review as it's a good tool for when you're down to two tempting answer choices for a Necessary Assumption question. Let's practice it: if we negate (C)—people with the tactile ability to discriminate symbols in Braille do *not* have an ability to discriminate similar patterns on a flat heated surface—how could we conclude that these readers will be able to easily adapt? We couldn't. Negating (C) destroys the argument.

2. PT32, S4, Q4

Psychiatrist: Take any visceral emotion you care to consider. There are always situations in which it is healthy to try to express that emotion. So, there are always situations in which it is healthy to try to express one's anger.

The conclusion of the argument follows logically if which one of the following is assumed?

  (A) Anger is always expressible.
  (B) Anger is a visceral emotion.
  (C) Some kinds of emotions are unhealthy to express.
  (D) All emotions that are healthy to express are visceral.
  (E) An emotion is visceral only if it is healthy to express.

(B) is correct.

The conclusion of this argument is rather clear: there are always situations in which it is healthy to try to express anger. The support for this is that there are always situations in which it's healthy to try to express any visceral emotion. If you didn't

already notice the term shift, take a look at the core:

There are always situations in which it's healthy to try to express any <u>visceral emotions.</u>   There are always situations in which it's healthy to try to express <u>anger.</u>

Is anger a visceral emotion? We are looking for a sufficient assumption that completely fills this gap. Let's look at those answers that don't:

(A) links anger and expression, but we still don't know if anger is a visceral emotion. Furthermore, this argument is not about whether emotions are *expressible* but whether it's healthy to *try* to express emotions.

(C) does not link anger to visceral emotions.

(D) is similar to (C)—where's the anger? These answers might be tempting if you had not boiled down the argument to its core. (D) links visceral emotions to the expression of emotions. We already know from the premise that if an emotion is visceral, it's healthy to try to express it, and (D) reverses that, telling us that if it's healthy to express it, it must be visceral—this reversal of the relationship does not validate the argument. Also, notice how (D) illicitly replaces the argument's focus on *trying* to express with the actual expression of the emotion.

(E) is similar to (C) in that there's no linkage to anger. It's similar to (D) in that it provides a useless link from an emotion being visceral to whether it is healthy to express the emotion. Like (D), (E) focuses on the expression of the emotion, and not on *trying* to express the emotion.

We're left with (B), which is actually both sufficient and necessary. It's sufficient to make the argument "work" and we know that (B) is necessary because if we were to negate it, the argument would be destroyed. Boom!

3. PT30, S2, Q15

During the recent economic downturn, banks contributed to the decline by loaning less money.

3

Prior to the downturn, regulatory standards for loanmaking by banks were tightened. Clearly, therefore, banks will lend more money if those standards are relaxed.

The argument assumes that

(A) the downturn did not cause a significant decrease in the total amount of money on deposit with banks which is the source of funds for banks to lend

(B) the imposition of the tighter regulatory standards was not a cause of the economic downturn

(C) the reason for tightening the regulatory standards was not arbitrary

(D) no economic downturn is accompanied by a significant decrease in the amount of money loaned out by banks to individual borrowers and to businesses

(E) no relaxation of standards for loanmaking by banks would compensate for the effects of the downturn

(A) is correct.

The conclusion of this question's argument is that if the regulatory standards for loanmaking are relaxed, banks will loan more money. Thus, the conclusion is a relationship: *relax loan rules → more loaning*. The support for this is that after the rules were tightened, the banks loaned less money. Later on in this book, we'll learn a lot more about conditional logic flaws. But for now it's sufficient to say that we should be suspicious of any conditional relationships that we meet in Assumption Family arguments. Of course, the overarching relationship that we should be wary of is the argument core. Does the premise really require (or definitively lead to) the conclusion? But, we should also be wary of implied relationships like the ones we see in this argument. The core is a bit tricky to grasp, but it could be represented as follows:

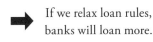

After loan rules tightened, banks loaned less. → If we relax loan rules, banks will loan more.

This may seem like a pretty reasonable argument,

but it's not! There are a few problems. First of all, do we know that the banks loaned less because the loanmaking rules were tightened? Maybe there was another reason they couldn't loan at that time. For a moment, let's ignore that and assume that we could say that the banks loaned less because the rules were tightened (*tightened loan rules → less* loaning). We still could not conclude *relax loan rules → more loaning*. The formal reason is that this is negated logic (just because A → B does not mean that NOT A → NOT B), but the common sense way of thinking about it is this: even though the tightened rules caused the banks to loan less (and remember that we're actually not convinced of this), we can't say that if those rules were relaxed the banks would loan more. Perhaps the banks would have to wait for something else to occur. Or perhaps banks will keep the purse strings tightened forever!

We have identified a couple of gaps in this argument. Now, what are we looking for? The question doesn't explicitly specify if we are to find a necessary or sufficient assumption, so we should be looking for a necessary assumption—something we know the argument is assuming. Let's take a look at the answer choices in real time:

(A) looks strange. It mentions the downturn, which isn't in our core. But it's too confusing to quickly assess, and necessary assumptions sometimes seem a bit off at first, so let's keep it.

(B) looks tempting. It evaluates a reason for the downturn. But we're not trying to explain the downturn! Eliminate this.

(C) is out of scope—we're not concerned with *why* the rules were tightened, but what effect the tightening had on loan activity.

(D) links downturns and loans; let's keep it.

(E) is out of scope. The argument is not about compensating for the effects of the downturn.

We're down to (A) and (D).

(A) rules out a different explanation for why the banks could not lend money during the economic downturn. Ruling out this reason makes it more likely that the reason was the tightened regulations. This is correct!

(D) asserts that whenever there is an economic downturn, there is no decrease in the amount of money loaned. That's suspicious since we learned that the recent economic downturn was in fact accompanied by a decrease in loans. Another suspicious aspect of this answer is that it introduces two new players, businesses and individuals. In fact, (D) is irrelevant to the argument.

4. PT33, S1, Q13

Ethicist: Studies have documented the capacity of placebos to reduce pain in patients who believe that they are receiving beneficial drugs. Some doctors say that they administer placebos because medically effective treatment reinforced by the placebo effect sometimes helps patients recover faster than good treatment alone. But administering placebos is nonetheless ethically questionable, for even if a placebo benefits a patient, a doctor might, for example, have prescribed it just to give the patient satisfaction that something was being done.

The ethicist's argument depends on which one of the following assumptions?

(A) A patient's psychological satisfaction is not a consideration in administering medical treatment.

(B) The motivation for administering a placebo can be relevant to the ethical justification for doing so.

(C) Medical treatment that relies on the placebo effect alone is ethically indefensible.

(D) The pain relief produced by the placebo effect justifies the deception involved in administering a placebo.

(E) Administering a placebo is not ethically justified if that treatment is not prescribed by a doctor.

Before you read this explanation, go ahead and try negating each answer choice and determine whether it destroys the argument. When it

comes to the negation technique, use it or lose it!

(B) is correct.

The conclusion of this argument is in the last sentence: administering placebos is ethically questionable. That's a strong conclusion! The reasoning is given in that same sentence: a doctor might have prescribed it just to give the patient satisfaction that something was being done. The first two sentences of the argument provide a lot of useful background information and very intelligent opposing points, but the core of this argument is all in the final sentence:

A doctor might prescribe a placebo only to give the patient satisfaction that something was being done. Administering a placebo is ethically questionable.

Notice that the conclusion discusses "administering" while the premise is about "prescribing." Perhaps the answer—a necessary assumption—will address this gap. However, there is a larger gap in this argument. What topic is mentioned in the conclusion that is not discussed in the premise? Ethics! We must assume something about what is and is not ethically questionable vis-à-vis prescribing drugs. It would be a waste of our time to try to predict the answer beyond this, since necessary assumptions can be rather unpredictable. With that in mind, let's look at the answer choices in real-time mode:

(A) looks good! While it does not mention ethics, it uses a broader term, "a consideration" that may include ethical evaluations, and it links that to something discussed in the premise, a patient's satisfaction.

(B) looks good too! It links ethics and the motivation for administering a placebo.

(C) is incorrect though tempting. The core is not about doctors prescribing *only* a placebo, or, to be as specific as the LSAT requires, it's not about a treatment relying *only* on the placebo effect. The

3

"only" in the argument refers to the only *reason* that the doctor prescribes the placebo, not the only *thing* the doctor prescribes—he or she may be prescribing many other drugs along with that placebo.

(D) may actually weaken the conclusion. If the deception is justified, why would the placebo be ethically questionable?

(E) is out of scope—we're only talking about placebos prescribed by a doctor.

Back to (A). On second thought, "considerations" is pretty vague. We're interested in ethics! Let's apply the negation test and get rid of the "not": A patient's psychological satisfaction is ~~not~~ a consideration in administering medical treatment. Does this disrupt the argument and its conclusion that administering a placebo may be ethically questionable? No! Even if the patient's feelings are a consideration, other considerations may be more important.

Indeed, (B) is correct. If we negate it—the motivation for administering a placebo is NOT relevant to the ethical justification for doing so— the argument falls apart. The premise supporting the conclusion is the motivation behind prescribing the medicine.

5. PT11, S2, Q22

Oil company representative: We spent more money on cleaning the otters affected by our recent oil spill than has been spent on any previous marine mammal rescue project. This shows our concern for the environment.

Environmentalist: You have no such concern. Your real concern is evident in your admission to the press that news photographs of oil-covered otters would be particularly damaging to your public image, which plays an important role in your level of sales.

The environmentalist's conclusion would be properly drawn if it were true that the

(A) oil company cannot have more than one motive for cleaning the otters affected by the oil spill

(B) otter population in the area of the oil spill could not have survived without the cleaning project

(C) oil company has always shown a high regard for its profits in choosing its courses of action

(D) government would have spent the money to clean the otters if the oil company had not agreed to do it

(E) oil company's efforts toward cleaning the affected otters have been more successful than have such efforts in previous projects to clean up oil spills

(A) is correct.

At first glance, this argument looks like one in which we're asked to find the point of disagreement—we'll learn about those questions later—but this is actually asking for a sufficient assumption. The oil company representative, who we'll refer to respectfully as "Oil Man," argues that his company is concerned about the environment. He supports this by pointing out that the company has spent more money on the current otter-and-oil fiasco than on any previous marine mammal rescue project.

The Environmentalist—and we'll call her just that—disagrees with the Oil Man, arguing that the company has no such concern. Her reasoning is that the company admitted that bad press about the oil-soaked otters would be bad publicity and thus damaging to sales.

The question asks about properly drawing the Environmentalist's conclusion, so we only need to focus on her argument. While it's not crucial to read the question stem before the stimulus, here's an example where it could save you a bit of work, since there's no need to dig into the Oil Man's argument other than to absorb it as background (and in case the Environmentalist's argument refers to it).

| Oil Co. concerned about effect of bad publicity about oil-covered otters. | → | In cleaning up the spill, Oil Co. is not concerned with the environment. |

If you had trouble seeing the gap in this argument, consider this analogy:

| Nurses are interested in earning as much money as possible when choosing which hospital to work at. | → | Nurses care only about earning money when choosing where to work. |

Just because a nurse, or an oil company, is concerned with one issue does not mean that there are not other concerns at play. The assumption is that caring about money precludes caring about the environment.

(A) provides the link that we need. It allows for only one motive for cleaning the oil-soaked otters. Note that this is a *sufficient* assumption. The argument does not require that there be room for only one motive. All that is needed is that the oil company's financial concern in the matter somehow prevents the existence of an environmental concern.

(B) is irrelevant to the Environmentalist's argument. In fact, neither party discusses the survival of the otters.

(C) is suspiciously extreme. Why would it be necessary that for all time the oil company has been very interested in profit?

(D) is out of scope. The Environmentalist's argument is not about whether anyone, particularly the government, would have spent the money.

(E) is also out of scope since it addresses the success of the project, not the company's motivations for doing the project.

6. PT22, S2, Q6

Astorga's campaign promises are apparently just an attempt to please voters. What she says she will do if elected mayor is simply what she has learned from opinion polls that voters want the new mayor to do. Therefore, voters are not being told what Astorga actually intends to do if she becomes mayor.

Which one of the following is a questionable assumption on which the argument relies?

(A) If she is elected mayor, Astorga will not be capable of carrying out the campaign promises she has made.

(B) The opinion polls on which Astorga's promises are based do not accurately reflect what voters want the new mayor to do.

(C) Most voters are unlikely to be persuaded by Astorga's campaign promises to vote for her in the mayoral election.

(D) Astorga has no strong opinions of her own about what the new mayor ought to do in office.

(E) Astorga does not actually intend, if elected, to do what she has learned from the public opinion polls that voters want the new mayor to do.

(E) is correct.

The conclusion of this argument is tough to identify! The first and last sentences include "apparently" and "therefore," words that often signal a conclusion. While it's initially tough to say which of those two the conclusion is, it is clear that the middle sentence is used as a premise. We can build up from there. There we learn that in her campaign, Astorga is saying that as mayor she would do certain things and that she learned from an opinion poll that voters would want the mayor to do those things. These facts could support the first sentence, the idea that her promises are just an attempt to please voters. But it could also be used to support the final sentence—that Astorga is not saying what she actually intends to do. Even if you apply the therefore test to the first and last sentences it will be difficult to identify which is the final conclusion. In this case, we'll rely on the "therefore" that begins the final sentence; indeed,

3

that is the final conclusion of this argument. This core could be represented as follows:

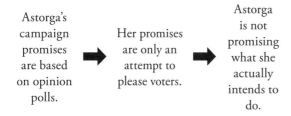

Or, the argument could be represented as follows:

Astorga's campaign promises are based on opinion polls. ➡ Her promises are only an attempt to please voters. ➡ Astorga is not promising what she actually intends to do.

If we use this second core, we should focus on the last connection, as that's where the assumption in question is likely to be. Looking at either core, notice that the final conclusion introduces the idea of intention, whereas the premise is about what is said. Can we definitively conclude Astorga doesn't intend to do the things she says, just because she apparently says them because they are what the voters want to hear? Perhaps Astorga is a woman who keeps her promises even if those promises are not based on her own opinions! With that in mind, let's look at the answer choices:

(A) is tempting but wrong. Notice this answer is about what she is *capable* of doing, whereas the argument was about her *intentions*.

(B) looks good! If those polls are wrong, then how can we draw any conclusion based on them? But this is actually the reverse of what we're trying to do. We want to support the argument, not destroy it! It's the negated assumption, not the assumption itself, that should destroy the argument.

(C) is out of scope since it is about voters being persuaded, not whether Astorga intends to carry out her campaign promises.

(D) is irrelevant. Whether Astorga intends to carry out her campaign promises does not depend on whether she has strong opinions of her own.

(E) helps fill the gap. If we negate this answer—Astorga *does* intend to do what she promised—then the given argument makes no sense.

7. PT17, S3, Q14

Many artists claim that art critics find it is easier to write about art that they dislike than to write about art that they like. Whether or not this hypothesis is correct, most art criticism is devoted to art works that fail to satisfy the critic. Hence it follows that most art criticism is devoted to works other than the greatest works of art.

The conclusion above is properly drawn if which one of the following is assumed?

(A) No art critic enjoys writing about art works that he or she dislikes intensely.

(B) All art critics find it difficult to discover art works that truly satisfy them.

(C) A work of art that receives extensive critical attention can thereby become more widely known than it otherwise would have been.

(D) The greatest works of art are never recognized as such until long after the time of their creation.

(E) The greatest works of art are works that inevitably satisfy all critics.

(E) is correct.

This problem is a great example of how narrowing our focus to an argument's core makes it much easier to evaluate answer choices. The conclusion is the last sentence and the support is the main clause in the sentence preceding it:

Most art criticism is devoted to art that fails to satisfy the critic. Most art criticism is devoted to works that are not the greatest works of art.

Once we've boiled down the argument to this, casting aside the irrelevant information in the first sentence and the opening clause in the second, the gap should be crystal clear. This argument assumes that art that doesn't satisfy the critic cannot be one of the greatest works of art. Before we look at the answer that fills this gap, let's watch the other answers fall victim to our stick-to-the-core approach:

(A) does not link to the conclusion about being one of the great works of art.

(B) falls short for the same reason as (A).

(C) suffers from the same affliction as (A) and (B); there's again no connection to whether art can be considered one of the greatest.

(D) does link to the conclusion, but (D) fails to link to the premise. (D) does not mention art not satisfying critics.

We're left with (E), the sufficient assumption we've been looking for all our lives! It provides us this connection: *great work of art* → *satisfying all critics*, and thus the contrapositive, *NOT satisfying all critics* → *NOT a great work of art*. This is exactly what we anticipated.

8. PT32, S4, Q7

Figorian Wildlife Commission: The development of wetlands in industrialized nations for residential and commercial uses has endangered many species. To protect wildlife we must regulate such development in Figoria: future wetland development must be offset by the construction of replacement wetland habitats. Thus, development would cause no net reduction of wetlands and pose no threat to the species that inhabit them.

Figorian Development Commission: Other nations have flagrantly developed wetlands at the expense of wildlife. We have conserved. Since Figorian wetland development might not affect wildlife and is necessary for growth, we should allow development. We have as much right to govern our own resources as countries that have already put their natural resources to commercial use.

Which one of the following is an assumption on which the argument advanced by the Figorian Wildlife Commission depends?

(A) More species have been endangered by the development of wetlands than have been endangered by any other type of development.
(B) The species indigenous to natural wetland habitats will survive in specially constructed replacement wetlands.
(C) In nations that are primarily agricultural, wetland development does not need to be regulated.
(D) Figorian regulation of development has in the past protected and preserved wildlife.
(E) The species that inhabit Figorian wetlands are among the most severely threatened of the designated endangered species.

(B) is correct.

At first this question seems quite difficult. It's unclear how the second argument relates to the first one. But, like another problem we saw earlier, we only need to examine the argument for which we're asked to find a necessary assumption. In this case, it's the Wildlife Commission's. The conclusion of that argument is that the development of wetlands would cause no net reduction of wetlands and pose no threat to the species in those wetlands. The support for this is that there should be a regulation that the construction of replacement wetlands offset any future wetland development. It's a pretty straightforward core:

Replacement wetlands will be built to offset wetland development. Wetland development will cause no net reduction of wetlands and will not threaten the species that inhabit them.

Reading like a debater, you might ask yourself whether that suggested regulation will actually be put in place. However, the conclusion is set within the hypothetical world in which the regulation is instituted. Notice that it states that future development "would" cause no net reduction, that is, if the regulation were to exist. If the conclusion had been that future development *will* not cause any net reduction, we would be justified in

3

considering this shift a significant gap.

A gap that does exist is whether the newly constructed wetlands could accomplish all that the Wildlife Commission's conclusion suggests they will. Would the animals that inhabit those wetlands be able to move to the new ones, and would they survive there? Maybe the act of being moved or some subtle difference between natural and man-made wetlands would render the slimy wetland species unable to survive the switch. (B) addresses this potential flaw (assumption). Does (B) completely assure us that there will be no net reduction of wetlands and no threat to the relevant species? No. Perhaps there are other problems—perhaps these constructed wetlands are unsustainable, inevitably draining dry after a few seasons. However, we're not looking for a sufficient assumption.

(A) is out of scope—the argument does not compare the impact of different types of developments.

(C) is out of scope. There's no discussion of agriculture in the argument.

(D) is out of scope, as the success of previous regulations is irrelevant to predictions for the impact of the regulation discussed in the argument. Whether past regulations had failed—that is, the negation of (D)—also proves to be irrelevant because those failed regulations may have been poorly designed.

(E) is out of scope. The argument does not mention how threatened the affected animals are.

9. PT29, S1, Q20

The price of a full-fare coach ticket from Toronto to Dallas on Breezeway Airlines is the same today as it was a year ago, if inflation is taken into account by calculating prices in constant dollars. However, today 90 percent of the Toronto-to-Dallas coach tickets that Breezeway sells are discount tickets and only 10 percent are full-fare tickets, whereas a year ago half were discount tickets and half were full-fare tickets. Therefore, on average, people pay less today in constant dollars for a

Breezeway Toronto-to-Dallas coach ticket than they did a year ago.

Which one of the following, if assumed, would allow the conclusion above to be properly drawn?

(A) A Toronto-to-Dallas full-fare coach ticket on Breezeway Airlines provides ticket-holders with a lower level of service today than such a ticket provided a year ago.

(B) A Toronto-to-Dallas discount coach ticket on Breezeway Airlines costs about the same amount in constant dollars today as it did a year ago.

(C) All full-fare coach tickets on Breezeway Airlines cost the same in constant dollars as they did a year ago.

(D) The average number of coach passengers per flight that Breezeway Airlines carries from Toronto to Dallas today is higher than the average number per flight a year ago.

(E) The criteria that Breezeway Airlines uses for permitting passengers to buy discount coach tickets on the Toronto-to-Dallas route are different today than they were a year ago.

(B) is correct.

This is a tricky argument to follow! We first learn that the "real" (inflation-adjusted) price of a specific airline ticket has stayed constant over the course of the year. This means that if inflation were 5% (!), then the ticket price would have risen 5% as well, leaving the "real" price unchanged.

Now, 90% of the tickets sold for this trip are discounted. A year ago only 50% were. The conclusion is that people are paying less on average for these tickets than a year ago, which would seem to make sense if more tickets today are sold at a discount. Here's the core of this argument:

Number of discounted Toronto-Dallas tickets rose from 50% to 90% (last year to today).

+

Price for regular ticket remained constant.

On average, people are paying less per Toronto-Dallas ticket today than a year ago.

3

At first glance, this sounds like a solid argument! But, this is an Assumption Family question, so we know there's a gap. Since this is a number-based argument, let's play with the numbers. How could we shift the numbers so that even though there are more discounted tickets sold, people are NOT paying less on average? It is not necessary that we actually predict how that could happen; it's enough to know that this is what the correct answer will probably resolve. With that in mind, let's look at the answer choices. Many of them can be eliminated, as usual, simply because they don't address the core:

(A) is about the level of service—out of scope!

(B) is about the discount amount—it's not immediately clear how this impacts the argument. Let's keep it.

(C) is about the cost of the tickets—looks useful. Let's keep it.

(D) is out of scope. We're not concerned with the number of passengers; the conclusion is about the average price paid.

(E) is about how the airline decided who would receive a discount—out of scope!

We're down to (B) and (C). (B) states that the amount of the discount has remained constant. While this isn't a Necessary Assumption question, let's consider the negation of this and see if it calls the argument into question (note that while negation is technically a tool for evaluating necessary assumptions, it can also be useful for grasping other assumptions). What if the discount ticket did NOT cost the same amount this year as last? Let's say it used to be $80 (with the usual

ticket being $150), but now it's $140. Even if a lot more people are enjoying the new discount, since it's no longer a significant discount, the effect on the average price paid would be minimal. But, as (B) suggests, if the discounted tickets were locked at a certain price, then a significant increase in the number of people receiving that discount would lower the average price paid. (B) looks like a useful assumption! (For the logic geeks out there, another version of a negated (B) scenario is that the discount tickets are even cheaper this year than last year, a change that would actually support the argument. That's why the negation test, as used here for a sufficient assumption, is simply a tool for considering what role an assumption might play and one can't be as formulaic about whether it directly destroys the argument).

(C) has two problems with it. First of all, since we already know that the regular tickets cost the same amount, this is a premise booster. If you read with a close eye, you also might have noticed that (C) is about *all* full-fare coach tickets. This argument is about only the Toronto-to-Dallas route.

Challenge Questions

10. PT30, S2, Q11

Teacher to a student: You agree that it is bad to break promises. But when we speak to each other we all make an implicit promise to tell the truth, and lying is the breaking of that promise. So even if you promised Jeanne that you would tell me she is home sick, you should not tell me that, if you know that she is well.

Which one of the following is an assumption on which the teacher's argument depends?

(A) Most people always tell the truth.
(B) It is sometimes better to act in a friend's best interests than to keep a promise to that friend.
(C) Breaking a promise leads to worse consequences than does telling a lie.
(D) Some implicit promises are worse to break than some explicit ones.
(E) One should never break a promise.

(D) is correct.

One can imagine that this student is not enjoying this conversation! If he's an LSAT student, he's found the conclusion of the teacher's argument: even if he promised Jeanne that he'd tell the teacher that Jeanne is home sick, the student should not say that to the teacher if Jeanne is actually well. Why not? According to the teacher, it is bad to break a promise and lying is breaking a promise since there's an implicit promise to tell the truth whenever people speak to each other. The core of this argument, is as follows:

There is an implicit promise to tell the truth when speaking to another + it is bad to break a promise.	➡	You should not lie about Jeanne being home sick, even if you promised to do so.

This is a tricky argument to evaluate. Remember that our job is not to evaluate the premises. We must accept, for example, that there is an implicit promise to tell the truth when speaking with others. Instead, we must read like a debater and consider why the student might be justified in lying to the teacher. This isn't that hard to do if you put yourself in the poor student's shoes. He's actually made a promise to lie on Jeanne's behalf. He would be breaking *that* promise if he tells the teacher the truth. What a bind! More importantly for solving this question, what a gap! How is this student to decide which promise he should honor? This is what (D) resolves so that the teacher's argument is valid. If we negate (D)—there are no implicit promises that are worse to break than any explicit ones—we'd be left wondering why the student should honor the implicit promise when it's not worse to break that than to break the explicit one he made to Jeanne.

(A) is out of scope. We don't care what most people are doing.

(B) is tempting since it seems to address the conflict between the competing promises. But in fact, it is out of scope since the argument is not

about best interests. Furthermore, we can't say whether lying for Jeanne is in her best interest.

(C) is about consequences, making this answer out of scope as well.

(E) is quite tempting. It sounds like the sort of thing the teacher would agree with. "Don't lie to me," the teacher might say, "You've made an implicit promise to tell the truth when speaking to me, and *you should never break a promise!*" However, the student, if he had his LSAT wits about him, would reply, "But you're asking me to break my promise to Jeanne!" Indeed, the argument actually requires us to assume, as (D) notes, that one *should* break certain promises in order to honor others.

11. PT28, S3, Q16

Historian: We can learn about the medical history of individuals through chemical analysis of their hair. It is likely, for example, that Isaac Newton's psychological problems were due to mercury poisoning; traces of mercury were found in his hair. Analysis is now being done on a lock of Beethoven's hair. Although no convincing argument has shown that Beethoven ever had a venereal disease, some people hypothesize that venereal disease caused his deafness. Since mercury was commonly ingested in Beethoven's time to treat venereal disease, if researchers find a trace of mercury in his hair, we can conclude that this hypothesis is correct.

Which one of the following is an assumption on which the historian's argument depends?

(A) None of the mercury introduced into the body can be eliminated.
(B) Some people in Beethoven's time did not ingest mercury.
(C) Mercury is an effective treatment for venereal disease.
(D) Mercury poisoning can cause deafness in people with venereal disease.
(E) Beethoven suffered from psychological problems of the same severity as Newton's.

(B) is correct.

There's a lot of information in this argument, so let's get to the core! The conclusion is that researchers finding traces of mercury in Beethoven's hair would confirm the hypothesis that venereal disease caused his deafness. The support for this is that mercury was commonly ingested in Beethoven's time to treat venereal disease. All the information about Newton is irrelevant to the core, which is simply this:

Mercury commonly ingested in B's time to treat VD. If mercury found in B's hair, he became deaf because of VD.

We're looking for a Necessary Assumption, but it's difficult to see the gap in this argument. Realistically, even those who answered this question correctly likely realized the relevant gap only upon seeing it in the answer choice. To see the gap that (B) hinges upon, let's debate the conclusion. Why might it be that finding mercury would NOT confirm the scandalous Beethoven-went-deaf-because-of-VD hypothesis? Perhaps we all have traces of mercury in us. Or, more specifically, perhaps everyone at that time was ingesting mercury. If we negate (B)—everyone in Beethoven's time ingested mercury—confirming that he ingested mercury would not confirm that he ingested it to treat venereal disease. Thus, (B) is necessary; it's required that some people did not ingest mercury in Beethoven's time, otherwise finding some mercury traces in his hair would indicate nothing other than the fact that he lived in the time when everyone ingested mercury.

(A) is not helpful to this argument. It would not be problematic for the argument if the negation of (A) were true, that is, that some of the mercury introduced into the body can be eliminated. Interestingly, it wouldn't be a problem for this argument if *all* the mercury introduced into the body could be eliminated since the argument is based on finding mercury traces and drawing a conclusion from that. The argument does not suggest that *not* finding traces of mercury would lead to any conclusion.

(C) is out of scope. The argument is not concerned with whether mercury can actually treat venereal disease.

(D) is very tempting. One might think that this is required because if mercury poisoning cannot cause deafness in people with venereal disease, then why would we be able to conclude that Beethoven went deaf because of the mercury he ingested? But look back at the argument and notice the small but definitive difference in focus. What does the argument suggest caused Beethoven's deafness? It wasn't the mercury but the venereal disease! The mercury would indicate only that he has the disease. The background about Newton may lead us to think this argument is about mercury poisoning causing problems, but the core of the argument is about something else.

(E) is clearly out of scope—there's no comparison being made between Newton and Beethoven.

12. PT33, S1, Q19

Historian: The spread of literacy informs more people of injustices and, in the right circumstances, leads to increased capacity to distinguish true reformers from mere opportunists. However, widespread literacy invariably emerges before any comprehensive system of general education; thus, in the interim, the populace is vulnerable to clever demagogues calling for change. Consequently, some relatively benign regimes may ironically be toppled by their own "enlightened" move to increase literacy.

Which one of the following is an assumption on which the historian's argument depends?

(A) A demagogue can never enlist the public support necessary to topple an existing regime unless a comprehensive system of general education is in place.

(B) Without literacy there can be no general awareness of the injustice in a society.

(C) Any comprehensive system of general education will tend to preserve the authority of benign regimes.

(D) A lack of general education affects the ability to differentiate between legitimate and illegitimate calls for reform.

(E) Any benign regime that fails to provide comprehensive general education will be toppled by a clever demagogue.

(D) is correct.

This is quite a tricky argument to follow! The conclusion is that some good regimes may be toppled by their efforts to increase literacy. The reasoning is that when the populace is literate but there is still no general education system, it is vulnerable to calls for change by demagogues, political opportunists playing on popular sentiment.

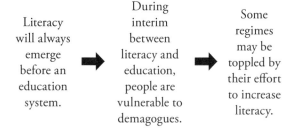

Notice that in the middle of the second sentence we encounter the intermediate conclusion. The "thus" is a clue that the rest of the sentence is a conclusion based on what we've just learned. What makes it an intermediate conclusion is that this conclusion is then used (Consequently…") to draw yet another conclusion.

Even when stripped to its core, this is a tough argument to evaluate. With a two-step argument like this, the assumption that the question hinges upon is usually between the premise or premises that directly lead to the final conclusion. In this case, one gap we find is that being vulnerable to a demagogue will actually lead, at least some of the time, to the toppling of a regime. Maybe demagogues are actually ineffective even if they attract the uneducated (yet literate) masses.

It turns out, however, that this question's answer hinges on the connection between the first premise and the intermediate conclusion. The argument assumes that literate people who lack an education will be vulnerable to demagogues. (D) is a necessary assumption that addresses this gap. If we negate this answer—a lack of general

education does NOT affect the ability to discern whether a call for change is legitimate—then how can we conclude that literate people will be more vulnerable to demagogues until a general education system is put in place? With a negated (D), the lack of education is irrelevant to people's ability to distinguish true reformers from mere opportunists.

(A) is tempting. It seems to address the gap we identified between the intermediate conclusion and the final one: can a demagogue actually topple a regime? However, (A) is the reverse of what we want! It states that a demagogue can *never* do what it takes to topple a regime.

(B) does not link either conclusion to the premises that support them. Furthermore, it's suspiciously strong. Indeed, the argument does not depend on it being true that if there were *no* literacy there would be *no* general awareness of injustice. Finally, (B) is essentially a premise booster since we already have been told that increased literacy informs *more* people of injustices.

(C) is tempting. It links education to the preservation of the benign regimes. The argument concludes that a lack of education leads to some of those regimes being toppled, but that does not require that having an education will definitely protect those regimes. It is not necessary that *any* education system can protect a benign regime; the argument could be valid even if there were a few education systems that did not.

Another problem with (C) is that it suggests we can use the negation of a relationship to support that relationship. We'll learn more about this later in the book, but in short, we cannot support *lack of education* → *some regimes toppling* by asserting that *NOT lack of education* → *NOT tend to topple*. Analogously, if we want to argue that *money* → *wild vacation*, it is not helpful that *NO money* → *NOT a wild vacation*. Even if the latter relationship is true, we don't know that having money will definitely lead to a wild vacation since there could be other factors that prevent a wild vacation (like inviting along grandma).

(E) is also very tempting! If we're trying to

support the idea that *lack of education → some regimes toppling*, it seems reasonable that *any lack of education → toppling regime*. However, this is more support than we need. The conclusion is only that *some* benign regimes will topple, not that *all* of them will. Negating this answer choice will reveal that it is more than required: not all regimes that fail to provide a comprehensive general education will be toppled by a clever demagogue. The conclusion is "soft" enough to allow for some regimes that don't provide a comprehensive general education to remain un-toppled.

Again, note that this is a rare argument in which the assumption that is tested is not one that connects to the main conclusion. While knowing how the LSAT tends to work is useful, flexibility is always key!

13. PT33, S3, Q21

Some government economists view their home countries as immune to outside influence. But economies are always open systems; international trade significantly affects prices and wages. Just as physicists learned the shortcomings of a mechanics based on idealizations such as the postulation of perfectly frictionless bodies, government economists must look beyond national borders if their nations' economies are to prosper.

The argument's conclusion follows logically if which one of the following is assumed?

  (A) A national economy cannot prosper unless every significant influence on it has been examined by that nation's government economists.

  (B) Economics is weakly analogous to the physical sciences.

  (C) Economic theories relying on idealizations are generally less accurate than economic theories that do not rely on idealizations.

  (D) International trade is the primary significant variable influencing prices and wages.

  (E) Some government economists have been ignoring the effects of international trade on prices and wages.

(A) is correct.

This argument concludes that if their nations' economies are to prosper, economists must look beyond their national borders. Why? Because, the argument asserts, economies are open systems that are affected by international trade. It can be hard to see the gap in this argument without boiling it down to the core and noticing what is discussed in the conclusion that is not mentioned in the premise:

Economies are open systems, affected by international influences.		Prosperous national economies require government economists to look beyond their national borders (when viewing their nations' economies).

When stripped to its core, it is clear that the economists are mentioned only in the conclusion. Why are the actions of the government economists relevant to the success of their nations' economies? (Some anarchists might argue that government economists are irrelevant at best!)

(A) is a sufficient assumption that allows the conclusion to be drawn. At first (A) may seem too extreme, but a sufficient assumption can go beyond the specific scope of the argument. In this case, (A) states that if a nation's economy is to prosper, the government economists of that nation must examine every significant influence affecting that economy. In other words, *economy prosper → economists have complete view*. Since we learn that economies are affected by international influences, we can amend this to be *economy prosper → economists have complete view, including international influences*, which is essentially the argument's conclusion.

(B) is tempting if you mistakenly think that the discussion of physicists and their realizations is relevant to the core of the argument.

(C) is similar to (B) in that it plays on a similar misreading of the argument. There's no discussion of idealizations in the core of the argument.

3

Idealizations are only discussed in relation to physicists.

(D) is suspiciously extreme. More importantly, it doesn't link to the conclusion about what government economists must do if an economy is to be successful. If anything, it links aspects of the premise to each other.

(E) is irrelevant because the argument does not state that there are national economies that are currently not prospering. It is a tempting answer if you think that the recommendation that people must eat spinach if they are to be strong is somehow strengthened by the idea that some people are currently not eating spinach. However, whether people are not eating spinach (or are ignoring international factors) is irrelevant.

> If you'd like more practice on iden-tifying assumptions, try playing "P + A = C" in the LSAT Arcade: (www.manhattanlsat.com/arcade)

_14. PT20, S1, Q20_

Some people have been promoting a new herbal mixture as a remedy for the common cold. The mixture contains, among other things, extracts of the plants purple coneflower and goldenseal. A cold sufferer, skeptical of the claim that the mix-ture is an effective cold remedy, argued, "Suppose that the mixture were an effective cold remedy. Since most people with colds wish to recover quickly, it follows that almost everybody with a cold would be using it. Therefore, since there are many people who have colds but do not use the mixture, it is obviously not effective."

Each of the following is an assumption required by the skeptical cold sufferer's argument EXCEPT:

(A) Enough of the mixture is produced to provide the required doses to almost eve-rybody with a cold.

(B) The mixture does not have side effects severe enough to make many people who have colds avoid using it.

(C) The mixture is powerful enough to pre-vent almost everybody who uses it from contracting any further colds.

(D) The mixture is widely enough known that almost everybody with a cold is aware of it.

(E) There are no effective cold remedies avail-able that many people who have colds prefer to the mixture.

(C) is the correct answer.

What a tricky problem! It's not particularly tough to find the conclusion of the cold sufferer's argument: the mixture is an ineffective cold remedy. And it's not tough to identify her reasoning: there are many people who don't use the mixture, and most people with colds want to recover quickly and would be using the mixture if it were effective. What is tough is that four of the answer choices are Necessary Assumptions—assumptions that we often cannot predict and that may strike us as irrelevant if we don't pause to consider them. Let's stick to the core:

If a remedy were effective, most cold sufferers would use it

+

there are many people not using it.

→ The mixture is not an effective cold remedy.

Finally, the way this argument works is that it establishes a rule: _remedy effective → most people use_ and then triggers the contrapositive: _NOT most people use → remedy NOT effective._ The use of a contrapositive is a valid logical move, so the problem (i.e., the missing assumption) in this argument must be the rule that if a remedy is effective, most people would use it. It isn't difficult to imagine reasons a cold sufferer would not use an effective remedy. For example, perhaps it's expensive, illegal, dangerous, or distasteful.

When we're looking at the answer choices for this type of EXCEPT problem, it's crucial to work from wrong-to-right and to remind yourself of your mission.

(A) is incorrect because it addresses a potential gap in the argument. Perhaps the reason that people are not using the remedy is not that it is ineffective but that it is not widely available. Good assumption, so eliminate.

(B) addresses another reason people may not choose this otherwise effective remedy: it has severe side effects. Eliminate it.

(C) is complex. It's unclear how preventing future colds is relevant to this discussion. Perhaps it explains why a limited number of people use the mixture. Keep it.

(D) is incorrect because, like (A) and (B), it eliminates a reason people might not use the mixture. If nobody knows about the mixture, then how would they choose it?

(E) may be tricky to place within the argument, but it is in fact relevant. Perhaps, it suggests, there is another remedy that is effective and that people prefer to the herbal mixture. If that were so, then it would explain why many people are not using the herbal mixture even though it is effective. (E) prevents that possibility, so we can eliminate it.

That leaves us with (C). This is correct because it is irrelevant to the argument. To prove its irrelevancy, negate it: the mixture is not powerful enough to prevent people from catching further colds. This doesn't mean that the remedy is effective or not. The argument doesn't suggest that for a remedy to be considered effective it must inoculate people from all future colds. That would be quite a cold remedy!

3

Chapter *of* 4

Logical Reasoning

Identify a Flaw Questions

Getting Familiar

To start, go ahead and try these four Identify a Flaw questions. Give yourself no more than six minutes total. We'll revisit these questions later on in the chapter.

PT36, S1, Q12

The consumer price index is a measure that detects monthly changes in the retail prices of goods and services. The payment of some government retirement benefits is based on the consumer price index so that those benefits reflect the change in the cost of living as the index changes. However, the consumer price index does not consider technological innovations that may drastically reduce the cost of producing some goods. Therefore, the value of government benefits is sometimes greater than is warranted by the true change in costs.

The reasoning in the argument is most vulnerable to the criticism that the argument

(A) fails to consider the possibility that there are years in which there is no change in the consumer price index

(B) fails to make explicit which goods and services are included in the consumer price index

(C) presumes, without providing warrant, that retirement benefits are not generally used to purchase unusual goods

(D) uncritically draws an inference from what has been true in the past to what will be true in the future

(E) makes an irrelevant shift from discussing retail prices to discussing production costs

PT14, S2, Q22

Gallery owner: Because this painting appears in no catalog of van Gogh's work, we cannot guarantee that he painted it. But consider: the subject is one he painted often, and experts agree that in his later paintings van Gogh invariably used just such broad brushstrokes and distinctive combinations of colors as we find here. Internal evidence, therefore, makes it virtually certain that this is a previously uncataloged, late van Gogh, and as such, a bargain at its price.

The reasoning used by the gallery owner is flawed because it

(A) ignores the fact that there can be general agreement that something is the case without its being the case

(B) neglects to cite expert authority to substantiate the claim about the subject matter of the painting

(C) assumes without sufficient warrant that the only reason anyone would want to acquire a painting is to make a profit

(D) provides no evidence that the painting is more likely to be an uncataloged van Gogh than to be a painting by someone else who painted that particular subject in van Gogh's style

(E) attempts to establish a particular conclusion because doing so is in the reasoner's self interest rather than because of any genuine concern for the truth of the matter

PT34, S2, Q9

A university study reported that between 1975 and 1983 the length of the average workweek in a certain country increased significantly. A governmental study, on the other hand, shows a significant decline in the length of the average workweek for the same period. Examination of the studies shows, however, that they used different methods of investigation; thus there is no need to look further for an explanation of the difference in the studies' results.

The argument's reasoning is flawed because the argument fails to

(A) distinguish between a study produced for the purposes of the operation of government and a study produced as part of university research

(B) distinguish between a method of investigation and the purpose of an investigation

(C) recognize that only one of the studies has been properly conducted

(D) recognize that two different methods of investigation can yield identical results

(E) recognize that varying economic conditions result in the average workweek changing in length

PT32, S1, Q10

To accommodate the personal automobile, houses are built on widely scattered lots far from places of work and shopping malls are equipped with immense parking lots that leave little room for wooded areas. Hence, had people generally not used personal automobiles, the result would have to have been a geography of modern cities quite different from the one we have now.

The argument's reasoning is questionable because the argument

(A) infers from the idea that the current geography of modern cities resulted from a particular cause that it could only have resulted from that cause

(B) infers from the idea that the current geography of modern cities resulted from a particular cause that other facets of modern life resulted from that cause

(C) overlooks the fact that many technological innovations other than the personal automobile have had some effect on the way people live

(D) takes for granted that shopping malls do not need large parking lots even given the use of the personal automobile

(E) takes for granted that people ultimately want to live without personal automobiles

4

Introduction

Let's begin this chapter by evaluating a simple argument:

Cats are friendlier than dogs.   Cats make for the best pets.

What's wrong with this argument? Perhaps you might think...

1. No! Dogs are friendlier than cats.
2. Cats and dogs are about as friendly as one another.
3. There is no accurate way to measure the friendliness of animals.
4. Friendliness is not the primary consideration for what makes a best pet.
5. There are other characteristics aside from friendliness, such as loyalty, that help determine a best pet.
6. Dogs make for the best pets.
7. There are pets other than cats and dogs that ought to be considered.
8. There is no way to crown a definitive "best pet."

All of these criticisms of the argument could, in real life, be valid. However, only some of these are representative of the types of *reasoning* flaws that you are typically asked to identify on the LSAT. Take a look through the list again if you'd like and see if you can determine which ones represent reasoning flaws.

For Identify a Flaw questions, you are not being asked to evaluate the validity of the premises, nor are you being asked, in any direct way, to evaluate the validity of the conclusion in and of itself. Rather, your task is to identify flaws in the relationship between the premises and the conclusion.

If you analyze the eight typical reactions above, you should see that the first three seem to question the validity of the premise on its own. #6 and #8 seem to question the validity of the conclusion on its own. Only #4, #5, and #7 represent flaws that call the relationship *between* the premise and the conclusion into question. These are the types of flaws you are consistently asked to identify on the LSAT.

If the previous few chapters have helped you get stronger at recognizing issues between premises and conclusion, this chapter should add to and reinforce that understanding. The reasoning skills required for Identify a Flaw questions are almost identical to those required for Assumption questions. In fact, these two question types can be considered two sides of the same coin.

It's a Flaw to Assume

For both Assumption and Identify a Flaw questions, we are expected to evaluate the connection between the evidence presented and the conclusion reached. There will *always* be a gap in this connection, and any such gap can be considered either as an unstated assumption or a flaw.

Let's use the earlier example to illustrate:

MANHATTAN
LSAT

Cats are friendlier than dogs. → Cats make for the best pets.

The author is making several assumptions in using this premise to support this conclusion, and most likely some of these assumptions are pretty obvious to you. He's assuming that friendliness is what determines a best pet (perhaps loyalty, intelligence, obedience, or protectiveness are factors). He's also assuming that there aren't animals other than cats and dogs that warrant consideration. Consider how an assumption can be presented as a flaw with just a few changes in wording:

"The author *assumes* that friendliness is the primary characteristic that defines a best pet."

Can be changed to…

"The author *takes for granted* that friendliness is the primary characteristic that defines a best pet."

"The author *assumes* no other pets need to be considered for best pet."

Can be changed to…

"The author *fails to consider* other pets for best pet."

Therefore, the work you've put into mastering Assumption questions should serve you well for Identify a Flaw questions. Remember that, in a general sense, assumptions play two broad roles—they either help to match up the premises and the conclusion (How does *friendliness* relate to *best* pet?), or they address other considerations relevant to the conclusion (What other pets need to be considered?).

We can use our understanding of these roles to shape how we think of Identify a Flaw questions. The right answer to any Identify a Flaw question will address one or both of the following concerns:

1. Is there a premise–conclusion mismatch?
2. What other factors has the author failed to consider in reaching his or her conclusion?

Let's discuss both issues in depth.

1. Is There a Premise–Conclusion Mismatch?

In the last chapter, we discussed "term" and "concept" shifts. Note that there will *always* be term and concept shifts between the premises and the conclusion (otherwise we'd just have the same sentence written twice!). What we want to be on the lookout for are the term or concept shifts that are significant enough to make us doubt that the premise is sufficient to validate the conclusion.

Here are a few examples of term and concept shifts that would be significant enough to warrant our suspicion:

P: People who floss **regularly** tend to have fewer gum problems later in life.
C: If you'd like to have fewer gum problems later in life, we recommend that you floss **daily**.
Who knows if daily flossing is the type of regular flossing that is good for you? Maybe flossing every 12 hours, or alternatively every three days, is the key.

P: The majority **of voters** will be Democrats.
C: Therefore, the Democratic candidate **will receive the most votes**.
Who knows if the Democratic voters will vote for this Democratic candidate?

P: Some of the judges **were surprised** by the flavors in the cake.
C: It's likely that they **will give it a low score**.
Maybe they were pleasantly surprised?

P: There are a lot more boys in this year's class than there were in last year's.
C: The girls will constitute a smaller proportion of this year's class.
For now, we'll leave it up to you to figure out what's wrong here.

If you are having trouble seeing these mismatches, there will be many more examples to come. If you think you've got it, great. Chances are, if you see a mismatch like this, the right answer will address it in one way or another. Now, the next thing to consider is, "How do the test writers make it more of a challenge to identify this mismatch?"

Let's use an example from earlier to discuss:

PT36, S1, Q12

> The consumer price index is a measure that detects monthly changes in the retail prices of goods and services. The payment of some government retirement benefits is based on the consumer price index so that those benefits reflect the change in the cost of living as the index changes. However, the consumer price index does not consider technological innovations that may drastically reduce the cost of producing some goods. Therefore, the value of government benefits is sometimes greater than is warranted by the true change in costs.
>
> The reasoning in the argument is most vulnerable to the criticism that the argument
>
> (A) fails to consider the possibility that there are years in which there is no change in the consumer price index
>
> (B) fails to make explicit which goods and services are included in the consumer price index
>
> (C) presumes, without providing warrant, that retirement benefits are not generally used to purchase unusual goods
>
> (D) uncritically draws an inference from what has been true in the past to what will be true in the future
>
> (E) makes an irrelevant shift from discussing retail prices to discussing production costs

We are asked to identify the criticism to which the argument is MOST vulnerable. Keep in mind that typically, even when an Identify a Flaw question is asked in relative terms—"most vulnerable" seems to indicate that we may compare multiple flaws—there will be just one answer choice that actually represents a flaw in the argument.

Let's model the reading process as it might play out in real time:

> The consumer price index is a measure that detects monthly changes in the retail prices of goods and services.

This is background information. The argument is about the consumer price index.

> The payment of some government retirement benefits is based on the consumer price index so that those benefits reflect the change in the cost of living as the index changes.

This is also background. This sentence links the consumer price index to government retirement benefits.

> However, the consumer price index does not consider technological innovations that may drastically reduce the cost of producing some goods.

The "however" sets up a contrast—the consumer price index doesn't consider this other factor. It's unclear at this point why this contrast is important.

> Therefore, the value of government benefits is sometimes greater than is warranted by the true change in costs.

This is definitely the author's main point.

In terms of the general structure of the argument, what we have is *background-background-counter to that background-"therefore" a conclusion.* The conclusion is a consequence of the previous sentence:

"However, the consumer price index does not consider technological innovations that may drastically reduce the cost of producing some goods."

At this point, we have a sense of the argument core:

> Consumer price index doesn't consider tech innovations that may drastically reduce cost of producing some goods. Value of government benefits sometimes greater than is warranted by true change in costs.

It is often true, particularly for challenging questions, that even though the reasoning issues are in the core, the key to understanding these issues lies outside the core. That is, it is in the other information (the background, or opposing points) that we come to understand the significance of issues in the core.

What is the relevance of this premise to the conclusion? Well, the benefits are based on the consumer price index. The author is saying there is a problem here—the consumer price index doesn't represent potential reductions in production costs.

Is this really a problem? In the background information, we learn that benefits are based on the index so that they reflect changes in the cost of living. This makes perfect sense. After all, the benefits are presumably meant to be used for *living costs.* Are the benefits flawed because the index doesn't reflect *production* costs?

No. It's not. And there's the gap. The author inserts production costs into an argument that doesn't seem to warrant discussion of that factor.

Ideally, for most Identify a Flaw questions, you want to go into the answer choices with this type of very clear sense of what the flaw or flaws are in an argument. Even so, as you evaluate the answers, you want to make sure to work from wrong to right. That is, even if you have a strong prediction about the right answer, you want to, in your first time through the answer choices, be on the lookout for reasons why four of the five answers are wrong. This is the most effective and efficient way to arrive at the right choice.

Let's rewrite the core here and evaluate the answer choices one at a time:

Consumer price index doesn't consider tech innovations that may drastically reduce cost of producing some goods. 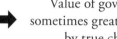 Value of government benefits sometimes greater than is warranted by true change in costs.

   (A) fails to consider the possibility that there are years in
       which there is no change in the consumer price index

Whether the index varies or stays the same has no direct bearing on whether production costs should be reflected in retirement benefits. We can eliminate this quickly.

   (B) fails to make explicit which goods and services are
       included in the consumer price index

This also has no direct bearing on the core. We don't need to know about every single item on the index in order to evaluate this particular argument involving the index. We can eliminate this quickly.

   (C) presumes, without providing warrant, that retirement
       benefits are not generally used to purchase unusual goods

This answer choice connects to the core in an interesting albeit indirect way—we can imagine that the consumer price index might be based on items that are usually purchased. Still, this answer choice has no direct bearing on the conclusion. Whether benefits are used for usual or unusual goods has no direct impact on whether production costs should be reflected in retirement benefits.

   (D) uncritically draws an inference from what has been true in
       the past to what will be true in the future

This argument does not use evidence from the past to claim that something will be true in the future. We can quickly eliminate this too.

We're down to just one:

   (E) makes an irrelevant shift from discussing retail prices to
       discussing production costs

This is the answer we anticipated. The fact that the consumer price index doesn't reflect changes in production costs is irrelevant to the issue of how the consumer price index is used to set benefits.

Consider now how the writers made it more of a challenge for you to identify the mismatch in the core. One challenge was the volume of information—it was imperative that you prioritized correctly. The second was that, in order to fully understand the elements discussed in the core, we had to reference the background information.

Let's take a look at another example. See if you can spot the significant shift between the premises and the conclusion in the argument before you evaluate the answer choices.

4

> *PT16, S3, Q24*
>
> A birth is more likely to be difficult when the mother is over the age of 40 than when she is younger. Regardless of the mother's age, a person whose birth was difficult is more likely to be ambidextrous than is a person whose birth was not difficult. Since other causes of ambidexterity are not related to the mother's age, there must be more ambidextrous people who were born to women over 40 than there are ambidextrous people who were born to younger women.
>
> The argument is most vulnerable to which one of the following criticisms?
>
> (A) It assumes what it sets out to establish.
> (B) It overlooks the possibility that fewer children are born to women over 40 than to women under 40.
> (C) It fails to specify what percentage of people in the population as a whole are ambidextrous.
> (D) It does not state how old a child must be before its handedness can be determined.
> (E) It neglects to explain how difficulties during birth can result in a child's ambidexterity.

What's the author's conclusion?

> …there must be more ambidextrous people who were born to women over 40 than there are ambidextrous people who were born to younger women.

How does he try to prove it? In this case, we can see that there are two premises that work together to support the conclusion:

> A birth is more likely to be difficult when the mother is over the age of 40 than when she is younger.

and…

A person whose birth was difficult is more likely to be ambidextrous than is a person whose birth was not difficult.

Thus, we can think about the core as follows:

Over-40 mother more likely to have difficult birth than when younger.

\+

A person with difficult birth more likely to be ambidextrous.

➡ More ambidextrous people born to women over 40 than to younger women.

Do you notice the mismatch? Think about it before reading on.

From these two premises, what can we conclude about people who are born to women over 40? Perhaps mothers over 40 are more *likely* to give birth to ambidextrous children, but that does not have to mean that they will be giving birth to a greater *number* of ambidextrous children. Notice that the conclusion is about the total number. Whether mothers over 40 give birth to a greater number of children would also depend on the proportion of children who are born to women over 40. If 50 percent of all children are born to women over 40, this argument makes a lot of sense. If 1% of all children are born to women over 40, well, the argument becomes significantly more dubious.

The point is not that you need to come up with hypothetical situations (though they can often be helpful in clarifying the specific mismatch). More important is that we recognize the mismatch between a likelihood and a total number, and that we recognize that the author has assumed a direct connection where there isn't one.

The correct answer, (B), reflects the consequences of this mismatch.

(B) It overlooks the possibility that fewer children are born to women over 40 than to women under 40.

None of the other answer choices address the gap between likelihood and amount.

Let's look back at an example we presented earlier:

P: There are a lot more boys in this year's class than there were in last year's.
C: The girls will constitute a smaller proportion of this year's class.

In this case, notice that the premise is about actual numbers, and the conclusion is about a proportion. As in the previous problem, this leads to a mismatch. We know nothing about the number of girls in this year's class—perhaps it has increased too, even more than the number of boys. In that case, the conclusion about the proportion could be incorrect.

The faulty link between proportion and amount is just one of the many issues that can be more easily spotted if you are consistently on the lookout for mismatches between the premise and the conclusion.

Now let's discuss the second of our primary concerns.

2. What Else Needs to Be Considered in Order to Evaluate the Conclusion?

Let's start this part of the discussion by evaluating another simple argument:

Janice is strong.   Janice is athletic.

Hopefully, you are reading with a critical eye and can see immediately that this argument is flawed. You can say that the flaw has to do with a mismatch between premise and conclusion—strong and athletic are not the same thing—and that would be 100% correct.

Another way to think about this flaw is that being strong is just one *part* of being athletic. What we commonly consider as being athletic often *also* entails speed and coordination, along with other traits. Many LSAT arguments are flawed because the author considers only one or two of what ought to be many determining factors.

Let's look at another simple example:

Janice is strong.   She must work out daily.

This is also a flawed argument because the author failed to consider alternatives, but in this case, it's a different type of consideration that has been forgotten: for what other reasons, and through what other means, could she be or get strong? Maybe she was born strong. Maybe she takes supplements to build muscle mass. We can't ignore these possibilities.

Take a look at one more argument. Identify the core, and try to figure out what else might be relevant to the conclusion.

> *PT19, S4, Q3*
>
> The number of calories in a gram of refined cane sugar is the same as in an equal amount of fructose, the natural sugar found in fruits and vegetables. Therefore, a piece of candy made with a given amount of refined cane sugar is no higher in calories than a piece of fruit that contains an equal amount of fructose.

We can think of the argument core as follows:

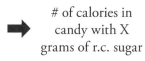

What is the author failing to consider? Think about it for a second before reading on.

A piece of candy is going to have calories that come from ingredients *other* than sugar. A piece of fruit will have calories that come from elements *other* than fructose. That is, calories from sugar are just one part of the total calories for a piece of candy, and calories from fructose are just one part of the total calories for a piece of fruit. Maybe the other ingredients in the candy have a lot more calories than the non-fructose parts of the piece of fruit.

Let's take a look at the answer choices that came with this argument. Evaluate each one relative to the core before reading the comments.

> (A) fails to consider the possibility that fruit might contain noncaloric nutrients that candy does not contain

Most of this answer sounds attractive, but since we're concerned with the number of calories, noncaloric nutrients are of no consequence.

> (B) presupposes that all candy is made with similar amounts of sugar

We're comparing candy and fruit with equivalent amounts of sugar and fructose rather than, say, two pieces of candy made with unknown amounts of sugar, and therefore the author does not need to assume this to be true.

> (C) confuses one kind of sugar with another

This is not the case. Notice it has little to do with our core.

> (D) presupposes what it sets out to establish, that fruit does not differ from sugar-based candy in the number of calories each contains

What this answer means is that the argument is using the conclusion to justify the conclusion. This is not the case. Furthermore, the actual conclusion is not simply comparing the calories in fruit and candy, but in a piece of fruit and a piece of candy that have respectively equal amounts of fructose and sugar.

> (E) overlooks the possibility that sugar might not be the only calorie-containing ingredient in candy or fruit

This is the answer we anticipated, and it is correct. The primary flaw in this argument was a failure to consider other relevant issues.

Now let's look back at an example from earlier in the chapter. Try solving it again if you'd like, and make sure to identify the flaw before moving on to the answer choices.

PT14, S2, Q22

Gallery owner: Because this painting appears in no catalog of van Gogh's work, we cannot guarantee that he painted it. But consider: the subject is one he painted often, and experts agree that in his later paintings van Gogh invariably used just such broad brushstrokes and distinctive combinations of colors as we find here. Internal evidence, therefore, makes it virtually certain that this is a previously uncataloged, late van Gogh, and as such, a bargain at its price.

The reasoning used by the gallery owner is flawed because it

(A) ignores the fact that there can be general agreement that something is the case without its being the case

(B) neglects to cite expert authority to substantiate the claim about the subject matter of the painting

(C) assumes without sufficient warrant that the only reason anyone would want to acquire a painting is to make a profit

(D) provides no evidence that the painting is more likely to be an uncataloged van Gogh than to be a painting by someone else who painted that particular subject in van Gogh's style

(E) attempts to establish a particular conclusion because doing so is in the reasoner's self interest rather than because of any genuine concern for the truth of the matter

The gallery owner's ultimate point is that the painting is a bargain at its price (by the way, what price?). How does he get there? Through the use of an intermediate conclusion: evidence makes it almost certain that the work is indeed a van Gogh. What's the evidence? The subject matter, stroke style, and color combinations match those of his other works.

We can think of the argument core as follows:

Subject matter, broad brushstrokes, and color combinations match van Gogh's work. → Painting is almost certainly van Gogh. → Painting is a bargain at its price.

In this argument, there are significant assumptions made at each point of connection.

In going from the intermediate conclusion to the conclusion, we are assuming that the painting being almost certainly a van Gogh is sufficient to conclude that the price of the painting, about which we have been given no information, is a bargain. We all know that van Gogh paintings are some of the most expensive in the world, but imagine if the price in question is $500 million. Is that still a bargain? We don't have enough information to say one way or the other.

There is an even more glaring jump from the original premise to the intermediate conclusion. We need to ask ourselves, are the three common characteristics mentioned (subject matter, brushstrokes, color combinations) enough to prove the painting to be a van Gogh? *What else needs to be considered?*

For one, surely, there are better, more specific ways to authenticate a van Gogh. It is the 21st century after all.

Furthermore, note that these are very broad and common characteristics—characteristics that paintings from other painters might share. Is it possible that another painter happened to paint similar subjects with broad strokes? Certainly. It's also easily plausible that it's a painting done deliberately in the style of van Gogh. He is an often studied and imitated artist.

The correct answer could have addressed any of these reasons to doubt the connections between the premises, the intermediate conclusion, and the final conclusion, and it happened to address a broad one: the evidence is simply not sufficient to prove that van Gogh painted the picture—someone else could have painted the picture in a style similar to his.

The correct answer is (D): provides no evidence that the painting is more likely to be an uncataloged van Gogh than to be a painting by someone else who painted that particular subject in van Gogh's style.

You might be asking at this point, *"But wait... Doesn't (D) bring in outside information? How is it not out of scope?"*

One of the best things you can do during the course of your studies is to develop solid instincts about which answers are "in scope" and which are "out of scope." In this case, (D), the correct answer, brings up other artists, and perhaps this made the answer less attractive to you at first.

Many test-takers rely on matching up key words in the answer choices with those in the argument to determine what is "in scope." While this might be helpful some of the time, it is not a reliable strategy. In fact, it will often be true that answers that can be considered out of scope will involve many key words that match those in the argument, and answers that will be in scope, like (D) here, will bring up elements that are not in the original argument.

The decision is not how the answer relates to the argument as a whole; for Assumption Family questions, the decision of in-scope and out-of-scope has to do with the relationship between the answer choice and the core. The answer is in-scope if you can see some relation between that answer and the core. It is out-of-scope if you can't. In this case, we can see that it is relevant to consider other painters when deciding whether or not van Gogh painted the picture.

Finding the core and evaluating the flaw or flaws in the core will set us up not only to find the right answer but also to quickly eliminate out-of-scope wrong answers. Very often, wrong answers are built using terms and ideas from other parts of the argument. If you don't know where to focus, these answer choices will seem much more attractive. If you are zeroed in on the core, you can more easily make quick eliminations.

Let's evaluate the incorrect answers. For Identify a Flaw questions, the majority of incorrect answers will have no direct connection to the core, or to the flaws that the argument is designed for us to anticipate. To illustrate the point, let's compare the answer choices to the core of the van Gogh argument:

Subject matter, broad brushstrokes, and color combinations match van Gogh's work. ➡ Painting is almost certainly van Gogh. ➡ Painting is a bargain at its price.

(A) ignores the fact that there can be general agreement that something is the case without its being the case

There is no general agreement being used as a premise, nor is general agreement something that is required in order for the conclusion to be true.

(B) neglects to cite expert authority to substantiate the claim about the subject matter of the painting

We have no indication that expert authority is required for the argument to be sound, let alone specifically required for validating a match of subject matter. Don't be tempted into thinking that we've got to justify the premise!

(C) assumes without sufficient warrant that the only reason anyone would want to acquire a painting is to make a profit

Profit is not relevant to the core.

(E) attempts to establish a particular conclusion because doing so is in the reasoner's self interest rather than because of any genuine concern for the truth of the matter

If you are the suspicious type, this answer might be attractive to you (the owner just wants to turn a buck!). Because of this, (E) is probably the most attractive of the wrong choices. But we've been given no indication at all that the owner is unscrupulous, and it's not our task to figure out whom we should be suspicious of. (E) may represent a tempting ulterior motive, but it does not represent a flaw in the reasoning used in the argument core.

4

Let's look at one more example for which it can be useful to think about "what else." Take 1:20 to try this question on your own first. Make sure to read like a debater and try to identify at least one flaw before moving on to the answer choices.

PT33, S3, Q15

Scientists hoping to understand and eventually reverse damage to the fragile ozone layer in the Earth's upper atmosphere used a spacecraft to conduct crucial experiments. These experiments drew criticism from a group of environmentalists who observed that a single trip by the spacecraft did as much harm to the ozone layer as a year's pollution by the average factory, and that since the latter was unjustifiable so must be the former.

The reasoning in the environmentalists' criticism is questionable because it

(A) treats as similar two cases that are different in a critical respect

(B) justifies a generalization on the basis of a single instance

(C) fails to distinguish the goal of reversing harmful effects from the goal of preventing those harmful effects

(D) attempts to compare two quantities that are not comparable in any way

(E) presupposes that experiments always do harm to their subjects

We can represent the core of the environmentalists' argument as follows:

Harm spacecraft does to ozone is equal
to that a factory does in a year.

+

Harm from factory is unjustifiable.

➡ Harm spacecraft does to ozone
unjustifiable.

To evaluate this, let's read like a debater. Think up a reason that the harm done by the spacecraft *is* justifiable. Yes, the spacecraft trip damaged the ozone layer, but...perhaps the experiments led to important breakthroughs and to methods for repairing the ozone layer. Right! Just because something causes some harm doesn't mean it's harmful overall—there are plenty of medicines that we consider beneficial regardless of their nasty side-effects.

The point is this: in evaluating whether something is justifiable or not, we must consider the *benefits* as well as the harms. This is the flaw in the argument. The author hasn't considered the relative differences in the benefits that a spacecraft mission—*to study the ozone*—and a factory might have in determining whether the action is justified. The author has come to a conclusion based on an incomplete equation.

While we might expect the correct answer to say something like "ignores the potential environmental benefits of conducting the experiments," the answer describes the flaw in a more abstract manner— another confirmation that we should work from wrong-to-right and not simply match words.

MANHATTAN
LSAT

The correct answer is (A): treats as similar two cases that are different in a critical respect.

The author compares the harm from factories with harm caused by a spacecraft mission without considering the relative benefits, and one benefit specifically—the mission can give us information valuable in healing the ozone, whereas the harm a factory does can't benefit the ozone in any obvious way.

Let's take a quick look at the incorrect answers, and relate them to the core:

> Harm spacecraft does to ozone is equal
> to that a factory does in a year.   **➡**   Harm spacecraft does to ozone
> \+   unjustifiable.
> Harm from factory is unjustifiable.

(B) justifies a generalization on the basis of a single instance

It's not clear what the generalization is, nor is it clear what the single instance is. This answer isn't relevant to this argument.

(C) fails to distinguish the goal of reversing harmful effects
from the goal of preventing those harmful effects

This is a tempting answer, but it does not directly address the issue of whether the harm is justifiable or not. Distinguishing between reversing and preventing harmful effects may be helpful in comparing two approaches to fighting ozone harm, but such a distinction would not prove or disprove that the harm the spacecraft does is justifiable.

(D) attempts to compare two quantities that are not
comparable in any way

It is true the argument compares the pollution caused by two elements (spacecraft and factories) that otherwise don't naturally match up together, but the argument does not compare two quantities that are not comparable. Furthermore, "in any way" is too extreme.

(E) presupposes that experiments always do harm to their
subjects

Doing harm to subjects is not relevant to the core.

To review, we know that for all Flaw questions there is going to be something wrong with the reasoning in the core of the argument. Therefore, we want to read with as critical an eye as possible. Look at the flaw from two perspectives—in terms of a mismatch, and in terms of what else needs to be considered—to better understand the issues in an argument in a clear and specific way.

Keep in mind that even though flaws can often more easily be seen from one perspective or another, our two perspectives—what is the mismatch and what else needs to be considered—are not meant to be separate or opposite. In fact, there is great overlap between the two.

Consider two simple arguments we've discussed in depth:

Cats are friendlier than dogs. ➡ Cats make for the best pets.

Janice is strong. ➡ Janice is athletic.

Note that in both cases, there are flaws that can be considered from either perspective. It is correct to say that being a friendly pet and being the best pet are not the same thing. It also correct to say that the author has failed to consider other pet types. The same dual perspective holds true for the second argument. It is correct to say that strong and athletic are not the same thing. It is also correct to say that being strong is only one part of being athletic, and that other issues need to be considered.

Your goal is not to categorize the flaw as fitting into one category or another. Your goal is to use both perspectives to understand the flaw as clearly as you can.

Causation Flaws

The most common reasoning flaws you'll see in Identify a Flaw questions are those that involve causation. Any claim of one element having a direct impact on another can be considered a claim of causation. Here are a few examples of causation claims:

"The success of the research project was due in part to the amount of money invested."
"The dishwashing soap is what removed the stain."
"Eating blueberries lowers one's chances of developing heart disease."

In each of the above examples, the impact that one element or idea has on another is stated directly. Note that on the LSAT, issues of causation will appear in two main ways—they will either be stated explicitly in the conclusion, or they will be implicitly involved in the connection that is assumed between the premises to the conclusion.

Let's use two simple arguments to clarify the difference:

Explicit:	Implicit:
"Ted didn't sleep well the night before the exam and performed poorly. Therefore, it's clear that his lack of sleep had a direct impact on his performance."	"Ted didn't sleep well the night before the exam and performed poorly. He would have performed better if he could have gotten more sleep."

The arguments are very similar, and they both involve a claim about causation. Notice in the first example that the causation claim is stated explicitly: "His lack of sleep had a **direct impact**...."

In the second example, that claim is never explicitly stated. Rather, it is implied. The author is making an unstated assumption in using the evidence to validate the conclusion—he is assuming that lack of sleep must have had some impact on Ted's performance.

In either situation, you should be very suspicious of the causation reasoning. For Identify a Flaw questions, almost all claims of causation that appear either explicitly in the conclusion or implicitly in the assumptions made by the author can and should be considered faulty. In these cases, the evidence provided will not be sufficient to validate the claim of causation.

This is a very important point to remember because the writers of the exam will do their best to make these claims of causation seem sound. In fact, some of the most challenging questions involving causation are challenging because the argument seems so very reasonable. Therefore, go in knowing that you should be suspicious! Consider the following example:

> Studies indicate that older antelope are, on average, more cautious than younger antelope. This proves that getting older causes antelope to become more cautious.

This argument seems pretty sound, right? Older antelope are more cautious, so it must be true that getting older is what *causes* these antelope to become more cautious, right?

When we are given a claim that "A," in this case getting older, has some direct impact on "B," in this case becoming more cautious, and the argument *seems* sound, we can walk through the following checklist:

1. Does the reverse make some sense too? Could B have a direct impact on A? Instead of age having some impact on the amount of caution, could it be that the amount of caution has some impact on getting older? Hmmm. Perhaps it seems unlikely, but see if you can imagine how this might be true and we'll come back to it later.

2. Could it be that something else impacts both A and B? It could be that certain antelope happen to have these two characteristics—older age and more cautiousness—but that these characteristics do not cause, or have any sort of impact, on one another. As an analogy, a certain car may have dents on the exterior, and stains on the interior, but these two characteristics could very well have nothing to do with one another.

3. Could it be that A and B have no impact on one another? It could be that certain antelope happen to have these two characteristics—older age and more cautiousness—but that these characteristics have nothing to do with causing, or having any sort of impact, on one another. As an analogy, state parks in Idaho always have both entrance fees and trees, but while trees and fees may rhyme, they have no causal relationship.

Now, let's go back to the first consideration, "Could B cause A?" Could cautiousness have some direct impact on getting older? It might seem unlikely at first, but consider a herd of antelope, and consider in particular the young in the group. Imagine that some of these young are cautious, and some of them are not. We've all seen nature shows—what might happen to some of these less cautious antelope? Chances are, they are more likely to run into unpleasant circumstances.

We are told that older antelope are, on average, more cautious. Could this be because, on average, more cautious antelope are more likely to survive to an older age? That is, instead of caution increasing with age, it's possible that caution is what allows the antelope to reach old age—it's possible that *B causes A*.

4

Keep in mind that our job is not to evaluate which mode of causation is more likely, although having instincts in this regard can certainly be beneficial. It is more important that we simply recognize that the argument is flawed in assuming one path of causation when multiple paths are possible.

If you had trouble seeing some of the alternative paths, that's perfectly understandable. Getting in the habit of asking the above three questions whenever you run into a claim of causation should help you develop better instincts about possible alternative modes of causation. Even when we can't imagine specific alternatives, we'll be in great shape to answer questions. We can feel confident that we can get the question correct as long as we can do two things:

1. recognize the claim or assumption about causation that the author makes, and
2. stay open-minded to answer choices that present information about possible alternative modes of causation.

Let's look at an example from earlier to illustrate:

PT39, S4, Q20

Some people believe that good health is due to luck. However, studies from many countries indicate a strong correlation between good health and high educational levels. Thus research supports the view that good health is largely the result of making informed lifestyle choices.

The reasoning in the argument is most vulnerable to criticism on the grounds that the argument

(A) presumes, without providing justification, that only highly educated people make informed lifestyle choices

(B) overlooks the possibility that people who make informed lifestyle choices may nonetheless suffer from inherited diseases

(C) presumes, without providing justification, that informed lifestyle choices are available to everyone

(D) overlooks the possibility that the same thing may causally contribute both to education and to good health

(E) does not acknowledge that some people who fail to make informed lifestyle choices are in good health

Note that the conclusion of the argument is an explicit claim of causation: "Thus research supports the view that good health is largely *the result* of making informed lifestyle choices." That is, making informed lifestyle choices has a direct impact on good health.

The evidence in this argument states a correlation between good health and high educational levels. What this means is that there is some statistical evidence that connects the people who happen to have good health and the people who happen to have high educational levels. Statistically speaking, having one changes the percentage chance that you have the other.

However, correlation is never sufficient to prove causation. That is, just because we know that there is a correlation between good health and high educational levels doesn't mean we know that good health is a part of the *reason* for high educational levels, or vice-versa. Perhaps both are consequences of another characteristic, such as living in a particular location. Or perhaps there is no causal connection, direct or indirect, between the two.

Let's think about our three questions:

1. Could it be the other way around? Does "B" impact "A"?
2. Could something else impact both "A" and "B"?
3. Could it be that "A" and "B" have no direct or indirect impact on one another?

We know that the correct answer will typically address one of these issues.

1. Could having good health help one make informed lifestyle choices? Maybe, but it is not likely. Regardless, we want to stay open-minded to this possibility when we evaluate the answer choices.

2. Could something else impact both good health and informed lifestyle choices? Absolutely. As stated before, where a person lives is just one example of something that could have an impact on the likelihood of both.

3. Could having good health and making informed lifestyle choices have no impact (or, in this case, a small impact) on one another? Yes. We've got a pretty strong conclusion here ("is largely the result"), and not enough evidence to back it up.

The correct answer for this question is (D): overlooks the possibility that the same thing may causally contribute both to education and to good health. The right answer addresses the second of the above concerns. But it was wise to remain open to the idea that it could have been any of them.

Did you notice that this argument also contains a term shift? The argument shifts from "high educational levels" to "informed lifestyle decisions." The correct answer to this Flaw question could have pointed out this mismatch as well.

Let's quickly discuss the incorrect answers:

(A) presumes, without providing justification, that only highly educated people make informed lifestyle choices

This is a tempting answer because it addresses the mismatch between education levels and informed lifestyle decisions. However, the word "only" makes this answer choice too strong. The argument involves generalizations—in shifting terms, the author is assuming a relationship between education and informed lifestyle choices, but not an exclusive one as this answer choice states.

(B) overlooks the possibility that people who make informed lifestyle choices may nonetheless suffer from inherited diseases

It may be true that they suffer from inherited diseases, but we've been given no indication that the rate of inherited diseases is different for the groups—those who don't make informed lifestyle choices may also suffer from inherited diseases, and so it's unclear what impact this information has on the argument being made.

(C) presumes, without providing justification, that informed
      lifestyle choices are available to everyone

Whether the choices are available to everyone is not mentioned in the argument and has no direct bearing on it.

(E) does not acknowledge that some people who fail to make
      informed lifestyle choices are in good health

The author does not conclude that only people who make informed lifestyle choices are healthy. The conclusion is that such choices are the major factor in good health.

Let's take a look at another question that involves an explicit claim of causation. Try to anticipate potential answers, and see if one of the answer choices matches your prediction.

PT22, S2, Q10

The only motives that influence all human actions arise from self-interest. It is clear, therefore, that self-interest is the chief influence on human action.

The reasoning in the argument is fallacious because the argument

(A) denies that an observation that a trait is common to all the
      events in a pattern can contribute to a causal explanation
      of the pattern
(B) takes the occurrence of one particular influence on a
      pattern or class of events as showing that its influence
      outweighs any other influence on those events
(C) concludes that a characteristic of a pattern or class of
      events at one time is characteristic of similar patterns or
      classes of events at all times
(D) concludes that, because an influence is the paramount
      influence on a particular pattern or class of events, that
      influence is the only influence on that pattern or class of
      events
(E) undermines its own premise that a particular attribute
      is present in all instances of a certain pattern or class of
      events

In this argument, the author makes a very strong claim of causation—self-interest *is the chief influence* on human action. The evidence might seem very strong—self-interest is the *only* motive that influences *all* human actions!

But does that mean it's the *chief* influence?

Well, fortunately, we can use our familiarity with the exam to our advantage here. We know there's something wrong with the argument. So, what we're thinking is:

"Is it possible that self-interest is a part of every action, but *not* the chief influence?"

Absolutely. Perhaps, looking at the argument from this critical perspective, it might be easier to see how one characteristic or element may always be present in another, but not the chief influence. Imagine a dinner where the only thing that is common to all dishes is salt and pepper. Would we say that salt and pepper are the chief flavors in the meal? Not necessarily. Even though self-interest is always there, perhaps something else, such as a desire to have a positive impact on the lives of others, has a much stronger influence on our actions.

The flaw in the argument is that the author assumes that just because self-interest is a part of every action, it must be the chief influence in every action.

Answer choice (B), the correct answer, addresses this issue: takes the occurrence of one particular influence on a pattern or class of events as showing that its influence outweighs any other influence on those events.

The answer is worded in a challenging way, but it essentially gives us the information we expect. The argument is flawed in that it assumes that how *often* a characteristic appears translates to how *strong* an influence that characteristic is.

Let's break down the incorrect answer choices:

(A) denies that an observation that a trait is common to all the events in a pattern can contribute to a causal explanation of the pattern

This answer choice is very attractive because it can easily be misread, but notice that what it is saying is that the author denies that self-interest can have an influence—this answer choice is actually the opposite of what we are looking for.

(C) concludes that a characteristic of a pattern or class of events at one time is characteristic of similar patterns or classes of events at all times

This is not what is happening in the argument. The author is not concluding that a characteristic that appeared once appears always.

(D) concludes that, because an influence is the paramount influence on a particular pattern or class of events, that influence is the only influence on that pattern or class of events

This answer choice is about whether a chief influence is necessarily the only influence. We are interested in whether the sole common influence is necessarily the chief influence.

(E) undermines its own premise that a particular attribute
is present in all instances of a certain pattern or class of
events

The premise is not undermined, and so we can eliminate this choice.

Let's take a look at another problem. Here, no claim of causation is stated explicitly, but the argument does have a causation issue. See if you can spot it before looking at the answer choices:

4

<u>PT14, S4, Q18</u>

According to a government official involved in overseeing
airplane safety during the last year, over 75 percent of the voice
recorder tapes taken from small airplanes involved in relatively
minor accidents record the whistling of the pilot during the
fifteen minutes immediately preceding the accident. Even such
minor accidents pose some safety risk. Therefore, if passengers
hear the pilot start to whistle they should take safety
precautions, whether instructed by the pilot to do so or not.

The argument is most vulnerable to criticism on the grounds
that it

(A) accepts the reliability of the cited statistics on the authority
of an unidentified government official

(B) ignores the fact that in nearly one quarter of these
accidents following the recommendation would not have
improved passengers' safety

(C) does not indicate the criteria by which an accident is
classified as "relatively minor"

(D) provides no information about the percentage of all small
airplane flights during which the pilot whistles at some
time during that flight

(E) fails to specify the percentage of all small airplane flights
that involve relatively minor accidents

For the previous two questions, we looked at arguments that have an explicit claim of causation—more specifically, arguments with causation conclusions that we are meant to evaluate and ultimately find fault with.

However, sometimes the causation flaw is not explicit—it exists in a faulty, *unstated* assumption that the author has made. That's the case in this problem. Notice that the conclusion does not contain a claim of causation. However, the author is assuming a causal relationship in reaching his conclusion.

To illustrate, let's separate out the argument core:

In over 75% of minor accidents, pilot   If passenger hears whistling,
of small plane recorded whistling   should take safety precautions

The conclusion, in this case, is a suggestion of what one should do. If a passenger hears whistling, he or she should take safety precautions.

Why? How did the author reach this conclusion? What was his reasoning? What did he assume, or, more specifically, how did he interpret the evidence?

In reaching the conclusion that the passenger should take safety precautions, the author is implying that the whistling is indicative of a greater likelihood of danger—in other words, that whistling has some impact on the chances of being in an accident.

Is this assumption about causation sound? Let's run it through our questions:

1. Could it be reversed? Could the likelihood of being in an accident make one whistle more? Not likely.

2. Could there be some other influence on both? Perhaps boredom makes one whistle, and makes one more likely to get in accidents, but that's a stretch.

3. Could it be that there is no connection between the two? Absolutely! It can just be a coincidence, or there could be some alternative explanation. Imagine, for instance, that over 75% of pilots just happen to always whistle while they fly. If that's the case, the author couldn't make the case that hearing whistling increases the likelihood of being in an accident.

The correct answer choice, (D), addresses this issue: provides no information about the percentage of all small airplane flights during which the pilot whistles at some time during that flight.

Without this information, we can't prove that whistling represents an increased likelihood of getting in an accident.

Let's take a look at the incorrect answers:

> (A) accepts the reliability of the cited statistics on the authority of an unidentified government official

Notice that this answer choice puts into question the validity of our premise. That's not our job here. This does not represent a reasoning flaw, and we are looking for reasoning flaws only.

> (B) ignores the fact that in nearly one quarter of these accidents following the recommendation would not have improved passengers' safety

The argument is not about what happens after passengers take the recommended safety precautions, but rather whether they should take those precautions when they hear whistling. Furthermore, is a recommendation unwarranted if it helps improve safety only 75% of the time?

> (C) does not indicate the criteria by which an accident is classified as "relatively minor"

This answer choice is not directly relevant to the reasoning in the argument.

> (E) fails to specify the percentage of all small airplane flights that involve relatively minor accidents

This is a tempting answer, but ultimately out of scope. This answer choice is about the percentage of small airplane flights that involve minor accidents. Whether this percentage is 0.1% or 90%, it does not impact the relationship between whistling and the likelihood of getting in an accident.

Let's finish by revisiting a very unusual example of a problem involving causation:

4

PT32, S1, Q10

To accommodate the personal automobile, houses are built on widely scattered lots far from places of work and shopping malls are equipped with immense parking lots that leave little room for wooded areas. Hence, had people generally not used personal automobiles, the result would have to have been a geography of modern cities quite different from the one we have now.

The argument's reasoning is questionable because the argument

(A) infers from the idea that the current geography of modern cities resulted from a particular cause that it could only have resulted from that cause

(B) infers from the idea that the current geography of modern cities resulted from a particular cause that other facets of modern life resulted from that cause

(C) overlooks the fact that many technological innovations other than the personal automobile have had some effect on the way people live

(D) takes for granted that shopping malls do not need large parking lots even given the use of the personal automobile

(E) takes for granted that people ultimately want to live without personal automobiles

In this argument, the causal relationship is not given to us as a conclusion, nor is it something simply assumed by the author. Notice that it is given to us explicitly as a *premise*. What is the cause? We need to accommodate personal automobiles. What is the effect? A variety of consequences to our living environment. Note that because this cause and effect relationship is given to us as a premise, it is *not* our job, in this case, to evaluate its validity. Rather, we're meant to evaluate its relationship to the conclusion. Let's take a look at the argument core:

We've designed our geography to accommodate the automobile   Without personal automobiles, our geography would be quite different.

Note that the flaw here is not in assuming the validity of one cause, but rather in seeing that one cause as the *only* potential cause. The author states that without personal automobiles, the geography of modern cities *would be* quite different. We know that personal automobiles have led us to a certain type of geography, but are they the only cause that could have led to that geography? Do we know for sure that the geography of modern cities would be different without the personal automobile?

It's possible, but far from certain. We can imagine, perhaps, that we could have evolved to have personal motorcycles, or helicopters, and perhaps the geography would then have resulted in something similar. The flaw in this argument is that the author assumes one cause to be the only cause. Answer choice (A), the correct answer, addresses this issue:

(A) infers from the idea that the current geography of modern
     cities resulted from a particular cause that it could only
     have resulted from that cause

We could also look at this through the lens of more formal conditional logic. The premise tells us that *cars → cities built the way they are*, and (A) suggests that *NO cars → cities NOT built the way they are*. It is logically invalid to simply negate both sides of a conditional statement.

Let's take a look at the incorrect answer choices:

(B) infers from the idea that the current geography of modern
     cities resulted from a particular cause that other facets of
     modern life resulted from that cause

Other facets of modern life are out of scope.

(C) overlooks the fact that many technological innovations
     other than the personal automobile have had some effect
     on the way people live

This gives us other causes, but not *causes for a certain geography. Rather, this answer proposes causes for "the way people live." This would be a good answer if it were worded slightly differently: "overlooks the fact that many technological innovations other than the personal automobile [other causes!] have had some effect on geography."*

(D) takes for granted that shopping malls do not need large
     parking lots even given the use of the personal automobile

This answer might be attractive if it is misread, but note that it says that the argument takes for granted that shopping malls do not need large parking lots—this is the reverse of what the author discusses, and it is not something that is therefore taken for granted.

(E) takes for granted that people ultimately want to live
     without personal automobiles

What people want is irrelevant.

The Last Hurdle: Digging Out the Correct Answer

Okay. You've read through the argument, identified the core, and you have a good understanding of the gap or flaw. Are you done with the heavy lifting? For the most part, yes. But the test writers can throw a few more challenges your way. Let's take a look at two ways that the LSAT makes the right answer harder to identify.

To begin, go ahead and try the following two questions. Give yourself 2:40 to 3:00.

4

PT34, S2, Q3

Restaurant manager: In response to requests from our patrons for vegetarian main dishes, we recently introduced three: an eggplant and zucchini casserole with tomatoes, brown rice with mushrooms, and potatoes baked with cheese. The first two are frequently ordered, but no one orders the potato dish, although it costs less than the other two. Clearly, then, our patrons prefer not to eat potatoes.

Which one of the following is an error of reasoning in the restaurant manager's argument?

(A) concluding that two things that occur at the same time have a common cause

(B) drawing a conclusion that is inconsistent with one premise of the argument

(C) ignoring possible differences between what people say they want and what they actually choose

(D) attempting to prove a claim on the basis of evidence that a number of people hold that claim to be true

(E) treating one of several plausible explanations of a phenomenon as the only possible explanation

PT34, S2, Q9

A university study reported that between 1975 and 1983 the length of the average workweek in a certain country increased significantly. A governmental study, on the other hand, shows a significant decline in the length of the average workweek for the same period. Examination of the studies shows, however, that they used different methods of investigation; thus there is no need to look further for an explanation of the difference in the studies' results.

The argument's reasoning is flawed because the argument fails to

(A) distinguish between a study produced for the purposes of the operation of government and a study produced as part of university research

(B) distinguish between a method of investigation and the purpose of an investigation

(C) recognize that only one of the studies has been properly conducted

(D) recognize that two different methods of investigation can yield identical results

(E) recognize that varying economic conditions result in the average workweek changing in length

Challenge #1: Abstract Language

A common way that test writers will try to challenge you is to write the answer choices using generalized, or abstract, language. Most of these answer choices will refer to the underlying reasoning or logic in the argument, and it makes perfect sense that these questions would work this way. After all, you are being tested on your ability to evaluate the underlying reasoning or logic—whether the argument is specifically about potatoes or workweeks is secondary to the test writer.

The great news is that reading for the core, and for structural flaws, in the manner that we've recommended up to this point, is the ideal way to prepare to evaluate an abstract or generalized answer choice.

The bad news is that for many of these questions, it is almost impossible to identify the correct answer if you haven't anticipated it. Most of the answer choices will sound very attractive, and most of the incorrect answers will be answers that could be correct for other arguments. This makes it even more important that you are strong at finding the core, and recognizing common flaws.

Let's look back at one of our two examples to review this issue more in depth:

> *PT34, S2, Q3*
>
> Restaurant manager: In response to requests from our patrons for vegetarian main dishes, we recently introduced three: an eggplant and zucchini casserole with tomatoes, brown rice with mushrooms, and potatoes baked with cheese. The first two are frequently ordered, but no one orders the potato dish, although it costs less than the other two. Clearly, then, our patrons prefer not to eat potatoes.
>
> Which one of the following is an error of reasoning in the restaurant manager's argument?
>
> (A) concluding that two things that occur at the same time have a common cause
> (B) drawing a conclusion that is inconsistent with one premise of the argument
> (C) ignoring possible differences between what people say they want and what they actually choose
> (D) attempting to prove a claim on the basis of evidence that a number of people hold that claim to be true
> (E) treating one of several plausible explanations of a phenomenon as the only possible explanation

We can think of the argument core as follows:

No one orders the potato dish   Our patrons prefer not to eat potatoes

Did you see a flaw when you read the argument initially? The author concludes that the patrons must not prefer potatoes, and the evidence he presents is that no one orders the potato dish. Could there be another reason no one orders the potato dish? Could it be the way that it's prepared? Perhaps the chef thinks capers go well with potatoes, but patrons don't. Perhaps patrons don't like the cheese that is being used. Perhaps people prefer to eat potatoes at home, or only as an accompaniment with meat.

As we've discussed before, it is not necessary for you to take the time to come up with these alternatives. What is important is that you recognize the fault in the reasoning: in using this evidence to validate the conclusion, the author has failed to consider other reasons why patrons don't order the potato dish—the author is thinking of one explanation as the only possible explanation. Answer choice (E), the correct answer, says just that: treating one of several plausible explanations of a phenomenon as the only possible explanation.

Let's discuss the incorrect answers:

(A) concluding that two things that occur at the same time have a common cause

This is a fault that is common to many arguments that appear in Identify a Flaw questions, but this is not a fault of this particular argument. We are not considering two things that happen at the same time. When facing abstract flaw answers, stand your ground. Check that the answer corresponds with the argument. Did the argument really claim that? Did it conclude that? Often these abstract answers refer to claims and conclusions that are simply not in the argument.

(B) drawing a conclusion that is inconsistent with one premise of the argument

This is not representative of a common fault that appears in flaw arguments, and it's not representative of a flaw in this particular argument. Stand your ground! There is no inconsistency between the premise and the conclusion.

(C) ignoring possible differences between what people say they want and what they actually choose

This answer choice addresses a more specific flaw. However, it's not a flaw in this argument—there is no confusion of what people say they want and what they choose. The argument is about what people actually want and what they choose.

(D) attempting to prove a claim on the basis of evidence that a number of people hold that claim to be true

We are not told that a number of people believe that the patrons don't like potatoes.

Remember, the key to recognizing correct answers written in an abstract or generalized way is to read for the core and anticipate the reasoning flaw. When stuck between a couple of answer choices, do not simply compare them against one another—this will lead you nowhere! Instead, compare each one to the argument core. Figure out which one best applies to the situation in the argument, and to your understanding of the core.

Here are some more examples of the types of abstract language answers you may face on the exam:

Abstract Answer	In Our Words...	Example
It assumes without warrant that a condition under which a phenomenon is said to occur is the only condition under which that phenomenon occurs.	The argument assumes that one way is the only way.	*When businesses on Main Street fail there is commercial space available in the downtown district. Since there is commercial space available in the downtown district, it must be true that businesses on Main Street failed.* *(Maybe there's another reason space is available.)*
Presumes that a condition necessary for an outcome is sufficient for that outcome.	The argument assumes that because something is required for an outcome to be true, it guarantees that the outcome will be true.	*All NFL linemen weigh over two hundred pounds. Since Ted weighs over two hundred pounds, he must be an NFL lineman.* *(Not everyone who is over two hundred pounds is an NFL linebacker!)*
Takes for granted that if one phenomenon co-occurs with another, then the two phenomena must be causally related.	The argument assumes from a correlation that there must be a cause and effect relationship.	*Those who have a computer at home have higher incomes on average than those who do not have a computer at home. Thus, having a computer at home leads to a higher income.* *(Having a computer and a higher income can both be due to other factors, or they can have no causal connection.)*
It sets up a dichotomy between alternatives that are not known to be exclusive.	The argument assumes a limited number of possibilities when there could be more.	*Since those who love our show already watch it and those who hate our show can't be convinced to watch it, advertising will have no impact on our viewership totals.* *(What about those who don't have a strong opinion about the show, or have never heard of it?)*
Takes for granted that a claim is false based on evidence about the source of the claim rather than any evidence about the claim itself.	The argument makes assumptions about a claim based on the trustworthiness of the source.	*Company X claims that its chemical products are completely safe for use at home. This is absurd, since Company X is only concerned with profits and cannot be trusted.* *(Even if the company is only concerned with profits, the chemical product can still be completely safe.)*
Infers from a claim about a single instance of a class that the class must itself possess that characteristic.	The argument assumes that what is true of the parts is true of the whole.	*The top scorer in the league is on the Cosmos. Therefore, the Cosmos must have scored more goals than any other team in the league.* *(One star player does not make a team. What about the other players?)*

4

| Too hastily draws a conclusion about what is a matter of fact from evidence that suggests a mere suspicion. | The argument assumes that an opinion is enough to prove the point being made. | *John believes that he'll get a "B" in biology this semester, so when his grades are released late next week, his biology grade will in fact report a "B."*

(Oh, if only life were that easy! How do we know that John's belief is correct?) |
| Confuses a relative comparison about one aspect of two different phenomena for an absolute claim about the two phenomena. | The argument assumes that a comparison allows us to infer something absolute. | *Training a lion is safe, as anyone can see by simple comparison: those who train sharks are twice as likely to get injured as those who train lions.*

(Just because something is safer than training sharks does not mean it is actually safe!) |

Challenge #2: From Another Point of View

Sometimes you will do everything correctly and come to understand the flaw or flaws perfectly, and you get to the answer choices and *still*…none of the answers fit what you are looking for! What could be wrong?

Perhaps that didn't happen to you with this next problem, but in any case, let's use it to illustrate the issue:

PT34, S2, Q9

A university study reported that between 1975 and 1983 the length of the average workweek in a certain country increased significantly. A governmental study, on the other hand, shows a significant decline in the length of the average workweek for the same period. Examination of the studies shows, however, that they used different methods of investigation; thus there is no need to look further for an explanation of the difference in the studies' results.

The argument's reasoning is flawed because the argument fails to

(A) distinguish between a study produced for the purposes of the operation of government and a study produced as part of university research

(B) distinguish between a method of investigation and the purpose of an investigation

(C) recognize that only one of the studies has been properly conducted

(D) recognize that two different methods of investigation can yield identical results

(E) recognize that varying economic conditions result in the average workweek changing in length

Here is a simplified version of the core:

the two studies used different
methods of investigation no need to look further for an
explanation of the difference in
the studies' results

Do you spot a flaw in the reasoning here? It's actually very similar to that in the previous argument—
the author assumes one reason when others could be plausible. In this case, he assumes that because
two studies used different methods of investigation, this was *the* reason for the difference in the studies'
results. Couldn't it be that, though the methods of investigation were different, something else could
have caused the difference in the results?

We go in anticipating an answer that addresses this issue. One way it could be worded is that *"the
author fails to recognize that there could be other reasons for differences in the studies' results."*

Unfortunately, we don't have that in the answer choices! Let's review what we've got:

The argument's reasoning is flawed because the argument fails
to

(A) distinguish between a study produced for the purposes of
the operation of government and a study produced as part
of university research

*We're not told that the governmental study was done for the purposes of the operation of the government, and
the author does recognize differences between the two studies discussed.*

(B) distinguish between a method of investigation and the
purpose of an investigation

*The argument doesn't involve the purpose of the investigation. Look back at the argument: there is no gap
between method and purpose.*

(C) recognize that only one of the studies has been properly
conducted

We've been given no claim or evidence that either of the studies was properly or improperly conducted.

(D) recognix ze that two different methods of investigation
can yield identical results

*This is in the ballpark of our core, but certainly isn't what we anticipated. Still, it's the best we've seen so far,
so let's keep it.*

(E) recognize that varying economic conditions result in the
average workweek changing in length

The argument is not about the causes *of the changes in the workweek, but rather the discrepancy in the results reported in two different studies about these changes. This answer does not represent issues with this core.*

The only viable answer is (D), but could it be correct? Let's look at it one more time:

> (D) (the argument fails to) recognize that two different
> methods of investigation can yield identical results

What does this mean, exactly? The author doesn't consider the fact that you can use two different methods of investigation and end up with the same result.

Isn't this simply a different perspective on the flaw that we saw initially? The author is mistakenly assuming a one-to-one connection between methods and results. Different methods, the argument assumes, will of course lead to different results. We can think of the flaw as failing to consider other ways to end up with different results, or we can think of the flaw as failing to consider that different methods can yield the same result.

Note that this is very different from an answer that reverses the logic, and it is not equivalent to a conditional logic contrapositive (which will be discussed in great detail in Chapter 8). It is simply a different perspective—a view from another angle—of a flaw that you are expected to anticipate.

Conclusion

Let's review the steps required for success on Identify a Flaw questions:

1. Read for the core. Like assumption questions, Identify a Flaw questions are designed to test your ability to evaluate the relationship between the supporting evidence and the conclusion—so make sure you zero in on the core.

2. See the gap and anticipate the flaw. No matter how sound the core may seem, we know it will contain a flaw. Two considerations that are helpful in identifying flaws are "What is the mismatch?" and "What else has the author failed to consider?"

3. Beware of all claims of causation! Recognize when the author is making an explicit or implicit claim of causation and always consider other causation possibilities.

4. Don't be scared off by challenging correct answers. Be prepared for answers that use abstract language, or present the flaw from a slightly different perspective.

DRILL IT: Identify a Flaw Questions

Give yourself no more than 20 minutes to complete the following problems.

1. PT16, S2, Q10

A fundamental illusion in robotics is the belief that improvements in robots will liberate humanity from "hazardous and demeaning work." Engineers are designing only those types of robots that can be properly maintained with the least expensive, least skilled human labor possible. Therefore, robots will not eliminate demeaning work—only substitute one type of demeaning work for another.

The reasoning in the argument is most vulnerable to the criticism that it

(A) ignores the consideration that in a competitive business environment some jobs might be eliminated if robots are not used in the manufacturing process

(B) assumes what it sets out to prove, that robots create demeaning work

(C) does not specify whether or not the engineers who design robots consider their work demeaning

(D) attempts to support its conclusion by an appeal to the emotion of fear, which is often experienced by people faced with the prospect of losing their jobs to robots

(E) fails to address the possibility that the amount of demeaning work eliminated by robots might be significantly greater than the amount they create

2. PT14, S4, Q20

Monroe, despite his generally poor appetite, thoroughly enjoyed the three meals he ate at the TipTop Restaurant, but, unfortunately, after each meal he became ill. The first time he ate an extra large sausage pizza with a side order of hot peppers; the second time he took full advantage of the all-you-can-eat fried shrimp and hot peppers special; and the third time he had two of TipTop's giant meatball sandwiches with hot peppers. Since the only food all three meals had in common was the hot peppers, Monroe concludes that it is solely due to TipTop's hot peppers that he became ill.

Monroe's reasoning is most vulnerable to which one of the following criticisms?

(A) He draws his conclusion on the basis of too few meals that were consumed at TipTop and that included hot peppers.

(B) He posits a causal relationship without ascertaining that the presumed cause preceded the presumed effect.

(C) He allows his desire to continue dining at TipTop to bias his conclusion.

(D) He fails to establish that everyone who ate TipTop's hot peppers became ill.

(E) He overlooks the fact that at all three meals he consumed what was, for him, an unusually large quantity of food.

4

3. PT14, S2, Q10

The government of Penglai, an isolated island, proposed eliminating outdoor advertising except for small signs of standard shape that identify places of business. Some island merchants protested that the law would reduce the overall volume of business in Penglai, pointing to a report done by the government indicating that in every industry the Penglai businesses that used outdoor advertising had a larger market share than those that did not.

Which one of the following describes an error of reasoning in the merchants' argument?

(A) presupposing that there are no good reasons for restricting the use of outdoor advertising in Penglai

(B) assuming without giving justification that the outdoor advertising increased market share by some means other than by diverting trade from competing businesses

(C) ignoring the question of whether the government's survey of the island could be objective

(D) failing to establish whether the marketshare advantage enjoyed by businesses employing outdoor advertising was precisely proportionate to the amount of advertising

(E) disregarding the possibility that the government's proposed restrictions are unconstitutional

4. PT19, S2, Q14

Herbalist: Many of my customers find that their physical coordination improves after drinking juice containing certain herbs. A few doctors assert that the herbs are potentially harmful, but doctors are always trying to maintain a monopoly over medical therapies. So there is no reason not to try my herb juice.

The reasoning in the herbalist's argument is flawed because the argument

(A) attempts to force acceptance of a claim by inducing fear of the consequences of rejecting that claim

(B) bases a conclusion on claims that are inconsistent with each other

(C) rejects a claim by attacking the proponents of the claim rather than addressing the claim itself

(D) relies on evidence presented in terms that presuppose the truth of the claim for which the evidence is offered

(E) mistakes the observation that one thing happens after another for proof that the second thing is the result of the first

5. PT19, S2, Q23

A museum director, in order to finance expensive new acquisitions, discreetly sold some paintings by major artists. All of them were paintings that the director privately considered inferior. Critics roundly condemned the sale, charging that the museum had lost first-rate pieces, thereby violating its duty as a trustee of art for future generations. A few months after being sold by the museum, those paintings were resold, in an otherwise stagnant art market, at two to three times the price paid to the museum. Clearly, these prices settle the issue, since they demonstrate the correctness of the critics' evaluation.

The reasoning in the argument is vulnerable to the criticism that the argument does which one of the following?

(A) It concludes that a certain opinion is correct on the grounds that it is held by more people than hold the opposing view.

(B) It rejects the judgment of the experts in an area in which there is no better guide to the truth than expert judgment.

(C) It rejects a proven means of accomplishing an objective without offering any alternative means of accomplishing that objective.

(D) It bases a firm conclusion about a state of affairs in the present on somewhat speculative claims about a future state of affairs.

(E) It bases its conclusion on facts that could, in the given situation, have resulted from causes other than those presupposed by the argument.

6. PT19, S4, Q6

Videocassette recorders (VCRs) enable people to watch movies at home on videotape. People who own VCRs go to movie theaters more often than do people who do not own VCRs. Contrary to popular belief, therefore, owning a VCR actually stimulates people to go to movie theaters more often than they otherwise would.

The argument is most vulnerable to criticism on the grounds that it

(A) concludes that a claim must be false because of the mere absence of evidence in its favor

(B) cites, in support of the conclusion, evidence that is inconsistent with other information that is provided

(C) fails to establish that the phenomena interpreted as cause and effect are not both direct effects of some other factor

(D) takes a condition that by itself guarantees the occurrence of a certain phenomenon to be a condition that therefore must be met for that phenomenon to occur

(E) bases a broad claim about the behavior of people in general on a comparison between two groups of people that together include only a small proportion of people overall

4

7. PT20, S1, Q10

Premiums for automobile accident insurance are often higher for red cars than for cars of other colors. To justify these higher charges, insurance companies claim that, overall, a greater percentage of red cars are involved in accidents than are cars of any other color. If this claim is true, then lives could undoubtedly be saved by banning red cars from the roads altogether.

The reasoning in the argument is flawed because the argument

(A) accepts without question that insurance companies have the right to charge higher premiums for higher-risk clients

(B) fails to consider whether red cars cost the same to repair as cars of other colors

(C) ignores the possibility that drivers who drive recklessly have a preference for red cars

(D) does not specify precisely what percentage of red cars are involved in accidents

(E) makes an unsupported assumption that every automobile accident results in some loss of life

8. PT21, S2, Q5

Irrigation runoff from neighboring farms may well have increased the concentration of phosphorus in the local swamp above previous levels, but the claim that the increase in phosphorus is harming the swamp's native aquatic wildlife is false; the phosphorus concentration in the swamp is actually less than that found in certain kinds of bottled water that some people drink every day.

The argument is vulnerable to criticism on the ground that it

(A) makes exaggerations in formulating the claim against which it argues

(B) bases its conclusion on two contradictory claims

(C) relies on evidence the relevance of which has not been established

(D) concedes the very point that it argues against

(E) makes a generalization that is unwarranted because the sources of the data on which it is based have not been specified

9. PT33, S3, Q5

The radiation absorbed by someone during an ordinary commercial airline flight is no more dangerous than that received during an ordinary dental X-ray. Since a dental X-ray does negligible harm to a person, we can conclude that the radiation absorbed by members of commercial airline flight crews will also do them negligible harm.

A flaw in the argument is its failure to consider that

(A) there may be many forms of dangerous radiation other than X-rays and the kinds of radiation absorbed by members of commercial airline flight crews

(B) receiving a dental X-ray may mitigate other health risks, whereas flying does not

(C) exposure to X-rays of higher intensity than dental X-rays may be harmful

(D) the longer and the more often one is exposed to radiation, the more radiation one absorbs and the more seriously one is harmed

(E) flying at high altitude involves risks in addition to exposure to minor radiation

10. PT36, S1, Q19

Although it has been suggested that Arton's plays have a strong patriotic flavor, we must recall that, at the time of their composition, her country was in anything but a patriotic mood. Unemployment was high, food was costly, and crime rates were soaring. As a result, the general morale of her nation was at an especially low point. Realizing this, we see clearly that any apparent patriotism in Arton's work must have been intended ironically.

The reasoning above is questionable because it

(A) posits an unstated relationship between unemployment and crime

(B) takes for granted that straightforward patriotism is not possible for a serious writer

(C) takes for granted that Arton was attuned to the predominant national attitude of her time

(D) overlooks the fact that some citizens prosper in times of high unemployment

(E) confuses irony with a general decline in public morale

Challenge Questions

11. PT36, S3, Q13

While it was once believed that the sort of psychotherapy appropriate for the treatment of neuroses caused by environmental factors is also appropriate for schizophrenia and other psychoses, it is now known that these latter, more serious forms of mental disturbance are best treated by biochemical—that is, medicinal—means. This is conclusive evidence that psychoses, unlike neuroses, have nothing to do with environmental factors but rather are caused by some sort of purely organic condition, such as abnormal brain chemistry or brain malformations.

The argument is vulnerable to criticism because it ignores the possibility that

(A) the organic conditions that result in psychoses can be caused or exacerbated by environmental factors

(B) the symptoms of mental disturbance caused by purely organic factors can be alleviated with medicine

(C) organic illnesses that are nonpsychological in nature may be treatable without using biochemical methods

(D) the nature of any medical condition can be inferred from the nature of the treatment that cures that condition

(E) organic factors having little to do with brain chemistry may be at least partially responsible for neuroses

12. PT18, S4, Q9

Brain scans of people exposed to certain neurotoxins reveal brain damage identical to that found in people suffering from Parkinson's disease. This fact shows not only that these neurotoxins cause this type of brain damage, but also that the brain damage itself causes Parkinson's disease. Thus brain scans can be used to determine who is likely to develop Parkinson's disease.

The argument contains which one of the following reasoning errors?

(A) It fails to establish that other methods that can be used to diagnose Parkinson's disease are less accurate than brain scans.

(B) It overestimates the importance of early diagnosis in determining appropriate treatments for people suffering from Parkinson's disease.

(C) It mistakes a correlation between the type of brain damage described and Parkinson's disease for a causal relation between the two.

(D) It assumes that people would want to know as early as possible whether they were likely to develop Parkinson's disease.

(E) It neglects to specify how the information provided by brain scans could be used either in treating Parkinson's disease or in monitoring the progression of the disease.

4

4

13. PT16, S3, Q11

A controversial program rewards prison inmates who behave particularly well in prison by giving them the chance to receive free cosmetic plastic surgery performed by medical students. The program is obviously morally questionable, both in its assumptions about what inmates might want and in its use of the prison population to train future surgeons. Putting these moral issues aside, however, the surgery clearly has a powerful rehabilitative effect, as is shown by the fact that, among recipients of the surgery, the proportion who are convicted of new crimes committed after release is only half that for the prison population as a whole.

A flaw in the reasoning of the passage is that it

(A) allows moral issues to be a consideration in presenting evidence about matters of fact

(B) dismisses moral considerations on the grounds that only matters of fact are relevant

(C) labels the program as "controversial" instead of discussing the issues that give rise to controversy

(D) asserts that the rehabilitation of criminals is not a moral issue

(E) relies on evidence drawn from a sample that there is reason to believe is unrepresentative

14. PT36, S1, Q10

Cotrell is, at best, able to write magazine articles of average quality. The most compelling pieces of evidence for this are those few of the numerous articles submitted by Cotrell that are superior, since Cotrell, who is incapable of writing an article that is better than average, must obviously have plagiarized superior ones.

The argument is most vulnerable to criticism on which one of the following grounds?

(A) It simply ignores the existence of potential counterevidence.

(B) It generalizes from atypical occurrences.

(C) It presupposes what it seeks to establish.

(D) It relies on the judgment of experts in a matter to which their expertise is irrelevant.

(E) It infers limits on ability from a few isolated lapses in performance.

15. PT16, S2, Q22

Director of personnel: Ms. Tours has formally requested a salary adjustment on the grounds that she was denied merit raises to which she was entitled. Since such grounds provide a possible basis for adjustments, an official response is required. Ms. Tours presents compelling evidence that her job performance has been both excellent in itself and markedly superior to that of others in her department who were awarded merit raises. Her complaint that she was treated unfairly thus appears justified. Nevertheless, her request should be denied. To raise Ms. Tours's salary because of her complaint would jeopardize the integrity of the firm's merit-based reward system by sending the message that employees can get their salaries raised if they just complain enough.

The personnel director's reasoning is most vulnerable to criticism on the grounds that it

(A) fails to consider the possibility that Ms. Tours's complaint could be handled on an unofficial basis

(B) attempts to undermine the persuasiveness of Ms. Tours's evidence by characterizing it as "mere complaining"

(C) sidesteps the issue of whether superior job performance is a suitable basis for awarding salary increases

(D) ignores the possibility that some of the people who did receive merit increases were not entitled to them

(E) overlooks the implications for the integrity of the firm's merit-based reward system of denying Ms. Tours's request

SOLUTIONS: Identify a Flaw Questions

1. PT16, S2, Q10

A fundamental illusion in robotics is the belief that improvements in robots will liberate humanity from "hazardous and demeaning work." Engineers are designing only those types of robots that can be properly maintained with the least expensive, least skilled human labor possible. Therefore, robots will not eliminate demeaning work—only substitute one type of demeaning work for another.

The reasoning in the argument is most vulnerable to the criticism that it

(A) ignores the consideration that in a competitive business environment some jobs might be eliminated if robots are not used in the manufacturing process

(B) assumes what it sets out to prove, that robots create demeaning work

(C) does not specify whether or not the engineers who design robots consider their work demeaning

(D) attempts to support its conclusion by an appeal to the emotion of fear, which is often experienced by people faced with the prospect of losing their jobs to robots

(E) fails to address the possibility that the amount of demeaning work eliminated by robots might be significantly greater than the amount they create

(E) is correct.

The author's final conclusion is that though robots will save humans from doing work that is considered demeaning, this work will be made up for by the demeaning work of maintaining those same robots.

We can think of the core of this argument as follows:

Robots are designed to require least skilled/expensive human labor for maintenance		demeaning human work of maintaining robots = demeaning human work taken over robots

This is a tricky question because in addition to the mismatch between two explicit ideas, "least expensive, least skilled" labor and "demeaning" labor, there is a mismatch between implicit facets of that labor. Let's deal with the explicit mismatch first. Is cheap, unskilled work necessarily demeaning? A lot of hardworking people might disagree.

Also, because the author is making a strong statement about the interchangeability of two things, a good place to start is to ask if those two things are truly comparable; if one thing truly substitutes for another in a society, then many aspects of those things must "line up." (For example, personal jets have the same function as personal automobiles do—to transport people from one place to another. Has the personal jet taken over the role of the personal automobile in our society? No, because not everyone can afford a personal jet! The vehicles' individual functions may be similar, but their roles in society are quite different.) Will the old work taken away be cancelled out by the new work created? There are several ways in which these two types of labor may not be interchangeable—if one comes to mind right away, great. If not, just keep in mind that the correct answer could deal with the nature of that comparison.

Let's take a look at the answer choices:

(A) is out of scope. the author is making a sweeping statement about the nature of human labor in our society, not just about "some jobs" in the "manufacturing process." While jobs may or may not be lost, this is not relevant to the author's conclusion.

4

(B) is tempting, because of the explicit mismatch we mentioned above. But is "robots create demeaning work" the argument's conclusion? No, the main point is that the work taken away will be cancelled out by the work added.

(C) has no bearing on the conclusion. Whether the engineers consider a type of work demeaning does not tell us whether the work is demeaning; it also does not relate to the "work taken away = work added" conclusion. Finally, the work that engineering designers do may not be the work that robots would do.

(D) is both factually incorrect and has no bearing on the conclusion. There is no direct appeal to people afraid of losing their jobs and, even if there were, it would not address the "work taken away = work added" conclusion.

This leaves us with (E), which is similar to the implicit "comparableness of work" issue we predicted. If the type of work is comparable ("demeaning"), then we also need the quantity of that work to be comparable for the conclusion to hold true. If robots take over 1,000,000 demeaning jobs but require 1 person to do unskilled maintenance, then the "work taken away = work added" conclusion does not hold.

Therefore, (E) is the correct answer.

2. PT14, S4, Q20

Monroe, despite his generally poor appetite, thoroughly enjoyed the three meals he ate at the TipTop Restaurant, but, unfortunately, after each meal he became ill. The first time he ate an extra large sausage pizza with a side order of hot peppers; the second time he took full advantage of the all-you-can-eat fried shrimp and hot peppers special; and the third time he had two of TipTop's giant meatball sandwiches with hot peppers. Since the only food all three meals had in common was the hot peppers, Monroe concludes that it is solely due to TipTop's hot peppers that he became ill.

Monroe's reasoning is most vulnerable to which one of the following criticisms?

(A) He draws his conclusion on the basis of too few meals that were consumed at Tip-Top and that included hot peppers.

(B) He posits a causal relationship without ascertaining that the presumed cause preceded the presumed effect.

(C) He allows his desire to continue dining at TipTop to bias his conclusion.

(D) He fails to establish that everyone who ate TipTop's hot peppers became ill.

(E) He overlooks the fact that at all three meals he consumed what was, for him, an unusually large quantity of food.

(E) is correct.

Monroe is proposing that one event is "due to" something else—in other words, the first event is caused by the second. Anytime we see a causation argument, we can think through our causation checklist:

1. Does the reverse make some sense too? Could B have a direct impact on A? Could the fact that he ate peppers have been caused by his later illness? Probably not.

2. Could it be that something else impacts both A and B? Could some condition that predisposed him to order peppers also be responsible for making him ill? Possible, but unlikely.

3. Could it be that A and B have no impact on one another? Could the fact that he had peppers and got ill be unrelated? Absolutely! There were no meals that he ate that did not involve peppers. What if something completely unrelated made him sick? The temperature of the room? The air freshener? Notice that the argument mentions that Monroe generally has a "poor appetite." But the quantity of food he finished at TipTop is pretty staggering—an extra large pizza, all-you-can-eat shrimp, and a giant meatball sub. What if eating all those jumbo meals—not the side of peppers he had with every meal—made him sick?

(A) is tempting because "small sample size" can be a flaw of an experiment. However, this choice does not account for any meals that did not contain hot peppers. Even if he had 100 TipTop meals that included hot peppers, this would not address the concern we identified above.

(B) is factually inaccurate (although it may be hard to tell because of the deliberately abstract language). Stand your ground! The author does posit ("put forth") a causal relationship, but we know that the presumed cause (eating peppers) happened before the presumed effect (getting sick).

(C) is not supported by the argument. We have no way of knowing whether he wants to dine at TipTop in the future.

(D) has no bearing on the argument. We don't care if everyone became ill, only if Monroe did (and what the cause of that illness was).

(E) is exactly what we predicted above. Even if we had missed the size of his meals on our first read, examining choice (E) reveals that this choice gives us another possible explanation for why he both ate peppers and got ill after his meals.

3. PT14, S2, Q10

The government of Penglai, an isolated island, proposed eliminating outdoor advertising except for small signs of standard shape that identify places of business. Some island merchants protested that the law would reduce the overall volume of business in Penglai, pointing to a report done by the government indicating that in every industry the Penglai businesses that used outdoor advertising had a larger market share than those that did not.

Which one of the following describes an error of reasoning in the merchants' argument?

(A) presupposing that there are no good reasons for restricting the use of outdoor advertising in Penglai

(B) assuming without giving justification that the outdoor advertising increased market share by some means other than by diverting trade from competing businesses

(C) ignoring the question of whether the government's survey of the island could be objective

(D) failing to establish whether the market-share advantage enjoyed by businesses employing outdoor advertising was precisely proportionate to the amount of advertising

(E) disregarding the possibility that the government's proposed restrictions are unconstitutional

(B) is correct.

While causality is not explicitly mentioned here, the merchants' objection to the proposed law is based on what they perceive to be a causal link between signage size and business volume: bigger signage has a direct impact on bigger market share. This is not necessarily a true causal relationship—what if, for example, companies with bigger market share are the only ones who can afford bigger signs? The flaw might deal with this correlation/causation gap.

Also, always look carefully at the wording of the conclusion: "the law would reduce the overall volume of business" on the island. Could there be a language mismatch here? "Market share" is a percentage of overall volume. In other words, a larger market share doesn't necessarily mean more overall business for the island, it just means a bigger piece of the existing pie. The correct answer could also address this mismatch.

Let's go to the answers.

(A) has no bearing on the conclusion. The argument concerns the economic effect of restricting advertising; whether that restriction is justified is irrelevant.

(C) is tempting because the survey's objectivity is not, in fact, addressed. But either way, there is not enough information to say this is an error. If the survey is objective, the flaws we came up with above still hold. If the survey is not objective, we can't make any conclusion (since we don't know what the true results of an objective survey would be). Eliminate it.

4

(D) is tempting because it is related to the argument's causality/causation claim, which is clearly flawed. However, knowing that sign sizes and market share were proportional would not prove causation; it would only give us more specific information about the correlation. Eliminate.

(E) has no bearing on the conclusion. The argument's scope is restricted to the economic effect of smaller signs; constitutionality is irrelevant.

At first glance, (B) may seem too specific to be our flaw, especially if we fixated on the causality flaw first. But upon closer inspection, (B) directly addresses the mismatch between the "overall volume" of island business and "market share." If bigger advertising did in fact increase market share, but did so only by stealing business from other competitors on the island, then the overall volume of business on the island was unaffected. Therefore, the merchants' argument (even if the problematic causal relationship is true), won't hold water. (B) is our answer.

_4. PT19, S2, Q14_

Herbalist: Many of my customers find that their physical coordination improves after drinking juice containing certain herbs. A few doctors assert that the herbs are potentially harmful, but doctors are always trying to maintain a monopoly over medical therapies. So there is no reason not to try my herb juice.

The reasoning in the herbalist's argument is flawed because the argument

(A) attempts to force acceptance of a claim by inducing fear of the consequences of rejecting that claim

(B) bases a conclusion on claims that are inconsistent with each other

(C) rejects a claim by attacking the proponents of the claim rather than addressing the claim itself

(D) relies on evidence presented in terms that presuppose the truth of the claim for which the evidence is offered

(E) mistakes the observation that one thing happens after another for proof that the second thing is the result of the first

(C) is correct.

The conclusion uses very strong wording: "there is no reason not to try my herb juice." This is an absolute statement, so be suspicious—claims this strong must be backed up with equally strong evidence. Has the argument addressed all possible reasons not to try the herb juice? No way. (Side note: be very careful and picky when dealing with double negatives...the conclusion does not say "you should try my herb juice"—it only says there is no reason not to try it.)

There is also a hidden causal claim here. There is one reason given for not trying the juice (a few doctors claim herb juice might be harmful), and that reason is shot down for the reason that those doctors are trying to maintain a monopoly on therapies. This assumes doctors warn against herb juice only because of self-interest. Is this necessarily true? No; the two things could be unrelated—if a personal trainer tells you exercise is good because he wants you to train with him, that doesn't necessarily mean that exercise is bad.

Let's look at the answers with these potential flaws in mind.

(A) is factually inaccurate, but may be tempting because of the abstract language. Look at each word specifically— the consequences of rejecting the herb juice are not addressed at all. Eliminate it.

(B) is inaccurate. Are there any claims that are inconsistent with each other? You could argue that the doctors' warnings and the author's claims are in opposition, but the author isn't using those inconsistencies to prove his argument; he shoots down the doctors' objections. Eliminate it.

(D) is confusingly written, but inaccurate. Does the evidence provided ("many of my customers find that their physical coordination improves after drinking juice containing herbs") presuppose the conclusion ("there is no reason not to try my herb juice") to be true? No. Don't allow deliberately abstract language to overwhelm you—break it down into smaller digestible pieces. Eliminate it.

(E) is tempting because there is no proven causal link between the herb juice and subsequent improved coordination. However, remember that our answer must relate back to the conclusion. Even if the herb juice does not cause improved coordination, does that mean there is no reason not to try it? No. Eliminate it.

That leaves us with (C), the only choice that addresses a specific reason not to try the juice. Doctors claim that herb juice might be dangerous, and the author rebuts this claim by criticizing doctors in general (by saying they want to maintain a monopoly). But the author never addresses the claim that herb juice might be dangerous—a very clear reason not to try his herb juice. (C) is our answer.

5. PT19, S2, Q23

A museum director, in order to finance expensive new acquisitions, discreetly sold some paintings by major artists. All of them were paintings that the director privately considered inferior. Critics roundly condemned the sale, charging that the museum had lost first-rate pieces, thereby violating its duty as a trustee of art for future generations. A few months after being sold by the museum, those paintings were resold, in an otherwise stagnant art market, at two to three times the price paid to the museum. Clearly, these prices settle the issue, since they demonstrate the correctness of the critics' evaluation.

The reasoning in the argument is vulnerable to the criticism that the argument does which one of the following?

(A) It concludes that a certain opinion is correct on the grounds that it is held by more people than hold the opposing view.

(B) It rejects the judgment of the experts in an area in which there is no better guide to the truth than expert judgment.

(C) It rejects a proven means of accomplishing an objective without offering any alternative means of accomplishing that objective.

(D) It bases a firm conclusion about a state of affairs in the present on somewhat speculative claims about a future state of affairs.

(E) It bases its conclusion on facts that could, in the given situation, have resulted from causes other than those presupposed by the argument.

(E) is correct.

Here the author's point is that the critics' evaluation—that the museum had lost first-rate pieces—is correct.

The price is, for her, what settles it—and we know that the price that the paintings resold for was two to three times the price the museum sold them for. We can think of an abbreviated core as follows:

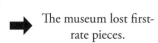

Museum sold artwork at much lower price than that at which artwork was resold ➡ The museum lost first-rate pieces.

There are many gaps to consider here. One, price does not define what a first-rate piece is, especially when it comes to what will be considered first-rate in the future. And we have very little information about whether the price was significant or not. Furthermore, there is an insinuation that the museum undervalued the paintings, but that isn't necessarily true. Perhaps, in the few months between the two sales, other factors caused the price of paintings in general, or paintings of a particular artist, to jump in unexpected ways?

(A) is factually inaccurate. The author never compares the number of people holding any of the views mentioned in the argument.

(B) has no bearing on the conclusion. We have no way of knowing whether there is "no better guide" than expert judgment, and even if we did, who are the experts in this case—the critics or the director? Eliminate it.

4

(C) is tempting because it addresses the fact that director wanted to purchase new works. However, this answer has no bearing on the critics' contention, and thus doesn't represent a flaw in the core of this argument.

(D) is tempting because we may have noticed a flaw in the argument about art price stability (high prices at one point does not guarantee high prices in the future). However, the argument does not make claims about the future value of the sold paintings, so this choice is factually inaccurate. Eliminate it.

(E) is correct. It represents the second of the issues we discussed—the change in price could be due to reasons other than the paintings indeed being first-rate.

6. PT19, S4, Q6

Videocassette recorders (VCRs) enable people to watch movies at home on videotape. People who own VCRs go to movie theaters more often than do people who do not own VCRs. Contrary to popular belief, therefore, owning a VCR actually stimulates people to go to movie theaters more often than they otherwise would.

The argument is most vulnerable to criticism on the grounds that it

(A) concludes that a claim must be false because of the mere absence of evidence in its favor

(B) cites, in support of the conclusion, evidence that is inconsistent with other information that is provided

(C) fails to establish that the phenomena interpreted as cause and effect are not both direct effects of some other factor

(D) takes a condition that by itself guarantees the occurrence of a certain phenomenon to be a condition that therefore must be met for that phenomenon to occur

(E) bases a broad claim about the behavior of people in general on a comparison between two groups of people that together include only a small proportion of people overall

(C) is correct.

The conclusion here is based on an observation about the frequency with which two events occur together (owning a VCR and going to the movies more often)—a classic causality question! Remember our checklist?

1. Does the reverse make some sense too? Could B have a direct impact on A? Could going to the movies more often make people want to own a VCR? Sure—if they like the movies they see maybe they want to watch them again at home.

2. Could it be that something else impacts both A and B? Could these two events have a separate cause? How about a general love of movies? Or higher disposable income?

As soon as we identify a classic causality flaw in this type of question we probably have enough information to proceed to the choices—no reason to predict every possible alternative.

(A) is factually inaccurate. The author presents evidence contrary to the "popular belief" (although whether we agree with that evidence or not is up for debate).

(B) is factually inaccurate. There is nothing inconsistent about the information provided— "popular belief" may be inconsistent with the evidence, but belief is not evidence!

(D) is factually inaccurate. Don't be put off by the abstract language—break it down: is the author saying that people MUST own a VCR in order to go to the movies more often? No; eliminate it.

(E) is tempting because the author does make a claim about general behavior, but the groups of people mentioned are *not* a small proportion of the overall population. Owning a VCR and not owning a VCR are mutually exclusive—together, the groups of people that fall into those categories make up 100% of the population. Eliminate it.

This leaves us with (C), which is exactly one of the flaws we mentioned above (option 2).

7. PT20, S1, Q10

Premiums for automobile accident insurance are often higher for red cars than for cars of other colors. To justify these higher charges, insurance companies claim that, overall, a greater percentage of red cars are involved in accidents than are cars of any other color. If this claim is true, then lives could undoubtedly be saved by banning red cars from the roads altogether.

The reasoning in the argument is flawed because the argument

   (A) accepts without question that insurance companies have the right to charge higher premiums for higher-risk clients
   (B) fails to consider whether red cars cost the same to repair as cars of other colors
   (C) ignores the possibility that drivers who drive recklessly have a preference for red cars
   (D) does not specify precisely what percentage of red cars are involved in accidents
   (E) makes an unsupported assumption that every automobile accident results in some loss of life

(C) is correct.

The author's final conclusion is that lives could be saved by banning red cars. The reasoning used is the claim that a greater percentage of red cars are involved in accidents than are cars of any other color. We can think of the core of this argument as follows:

Red color cars have highest likelihood of accident Lives could be saved by banning red cars.

Notice that in this case, the conclusion doesn't explicitly mention causation. However, causation is implied in the *reasoning* the author uses to connect evidence to conclusion. Why does the author think lives could be saved by banning red cars? Because he assumes that the car being

red has some impact on lives being saved or lost. Remember that in evaluating any claim of causation, it is helpful to think about the potential for the reverse causation and also about no causal relationship at all.

Since the author is assuming that the color being red has an impact on the likelihood of an accident, we want to ask ourselves…

(1) Is it possible that having a higher likelihood of having an accident impacts whether the car is red?

This may seem implausible at first, but it actually makes a lot of sense. Perhaps those who are more inclined to drive in a manner that leads to accidents are more likely to buy red cars.

(2) Is it possible that the color red and the likelihood of being in an accident have no direct impact on one another?

Absolutely. Imagine that the most popular car in the world also happens to be the most dangerous, and it happens to only come in red. In that case, the color of the car could have no causal relation to the likelihood of an accident.

It's not essential that you come up with exact reasons why alternative modes of causation are possible during the course of the actual exam. However, it is critical that you recognize that alternative modes are indeed possible, and that the author is flawed in assuming one particular path of causation.

There is also a mismatch between premise and conclusion having to do with "accidents" versus "deaths." It's possible certain cars are more likely to lead to accidents, but less likely to lead to *fatal* accidents. A correct answer could address this flaw as well.

With that in mind, let's take a look at the answer choices:

(A) has no bearing on whether lives will be saved by banning red cars and therefore can be eliminated quickly. Whether insurance companies have this right is not what is at issue.

(B) has no bearing on whether lives will be saved by banning red cars and can be eliminated quickly.

(D) is tempting, in part because such information would be helpful for us in understanding the argument. However, a precise percentage is not *required* for this argument to hold, and thus this answer doesn't represent a reasoning flaw in this argument.

(E) sounds a lot like the second issue we predicted, and therefore is probably the most tempting incorrect answer.

If we carefully inspect each word in (E), the term "every" jumps out at us. Certainly, the author is assuming a connection between accidents and loss of life, but is he assuming every accident results in loss of life? No.

That leaves us with answer (C): "ignores the possibility that drivers who drive recklessly have a preference for red cars." This sounds exactly like an alternate mode of causation that we predicted.

If we inspect each word in (C), nothing jumps out as questionable, and (C) makes a lot of sense. In assuming one path of causation, the author is ignoring this other possibility.

Therefore, (C) is the correct answer.

8. PT21, S2, Q5

Irrigation runoff from neighboring farms may well have increased the concentration of phosphorus in the local swamp above previous levels, but the claim that the increase in phosphorus is harming the swamp's native aquatic wildlife is false; the phosphorus concentration in the swamp is actually less than that found in certain kinds of bottled water that some people drink every day.

The argument is vulnerable to criticism on the ground that it

    (A) makes exaggerations in formulating the claim against which it argues

    (B) bases its conclusion on two contradictory claims

    (C) relies on evidence the relevance of which has not been established

    (D) concedes the very point that it argues against

    (E) makes a generalization that is unwarranted because the sources of the data on which it is based have not been specified

(C) is correct.

If the author flat-out declares another claim is true or false, that declaration is often the argument's main conclusion. What is the evidence used to prove that the claim about phosphorus's harmfulness to the swamp's native aquatic life is *false*? The fact that phosphorus in the swamp is less than phosphorus in certain common kinds of bottled water.

Do you see the mismatch? Whenever two things are compared, make sure those quantities are actually similar. Could water appropriate for human consumption contain higher phosphorus than water appropriate for a swamp's wildlife? Certainly—they are used for completely different functions; one is exclusively for drinking and one is pervasive throughout an entire ecosystem.

Keeping that mismatch in mind, let's look at our choices:

(A) is inaccurate; the claim against which the author argues is simply stated: "increase in phosphorus is harming the swamp's native aquatic wildlife"—there is no exaggeration.

(B) is tempting because there are two contradictory claims presented, but the conclusion of the argument denies one of these claims in favor of the other, rather than basing its conclusion on both. Eliminate it.

(D) is incorrect because ceding a point to the opposition is not a flaw—stating a premise counter to the conclusion, then demonstrating why (despite that counter-premise) the conclusion still holds, is a technique often used in sophisticated arguments. Eliminate it.

MANHATTAN
LSAT

(E) is tempting because the sources of the data are indeed not disclosed. However, you cannot dispute the accuracy of information presented in the premises. If the argument says something is a fact, then you must assume it is true (otherwise you could argue with *everything* simply by saying there isn't documentation for why that thing is true).

That leaves (C), which addresses the mismatch in comparability we discussed above. Unlike choice (E), which says we can't prove a conclusion without a specific *source,* choice (C) directly addresses the fact that the information itself (which we must assume is true because it is presented as true in the argument) may not be relevant to the argument. That's our answer.

9. PT33, S3, Q5

The radiation absorbed by someone during an ordinary commercial airline flight is no more dangerous than that received during an ordinary dental X-ray. Since a dental X-ray does negligible harm to a person, we can conclude that the radiation absorbed by members of commercial airline flight crews will also do them negligible harm.

A flaw in the argument is its failure to consider that

(A) there may be many forms of dangerous radiation other than X-rays and the kinds of radiation absorbed by members of commercial airline flight crews

(B) receiving a dental X-ray may mitigate other health risks, whereas flying does not

(C) exposure to X-rays of higher intensity than dental X-rays may be harmful

(D) the longer and the more often one is exposed to radiation, the more radiation one absorbs and the more seriously one is harmed

(E) flying at high altitude involves risks in addition to exposure to minor radiation

(D) is correct.

Did you spot the mismatch? There are two things being compared in the conclusion—are

they truly comparable? The argument discusses single occurrences of events (an X-ray, a flight) then makes a conclusion about the damage made to multiple people who will undergo multiple occurrences of such events—a mismatch! Smoking a single cigarette may not kill someone, but smoking a single cigarette every waking hour for 20 years might.

(A) is tempting because it seemingly addresses an "alternate consideration" (other types of radiation), but look closely at the first premise. The sentence explicitly states: "The radiation absorbed…," which covers all kinds of radiation, not just X-ray radiation. Also, the conclusion deals with radiation damage to flight crews, so we only care about the "the kinds of radiation absorbed" by these people. Eliminate it.

(B) has no bearing on the conclusion, because we only care about the risk associated with radiation to flight crews, not other types of risk.

(C) has no bearing on the conclusion. The first premise explicitly compares radiation exposure during an X-ray to radiation exposure during a flight, so higher levels are irrelevant.

(E) has no bearing on the conclusion, because we only care about the risk associated with radiation to flight crews, not other types of risk.

Choice (D) addresses the mismatch between the two quantities we are comparing—if the effect of radiation exposure is cumulative, it is quite possible that a flight crew member, who is repeatedly exposed to radiation, could be harmed more than the average person who only infrequently gets a dental X-ray.

10. PT36, S1, Q19

Although it has been suggested that Arton's plays have a strong patriotic flavor, we must recall that, at the time of their composition, her country was in anything but a patriotic mood. Unemployment was high, food was costly, and crime rates were soaring. As a result, the general morale of her nation was at an especially low point. Realizing this, we see clearly that any apparent patriotism in

4

Arton's work must have been intended ironically.

The reasoning above is questionable because it

(A) posits an unstated relationship between unemployment and crime

(B) takes for granted that straightforward patriotism is not possible for a serious writer

(C) takes for granted that Arton was attuned to the predominant national attitude of her time

(D) overlooks the fact that some citizens prosper in times of high unemployment

(E) confuses irony with a general decline in public morale

(C) is correct.

Why does the author conclude that "clearly… any apparent patriotism in Arton's work must have been intended ironically"? He draws that conclusion from the fact that the *country*'s morale was low, and that it was not in a patriotic mood. There is a big mismatch here—does a citizen of a country necessarily reflect the overall mood of that country? Absolutely not. Let's look at the answers:

(A) has no bearing on the conclusion. Whether unemployment and crime are related has no effect on the core of the argument.

(B) is factually incorrect. The argument never implies this (and that word "not possible" creates a very extreme sentiment!).

(D) is tempting because this choice addresses the possibility that there may be exceptions to the general mood of the country. However, unemployment is only one of many facts cited as evidence for the generally low morale of the country. We must still accept at face value the premise that the "morale of her nation was at an especially low point." This choice actually has no bearing on our conclusion.

(E) is tempting because it seems to address the mismatch between Arton's mood and the public's mood. However, remember to look at each word with ruthless specificity. Is "irony" itself being

confused with low morale? No—the author is making a conclusion *about* irony based on low morale. Eliminate it.

Choice (C) properly addresses the mismatch between Arton's mood and the country's mood. If she was *not* attuned to the predominant national attitude, she may have sincerely expressed patriotism, rather than ironically expressing it.

Challenge Questions

11. PT36, S3, Q13

While it was once believed that the sort of psychotherapy appropriate for the treatment of neuroses caused by environmental factors is also appropriate for schizophrenia and other psychoses, it is now known that these latter, more serious forms of mental disturbance are best treated by biochemical—that is, medicinal—means. This is conclusive evidence that psychoses, unlike neuroses, have nothing to do with environmental factors but rather are caused by some sort of purely organic condition, such as abnormal brain chemistry or brain malformations.

The argument is vulnerable to criticism because it ignores the possibility that

(A) the organic conditions that result in psychoses can be caused or exacerbated by environmental factors

(B) the symptoms of mental disturbance caused by purely organic factors can be alleviated with medicine

(C) organic illnesses that are nonpsychological in nature may be treatable without using biochemical methods

(D) the nature of any medical condition can be inferred from the nature of the treatment that cures that condition

(E) organic factors having little to do with brain chemistry may be at least partially responsible for neuroses

(A) is correct.

Did you spot the many uses of extreme language

in this argument? Let's look at the conclusion first. The phrase "this is conclusive evidence that" lets us know that a conclusion is coming:

"…psychoses, unlike neuroses, have **NOTHING** to do with environmental factors but rather are caused by some sort of **PURELY** organic condition."

What is the evidence for this extreme claim? The argument starts with a counterpremise ("while.."), then lists its star witness—an observation about the *best* treatment for schizophrenia and other psychoses. The core of the argument looks like this:

schizophrenia and other psychoses are **BEST** treated by biochemical/ medicinal means psychoses have **NO** environmental causes and **ONLY** organic causes

Notice the mismatch in extreme language of the premise and the conclusion—are "best" and "only" the same thing? Just because biochemical treatment is most effective, does that mean no other treatments are effective at all? The alternative treatments may still work, but just not as well as biochemical treatments. And just because a medicinal treatment is effective, does that mean the condition is caused *only* by biology? No—for example, some people take drugs to alleviate the effects of environmental stress. There are several logic gaps here. There's no need to identify them all—just have a sense of one or two big ones when going to the answers.

(B) has no bearing on the conclusion. The author would probably agree that this choice is true—if psychoses are caused by organic factors, and psychoses are treatable by medicine, then medicine can treat conditions caused by organic factors. But we want to find the *flaw* in the argument. Eliminate it.

(C) has no bearing on the conclusion. We are not concerned with nonpsychological illnesses.

(D) is tempting because the author does make an assumption about the link between the type

of treatment and the cause of a condition. But notice that little word "any." Does the author make an assumption about *any* condition? No, he only makes one about this particular subgroup. Eliminate it.

(E) has no bearing on the conclusion. The author's claim concerns organic factors—whether they are related to brain chemistry is irrelevant. The phrase "such as" in the conclusion triggers *examples* of organic causes, not the *only* types of organic causes. Eliminate it.

Choice (A) addresses the alternate possibility that environmental factors may have an effect on psychoses (either by making the condition worse or by ultimately *causing* organic conditions that in turn cause psychoses). This is our answer.

12. PT18, S4, Q9

Brain scans of people exposed to certain neurotoxins reveal brain damage identical to that found in people suffering from Parkinson's disease. This fact shows not only that these neurotoxins cause this type of brain damage, but also that the brain damage itself causes Parkinson's disease. Thus brain scans can be used to determine who is likely to develop Parkinson's disease.

The argument contains which one of the following reasoning errors?

(A) It fails to establish that other methods that can be used to diagnose Parkinson's disease are less accurate than brain scans.

(B) It overestimates the importance of early diagnosis in determining appropriate treatments for people suffering from Parkinson's disease.

(C) It mistakes a correlation between the type of brain damage described and Parkinson's disease for a causal relation between the two.

(D) It assumes that people would want to know as early as possible whether they were likely to develop Parkinson's disease.

(E) It neglects to specify how the information provided by brain scans could be used either in treating Parkinson's disease or in monitoring the progression of the disease.

(C) is correct.

The conclusion of this argument claims that a brain scan can help predict Parkinson's. Notice that the word "causes" shows up twice, to link two different correlations (exposure to neurotoxins + Parkinson's-type brain damage and brain damage + Parkinson's). Let's go to our causation checklist:

1. Does the reverse make some sense too? Could B have a direct impact on A?

We have two different causation claims, so check each independently. Could brain damage cause exposure to neurotoxins? Probably not. But could Parkinson's cause brain damage? It's possible.

2. Could it be that something else impacts both A and B?

Could something else impact both exposure to neurotoxins and brain damage? Perhaps not likely but still possible—an explosion could expose someone to both neurotoxins and a physical accident that caused brain damage. Could something else cause both Parkinson's and brain damage? Sure; genetics, another disease, and non-neurotoxin chemicals are some possible candidates.

3. Could it be that A and B have no impact on one another?

Could the neurotoxins and brain damage, or the brain damage and Parkinson's, be completely unrelated? Absolutely. And could both of these relationships be unrelated to each other? Yes—just because a type of brain damage is similar to Parkinson's brain damage, that does not mean the first type is Parkinson's brain damage.

We're not suggesting that you identify every single one of these alternate models. After you identified one possible alternative, it is probably smart to move on to the answers so you can keep a brisk pace under time pressure (but keep that general flaw in mind!).

(A) has no bearing on the conclusion. We don't care about whether this method is more or less accurate than other methods; we only care if it works.

(B) has no bearing on the conclusion. The argument does not discuss treatment.

(D) has no bearing on the argument, which deals with whether brain scans can be used, not whether people will want to use them

(E) has no bearing on the conclusion. The argument does not discuss treatment or monitoring progression.

Choice (C) is the final causation flaw we identified above. Even if you stop before identifying all the flaws, and this flaw is not the specific one you saw first, you can quickly check to see that this statement is true.

13. PT16, S3, Q11

A controversial program rewards prison inmates who behave particularly well in prison by giving them the chance to receive free cosmetic plastic surgery performed by medical students. The program is obviously morally questionable, both in its assumptions about what inmates might want and in its use of the prison population to train future surgeons. Putting these moral issues aside, however, the surgery clearly has a powerful rehabilitative effect, as is shown by the fact that, among recipients of the surgery, the proportion who are convicted of new crimes committed after release is only half that for the prison population as a whole.

A flaw in the reasoning of the passage is that it

(A) allows moral issues to be a consideration in presenting evidence about matters of fact

(B) dismisses moral considerations on the grounds that only matters of fact are relevant

(C) labels the program as "controversial" instead of discussing the issues that give rise to controversy

(D) asserts that the rehabilitation of criminals is not a moral issue

(E) relies on evidence drawn from a sample that there is reason to believe is unrepresentative

(E) is correct.

The conclusion that the surgery has "a powerful rehabilitative effect" contains a word that lets us know the author is asserting a causal relationship —"effect." Does surgery truly cause lower rates of recidivism? Let's go to our checklist:

1. Does the reverse make some sense too? Could B have a direct impact on A?

Could the lower rate of recidivism cause the surgery? Because one event happens later in time than the other, it is unlikely that the later event caused the earlier event (unless you believe in time travel!).

2. Could it be that something else impacts both A and B?

Could something else, however, have caused both surgery and a lower rate of recidivism? Prisoners were "awarded" surgery for good behavior—could this good behavior (or some underlying factor that caused the good behavior) also be responsible for fewer crimes committed after release? Absolutely.

This is a pretty big flaw, and probably enough for us to go on when attacking the answers. Let's look at the choices. Many of them address the morality/controversy of the surgery. A large portion of the argument text deals with the moral implications of the surgery, but notice that the conclusion itself begins with the phrase "putting moral issues aside." This may help us do some rapid elimination.

(A) has no bearing on the argument. Morality is irrelevant to the primary conclusion of this argument.

(B) is tempting because it directly addresses the fact that the author sweeps morality aside. However, you must deal with the conclusion as given, and the conclusion as given excludes morality.

(C) has no bearing on the argument. The controversy is not relevant to the asserted causal link.

(D) has no bearing on the argument, and is factually inaccurate. The author never states that rehabilitation is not a moral issue.

This leaves us with (E), which may not seem at first to address the causation flaw we found. But take a closer look. How could the sample of prisoners be considered unrepresentative? The group that receives surgery is selected by good behavior, and is therefore not a clear control group to compare against the general population that does not receive the surgery. It is potentially difficult to separate the ultimate cause of the surgery (better behavior in prison) from the ultimate result (better behavior outside of prison). Therefore, (E) is our answer.

_14. PT36, S1, Q10_

Cotrell is, at best, able to write magazine articles of average quality. The most compelling pieces of evidence for this are those few of the numerous articles submitted by Cotrell that are superior, since Cotrell, who is incapable of writing an article that is better than average, must obviously have plagiarized superior ones.

The argument is most vulnerable to criticism on which one of the following grounds?

(A) It simply ignores the existence of potential counterevidence.

(B) It generalizes from atypical occurrences.

(C) It presupposes what it seeks to establish.

(D) It relies on the judgment of experts in a matter to which their expertise is irrelevant.

(E) It infers limits on ability from a few isolated lapses in performance.

(C) is correct.

Which of the statements is the conclusion? The words *"pieces of evidence"* and *"since"* in the second sentence signal that this second sentence contains premises that support something else.

4

The conclusion, therefore, is the *first* sentence.

The core of the argument is as follows:

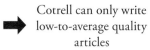

("evidence") Cotrell submitted a few superior articles

+

("since") Cotrell is incapable of writing a better-than-average article, he must have plagiarized

➡ Cotrell can only write low-to-average quality articles

When we break down the core, it is easier to see that the conclusion merely restates part of the second premise, without additional support.

(A) is factually inaccurate. The argument cites counterevidence (the few superior articles), but attempts to use that counterevidence to support the conclusion. Eliminate it.

(B) is factually inaccurate. There are "atypical occurrences" mentioned (the superior articles), but rather than generalizing from these occurrences, the author attempts to prove the opposite of what they would imply. (A generalization from these occurrences would suggest that Cotrell is able to write superior articles.) Eliminate it.

(D) is factually inaccurate. There are no experts cited in this argument.

(E) is tempting because the first part of the answer ("infers limits on ability") is correct, but this conclusion is not drawn from isolated lapses in performance, but from isolated superior performances. Read every word of each choice carefully—the test writers may try to sneak something into the end of an otherwise tempting choice that makes it wrong. Eliminate it.

Choice (C) points out the similarity between the conclusion and second premise. The argument assumes the idea that Cotrell writes only low-to-average articles is true, and then uses that idea to prove that the statement "Cotrell writes only low-to-average articles" is true. (C) is our answer.

Notice how short the argument and answer choices are—abstract language can make a seemingly simple question very tricky. When dealing with abstract language, which the test writers deliberately employ to confuse test-takers, don't let any small words off the hook—get more specific!

15. PT16, S2, Q22

Director of personnel: Ms. Tours has formally requested a salary adjustment on the grounds that she was denied merit raises to which she was entitled. Since such grounds provide a possible basis for adjustments, an official response is required. Ms. Tours presents compelling evidence that her job performance has been both excellent in itself and markedly superior to that of others in her department who were awarded merit raises. Her complaint that she was treated unfairly thus appears justified. Nevertheless, her request should be denied. To raise Ms. Tours's salary because of her complaint would jeopardize the integrity of the firm's merit-based reward system by sending the message that employees can get their salaries raised if they just complain enough.

The personnel director's reasoning is most vulnerable to criticism on the grounds that it

(A) fails to consider the possibility that Ms. Tours's complaint could be handled on an unofficial basis

(B) attempts to undermine the persuasiveness of Ms. Tours's evidence by characterizing it as "mere complaining"

(C) sidesteps the issue of whether superior job performance is a suitable basis for awarding salary increases

(D) ignores the possibility that some of the people who did receive merit increases were not entitled to them

(E) overlooks the implications for the integrity of the firm's merit-based reward system of denying Ms. Tours's request

(E) is correct.

The personnel director concludes that although Ms. Tours was unjustly underpaid, correcting that error would undermine the integrity of the merit system. We can think of the core of the argument in the following way:

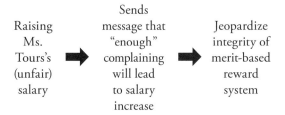

Why does the personnel director think the integrity of the merit-based reward system would be compromised? There is a clear mismatch between the wording of the conclusion ("just complain enough") and the wording of the premises ("compelling evidence" and "justified" complaint). Additionally, if "integrity" of the merit-based reward system is our ultimate goal, wouldn't this goal be threatened by the unfair violation of merit-based rewards in Ms. Tours's case? Let's look at the choices.

(A) has no bearing on the conclusion. Even if Ms. Tours's salary could be raised "unofficially," the effect on the public perception of the merit-based system would not be improved. In fact, it might be compromised further, since backchannel ways of fixing problems are probably not the best way to demonstrate integrity. Also, the author states that "an official response is required."

(B) is tempting, because it addresses the mismatch between "compelling evidence" and "just complain enough." However, does the director actually attempt to undermine the persuasiveness of Ms. Tours' evidence? No. In fact, he calls the evidence "compelling" and her claim "justified." Eliminate it.

(C) is tempting because the author does not explicitly state that superior performance is grounds for merit-based increases. However, he does state that Ms. Tours's claim of unfair treatment is justified. The issue is not whether she is entitled to a merit-based increase, but whether the fair awarding of that increase would undermine the system. Eliminate it.

(D) has no bearing on the conclusion. We are only concerned with the effect of Ms. Tours's potential salary increase; we don't care about the salary increases of others.

While choice (E) does not address the more obvious vocabulary mismatch between "just complain enough" and "compelling evidence," it does address the second concern we identified. If integrity is what we are after, then choosing to uphold something that we know is unfair will undermine that same integrity. This is our answer.

4

Chapter 5

of

Logical Reasoning

The Problem-Solving Process for Assumption Family Questions

Introduction

Assumption and Identify a Flaw are two of the most important question types that appear in the Logical Reasoning section. Now that you've had a chance to study both of them in depth, how do you feel?

Hopefully, you're excited about the fact that you now know more about the nature of these questions than you did before. However, this added knowledge can also be a burden. Perhaps these questions feel harder because you now realize just how much there is for you to think about!

Now is a good time to pause and consider your *process*. Your process is the strategy you use to arrive at an answer. Perhaps a more effective way to think about process is that it is the manner in which you choose to apply your understanding and judgment.

It's impossible to predict the key idea or spark of inspiration that will unlock any one particular logical reasoning problem. However, for all logical reasoning problems, the types of issues that need to be considered, and the ideal order in which one ought to consider them, are defined. That is, for every type of problem, there is a common set of decisions to be made, and a logical order in which to make these decisions. Therefore, a process that helps you think about the right issues at the right time can be a powerful tool.

For all Assumption Family questions—Assumption, Identify a Flaw, Strengthen, Weaken, and Principle (support) questions—the recommended process is the same. Let's take a look at that process in two parts:

1. Preparing to answer the question
2. Evaluating the answer choices

In future chapters, we'll discuss how this process can be adjusted for non-Assumption Family questions.

Preparing to Answer the Question

To get started, let's take a look at arguments and question stems for four Assumption and Identify a Flaw problems that appeared in one section of the October 2002 exam.

After you've read each one, please write down whatever you think is most important to know about the particular argument. See if you can perhaps correctly predict the key to identifying the correct answer.

PT38, S4, Q8

Politician: My opponent says our zoning laws too strongly promote suburban single-family dwellings and should be changed to encourage other forms of housing like apartment buildings. Yet he lives in a house in the country. His lifestyle contradicts his own argument, which should therefore not be taken seriously.

The politician's reasoning is most vulnerable to criticism on the grounds that

PT38, S4, Q16

People who do not believe that others distrust them are confident in their own abilities, so people who tend to trust others think of a difficult task as a challenge rather than a threat, since this is precisely how people who are confident in their own abilities regard such tasks.

The conclusion above follows logically if which one of the following is assumed?

PT38, S4, Q14

Reducing speed limits neither saves lives nor protects the environment. This is because the more slowly a car is driven, the more time it spends on the road spewing exhaust into the air and running the risk of colliding with other vehicles.

The argument's reasoning is flawed because the argument

PT38, S4, Q22

In humans, ingested protein is broken down into amino acids, all of which must compete to enter the brain. Subsequent ingestion of sugars leads to the production of insulin, a hormone that breaks down the sugars and also rids the bloodstream of residual amino acids, except for tryptophan. Tryptophan then slips into the brain uncontested and is transformed into the chemical serotonin, increasing the brain's serotonin level. Thus, sugars can play a major role in mood elevation, helping one to feel relaxed and anxiety-free.

Which one of the following is an assumption on which the argument depends?

We'll take a look at the answer choices for these problems in just a bit. For now, let's use these arguments to break down and illustrate the first steps in your process.

A Series of Decisions

It's helpful to think about your process in terms of a series of decisions to be made. For *all* Logical Reasoning problems, this will be your first one:

DECISION #1: What is my task?

We recommend that you begin every logical reasoning problem by reading the question stem.

Perhaps most important among the reasons for doing so is that the question stem can help you anticipate the *type* of argument that you are about to read. For all Assumption Family questions, you know that the argument you are about to read will:

- Present a set of premises meant to support one main point.
- Have gaps in the reasoning used.
- Have a correct answer that addresses these gaps in one way or another.

Knowing all this can give you a tremendous head start on Assumption Family questions. Other question prompts will require a different mind-set, so it's important that you consider the question stem first.

Let's take a look at the two Assumption question prompts from the arguments you just evaluated:

1. "The conclusion above follows logically if which one of the following is assumed?"
2. "Which one of the following is an assumption on which the argument depends?"

Your understanding of the difference between the two will be most important when you evaluate the answer choices (more on this later), but it can also help you, in subtle ways, anticipate what you are about to read.

The first question stem requires us to find an answer that would make the argument *logical*. Remember, the LSAT has a very narrow definition of logic—we need an answer that will make the argument airtight. The right answer will completely fill whatever gap exists, or, in some cases, give us even more than we need to fill that gap. Remember from the Assumptions chapter that we call this a *sufficient assumption*.

A consequence of this is that you, the test-taker, know that there is going to be a clearly defined gap *to be filled*. You will not be presented with an argument that has an open ended, or vague, gap, because one concise answer is going to have to make the argument airtight. Very often, this gap will be recognizable because of a term shift (a change of subject matter or attribute) between the premise and the conclusion. In arguments that involve a logical chain, there will be one clear link missing, and the right answer will supply this link. For these reasons, you should *expect* to know, before going into the answer choices, the exact gap that needs to be filled.

The second question stem asks for a different type of assumption—something that must be true if the argument is to be true, but something that, in and of itself, doesn't have to make the argument "perfect." We're looking for something that at the least partially fills the gap. Remember from the Assumptions lesson that we call this a *necessary assumption*.

Consequently, you, the test-taker, have a smaller burden in terms of having to define the gap clearly. Perhaps the argument has a clearly definable gap, and, if so, of course it's to your advantage to understand it as such. But many of these arguments have multiple gaps, or gaps that are less clearly definable. For these problems, your main goal is still to understand the core as well as you can, but you should not necessarily *expect* to know what function the right answer will play.

It's also helpful to know that the second type of assumption, the necessary assumption, is asked for far more often than the sufficient assumption. It's what you want to consider as your default, or standard, Assumption problem.

It might be helpful now to compare some of the thoughts listed above to those you had as you read the question stems earlier. Did reading the question stems originally give you this type of head start? If so, fantastic! If not, make a conscious effort to devote extra focus to every question stem that you read, until the defining of your task is intuitively the first part of your process.

Finally, don't be afraid to revisit the question stem as you evaluate the answer choices. In fact, make a habit of it. Because you will primarily be focused on comparing answer choices against the argument itself, it's going to be very easy to forget if you are looking for something that strengthens, weakens, fills a gap, or represents a flaw. It's true that all of these Assumption Family questions require us to think about the assumptions or gaps in an argument, but each question type presents us with a unique task. The last thing you want to do is pick the right answer for the wrong question.

Once you have decided what your task is, you're ready to move on to the argument itself. If you are reading an argument for an Assumption Family question, you must deal with this next issue before you deal with all the rest.

DECISION #2: What is the conclusion?

This should be your primary focus as you read through an argument for the first time.

In previous chapters, we've stressed the importance of not just trying to understand the meaning of each sentence or clause in an argument but also the *function*—whether it supports or goes against the main point, is the main point, or serves as background information. It is impossible to assign these roles without first having an understanding of the author's main point, and so it makes sense that finding the conclusion should be your first priority.

Also in previous chapters, we've discussed the defining characteristics of conclusions. Conclusions are always opinions, not facts or truths. When an argument has multiple opinions or predictions, the conclusion is the primary opinion or prediction—the one that all others are meant to lead to. Conclusions are often signaled by words such as "thus" and "therefore," and conclusions also frequently come after a counterpoint and a pivot word, such as "however."

In some arguments, it's easy to see which part the conclusion is. In others, the test writers make your task far more difficult. It's important, in these situations, to take the time to get it right.

In Chapter 2, we discussed the many challenges associated with determining the parts of an argument. We'll revisit two particular challenges here, both related to the task of identifying the main conclusion:

(1) the use of an intermediate conclusion, and (2) the use of borrowed language. Let's take a quick look at an example from earlier that illustrates both of these challenges.

PT38, S4, Q8

> Politician: My opponent says our zoning laws too strongly promote suburban single-family dwellings and should be changed to encourage other forms of housing like apartment buildings. Yet he lives in a house in the country. His lifestyle contradicts his own argument, which should therefore not be taken seriously.

In this case, we have two opinions presented in the final sentence—the opponent's lifestyle contradicts his own argument, and the opponent's argument should not be taken seriously.

When dealing with two different opinions, you can identify the final conclusion based on order—which consequence comes last. One simple way to do this is to use the "Therefore Test."

Case 1: The opponent's argument should not be taken seriously. THEREFORE, the opponent's lifestyle contradicts his own argument.

This makes little sense. Let's try it the other way around.

Case 2: The opponent's lifestyle contradicts his own argument. THEREFORE, the opponent's argument should not be taken seriously.

Much better. So, "The opponent's argument should not be taken seriously" should be considered the final conclusion.

Another way that test writers will make it more difficult for you to identify the main conclusion is to borrow language from other parts of the argument. This is often done through the use of a pronoun, a pivot, or a clause that is meant to refer to a different part of the argument.

Notice the wording of the final conclusion: "The opponent's argument should not be taken seriously." In order to fully understand what this means, we have to know what the opponent's argument is, and it's stated earlier in the argument: "…our zoning laws…should be changed to encourage other forms of housing like apartment buildings."

Once you have a clear sense of the author's conclusion, you are ready to move on to the next decision point.

DECISION #3: How is this conclusion supported?

Everything in the argument other than the conclusion is intended to support the conclusion, oppose the conclusion, or serve as background information. A clear understanding of the conclusion should clarify certain distinctions, such as that between supporting and opposing points, but other distinctions can remain vague and somewhat subjective. For example, it may be difficult to decide whether a certain clause is meant to support the conclusion or serve as background information, or do a little bit of both. Don't dwell on this. Generally, in these situations, identifying the answer will not require such distinctions.

What *is* essential is that you identify the *primary* premise(s) meant to support the conclusion. These are the premises that, combined with the conclusion, create the argument core. Simpler arguments will often have one premise, but others can have two or (rarely) three premises that complement each other or link together to lead to the final conclusion. For the vast majority of Assumption Family questions, the right answer will have something to do with the relationship between these supporting premises and the conclusion. A clear understanding of the core is essential for quickly recognizing correct answers and weeding out incorrect ones.

Sometimes, you will be able to see the argument core after just one read. The argument will be simple enough for you to keep all the pieces in mind at once, and you will understand it well enough so that you can easily recognize the function of each component. Other times, you will have to go back and reread certain parts of the argument after you've identified the conclusion. Finally, sometimes you will have to read an argument a third time in order to identify the core.

In general, time spent trying to identify the core is time well spent, so give yourself some slack when you need to. However, be mindful that you don't waste time trying to absorb details of parts of the argument that are *not* in the core. These details are far less likely to be relevant to the correct answer, and an incomplete understanding of these secondary details can distract you and tempt you toward incorrect answer choices. If you are still having trouble finding the argument core on a regular basis, it may help to revisit Chapter 2.

Often, you will find yourself (and us) identifying the conclusion and the premise at the same time. That's fine. In general, as the argument becomes more complex, slow down and separate the steps.

DECISION #4: What is(are) the gap(s)?

For every argument for every Assumption Family question, there will be a gap between the premises presented and the conclusion reached. That is, there will be some flaw in terms of how the author is trying to make his or her point. The correct answer will relate to an issue in this reasoning.

In your process, always pause after you identify the argument core to consider the gap. Compare the subject in the premise to the subject in the conclusion. How are they related? Does the relationship make sense? Compare the attribute in a premise to an attribute in the conclusion. How similar or different are they?

Look for strong words in the conclusion and use them to turn the conclusion into a question. If the conclusion is "only cars equipped with brakes using the new technology should be considered safe," you should think: "Is it *only* those cars?" If the argument concludes that "it is because of our high protein diet that more people generally have shorter lives," you should challenge that with: "Does it have to be *because* of the high protein diet?" Remember, read like a debater! This will help you identify gaps.

If you correctly identify the gap or gaps in an argument, you'll put yourself in the perfect position to answer the question correctly. In fact, it'll often be true that you'll be able to predict the right answer. Unfortunately, no matter how much you prepare, there will be times when you don't see the gap clearly, even if you are at the 180 level. Still, even when you don't clearly see the gap, having searched for it will always be beneficial, because the action places your thinking firmly in the middle of the argument core, and that's where you want to be focused as you evaluate the answer choices.

Let's now deconstruct the four arguments we saw earlier to see how a consistent process can help prepare you to evaluate the answer choices:

PT38, S4, Q8

Politician: My opponent says our zoning laws too strongly promote suburban single-family dwellings and should be changed to encourage other forms of housing like apartment buildings. Yet he lives in a house in the country. His lifestyle contradicts his own argument, which should therefore not be taken seriously.

The politician's reasoning is most vulnerable to criticism on the grounds that

DECISION #1: What is my task?

This is an Assumption Family question: Identify a Flaw.

DECISION #2: What is the conclusion?

The author's conclusion is that the opponent's argument should not be taken seriously. We know what the opponent's argument is—that zoning laws should be changed to encourage other forms of housing. We're ready to move on.

DECISION #3: How is this conclusion supported?

The primary evidence presented is that his lifestyle contradicts his own argument—he lives in a house in the country.

We can see the argument core as follows:

Lifestyle contradicts argument *Argument shouldn't be taken seriously.*

DECISION #4: What is the gap?

While in real life we often say "practice what you preach" as way of criticism, there's no rule that says arguments shouldn't be taken seriously if the person making the argument acts in an inconsistent manner—that is, we have no reason at all to believe that there is any connection between where the opponent lives and the issue of whether his argument should be taken seriously. This is our gap. Since this is an Identify a Flaw question, we want to expose this gap, and we should have a pretty clear sense of what role the right answer is going to play: it's going to address the fact that where the opponent chooses to live is not a significant factor in evaluating the opponent's argument.

PT38, S4, Q16

People who do not believe that others distrust them are confident in their own abilities, so people who tend to trust others think of a difficult task as a challenge rather than a threat, since this is precisely how people who are confident in their own abilities regard such tasks.

The conclusion above follows logically if which one of the following is assumed?

DECISION #1: What is my task?

This is an Assumption Family question. An Assumption question to be more precise, and, furthermore, one that requires a sufficient assumption—we will need to identify an answer that completely fills the gap and makes the argument logically sound. Therefore, we know we're going to see an argument that has a clearly defined gap.

DECISION #2: What is the conclusion?

The conclusion is stated in the middle of the argument, with reasoning before and after:

"So people who tend to trust others think of a difficult task as a challenge rather than a threat…."

Notice, the previous argument was far more grounded in reality, or at least a fictional version of reality. This is more of a philosophical conclusion—it's tempting to interpret it based on your real-life experiences, but you want to avoid thinking about the problem that way. Remember, it's not the truth of the conclusion that we are evaluating (maybe you disagree with this conclusion, but it doesn't matter). We're evaluating the connection between the premises and the conclusion.

DECISION #3: How is this conclusion supported?

This is a short argument, and we can see that it's one where parts are meant to "link" with one another in a complementary fashion. Let's try to understand the relationships more clearly.

The two premises presented are:

1. People who do not believe that others distrust them are confident in their own abilities.
2. People who are confident in their own abilities think of a difficult task as a challenge rather than a threat.

These ideas are supposed to "link" to the conclusion, but we know there is going to be a gap here—a missing link.

DECISION #4: What is the gap?

How do these two premises complement each other? Notice the two statements have a common element (are confident in their own abilities) and we can use this common element to link these statements up.

Since people who do not believe that others distrust them *are confident in their own abilities,* and *those who are confident in their own abilities* think of a difficult task as a challenge rather than a threat, we can say that…

"People who do not believe others distrust them think of a difficult task as a challenge rather than a threat."

But that's not what the author's conclusion says. It says:

"So people WHO TEND TO TRUST OTHERS think of a difficult task as a challenge rather than a threat."

What's the difference? It's between those who do not believe others distrust them and those who tend to trust others. These are similar ideas, but they are not the same.

In order for this argument to be sound, we need to show that people who do not believe others distrust them are people who tend to trust others. That's what the right answer will likely do.

PT38, S4, Q14

> Reducing speed limits neither saves lives nor protects the environment. This is because the more slowly a car is driven, the more time it spends on the road spewing exhaust into the air and running the risk of colliding with other vehicles.
>
> The argument's reasoning is flawed because the argument

DECISION #1: What is my task?

We can see that this is an Assumption Family question—an Identify a Flaw question to be more specific.

DECISION #2: What is the conclusion?

The conclusion is twofold: reducing speed limits neither saves lives nor protects the environment.

DECISION #3: How is this conclusion supported?

The two parts of the conclusion are supported by separate premises:

"The more slowly a car is driven, the more time it spends on the road spewing exhaust into the air" is meant to support the idea that reducing speed limits doesn't protect the environment.

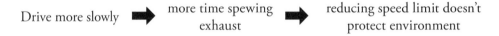

"...running the risk of colliding with other vehicles" is meant to support the idea that reducing speed limits doesn't save lives.

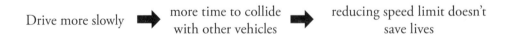

DECISION #4: What are the gaps?

There are some pretty wide gaps here between the premises presented and the two conclusions reached. For both conclusions, the support is too simple and limited to prove the larger generalization.

There are many reasons that would make the first argument core faulty (other ways that fast driving is bad for the environment, the relative amounts of exhaust that come out at different speeds, etc.) and many considerations that could make the second core faulty (accidents at slower speeds are probably less dangerous, and perhaps driving at slower speeds helps one avoid accidents in general).

We've got a very good sense of the problems with this argument. We're ready to move on to the answer choices.

PT38, S4, Q22

In humans, ingested protein is broken down into amino acids, all of which must compete to enter the brain. Subsequent ingestion of sugars leads to the production of insulin, a hormone that breaks down the sugars and also rids the bloodstream of residual amino acids, except for tryptophan. Tryptophan then slips into the brain uncontested and is transformed into the chemical serotonin, increasing the brain's serotonin level. Thus, sugars can play a major role in mood elevation, helping one to feel relaxed and anxiety-free.

Which one of the following is an assumption on which the argument depends?

DECISION #1: What is my task?

This is an Assumption Family question. A Necessary Assumption question—we're looking for something that must be true for the conclusion to be true.

As we start reading, we're thinking about…

DECISION #2: What is the conclusion?

Though the subject matter is challenging, the structure of the writing is not. We're given a series of incidents that lead to one another and eventually to the conclusion, which comes at the end of the paragraph:

Thus, sugars can play a major role in mood elevation, helping one to feel relaxed and anxiety-free.

We're ready to move on.

DECISION #3: How is the conclusion supported?

We can see that the primary premise comes right before the conclusion:

Tryptophan then slips into the brain uncontested and is transformed into the chemical serotonin, increasing the brain's serotonin level.

Tryptophan slips into brain, increasing serotonin level sugars can play a major role in mood elevation, helping one to feel relaxed and anxiety-free

One could argue that the core should include elements mentioned in the previous sentence, which gives us more specific information about how sugar impacts tryptophan (it does so by ridding the bloodstream of other amino acids, allowing the tryptophan to slip into the bloodstream uncontested). And that would be 100% valid. However, it's often true that we don't need to link together every premise that we've been given, especially when there is a clear gap between the last premise and the conclusion, which is the case here. So, we can jump to…

DECISION #4: What is the gap?

The premises end with the tryptophan increasing the brain's serotonin level. But the conclusion is about mood elevation, specifically about one feeling relaxed and worry-free.

Yet we've been told nothing about how serotonin affects mood! This is a huge gap, and it's more than likely the right answer will address it.

Now is a good time to think about how you read the arguments originally. Take a look at the notes you wrote down. Did you put yourself in an ideal position to evaluate the answer choices? Consider now—are there any parts of this process that you routinely shortchange or overlook? On the flip side, are their other things that you focus on that now seem to be less important?

Here are the four arguments once again, this time with the answer choices. Evaluate each argument once more, then select the correct answer.

PT38, S4, Q8

Politician: My opponent says our zoning laws too strongly promote suburban single-family dwellings and should be changed to encourage other forms of housing like apartment buildings. Yet he lives in a house in the country. His lifestyle contradicts his own argument, which should therefore not be taken seriously.

The politician's reasoning is most vulnerable to criticism on the grounds that

(A) its characterization of the opponent's lifestyle reveals the politician's own prejudice against constructing apartment buildings

(B) it neglects the fact that apartment buildings can be built in the suburbs just as easily as in the center of the city

(C) it fails to mention the politician's own living situation

(D) its discussion of the opponent's lifestyle is irrelevant to the merits of the opponent's argument

(E) it ignores the possibility that the opponent may have previously lived in an apartment building

PT38, S4, Q16

People who do not believe that others distrust them are confident in their own abilities, so people who tend to trust others think of a difficult task as a challenge rather than a threat, since this is precisely how people who are confident in their own abilities regard such tasks.

The conclusion above follows logically if which one of the following is assumed?

(A) People who believe that others distrust them tend to trust others.

(B) Confidence in one's own abilities gives one confidence in the trustworthiness of others.

(C) People who tend to trust others do not believe that others distrust them.

(D) People who are not threatened by difficult tasks tend to find such tasks challenging.

(E) People tend to distrust those who they believe lack self-confidence.

PT38, S4, Q14

Reducing speed limits neither saves lives nor protects the environment. This is because the more slowly a car is driven, the more time it spends on the road spewing exhaust into the air and running the risk of colliding with other vehicles.

The argument's reasoning is flawed because the argument

(A) neglects the fact that some motorists completely ignore speed limits

(B) ignores the possibility of benefits from lowering speed limits other than environmental and safety benefits

(C) fails to consider that if speed limits are reduced, increased driving times will increase the number of cars on the road at any given time

(D) presumes, without providing justification, that total emissions for a given automobile trip are determined primarily by the amount of time the trip takes

(E) presumes, without providing justification, that drivers run a significant risk of collision only if they spend a lot of time on the road

PT38, S4, Q22

In humans, ingested protein is broken down into amino acids, all of which must compete to enter the brain. Subsequent ingestion of sugars leads to the production of insulin, a hormone that breaks down the sugars and also rids the bloodstream of residual amino acids, except for tryptophan. Tryptophan then slips into the brain uncontested and is transformed into the chemical serotonin, increasing the brain's serotonin level. Thus, sugars can play a major role in mood elevation, helping one to feel relaxed and anxiety-free.

Which one of the following is an assumption on which the argument depends?

(A) Elevation of mood and freedom from anxiety require increasing the level of serotonin in the brain.

(B) Failure to consume foods rich in sugars results in anxiety and a lowering of mood.

(C) Serotonin can be produced naturally only if tryptophan is present in the bloodstream.

(D) Increasing the level of serotonin in the brain promotes relaxation and freedom from anxiety.

(E) The consumption of protein-rich foods results in anxiety and a lowering of mood.

5

Evaluating the Answer Choices

Okay, we've read the argument. We've zeroed in on the most important components, and we've put ourselves in the right position to answer the question.

One more look at the question stem and…

Here we go. As we evaluate the answer choices for the first time, our primary consideration is going to be:

DECISION #5: Which answer choices are clearly wrong?

It can be argued that being skilled at recognizing wrong answers is more important than being skilled at recognizing right answers. After all, 80 percent of the answers you evaluate are going to be wrong!

Many test-takers evaluate answer choices by looking for the right answer *and* eliminating wrong answers all at once. For most people, this is an inefficient strategy.

Certainly, there will be problems for which the right answer will jump out at you, and you'll be able to pick it and move on quickly. However, your general mind-set should not be "Which answer is correct and which are incorrect?" but rather "Which answer choices are clearly wrong?"

Though it may seem like a small difference, it is a significant one: if you are focused on finding reasons why answer choices are wrong, you will be able to spot problems far more efficiently. Furthermore, working from wrong to right will help ensure that you focus your attention appropriately and spend the majority of your time evaluating the most attractive answer choices.

The biggest payoff will be on the most challenging questions. For these problems, right answers are often written in an unpredictable fashion. Furthermore, tempting wrong answers are often variations on incorrect suppositions that the test-taker might have. Working in a disciplined fashion from wrong to right can significantly impact your accuracy rate on these most challenging questions.

In eliminating answer choices for Assumption Family questions, there are two main considerations that can help you weed out incorrect choices:

1. Be suspicious of answer choices you cannot relate to the conclusion. For Assumption Family questions, we are trying to relate an answer choice to a clearly defined argument core, and, more specifically, to a gap we see. However, sometimes we see the argument core or gap incorrectly, and for some arguments this core is vague to begin with. For the first round of eliminations, it makes sense to be less rigid about the argument core.

Whether you see the core clearly or not, you should always be able to identify the correct conclusion. Furthermore, the test-writers create many incorrect answers that have nothing to do with the conclusion (and, therefore, nothing to do with any core that can be imagined).

The right answer must relate in some way to the main point of the argument. If you see that an answer does not, or, as is commonly the case, you see that an answer choice relates to an incorrect interpretation of the conclusion, you can eliminate it.

Keep in mind that many incorrect answers are created through misinterpretations of secondary parts of an argument. Test-takers who try to read all parts of an argument with equal attention are more easily duped by these wrong choices. Focusing in on the argument core, and specifically the conclusion, will help you recognize these incorrect choices more easily.

2. Recognize incorrect answers that may be relevant to a different question stem. For Assumption questions, there will be often be answers that would be correct for Identify a Flaw questions, and vice versa. It's the same with Strengthen and Weaken questions. Furthermore, they will make it more challenging for you through the use of double negatives and contrasting perspectives. Don't lose sight of your task, and don't hesitate to revisit the question stem whenever necessary.

For your first round of eliminations, you want to make sure to defer judgment on answer choices that you cannot confidently eliminate. Once you eliminate an answer choice, you are never going to look at it again.

A good criterion for what you should eliminate and what you should not: for each wrong answer you eliminate in the first go-around, you should be able to pinpoint the exact reason why it is wrong. If it *seems* wrong but you don't know exactly why, keep it around. This is especially true if you are frequently tripped up by the wording used on the LSAT. Answers that feel this way can often be right answers in disguise.

Do you feel like you can't find exact reasons why wrong answers are wrong? That's understandable, especially if you haven't thought about the answer choices in this way before. When reviewing questions after timed practice, be as specific as possible about why answer choices are wrong. Find at least one definitive reason for every wrong answer you encounter. Soon enough, you will become much better at identifying the common ways in which the LSAT creates incorrect answer choices.

Once you have eliminated the clearly wrong choices, typically you will be left with just one, two, or three answers remaining. You will be ready to make…

DECISION #6: What is the best available answer?

Left with answers that you can't confidently eliminate, you must now select the best available answer. Often, this decision will be less clear-cut than the first round of eliminations. You might find reasons why you like and dislike each of the remaining answer choices. Keep in mind that your job is not to find the *ideal* answer, but rather the best available answer.

Of all the decisions that you have to make during the course of any one problem, this is the most subtle and difficult. More than ever, no one route can guarantee success. You want to stay as flexible and open-minded as you can, and be ready to consider both why answers might be wrong and why answers might be right. Still, there are some common issues that you will find yourself considering. Here's a basic chain of reasoning you can lean on whenever you feel challenged in making the final call:

1. Compare the answer choices against the argument core. This may seem obvious, but, down to two answers, we've seen many students pick the answer that "sounds more like a right answer," or pick an answer by comparing the answer choice against one another. Remember that your task is to match the answer with the argument.

2. Remember and utilize the exact question category. If we are looking for an assumption that makes the argument true, or the *most* significant flaw, we should lean towards answer choices that clearly have a *strong* impact on the conclusion.

If we are looking for a Necessary Assumption, we should look for an answer that is required. We want to be careful to avoid answers that are more creative or stronger than need be (answers that go beyond helping to fill the gap).

3. Vet the right answer as much as possible. Prove to yourself that the right answer is right. Imagine the story that connects the answer choice to the conclusion. If you can't imagine it, it's a good sign the answer isn't correct.

For a Necessary Assumption, you can perform the negation test: if it's a Necessary Assumption, the opposite of that assumption should invalidate the argument. The negation test is less effective for Sufficient Assumption questions.

4. Consider each word of the answer. If you can't justify why one answer is right, do your best to find one thing wrong with the wrong answer. Check every noun, verb, and modifier against the original argument. And check the orientation of the elements—often the most attractive incorrect answers are those that reverse cause and effect. Select the answer that is least wrong.

Let's go back to the four problems to discuss how this process might play out in real time:

PT38, S4, Q8

Politician: My opponent says our zoning laws too strongly promote suburban single-family dwellings and should be changed to encourage other forms of housing like apartment buildings. Yet he lives in a house in the country. His lifestyle contradicts his own argument, which should therefore not be taken seriously.

The politician's reasoning is most vulnerable to criticism on the grounds that

(A) its characterization of the opponent's lifestyle reveals the politician's own prejudice against constructing apartment buildings

(B) it neglects the fact that apartment buildings can be built in the suburbs just as easily as in the center of the city

(C) it fails to mention the politician's own living situation

(D) its discussion of the opponent's lifestyle is irrelevant to the merits of the opponent's argument

(E) it ignores the possibility that the opponent may have previously lived in an apartment building

Remember what we identified as the core:

Lifestyle contradicts argument   ➡   Argument shouldn't be taken seriously.

Also remember we had a pretty good sense of the role that the right answer would play: it should address the fact that where the opponent chooses to live is not directly relevant to his opinion about the law in question.

DECISION #5: Which answer choices are clearly wrong?

We want to quickly eliminate answers that are clearly wrong. On the first go-around, perhaps we quickly eliminate (B), (C), and (E). (D) looks like the answer we predicted, but let's hold off on evaluating it fully for now.

(B) involves subjects (apartment buildings, suburbs, city center) that are in the argument, but it doesn't make a point that helps us judge whether the evidence presented should discourage us from taking the opponent's argument seriously.

(C) is tempting if we get creative, but has no direct bearing on the conclusion. The argument core involves the opponent's lifestyle, not the author's.

(E) has no direct bearing on the conclusion. Again, in order to try to make it relevant, we would have to get creative. The opponent could have lived in an apartment in the past, but it's unclear how this would impact the author's point.

DECISION #6: What is the best available answer?

Down to two choices, let's evaluate them more in depth:

(A) is somewhat tempting, but, when we match up all the subjects and attributes, there's a problem with the end of this answer choice—prejudice against apartment buildings. It's unclear if the author is prejudiced against apartment buildings—we only know that he is against the opponent's opinion. This goes beyond the conclusion in question.

Answer choice (D) looked good from the beginning. Now let's verify it.

> (D) its discussion of the opponent's lifestyle is irrelevant to the merits of the opponent's argument

This answer's subject matter matches that in the argument, and the relationship between lifestyle and argument is characterized as predicted. We can select (D) and move on.

PT38, S4, Q16

People who do not believe that others distrust them are confident in their own abilities, so people who tend to trust others think of a difficult task as a challenge rather than a threat, since this is precisely how people who are confident in their own abilities regard such tasks.

The conclusion above follows logically if which one of the following is assumed?

(A) People who believe that others distrust them tend to trust others.
(B) Confidence in one's own abilities gives one confidence in the trustworthiness of others.
(C) People who tend to trust others do not believe that others distrust them.
(D) People who are not threatened by difficult tasks tend to find such tasks challenging.
(E) People tend to distrust those who they believe lack self-confidence.

Remember the gap we saw in the original argument.

The premises link together so that we can infer, "People *who do not believe others distrust them* think of a difficult task as a challenge rather than a threat." But the author's conclusion states, "So people *who tend to trust others* think of a difficult task as a challenge rather than a threat."

Notice the difference in subject matter between people who do not believe others distrust them and those who tend to trust others. We need to connect these ideas, and we need to connect them in the right order. For this argument to be sound, we need to show that those who do not believe others distrust them are people who tend to trust others.

DECISION #5: Which answer choices are clearly wrong?

If we did not have a good sense of the core, and the "link" that is missing, all the answer choices might seem attractive, because they all involve relationships between elements that are mentioned in the text. However, we know which specific pieces we need to link up in order to make the argument completely sound—people who do not believe others distrust them and people who tend to trust others.

We can eliminate (B), (D), and (E), because none of them provide the particular link this argument needs.

DECISION #6: What is the best available answer?

(A) and (C) seem similar, but they're actually not. Read (A) closely. It links those who BELIEVE that others distrust them and those who tend to trust others. We want to connect those who do NOT believe that others distrust them and those who tend to trust others.

(C) provides the correct link and is therefore the correct answer.

PT38, S4, Q14

Reducing speed limits neither saves lives nor protects the environment. This is because the more slowly a car is driven, the more time it spends on the road spewing exhaust into the air and running the risk of colliding with other vehicles.

The argument's reasoning is flawed because the argument

(A) neglects the fact that some motorists completely ignore speed limits

(B) ignores the possibility of benefits from lowering speed limits other than environmental and safety benefits

(C) fails to consider that if speed limits are reduced, increased driving times will increase the number of cars on the road at any given time

(D) presumes, without providing justification, that total emissions for a given automobile trip are determined primarily by the amount of time the trip takes

(E) presumes, without providing justification, that drivers run a significant risk of collision only if they spend a lot of time on the road

Remember that there were two related points made in this argument, and that there were distinct premises meant to support each point:

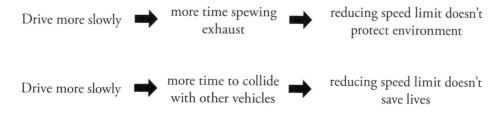

There are wide gaps here between the premises presented and the two conclusions reached. For both conclusions, the premises are too simple and limited to prove the larger generalization. There are many reasons we can think of that would make the first argument core faulty (other ways that faster driving is bad for the environment, the relative amounts of exhaust that come out at different speeds, etc.) and many considerations that could make the second core faulty (accidents at slower speeds are probably less dangerous, and perhaps driving at slower speeds helps one avoid accidents in general). We're in a good place for evaluating answer choices.

DECISION #5: Which answer choices are clearly wrong?

Perhaps the answers we eliminate first are (B), (C), and (E).

(B) is clearly outside the scope of our argument. The other benefits aren't relevant here.

(C) slightly reworded might be the right answer to a Strengthen question. It doesn't represent a flaw in the argument, because it doesn't show that going slower is less dangerous or not as bad for the environment.

(E) might be attractive if you miss the word "only." However, if you catch it, it's a good tip-off that this answer is incorrect. That doesn't have to be the "only" reason for the increased risk of collision.

DECISION #6: What is the best available answer?

(A) is not an answer we predicted, but it seems connected to both the premises and the conclusion. If some motorists ignore speed limits, this must impact the effect that speed limits have. But what would the impact be? Can we connect this impact to changes in safety or environmental concerns? It's tough to see how.

(D) is the type of answer we expected.

Let's look at it one more time: "presumes, without providing justification, that total emissions for a given automobile trip are determined primarily by the amount of time the trip takes."

Notice that the author is making a generalization about the environmental impact just based on the amount of time spent driving. This is an issue that we anticipated. We can double-check every word against the argument—nothing is inconsistent. Let's pick (D) and move on.

PT38, S4, Q22

In humans, ingested protein is broken down into amino acids, all of which must compete to enter the brain. Subsequent ingestion of sugars leads to the production of insulin, a hormone that breaks down the sugars and also rids the bloodstream of residual amino acids, except for tryptophan. Tryptophan then slips into the brain uncontested and is transformed into the chemical serotonin, increasing the brain's serotonin level. Thus, sugars can play a major role in mood elevation, helping one to feel relaxed and anxiety-free.

Which one of the following is an assumption on which the argument depends?

(A) Elevation of mood and freedom from anxiety require increasing the level of serotonin in the brain.
(B) Failure to consume foods rich in sugars results in anxiety and a lowering of mood.
(C) Serotonin can be produced naturally only if tryptophan is present in the bloodstream.
(D) Increasing the level of serotonin in the brain promotes relaxation and freedom from anxiety.
(E) The consumption of protein-rich foods results in anxiety and a lowering of mood.

After the original read, the gap was pretty clear. The evidence ends with tryptophan increasing the brain's serotonin level, but the conclusion is about mood elevation, specifically about one feeling relaxed and worry-free.

Tryptophan slips into brain, increasing serotonin level ➡ sugars can play a major role in mood elevation, helping one to feel relaxed and anxiety-free

We've been told nothing about how serotonin affects mood. We're ready to evaluate.

DECISION #5: Which answer choices are clearly wrong?

Perhaps the answers to eliminate first are (B), (C), and (E).

(B) goes far beyond the text. We don't *need* to know this is true in order for the argument to be sound.

(C) might be attractive if it weren't for the "only." In order for the argument to be sound, we don't need to know that this is the "only" way for serotonin to be produced. Furthermore, there's no connection to the issue of changing mood.

(E) states the complete opposite of the author's point.

DECISION #6: What is the best available answer?

We are down to (A) and (D), and the key is a correct understanding of the question stem. We are looking for a necessary assumption—something that must be true in order for the argument to be true.

In this light, (D) looks far more attractive than (A).

The word "require" in (A) is too strong. We don't have to show that improvement in mood requires increasing serotonin to show that serotonin plays a major role.

If we were looking for a sufficient answer—that is, an answer that doesn't have to be true, but, if it were true, would make the argument perfectly sound—(A) would be a much more attractive answer. But that's not the case here.

Let's revisit (D) again:

(D) Increasing the level of serotonin in the brain promotes relaxation and freedom from anxiety.

Does this prove the point that serotonin plays a *major* role? No. However, in order for serotonin to play a major role, it must play at least some role, and that's what this answer states.

Remember, the right answer to a question that asks for an assumption that must be true does not have to make the argument perfect.

To verify our answer, consider its opposite (negate it): "Increasing the level of serotonin in the brain does NOT promote relaxation and freedom from anxiety." Notice, the opposite of a Necessary Assumption invalidates the argument. That proves that the original assumption was necessary.

The correct answer is (D).

Conclusion

In this chapter, we've broken down the general problem-solving process for all Assumption Family questions. The six decisions that need to be made correctly in order to solve an Assumption Family question are:

1. What is my task?
2. What is the conclusion?
3. How is that conclusion supported?
4. What is the gap?
5. Which answer choices are clearly wrong?
6. What is the best available answer?

DRILL IT: Assumption Family Questions

Here are the three remaining Assumption and Identify a Flaw questions from the fourth section of the October 2002 exam.

For the purposes of this exercise, don't worry about timing. Take as much time as you need. Consider each question carefully and deliberately. Use this exercise as a chance to reflect on your process. Make sure to make your six decisions in order, and, at each point along the way, do your best not to move on to the next step until you're completely ready. After each problem, compare the thoughts you had with those in the solution.

1. PT38, S4, Q6

In any field, experience is required for a proficient person to become an expert. Through experience, a proficient person gradually develops a repertory of model situations that allows an immediate, intuitive response to each new situation. This is the hallmark of expertise, and for this reason computerized "expert systems" cannot be as good as human experts. Although computers have the ability to store millions of bits of information, the knowledge of human experts, who benefit from the experience of thousands of situations, is not stored within their brains in the form of rules and facts.

The argument requires the assumption of which one of the following?

(A) Computers can show no more originality in responding to a situation than that built into them by their designers.
(B) The knowledge of human experts cannot be adequately rendered into the type of information that a computer can store.
(C) Human experts rely on information that can be expressed by rules and facts when they respond to new situations.
(D) Future advances in computer technology will not render computers capable of sorting through greater amounts of information.
(E) Human experts rely heavily on intuition while they are developing a repertory of model situations.

DECISION #1: What is my task?

We're looking for an assumption that must be true for the argument to be true. A Necessary Assumption.

DECISION #2: What is the conclusion?

Computerized "expert systems" cannot be as good as human experts.

DECISION #3: How is the conclusion supported?

The part before the conclusion is cited as the main reason. However, the information that follows the conclusion is also significant, and adds to our understanding.

Taken together, what we know is…

Human experts have a repertory of model situations

+

information is not stored as rules and facts in human brain

➡ Computerized "expert systems" cannot be as good as human experts.

DECISION #4: What is the gap?

There are lots of gaps in this argument, both in terms of the way the premises are meant to connect to one another, and in the way the premises are collectively meant to connect to the conclusion.

We're not actually told that human knowledge cannot be transferred to a computer—it's implied. But in making the implication, the author is assuming that computers can only understand rules and facts. Furthermore, the author is making a claim that since one type of expert (human) becomes an expert one way (by developing this repertory), that another type of expert (computer) can only become an expert the same way.

It's fine if you didn't have these specific thoughts as you solved the question. As mentioned before, this is an argument that is flawed in various and vague ways. What is most important is that you recognize the argument core, and use it to evaluate the answer choices.

DECISION #5: Which answer choices are clearly wrong?

(A) and (B) both seem attractive.

We can get rid of (C), (D), and (E) quickly.

(C) is an incorrect interpretation of a premise.

(D) is incorrect because the amount of information a computer can sort through is not in question, but rather the type of information.

(E) gives us more information about a premise, but bears no relation to the argument core.

MANHATTAN
LSAT

DECISION #6: What is the best available answer?

Let's review (A) and (B) carefully:

        (A) Computers can show no more originality in responding to a situation than that built into them by their designers.

        (B) The knowledge of human experts cannot be adequately rendered into the type of information that a computer can store.

The reason (A) is attractive is that if computers could show more originality, maybe they could become experts in an unexpected way. But must it be true that computers could not show more originality for this argument to be sound? Maybe computers could show a little originality, but not enough to become an expert. This doesn't seem like something that must be true.

(B) is pretty close to something we predicted.

Let's verify it. Since it's a Necessary Assumption question, we know that the opposite of this assumption should really hurt the argument. Here's what the opposite would look like: "The knowledge of human experts CAN be adequately rendered into the type of information that a computer can store." We know this would hurt the author's main point.

(B) doesn't make the author's argument perfect, but it is something that must be true in order for the argument to be valid.

2. PT38, S4, Q20

Shy adolescents often devote themselves totally to a hobby to help distract them from the loneliness brought on by their shyness. Sometimes they are able to become friends with others who share their hobby. But if they lose interest in that hobby, their loneliness may be exacerbated. So developing an all-consuming hobby is not a successful strategy for overcoming adolescent loneliness.

Which one of the following assumptions does the argument depend on?

(A) Eventually, shy adolescents are going to want a wider circle of friends than is provided by their hobby.
(B) No successful strategy for overcoming adolescent loneliness ever intensifies that loneliness.
(C) Shy adolescents will lose interest in their hobbies if they do not make friends through their engagement in those hobbies.
(D) Some other strategy for overcoming adolescent loneliness is generally more successful than is developing an all-consuming hobby.
(E) Shy adolescents devote themselves to hobbies mainly because they want to make friends.

MANHATTAN
LSAT

DECISION #1: What is my task?

We're looking for an assumption that must be true for the argument to be true. A Necessary Assumption.

DECISION #2: What is the conclusion?

It comes right at the end: "Developing an all-consuming hobby is not a successful strategy for overcoming adolescent loneliness."

DECISION #3: How is the conclusion supported?

We've got a series of premises that link to one another:

Shy adolescents often devote themselves totally to a hobby to help distract them from the loneliness brought on by their shyness. Sometimes they are able to become friends with others who share their hobby. But if they lose interest in that hobby, their loneliness may be exacerbated.

And that last part is meant to connect to the conclusion. Here's the argument core:

If they lose interest in that hobby, their loneliness may be exacerbated. Developing an all-consuming hobby is not a successful strategy for overcoming adolescent loneliness.

DECISION #4: What is the gap?

Though we may choose to reread the entire argument just to ground ourselves before going into the answer choices, looking at just the argument core should make the issue obvious:

The premises lead to negative consequences in only some instances (notice the "if" and the "may be"), and the conclusion is far more definitive ("is"). Is the fact that there's a negative impact sometimes enough to conclude that developing an all-consuming hobby is never a successful strategy?

We should lean towards an answer choice that addresses this issue.

DECISION #5: Which answers choices are clearly wrong?

(C) and (E) seem to have no direct relationship to the conclusion, and we can eliminate these quickly.

(C) is about these adolescents losing interest in their hobbies—that's not what the conclusion is about.

(E) is easy to eliminate if you notice the "mainly"—this type of determination is not relevant to our conclusion.

DECISION #6: What is the best available answer?

(A) seems really attractive because, if it's true, it seems like it would make the argument stronger. If shy adolescents are going to want more friends, then perhaps developing this hobby is a bad idea.

But wait—our primary purpose here isn't to strengthen the argument (though an Assumption answer always does). It's to identify something that must be true in order for the argument to be valid.

Does (A) have to be true in order for the argument to be valid? Not necessarily. If we look at (A) closer, perhaps we also become suspicious of the "eventually" (When? During college? Would that be relevant to this argument?). Let's get rid of (A).

(B) doesn't sound right. The "no" is too extreme. But let's think about it carefully just to be sure. Remember the gap we anticipated: "If it causes problems for some, it shouldn't be adopted." If we think about (B) and compare it to the gap, it actually seems pretty closely related, though in a twisted sort of way. Let's leave it for now.

(D) sounded really good on the first go-around, but remember what we considered for (A): does (D) have to be true in order for the argument to be sound? Even if there were no better strategies, we could still say that this strategy is ineffective. We can eliminate (D).

Let's go back to (B):

> (B) No successful strategy for overcoming adolescent
>   loneliness ever intensifies that loneliness.

What it's really saying is that if something is a successful strategy, it never intensifies loneliness. So what would that mean for a strategy that sometimes intensifies loneliness? It must not be a successful strategy.

That's exactly what we were looking for. (B) is correct.

MANHATTAN
LSAT

3. PT38, S4, Q21

Political scientist: As a political system, democracy does not promote political freedom. There are historical examples of democracies that ultimately resulted in some of the most oppressive societies. Likewise, there have been enlightened despotisms and oligarchies that have provided a remarkable level of political freedom to their subjects.

The reasoning in the political scientist's argument is flawed because it

(A) confuses the conditions necessary for political freedom with the conditions sufficient to bring it about

(B) fails to consider that a substantial increase in the level of political freedom might cause a society to become more democratic

(C) appeals to historical examples that are irrelevant to the causal claim being made

(D) overlooks the possibility that democracy promotes political freedom without being necessary or sufficient by itself to produce it

(E) bases its historical case on a personal point of view

5

DECISION #1: What is my task?

This is an Assumption Family question. It's an Identify a Flaw question to be more specific.

DECISION #2: What is the conclusion?

Given to us right at the beginning: "As a political system, democracy does not promote political freedom."

DECISION #3: How is the conclusion supported?

The two premises that follow work in a complementary fashion.

Some democracies have been oppressive.
Some non-democracies have provided great freedom.

Together, they are meant to show that whether a country is democratic has no direct impact on the amount of freedom a country has.

DECISION #4: What is the gap?

The gap seems pretty clear. Take the following analogy:

> Some smokers do not get lung cancer.
> Some non-smokers do get lung cancer.
> So, smoking does not affect the likelihood of getting lung cancer.

Of course we know that smoking doesn't guarantee lung cancer, and of course we know that having lung cancer doesn't necessarily mean that you are a smoker, but does that mean that smoking doesn't impact your odds of getting lung cancer? In this analogous argument, the author fails to consider that smoking could indeed impact the odds of getting lung cancer even if smoking doesn't guarantee it, and even if smoking isn't necessary to get it.

The same sort of issue is present in the democracy example. Democracy may not guarantee freedom, and democracy may not be necessary for freedom, but does that mean that democracy doesn't improve the odds of having a free society?

We see the issue. Time to dive into the choices.

DECISION #5: Which answer choices are clearly wrong?

(A) involves conditional logic language that seems relevant. Too much to consider for now. Let's leave it.

We can eliminate (B), (C), and (E) quickly.

(B) matches some of the subjects in the argument, but orients them in a way that's not helpful for proving the author's point. We're interested in whether democracy promotes freedom, NOT whether increases in freedom promote democracy.

(C) is wrong because "irrelevant" is much too strong. The historical examples might not be enough to prove the point, but they are not irrelevant.

(E) is suggesting the argument contains a bias. Though the argument may be limited, it's tough to see a personal bias.

(D) also involves conditional language—let's leave it for now.

DECISION #6: What is the best available answer?

Let's go back to (A) and reread it to check if it is indeed correct: "confuses the conditions necessary for political freedom with the conditions sufficient to bring it about"

Remember our previous analysis of the gap: democracy may not guarantee (be sufficient for) freedom, and democracy may not be necessary for freedom, but that doesn't mean that democracy doesn't improve the odds of having a free society. So, it's not that the argument is "confusing" the necessary conditions and the sufficient conditions, but rather that the argument is taking the fact that democracy is NEITHER necessary NOR sufficient in order to show that democracy doesn't impact freedom.

Let's look at (D) one more time:

> (D) overlooks the possibility that democracy promotes political
>   freedom without being necessary or sufficient by itself to
>   produce it

Ah, yes. The argument fails to consider ("overlooks the possibility") that democracy could affect freedom even if democracy is neither necessary nor sufficient to have freedom. (D) is the correct answer.

Again, these solutions are not meant to represent the exact thoughts you are meant to have during the course of a problem. There's no one way to think about a problem, and no two people will think about a problem in exactly the same way. However, these solutions can help you evaluate your own process. Consider again—are there any parts to this process that you routinely shortchange or overlook? On the flip side, are there other things that you focus on that now seem less important? As you learn about the other question types in the chapters to come, keep mindful of the ideal process for each question type, and make sure your process helps you think about the right thing at the right time.

5

Chapter 6 of Logical Reasoning

Strengthen and Weaken Questions

Getting Familiar

To start, go ahead and try these four Strengthen and Weaken questions. Give yourself no more than six minutes total. We'll revisit these questions later on in the chapter.

PT38, S4, Q15

Loggerhead turtles live and breed in distinct groups, of which some are in the Pacific Ocean and some are in the Atlantic. New evidence suggests that juvenile Pacific loggerheads that feed near the Baja peninsula hatch in Japanese waters 10,000 kilometers away. Ninety-five percent of the DNA samples taken from the Baja turtles match those taken from turtles at the Japanese nesting sites.

Which one of the following, if true, most seriously weakens the reasoning above?

(A) Nesting sites of loggerhead turtles have been found off the Pacific coast of North America several thousand kilometers north of the Baja peninsula.

(B) The distance between nesting sites and feeding sites of Atlantic loggerhead turtles is less than 5,000 kilometers.

(C) Loggerhead hatchlings in Japanese waters have been declining in number for the last decade while the number of nesting sites near the Baja peninsula has remained constant.

(D) Ninety-five percent of the DNA samples taken from the Baja turtles match those taken from Atlantic loggerhead turtles.

(E) Commercial aquariums have been successfully breeding Atlantic loggerheads with Pacific loggerheads for the last five years.

PT29, S4, Q24

Medical researcher: As expected, records covering the last four years of ten major hospitals indicate that babies born prematurely were more likely to have low birth weights and to suffer from health problems than were babies not born prematurely. These records also indicate that mothers who had received adequate prenatal care were less likely to have low birth weight babies than were mothers who had received inadequate prenatal care. Adequate prenatal care, therefore, significantly decreases the risk of low birth weight babies.

Which one of the following, if true, most weakens the medical researcher's argument?

(A) The hospital records indicate that many babies that are born with normal birth weights are born to mothers who had inadequate prenatal care.

(B) Mothers giving birth prematurely are routinely classified by hospitals as having received inadequate prenatal care when the record of that care is not available.

(C) The hospital records indicate that low birth weight babies were routinely classified as having been born prematurely.

(D) Some babies not born prematurely, whose mothers received adequate prenatal care, have low birth weights.

(E) Women who receive adequate prenatal care are less likely to give birth prematurely than are women who do not receive adequate prenatal care.

PT36, S1, Q8

It has been claimed that television networks should provide equal time for the presentation of opposing views whenever a television program concerns scientific issues—such as those raised by the claims of environmentalists—about which people disagree. However, although an obligation to provide equal time does arise in the case of any program concerning social issues, it does so because social issues almost always have important political implications and seldom can definitely be settled on the basis of available evidence. If a program concerns scientific issues, that program gives rise to no such equal time obligation.

Which one of the following, if true, most seriously weakens the argument?

(A) No scientific issues raised by the claims of environmentalists have important political implications.

(B) There are often more than two opposing views on an issue that cannot be definitely settled on the basis of available evidence.

(C) Some social issues could be definitely settled on the basis of evidence if the opposing sides would give all the available evidence a fair hearing.

(D) Many scientific issues have important political implications and cannot be definitely settled on the basis of the available evidence.

(E) Some television networks refuse to broadcast programs on issues that have important political implications and that cannot be definitely settled by the available evidence.

PT37, S2, Q20

Antarctic seals dive to great depths and stay submerged for hours. They do not rely solely on oxygen held in their lungs, but also store extra oxygen in their blood. Indeed, some researchers hypothesize that for long dives these seals also store oxygenated blood in their spleens.

Each of the following, if true, provides some support for the researchers' hypothesis EXCEPT:

(A) Horses are known to store oxygenated blood in their spleens for use during exertion.

(B) Many species of seal can store oxygen directly in their muscle tissue.

(C) The oxygen contained in the seals' lungs and bloodstream alone would be inadequate to support the seals during their dives.

(D) The spleen is much larger in the Antarctic seal than in aquatic mammals that do not make long dives.

(E) The spleens of Antarctic seals contain greater concentrations of blood vessels than are contained in most of their other organs.

6

One Extra Layer

Thus far, we've looked at two Assumption Family question types—Assumption and Identify a Flaw—and we've discussed the general process for attacking Assumption Family problems. Hopefully, you are feeling more and more comfortable with identifying the argument core and evaluating the issues that it might present.

We will continue to reinforce those skills in this chapter. Like Assumption and Identify a Flaw questions, Strengthen and Weaken questions test your ability to evaluate the reasoning in an argument—that is, the connection between the premises and the conclusion. However, Strengthen and Weaken questions present us with an additional and unique challenge. Whereas Assumption and Identify a Flaw questions primarily require us to *identify* the argument core and *assess* it, Strengthen and Weaken questions require us to *identify, assess,* and then consider ways to *address* the issues in the argument core. For Assumption and Identify a Flaw questions, we select answers that directly represent our understanding of the reasoning within the argument. For Strengthen and Weaken questions, we must consider how different bits of *new* information might relate to that reasoning.

Let's use a simple example to illustrate the impact of this additional layer. Consider the following argument:

> Sally owns more cookbooks than Finn. Therefore, Sally is a better cook than Finn.

It's clear the argument is flawed, but success on the LSAT requires that we understand this type of flaw in a specific way. The subjects, Sally and Finn, don't change from premise to conclusion, but what is discussed about these subjects does:

Sally **owns more cookbooks**
than Finn   Sally **is a better cook**
than Finn

What are the gaps or flaws?

For one, the argument is assuming that *owning* more cookbooks equates to *being* a better cook. This is a pretty big assumption. One needs to do more than *own* cookbooks to be a good cook—at the least, one should probably *read* them. And learn from them. And incorporate what is learned into the cooking. Furthermore, the number of cookbooks is not indicative of the knowledge these books have to offer—it's likely that one great cookbook has more valuable information than 10 bad ones.

We can also say that the argument is assuming that owning more cookbooks is enough, by itself, to justify the conclusion. That is, that there are no other factors that significantly influence how well Sally and Finn cook. Again, that's a pretty big assumption. We know from our own lives that there are plenty of other factors that could be considered here: experience in the kitchen, teachers, parents, natural aptitude, taste, and even exposure to various foods of various cultures.

We can generalize the flaws in the argument as follows:

1. The author takes for granted that owning more cookbooks has a direct impact on being a better cook.
2. The author fails to consider that other factors could be involved in determining who is the better cook.

MANHATTAN
LSAT

Most commonly, correct answers to Strengthen questions help the argument by helping to plug a gap in the core. This gap can relate to how the elements of the premise and conclusion equate to one another, or to the "What else?" the author should have considered but didn't. Correct answers to Weaken questions will most commonly expose these gaps.

With that in mind, take a look at some ways that we might strengthen or weaken the argument, by helping to plug one of the two gaps we just discussed:

Assumption	Valid Strengthen Answers	Valid Weaken Answers
Owning more cookbooks is related to being a better cook.	The number of cookbooks one owns is an accurate gauge of how much one knows about cooking. Owning cookbooks inspires people to practice cooking, and, in turn, to become better cooks. In Sally's collection are some of the greatest cookbooks in the world, and she has read and learned from them.	Sally has not read any of her cookbooks. None of Sally's cookbooks describe anything aside from different ways of decorating gingerbread houses. People often misread cookbooks and end up becoming worse cooks after reading them.
There are not other significant factors in being a good cook.	A recent study found that owning cookbooks was the most significant factor in determining a person's understanding of cooking. Experience in the kitchen and exposure to foods of other cultures are not factors that significantly influence knowledge of cooking.	Finn is a cooking school instructor and the books Sally owns were written by Finn. Finn has been apprenticing for a world-renowned chef for the past three years. Sally was born without taste buds and cannot accurately gauge the flavor of her cooking.

Keep in mind two factors in thinking about the above samples:

1. You do not have to consider whether the answer could be valid in real life or not. In fact, most question stems will explicitly ask that you consider the answers as if they are true.

So, even if you think it's not possible that reading cookbooks might make Sally a worse cook, it's not your job here to make that judgment. Even if you know that it's rare for people not to have taste buds, when evaluating an answer you should work off the assumption that the statement is true.

2. A Strengthen answer doesn't have to make the argument perfect, and a Weaken answer doesn't have to destroy the argument entirely. In fact, for some of the most challenging questions, a Strengthen answer will still leave the argument with significant gaps, and a Weaken answer may address the slightest of many issues in the core.

Consider this Weaken answer:

> *Finn is a cooking school instructor and the books Sally owns were written by Finn.*

Does this mean Sally isn't a better cook than Finn? Does this prove Finn is a better cook? No, certainly not if we are considering this with the strict reasoning eye the LSAT requires. Finn can be an instructor and a book writer—and a terrible cook! It's possible Sally has never been to cooking school but is a phenomenal cook (we all know people like this in real life).

Furthermore, this answer has some characteristics that would, with good reason, cause us to shy away from it if it appeared on an Assumption or Identify a Flaw problem. If we think about one component of the answer—Finn teaches cooking—is this something that could play a critical role in an Assumption or Flaw answer? No. In making his argument, the author need not assume one thing or another about whether Finn teaches cooking, nor would any assumption about Finn teaching cooking be sufficient to make the argument sound. It's also not a flaw that, in reaching his conclusion, the author didn't consider whether Finn teaches cooking. There is no way that the author could anticipate that that is something he would have to consider, and, more importantly, because it's not an assumption that is required, it wouldn't be a flaw in reasoning not to consider it.

So, why could this be the correct answer to a Weaken question? Because it dents an assumption the author is making. In thinking that the evidence is sufficient to prove the conclusion, the author is assuming that the relative number of cookbooks Sally and Finn respectively own is enough, by itself, to determine which of the two is the better cook—the author is assuming that there *must* be no other significant factors. An answer choice such as this one exposes the issue with that assumption simply by showing that there *could* be other factors.

6

This leads us to a subtle but significant point. The answers to Strengthen and Weaken questions can address an assumption by bringing in new and unexpected information, like the lack of taste buds or being a cooking instructor. Because answer choices can bring in new information, it is often true that correct answers to these questions will relate less obviously to the argument core than most Assumption and Flaw answers do. In a certain way, this is similar to what we face with some questions asking for a necessary assumption; the correct answer to those can address an obvious gap in an unpredictable manner, or address a gap that is itself unpredictable.

This freedom of scope is important on two fronts. First, you want to cast a wider net when it comes to thinking about what could be the right answer to a Strengthen or Weaken question. The answer's relation to the core can be less obvious than for other Assumption Family questions. We've also noticed that correct Strengthen and Weaken answers are more likely than correct Assumption and Flaw answers to address secondary, or perhaps less significant, gaps in the reasoning of the argument.

Second, you want to make sure that the skills you develop for connecting tangential answers does not take away from the sharp eye you've developed for spotting ones that are truly out of scope. Right answers to Assumption and Flaw questions tend to relate more directly to the core—and a lot of the work we've done has been designed to help you better separate the answers that relate to the core from the answers that don't. We'd hate for the work you do on Strengthen and Weaken questions to take away from the work you've done on Assumption and Flaw questions. Again, if you think of Strengthen and Weaken questions as questions that add an additional layer to the tasks required of you in Assumption and Flaw questions, you can keep these characteristics clear.

Consider this potential weakener of our argument about Sally owning more cookbooks than Finn and thus being a better cook than him:

Finn is a good cook.

Why is this not a correct weakener? For one, it doesn't tell us if Finn is a *better* cook than Sally is. Also—and this is crucial—Finn being a good cook does not weaken the connection between the premises and conclusion. Our job is not to weaken the conclusion but to weaken the *argument*. We'll look at some rare questions where we're specifically asked to weaken the conclusion, but for the overwhelming majority of Strengthen and Weaken questions we're expected to focus on the *reasoning*.

Let's now practice our process on a real LSAT question. Remember to identify the conclusion, evaluate the premises, find the gaps and flaws, and choose an answer that addresses one of those gaps or flaws.

PT36, S1, Q25

A 1991 calculation was made to determine what, if any, additional health-care costs beyond the ordinary are borne by society at large for people who live a sedentary life. The figure reached was a lifetime average of $1,650. Thus people's voluntary choice not to exercise places a significant burden on society.

Which one of the following, if true and not taken into account by the calculation, most seriously weakens the argument?

(A) Many people whose employment requires physical exertion do not choose to engage in regular physical exercise when they are not at work.
(B) Exercise is a topic that is often omitted from discussion between doctor and patient during a patient's visit.
(C) Physical conditions that eventually require medical or nursing-home care often first predispose a person to adopt a sedentary life-style.
(D) Individuals vary widely in the amount and kind of exercise they choose, when they do exercise regularly.
(E) A regular program of moderate exercise tends to increase circulation, induce a feeling of well-being and energy, and decrease excess weight.

In the previous chapter, we deconstructed a thought process that aligns with, and works effectively for, almost all Assumption Family questions. Let's use it to break down this problem.

DECISION #1: What is my task?

We're asked to find an answer that most weakens the argument. We know this is an Assumption Family question, and we're going to need to understand the argument core well in order to efficiently arrive at the correct answer.

DECISION #2: What is the conclusion?

Let's model how this process might go in real time:

> A 1991 calculation was made to determine what, if any, additional health-care costs beyond the ordinary are borne by society at large for people who live a sedentary life.

This is background information. It gives us the context for the argument.

> The figure reached was a lifetime average of $1,650.

Still background? Unclear what role this plays.

> Thus people's voluntary choice not to exercise places a significant burden on society.

This is definitely the conclusion. It is the author's main point, and, in fact, it's the only claim in the argument.

DECISION #3: How is this conclusion supported?

Once we identify the conclusion, it's easier to see that the information in the previous sentence—that the figure reached was a lifetime average of $1,650—is being used to support that conclusion. Furthermore, the sentence before that tells us what "the figure" stands for: "additional health-care costs beyond the ordinary that are borne by society at large for people who live a sedentary life." Thus, we can think of the argument core as follows:

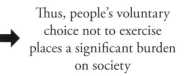

Additional health-care costs beyond the ordinary borne by society at large for people who live a sedentary life averages $1,650 → Thus, people's voluntary choice not to exercise places a significant burden on society

DECISION #4: What is the gap?

Perhaps you notice the mismatch between the people who are discussed in the premises and those who are discussed in the conclusion.

The premises are specifically about people who live a sedentary life.

The conclusion is specifically about people who voluntarily choose not to exercise.

Do we know that those who live a sedentary life do so because they *choose* not to exercise? Absolutely not! There are a variety of other reasons why people *must* live a sedentary life. This is a significant mismatch, and it is very likely the correct answer will have to address this discrepancy.

Furthermore, it's unclear whether an average of $1,650 represents a significant burden. We've been given no tools to decide. A correct weaken answer could expose this gap by showing us why, for any of a variety of reasons, this would NOT be a significant burden.

With a clear understanding of these gaps, we are ready to evaluate the answer choices.

DECISION #5: Which answer choices are clearly wrong?

> (A) Many people whose employment requires physical exertion do not choose to engage in regular physical exercise when they are not at work.

This answer is about an apparently related subject. Let's keep it for now.

(B)   Exercise is a topic that is often omitted from discussion
        between doctor and patient during a patient's visit.

*In real life this might be relevant to the discussion, but, for the purposes of the LSAT, this is completely out of
scope. We can eliminate this quickly.*

(C)   Physical conditions that eventually require medical or
        nursing-home care often first predispose a person to adopt
        a sedentary life-style.

*This answer relates directly to a gap we saw initially in the argument—the idea that the sedentary lifestyle
must be voluntary. This is evidence that shows that perhaps the sedentary lifestyle is not always voluntary.
Let's keep it.*

(D)   Individuals vary widely in the amount and kind of exercise
        they choose, when they do exercise regularly.

We're interested in people who do not *exercise. And this answer doesn't address core issues. Let's eliminate it.*

(E)   A regular program of moderate exercise tends to increase
        circulation, induce a feeling of well-being and energy, and
        decrease excess weight.

And for the same reasons as (D), this answer can be eliminated quickly as well.

DECISION #6: What is the best available answer?

Keep in mind that even when a question asks for an answer that MOST weakens, there will typically
only be one answer that actually weakens. This is the same for Strengthen questions as well. Down
to two answers, your focus ought not to be on which one weakens more, but rather, on which answer
actually does weaken, and which one does not. Let's evaluate the remaining choices one more time:

(A)   Many people whose employment requires physical exertion
        do not choose to engage in regular physical exercise when
        they are not at work.

*Does this answer help convince us that voluntarily lack of exercise doesn't place a significant burden on
society? Perhaps indirectly, but the connection certainly isn't clear.*

More importantly, keep in mind that the author is claiming that his conclusion is true because of additional
health-care costs due to people who live a sedentary life. *Those mentioned in this answer are not ones who live
a sedentary lifestyle! This answer has no clearly definable impact on the reasoning—the connection between
premise and conclusion—in this argument.*

That leaves us with (C), the correct answer. Let's take one more look at it:

(C)   Physical conditions that eventually require medical or
        nursing-home care often first predispose a person to adopt
        a sedentary life-style.

6

Does this answer destroy the argument? No. Perhaps such physical conditions as those described in this answer choice are exceedingly rare, and perhaps the vast majority of people adopt a sedentary lifestyle voluntarily, in which case the argument still could be pretty strong (at least in respect to the "voluntary" aspect). However, this answer does weaken the reasoning within the argument. It shows that something the author is assuming to be true—that people choose *to be sedentary—may in fact not be.*

Let's take a look at another question. Try solving it and analyzing the answers you didn't choose before reading further.

<u>PT36, S3, Q2</u>

Several companies will soon offer personalized electronic news services, delivered via cable or telephone lines and displayed on a television. People using these services can view continually updated stories on those topics for which they subscribe. Since these services will provide people with the information they are looking for more quickly and efficiently than printed newspapers can, newspaper sales will decline drastically if these services become widely available.

Which one of the following, if true, most seriously weakens the argument?

(A) In reading newspapers, most people not only look for stories on specific topics but also like to idly browse through headlines or pictures for amusing stories on unfamiliar or unusual topics.

(B) Companies offering personalized electronic news services will differ greatly in what they charge for access to their services, depending on how wide a range of topics they cover.

(C) Approximately 30 percent of people have never relied on newspapers for information but instead have always relied on news programs broadcast on television and radio.

(D) The average monthly cost of subscribing to several channels on a personalized electronic news service will approximately equal the cost of a month's subscription to a newspaper.

(E) Most people who subscribe to personalized electronic news services will not have to pay extra costs for installation since the services will use connections installed by cable and telephone companies.

The core of this argument comes at the end:

These (electronic news) services will provide people with the information they are looking for more quickly and efficiently than printed newspapers can newspaper sales will decline drastically if these services become widely available.

Perhaps, at least the first time through, this argument seems pretty sound! However, since it's an Assumption Family question, we know it's got to have some issues, and, in this case, it's helpful to think about the conclusion in terms of "What else?" Why else do people buy and read papers? Do people primarily read newspapers searching for stuff they already know about?

No.

People often read with no idea of what's going to be in the paper—we read in part *to see* what's in the paper. People also buy newspapers for other reasons—for the crossword or for coupons, for example. The fact that people can identify information they are looking for faster through other forms is not the sole characteristic that needs to be considered in determining whether newspaper sales will drastically decrease.

Let's evaluate the answer choices:

> (A) In reading newspapers, most people not only look for stories on specific topics but also like to browse idly through headlines or pictures for amusing stories on unfamiliar or unusual topics.

Perhaps you predicted this, or perhaps you didn't. In either case, you ought to be able to recognize that this answer presents an alternative reason that needs to be considered when thinking about whether newspaper sales will drastically decline. If (A) is true, people may want to continue buying the paper.

> (B) Companies offering personalized electronic news services will differ greatly in what they charge for access to their services, depending on how wide a range of topics they cover.

A comparison within companies offering personalized electronic news services (as opposed to a comparison between such companies and newspapers) is of no relevance to this argument. We can quickly eliminate this answer choice.

> (C) Approximately 30 percent of people have never relied on newspapers for information but instead have always relied on news programs broadcast on television and radio.

It's unclear how this relates to the conclusion. We're concerned about the people who do *currently buy newspapers. Will they switch to the new medium? This answer is out of scope.*

> (D) The average monthly cost of subscribing to several channels on a personalized electronic news service will approximately equal the cost of a month's subscription to a newspaper.

Ahh. This answer perhaps brings to light a potential gap in the argument. Perhaps newspaper sales won't decline because electronic services will be more costly. However, this answer choice states the opposite, it states that the costs are equal. *This answer eliminates a potential gap we didn't see initially. In doing so, it* strengthens *the argument.*

6

(E) Most people who subscribe to personalized electronic news
     services will not have to pay extra costs for installation
     since the services will use connections installed by cable
     and telephone companies.

*This answer touches on the same issue as (D)—cost. But again, it doesn't weaken the argument because it's
information about how people* won't *have to pay additional costs to switch away from the paper.*

(A) is the best available answer, and it is the correct answer.

Hopefully these two questions have helped place Strengthen and Weaken questions in context relative
to the Assumption Family questions discussed in previous chapters. Keep in mind, though, that there
is more variation in Strengthen and Weaken questions than there is in both Assumption and Identify a
Flaw questions. The arguments have gaps that are less absolute—often wider and often harder to clearly
define, and the connection between argument and answer choice, for reasons discussed above, can be
less obvious.

6

Let's look at one more challenging example, one that you tried at the start of the chapter:

PT38, S4, Q15

Loggerhead turtles live and breed in distinct groups, of which some are in the Pacific Ocean and some are in the Atlantic. New evidence suggests that juvenile Pacific loggerheads that feed near the Baja peninsula hatch in Japanese waters 10,000 kilometers away. Ninety-five percent of the DNA samples taken from the Baja turtles match those taken from turtles at the Japanese nesting sites.

Which one of the following, if true, most seriously weakens the reasoning above?

(A) Nesting sites of loggerhead turtles have been found off the Pacific coast of North America several thousand kilometers north of the Baja peninsula.

(B) The distance between nesting sites and feeding sites of Atlantic loggerhead turtles is less than 5,000 kilometers.

(C) Loggerhead hatchlings in Japanese waters have been declining in number for the last decade while the number of nesting sites near the Baja peninsula has remained constant.

(D) Ninety-five percent of the DNA samples taken from the Baja turtles match those taken from Atlantic loggerhead turtles.

(E) Commercial aquariums have been successfully breeding Atlantic loggerheads with Pacific loggerheads for the last five years.

We can take what the new evidence *suggests* as the conclusion of the argument: juvenile Pacific loggerheads that feed near the Baja peninsula hatch in Japanese waters 10,000 kilometers away. What is the reasoning given? DNA. Ninety-five percent of the DNA samples taken from the Baja turtles match those taken from turtles at the Japanese nesting sites.

We can think of the core as follows:

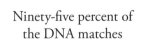

Ninety-five percent of the DNA matches ➡ Pacific loggerhead turtles that feed near the Baja peninsula hatch in Japanese waters 10,000 kilometers away

What would we need to know in order for this argument to be valid? We would need to know that a 95 percent match is significant *enough* to prove the connection. Perhaps these loggerheads also have a 95 percent DNA match with cabbage (unlikely, we realize). We don't know the exact significance of 95 percent, not based on the information we are given. Therefore, we can say the author is *assuming* that 95 percent is enough of a match to prove a relation. It's likely an answer meant to weaken will exploit this assumption.

One of the things that makes this question more challenging is that several of the answer choices are very attractive. Let's look at them in depth:

(A) Nesting sites of loggerhead turtles have been found off the Pacific coast of North America several thousand kilometers north of the Baja peninsula.

This answer choice doesn't address the exact gap we identified, but it does present an intriguing, alternative location from which these turtles in question could have come. Perhaps the turtles came from somewhere else…

But there is no proof that these sites are more likely places for the turtles to have been born, and, more significantly, this answer does not address any gap in reasoning between the premise and conclusion. We're looking for something that shows us that the DNA evidence is perhaps not as significant as the author believes.

(B) The distance between nesting sites and feeding sites of Atlantic loggerhead turtles is less than 5,000 kilometers.

This answer is related to an opposing point presented in the argument (the distance between the Baja peninsula and Japanese waters is over 10,000 kilometers). However, does this particular distance being 5,000 kilometers mean that 5,000 kilometers is a norm, or a maximum? Not at all. Therefore, this doesn't help us evaluate the reasoning in the argument, and this answer has no direct bearing on the conclusion.

(C) Loggerhead hatchlings in Japanese waters have been declining in number for the last decade while the number of nesting sites near the Baja peninsula has remained constant.

This is another somewhat tempting answer, but we haven't been told, or been given any indication, that all the hatchlings from Japanese waters come to the Baja peninsula. Therefore, it's unclear what relevance this decline would have for those particular turtles. Perhaps the decline in numbers is connected to turtles that end up going elsewhere. We can eliminate it.

(D) Ninety-five percent of the DNA samples taken from the Baja turtles match those taken from Atlantic loggerhead turtles.

It's unclear what this answer means in terms of where the Baja turtles came from.

The point of this answer is NOT that the turtles in question could have come from the Atlantic. We are told explicitly in the argument that Atlantic turtles and Pacific turtles are distinct.

However, this is a clever way to address the gap that we identified. If the turtles in the Baja peninsula have just as strong a DNA match with the Atlantic turtles—turtles that we know for certain are a distinct group—as they do with the Japanese hatchlings, this puts a big dent into the premise-conclusion relationship. This makes it seem the DNA evidence is NOT strong enough to justify the conclusion. (D) seems like the correct answer.

(E) Commercial aquariums have been successfully breeding Atlantic loggerheads with Pacific loggerheads for the last five years.

This is out of scope. We can eliminate it quickly, leaving us with (D).

Notice that the right answer is the one that is most directly relevant to the *gap* that we identified—specifically the author's assumption that a 95 percent DNA match is adequate proof that the Baja turtles hatched in Japanese waters. If we were just to look for an answer that matches "keywords," we'd be in trouble here. Without a clear understanding of the argument core, and the gap therein, it's very difficult to see which answers can play a more significant role than others.

Unique Strengthen and Weaken Questions

Though most—in fact, almost all—Strengthen and Weaken questions will develop in a manner that is fairly consistent with other Assumption Family questions, as exampled by the problems above, there are certain Strengthen and Weaken questions that do not agree neatly with what we traditionally associate with Assumption Family questions. Again, these questions are fairly rare, but it's important that you are familiar with their characteristics:

Argument, Minus Core

Take a look at the following question. In addition to solving it, consider what makes this argument different from others we've been looking at.

PT 43, S2, Q8

Criminologist: Increasing the current prison term for robbery will result in no significant effect in discouraging people from committing robbery.

Each of the following, if true, supports the criminologist's claim EXCEPT:

(A) Many people who rob are motivated primarily by thrill-seeking and risk-taking.

(B) An increase in the prison term for embezzlement did not change the rate at which that crime was committed.

(C) Prison terms for robbery have generally decreased in length recently.

(D) Most people committing robbery believe that they will not get caught.

(E) Most people committing robbery have no idea what the average sentence for robbery is.

This is an EXCEPT question. There is a specific way that we want you to approach EXCEPT questions, and we'll discuss this approach in greater detail later in the chapter.

For now, let's focus on the argument. Did you notice something unique about it? We're given a conclusion, but nothing else!

There is no supporting premise and, therefore, no *reasoning* to evaluate, strengthen, or weaken. Notice the question stem itself makes no mention of "author's reasoning" or "argument," it simply asks us to evaluate the answers relative to the conclusion. Again, this type of question is fairly rare, but it does show up once every few exams. So, if you see an argument on the exam that just doesn't seem to have a core, don't force it.

Let's finish considering this question.

This is really a conclusion about causation—the author is saying that a certain trigger (lengthening sentences) *won't* have a particular direct impact (discouragement) on a certain action (robbery).

How do we strengthen such an argument? In one of two ways:

1. By showing that there is indeed little or no causal connection between lengthening term sentences and discouraging crime.
2. By showing that there are other factors that more strongly influence the rate of robbery (and in so doing showing that the particular trigger in question is not primary, or significant, to the likelihood of the outcome).

Let's take a look at the answer choices:

(A) Many people who rob are motivated primarily by thrill-seeking and risk-taking.

This addresses the second of our concerns. If this is the primary reason people are robbing, the increase in jail term is less likely to have an impact. This strengthens the claim.

(B) An increase in the prison term for embezzlement did not change the rate at which that crime was committed.

This addresses the first of our concerns. In a similar scenario, we can see that a lengthening of the term didn't impact the rate of crime. This strengthens the claim.

(C) Prison terms for robbery have generally decreased in length recently.

So what? Would an increase deter crime or not? The impact of this answer is unclear.

(D) Most people committing robbery believe that they will not get caught.

If this is true, it's likely robbers are not thinking about prison term length. This would also strengthen the conclusion.

(E) Most people committing robbery have no idea what the
      average sentence for robbery is.

This addresses the first of our issues. If people don't know how long the term is, it won't matter to them if it is lengthened. This strengthens the claim that increasing the term won't deter crime.

Four of the answers clearly strengthen the conclusion. (C) has an uncertain impact on the conclusion, and is therefore the correct answer.

Beware of Claims within Premises

Another way in which Strengthen and Weaken questions can differ from other typical Assumption Family questions is that they can address the validity of a claim made within a premise. That is, a correct answer can strengthen or weaken something that the premise assumes to be true.

To illustrate, let's take a look at the following example:

My child says she   Therefore, my child
can see ghosts   can see ghosts

Notice, as with all other premises for Assumption Family questions, the truth of the *full* premise is not what needs evaluating—we should take it to be true that the child does indeed say this. Our job is not to evaluate whether the child said she can see ghosts.

What needs to be evaluated here is the claim *within* the premise—the child's claim that she can see ghosts. This is suspect. Perhaps she is seeing shadows. A strengthen answer might validate the fact that she does indeed see ghosts, and a weaken answer might give a reason to believe she does not see ghosts.

Again, we want to be clear—it is not necessary for you to evaluate the truth of the vast majority of claims you see within premises—in fact, in general this will distract you from the far more important task, which is to evaluate the relationship *between* the premises and the conclusion. However, for certain Strengthen and Weaken questions—you'll see no more than one such problem on your exam—you may need to evaluate the truth of elements within a premise.

Let's take a look at an example from the "Getting Familiar" section:

PT29, S4, Q24

Medical researcher: As expected, records covering the last four years of ten major hospitals indicate that babies born prematurely were more likely to have low birth weights and to suffer from health problems than were babies not born prematurely. These records also indicate that mothers who had received adequate prenatal care were less likely to have low birth weight babies than were mothers who had received inadequate prenatal care. Adequate prenatal care, therefore, significantly decreases the risk of low birth weight babies.

Which one of the following, if true, most weakens the medical researcher's argument?

(A) The hospital records indicate that many babies that are born with normal birth weights are born to mothers who had inadequate prenatal care.

(B) Mothers giving birth prematurely are routinely classified by hospitals as having received inadequate prenatal care when the record of that care is not available.

(C) The hospital records indicate that low birth weight babies were routinely classified as having been born prematurely.

(D) Some babies not born prematurely, whose mothers received adequate prenatal care, have low birth weights.

(E) Women who receive adequate prenatal care are less likely to give birth prematurely than are women who do not receive adequate prenatal care.

The medical researcher gives us a lot of information, then arrives at his main point at the end of the argument: Adequate prenatal care significantly decreases the risk of low birth weight babies.

Like many long arguments, this one has its core at the end. The first sentence perhaps gives us more information about the subjects in the conclusion, and the consequences of the conclusion, but it has no bearing on the reasoning used to reach the conclusion.

The primary evidence he uses comes in the sentence prior to the conclusion, and we can think of the argument core as follows:

Records indicate mothers who received adequate prenatal care are less likely to give birth to low birth weight babies than mothers who received inadequate prenatal care Adequate prenatal care significantly decreases risk of low birth weight babies

If we heard this argument in real life, it might seem very reasonable to many of us. In critical debater mode, perhaps you noticed a jump from correlation (in the premise) to causation (in the conclusion). It could be true that there is a correlation between adequate prenatal care and the likelihood of giving birth to a low birth weight baby, but that the prenatal care has no direct impact on that outcome. Perhaps another element—such as mother's diet—is most important to birth weight, and those who are likely to follow the proper diet, for a variety of indirect reasons, such as socioeconomic status, happen to be those who get adequate prenatal care. If that were the case, it would be incorrect to say that the prenatal care is what decreases risk.

Let's evaluate the answer choices to see which ones weaken the conclusion:

(A) The hospital records indicate that many babies that are born with normal birth weights are born to mothers who had inadequate prenatal care.

The fact that "many" babies are born of normal weight to mothers who had inadequate prenatal care does not impact the relative *likelihood of giving birth to low birth weight babies. This can be a tricky concept to understand, so let's take a look at a simpler example.*

Suppose that at a certain ice cream shop those who order the sundae are far more likely to request peanuts than those who order the banana split. This would not mean that all those who order the sundae request peanuts—just that ordering the sundae makes the request more likely. We can image the following results for 100 orders:

	Requested Peanuts	Didn't Request Peanuts
Ordered Sundae	40	10
Ordered Banana Split	10	40

In the above situation, it's true that *many* people who ordered the banana split requested peanuts, but it doesn't change the fact that those who ordered the sundae *were more likely* to request peanuts.

The same thing is happening with answer (A). Even if those who get inadequate care give birth to many normal weight babies, it's unclear what impact this has on the conclusion, so we can eliminate it.

(B) Mothers giving birth prematurely are routinely classified by hospitals as having received inadequate prenatal care when the record of that care is not available.

This doesn't address a gap we discussed, but it does impact the premise—it provides an alternative reason for why the difference between likelihoods exists. Let's keep it for now.

(C) The hospital records indicate that low birth weight babies were routinely classified as having been born prematurely.

It's tough to see how this impacts the argument. This answer addresses the relationship between low birth weight and prematurity, but it does not address the relationship between prenatal care and birth weight. Let's eliminate it.

(D) Some babies not born prematurely, whose mothers received adequate prenatal care, have low birth weights.

This answer is similar to (A). "Some" is very vague, and so this gives us no insight into the relative likelihood for the different groups.

(E)   Women who receive adequate prenatal care are less likely
      to give birth prematurely than are women who do not
      receive adequate prenatal care.

*If anything, this answer would strengthen the argument by connecting the factors in the premise and giving
another reason why women who receive adequate prenatal care are going to be less likely to give birth to a low
weight baby.*

We can eliminate this answer because it certainly doesn't weaken.

That leaves us only with answer choice (B). It certainly wasn't what we expected, but it does impact the
conclusion. Let's review it one more time:

(B)   Mothers giving birth prematurely are routinely classified
      by hospitals as having received inadequate prenatal care
      when the record of that care is not available.

In what way does this specifically impact our core? It's essentially telling us that the records *themselves are
not accurate. In other words, the support for the conclusion is not reliable! This answer choice weakens the
reliability of a premise, and thus the argument. Usually we expect an answer that more obviously attacks
the connection between the premise and conclusion, but we should expect some curveballs in Strengthen and
Weaken questions.*

Here's another question with a similar issue. Try it completely before reading further.

<u>*PT44, S2, Q20*</u>

Scientist: My research indicates that children who engage in
impulsive behavior similar to adult thrill-seeking behavior are
twice as likely as other children to have a gene variant that
increases sensitivity to dopamine. From this, I conclude that
there is a causal relationship between this gene variant and an
inclination toward thrill-seeking behavior.

Which one of the following, if true, most calls into question
the scientist's argument?

(A)   Many impulsive adults are not unusually sensitive to
      dopamine.
(B)   It is not possible to reliably distinguish impulsive behavior
      from other behavior.
(C)   Children are often described by adults as engaging
      in thrill-seeking behavior simply because they act
      impulsively.
(D)   Many people exhibit behavioral tendencies as adults that
      they did not exhibit as children.
(E)   The gene variant studied by the scientist is correlated
      with other types of behavior in addition to thrill-seeking
      behavior.

6

Here's the argument core:

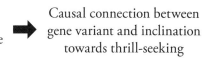

Research indicates children who engage in impulsive behavior similar to adult thrill-seeking twice as likely to have gene variant → Causal connection between gene variant and inclination towards thrill-seeking

Once again, this argument is one that would seem quite reasonable in real life. Reading as a debater, perhaps you notice the causal flaw—correlation doesn't prove causation! Perhaps the likelihood is twice as great, but maybe there is another explanation, and there is no causal relationship between the two at all.

Let's evaluate the answer choices:

(A) Many impulsive adults are not unusually sensitive to dopamine.

This answer choice is very similar to a couple from the previous example—"many" does not, in any direct way, impact the likelihood of a characteristic in one group versus another. We can eliminate this quickly.

(B) It is not possible to reliably distinguish impulsive behavior from other behavior.

Hmmm. Interesting. Certainly doesn't have to do with any issue we saw, but, if this were true, it might weaken the argument. Let's keep it.

(C) Children are often described by adults as engaging in thrill-seeking behavior simply because they act impulsively.

This may be true, but it is irrelevant to the facts of this argument. The research was not based on such adult characterizations. We can eliminate this.

(D) Many people exhibit behavioral tendencies as adults that they did not exhibit as children.

The research is about children—tendencies that develop later are irrelevant. Eliminate it.

(E) The gene variant studied by the scientist is correlated with other types of behavior in addition to thrill-seeking behavior.

This answer, if anything, would strengthen the connection between the genes and the behavior. We can eliminate it.

Once again, we're left with just one viable answer. Let's evaluate it again:

(B) It is not possible to reliably distinguish impulsive behavior from other behavior.

What would the significance of this answer be? If it's not possible to reliably distinguish impulsive behavior, the research is far less likely to be accurate. If the research is not accurate, it doesn't provide compelling support for the conclusion.

(B) is correct.

This last problem is a perfect example of a difficult Strengthen and Weaken question. The right answer is tough to predict and is presented in a surprising manner. For this type of question, it is critical that you stay open-minded as you evaluate the answer choices. With that in mind, your elimination process becomes even more critical, so let's discuss it in more depth.

The Elimination Process for Strengthen and Weaken Questions

The characteristics of incorrect answers for Strengthen and Weaken questions are fairly consistent with the characteristics of incorrect answers for other Assumption Family questions, and they are answers that are flawed either because of language issues or reasoning issues.

We've already discussed many incorrect answers in this chapter—let's try to organize our understanding of them. You can think of almost all wrong answers to Strengthen and Weaken questions as falling into one of three categories:

1. The answer has no direct bearing on the conclusion. Often, these answers are related to a vague, or slightly incorrect, understanding of the author's point. If you don't have a clear sense of the core, or if you've generalized beyond what the author is specifically discussing, you'll be in trouble with these. If you do have a strong sense of the core, you can often spot an incorrect answer that falls in this category because there is a subtle but significant shift (often a mismatch of terms) between the argument and the answer.

If you have a clear understanding of the core and, most importantly, the conclusion, these answers can be the simplest to eliminate. They also happen to be the most common wrong choices.

2. The answer has an unclear bearing on the conclusion. A slightly more tempting wrong answer is one that is related to the elements of the conclusion, but has an unclear impact on the author's point. We'll discuss these types of answers in more depth in the "EXCEPT" section. These answers may discuss the same subject matter as the argument, but in a manner that doesn't relate directly to the point that the author is making or to the reasoning that the author is using to reach that conclusion. If you can't see how the answer impacts the author's point, or if you can see the answer either strengthening or weakening the argument, depending on how you interpret the answer choice or on what assumptions you make, that's a good sign it neither strengthens nor weakens.

3. The answer plays the opposite role relative to the argument. Let's imagine you are given a Strengthen question, you read through the argument, immediately see one significant flaw, then go to the answer choices. Answers (A) through (C) have no direct impact on the author's point. You get to (D)—it is an example that accurately and absolutely proves the flaw you saw in the argument, and so you pick it…

But wait… wouldn't that mean (D) weakens the argument? We're supposed to strengthen!

As we've said before, answers that express an assumption when we should be looking for a flaw, or answers that weaken an argument when we're looking for something that should strengthen—answers that play the opposite role of what we're looking for—can often be the most tempting and most attractive. This is particularly true for "EXCEPT" questions!

Let's take a look at a real LSAT question. For each wrong choice, take the extra time to try to determine exactly why it is incorrect.

> *PT36, S3, Q7*
>
> Medical doctor: Sleep deprivation is the cause of many social ills, ranging from irritability to potentially dangerous instances of impaired decision making. Most people today suffer from sleep deprivation to some degree. Therefore we should restructure the workday to allow people flexibility in scheduling their work hours.
>
> Which one of the following, if true, would most strengthen the medical doctor's argument?
>
> (A) The primary cause of sleep deprivation is overwork.
> (B) Employees would get more sleep if they had greater latitude in scheduling their work hours.
> (C) Individuals vary widely in the amount of sleep they require.
> (D) More people would suffer from sleep deprivation today than did in the past if the average number of hours worked per week had not decreased.
> (E) The extent of one's sleep deprivation is proportional to the length of one's workday.

The argument begins with a general statement about the consequences of sleep deprivation. The second sentence shows how widespread the issue is, and the author's conclusion comes at the end.

We can think of the core of the doctor's argument as follows:

Most people today suffer from sleep deprivation

+

Sleep deprivation is the cause of many social ills

➡ Should restructure workday to allow more flexibility in scheduling work hours

There is a fairly big gap in this argument. It's unclear what the relationship is between sleep deprivation and flexibility in scheduling work hours.

It's easy to misinterpret, or generalize, this argument to mean that workdays should be set up in such a way as to prevent people from overworking and not getting enough sleep. Notice though that that's

NOT what this argument says. If you thought of the conclusion in this way, many of the answer choices could have seemed a lot more attractive than they should have.

Let's go through them now:

> (A) The primary cause of sleep deprivation is overwork.

This may be true, but it's unclear what overwork has to do with flexibility in the schedule. This answer is not relevant to the conclusion.

> (B) Employees would get more sleep if they had greater latitude in scheduling their work hours.

This answer seems to help bridge the gap between elements in the premises (amount of sleep) and the conclusion (flexibility). Let's keep it for now.

> (C) Individuals vary widely in the amount of sleep they require.

It's unclear what impact, if any, this could have on our conclusion. We can eliminate it.

> (D) More people would suffer from sleep deprivation today than did in the past if the average number of hours worked per week had not decreased.

Again, if you had generalized the conclusion to be about a workload that allowed for more sleep, this answer would seem tempting. However, it's unclear what connection there is between a decrease in work hours and the flexibility in hours discussed in the conclusion. You can have flexible work hours and still work a lot!

> (E) The extent of one's sleep deprivation is proportional to the length of one's workday.

Again, it's unclear what impact this has on an argument that has to do with flexibility.

That leaves us with (B), the correct answer. Let's review it one more time:

> (B) Employees would get more sleep if they had greater latitude in scheduling their work hours.

How does this strengthen the argument, exactly? If (B) is true, then giving more flexibility would allow employees to not be as sleep deprived. This is a good thing, since we're told that sleep deprivation is the cause of many social ills. This answer connects the premises to the conclusion, and helps the premises justify that conclusion.

Note that in this case, there was only one answer that had any direct bearing at all on the conclusion. A careful understanding of the core should have helped you knock off the incorrect choices fairly quickly.

Here's another challenging problem for which many incorrect choices will have no relation to the core. Try to eliminate these answers first, before moving on to decide which answer choice is correct.

PT16, S3, Q18

Because dinosaurs were reptiles, scientists once assumed that, like all reptiles alive today, dinosaurs were cold-blooded. The recent discovery of dinosaur fossils in the northern arctic, however, has led a number of researchers to conclude that at least some dinosaurs might have been warm-blooded. These researchers point out that only warm-blooded animals could have withstood the frigid temperatures that are characteristic of arctic winters, whereas cold-blooded animals would have frozen to death in the extreme cold.

Which one of the following, if true, weakens the researchers' argument?

(A) Today's reptiles are generally confined to regions of temperate or even tropical climates.
(B) The fossils show the arctic dinosaurs to have been substantially smaller than other known species of dinosaurs.
(C) The arctic dinosaur fossils were found alongside fossils of plants known for their ability to withstand extremely cold temperatures.
(D) The number of fossils found together indicates herds of dinosaurs so large that they would need to migrate to find a continual food supply.
(E) Experts on prehistoric climatic conditions believe that winter temperatures in the prehistoric northern arctic were not significantly different from what they are today.

Before reading the explanation, please think again about the answer choices that do not relate to the argument core and notate them in some way.

We can think of the core of this argument as follows:

Dinosaur fossils discovered in
northern arctic

+   ➔   Some dinosaurs were warm-
                                        blooded
Only warm-blooded animals
can withstand artic winters

You may have considered the core slightly differently, but by this point your understanding of the core should in general be consistent with ours.

What are the gaps in this argument?

For one, perhaps the winters may have been different when the dinosaurs were around. Perhaps arctic winters weren't as cold back then as they are now, and cold-blooded dinosaurs could have survived. For another, perhaps the dinosaurs migrated north in the warmer summer, and migrated to warmer areas in the south for the winter. In this case, they wouldn't need to survive arctic winters.

Simple enough, perhaps, to see the issues once the argument is dissected, but we know this is a difficult argument to understand the first time through. We can do ourselves a big favor by first getting rid of answers that do not impact the reasoning in any way.

Here are two answer choices we feel you can eliminate even when you don't have a perfect understanding of the core, answer choices that simply have no relationship to the reasoning in the argument:

> (A) Today's reptiles are generally confined to regions of temperate or even tropical climates.

Does this generalization have any impact on our conclusion? No. The fact that the reptiles generally live in temperate or tropical climates has no impact on our argument—this doesn't mean reptiles don't live in cold climates. Furthermore, we're assuming a lot in connecting the behavior of reptiles today with the behavior of dinosaurs.

> (B) The fossils show the arctic dinosaurs to have been substantially smaller than other known species of dinosaurs.

It's unclear what relevance the size of the dinosaurs has for this argument. So what if they were small? Perhaps you can imagine some relationship between size and heat retention. However, that requires assumptions that go too far beyond the text.

The other answer choices are a bit more tempting. Let's evaluate them in depth:

> (C) The arctic dinosaur fossils were found alongside fossils of plants known for their ability to withstand extremely cold temperatures.

Hmmm. If this is true, it would seem the dinosaurs died during very cold temperatures. It supports the idea, perhaps, that the dinosaurs died in the winter. Let's leave it for now.

But wait a minute! That would make it so the author's argument sounds better, and we're looking to weaken. We can eliminate this answer because it plays a reverse role.

By the way, we can also eliminate this answer because it doesn't actually indicate whether these plants (and thus the dinosaurs) actually died in extremely cold temperatures; we simply know that these plants were capable of withstanding cold temperatures. If you noticed this, perhaps you also noticed that this answer has no direct bearing on the conclusion—that some dinosaurs may have been warm-blooded. It's often true that answers are wrong for multiple reasons.

> (D) The number of fossils found together indicates herds of dinosaurs so large that they would need to migrate to find a continual food supply.

The first part, about the size of the herds, makes this answer seem out of scope, but the second part is relevant—these herds migrated. If they migrated, perhaps they were in the north only during the summer months. Notice how this answer seems out of scope, but actually helps to break the bond between premise and conclusion. Thus, this answer weakens the author's argument by deflecting the impact of evidence the author uses to prove that there were warm-blooded dinosaurs.

(D) is correct. Let's finish this off by looking at (E):

> (E) Experts on prehistoric climatic conditions believe that winter temperatures in the prehistoric northern arctic were not significantly different from what they are today.

This is a very tempting answer. Of all the choices, this one addresses a gap in the argument most directly. However, notice that this is an answer that would strengthen *the argument. It's another answer that's the opposite of what we're looking for.*

Clearly, this is a difficult question, especially if you didn't anticipate the gap about migration when you initially read the argument. However, even if you didn't see the gap, an answer like (D) should be attractive to you, because it presents an alternative explanation for why bones could be found in an area where dinosaurs seemingly shouldn't be able to survive the winter—*because the dinosaurs migrated.* In so doing, it directly addresses a gap in the core. Does it make it so that the argument is 100 percent wrong? Absolutely not. Is it the type of answer we expect you can predict every time? Absolutely not. Again, having the ability to quickly eliminate answers that don't directly relate to the core will give you a better chance of zeroing in on such an unlikely correct answer.

6

Here is a final question you tried earlier. Take the time to solve it again and to classify the wrong answer choices before moving forward.

PT36, S1, Q8

It has been claimed that television networks should provide equal time for the presentation of opposing views whenever a television program concerns scientific issues—such as those raised by the claims of environmentalists—about which people disagree. However, although an obligation to provide equal time does arise in the case of any program concerning social issues, it does so because social issues almost always have important political implications and seldom can definitely be settled on the basis of available evidence. If a program concerns scientific issues, that program gives rise to no such equal time obligation.

Which one of the following, if true, most seriously weakens the argument?

(A) No scientific issues raised by the claims of environmentalists have important political implications.

(B) There are often more than two opposing views on an issue that cannot be definitely settled on the basis of available evidence.

(C) Some social issues could be definitely settled on the basis of evidence if the opposing sides would give all the available evidence a fair hearing.

(D) Many scientific issues have important political implications and cannot be definitely settled on the basis of the available evidence.

(E) Some television networks refuse to broadcast programs on issues that have important political implications and that cannot be definitely settled by the available evidence.

It's very easy to get distracted in this argument, because it is long, and because the author uses claims that we might disagree with. It's great to read like a debater, but be sure to apply that to the entire core, not just to the premises or just to the conclusion.

Let's evaluate the argument core:

There is obligation to provide equal time for programs involving social issues because they almost always have important political implications and can rarely be solved with available evidence. If program is about scientific issues, there is no such equal time obligation.

MANHATTAN
LSAT

There are many flaws with this argument, and it's dangerous to be overly specific. For example, it's unclear exactly which obligation "no such equal time obligation" refers to—the obligation for equal time, or the obligation for equal time *because* of these same reasons.

Furthermore, the argument has many gaps. Can't a program be both scientific and social? How do we know scientific problems don't have the characteristics the author describes? Depending on how you read that conclusion, who is to say an obligation doesn't exist to present equal sides for scientific issues *for other reasons*?

Again, because the argument is vague and heavily flawed, we want to cast a wide net in terms of what could strengthen or what could weaken. Indeed, it will be far more effective to start by finding reasons why four of the answers don't work.

Let's review the answers one at a time:

(A) No scientific issues raised by the claims of environmentalists have important political implications.

This seems to be something the author is assuming, and we know the author is wrong in assuming this— and so this answer can be very tempting. However, this answer is NOT one that, if true, would weaken the argument. If this were true, the argument would be strengthened. We must be careful to be clear about our task. If we are, we can eliminate this answer.

(B) There are often more than two opposing views on an issue that cannot be definitely settled on the basis of available evidence.

This may be true, but it has an unclear impact on our conclusion, because we don't know that scientific issues have views that definitely cannot be settled on the basis of available evidence. Though we are told that people disagree on scientific issues, that's not the same thing, and it would be an assumption to say these people definitely could not settle the dispute using all the available evidence. Furthermore, why does it matter if the number of opposing views is two or more than two? We can eliminate this answer.

(C) Some social issues could be definitely settled on the basis of evidence if the opposing sides would give all the available evidence a fair hearing.

This answer has no bearing on the author's conclusion about scientific *issues and can be eliminated quickly. If you were tempted by this answer, make sure you keep your eyes on the core.*

(D) Many scientific issues have important political implications and cannot be definitely settled on the basis of the available evidence.

This answer directly addresses the gap, and, if this were true, then the author's point would be weakened. Scientific issues would have the same characteristics that obligate networks to air equal time for social issues.

(E) Some television networks refuse to broadcast programs on issues that have important political implications and that cannot be definitely settled by the available evidence.

6

Whether they "refuse" is irrelevant to this argument (this is a mismatch with "obligation") and you can quickly eliminate this answer.

(D) is correct.

To be clear, we do not want you to spend precious time during the exam categorizing incorrect choices. However, we think it's very useful for you to go into the exam knowing, in as clear a way as possible, why wrong answer choices are wrong. In reviewing your work, even for problems that you confidently answered correctly, take the time to consider exactly how each wrong choice is "made" incorrect. A strong sense of how wrong answers are built will allow you to go through Strengthen and Weaken questions more efficiently and effectively.

EXCEPT

EXCEPT questions can often be some of the most challenging questions in a Logical Reasoning section. They cause careless errors, are easily misunderstood, and can cause us to get all twisted around.

It's understandable! EXCEPT questions require us to think in the reverse of what we've grow accustomed to doing for solving other types of problems. Answers that directly relate to core, and clearly strengthen or weaken—answers that we typically ought to be attracted to—are going to be the ones we'll generally want to eliminate.

Therefore, it's important that you consider EXCEPT questions as a distinct subcategory of Strengthen and Weaken, and that you practice a process that is specific to these types of questions.

Here are a few key points to remember:

1. Make sure you clearly understand what you are looking for. Let's take a look at a typical phrasing of an EXCEPT question:

> "Each of the following, if true, would weaken the argument EXCEPT:"

A common misconception is that the answer choices for such a question will break down as follows: four answer choices that weaken and one answer choice that strengthens.

It's critical to remember that the right answer to this type of question need not, and often will not, strengthen the conclusion. The right answer will simply be the only one that *does not weaken*. It may strengthen, or it may have no direct bearing on the conclusion. For the most challenging questions, the tendency will be that the right answer has no clearly discernable impact on the conclusion. So, remember that there are three categories of answers:

| **Weaken** | **No/Unclear bearing** | **Strengthen** |

For a question such as "Each of the following, if true, would strengthen the argument EXCEPT," four answers will strengthen, and the right answer will either weaken or, more commonly, have no clearly discernable impact on the conclusion.

How can this be? How can the LSAT outsmart you with answers that don't have an impact on the conclusion, and how can it do so to such a degree that these can be some of the most challenging questions on the exam? The key to these well-cloaked answers is that they will relate directly to some other part of the argument, often the primary premise, but not in a way that impacts the author's point. Remember, your job in most Strengthen and Weaken questions is to strengthen or weaken the *argument*, not the premises or conclusion alone. Your ability to recognize and focus in on the argument core is critical.

To illustrate, let's go back to the sample argument that started the chapter:

Sally **owns more cookbooks** than Finn Sally **is a better cook** than Finn

Here are a few examples of answers that, if true, would strengthen the argument:

> "The number of cookbooks one owns is an accurate gauge of how much one knows about cooking."

> "Owning cookbooks inspires people to practice cooking, and, in turn, to become better cooks."

> "Experience in the kitchen and exposure to foods of other cultures are not factors that significantly influence knowledge of cooking."

Here are a few examples of answers that would, if true, weaken the argument:

> "Sally has not read any of her cookbooks."

> "Sally often misreads cookbooks and ends up becoming a worse cook after reading them."

> "Sally was born without taste buds and cannot accurately gauge the flavor of her cooking."

Each of these answers has a direct impact on the conclusion either because it supports the reasoning used in connecting the premise to the conclusion, or because it exposes gaps in this reasoning. We can see how each of these answers would have a direct impact on our judgment of whether Sally is a better cook than Finn.

Now here is an answer that *seems* related to the argument, but neither strengthens nor weakens the author's reasoning:

> "Sally unexpectedly got all the cookbooks from her mother when her mother moved into a smaller house."

Note that this answer relates directly to our premise—in fact, it gives us a reason *why* our premise is true.

But does this answer impact the author's conclusion? Does it impact the reasoning used? Not in a clear, direct way.

The fact that Sally inherited the books could mean she didn't have any interest in owning them, or it could mean she wanted the books. If we try to connect this answer to the argument in a way that impacts whether Sally is a better cook than Finn, we could only do so by adding significant conjectures, or assumptions. Therefore, we can say that this answer does not have a clearly definable impact on our argument.

Let's now take a look back at a question from the start of the chapter. Please solve it again now so that your process will be fresh in your mind as we continue the discussion:

PT37, S2, Q20

Antarctic seals dive to great depths and stay submerged for hours. They do not rely solely on oxygen held in their lungs, but also store extra oxygen in their blood. Indeed, some researchers hypothesize that for long dives these seals also store oxygenated blood in their spleens.

Each of the following, if true, provides some support for the researchers' hypothesis EXCEPT:

(A) Horses are known to store oxygenated blood in their spleens for use during exertion.
(B) Many species of seal can store oxygen directly in their muscle tissue.
(C) The oxygen contained in the seals' lungs and bloodstream alone would be inadequate to support the seals during their dives.
(D) The spleen is much larger in the Antarctic seal than in aquatic mammals that do not make long dives.
(E) The spleens of Antarctic seals contain greater concentrations of blood vessels than are contained in most of their other organs.

We discussed earlier that arguments for Strengthen and Weaken questions can stray farther from the norm than arguments for Assumption and Identify a Flaw questions—this isn't very common, but here's an example of an argument that doesn't fit the argument core model.

We could think of the core in this way:

Seals stay submerged for hours

+

Don't rely solely on oxygen in lungs   ➡   Store oxygenated blood in spleens

+

Store oxygen in blood

However, a *more* accurate representation of this argument is that the first two sentences present background for a hypothesis that doesn't have a supporting premise. Here we have another argument without a core:

>   Seals store oxygenated blood in their spleens.

Again, we want to stress that being asked to strengthen or weaken an argument without a premise-conclusion is fairly unusual. Something you should expect to see no more than once, if that, on any given exam. By the way, it's no coincidence that both "core-free" arguments we've discussed in this chapter have come in the form of EXCEPT questions. Also, note that we were given a subtle clue in the way the question is asked:

>   "Each of the following, if true, **provides some support for the researchers'
>   hypothesis** EXCEPT:"

The words in bold are of note because of what is *missing*—typically we are asked to evaluate what would strengthen or weaken *reasoning*, or an *argument*. In this case, we're asked to identify answers that simply support the *hypothesis,* or conclusion. We know we just need to compare the answers to the conclusion.

Now it's time to look at the answer choices. Your frame of mind is critical to your success and efficiency. Here's our second tip:

2. Eliminate the four that weaken or strengthen! This may seem like obvious advice—incredibly obvious advice, perhaps. However, the reason we make a point of stating this is that by the time you are done practicing all the Strengthen and Weaken questions that we hope you will practice, your default mind-set is going to be to look for the one answer that weakens or the one answer that strengthens. If you are not careful, this habit will slow you down or distract you on EXCEPT questions.

It is important that you change your mind-set for EXCEPT questions. What you know going in to the answer choices is that almost all of the answers, 80 percent, in fact, will strengthen or will weaken.

Let's focus in on the hypothesis one more time before going into the answer choices:

>   Seals store oxygenated blood in their spleens.

We know almost all the answers will support this idea, and we want to cast a wide net. Let's evaluate each in depth:

>   (A) Horses are known to store oxygenated blood in their
>   spleens for use during exertion.

This strengthens the argument because it shows that such a thing—an animal storing oxygenated blood in its spleen—is possible.

It's important to note that this is the type of answer that most likely would be considered out of scope for an Assumption or Identify a Flaw question. The author doesn't need to assume anything about horses to make her claim about seals, nor is it a flaw that she didn't. This is another example of how answers that strengthen or weaken can feel a bit further separated from the text than answers that represent assumptions or flaws.

> (B) Many species of seal can store oxygen directly in their
>   muscle tissue.

How does this impact the conclusion? It's unclear. Let's leave it for now.

> (C) The oxygen contained in the seals' lungs and bloodstream
>   alone would be inadequate to support the seals during
>   their dives.

This strengthens the conclusion. It means that they need to store oxygen someplace else, and that supports the idea that they could store it in the spleen.

> (D) The spleen is much larger in the Antarctic seal than in
>   aquatic mammals that do not make long dives.

This also strengthens. If the spleen for these seals is larger, it's possible this difference is due to using the spleen for storing oxygenated blood.

> (E) The spleens of Antarctic seals contain greater
>   concentrations of blood vessels than are contained in most
>   of their other organs.

This also strengthens. This difference in the spleen is more evidence that the spleens are used to store extra oxygen.

In the initial read, you may have felt that many of these answers did not strengthen the argument. If so, it's likely you are setting the bar too high. Remember that answers that strengthen need not make an argument perfect, or anywhere near that. Especially for an EXCEPT question, strengthen answers simply have to give you a stronger sense that the conclusion is true than that the conclusion is false.

There is only one answer that doesn't have *any* discernable impact on the conclusion:

> (B) Many species of seal can store oxygen directly in their
>   muscle tissue.

This is the correct answer. How does the fact that seals can store oxygen in their muscles support the idea that they can store it in their spleens? It doesn't.

Let's try another challenging example:

PT33, S1, Q20

Recently discovered prehistoric rock paintings on small islands off the northern coast of Norway have archaeologists puzzled. The predominant theory about northern cave paintings was that they were largely a description of the current diets of the painters. This theory cannot be right, because the painters must have needed to eat the sea animals populating the waters north of Norway if they were to make the long journey to and from the islands, and there are no paintings that unambiguously depict such creatures.

Each of the following, if true, weakens the argument against the predominant theory about northern cave paintings EXCEPT:

(A) Once on these islands, the cave painters hunted and ate land animals.

(B) Parts of the cave paintings on the islands did not survive the centuries.

(C) The cave paintings that were discovered on the islands depicted many land animals.

(D) Those who did the cave paintings that were discovered on the islands had unusually advanced techniques of preserving meats.

(E) The cave paintings on the islands were done by the original inhabitants of the islands who ate the meat of land animals.

The author's conclusion is that the predominant theory cannot be right, and this predominant theory is that northern cave paintings were largely a description of the current diets of the painters. The premises are given in the sentence that follows in the argument, and we can think of the argument core as follows:

Needed to eat sea animals
during journey to islands

+

No unambiguous paintings
of sea animals

➡   False that cave paintings
largely describe current
diets of painters.

There are some significant gaps in the argument—we don't actually know anything about the diets of the painters once they are on the island, and we don't know if the paintings that have been discovered are representative of *all* the paintings on the island. It's certainly helpful to consider these gaps as we go into the answer choices.

We want to make sure to focus on eliminating answers that weaken this core. In this case—because we are asked specifically to weaken a claim that another claim is false—it's especially easy to get turned around. To keep focused, remember that the conclusion of the argument is that the paintings were not based on the diet.

Let's evaluate the answer choices carefully:

> (A) Once on these islands, the cave painters hunted and ate land animals.

This shows that the painters could have painted their current diet, but that diet just didn't consist of seafood. Therefore, it weakens the author's claim. Let's eliminate it.

> (B) Parts of the cave paintings on the islands did not survive the centuries.

This shows that the evidence provided might be limited or unrepresentative, and therefore weakens the argument. Maybe they did paint sea animals, but those paintings have been lost. Let's eliminate it.

> (C) The cave paintings that were discovered on the islands depicted many land animals.

This answer seems less directly connected to the core than the first two. Let's leave it for now.

> (D) Those who did the cave paintings that were discovered on the islands had unusually advanced techniques of preserving meats.

At first this seems out of scope, but (D) offers another explanation for how, perhaps, the food the painters were eating, and consequently painting, could have been something other than seafood. It calls into question the idea that the long journey required eating fish.

> (E) The cave paintings on the islands were done by the original inhabitants of the islands who ate the meat of land animals.

If they were done by people who didn't need to travel to get to the island, one of the premises is made irrelevant. This answer presents the possibility that even though the painters didn't paint seafood they could have still painted the food they ate.

Once again, we're left with one answer that didn't get cut. Let's look at it one more time:

> (C) The cave paintings that were discovered on the islands depicted many land animals.

Does this prove that the premises don't connect to the conclusion? It could if you, as the reader, assume that the painters ate land animals. But it could also strengthen the conclusion if the painters did not eat the land animals (maybe the only land animals were ones that aren't nice to eat, or maybe the painters were vegans). Notice that, in order to determine whether this answer strengthens or weakens, we need a lot of conjecture. This is an answer that has an uncertain bearing on the conclusion, and it is therefore correct.

Conclusion

Strengthen and Weaken questions are still Assumption Family questions, and the skills you've developed for Assumption and Identify a Flaw questions should help you here. Here are some additional considerations specific to Strengthen and Weaken questions:

1. One extra layer. For Assumption and Identify a Flaw questions, we are expected to identify and assess the core. For Strengthen and Weaken questions, we also must *address* gaps in the core. The answers to Strengthen and Weaken questions may feel less directly connected to the argument than answers to Assumption and Identify a Flaw, and also less predictable.

2. Unique arguments. Strengthen and Weaken arguments have more of a tendency to vary from the norm than other Assumption Family questions. It's critical to be flexible. Beware of arguments without cores and of claims within premises.

3. The elimination process. Because the right answers are less predictable, your elimination process is crucial. Eliminate answers that don't relate to the core, have an indeterminate relationship to the core, or—and this one can be tricky to spot—play an opposite role.

4. EXCEPT questions. Make sure to change your process for EXCEPT questions. Eliminate the four answer choices that strengthen or weaken. The right answer will often relate to the elements in the argument, but have no clearly discernable bearing on the author's point.

6

DRILL IT: Strengthen and Weaken Questions

Give yourself no more than 20 minutes to complete the following problems.

1. PT29, S1, Q3

There should be a greater use of gasohol. Gasohol is a mixture of alcohol and gasoline, and has a higher octane rating and fewer carbon monoxide emissions than straight gasoline. Burning gasohol adds no more carbon dioxide to the atmosphere than plants remove by photosynthesis.

Each of the following, if true, strengthens the argument above EXCEPT:

(A) Cars run less well on gasoline than they do on gasohol.

(B) Since less gasoline is needed with the use of gasohol, an energy shortage is less likely.

(C) Cars burn on the average slightly more gasohol per kilometer than they do gasoline.

(D) Gasohol is cheaper to produce and hence costs less at the pump than gasoline.

(E) Burning gasoline adds more carbon dioxide to the atmosphere than plants can remove.

2. PT29, S1, Q16

We can learn about the living conditions of a vanished culture by examining its language. Thus, it is likely that the people who spoke Proto-Indo-European, the language from which all Indo-European languages descended, lived in a cold climate, isolated from ocean or sea, because Proto-Indo-European lacks a word for "sea," yet contains words for "winter," "snow," and "wolf."

Which one of the following, if true, most seriously weakens the argument?

(A) A word meaning "fish" was used by the people who spoke Proto-Indo-European.

(B) Some languages lack words for prominent elements of the environments of their speakers.

(C) There are no known languages today that lack a word for "sea."

(D) Proto-Indo-European possesses words for "heat."

(E) The people who spoke Proto-Indo-European were nomadic.

3. PT29, S4, Q20

Amphibian populations are declining in numbers worldwide. Not coincidentally, the earth's ozone layer has been continuously depleted throughout the last 50 years. Atmospheric ozone blocks UV-B, a type of ultraviolet radiation that is continuously produced by the sun, and which can damage genes. Because amphibians lack hair, hide, or feathers to shield them, they are particularly vulnerable to UV-B radiation. In addition, their gelatinous eggs lack the protection of leathery or hard shells. Thus, the primary cause of the declining amphibian population is the depletion of the ozone layer.

Each of the following, if true, would strengthen the argument EXCEPT:

(A) Of the various types of radiation blocked by atmospheric ozone, UV-B is the only type that can damage genes.

(B) Amphibian populations are declining far more rapidly than are the populations of nonamphibian species whose tissues and eggs have more natural protection from UV-B.

(C) Atmospheric ozone has been significantly depleted above all the areas of the world in which amphibian populations are declining.

(D) The natural habitat of amphibians has not become smaller over the past century.

(E) Amphibian populations have declined continuously for the last 50 years.

4. PT30, S2, Q3

Opponents of peat harvesting in this country argue that it would alter the ecological balance of our peat-rich wetlands and that, as a direct consequence of this, much of the country's water supply would be threatened with contamination. But this cannot be true, for in Ireland, where peat has been harvested for centuries, the water supply is not contaminated. We can safely proceed with the harvesting of peat.

Which one of the following, if true, most strengthens the argument?

(A) Over hundreds of years, the ecological balance of all areas changes slowly but significantly, sometimes to the advantage of certain flora and fauna.

(B) The original ecology of the peat-harvesting areas of Ireland was virtually identical to that of the undisturbed wetlands of this country.

(C) The activities of other industries in coming years are likely to have adverse effects on the water supply of this country.

(D) The peat resources of this country are far larger than those of some countries that successfully harvest peat.

(E) The peat-harvesting industry of Ireland has been able to supply most of that country's fuel for generations.

5. PT30, S4, Q11

High school students who feel that they are not succeeding in school often drop out before graduating and go to work. Last year, however, the city's high school dropout rate was significantly lower than the previous year's rate. This is encouraging evidence that the program instituted two years ago to improve the morale of high school students has begun to take effect to reduce dropouts.

Which one of the following, if true about the last year, most seriously weakens the argument?

(A) There was a recession that caused a high level of unemployment in the city.

(B) The morale of students who dropped out of high school had been low even before they reached high school.

(C) As in the preceding year, more high school students remained in school than dropped out.

(D) High schools in the city established placement offices to assist their graduates in obtaining employment.

(E) The antidropout program was primarily aimed at improving students' morale in those high schools with the highest dropout rates.

6. PT32, S1, Q20

Current maps showing the North American regions where different types of garden plants will flourish are based on weather data gathered 60 years ago from a few hundred primitive weather stations. New maps are now being compiled using computerized data from several thousand modern weather stations and input from home gardeners across North America. These maps will be far more useful.

Each of the following, if true, helps to support the claim that the new maps will be more useful EXCEPT:

(A) Home gardeners can provide information on plant flourishing not available from weather stations.

(B) Some of the weather stations currently in use are more than 60 years old.

(C) Weather patterns can be described more accurately when more information is available.

(D) Weather conditions are the most important factor in determining where plants will grow.

(E) Weather patterns have changed in the past 60 years.

6

_7. PT30, S4, Q12_

The television show Henry was not widely watched until it was scheduled for Tuesday evenings immediately after That's Life, the most popular show on television. During the year after the move, Henry was consistently one of the ten most-watched shows on television. Since Henry's recent move to Wednesday evenings, however, it has been watched by far fewer people. We must conclude that Henry was widely watched before the move to Wednesday evenings because it followed That's Life and not because people especially liked it.

Which one of the following, if true, most strengthens the argument?

(A) Henry has been on the air for three years, but That's Life has been on the air for only two years.

(B) The show that replaced Henry on Tuesdays has persistently had a low number of viewers in the Tuesday time slot.

(C) The show that now follows That's Life on Tuesdays has double the number of viewers it had before being moved.

(D) After its recent move to Wednesday, Henry was aired at the same time as the second most popular show on television.

(E) That's Life was not widely watched during the first year it was aired.

_8. PT32, S1, Q12_

Navigation in animals is defined as the animal's ability to find its way from unfamiliar territory to points familiar to the animal but beyond the immediate range of the animal's senses. Some naturalists claim that polar bears can navigate over considerable distances. As evidence, they cite an instance of a polar bear that returned to its home territory after being released over 500 kilometers (300 miles) away.

Which one of the following, if true, casts the most doubt on the validity of the evidence offered in support of the naturalists' claim?

(A) The polar bear stopped and changed course several times as it moved toward its home territory.

(B) The site at which the polar bear was released was on the bear's annual migration route.

(C) The route along which the polar bear traveled consisted primarily of snow and drifting ice.

(D) Polar bears are only one of many species of mammal whose members have been known to find their way home from considerable distances.

(E) Polar bears often rely on their extreme sensitivity to smell in order to scent out familiar territory.

9. PT32, S1, Q17

Detective: Because the embezzler must have had specialized knowledge and access to internal financial records, we can presume that the embezzler worked for XYZ Corporation as either an accountant or an actuary. But an accountant would probably not make the kind of mistakes in ledger entries that led to the discovery of the embezzlement. Thus it is likely that the embezzler is one of the actuaries.

Each of the following weakens the detective's argument EXCEPT:

(A) The actuaries' activities while working for XYZ Corporation were more closely scrutinized by supervisors than were the activities of the accountants.

(B) There is evidence of breaches in computer security at the time of the embezzlement that could have given persons outside XYZ Corporation access to internal financial records.

(C) XYZ Corporation employs eight accountants, whereas it has only two actuaries on its staff.

(D) An independent report released before the crime took place concluded that XYZ Corporation was vulnerable to embezzlement.

(E) Certain security measures at XYZ Corporation made it more difficult for the actuaries to have access to internal financial records than for the accountants.

10. PT37, S4, Q2

The vomeronasal organ (VNO) is found inside the noses of various animals. While its structural development and function are clearer in other animals, most humans have a VNO that is detectable, though only microscopically. When researchers have been able to stimulate VNO cells in humans, the subjects have reported experiencing subtle smell sensations. It seems, then, that the VNO, though not completely understood, is a functioning sensory organ in most humans.

Which one of the following, if true, most weakens the argument?

(A) It is not known whether the researchers succeeded in stimulating only VNO cells in the human subjects' noses.

(B) Relative to its occurrence in certain other animals, the human VNO appears to be anatomically rudimentary and underdeveloped.

(C) Certain chemicals that play a leading role in the way the VNO functions in animals in which it is highly developed do not appear to play a role in its functioning in humans.

(D) Secondary anatomical structures associated with the VNO in other animals seem to be absent in humans.

(E) For many animal species, the VNO is thought to subtly enhance the sense of smell.

6

Challenge Questions

11. PT29, S4, Q11

Sometimes when their trainer gives the hand signal for "Do something creative together," two dolphins circle a pool in tandem and then leap through the air simultaneously. On other occasions the same signal elicits synchronized backward swims or tail-waving. These behaviors are not simply learned responses to a given stimulus. Rather, dolphins are capable of higher cognitive functions that may include the use of language and forethought.

Which one of the following, if true, most strengthens the argument?

(A) Mammals have some resemblance to one another with respect to bodily function and brain structure.
(B) The dolphins often exhibit complex new responses to the hand signal.
(C) The dolphins are given food incentives as part of their training.
(D) Dolphins do not interact with humans the way they interact with one another.
(E) Some of the behaviors mentioned are exhibited by dolphins in their natural habitat.

12. PT30, S4, Q18

People who have political power tend to see new technologies as a means of extending or protecting their power, whereas they generally see new ethical arguments and ideas as a threat to it. Therefore, technical ingenuity usually brings benefits to those who have this ingenuity, whereas ethical inventiveness brings only pain to those who have this inventiveness.

Which one of the following statements, if true, most strengthens the argument?

(A) Those who offer new ways of justifying current political power often reap the benefits of their own innovations.
(B) Politically powerful people tend to reward those who they believe are useful to them and to punish those who they believe are a threat.
(C) Ethical inventiveness and technical ingenuity are never possessed by the same individuals.
(D) New technologies are often used by people who strive to defeat those who currently have political power.
(E) Many people who possess ethical inventiveness conceal their novel ethical arguments for fear of retribution by the politically powerful.

13. PT30, S2, Q21

The new agriculture bill will almost surely fail to pass. The leaders of all major parties have stated that they oppose it.

Which one of the following, if true, adds the most support for the prediction that the agriculture bill will fail to pass?

(A) Most bills that have not been supported by even one leader of a major party have not been passed into law.
(B) Most bills that have not been passed into law were not supported by even one member of a major party.
(C) If the leaders of all major parties endorse the new agriculture bill, it will pass into law.
(D) Most bills that have been passed into law were not unanimously supported by the leaders of all major parties.
(E) Most bills that have been passed into law were supported by at least one leader of a major party.

14. PT30, S4, Q20

Consumer advocate: The introduction of a new drug into the marketplace should be contingent upon our having a good understanding of its social impact. However, the social impact of the newly marketed antihistamine is far from clear. It is obvious, then, that there should be a general reduction in the pace of bringing to the marketplace new drugs that are now being tested.

Which one of the following, if true, most strengthens the argument?

(A) The social impact of the new antihistamine is much better understood than that of most new drugs being tested.

(B) The social impact of some of the new drugs being tested is poorly understood.

(C) The economic success of some drugs is inversely proportional to how well we understand their social impact.

(D) The new antihistamine is chemically similar to some of the new drugs being tested.

(E) The new antihistamine should be on the market only if most new drugs being tested should be on the market also.

15. PT34, S2, Q12

The five senses have traditionally been viewed as distinct yet complementary. Each sense is thought to have its own range of stimuli that are incapable of stimulating the other senses. However, recent research has discovered that some people taste a banana and claim that they are tasting blue, or see a color and say that it has a specific smell. This shows that such people, called synesthesiacs, have senses that do not respect the usual boundaries between the five recognized senses.

Which one of the following statements, if true, most seriously weakens the argument?

(A) Synesthesiacs demonstrate a general, systematic impairment in their ability to use and understand words.

(B) Recent evidence strongly suggests that there are other senses besides sight, touch, smell, hearing, and taste.

(C) The particular ways in which sensory experiences overlap in synesthesiacs follow a definite pattern.

(D) The synesthetic phenomenon has been described in the legends of various cultures.

(E) Synesthesiacs can be temporarily rid of their synesthetic experiences by the use of drugs.

6

SOLUTIONS: Strengthen and Weaken Questions

1. PT29, S1, Q3

There should be a greater use of gasohol. Gasohol is a mixture of alcohol and gasoline, and has a higher octane rating and fewer carbon monoxide emissions than straight gasoline. Burning gasohol adds no more carbon dioxide to the atmosphere than plants remove by photosynthesis.

Each of the following, if true, strengthens the argument above EXCEPT:

(A) Cars run less well on gasoline than they do on gasohol.
(B) Since less gasoline is needed with the use of gasohol, an energy shortage is less likely.
(C) Cars burn on the average slightly more gasohol per kilometer than they do gasoline.
(D) Gasohol is cheaper to produce and hence costs less at the pump than gasoline.
(E) Burning gasoline adds more carbon dioxide to the atmosphere than plants can remove.

(C) is correct.

Here, the author's conclusion is that there should be a greater use of gasohol. The support given is that gasohol is higher in octane and has fewer emissions than gasoline. Also, burning gasohol adds no more carbon to the atmosphere than plants remove.

This is a simple argument with a wide range of potential "strengtheners" (there might be a thousand additional reasons to use more gasohol), so we should keep our minds open and focus on eliminating choices that strengthen the conclusion.

(A) adds a reason that gasohol is superior to gasoline. This strengthens.

(B) tells us that gasohol use reduces the likelihood of an energy shortage. Since energy shortages are undesirable, this is a good thing for gasohol and therefore strengthens the argument.

(C) weakens the argument by saying that gasohol is a less efficient fuel than gasoline. This is definitely our answer, but let's rule out the other two just to be sure.

(D) says gasohol is cheaper. This strengthens.

(E) is a tempting choice. At first glance, it doesn't seem to say anything about gasohol. However, by stating that gasoline adds *more* carbon to the atmosphere than plants can remove, the case for using gasohol, which we know adds less carbon, is strengthened.

2. PT29, S1, Q16

We can learn about the living conditions of a vanished culture by examining its language. Thus, it is likely that the people who spoke Proto-Indo-European, the language from which all Indo-European languages descended, lived in a cold climate, isolated from ocean or sea, because Proto-Indo-European lacks a word for "sea," yet contains words for "winter," "snow," and "wolf."

Which one of the following, if true, most seriously weakens the argument?

(A) A word meaning "fish" was used by the people who spoke Proto-Indo-European.
(B) Some languages lack words for prominent elements of the environments of their speakers.
(C) There are no known languages today that lack a word for "sea."
(D) Proto-Indo-European possesses words for "heat."
(E) The people who spoke Proto-Indo-European were nomadic.

(B) is correct.

The author's conclusion is that the people who spoke Proto-Indo-European lived in a cold climate, isolated from the ocean. The only reasons given are the presence of the words "winter," "snow," and "wolf" in that language, and the absence of the word "sea."

The gap here is fairly clear: what exactly is the connection between the presence or absence of certain words in a language and the presence or absence of the features that those words represent? Since our task is to weaken the argument, we essentially want to select an answer choice that makes it possible for a culture to lack words for the environments in which they live.

Let's look at the choices:

(A) is a trap designed to make us associate "fish" with the "sea." Fish can live in rivers, lakes, and ponds, however, and the Proto-Indo-Europeans might have had those words.

(B) weakens. If some languages lack words for prominent features of the speakers' environment, then it is possible that the Proto-Indo-Europeans *did* live by the sea and yet did not have a word for it.

(C) does not affect the argument about the environment in which the Proto-Indo-Europeans lived.

(D) has no bearing whatsoever.

(E) is a trap. Even if they were nomadic, they may still have lived in a cold climate isolated from the ocean. Therefore, this choice neither strengthens nor weakens.

3. PT29, S4, Q20

Amphibian populations are declining in numbers worldwide. Not coincidentally, the earth's ozone layer has been continuously depleted throughout the last 50 years. Atmospheric ozone blocks UV-B, a type of ultraviolet radiation that is continuously produced by the sun, and which can damage genes. Because amphibians lack hair, hide, or feathers to shield them, they are particularly vulnerable to UV-B radiation. In addition, their gelatinous eggs lack the protection of leathery or hard shells. Thus, the primary cause of the declining amphibian population is the depletion of the ozone layer.

Each of the following, if true, would strengthen the argument EXCEPT:

(A) Of the various types of radiation blocked by atmospheric ozone, UV-B is the only type that can damage genes.

(B) Amphibian populations are declining far more rapidly than are the populations of nonamphibian species whose tissues and eggs have more natural protection from UV-B.

(C) Atmospheric ozone has been significantly depleted above all the areas of the world in which amphibian populations are declining.

(D) The natural habitat of amphibians has not become smaller over the past century.

(E) Amphibian populations have declined continuously for the last 50 years.

(A) is correct.

"Primary" is a very important word on the LSAT, and one we should notice immediately. The author's conclusion is that the depletion of the ozone layer is the *primary* cause of the decline in amphibian populations. The reasons given are that (1) depleted atmosphere blocks less UV-B radiation, which is dangerous to amphibians, and (2) amphibian eggs have less protection than others.

We should focus on eliminating the four choices that strengthen the argument.

(A) does not seem to strengthen. Does it matter how many kinds of radiation damage genes? No! We know that UV-B does, and amphibians are vulnerable to it, and the atmosphere blocks it. To say that UV-B is the *only* kind of radiation that damages genes does not support that reasoning.

(B) strengthens the idea that UV-B is killing the amphibians. Eliminate it.

(C) strengthens by directly correlating depleted ozone with the locations of amphibian populations. Eliminate it.

(D) strengthens by ruling out an alternative explanation. We should always be on the lookout for choices like this when we are working with causal arguments. As soon as we recognize an

6

argument as causal (as in depletion of ozone had a direct impact on the decline of amphibians), we can anticipate potential strengthen and weaken answer choices. A weakening choice will suggest another cause, or an alternate mode of causation, while a strengthening choice will rule out other potential causes, or modes of causation.

In this argument, a decline in habitat size could very well be the primary cause for the demise of the amphibians. By ruling out that possibility, we strengthen the idea that depleted ozone *is* the cause. Eliminate it.

(E) strengthens by matching up the timelines of the ozone depletion and the amphibian decline. Eliminate it.

4. PT30, S2, Q3

Opponents of peat harvesting in this country argue that it would alter the ecological balance of our peat-rich wetlands and that, as a direct consequence of this, much of the country's water supply would be threatened with contamination. But this cannot be true, for in Ireland, where peat has been harvested for centuries, the water supply is not contaminated. We can safely proceed with the harvesting of peat.

Which one of the following, if true, most strengthens the argument?

(A) Over hundreds of years, the ecological balance of all areas changes slowly but significantly, sometimes to the advantage of certain flora and fauna.

(B) The original ecology of the peat-harvesting areas of Ireland was virtually identical to that of the undisturbed wetlands of this country.

(C) The activities of other industries in coming years are likely to have adverse effects on the water supply of this country.

(D) The peat resources of this country are far larger than those of some countries that successfully harvest peat.

(E) The peat-harvesting industry of Ireland has been able to supply most of that country's fuel for generations.

(B) is correct.

The author concludes that opponents of peat harvesting are wrong and that it is in fact safe to proceed. The basis for the argument is a comparison to Ireland. This is another common argument type that we should recognize immediately! When an argument is made by analogy, as it is here, there is a simple way to weaken and a simple way to strengthen: to weaken, make the comparison less sound (apples to oranges); to strengthen, make the comparison more sound (apples to apples).

So here, we can anticipate that a good answer choice will make the comparison to Ireland stronger by relating Ireland to the country in question in some important way.

(A) has no bearing.

(B) strengthens. This is exactly what we anticipated. If Ireland's ecology was originally identical to *this* country's, then the argument is better because the comparison is well made. If Ireland's ecology was nothing at all like this country's, the argument would be severely weakened.

(C) is out of scope—this conclusion is about the peat-harvesting industry and no other industries.

(D) is out of scope, though perhaps a bit tempting. First of all, we have no evidence that the size of the peat resources has anything to do with whether the peat can be harvested without contaminating the water. Another key is the word "some." The fact that the resources here are larger than those in *some* countries does not say much. If other countries can successfully handle an equal or greater amount of resources, then this country should be able to as well.

(E) is out of scope. The amount of fuel produced has nothing to do with the question of water contamination or the comparison to Ireland.

5. PT30, S4, Q11

High school students who feel that they are not succeeding in school often drop out before graduating and go to work. Last year, however, the city's high school dropout rate was significantly lower than the previous year's rate. This is encouraging evidence that the program instituted two years ago to improve the morale of high school students has begun to take effect to reduce dropouts.

Which one of the following, if true about the last year, most seriously weakens the argument?

(A) There was a recession that caused a high level of unemployment in the city.

(B) The morale of students who dropped out of high school had been low even before they reached high school.

(C) As in the preceding year, more high school students remained in school than dropped out.

(D) High schools in the city established placement offices to assist their graduates in obtaining employment.

(E) The antidropout program was primarily aimed at improving students' morale in those high schools with the highest dropout rates.

(A) is correct.

Let's take a look at the core:

Some high school students drop out and go to work

\+

last year the dropout rate was lower than the previous year

➡️ the morale program is reducing the number of dropouts.

There is definitely a "percentage vs. real numbers" flaw at work here, and we could go to the choices equipped with that perspective. What we find is that none of the choices address that issue. At that point, we might have to start over with (A) and reconsider things with an open mind. Another flaw to consider would be the causal nature of the program. What if something else was responsible for reducing the number of dropouts? That would be a clear way to weaken this argument.

(A) does exactly that. If unemployment was especially high, then students would not be able to drop out and find jobs. Therefore, they might be more likely to stay in school. *This* might explain the reduced number of dropouts.

(B) does not relate to the argument. Was the program effective at reducing dropouts or not?

(C) does not directly relate to the argument, either. It simply says that in both years, most students did not drop out.

(D) pretends to provide an incentive for the students to stay in school, which could potentially offer an alternative to the morale program. However, if most students who drop out do so to go to work, then we have no reason to believe that an employment program would be of any benefit to them.

(E) is irrelevant.

6. PT32, S1, Q20

Current maps showing the North American regions where different types of garden plants will flourish are based on weather data gathered 60 years ago from a few hundred primitive weather stations. New maps are now being compiled using computerized data from several thousand modern weather stations and input from home gardeners across North America. These maps will be far more useful.

Each of the following, if true, helps to support the claim that the new maps will be more useful EXCEPT:

(A) Home gardeners can provide information on plant flourishing not available from weather stations.

(B) Some of the weather stations currently in use are more than 60 years old.

(C) Weather patterns can be described more accurately when more information is available.

(D) Weather conditions are the most important factor in determining where plants will grow.

(E) Weather patterns have changed in the past 60 years.

(B) is correct.

Four of the answers will strengthen the claim that the new maps, drawn from information from modern weather stations and home gardeners, will be more useful than the old maps.

We want to eliminate the choices that strengthen:

(A) strengthens because the home gardeners are providing information for the new maps.

(B) definitely does not strengthen. It actually seems to weaken, though this is debatable. The pertinent issue regarding the weather stations is whether they are primitive or modern, which, as far as we know, may or may not have to do with their age. Just because the old maps were drawn over 60 years ago using primitive stations, this does not mean that *all* stations built more than 60 years ago were primitive. Perhaps the maps were drawn 60 years ago using the "primitive" stations built 200 years ago, and the new maps are being drawn using the "modern" stations built 70 years ago. So, at best, (B) does not affect the argument at all, and at worst, it weakens it. Let's leave it.

(C) definitely strengthens. Since the new maps utilize information from many more stations, and an additional source—home gardeners—we can infer that more information will be available.

(D) strengthens the "far more useful" part of our conclusion. Consider the opposite: if weather patterns are actually not important *at all*, then a weather map is useless, and a better weather map is equally useless.

(E) definitely strengthens. If the old maps are obsolete, the claim that the new maps will be more useful is supported.

Therefore, (B) is our answer.

7. PT30, S4, Q12

The television show *Henry* was not widely watched until it was scheduled for Tuesday evenings immediately after *That's Life*, the most popular show on television. During the year after the move, *Henry* was consistently one of the ten most-watched shows on television. Since *Henry's* recent move to Wednesday evenings, however, it has been watched by far fewer people. We must conclude that *Henry* was widely watched before the move to Wednesday evenings because it followed *That's Life* and not because people especially liked it.

Which one of the following, if true, most strengthens the argument?

(A) *Henry* has been on the air for three years, but *That's Life* has been on the air for only two years.
(B) The show that replaced *Henry* on Tuesdays has persistently had a low number of viewers in the Tuesday time slot.
(C) The show that now follows *That's Life* on Tuesdays has double the number of viewers it had before being moved.
(D) After its recent move to Wednesday, *Henry* was aired at the same time as the second most popular show on television.
(E) *That's Life* was not widely watched during the first year it was aired.

(C) is correct.

We are asked to strengthen the conclusion that the show *Henry* was widely watched because it followed *That's Life* rather than because people liked it. The evidence is that when *Henry* followed *That's Life*, it was widely watched, and since it was moved, it is watched by far fewer people.

We should anticipate that a correct answer will most likely give us additional evidence that *Henry's* placement after *That's Life* was essential to its success. A correct answer might also give us reason to believe that *Henry* was *not* watched because people especially liked it.

(A) does not tell us anything about *why* the show was popular or why it declined in popularity.

(B) tells us that the show now occupying *Henry's* old slot is not popular. This hints at the fact that following *That's Life* does not guarantee success, and therefore does not strengthen the argument.

(C) adds direct support to our conclusion. If another show has *doubled* its audience since being placed after *That's Life*, we have an additional reason to believe that *That's Life* contributed to *Henry's* popularity as well.

(D) offers an alternate explanation of perhaps why fewer people watched *Henry* after its move. It does not offer support for the author's conclusion.

(E) gives us a bit more information about the premise, but does not impact reasoning issues in the core in any way.

8. PT32, S1, Q12

Navigation in animals is defined as the animal's ability to find its way from unfamiliar territory to points familiar to the animal but beyond the immediate range of the animal's senses. Some naturalists claim that polar bears can navigate over considerable distances. As evidence, they cite an instance of a polar bear that returned to its home territory after being released over 500 kilometers (300 miles) away.

Which one of the following, if true, casts the most doubt on the validity of the evidence offered in support of the naturalists' claim?

  (A) The polar bear stopped and changed course several times as it moved toward its home territory.
  (B) The site at which the polar bear was released was on the bear's annual migration route.
  (C) The route along which the polar bear traveled consisted primarily of snow and drifting ice.
  (D) Polar bears are only one of many species of mammal whose members have been known to find their way home from considerable distances.
  (E) Polar bears often rely on their extreme sensitivity to smell in order to scent out familiar territory.

(B) is correct.

This is a slightly different-flavored Weaken question. Our task is to challenge the validity of the evidence itself, so in this case, we will emphasize the evidence in our analysis.

First of all, to fit the definition of navigation, the animal must find its way from *unfamiliar* territory to *familiar* territory *beyond* the range of its senses. Next, a polar bear returned home after being released 300 miles away.

It is very difficult to anticipate or imagine potential answer choices here, so with the evidence firmly in mind, let's go to the choices.

(A) ...so what? Nothing in the given definition of navigation says that changing direction is not allowed.

(B) weakens. If the place the bear was released was on its annual migration route, then that place is not unfamiliar. This is definitely our answer, but we'll check the others.

(C) ...so what?

(D) says other species can find their way home. If anything, this strengthens the claim being used as evidence.

(E) ...so what? In order for this to weaken, we would need to know that the bear actually used its sense of smell in *this* case. If this choice said something like "the bear could smell its home from where it was released," it would be a good answer, because one of the conditions that must be met is "beyond the range of the senses."

6

9. PT32, S1, Q17

Detective: Because the embezzler must have had specialized knowledge and access to internal financial records, we can presume that the embezzler worked for XYZ Corporation as either an accountant or an actuary. But an accountant would probably not make the kind of mistakes in ledger entries that led to the discovery of the embezzlement. Thus it is likely that the embezzler is one of the actuaries.

Each of the following weakens the detective's argument EXCEPT:

- (A) The actuaries' activities while working for XYZ Corporation were more closely scrutinized by supervisors than were the activities of the accountants.
- (B) There is evidence of breaches in computer security at the time of the embezzlement that could have given persons outside XYZ Corporation access to internal financial records.
- (C) XYZ Corporation employs eight accountants, whereas it has only two actuaries on its staff.
- (D) An independent report released before the crime took place concluded that XYZ Corporation was vulnerable to embezzlement.
- (E) Certain security measures at XYZ Corporation made it more difficult for the actuaries to have access to internal financial records than for the accountants.

(D) is correct.

In order to get this one right, we must stick to a disciplined process of elimination. Here's how that process might look:

First, the core:

The embezzler was either an actuary or an accountant

+

accountant would *probably* not make the kind of mistakes that were made

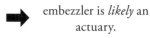 embezzler is *likely* an actuary.

Since this is an EXCEPT question, we should try to eliminate the answer choices that weaken.

(A) slightly weakens. If the actuaries were more closely scrutinized, it is reasonable to think that they are less likely to embezzle. Eliminate it.

(B) definitely weakens by suggesting that the embezzler may not have worked for the company at all. Eliminate it.

(C) is unclear. Does it matter how many of each kind they were? Leave it for now.

(D) does not weaken. Of course the company was vulnerable to embezzlement—embezzlement happened! The fact that a report was released does not weaken the idea that an actuary did the embezzling. Leave it for now.

(E) definitely weakens. Eliminate it.

Now, we're down to (C) and (D). It is unclear how (C) applies, and we know that (D) does not weaken. In a situation like this, which we will encounter many times in our LSAT adventures, we should choose (D) and move on.

To confidently eliminate (C), we must, as always, take another careful look at the wording of the argument's conclusion. It all comes down to simple math. If the embezzler is presumably either an accountant or an actuary, and there are eight accountants and only two actuaries, it seems to go against the idea that the embezzler was likely an actuary.

_10. PT37, S4, Q2_

The vomeronasal organ (VNO) is found inside the noses of various animals. While its structural development and function are clearer in other animals, most humans have a VNO that is detectable, though only microscopically. When researchers have been able to stimulate VNO cells in humans, the subjects have reported experiencing subtle smell sensations. It seems, then, that the VNO, though not completely understood, is a functioning sensory organ in most humans.

Which one of the following, if true, most weakens the argument?

(A) It is not known whether the researchers succeeded in stimulating only VNO cells in the human subjects' noses.

(B) Relative to its occurrence in certain other animals, the human VNO appears to be anatomically rudimentary and underdeveloped.

(C) Certain chemicals that play a leading role in the way the VNO functions in animals in which it is highly developed do not appear to play a role in its functioning in humans.

(D) Secondary anatomical structures associated with the VNO in other animals seem to be absent in humans.

(E) For many animal species, the VNO is thought to subtly enhance the sense of smell.

(A) is correct.

Let's start with the core:

When researchers have stimulated the VNO in humans, those humans have reported smell sensations ➡️ the VNO is a functioning sensory organ in most humans.

The word "most" really jumps out of the conclusion, and as this question is very early in the section, we might expect the answer choice to relate to this "obvious" issue. Let's go to the choices and see.

(A) is a bit unclear. "Only" is certainly an important word on the LSAT, and this choice definitely relates to the argument's evidence. Let's leave it for now.

(B) does not directly relate to the conclusion. It doesn't matter if human VNOs are less developed than animal VNOs. We might say that human ears are less developed than the ears of deer, but human ears are still functioning organs! Eliminate it.

(C) makes the same "comparison" mistake that (B) makes. The question at hand is whether the human VNO functions at all—not whether it functions as well as an animal VNO. Eliminate it.

(D) says nothing about whether the human VNO _functions_. It is entirely possible that it functions without those secondary structures, as we have no evidence that those secondary structures are required for functioning.

(E), if anything, strengthens the argument by making clearer the connection between the VNO and smell, and thus, in a small way, validating the argument's evidence.

This leaves us with (A). Really? Absolutely. This is an example of a "claim in the premise" problem. Remember the "premature babies/adequate care" argument? While we must always accept the claims themselves as fact—the researchers definitely stimulated the VNO—we occasionally see a question that brings our attention to little assumptions hidden in those claims. Think about (A). What if the researchers did _not_ stimulate _only_ the VNO when they did their research? What if they also stimulated a part of the brain responsible for smell? Well, this would make us much less certain that the VNO was responsible for the smell sensations, and suddenly we have a bad experiment on our hands. Therefore, since (A) creates the possibility that the research was imperfect, and the research is the only leg the conclusion has to stand on, (A) weakens the conclusion.

6

Challenge questions

_11. PT29, S4, Q11_

Sometimes when their trainer gives the hand signal for "Do something creative together," two dolphins circle a pool in tandem and then leap through the air simultaneously. On other occasions the same signal elicits synchronized backward swims or tail-waving. These behaviors are not simply learned responses to a given stimulus. Rather, dolphins are capable of higher cognitive functions that may include the user of language and forethought.

Which one of the following, if true, most strengthens the argument?

(A) Mammals have some resemblance to one another with respect to bodily function and brain structure.

(B) The dolphins often exhibit complex new responses to the hand signal.

(C) The dolphins are given food incentives as part of their training.

(D) Dolphins do not interact with humans the way they interact with one another.

(E) Some of the behaviors mentioned are exhibited by dolphins in their natural habitat.

(B) is correct.

This is a tricky problem. The core looks something like this:

When given a signal, sometimes the dolphins do X, sometimes do Y (these are not merely learned responses) dolphins are capable of higher cognitive functions.

Since our task is to strengthen the argument, we must focus on supporting the _connection_ between the evidence and the conclusion. In other words, we should make it more likely that these two examples, X and Y, are not learned responses, but examples of higher cognitive function.

(A) is too vague to be relevant to the argument.

A better, though not totally awesome, version of (A) might say something like, "the cognitive structures of dolphins are very similar to those of humans."

(B) adds more evidence and therefore strengthens. If the dolphins always did either X or Y, then we might begin to think that these were merely automatic responses. However, if the dolphins _often_ make _new_ and _complex_ responses, we have real evidence that they are doing more than merely responding to stimulus, which supports the idea that they are capable of higher cognitive function. This is probably our answer, but we should consider the other choices.

(C) is essentially irrelevant, though it seems to weaken. It is possible that the dolphins have higher cognitive capabilities _and_ get food in their training. This choice does not significantly strengthen or weaken.

(D) is irrelevant.

(E) is a tempting choice. If we examine it closely, though, we'll see that even if the dolphins happen to do those things in nature, the tricks could still be mere responses to stimulus. Wild dogs sit all the time. Many dogs also sit as a simple response to stimulus. In addition, we can see that the fact that the dolphins do these things in nature is not good evidence that the dolphins have "higher cognitive function."

_12. PT30, S4, Q18_

People who have political power tend to see new technologies as a means of extending or protecting their power, whereas they generally see new ethical arguments and ideas as a threat to it. Therefore, technical ingenuity usually brings benefits to those who have this ingenuity, whereas ethical inventiveness brings only pain to those who have this inventiveness.

Which one of the following statements, if true, most strengthens the argument?

(A) Those who offer new ways of justifying current political power often reap the benefits of their own innovations.

MANHATTAN
LSAT

(B) Politically powerful people tend to reward those who they believe are useful to them and to punish those who they believe are a threat.

(C) Ethical inventiveness and technical ingenuity are never possessed by the same individuals.

(D) New technologies are often used by people who strive to defeat those who currently have political power.

(E) Many people who possess ethical inventiveness conceal their novel ethical arguments for fear of retribution by the politically powerful.

(B) is correct.

Once again, we should consider the core as simply as possible before going to the choices:

The politically powerful see new tech as good and new ethics as threatening new tech brings benefits to those who have it, and new ethics bring pain to those who have them.

The gaps in this argument are fairly clear—the author is assuming that the politically powerful are the primary determinants of benefit and pain. Furthermore, the author is assuming that the politically powerful will bring benefit to those they see as bringing good, and pain to those they see as threatening.

As we evaluate the answers, let's remember that our job is to strengthen the argument:

(A) sounds appealing, but actually does not apply to the case at hand. "New *technology* as means of *extending or protecting*" is not quite the same as "new *ways* of *justifying*." And even if those terms were equivalent, the fact that this "often" benefits the creators does not add much support to the conclusion. How much is often? Ten percent of the time might be "often," but not often enough to help this conclusion. This is a weak choice that we should eliminate.

(B) is a much better choice than (A). For one thing, "tend to" means "most of the time," which

is much stronger than "often." Also, this choice has less language ambiguity than (A). It is totally reasonable to infer that people who invent new tech that can be used as a means to extend power are "useful" to those with power. And we can reasonably infer that "punishment" is roughly equivalent to "pain." Let's leave (B) for now.

(C) is an interesting choice in some ways, but it does not directly affect the argument, so we can safely eliminate it. The fact that no individual possesses both traits does not support the idea that individuals with one trait are usually benefitted while individuals with the other get only pain.

(D) seems to weaken, but actually says nothing about the individuals who *invent* the new technology, which is who the argument concerns. Perhaps those who invent the new tech still receive benefits from the powerful, while other people use the new tech to defeat the powerful. These kinds of group/subgroup distinctions are important on the LSAT.

(E) does not provide evidence that those with ethical inventiveness actually *receive* pain or punishment, nor does it provide evidence that those with technical inventiveness receive benefits. Eliminate it.

In the end, we are left with only (B), which by no means makes the argument rock-solid. It does, however, strengthen the argument more than the other choices.

13. PT30, S2, Q21

The new agriculture bill will almost surely fail to pass. The leaders of all major parties have stated that they oppose it.

Which one of the following, if true, adds the most support for the prediction that the agriculture bill will fail to pass?

(A) Most bills that have not been supported by even one leader of a major party have not been passed into law.

(B) Most bills that have not been passed into law were not supported by even one member of a major party.

(C) If the leaders of all major parties endorse the new agriculture bill, it will pass into law.

(D) Most bills that have been passed into law were not unanimously supported by the leaders of all major parties.

(E) Most bills that have been passed into law were supported by at least one leader of a major party.

The correct answer is (A).

Here is the core of this (short) argument:

All major party leaders oppose the bill therefore it will fail to pass.

The author is assuming that if all major party leaders oppose the bill, this is sufficient to ensure that the bill will fail to pass.

Our task is to strengthen this conclusion.

(A) matches the logic of the argument's particular case (the agriculture bill) with a general trend ("*most unsupported bills have not passed*"). In so doing, it adds validation to the underlying assumption, and therefore strengthens the argument.

(B) seems close, but uses the word "member," while our argument is about "leaders."

(C) is a reverse logic trap!

In order to firm up the argument, we need to know…

All major party leaders oppose the bill therefore it will fail to pass.

This answer represents a negation of that…

All major leaders endorse It will pass.

Therefore, it does not strengthen the argument.

(D) concerns subjects that are not directly related to the argument. The argument discusses a bill that is universally opposed, whereas (D) concerns bills that are opposed to some general level (not universally supported). These are two very different things. Furthermore, if we assumed (D) did relate to the argument, it would seem to weaken rather than strengthen it.

(E) is a very tempting choice, and at first glance may seem very similar to (A). However, the fact that most bills that pass are supported by at least one leader does not actually tell us anything about the odds of passing a bill that isn't supported by any leaders. It could be true that a very small percentage of all bills are not supported by any of the leaders, but that these all happen to get passed.

14. PT30, S4, Q20

Consumer advocate: The introduction of a new drug into the marketplace should be contingent upon our having a good understanding of its social impact. However, the social impact of the newly marketed antihistamine is far from clear. It is obvious, then, that there should be a general reduction in the pace of bringing to the marketplace new drugs that are now being tested.

Which one of the following, if true, most strengthens the argument?

(A) The social impact of the new antihistamine is much better understood than that of most new drugs being tested.

(B) The social impact of some of the new drugs being tested is poorly understood.

(C) The economic success of some drugs is inversely proportional to how well we understand their social impact.

(D) The new antihistamine is chemically similar to some of the new drugs being tested.

(E) The new antihistamine should be on the market only if most new drugs being tested should be on the market also.

(A) is correct.

Here's the core:

Introduction of drugs
to marketplace should
be contingent on
understanding social
impact

+

the social impact of a
certain antihistamine
(one already on the
market) is unclear

➡

there should be a
general reduction
in the pace of
bringing to market
new drugs now
being tested.

The word "general" in the conclusion immediately jumps out. Our task is to strengthen, most likely by supporting the connection of this particular antihistamine to the other drugs.

(A) does exactly what we want. If the social impact of the other drugs is understood even less than the antihistamine, then according to the argument, these other drugs should certainly not soon be brought to market. This is a good choice, so let's keep it.

(B) does not impact the argument in a clear way. It does not relate the antihistamine to the more general conclusion. Furthermore, the word "some" has a weak impact. Without knowing how prevalent the "some" is, it's tough to prescribe a general slowdown.

(C) is irrelevant—economic success does not play a role in the logic.

(D) may seem to strengthen if we read too quickly, but chemical similarity may or may not have anything to do with social impact. Therefore, eliminate it.

(E) is an error of reversed logic.

15. PT34, S2, Q12

The five senses have traditionally been viewed as distinct yet complementary. Each sense is thought to have its own range of stimuli that are incapable of stimulating the other senses. However, recent research has discovered that some people taste a banana and claim that they are tasting blue, or see a color and say that it has a specific smell. This shows that such people, called synesthesiacs, have senses that do not respect the usual boundaries between the five recognized senses.

Which one of the following statements, if true, most seriously weakens the argument?

(A) Synesthesiacs demonstrate a general, systematic impairment in their ability to use and understand words.

(B) Recent evidence strongly suggests that there are other senses besides sight, touch, smell, hearing, and taste.

(C) The particular ways in which sensory experiences overlap in synesthesiacs follow a definite pattern.

(D) The synesthetic phenomenon has been described in the legends of various cultures.

(E) Synesthesiacs can be temporarily rid of their synesthetic experiences by the use of drugs.

(A) is correct.

This is a tough problem, mostly because the correct answer seems outlandish.

The conclusion of the argument is that the synesthesiacs have senses that do not respect normal boundaries. The evidence given is a study in which these people claimed they ate a banana and tasted blue or smelled colors.

We might first go through the choices anticipating an answer choice that simply made it more likely that the senses of these people *did* in fact respect normal boundaries.

(A) is actually kind of funny, isn't it? Imagine a bunch of nonsensical mumblers sitting in a research room claiming that they can smell red. Words don't have anything to do with the senses, so we might eliminate this one.

(B) is irrelevant. Do the senses of the synesthesiacs, no matter how many they have, respect boundaries or not? Eliminate it.

(C) sounds pretty good. But what if the definite pattern is one that violates the normal boundaries? That would actually strengthen. Therefore, eliminate.

(D) simply states that synesthesiacs have been described in the past. However, while this may support the claim that synesthesiacs exist, it does not support the claim that their senses do not respect normal boundaries. Always pay attention to the exact wording of the conclusion, especially on difficult questions!

(E) says nothing about whether their senses respect normal boundaries.

Now what? We've eliminated them all! Go back to the top, reconsider the argument core, and go back to the choices with a more open mind.

Aha! Take another look at (A). If the synesthesiacs cannot understand or use words, then what are we to make of the evidence used in the argument? Of what value is their claim that they taste blue when they eat bananas if they don't know what "blue" or "taste" means? This is our answer. If (A) is true, it puts the validity of the evidence in question, and therefore weakens the argument. The others are all wrong for the reasons previously stated.

6

Chapter 7

of

Logical Reasoning

Principle Support
Questions

Getting Familiar

To start, go ahead and try these four Principle Support questions. Give yourself no more than six minutes total. We'll revisit these questions later on in the chapter.

PT20, S1, Q5

Archaeologist: A large corporation has recently offered to provide funding to restore an archaeological site and to construct facilities to make the site readily accessible to the general public. The restoration will conform to the best current theories about how the site appeared at the height of the ancient civilization that occupied it. This offer should be rejected, however, because many parts of the site contain unexamined evidence.

Which one of the following principles, if valid, justifies the archaeologist's argument?

(A) The ownership of archaeological sites should not be under the control of business interests.

(B) Any restoration of an archaeological site should represent only the most ancient period of that site's history.

(C) No one should make judgments about what constitutes the height of another civilization.

(D) Only those with a true concern for an archaeological site's history should be involved in the restoration of that site.

(E) The risk of losing evidence relevant to possible future theories should outweigh any advantages of displaying the results of theories already developed.

PT20, S4, Q24

Marianne is a professional chess player who hums audibly while playing her matches, thereby distracting her opponents. When ordered by chess officials to cease humming or else be disqualified from professional chess, Marianne protested the order. She argued that since she was unaware of her humming, her humming was involuntary and that therefore she should not be held responsible for it.

Which one of the following principles, if valid, most helps to support Marianne's argument against the order?

(A) Chess players who hum audibly while playing their matches should not protest if their opponents also hum.

(B) Of a player's actions, only those that are voluntary should be used as justification for disqualifying that player from professional chess.

(C) A person should be held responsible for those involuntary actions that serve that person's interests.

(D) Types of behavior that are not considered voluntary in everyday circumstances should be considered voluntary if they occur in the context of a professional chess match.

(E) Chess players should be disqualified from professional chess matches if they regularly attempt to distract their opponents.

MANHATTAN
LSAT

PT21, S3, Q17

An editorial in the Grandburg Daily Herald claims that Grandburg's voters would generally welcome the defeat of the political party now in control of the Grandburg City Council. The editorial bases its claim on a recent survey that found that 59 percent of Grandburg's registered voters think that the party will definitely be out of power after next year's city council elections.

Which one of the following is a principle that, if established, would provide the strongest justification for the editorial's conclusion?

(A) The way voters feel about a political party at a given time can reasonably be considered a reliable indicator of the way they will continue to feel about that party, barring unforeseeable political developments.

(B) The results of surveys that gauge current voter sentiment toward a given political party can legitimately be used as the basis for making claims about the likely future prospects of that political party.

(C) An increase in ill-feeling toward a political party that is in power can reasonably be expected to result in a corresponding increase in support for rival political parties.

(D) The proportion of voters who expect a given political possibility to be realized can legitimately be assumed to approximate the proportion of voters who are in favor of that possibility being realized.

(E) It can reasonably be assumed that registered voters who respond to a survey regarding the outcome of a future election will exercise their right to vote in that election.

PT37, S2, Q22

Political theorist: Many people believe that the punishment of those who commit even the most heinous crimes should be mitigated to some extent if the crime was motivated by a sincere desire to achieve some larger good. Granted, some criminals with admirable motives deserve mitigated punishments. Nonetheless, judges should never mitigate punishment on the basis of motives, since motives are essentially a matter of conjecture and even vicious motives can easily be presented as altruistic.

Which one of the following principles, if valid, most helps to justify the political theorist's reasoning?

(A) Laws that prohibit or permit actions solely on the basis of psychological states should not be part of a legal system.

(B) It is better to err on the side of overly severe punishment than to err on the side of overly lenient punishment.

(C) The legal permissibility of actions should depend on the perceivable consequences of those actions.

(D) No law that cannot be enforced should be enacted.

(E) A legal system that, if adopted, would have disastrous consequences ought not be adopted.

7

Principle Support Questions and the Assumption Family

At this point, we have covered just about all of the Assumption Family question types. Principle Support questions will round out our discussion of the Assumption Family.

It's important to know that there are actually two types of Principle questions on the LSAT. Principle Support questions, the topic of this chapter, require you to choose a principle that helps to justify, or support, the argument. Principle II (example) questions, the subject of a later chapter, ask you to select an example that matches a *given* principle. Principle II questions are NOT Assumption Family questions.

Principle I questions, on the other hand, function just like any other Assumption Family question. Thus, our process should be the same. It will be driven by the following six questions:

1. What is my task?
2. What is the author's conclusion?
3. How is that conclusion supported?
4. What is the gap?
5. Which answer choices are clearly wrong?
6. What is the best available answer?

In a sense, Principle I questions are Assumption questions in disguise. Here's a quick example:

> Dr. Singh is the best professor at Doug's college. Therefore, Doug should sign up for Dr. Singh's course.

This may seem like a great argument. It seems only natural to conclude that Doug should take a course with Dr. Singh, since she is the best. In fact, it's *so* reasonable that it may cause us to overlook a key assumption: that Doug should make his decision about which classes to take based on the quality of the professor. What if Dr. Singh teaches anthropology and Doug is a literature major? In order for the argument to be sound, we must assume that professor quality should be the deciding factor. Here's the argument core with the assumption inserted:

> Dr. Singh is the best professor at Doug's college. (When making decisions about which courses to take, one should consider professor quality before any other factor.) Therefore, Doug should sign up for Dr. Singh's course.

Notice that the assumption in this case can also be thought of as a general principle. Let's examine the concept of "principle" a bit more thoroughly.

Should We or Shouldn't We?

According to the Oxford American Dictionary, a principle is a fundamental proposition that serves as the foundation for a belief or behavior. In other words, principles are propositions that guide what we should and shouldn't think or do.

Let's look back again at the assumption, or principle, from the previous example: When making decisions about which courses to take, one should consider professor quality before any other factor. It's a proposition that guides how we should behave in a particular situation. It tells us what we should do.

On the LSAT, Principle Support questions will often have conclusions that dictate how one should or shouldn't act or behave. The correct answer will be a principle that strengthens, or supports, the opinion given in the conclusion. Here's a little exercise to illustrate the point. We'll give you an argument core. Take a second to think about what the assumption is, and then write a principle that bridges the gap. Here's the first one:

Many students in the class failed the final exam.   The teacher of the class should not be offered the standard end-of-year raise.

So, what's the principle that would support this argument? Take a second to think before reading on.

Here's the core with the principle inserted:

> Many students in the class failed the final exam. (Teachers who have students who failed the final exam should not be offered the standard end-of-year raise.) The teacher of the class should not be offered the standard end-of-year raise.

Is the principle more obvious than you had anticipated? Let's try another one:

The chair in the corner is an antique.   The chair in the corner should be sold at auction.

And here it is with the principle inserted:

> The chair in the corner is an antique. (Antiques should be sold at auction.) The chair in the corner should be sold at auction.

Okay, hopefully you've got the hang of it now. It's really not that hard, right? Well, we all know that it's never this easy on the LSAT. Let's put all this thinking to work on a question that you tried at the start of the chapter. We'll begin by looking only at the argument and the question stem itself. Remember, this is an Assumption Family question, so we'll want to use the following questions to guide our process:

1. What is my task?
2. What is the author's conclusion?
3. How is that conclusion supported?
4. What is the gap?
5. Which answer choices are clearly wrong?
6. What is the best available answer?

7

PT20, S1, Q5

Archaeologist: A large corporation has recently offered to provide funding to restore an archaeological site and to construct facilities to make the site readily accessible to the general public. The restoration will conform to the best current theories about how the site appeared at the height of the ancient civilization that occupied it. This offer should be rejected, however, because many parts of the site contain unexamined evidence.

Which one of the following principles, if valid, justifies the archaeologist's argument?

DECISION #1: What is my task?

In this case, the question asks us to choose a principle that justifies, or supports, the argument. Thus, this is a Principle Support question. We'll need to start by identifying the argument core.

DECISION #2: What is the author's conclusion?

DECISION #3: How is that conclusion supported?

Let's look at the components of the argument one more time with the above questions in mind:

A large corporation has recently offered to provide funding to restore an archaeological site and to construct facilities to make the site readily accessible to the general public.

Seems like background information so far.

The restoration will conform to the best current theories about how the site appeared at the height of the ancient civilization that occupied it.

More background. Where's the argument?

This offer should be rejected, however,

Aha. A clear conclusion—an expression of something we should do. But what exactly is the "offer" in question? Which "offer" should be rejected? We'll need to revisit the background information to find out. The offer was an offer by a large corporation to use the best current theories about how an archaeological site once appeared in order to restore the site and make it available to the public for viewing.

because many parts of the site contain unexamined evidence.

The word "because" is a clear indication that this portion of the argument is the support for the conclusion. So, the argument core is:

Many parts of site contain unexamined evidence.   Offer to restore the site according to current theories of how it once appeared and then open it up to public should be rejected.

DECISION #4: What is the gap?

Another way of asking this is: What's the principle that would support this argument? Think about it before reading on.

Why does the fact that there is unexamined evidence on-site make it inadvisable to open the site up to the public? There are two ways to think about the answer to this question:

1. Maybe presenting the archaeological site according to theories that are based on evidence that hasn't been fully examined might compromise the accuracy and integrity of the display.
2. Maybe presenting the site to the public while there is unexamined evidence inside will put that evidence in jeopardy (people might destroy or steal the evidence).

It's hard to know exactly which of the two issues the author has in mind, but we can anticipate both. If the author has the first point in mind, we can close that gap with the following principle:

> Many parts of site contain unexamined evidence. (We shouldn't open up sites for public viewing if the presentation of the site is based on an incomplete examination of evidence.) Offer to restore the site according to current theories of how it once appeared and then open it up to public should be rejected.

If the author has the second point in mind, we can close that gap as follows:

> Many parts of site contain unexamined evidence. (We shouldn't open up sites for public viewing if doing so could jeopardize the unexamined evidence.) Offer to restore site according to current theories of how it once appeared and open it up to public should be rejected.

Now, all of this is simply preparation for the answer choices. We don't know for certain that either of these principles will appear—perhaps the correct answer is something we haven't yet thought of. At this point, there's no need to fret over anticipating every single possible correct answer. We just want to be focused on the argument core and note any possible gaps that pop into our minds. And of course, we want to be *thinking* all of this, NOT writing it out as we've done here.

DECISION #5: Which answer choices are clearly wrong?

The easiest eliminations will be answers that aren't related to the argument core. Here's our core again:

7

Many parts of site contain unexamined evidence. Offer to restore the site according to current theories of how it once appeared and then open it up to public should be rejected.

(A) The ownership of archaeological sites should not be under the control of business interests.

This has nothing to do with whether the site should be opened up to the public before all evidence is examined. Eliminate it.

(B) Any restoration of an archaeological site should represent only the most ancient period of that site's history.

Great. But this answer mentions nothing about unexamined evidence (which could be from any time period) and its impact on whether the site should be restored and opened to the public. Get rid of it.

(C) No one should make judgments about what constitutes the height of another civilization.

Again, should it be restored and opened to the public? This answer fails to address the central issue of the core argument. Eliminate it.

(D) Only those with a true concern for an archaeological site's history should be involved in the restoration of that site.

Out of scope again. Eliminate it.

DECISION #6: What is the best available answer?

Well, we only have one answer left! We should check it quickly to be sure it's relevant:

(E) The risk of losing evidence relevant to possible future theories should outweigh any advantages of displaying the results of theories already developed.

Last man standing! It mentions unexamined evidence ("evidence relevant to possible future theories") and how the potential of losing this evidence is more important ("should outweigh") any advantage that could be gained by opening to the public now ("displaying results of theories already developed."). It's basically saying that the risk of losing the unexamined evidence is more important than displaying the stuff that's currently available. This is the only answer that addresses the core. Choose it and move on.

When we were preparing for the answers, we anticipated that a correct answer might address the danger of exposing the unexamined evidence to the public. Remember the second anticipation from earlier: We shouldn't open up sites for public viewing if doing so could jeopardize the unexamined evidence. Answer choice (E) certainly didn't match exactly, but it was based on the same notion—protecting the unexamined evidence should be the primary consideration.

Answer choice (E) might have felt too broad to you—why is it not discussing theories about the archeological site? The correct answers to principle questions often establish a rule about a general category that includes the topic of the argument. In some ways this might remind you of Sufficient Assumptions in that the correct answer might go beyond what you need, but still do the trick.

Now that you've got the hang of it, let's review the remaining three questions from the start of the chapter. Each one is progressively more difficult than the next. We'll work our way up.

Take another shot at this one before we discuss. Pay close attention to your process. Are you making the right decisions at the right time?

PT20, S4, Q24

Marianne is a professional chess player who hums audibly while playing her matches, thereby distracting her opponents. When ordered by chess officials to cease humming or else be disqualified from professional chess, Marianne protested the order. She argued that since she was unaware of her humming, her humming was involuntary and that therefore she should not be held responsible for it.

Which one of the following principles, if valid, most helps to support Marianne's argument against the order?

(A) Chess players who hum audibly while playing their matches should not protest if their opponents also hum.

(B) Of a player's actions, only those that are voluntary should be used as justification for disqualifying that player from professional chess.

(C) A person should be held responsible for those involuntary actions that serve that person's interests.

(D) Types of behavior that are not considered voluntary in everyday circumstances should be considered voluntary if they occur in the context of a professional chess match.

(E) Chess players should be disqualified from professional chess matches if they regularly attempt to distract their opponents.

DECISION #1: What is my task?

This question asks us to choose a principle to support the argument. Thus, this is a Principle Support question. This is an Assumption Family question.

DECISION #2: What is the author's conclusion?

DECISION #3: How is that conclusion supported?

Let's go line by line through the argument in order to identify the argument core:

> Marianne is a professional chess player who hums audibly while playing her matches, thereby distracting her opponents.

Just background information so far.

> When ordered by chess officials to cease humming or else be disqualified from professional chess, Marianne protested the order.

Still no arguments, just facts.

> She argued that since she was unaware of her humming, her humming was involuntary and that therefore she should not be held responsible for it.

This sentence gives us all the information we need to know. The word "since" is a language cue indicating support for something, and the word "therefore" clearly leads to the conclusion. The fact that Marianne is unaware of her own humming means that it is involuntary—done without conscious control. Thus, we can combine those two elements into one premise. They are essentially duplicate premises. So, our core is:

Marianne's humming is involuntary (she's unaware of it).   Marianne should not be held responsible for her humming.

DECISION #4: What is the gap?

This argument assumes that one should not be held responsible for actions that are involuntary. If you have a nervous, involuntary twitch that knocks a $25,000 vase off of your friend's coffee table, does that mean you shouldn't be held responsible for the cost of that vase? Not necessarily, right? We've spotted the gap. Now let's eliminate some answers.

DECISION #5: Which answer choices are clearly wrong?

> (A) Chess players who hum audibly while playing their matches should not protest if their opponents also hum.

Is the humming involuntary? Should they be held responsible for the humming? This answer has nothing to do with the argument core. Eliminate it.

> (B) Of a player's actions, only those that are voluntary should be used as justification for disqualifying that player from professional chess.

Hmm. This one feels a bit closer. It mentions "voluntary," and this idea of disqualification is related to holding someone responsible. Keep it for now.

> (C) A person should be held responsible for those involuntary actions that serve that person's interests.

This mentions "involuntary," and it also mentions holding someone responsible. Keep it for now.

(D) Types of behavior that are not considered voluntary in everyday circumstances should be considered voluntary if they occur in the context of a professional chess match.

But should someone be held responsible for these behaviors? Eliminate it.

(E) Chess players should be disqualified from professional chess matches if they regularly attempt to distract their opponents.

This answer is tempting if we are focused on the background information, but it mentions nothing about involuntary or voluntary behaviors. Get rid of it.

DECISION #6: What is the best available answer?

We're down to two answers: (B) and (C). If we simply bounce back and forth between the two remaining choices, they'll start to look more and more alike. That won't help us. A better strategy is to compare each choice against the argument core. Let's remind ourselves of the core quickly:

Marianne's humming is involuntary (she's unaware of it). Marianne should not be held responsible for her humming.

Remember, we decided that the argument assumes that one should not be held responsible for actions that are involuntary. Notice that (C) gives us the exact opposite!

(C) A person *should* be held responsible for those involuntary actions that serve that person's interests.

If Marianne's humming distracts her opponents, then her involuntary behavior is certainly serving her interests. Thus, according to (C) she should be held responsible! This isn't what we want.

(B) Of a player's actions, only those that are voluntary should be used as justification for disqualifying that player from professional chess.

Ah. Much better. Only voluntary actions (not involuntary actions) should be used to disqualify a chess player. In other words, one shouldn't be held responsible for involuntary actions. This is our answer.

Notice that the correct answer doesn't focus simply on humming but instead establishes a rule about the broader category of "behavior," which includes humming.

Let's do another one. Again, pay attention to your process, even if that means taking a bit more time than you normally would:

7

PT21, S3, Q17

An editorial in the Grandburg Daily Herald claims that Grandburg's voters would generally welcome the defeat of the political party now in control of the Grandburg City Council. The editorial bases its claim on a recent survey that found that 59 percent of Grandburg's registered voters think that the party will definitely be out of power after next year's city council elections.

Which one of the following is a principle that, if established, would provide the strongest justification for the editorial's conclusion?

(A) The way voters feel about a political party at a given time can reasonably be considered a reliable indicator of the way they will continue to feel about that party, barring unforeseeable political developments.

(B) The results of surveys that gauge current voter sentiment toward a given political party can legitimately be used as the basis for making claims about the likely future prospects of that political party.

(C) An increase in ill-feeling toward a political party that is in power can reasonably be expected to result in a corresponding increase in support for rival political parties.

(D) The proportion of voters who expect a given political possibility to be realized can legitimately be assumed to approximate the proportion of voters who are in favor of that possibility being realized.

(E) It can reasonably be assumed that registered voters who respond to a survey regarding the outcome of a future election will exercise their right to vote in that election.

DECISION #1: What is my task?

This question asks us to choose a principle to provide justification for the argument. Thus, this is a Principle Support question. This is an Assumption Family question.

DECISION #2: What is the author's conclusion?

DECISION #3: How is that conclusion supported?

Again, we'll go line by line through the argument in order to identify the argument core:

An editorial in the Grandburg Daily Herald claims that Grandburg's voters would generally welcome the defeat of the political party now in control of the Grandburg City Council.

This is a claim. Perhaps it's an opposing claim that the author will disagree with?

> The editorial bases its claim on a recent survey that found that 59 percent of Grandburg's registered voters think that the party will definitely be out of power after next year's city council elections.

Oh—"The editorial bases its claim...." This is just support for the editorial's claim. Pretty simple argument.

59% of Grandburg's registered voters think that the party in power will lose power in next year's election.   Grandburg's voters would generally welcome defeat of the party now in power of the city council.

DECISION #4: What is the gap?

This argument assumes that if a majority of people *think* something will happen, then a majority of people *welcome* that thing happening. We can think of a number of examples for which this sort of an argument doesn't hold. A majority of people might think that the world will become overpopulated at some point in the future, but does this necessarily mean that a majority of people would *welcome* an overpopulated world? Of course not! I think we see the problem with this argument. Let's move to the answer choices.

DECISION #5: Which answer choices are clearly wrong?

> (A) The way voters feel about a political party at a given time can reasonably be considered a reliable indicator of the way they will continue to feel about that party, barring unforeseeable political developments.

Not sure about this one. It seems relevant. Keep it for now.

> (B) The results of surveys that gauge current voter sentiment toward a given political party can legitimately be used as the basis for making claims about the likely future prospects of that political party.

We're interested in whether the editorial can use a poll of what voters think will happen to conclude how voters would feel about that phenomenon happening. This answer focuses on whether the voters' prediction will come true or not. Eliminate it.

> (C) An increase in ill-feeling toward a political party that is in power can reasonably be expected to result in a corresponding increase in support for rival political parties.

Completely out of scope. This argument is not about increasing support for rival parties. It's about whether thinking something will happen translates to wanting that thing to happen. Get rid of this.

7

(D) The proportion of voters who expect a given political possibility to be realized can legitimately be assumed to approximate the proportion of voters who are in favor of that possibility being realized.

Ah. This looks good. This relates expecting something to happen with being in favor of it happening. Let's keep this for now.

(E) It can reasonably be assumed that registered voters who respond to a survey regarding the outcome of a future election will exercise their right to vote in that election.

Whether or not they will vote is beside the point. This issue is whether thinking something will happen translates to wanting that thing to happen. Eliminate it.

DECISION #6: What is the best available answer?

We're down to two answers: (A) and (D). Remember, we want to compare each choice against the argument core. Let's remind ourselves of the core quickly:

| 59% of Grandburg's registered voters think that the party in power will lose power in next year's election. | | Grandburg's voters would generally welcome defeat of the party now in power of the city council. |

Again, the argument assumes that a majority of people *believing* something will happen suggests that a majority of people *welcome* that thing happening.

(A) The way voters feel about a political party at a given time can reasonably be considered a reliable indicator of the way they will continue to feel about that party, barring unforeseeable political developments.

This answer feels less attractive the second time through. It's nice to know that the way voters "feel" about a party is unlikely to change, but the way they "feel" about a political party tells us nothing about what they think will happen to that political party.

(D) The proportion of voters who expect a given political possibility to be realized can legitimately be assumed to approximate the proportion of voters who are in favor of that possibility being realized.

This one is correct. This clearly connects the voters' expectations (what they think will happen) with what they want to happen.

Take a second to read the core again, now with the principle inserted:

59% of Grandburg's registered voters think that the party in power will lose power in next year's election. (The proportion of voters who *expect* a given political possibility to be realized can legitimately be assumed to approximate the proportion of voters who are *in favor* of that possibility being realized.) Grandburg's voters would generally welcome defeat of the party now in power of the city council.

Now, some of you may be thinking that the correct answer choice is way too general for this argument. After all, the argument discusses voters in *Grandburg specifically*, not any or all voters in general as answer (D) might suggest. Also, the argument discusses *the party in power losing power*, not just any old political possibility as answer (D) indicates.

But, consider the fact that when we talk about "voters" generally, this includes Grandburg's voters. And when we talk about a "political possibility" in general, this includes the specific possibility, the party in power losing power, in Grandburg. Here's an analogous situation:

> The Blasters soccer team won two straight Riverville League Championships. Thus, the Blasters soccer team should be considered an exceptional team.

We could insert a very specific principle to support this argument:

> The Blasters soccer team won two straight Riverville League Championships. (If the Blasters soccer team won two straight Riverville League Championships, then the Blasters soccer team should be considered an exceptional team.) Thus, the Blasters soccer team should be considered an exceptional team.

That's a pretty straightforward, specific principle. But can we make it a bit more general?

> The Blasters soccer team won two straight Riverville League Championships. (If a team wins two straight championships, then that team should be considered exceptional.) Thus, the Blasters soccer team should be considered an exceptional team.

This principle is much more general, but it still helps the argument, doesn't it? After all, "team" in general would include the Blasters soccer team, and "championships" in general include the Riverville League Championships. We can take it even one step further:

> The Blasters soccer team won two straight Riverville League Championships. (An entity that accomplishes something two times in a row should be considered exceptional.) Thus, the Blasters soccer team should be considered an exceptional team.

This is an extremely general principle, but it still helps the argument. A general "entity" would include a soccer team, and "accomplishing something two times in a row" would certainly include winning two straight Riverville League Championships.

Let's go back to our original question. Here's the core one more time. Try to write the most general principle you possibly can to support this argument:

59% of Grandburg's registered voters think that the party in power will lose power in next year's election. Grandburg's voters would generally welcome defeat of the party now in power of the city council.

How'd you do? Don't read on until you've given it a try! Here's how we would write it:

> 59% of Grandburg's registered voters think that the party in power will lose power in next year's election. (If more than half of a group of people believe something will occur, then that group of people in general is in favor of that something occurring.) Grandburg's voters would generally welcome defeat of the party now in power of the city council.

This answer would have been just as correct as answer (D) above. So, keep in mind that for Principle questions, general or broad answer choices are often correct.

Okay, now on to the toughest of the four questions you saw to start the chapter. Try it again. Give yourself 1:30, and really pay attention to your process. Here we go!

PT37, S2, Q22

Political theorist: Many people believe that the punishment of those who commit even the most heinous crimes should be mitigated to some extent if the crime was motivated by a sincere desire to achieve some larger good. Granted, some criminals with admirable motives deserve mitigated punishments. Nonetheless, judges should never mitigate punishment on the basis of motives, since motives are essentially a matter of conjecture and even vicious motives can easily be presented as altruistic.

Which one of the following principles, if valid, most helps to justify the political theorist's reasoning?

(A) Laws that prohibit or permit actions solely on the basis of psychological states should not be part of a legal system.
(B) It is better to err on the side of overly severe punishment than to err on the side of overly lenient punishment.
(C) The legal permissibility of actions should depend on the perceivable consequences of those actions.
(D) No law that cannot be enforced should be enacted.
(E) A legal system that, if adopted, would have disastrous consequences ought not be adopted.

DECISION #1: What is my task?

This question asks us to choose a principle to provide justification for the theorist's reasoning. Thus, this is a Principle Support question. This is an Assumption Family question.

DECISION #2: What is the author's conclusion?

DECISION #3: How is that conclusion supported?

Again, we'll go line by line through the argument in order to identify the argument core.

> Political theorist: Many people believe that the punishment of those who commit even the most heinous crimes should be mitigated to some extent if the crime was motivated by a sincere desire to achieve some larger good.

"Many people believe…" sounds very much like an opposing point. So, many people believe that punishments should be lessened if there was some desire to achieve good. The author will likely disagree.

> Granted, some criminals with admirable motives deserve mitigated punishments.

"Granted…" The author is granting a point to the opposition, but she would do this only if there were a counter on the way!

> Nonetheless, judges should never mitigate punishment on the basis of motives,

"Nonetheless" is our pivot word, and we get the conclusion immediately following. The author believes judges should NEVER mitigate punishments on the basis of motive. Why does the author believe this?

> since motives are essentially a matter of conjecture and even vicious motives can easily be presented as altruistic.

The word "since" is an indication that this will be support for the conclusion. Judges should never mitigate punishments based on motive because motives are a matter of conjecture (we can only guess at people's true motives).

7

Motives are a matter of conjecture.   Judges should never mitigate punishments based on motives.

DECISION #4: What is the gap?

Hmm. This core is tricky. It seems to make sense, right? We can only guess at people's motives for committing heinous crimes, so judges should never weaken punishments based on motives. It's hard to see any gaps or flaws in this argument, but at least we have a clear sense for the argument core. We should be able to eliminate answer choices that deviate from the core. Let's give it a try.

DECISION #5: Which answer choices are clearly wrong?

> (A) Laws that prohibit or permit actions solely on the basis of psychological states should not be part of a legal system.

This answer addresses criteria for determining whether certain laws should be a part of a legal system. But does "psychological states" include motives? How does this answer connect us to a conclusion about the leniency of punishments? This answer doesn't match our core. Eliminate it.

(B) It is better to err on the side of overly severe punishment
     than to err on the side of overly lenient punishment.

This doesn't seem right, but it does comment on varying degrees of punishment. Let's keep it for now.

(C) The legal permissibility of actions should depend on the
     perceivable consequences of those actions.

Uhhh… not sure. This seems related as well. "The perceivable consequences of actions…" This means things we don't have to guess at, the opposite of conjecture. Better keep it for now.

(D) No law that cannot be enforced should be enacted.

Okay, we can get rid of this one. This passage has nothing to do with whether laws should be enacted, but rather whether punishments should be mitigated. Those are two different things. Eliminate it.

(E) A legal system that, if adopted, would have disastrous
     consequences ought not be adopted.

Adopting a legal system? Way out of scope. We need something related to whether punishments should be mitigated. Get rid of this.

DECISION #6: What is the best available answer?

We're down to two answers: (B) and (C). Remember, we want to compare each choice against the argument core. Let's remind ourselves of the core quickly:

Motives are a matter of conjecture.   Judges should never mitigate
                                                                punishments based on motives.

We hadn't anticipated a certain answer, but having a strong sense for the core has helped us eliminate three answers, and it will help us decide between the final two.

(C) The legal permissibility of actions should depend on the
     perceivable consequences of those actions.

Ohhh. This discusses the legal permissibility of actions—whether actions are legal or not. After reviewing the core one more time, we're reminded that we're interested in the severity of punishments, NOT the legal permissibility of actions. This one doesn't seem to work.

(B) It is better to err on the side of overly severe punishment
     than to err on the side of overly lenient punishment.

But this doesn't seem right either! Okay, let's break this down by going back to the argument core. Essentially, it's saying that if we're not sure of the motivation for the crime (maybe the motivation was to do something good), we should keep punishments severe. Isn't this counterintuitive? Wouldn't it make more sense to be cautious when doling out punishment, to be more lenient in the face of uncertainty just in case we got it all wrong? It would, but the conclusion goes in the other direction—the punishment should NOT be mitigated, even in the face of uncertainty.

MANHATTAN
LSAT

In order to justify this conclusion, we'd need some principle that states that it's better to be overly severe than too lenient. In other words, we should err on the side of being too harsh. If that's an underlying principle, then it would make sense to conclude that we shouldn't mitigate the punishment, even in the face of uncertainty. Let's look at the core with the principle inserted:

> *Motives are a matter of conjecture. (It is better to err on the side of overly severe punishment than to err on the side of overly lenient punishment.) Judges should never mitigate punishments based on motives.*

(B) is correct! Wow. Tough question! We can see now that this answer choice would be very difficult to anticipate in advance, but we can make a lot of progress by identifying the core and then eliminating answers that stray from the core.

Conclusion

Principle Support questions are Assumption Family questions. We must treat them as such. The same six-step process that we covered a few chapters ago applies:

1. What is my task?
2. What is the author's conclusion?
3. How is that conclusion supported?
4. What is the gap?
5. Which answer choices are clearly wrong?
6. What is the best available answer?

If this process is taking longer than you'd like, that's understandable. However, keep in mind that these are all *necessary* steps—that is, if we were to shortchange any part of this process, we would have to answer questions with an incomplete understanding. So, we encourage you to keep at it. We're confident that it is through this process that you can best develop an effective approach that will lead to quicker and more accurate answers.

7

DRILL IT: Principle Support Questions

Give yourself no more than 11 minutes to complete the following problems.

1. PT11, S2, Q10

The labeling of otherwise high-calorie foods as "sugarfree," based on the replacement of all sugar by artificial sweeteners, should be prohibited by law. Such a prohibition is indicated because many consumers who need to lose weight will interpret the label "sugarfree" as synonymous with "low in calories" and harm themselves by building weight-loss diets around foods labeled "sugarfree." Manufacturers of sugarfree foods are well aware of this tendency on the part of consumers.

Which one of the following principles, if established, most helps to justify the conclusion in the passage?

(A) Product labels that are literally incorrect should be prohibited by law, even if reliance on those labels is not likely to cause harm to consumers.

(B) Product labels that are literally incorrect, but in such an obvious manner that no rational consumer would rely on them, should nevertheless be prohibited by law.

(C) Product labels that are literally correct but cannot be interpreted by the average buyer of the product without expert help should be prohibited by law.

(D) Product labels that are literally correct but will predictably be misinterpreted by some buyers of the product to their own harm should be prohibited by law.

(E) Product labels that are literally correct, but only on one of two equally accurate interpretations, should be prohibited by law if buyers tend to interpret the label in the way that does not match the product's actual properties.

2. PT11, S2, Q6

Cigarette smoking has been shown to be a health hazard; therefore, governments should ban all advertisements that promote smoking.

Which one of the following principles, if established, most strongly supports the argument?

(A) Advertisements should not be allowed to show people doing things that endanger their health.

(B) Advertisers should not make misleading claims about the healthfulness of their products.

(C) Advertisements should disclose the health hazards associated with the products they promote.

(D) All products should conform to strict government health and safety standards.

(E) Advertisements should promote only healthful products.

3. PT33, S3, Q6

The recent cleaning of frescoes in the Sistine Chapel has raised important aesthetic issues. Art historians are now acutely aware that the colors of the works they study may differ from the works' original colors. Art historians have concluded from this that interpretations of the frescoes that seemed appropriate before the frescoes' restoration may no longer be appropriate.

Which one of the following principles, if valid, most helps to justify the art historians' reasoning?

(A) The appropriateness of an interpretation of an artwork is relative to the general history of the period in which the interpretation is made.

(B) The restoration of an artwork may alter it such that it will have colors that the artist did not intend for it to have.

(C) The colors of an artwork are relevant to an appropriate interpretation of that work.

(D) Art historians are the best judges of the value of an artwork.

(E) Interpretations of an artwork are appropriate if they originated during the period when the work was created.

7

4. PT28, S1, Q4

Dental researcher: Filling a cavity in a tooth is not a harmless procedure: it inevitably damages some of the healthy parts of the tooth. Cavities are harmful only if the decay reaches the nerves inside the tooth, and many cavities, if left untreated, never progress to that point. Therefore, dentists should not fill a cavity unless the nerves inside the tooth are in imminent danger from that cavity.

Which one of the following principles, if valid, most strongly supports the researcher's reasoning?

(A) Dentists should perform any procedure that is likely to be beneficial in the long term, but only if the procedure does not cause immediate damage.

(B) Dentists should help their patients to prevent cavities rather than waiting until cavities are present to begin treatment.

(C) A condition that is only potentially harmful should not be treated using a method that is definitely harmful.

(D) A condition that is typically progressive should not be treated using methods that provide only temporary relief.

(E) A condition that is potentially harmful should not be left untreated unless it can be kept under constant surveillance.

Challenge Problems

5. PT29, S1, Q19

Arbitrator: The shipping manager admits that he decided to close the old facility on October 14 and to schedule the new facility's opening for October 17, the following Monday. But he also claims that he is not responsible for the business that was lost due to the new facility's failing to open as scheduled. He blames the contractor for not finishing on time, but he too, is to blame, for he was aware of the contractor's typical delays and should have planned for this contingency.

Which one of the following principles underlies the arbitrator's argument?

(A) A manager should take foreseeable problems into account when making decisions.

(B) A manager should be able to depend on contractors to do their jobs promptly.

(C) A manager should see to it that contractors do their jobs promptly.

(D) A manager should be held responsible for mistakes made by those whom the manager directly supervises.

(E) A manager, and only a manager, should be held responsible for a project's failure.

7

<u>6. PT29, S1, Q22</u>

Editorial: The government claims that the country's nuclear power plants are entirely safe and hence that the public's fear of nuclear accidents at these plants is groundless. The government also contends that its recent action to limit the nuclear industry's financial liability in the case of nuclear accidents at power plants is justified by the need to protect the nuclear industry from the threat of bankruptcy. But even the government says that unlimited liability poses such a threat only if injury claims can be sustained against the industry; and the government admits that for such claims to be sustained, injury must result from a nuclear accident. The public's fear, therefore, is well founded.

Which one of the following principles, if valid, most helps to justify the editorial's argumentation?

(A) If the government claims that something is unsafe then, in the absence of overwhelming evidence to the contrary, that thing should be assumed to be unsafe.

(B) Fear that a certain kind of event will occur is well founded if those who have control over the occurrence of events of that kind stand to benefit financially from such an occurrence.

(C) If a potentially dangerous thing is safe only because the financial security of those responsible for its operation depends on its being safe, then eliminating that dependence is not in the best interests of the public.

(D) The government sometimes makes unsupported claims about what situations will arise, but it does not act to prevent a certain kind of situation from arising unless there is a real danger that such a situation will arise.

(E) If a real financial threat to a major industry exists, then government action to limit that threat is justified.

<u>7. PT28, S3, Q18</u>

The human brain and its associated mental capacities evolved to assist self-preservation. Thus, the capacity to make aesthetic judgments is an adaptation to past environments in which humans lived. So an individual's aesthetic judgments must be evaluated in terms of the extent to which they promote the survival of that individual.

Which one of the following is a principle that would, if valid, provide the strongest justification for the reasoning above?

(A) All human adaptations to past environments were based on the human brain and its associated mental capacities.

(B) Human capacities that do not contribute to the biological success of the human species cannot be evaluated.

(C) If something develops to serve a given function, the standard by which it must be judged is how well it serves that function.

(D) Judgments that depend on individual preference or taste cannot be evaluated as true or false.

(E) Anything that enhances the proliferation of a species is to be valued highly.

8. PT17, S3, Q8

Political advocate: Campaigns for elective office should be subsidized with public funds. One reason is that this would allow politicians to devote less time to fundraising, thus giving campaigning incumbents more time to serve the public. A second reason is that such subsidies would make it possible to set caps on individual campaign contributions, thereby reducing the likelihood that elected officials will be working for the benefit not of the public but of individual large contributors.

Critic: This argument is problematic: the more the caps constrain contributions, the more time candidates have to spend finding more small contributors.

Which one of the following principles, if established, provides a basis for the advocate's argument?

(A) If complete reliance on private funding of some activity keeps the public from enjoying a benefit that could be provided if public funds were used, such public funds should be provided.

(B) If election campaigns are to be funded from public funds, terms of office for elected officials should be lengthened.

(C) If in an election campaign large contributions flow primarily to one candidate, public funds should be used to support the campaigns of that candidate's rivals.

(D) If public funding of some activity produces a benefit to the public but also inevitably a special benefit for specific individuals, the activity should not be fully funded publicly but in part by the individuals deriving the special benefit.

(E) If a person would not have run for office in the absence of public campaign subsidies, this person should not be eligible for any such subsidies.

SOLUTIONS: Principle Support Questions

1. PT11, S2, Q10

The labeling of otherwise high-calorie foods as "sugarfree," based on the replacement of all sugar by artificial sweeteners, should be prohibited by law. Such a prohibition is indicated because many consumers who need to lose weight will interpret the label "sugarfree" as synonymous with "low in calories" and harm themselves by building weight-loss diets around foods labeled "sugarfree." Manufacturers of sugarfree foods are well aware of this tendency on the part of consumers.

Which one of the following principles, if established, most helps to justify the conclusion in the passage?

(A) Product labels that are literally incorrect should be prohibited by law, even if reliance on those labels is not likely to cause harm to consumers.

(B) Product labels that are literally incorrect, but in such an obvious manner that no rational consumer would rely on them, should nevertheless be prohibited by law.

(C) Product labels that are literally correct but cannot be interpreted by the average buyer of the product without expert help should be prohibited by law.

(D) Product labels that are literally correct but will predictably be misinterpreted by some buyers of the product to their own harm should be prohibited by law.

(E) Product labels that are literally correct, but only on one of two equally accurate interpretations, should be prohibited by law if buyers tend to interpret the label in the way that does not match the product's actual properties.

(D) is correct.

Many consumers will harm themselves by mistakenly building diets around sugarfree foods

+

Manufacturers of sugarfree foods are well aware of this tendency

The labeling of otherwise high-calorie foods as "sugarfree" should be prohibited.

Wow, a product that truly has no sugar shouldn't be allowed to call itself "sugarfree," just because people will misinterpret that label? The author is making a pretty big assumption here: even if a label is true, it should be prohibited if consumers tend to harm themselves by misinterpreting it. We're looking for a principle that expresses that assumption.

(A) is about labels that are literally *incorrect*; the argument is about labels that are literally *correct*. Eliminate it.

(B) is also about literally incorrect answers. Eliminate it.

(C) looks better, as it deals with the prohibition of literally correct labels. However, this argument is about labels that consumers will misinterpret *to their own harm*, not about whether consumers can interpret the labels without expert help.

(E) comes out of left field with its mention of "two equally accurate interpretations." That has nothing to do with this argument!

We're left with answer (D): *Product labels that are literally correct but will predictably be misinterpreted by some buyers of the product to their own harm should be prohibited by law.*

This looks like a winner! It covers all our bases: these sugarfree labels make a true claim, so they are "literally correct," but the manufacturers are well aware that "some buyers" (this matches with "many consumers") will misinterpret them "to their own harm"—therefore, they should be prohibited.

So (D) is correct.

MANHATTAN
LSAT

7

2. PT11, S2, Q6

Cigarette smoking has been shown to be a health hazard; therefore, governments should ban all advertisements that promote smoking.

Which one of the following principles, if established, most strongly supports the argument?

(A) Advertisements should not be allowed to show people doing things that endanger their health.

(B) Advertisers should not make misleading claims about the healthfulness of their products.

(C) Advertisements should disclose the health hazards associated with the products they promote.

(D) All products should conform to strict government health and safety standards.

(E) Advertisements should promote only healthful products.

(E) is correct.

This is a very straightforward argument—all core, no clutter:

Cigarette smoking has been shown to be a health hazard		Governments should ban all advertisements that promote smoking.

The logical gap here is likewise not too difficult to spot. The author of this argument assumes that if something is a health hazard, governments should ban advertisements that promote it. We can be confident that the correct answer will be a principle that expresses that assumption.

(A) is very tempting and probably made it through your first pass through the answer choices. It seems to suggest that advertisements shouldn't promote unhealthy acts, but it doesn't. Take a look at the subtle shift: from "promote" in the argument to "show people doing things" in the answer choice. This difference leaves large gaps in the argument—one could show someone smoking without promoting the act. In fact, an advertisement could use an image of a smoker to suggest that smoking is a health hazard. Another

gap that this answer leaves is that if advertisers were to abide by the principle in (A), they could still create ads that promote smoking by not including any images of people smoking.

(B) has nothing to do with whether the advertisements should be banned, and the argument never says anything about misleading claims, so we can eliminate it easily.

(C) is incorrect for the same reason: the argument is about whether governments should ban cigarette advertisements, not about what kinds of claims those advertisements should make.

(D) doesn't even address the issue of advertisements, so it's even further out of scope! Get rid of it.

So we're down to (E): *Advertisements should promote only healthful products.*

(E) is a broad rule that is more than we need to fill the argument's gap—and that's just fine on Principle Support questions. It's a bit confusing that the principle in (E) outlines what advertisements should promote, and that it prohibits the promotion of products that are neutral in terms of health (like a pair of socks). But if advertisers are limited to promoting healthful acts, then they're not allowed to promote unhealthful acts, a principle that makes the argument valid.

Therefore, (E) is the correct answer.

3. PT33, S3, Q6

The recent cleaning of frescoes in the Sistine Chapel has raised important aesthetic issues. Art historians are now acutely aware that the colors of the works they study may differ from the works' original colors. Art historians have concluded from this that interpretations of the frescoes that seemed appropriate before the frescoes' restoration may no longer be appropriate.

Which one of the following principles, if valid, most helps to justify the art historians' reasoning?

(A) The appropriateness of an interpretation of an artwork is relative to the general history of the period in which the interpretation is made.

(B) The restoration of an artwork may alter it such that it will have colors that the artist did not intend for it to have.

(C) The colors of an artwork are relevant to an appropriate interpretation of that work.

(D) Art historians are the best judges of the value of an artwork.

(E) Interpretations of an artwork are appropriate if they originated during the period when the work was created.

(C) is correct.

| Restoration of frescoes revealed original colors that differ from those studied before the restoration | → | Interpretations that seemed appropriate before may no longer be appropriate. |

Why would the art historians conclude that the old interpretations may no longer be appropriate? They must be assuming that an appropriate interpretation of a work of art has something to do with the colors in that work; if the colors have changed, maybe what qualifies as an appropriate interpretation has also changed.

(A) is way out of scope. It doesn't address the color issue, and the argument has nothing to do with "the general history of the period."

(B) has no bearing on whether the older interpretations are appropriate; artist's intent doesn't factor in here.

(D) has even less to do with the core. The argument is about whether the old interpretations are appropriate, not at all about the value of a work or who the best judges are.

(E) at least deals with the appropriateness of interpretations, but it doesn't help us get from the color-difference issue to the conclusion that the pre-restoration interpretations may no longer be appropriate. In fact, it doesn't allow us to deem any interpretations inappropriate, because this answer choice only identifies interpretations that *are* appropriate.

That leaves answer (C): *The colors of an artwork are relevant to an appropriate interpretation of that work.*

Hmm. Boring, but it gets the job done! If the colors of an artwork are relevant to interpreting it appropriately, then the fact that the pre-restoration interpretations were based on different colors could mean that those interpretations are no longer appropriate, given the newly revealed original colors.

Therefore, (C) is correct.

4. PT28, S1, Q4

Dental researcher: Filling a cavity in a tooth is not a harmless procedure: it inevitably damages some of the healthy parts of the tooth. Cavities are harmful only if the decay reaches the nerves inside the tooth, and many cavities, if left untreated, never progress to that point. Therefore, dentists should not fill a cavity unless the nerves inside the tooth are in imminent danger from that cavity.

Which one of the following principles, if valid, most strongly supports the researcher's reasoning?

(A) Dentists should perform any procedure that is likely to be beneficial in the long term, but only if the procedure does not cause immediate damage.

(B) Dentists should help their patients to prevent cavities rather than waiting until cavities are present to begin treatment.

(C) A condition that is only potentially harmful should not be treated using a method that is definitely harmful.

(D) A condition that is typically progressive should not be treated using methods that provide only temporary relief.

(E) A condition that is potentially harmful should not be left untreated unless it can be kept under constant surveillance.

(C) is correct.

responsible for its operation depends on its being safe, then eliminating that dependence is not in the best interests of the public.

(D) The government sometimes makes unsupported claims about what situations will arise, but it does not act to prevent a certain kind of situation from arising unless there is a real danger that such a situation will arise.

(E) If a real financial threat to a major industry exists, then government action to limit that threat is justified.

(D) is correct.

This one is a real mouthful! As always, we should start by finding the conclusion. In this case, thankfully, it's pretty easy to spot: the public's fear of nuclear accidents is well founded. Now, what is that conclusion based on? Well, we're told that the government has limited the nuclear industry's financial ability in order to protect it from bankruptcy. Then we're told that, by the government's own admission, bankruptcy is only a threat if injury claims can be sustained, and that injury claims can only be sustained in the event of a nuclear accident. If we condense that second statement, we end up with a two-premise core that looks like this:

The government has limited the nuclear industry's financial liability to protect it from bankruptcy

+

The government admits that bankruptcy is only a threat if nuclear accidents occur

→ The public's fear of nuclear accidents is well founded.

So, even though the government claims that the nuclear power plants are safe, it has taken actions to protect those plants from a situation that could only occur as a result of a nuclear accident. From this, the argument concludes that the public is right to be afraid of nuclear accidents. The basic assumption, then, is that the government wouldn't make efforts to limit the consequences of a situation unless there was actually a chance of that situation occurring.

Now, even in condensed form, that's still a lot to keep track of. So as we consider the answer choices, let's remember to make things easier by really focusing on how they relate to the core. The correct answer *must* help us conclude that the public's fear is well founded.

(A) can be easily eliminated because the government doesn't claim that anything is unsafe; it does the exact opposite!

(B) addresses the issue of whether the fear is well founded, but nowhere does the argument suggest that those who have control over nuclear accidents (who would that be, anyway?) stand to benefit from them. Limiting your financial liability just means there's a limit to how much money you *lose*; it doesn't mean you're profiting.

(C) is out of scope; the argument is about whether the public's fear is justified, not about the best interests of the public.

(E) is similarly out of scope. The question is not whether the government's action is justified, but rather, should we be afraid of nuclear accidents?

That leaves (D): *The government sometimes makes unsupported claims about what situations will arise, but it does not act to prevent a certain kind of situation from arising unless there is a real danger that such a situation will arise.*

This looks a lot like the assumption we identified earlier. The government does not act to prevent *bankruptcy* from arising unless there is a real danger that it will arise. And, according to the argument, bankruptcy is only a danger if a nuclear accident occurs. If this principle is true, then the public would have good reason to fear nuclear accidents, despite the government's "unsupported claims" to the contrary.

So (D) is correct.

7 *PT28, S3, Q18*

The human brain and its associated mental capacities evolved to assist self-preservation. Thus, the capacity to make aesthetic judgments is an adaptation to past environments in which humans lived. So an individual's aesthetic judgments must be evaluated in terms of the extent to which they promote the survival of that individual.

Which one of the following is a principle that would, if valid, provide the strongest justification for the reasoning above?

(A) All human adaptations to past environments were based on the human brain and its associated mental capacities.

(B) Human capacities that do not contribute to the biological success of the human species cannot be evaluated.

(C) If something develops to serve a given function, the standard by which it must be judged is how well it serves that function.

(D) Judgments that depend on individual preference or taste cannot be evaluated as true or false.

(E) Anything that enhances the proliferation of a species is to be valued highly.

(C) is correct.

This argument does us the favor of making its logical structure fairly clear through the use of the keywords "thus" and "so," which we know mean "therefore." Since there are *two* "therefore" moments, we know we're dealing with an intermediate conclusion, and we can map the core like this:

The human brain and its capacities evolved for self-preservation	➡	The capacity to make aesthetic judgments is an environmental adaptation	➡	Individual's aesthetic judgements must be evaluated in terms of self-preservation

It's always important that we recognize the presence of an intermediate conclusion, because as we saw two problems ago, it's possible for the correct answer to fit between the premise and the

intermediate conclusion. In this case, though, there doesn't appear to be a gap there; since the capacity to make aesthetic judgments is clearly a mental capacity, the first half of the argument is actually logically valid.

So let's turn our attention to the second half of the argument. Does it really make sense to evaluate aesthetic judgments in terms of their contribution to a person's survival? The Post-it® Note was originally invented to mark pages in a hymn book; must we evaluate them as bookmarks every time we leave a note on the refrigerator? ("PLEASE wash the dishes!") Only if we assume that things should be evaluated in terms of their original reason for being. We're looking for a principle that establishes this assumption.

(A) leads with the always-suspicious word "all." Whether *all* adaptations were based on the human brain is irrelevant to the question of evaluating aesthetic judgments.

(B) is about what *cannot* be evaluated, but the argument is about how something *should* be evaluated.

(D) is out of scope, because the argument has nothing to do with evaluating judgments as true or false.

(E) is also out of scope. The argument never says we should value aesthetic judgments, or anything else, for that matter, highly. For all we know, the author thinks evolutionary adaptations stink!

That leaves answer (C): *If something develops to serve a given function, the standard by which it must be judged is how well it serves that function.*

Ah, this looks better. If we accept this principle, then the standard by which aesthetic judgments must be evaluated is indeed the extent to which they promote an individual's survival, because the capacity to make these judgments originally developed for that purpose.

Therefore, (C) is correct.

MANHATTAN
LSAT

8. PT17, S3, Q8

Political advocate: Campaigns for elective office should be subsidized with public funds. One reason is that this would allow politicians to devote less time to fundraising, thus giving campaigning incumbents more time to serve the public. A second reason is that such subsidies would make it possible to set caps on individual campaign contributions, thereby reducing the likelihood that elected officials will be working for the benefit not of the public but of individual large contributors.

Critic: This argument is problematic: the more the caps constrain contributions, the more time candidates have to spend finding more small contributors.

Which one of the following principles, if established, provides a basis for the advocate's argument?

   (A) If complete reliance on private funding of some activity keeps the public from enjoying a benefit that could be provided if public funds were used, such public funds should be provided.

   (B) If election campaigns are to be funded from public funds, terms of office for elected officials should be lengthened.

   (C) If in an election campaign large contributions flow primarily to one candidate, public funds should be used to support the campaigns of that candidate's rivals.

   (D) If public funding of some activity pro- duces a benefit to the public but also inevitably a special benefit for specific individuals, the activity should not be fully funded publicly but in part by the individuals deriving the special benefit.

   (E) If a person would not have run for office in the absence of public campaign subsidies, this person should not be eligible for any such subsidies.

(A) is correct.

This is an unusual argument. The advocate begins with the conclusion that campaigns for elective office should be subsidized with public funds. He then offers two "reasons," that is, *premises,* in support of this claim.

So far, so good. Where this argument departs from the norm is that each premise is actually a mini-argument unto itself. Public funds would allow politicians to spend less time fundraising, *thus* giving them more time to serve the public; subsidies would allow caps to be set on contributions, *thereby* reducing the chances of politicians working for large contributors. Each premise contains a logical movement that we ought to keep track of. Here's our core:

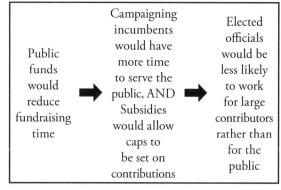

Since we have three "therefores," we have three places to look for logical gaps. In the first premise, the advocate assumes that the time saved by less fundraising wouldn't get eaten up by some other activity—for example, maybe campaigning incumbents would end up wasting *more* time filling out paperwork for public funding. In the second premise, the advocate assumes that the likelihood of an official working for individual donors would decrease as the maximum allowable donation decreases. But what if the new caps on contributions were still far above the maximum amounts actually given?

Finally, there's the more run-of-the-mill gap between the premises and the conclusion: the advocate assumes that if a method of campaign funding would have these two benefits, then it should be adopted.

By the way, what's going on with the critic's rejoinder? The critic actually identifies and negates another assumption: that the caps mentioned in the second premise wouldn't negate the time-saving effect mentioned in the first. It turns out, though, that we don't really care about this part of the stimulus, because the question is asking us to identify a principle underlying the *advocate's* argument. The critic's opinion is therefore irrelevant.

Let's take a look at the answer choices:

(B) is way out of scope. The argument is about implementing public funding, not about lengthening terms in office.

(C) makes a comparison between the funds received by a candidate and his rivals that the argument doesn't make. The advocate's point is just that public funds should be used, not that they should be distributed in a particular way.

(D) is a mess. The advocate doesn't say that public funding would produce a special benefit for specific individuals, nor does he say anything about the optimal balance between public and private funding.

(E) is about who should be eligible for public funding, but the argument is simply about whether public funding should be used.

We're down to (A): *If complete reliance on private funding of some activity keeps the public from enjoying a benefit that could be provided if public funds were used, such public funds should be provided.*

Well, this one looks pretty good, since it addresses the position that "public funds should be provided." You may be hung up by the phrase "complete reliance on private funding," but this is actually supported by the language in the argument: if the advocate's point is that public funding ought to be provided, because it *would* have certain effects, then we can infer that such funds are not currently being provided. It's accurate to describe the absence of public funding as complete reliance on private funding, since that's the only other kind.

So, if the lack of public funding is preventing the public from enjoying benefits—more attention and less favoritism from their elected officials—then public funding should be used. Looks good!

So, (A) is correct.

Chapter 8
of **Logical Reasoning**

Conditional Logic

Introduction to Conditional Logic

Conditional logic. The phrase itself has been known to induce the sweats for many an LSAT test-taker. Yes, knowing and understanding conditional logic is important for your success on the LSAT, but it doesn't have to cause you undue anxiety. We got you started with the basics in Chapter 2, but we're going to start over from the beginning here to be sure that your foundation is solid. Then we'll take you through the tough stuff. By the end of this chapter, you'll be able to use your conditional logic skills to fight off some of the toughest logical reasoning questions out there. Let's get started.

Back to the Basics

(NOTE: If you truly understand simple conditional statements and their contrapositives, you may skip to the Application section. Don't make this decision lightly, though. The review can't hurt.)

As promised, we're going to start at the beginning. Remember this example?

> When Jasmine wakes up early in the morning, she is not productive at work that day. Jasmine woke up early in the morning on Wednesday.
>
> If the above statements are true, which one of the following must also be true?
>
> (A) If Jasmine was unproductive at work on any particular day, then she must have woken up early on that day.
> (B) Jasmine was not productive at work on Wednesday.

This abbreviated Logical Reasoning question contains a conditional relationship. If condition X (waking up early) is met, then Y (unproductive at work) is guaranteed. Thus, if Jasmine woke up early on Wednesday, then we can infer that she was not productive at work on Wednesday. Answer (B) is correct.

Doesn't (A) seem correct too? In fact, it is NOT necessarily correct. Let's explore the ins and outs of conditional logic in order to fully understand why not.

What Is a Conditional Statement?

A conditional statement expresses a guaranteed outcome when a specific condition is met. The most basic type of conditional statement uses "If ... then" phrasing:

IF Jeremy eats a big lunch, **THEN** he won't be hungry for dinner.

IF John lives in San Francisco, **THEN** John lives in California.

IF Sue attends the concert, **THEN** her husband is at home babysitting the children.

IF Hiromi wins the election, **THEN** she had the most organized campaign.

It's important to note that conditional statements are sometimes disguised. As an example, consider this statement again:

When Jasmine wakes up early in the morning, she is not productive at work that day.

This statement is not written in If/Then form, but it indeed is a conditional statement. Again, when condition X (waking up early) is satisfied, then Y (unproductive at work) is *guaranteed*. A simple and effective way to think about all conditional statements is that they express guarantees. We can phrase this in If/Then form:

IF Jasmine wakes up early in the morning, **THEN** (it is guaranteed) she is not productive at work that day.

Sufficient vs. Necessary Condition

The "If" part of the conditional statement is called the *sufficient* condition because it is *sufficient,* or *enough by itself,* to guarantee the truth of the "Then" part of the statement. The "Then" part of the statement is called the *necessary* condition because, when the sufficient condition is true, it is required, or *necessary,* that the "Then" portion be true as well. To summarize:

Sufficient Condition: The "If" part of the statement. When satisfied, it is sufficient on its own to guarantee the outcome.

Necessary Condition: The "Then" part of the statement. It is guaranteed to be true when the sufficient condition is satisfied.

Note that while the sufficient condition is *sufficient* to guarantee the truth of the necessary condition, or outcome, it is not necessarily *required* to arrive at this outcome. This is a critical difference. Let's take a look at another very simple example to illustrate.

IF you buy me a gift, **THEN** I will be happy.

Buying me a gift guarantees my happiness, but is it the only thing that would make me happy? Not necessarily. Here are some other possibilities:

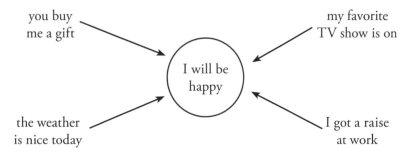

So, what can we conclude? Two things for now:

1. You giving me a gift is *sufficient* to guarantee that I will be happy (note the arrow signifying the guaranteed outcome).

2. You giving me a gift is *not required* to guarantee that I will be happy. If I am happy, this does NOT guarantee that you have given me a gift (maybe I'm happy for a different reason—maybe I got a raise, or maybe the weather is nice). In other words, the relationship doesn't necessarily work the other way around!

Conditional Inferences

Valid vs. Invalid

Before we get back to our "happiness" example, let's consider the following:

> **IF** Sally lives in Boston, **THEN** Sally lives in Massachusetts.

Based on real life understanding of U.S. geography, we know this statement to be true. Now consider the validity of the following inferences that could be made given the statement above:

> **1. Is the negative true?** If Sally does not live in Boston, then is it guaranteed that Sally does not live in Massachusetts?

> **2. Is the reverse true?** If Sally lives in Massachusetts, then is it guaranteed that Sally lives in Boston?

> **3. Is the negative AND reverse true?** If Sally does not live in Massachusetts, then is it guaranteed that Sally does not live in Boston?

This is a simpler case because you already know that Boston is not the only city or town in Massachusetts. You can probably see already that the first and second inferences are NOT valid. Even so, let's use our picture to illustrate (Worcester, Newton, and Cambridge are other cities in Massachusetts):

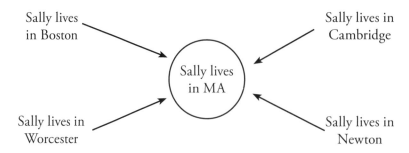

1. If Sally does not live in Boston, then is it guaranteed that Sally does not live in Massachusetts? No. After all, Sally could live in Newton, which would still put her in MA.

2. If Sally lives in Massachusetts, then is it guaranteed that Sally lives in Boston? This isn't necessarily true either. There are many places Sally could live, including Cambridge, Worcester, and

Newton, that are in Massachusetts but outside of Boston. Yes, Boston guarantees Massachusetts, but Massachusetts does not guarantee Boston!

3. If Sally does not live in Massachusetts, then is it guaranteed that Sally does not live in Boston? Yes! This, of course, MUST be true. If Sally does not live in the state of Massachusetts, it is not possible for her to live in Boston. This is the only inference of the bunch that is valid.

Let's now apply the same logic to the "happiness" example, which is a bit tougher:

IF you give me a gift, **THEN** I will be happy.

Now consider the following related inferences that might be made given the statement above:

1. The NEGATION: If you do not give me a gift, then I will not be happy.

2. The REVERSAL: If I am happy, then you have given me a gift.

3. The REVERSAL and NEGATION: If I am not happy, then you have not given me a gift.

Which of these inferences, if any, are valid? To evaluate our potential inferences, let's consider our picture again, remembering that there may be other sufficient conditions that would guarantee "my happiness."

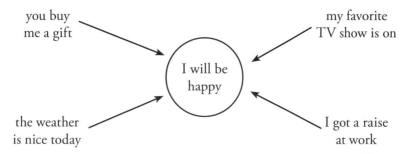

1. If you do not give me a gift, then I will not be happy. This, of course, is not necessarily true. Remember, while giving me a gift is *sufficient* to make me happy, it is not required. Maybe you haven't given me a gift, but perhaps I am happy because I got a raise at work today. Thus, this is an invalid inference.

2. If I am happy, then you have given me a gift. Remember, there could be other reasons why I am happy. This is an invalid inference.

3. If I am not happy, then you have not given me a gift. This MUST be true. Gift automatically guarantees happiness. So, if I am not happy, you could not have possibly given me a gift. This is the only valid inference of the bunch.

By now you may be noticing that the only correct inference, regardless of the original conditional statement, is one that reverses and negates the original.

We can reduce this complex train of thought to a reliable rule. To do so, let's start by organizing our thinking through the use of symbols. Let's use a G to symbolize "You buy me a gift" and an H to symbolize "I will be happy." The arrow indicates the "If ... then" relationship:

Statement	Symbols	Valid/Invalid	Description
If you give me a gift, then I will be happy.	**G ⟶ H**	**GIVEN**	**GIVEN**
1. If you do not give me a gift, then I will not be happy.	–G ⟶ –H	Invalid	Negate
2. If I am happy, then you have given me a gift.	H ⟶ G	Invalid	Reverse
3. If I am not happy, then you have not given me a gift.	–H ⟶ –G	VALID	REVERSE & NEGATE

You can see by looking at the symbols that the first inference simply negates the components of the original given statement. The second inference simply reverses the original components. The third inference both reverses and negates the components of the original statement. Thus, the only valid inference is one that reverses and negates the form of the original given statement. This is called the contrapositive.

Contrapositive: The valid inference derived by reversing and negating the components of the given conditional statement.

Let's generalize:

Statement	Symbols	Valid/Invalid	Description
If X, then Y.	**X ⟶ Y**	**GIVEN**	**GIVEN**
1. If not X, then not Y.	–X ⟶ –Y	Invalid	Negate
2. If Y, then X.	Y ⟶ X	Invalid	Reverse
3. If not Y, then not X.	–Y ⟶ –X	VALID	REVERSE & NEGATE

So, what have we learned? We've learned that *any time* we have a conditional statement, *we know with certainty* that the contrapositive statement is also true.

Revisiting Jasmine

Here's our example from the start of the chapter. Take a second now to think about why (A) is NOT a correct answer:

> When Jasmine wakes up early in the morning she is not productive at work that day. Jasmine woke up early in the morning on Wednesday.
>
> If the above statements are true, which one of the following must also be true?
>
> (A) If Jasmine was unproductive at work on any particular day, then she must have woken up early on that day.
>
> (B) Jasmine was not productive at work on Wednesday.

If you said that answer (A) illegally reverses the logic, you would be correct! Let's diagram the situation:

Statement	Symbols	Valid/Invalid	Description
IF wakes up early, THEN not productive.	E $\longrightarrow$ –P	**GIVEN**	**GIVEN**
1. If don't wake up early, then productive.	–E $\longrightarrow$ P	Invalid	Negate
2. If not productive, then woke up early.	–P $\longrightarrow$ E	Invalid	Reverse
3. If productive, then didn't wake up early.	P $\longrightarrow$ –E	VALID	REVERSE & NEGATE

Answer choice (A) is the equivalent of inference #2 in the table above. Bad inference!

Let's practice what we've learned so far.

8

DRILL IT: Conditional Statements and Contrapostives

Diagram each of the conditional statements below, then diagram the contrapositive relationship by reversing and negating the components of the original. Finally, use the contrapositive diagram to write a statement that expresses the valid inference made. Be sure to check your responses against the solutions after each one.

Example: GIVEN: If X is not selected, then Y is selected.

GIVEN DIAGRAM: $-X \longrightarrow Y$

CONTRAPOSITIVE DIAGRAM: $-Y \longrightarrow X$

VALID INFERENCE: If Y is not selected, then X is selected.

1. GIVEN: If Sid is on the committee, then Jana is on the committee.

GIVEN DIAGRAM:

CONTRAPOSITIVE DIAGRAM:

VALID INFERENCE:

2. GIVEN: If Raul is invited to the party, then Shaina is not invited to the party.

GIVEN DIAGRAM:

CONTRAPOSITIVE DIAGRAM:

VALID INFERENCE:

3. GIVEN: If Brooks is not on the bus, then Traiger is not on the bus.

GIVEN DIAGRAM:

CONTRAPOSITIVE DIAGRAM:

VALID INFERENCE:

4. GIVEN: If the tiger is not in the cage, then the lion is in the cage.

GIVEN DIAGRAM:

CONTRAPOSITIVE DIAGRAM:

VALID INFERENCE:

5. GIVEN: I will not go jogging if it is raining outside.

GIVEN DIAGRAM:

CONTRAPOSITIVE DIAGRAM:

VALID INFERENCE:

6. GIVEN: Yohei plays guitar if Juan plays drums.

GIVEN DIAGRAM:

CONTRAPOSITIVE DIAGRAM:

VALID INFERENCE:

7. GIVEN: If T is not chosen for the team, then N is not chosen for the team.

GIVEN DIAGRAM:

CONTRAPOSITIVE DIAGRAM:

VALID INFERENCE:

8. GIVEN: G is not selected for the club if F is selected for the club.

GIVEN DIAGRAM:

CONTRAPOSITIVE DIAGRAM:

VALID INFERENCE:

8

9. GIVEN: If Beethoven is played, then Mozart is also played.

GIVEN DIAGRAM:

CONTRAPOSITIVE DIAGRAM:

VALID INFERENCE:

10. GIVEN: Dmitry might play volleyball or squash, but he definitely can't play both.

GIVEN DIAGRAM:

CONTRAPOSITIVE DIAGRAM:

VALID INFERENCE:

SOLUTIONS: Conditional Statements and Contrapositives

1. GIVEN: If Sid is on the committee, then Jana is on the committee.

GIVEN DIAGRAM: S $\longrightarrow$ J

CONTRAPOSITIVE DIAGRAM: $-$J $\longrightarrow$ $-$S

VALID INFERENCE: If Jana is not on the committee, then Sid is not on the committee.

2. GIVEN: If Raul is invited to the party, then Shaina is not invited to the party.

GIVEN DIAGRAM: R $\longrightarrow$ $-$S

CONTRAPOSITIVE DIAGRAM: S $\longrightarrow$ $-$R

VALID INFERENCE: If Shaina is invited to the party, then Raul is not invited to the party.

3. GIVEN: If Brooks is not on the bus, then Traiger is not on the bus.

GIVEN DIAGRAM: $-$B$\longrightarrow$$-$T

CONTRAPOSITIVE DIAGRAM: T $\longrightarrow$ B

VALID INFERENCE: If Traiger is on the bus, then Brooks is on the bus.

4. GIVEN: If the tiger is not in the cage, then the lion is in the cage.

GIVEN DIAGRAM: $-$T$\longrightarrow$L

CONTRAPOSITIVE DIAGRAM: $-$L$\longrightarrow$ T

VALID INFERENCE: If the lion is not in the cage, then the tiger is in the cage.

5. GIVEN: *I will not go jogging if it is raining outside. = **If it is raining outside, then I will not go jogging.**

GIVEN DIAGRAM: R $\longrightarrow$ $-$J

CONTRAPOSITIVE DIAGRAM: J $\longrightarrow$ $-$R

VALID INFERENCE: If I go jogging, then it is not raining outside.

*Be careful with this one! Notice that the original given statement has a unique structure.

6. GIVEN: Yohei plays guitar if Juan plays drums. = **If Juan plays drums, then Yohei plays guitar.**

GIVEN DIAGRAM: JD $\longrightarrow$ YG

CONTRAPOSITIVE DIAGRAM: −YG $\longrightarrow$ −JD

VALID INFERENCE: If Yohei does not play guitar, then Juan does not play drums.

7. GIVEN: If T is not chosen for the team, then N is not chosen for the team.

GIVEN DIAGRAM: −T $\longrightarrow$ −N

CONTRAPOSITIVE DIAGRAM: N $\longrightarrow$ T

VALID INFERENCE: If N is chosen for the team, then T is chosen for the team.

8. GIVEN: G is not selected for the club if F is selected for the club. = **If F is selected for the club, then G is not selected.**

GIVEN DIAGRAM: F $\longrightarrow$ −G

CONTRAPOSITIVE DIAGRAM: G $\longrightarrow$ −F

VALID INFERENCE: If G is selected for the club, then F is not selected for the club.

9. GIVEN: If Beethoven is played, then Mozart is also played.

GIVEN DIAGRAM: B $\longrightarrow$ M

CONTRAPOSITIVE DIAGRAM: −M $\longrightarrow$ −B

VALID INFERENCE: If Mozart is not played, then Beethoven is not played.

10. GIVEN: Dmitry might play volleyball or squash, but he definitely can't play both.

GIVEN DIAGRAM: V $\longrightarrow$ −S or S $\longrightarrow$ −V

This is a tricky one! The conditional logic is hidden a bit here.

CONTRAPOSITIVE DIAGRAM: S $\longrightarrow$ −V or V $\longrightarrow$ −S

VALID INFERENCE: If Dmitry plays volleyball, then he does not play squash. And, if Dmitry plays squash, then he does not play volleyball.

Applying Conditional Logic 1: The Basics

Now that you've got the basics under your belt, let's see how an understanding of standard conditional statements and contrapositives can help you on an actual LSAT problem. Give yourself 1:20 to answer the following question.

PT36, S1, Q26

In the paintings by seventeenth-century Dutch artist Vermeer, we find several recurrent items: a satin jacket, a certain Turkish carpet, and wooden chairs with lion's-head finials. These reappearing objects might seem to evince a dearth of props. Yet we know that many of the props Vermeer used were expensive. Thus, while we might speculate about exactly why Vermeer worked with a small number of familiar objects, it was clearly not for lack of props that the recurrent items were used.

The conclusion follows logically if which one of the following is assumed?

(A) Vermeer often borrowed the expensive props he represented in his paintings.
(B) The props that recur in Vermeer's paintings were always available to him.
(C) The satin jacket and wooden chairs that recur in the paintings were owned by Vermeer's sister.
(D) The several recurrent items that appeared in Vermeer's paintings had special sentimental importance for him.
(E) If a dearth of props accounted for the recurrent objects in Vermeer's paintings, we would not see expensive props in any of them.

By now, you should be comfortable recognizing this as an Assumption Family question, and you should be familiar with the optimal approach for attacking such questions. Let's run through it.

DECISION #1: What is my task?

This question is asking us to select an assumption that would allow the conclusion to follow logically. In other words, we need a *sufficient* assumption.

(NOTE: We've now used the word *sufficient* in two different contexts: *sufficient* assumption and *sufficient* condition. Just as a reminder, a *sufficient* assumption is an assumption that is *enough* on its own to get to the conclusion. As we've just learned, a *sufficient* condition is a condition that is *enough* on its own to guarantee an outcome. While the term *sufficient* is used in two different contexts, the implication is the same in both: one thing is *sufficient*, or enough, on its own to lead to, guarantee, or require something else.)

DECISION #2: What is the author's conclusion?

DECISION #3: How is that conclusion supported?

> Let's read the argument again with the above questions in mind:

> In the paintings by seventeenth-century Dutch artist Vermeer, we find several recurrent items: a satin jacket, a certain Turkish carpet, and wooden chairs with lion's-head finials.

Background information so far.

> These reappearing objects might seem to evince a dearth of props.

"…might seem…" Sounds like the author is about to counter this viewpoint.

> Yet we know that many of the props Vermeer used were expensive.

Yes. The word "yet" is a pivot word. So, some might say that Vermeer used the same props over and over again because he was lacking in props, but the author is countering this viewpoint.

> Thus, while we might speculate about exactly why Vermeer worked with a small number of familiar objects, it was clearly not for lack of props that the recurrent items were used.

Okay, this is the conclusion. Vermeer was not lacking in props. He had plenty (and we know this because his props were expensive). So the argument core is:

Vermeer used expensive props. ➡ Vermeer was not lacking in props.

It's important that we really understand the logic behind this argument. Think about it. If your friend drove the same Porsche around for 10 years, would you conclude that he hadn't bought a new car because he was lacking in means? Probably not. He drives an expensive Porsche! You would likely conclude that he has plenty of money to get a different car if he wanted to. He's sticking with his Porsche, but it's probably not because he's lacking the means to get something else.

The same sort of logic is used here. Because Vermeer's props were expensive, the author concludes that Vermeer could have had access to other props if he wished. The question is, does this make a valid argument?

DECISION #4: What is the gap?

The author assumes that because the props were expensive he must have had access to many more props. So, in attempting to explain why Vermeer would use the same props repeatedly, the author rules out the possibility that he didn't have access to other props. This doesn't necessarily need to be the case. Maybe the expensive props were gifted to Vermeer and those were the only ones he had access to. Maybe he didn't have the money to buy new props because he spent all his money on those few expensive ones. Maybe he'd borrowed those props.

Okay, at this point we have a sense for what might come up in the answer choices.

DECISION #5: Which answer choices are clearly wrong?

The easiest eliminations will be answers that aren't related to the argument core. Here's our core again:

Vermeer used expensive props. Vermeer was not lacking in props.

(A) Vermeer often borrowed the expensive props he represented in his paintings.

Ooh, this is attractive! Be careful though. This actually weakens the argument. If he had borrowed the expensive props (likely because he couldn't purchase them on his own), it wouldn't make sense to conclude that he had the means to access many props. It would actually suggest that he WAS lacking in props. Eliminate it.

(B) The props that recur in Vermeer's paintings were always available to him.

This seems like it might work. It seems related to the conclusion. If they were always available to him, then he wasn't lacking in props. Keep it for now.

(C) The satin jacket and wooden chairs that recur in the paintings were owned by Vermeer's sister.

Again, this actually weakens the argument. If he had borrowed the expensive props, there would be reason to believe that he WAS lacking in props. Remember, correct assumption answers ought to strengthen the argument, not weaken it. Eliminate this answer.

(D) The several recurrent items that appeared in Vermeer's paintings had special sentimental importance for him.

This is attractive. Maybe he uses these props repeatedly because he's emotionally attached to them and NOT because he's lacking in props. This seems to help. Keep it for now.

(E) If a dearth of props accounted for the recurrent objects in Vermeer's paintings, we would not see expensive props in any of them.

This is the only answer choice that mentions both the expensive props and the lack of props ("dearth of props"). There seems to be a connection made between the two in this answer choice. Keep it.

DECISION #6: What is the best available answer?

We are down to three answer choices. When making a final decision, it's critical that we revisit the core. The correct answer will be the one that most clearly addresses the relationship between the premise and the conclusion:

Vermeer used   Vermeer was not
expensive props.   lacking in props.

(B) The props that recur in Vermeer's paintings were always
     available to him.

On second glance, (B) seems unrelated. The conclusion that Vermeer was not lacking in props refers to other props aside from the ones he used regularly. The fact that his recurring props were always available to him doesn't make it any more likely that he was not lacking in other props. Furthermore, what does this have to do with the cost of the props?

(D) The several recurrent items that appeared in Vermeer's
     paintings had special sentimental importance for him.

This might explain why he used those props over and over again, but it doesn't give us any more reason to argue that since the props he used were pricey he was not lacking in props. Maybe he used the same props over and over because he was sentimental about them, but maybe he was also lacking in other props! This answer is not enough to ensure that the conclusion follows logically from the premise.

Down to answer (E). Let's look at the core one more time:

Vermeer used   Vermeer was not
expensive props.   lacking in props.

We can think of this argument as having the structure "A. Therefore, B." The simplest sufficient assumption to any argument of this form is: "If A, then B." For the above argument, that would look like this: "If Vermeer used expensive props, then Vermeer was not lacking in props."

Let's imagine what this would look like inserted this into our argument:

Vermeer used expensive props. (If Vermeer used expensive props, then Vermeer was not lacking in props.) Thus, Vermeer was not lacking in props.

Notice the simple conditional statement would make the argument valid by connecting premise to conclusion.

Let's take a look at (E) one more time:

(E) If a dearth of props accounted for the recurrent objects in
     Vermeer's paintings, we would not see expensive props in
     any of them.

Let's try to think about this answer choice in simple "If/Then" terms:

"If a lack of props did account for recurring objects, then we
would not see expensive props."

Is this answer what we were looking for? Not exactly. But it seems related. Let's compare the conditional in this answer choice with the conditional we originally determined would be sufficient.

Sufficient Conditional: If Vermeer used expensive props, then Vermeer was not lacking in props. EP ⟶ –LP.

Conditional in (E): If a lack of props did account for recurring objects, then we would not see expensive props. LP ⟶ –EP.

Do you notice the relationship between the two? This answer is the contrapositive of what we need! If we reverse and negate it, we can infer the assumption that bridges the gap between the premise and conclusion. EP ⟶ –LP.

Perhaps (E) seemed somewhat relevant but a bit confusing, on your first read. When examined through the conditional logic lens, (E) is clearly correct.

The above question has a logical structure that is worth noting, since many Sufficient Assumption questions play on this form. Here it is again:

> Original Argument: A. Therefore, B.
> Sufficient Assumption: If A, then B. Make an assumption explicit.

The correct answer could be "If A, then B" or its contrapositive, "If not B, then not A."

Compound Conditional Statements

Compound conditional statements are statements that have a two-part *sufficient* condition (a two-part trigger such as "if X and Y, then…") and/or a two-part *necessary* condition (a two part outcome such as "…then Y or Z"). The following example has a two-part outcome:

> If M is selected, then both G and H must be selected.

What do we know? If M is selected, then G must be selected. Also, if M is selected, then H must be selected. We can deal with this by splitting the statement into two separate conditionals:

> If M is selected, then G is selected. (M ⟶ G)
> If M is selected, then H is selected. (M ⟶ H)

While this is the most common type of compound statement that you'll see, it's not the only type. Let's take a moment to define the four types of compound statements that are fair game on the LSAT, starting with the type discussed above.

1. AND in the outcome: If M is selected, then both G and H must be selected.

In this case, M, the sufficient condition, is enough to trigger *both* G and H. In other words, M alone is enough to trigger G, and M alone is enough to trigger H. Thus, we can split the compound statement into two simple statements as we've already learned to do:

If M is selected, then G is selected. (M ——► G)
If M is selected, then H is selected. (M ——► H)

Of course, from these two simple statements we can derive two contrapositives:

If G is not selected, then M is not selected. (–G ——► –M)
If H is not selected, then M is not selected. (–H ——► –M)

It's important to note that this type of compound statement won't always have the word "and" explicitly written in the outcome. For example:

If M is selected, then G is selected but H is not.

This is the same type of compound statement in disguise! Selecting M triggers two outcomes: G is selected AND H is *not* selected. We can split this up as follows:

M ——► G
M ——► –H

2. OR in the trigger: If M or G is selected, then H must be selected.

In this case, M on its own is enough to trigger H. We can say the same for G. *Either one* is enough to trigger the outcome, H. Thus, we can split this compound statement into two simple statements:

If M is selected, then H is selected. (M ——► H)
If G is selected, then H is selected. (G ——► H)

Again, we can generate contrapositives:

If H is not selected, then M is not selected. (–H ——► –M)
If H is not selected, then G is not selected. (–H ——► –G)

3. AND in the trigger: If M and G are selected, then H is selected.

Here, *both* M and G *together* are enough to trigger H, but we're not sure if either one *alone* is enough. Thus, we CANNOT split this statement into two parts. We must keep it together:

M + G ——► H

Oh boy. So how on earth can we take the contrapositive of a statement like this? Well, let's think about it. M and G together give us H. If we don't have H, then we couldn't have had M and G together. In other words, if we don't have H, either M is missing or G is missing (or both). –H means –M or –G. To find the contrapositive of a statement like this, reverse and negate the elements and SWAP "AND" for "OR":

–H ——► –M or –G

Note: It's important to know that "–M or –G" leaves open the possibility that neither is selected. It's not necessarily one or the other. For example, if you're told "Either Tamara or Igor will be invited," we know for certain that at least one of them must be invited. It's a small example of the difference between our everyday language and the legalistic language used by the LSAT—and law students!

4. OR in the outcome: If M is selected, then G or H is selected.

Notice that M is enough to trigger G or H, but not necessarily both. Thus, we CANNOT split this statement into two parts. We must keep it together:

M ⟶ G or H

Again, to find the contrapositive, reverse, negate, and SWAP "OR" for "AND" or vice versa:

−G + −H ⟶ −M

The last three compound statement types are quite rare on the LSAT, but you need to be prepared to deal with them if they do show up. Let's summarize the four types:

Type	Example	Strategy	Notation	Contrapositive	Frequency
AND as an outcome	If J, then K and L.	Split it up	J ⟶ K J ⟶ L	−K ⟶ −J −L ⟶ −J	Common
OR as a trigger	If M or N, then P.	Split it up	M ⟶ P N ⟶ P	−P ⟶ −M −P ⟶ −N	Rare
AND as a trigger	If R and S, then X.	Together	R + S ⟶ X	−X ⟶ −R or −S	Rare
OR as an outcome	If Q, then T or V.	Together	Q ⟶ T or V	−T + −V ⟶ −Q	Rare

Time to practice.

DRILL IT: Compound Conditional Statements

Convert each of the statements into conditional diagrams, and then derive contrapositive inferences. Be sure to check your responses against the solutions **after each exercise**.

Example: If X is selected, then both Y and Z are selected.

Conversions: Contrapositives:

X ⟶ Y   –Y ⟶ –X

X ⟶ Z   –Z ⟶ –X

1. If H is selected, then J is selected but G is not.

2. If K is selected, then neither M nor N is selected.

3. If both P and Q are on the team, then R is on the team.

4. If Paulson is selected, then Oster is selected but Vicenza is not.

5. If both X and Y are chosen, Z is chosen.

6. If the car is red or green, then it is a used car.

7. A good parent is both empathetic and sympathetic.

8. A country is economically healthy if it has both a skilled labor force and a competent government.

9. If one lives with both peace and love, then happiness is attainable.

8

SOLUTIONS: Compound Conditional Statements

1. If H is selected, then J is selected but G is not.

Conversions:	Contrapositives:
H $\longrightarrow$ J	–J $\longrightarrow$ –H
H $\longrightarrow$ –G	G $\longrightarrow$ –H

2. If K is selected, then neither M nor N is selected.

Be careful! "Neither/nor" is NOT the same as "or." "Neither/nor" is the same as neither one! We can translate "neither M nor N" to "not M *and* not N."

Conversions:	Contrapositives:
K $\longrightarrow$ –M	M $\longrightarrow$ –K
K $\longrightarrow$ –N	N $\longrightarrow$ –K

3. If both P and Q are on the team, then R is on the team.

Conversions:	Contrapositives:
P + Q $\longrightarrow$ R	–R $\longrightarrow$ –P or –Q

4. If Paulson is selected, then Oster is selected but Vicenza is not.

Conversions:	Contrapositives:
P $\longrightarrow$ O	–O $\longrightarrow$ –P
P $\longrightarrow$ –V	V $\longrightarrow$ –P

5. If both X and Y are chosen, Z is chosen.

Conversions:	Contrapositives:
X + Y $\longrightarrow$ Z	–Z $\longrightarrow$ –X or –Y

6. If the car is red or green, then it is a used car.

    Conversions: Contrapositives:

    R ——→ U   –U ——→ –R

    G ——→ U   –U ——→ –G

7. A good parent is both empathetic and sympathetic.

    Conversions: Contrapositives:

    GP ——→ E   –E ——→ –GP

    GP ——→ S   –S ——→ –GP

8. A country is economically healthy if it has both a skilled labor force and a competent government.

    Conversions: Contrapositives:

    SLF + CG ——→ EH   –EH ——→ –SLF or –CG

9. If one lives with both peace and love, then happiness is attainable.

    Conversions: Contrapositives:

    P + L ——→ HA   –HA ——→ –P or –L

Applying Conditional Logic 2: Compound Conditional Statements

Let's apply these skills to a real LSAT question. Take 1:20, and then we'll discuss.

PT22, S2, Q18

To classify a work of art as truly great, it is necessary that the work have both originality and far reaching influence upon the artistic community.

The principle above, if valid, most strongly supports which one of the following arguments?

(A) By breaking down traditional schemes of representation, Picasso redefined painting. It is this extreme originality that warrants his work being considered truly great.

(B) Some of the most original art being produced today is found in isolated communities, but because of this isolation these works have only minor influence, and hence cannot be considered truly great.

(C) Certain examples of the drumming practiced in parts of Africa's west coast employ a musical vocabulary that resists representation in Western notational schemes. This tremendous originality coupled with the profound impact these pieces are having on musicians everywhere, is enough to consider these works to be truly great.

(D) The piece of art in the lobby is clearly not classified as truly great, so it follows that it fails to be original.

(E) Since Bach's music is truly great, it not only has both originality and a major influence on musicians, it has broad popular appeal as well.

This question is a Principle question that requires us to find an answer that illustrates the given principle. This is a Principle Example question. We'll study these in the next chapter. Note that this is NOT the same as a Principle Support question (the kind we studied in the last chapter).

Did you recognize the given principle as a conditional statement? It's not written in traditional "If/Then" form, but it is a conditional statement nonetheless. A bit later, we'll discuss disguised conditionals in greater detail. For now, just know that the word "necessary" is a conditional trigger. It makes sense, right? Every conditional statement has a *necessary* component, or outcome. So, if one thing makes something else *necessary*, you've got a conditional situation on your hands. In this case, to be an example of truly great art (TGA), two things are necessary: (1) originality (O), and (2) far reaching influence on the artistic community (FRI). In other words:

If TGA, then both O and FRI.

TGA $\longrightarrow$ O + FRI

Look! A compound conditional statement! Now, we're looking for an answer choice that conforms to this principle, or conditional statement. What would a correct answer look like? Well, a correct answer might give us a TGA, and then describe how it is both O and FRI. Or, and this is the more likely scenario, a correct answer might play off of the contrapositive of this principle:

$$-O \text{ or } -FRI \longrightarrow -TGA$$

Since either –O, or –FRI, by itself, guarantees –TGA, we can split this conditional statement into two parts:

$$-O \longrightarrow -TGA$$
$$-FRI \longrightarrow -TGA$$

Maybe the answer will describe how a particular art is either not O, or not FRI, and then conclude that the art is not truly great. Let's look at the choices, but before we do, we'll revisit the principle one last time:

$$TGA \longrightarrow O + FRI$$
$$-O \longrightarrow -TGA$$
$$-FRI \longrightarrow -TGA$$

Any answer choice that conforms to any one of the three statements above will be a correct answer.

(A) By breaking down traditional schemes of representation, Picasso redefined painting. It is this extreme originality that warrants his work being considered truly great.

This says the work is O ("redefined painting"), so it must be TGA (O $\longrightarrow$ TGA). Does this fit the principle? No, it does not. Eliminate it.

(B) Some of the most original art being produced today is found in isolated communities, but because of this isolation these works have only minor influence, and hence cannot be considered truly great.

This says the work is O, but also that it is –FRI (not far-reaching). Because it is –FRI, it is –TGA. Does this match the principle? Indeed it does: –FRI $\longrightarrow$ –TGA.

(C) Certain examples of the drumming practiced in parts of Africa's west coast employ a musical vocabulary that resists representation in Western notational schemes. This tremendous originality coupled with the profound impact these pieces are having on musicians everywhere, is enough to consider these works to be truly great.

This is very tempting. The work is both O and has FRI. Thus, the answer states, it must be TGA: O + FRI $\longrightarrow$ TGA

Be careful. This is the exact reverse of the original principle! We can't simply reverse the terms. This is incorrect. While great art must be original and have a far reaching influence, a piece of art could have those characteristics and not be great.

(D) The piece of art in the lobby is clearly not classified as truly great, so it follows that it fails to be original.

–TGA ⟶ –O. This is a reversal of what we've got as well. Eliminate it.

(E) Since Bach's music is truly great, it not only has both originality and a major influence on musicians, it has broad popular appeal as well.

TGA ⟶ O + FRI + BPA. Oooh. This is very tempting. We seem to get the TGA ⟶ O + FRI that we need, but we have to be very careful here. Remember, FRI stands for "far reaching influence ON THE ARTISTIC COMMUNITY." Is that the same as "major influence on musicians?" Do musicians fully represent the artistic community? No. Furthermore, this answer choice adds in a third necessary element that is not mentioned in the original principle.

The correct answer is (B).

Only

From "If" to "Only If"

The word "only" could be the single most important word on the LSAT. It shows up all over the place. In the Logical Reasoning section of the exam, "only" is often a conditional logic trigger. To see how it comes into play, consider the following conditional statement:

Marcus wears a jacket if it is raining outside.

This is a pretty simple conditional relationship:

raining ⟶ Marcus wears a jacket

In other words, the rain is enough, or *sufficient,* to trigger Marcus wearing a jacket. Anytime it rains, Marcus wears a jacket. We know by now that the reverse is NOT necessarily true: If Marcus wears a jacket, that doesn't necessarily mean that it is raining. Maybe he's wearing a jacket because it's cold out. Or maybe he's wearing a jacket because he's trying it on for size.

Now let's consider a slightly different statement:

Marcus wears a jacket *only* if it is raining outside.

Which one of the following is a correct interpretation of this new statement?

(A) If Marcus wears a jacket, then it is raining outside. (J ⟶ R)
(B) If it is raining outside, then Marcus wears a jacket. (R ⟶ J)

Well, we know that Marcus wears a jacket *only* when it rains outside. So, he can't wear a jacket under any other circumstance. Thus, IF he is wearing a jacket, THEN we know for certain it must be raining! J ⟶ R. (A) is correct.

8

(B) is incorrect. Yes, Marcus wears a jacket *only* when it is raining (and no other time), but not necessarily *every* time it rains. R does not guarantee J. Let's review:

The standard conditional: Marcus wears a jacket if it is raining outside. (R ⟶ J)
With "only if": Marcus wears a jacket *only* if it is raining outside. (J ⟶ R)

So, the "only if" gives us the exact opposite relationship. Note that replacing the word "if" with "when" gives us the same structures. "If" and "when" are equivalent:

Marcus wears a jacket when it is raining outside. (R ⟶ J)
Marcus wears a jacket *only* when it is raining outside. (J ⟶ R)

"If and Only If"?

Now let's take it one step further:

Marcus wears a jacket *if, and only if,* it is raining outside.

This is an LSAT favorite. It's a conditional construction that throws many test-takers for a serious loop. However, with a bit of thinking, we can make sense of this construction without much trouble. In fact, you already know all you need to know in order to properly interpret this statement. This statement is the combination of two simpler statements:

Marcus wears a jacket   Marcus wears a jacket   Marcus wears a jacket
if it is raining outside   *only if* it is raining outside   *if, and only if,* it is
(R ⟶ J)   +   (J ⟶ R)   =   raining outside
                                                              (R ⟶ J, J ⟶ R)

As you can see, the "if and only if" construction actually gives us two conditional statements, the second of which is simply the reverse of the first. Remember that each of these will yield a contrapositive. In the end, we get four relationships:

R ⟶ J and the contrapositive –J ⟶ –R
J ⟶ R and the contrapositive –R ⟶ –J

Another way to express the sum of these relationships is:

R ⟷ J
–J ⟷ –R

For "if and only if" statements, the arrows work in both directions. Here are some other terms that indicate this bidirectional relationship:

A if, but only if, B.   A when, and only when, B.
A then B, and only then.   All A, and only A, are B.

Time to get some practice interpreting the word "only."

DRILL IT: Only

Choose all of the answer choices that are logically equivalent to the given statement. Keep in mind that there may be more than one correct answer for each question (or no correct answer at all!). Check your answers after each exercise.

Example (bold answers are correct):

If B, then A.

(A) B only if A.
(B) If A, then B.
(C) If not B, then not A.
(D) If not A, then not B. (the contrapositive!)

1. If Janet goes to the party, then Bill goes to the party.

    (A) If Janet does not go to the party, then Bill does not go.
    (B) Janet goes to the party only if Bill goes.
    (C) Bill goes to the party only if Janet goes.
    (D) If Bill does not go to the party, then Janet does not go.

2. The play is popular if ticket sales exceed 100.

    (A) Ticket sales for the play exceed 100 only if the play is popular.
    (B) Only if the play is popular do ticket sales for the play exceed 100.
    (C) If ticket sales exceed 100, then the play is popular.
    (D) If the play is not popular, then ticket sales do not exceed 100.

3. Only if the car is new is it in good shape.

    (A) The car is in good shape if, and only if, it is new.
    (B) The car is new if, and only if, it is in good shape.
    (C) If the car is in good shape, then it is new.
    (D) If the car is new, then it is in good shape.

4. John speaks when, and only when, he is asked to speak.

    (A) S $\longrightarrow$ AS, AS $\longrightarrow$ S
    (B) –AS $\longleftrightarrow$ S
    (C) –S $\longrightarrow$ –AS, –AS $\longrightarrow$ –S
    (D) –AS $\longleftrightarrow$ –S

5. Only the good die young.

    (A) good $\longrightarrow$ die young
    (B) –good $\longrightarrow$ –die young
    (C) One who dies young is good.
    (D) One who is not good never dies young.

8

SOLUTIONS: Only

1. If Janet goes to the party, then Bill goes to the party.

    (A) If Janet does not go to the party, then Bill does not go.

    (B) Janet goes to the party only if Bill goes.

    (C) Bill goes to the party only if Janet goes.

    (D) If Bill does not go to the party, then Janet does not go.

2. The play is popular if ticket sales exceed 100.

    (A) Ticket sales for the play exceed 100 only if the play is popular.

    (B) Only if the play is popular do ticket sales for the play exceed 100.

    (C) If ticket sales exceed 100, then the play is popular.

    (D) If the play is not popular, then ticket sales do not exceed 100.

3. Only if the car is new is it in good shape.

    (A) The car is in good shape if, and only if, it is new.

    (B) The car is new if, and only if, it is in good shape.

    (C) If the car is in good shape, then it is new.

    (D) If the car is new, then it is in good shape.

4. John speaks when, and only when, he is asked to speak.

    (A) S ⟶ AS, AS ⟶ S

    (B) –AS ⟷ S

    (C) –S ⟶ –AS, –AS ⟶ –S

    (D) –AS ⟷ –S

5. Only the good die young.

    (A) good ⟶ die young (Be careful. Only the good die young, but that doesn't mean ALL good people die young.)

    (B) –good ⟶ –die young

    (C) One who dies young is good.

    (D) One who is not good never dies young.

8

Applying Conditional Logic 3: Only, Must, and No

Here's an LSAT question that requires a strong understanding of what we just discussed. Give yourself 1:20 and then we'll go through it.

PT34, S2, Q10

Although the charter of Westside School states that the student body must include some students with special educational needs, no students with learning disabilities have yet enrolled in the school. Therefore, the school is currently in violation of its charter.

The conclusion of the argument follows logically if which one of the following is assumed?

(A) All students with learning disabilities have special educational needs.

(B) The school currently has no student with learning disabilities.

(C) The school should enroll students with special educational needs.

(D) The only students with special educational needs are students with learning disabilities.

(E) The school's charter cannot be modified in order to avoid its being violated.

Again, we're dealing with an Assumption question. Let's apply our approach:

DECISION #1: What is my task?

This question is asking us to select an assumption that would allow the conclusion to "follow logically." In other words, we need a *sufficient* assumption.

DECISION #2: What is the author's conclusion?

DECISION #3: How is that conclusion supported?

Let's read the argument again with the above questions in mind:

> Although the charter of Westside School states that the student body must include some students with special educational needs,

"Although" is a sign that we're about to get some contrary information.

> no students with learning disabilities have yet enrolled in the school.

And here it is. The charter states that the student body must include some special needs students, but as of yet the school does not have any students with learning disabilities. Hmm. Notice the difference between the two concepts: "special needs students" and "students with learning disabilities." Are these groups necessarily the same? We'll keep this in mind.

Therefore, the school is currently in violation of its charter.

This is obviously the conclusion. So the argument core is:

Charter requires SN students

+   ➡   school is in violation of its charter

no students with LD enrolled

DECISION #4: What is the gap?

We've already noticed the potential difference between special needs (SN) and learning disability (LD). If the school needs to have SN students to comply with its charter, and it doesn't have LD students, does that mean the school is in violation of the charter? There's something going on here with the connection between SN and LD. Our answer needs to address this.

DECISION #5: Which answer choices are clearly wrong?

The easiest eliminations will be answers that aren't related to the argument core. Here's our core again:

Charter requires SN students

+   ➡   school is in violation of its charter

no students with LD enrolled

(A) All students with learning disabilities have special educational needs.

This looks attractive. It makes a direct connection between LD and SN. Keep it for now.

(B) The school currently has no student with learning disabilities.

We already know this is true. This is one of our premises! This is a premise booster. Eliminate it.

(C) The school should enroll students with special educational needs.

This is tempting. It seems logical that they should enroll some special needs students. However, this isn't an assumption that would allow us to conclude that the school is currently *in violation of the charter. Unless the argument is about what should or should not be done, be careful of answers that express "should's" or "should not's." Eliminate it.*

(D) The only students with special educational needs are students with learning disabilities.

Here's another one that seems to connect SN with LD. Better keep it for now.

> (E) The school's charter cannot be modified in order to avoid
>   its being violated.

This is out of scope. We're looking for an assumption that would allow us to conclude that the school is currently in violation of the charter. Whether the charter could be modified is irrelevant.

DECISION #6: What is the best available answer?

Okay, so we're down to two answers, (A) and (D), and they both look very good. When we're down to two, we always want to revisit the core before making a final decision.

So, the argument assumes that if there are no LD, then there are no SN, right? We can express this in conditional form:

$$-LD \longrightarrow -SN$$

Look at (A) one more time, and try to translate it into a conditional statement:

> (A) All students with learning disabilities have special
>   educational needs.

Don't read on until you've given it a shot. Does it match the assumption we've written above?

This translates to "All LD are SN." (LD $\longrightarrow$ SN)

What do you think of (A) now? It's the exact negation of what we need! We need: $-LD \longrightarrow -SN$. Back to (D):

> (D) The only students with special educational needs are
>   students with learning disabilities.

Don't continue on until you've tried to translate this statement. It's an "only" statement, so be careful. This is a difficult statement. Let's look at a simpler, more intuitive one that uses the same structure:

> The only people who water ski are those who can swim.

We've got two choices, right? It's either W $\longrightarrow$ S, or S $\longrightarrow$ W. Which one is it? Well, consider it from the perspective of guarantees. Which one guarantees the other?

If you water ski, does that guarantee that you can swim? Yes, it does, because the only people who water ski are those who can swim.

If you can swim, does that guarantee that you water ski? No, it doesn't. A 5-year-old might be able to swim but not water ski. So, we have W $\longrightarrow$ S.

Back to (D) again.

>   (D) The only students with special educational needs are
>   students with learning disabilities.

This is saying that the only students with SN are those who also have LD. In other words, if you have SN, then it is a guarantee that you also have LD:

>   SN $\longrightarrow$ LD

Oh no! This doesn't match our predicted assumption, –LD $\longrightarrow$ –SN, either! Or does it? Try taking the contrapositive of (D). This is the correct answer.

The key to this question is correctly interpreting the "only" conditional in answer choice (D). It's a tricky one. The more comfortable you get with the word "only," the better off you'll be.

Beyond If/Then Triggers

We discussed the fact that "If/Then" phrasing indicates we're dealing with a conditional statement, but we also mentioned that disguised conditional statements won't contain the "If/Then" structure. For you to get the most out of your conditional logic knowledge on the LSAT, you'll need to learn to work with disguised conditionals. The key is the guarantee.

Looking for Guarantees

Have a look at this standard conditional statement:

>   If one is young, then one is happy.

According to this statement, being young guarantees happiness. Always. Without exception. Every time. We can express this exact idea in many different ways:

>   All young people are happy.
>   Being young assures happiness.
>   A young person is a happy person.

Each of these three statements conveys the exact same meaning as the original "If/Then" statement. Being young guarantees happiness. Always. Without exception. Every time. Thus, we can say these three statements are conditional statements, even though they may not look like it. When the LSAT gives us a conditional statement on a Logical Reasoning question, it will likely be disguised like this. How can we learn to recognize these disguised conditionals? We need to learn to recognize *words that imply a guarantee*. There are three main categories of such words. Here they are with examples for each. Notice that every disguised conditional statement can be translated to "If/Then" form:

1. Absolute modifiers (all, any, every, always, none, never)

    All engineers enjoy math. (If one is an engineer, then one enjoys math.)

    Any hamburger is worth $2. (If it is a hamburger, then it is worth $2.)

    Every good movie has a star actor. (If it is a good movie, then it has a star actor.)

    A new car **always** smells good. (If it is a new car, then it smells good.)

    None of the pies at the party had blueberry filling. (If it was a pie at the party, then it did not have blueberry filling.)

    Good soccer players are **never** good football players. (If one is a good soccer player, then one is not a good football player.)

2. Words of necessity (necessary, require, depend, assure, guarantee, must, is essential for)

    A large vocabulary is **necessary** to be a great writer. (If one is a great writer, one has a large vocabulary.)

    Success **requires** patience. (If a person is successful, then that person is patient.)

    Being happy **depends on** being healthy. (If a person is happy, then that person is healthy.)

    Repeated practice **assures** an error-free performance. (If one practices repeatedly, then one will have an error-free performance.)

    Buying a ticket online **guarantees** a seat on the bus. (If one buys a ticket online, then one will have a seat on the bus.)

    A good pizza **must** be hot. (If a pizza is good, then it is hot.)

    Experience **is essential for** humility. (If one is humble, one has experience.)

3. Verbs of certainty (is, are, will be, do, do not, has/have)

    A long story **is** a boring story. (If a story is long, then it is boring.)

    Oranges **are** fruits. (If it is an orange, then it is a fruit.)

    Mixing yellow and blue **does not** make red. (If yellow and blue are mixed, then red is not the result.)

    Dogs **have** fleas. (If it is a dog, then it has fleas.)

8

This is certainly not an exhaustive list of words that imply a guarantee, but it is a start, and it should put you in the right mind-set for recognizing the clues when they are present. Let's give it a try. Take 1:20 for this one.

PT11, S2, Q9

Any announcement authorized by the head of the department is important. However, announcements are sometimes issued, without authorization, by people other than the head of the department, so some announcements will inevitably turn out not to be important.

The reasoning is flawed because the argument

(A) does not specify exactly which communications are to be classified as announcements

(B) overlooks the possibility that people other than the head of the department have the authority to authorize announcements

(C) leaves open the possibility that the head of the department never, in fact, authorizes any announcements

(D) assumes without warrant that just because satisfying a given condition is enough to ensure an announcement's importance, satisfying that condition is necessary for its importance

(E) fails to distinguish between the importance of the position someone holds and the importance of what that person may actually be announcing on a particular occasion

This is an Assumption Family question. Let's follow the steps:

DECISION #1: What is my task?

This question is asking us to find a flaw.

DECISION #2: What is the author's conclusion?

DECISION #3: How is that conclusion supported?

Let's read the argument again with the above questions in mind:

Any announcement authorized by the head of the department is important.

This could be a premise (statement of fact) or a claim (an opinion). Regardless, it's a disguised conditional statement, with the absolute modifier "any" being the clue. If an announcement is authorized by the head of the department, then the announcement must be important.

AHD ⟶ I

(NOTE: Some people like to jot conditional statements down on the page in notation form, others don't. If you had trouble seeing that first sentence as a conditional, or if you generally prefer to work in diagram form, go ahead and get in the habit of putting conditionals on the paper using your own notation. It's fine if you choose not to write it down, as long as you can "hold" the logical information in your head as you continue reading.)

> However, announcements are sometimes issued, without authorization, by people other than the head of the department,

Now, you've learned that "however" generally signals that the author disagrees with the part coming before it, but in this case "however" is not really used in the traditional way. It's used to introduce a contrast, not a difference in opinion.

Consider this analogous structure:

> *James empties the trash on Thursdays. However, Janet empties the trash on Fridays.*

The "however" doesn't introduce a difference in opinion, but rather just a contrasting point. Important distinction!

So far we know that announcements authorized by the head of the department are important, and some announcements are NOT authorized by the head of the department:

> $AHD \longrightarrow I$
> Some $-AHD$

> so some announcements will inevitably turn out not to be important.

This is the conclusion. So the argument looks like this:

> $AHD \longrightarrow I$
> Some $-AHD \longrightarrow$ Some $-I$

Another way to say this is:

> *AHD guarantees I.*
> *So, −AHD means −I.*

Do you notice anything fishy here? Try to figure it out before reading on.

DECISION #4: What is the flaw?

This argument presents a conditional relationship, and then concludes that the negation must also be true! Here's an analogy:

> All children like ice cream. Bob is not a child. Thus, Bob does not like ice cream.

This doesn't make logical sense. It's perfectly reasonable that Bob could be an adult who likes ice cream. This argument illegally negates the logic of the conditional statement.

DECISION #5: Which answer choices are clearly wrong?

      (A) does not specify exactly which communications are to be classified as announcements

Out of scope. The conclusion deals with the importance of certain announcements. This answer choice gives us nothing about importance. Eliminate it.

      (B) overlooks the possibility that people other than the head of the department have the authority to authorize announcements

It's irrelevant whether other people have the authority to authorize announcements. What's important is whether an announcement can be deemed important when people who do NOT have authority issue these announcements. Remember, stay close to the conclusion. The conclusion is about the importance of unauthorized announcements. Our answer is bound to have the word "important" in it, one way or another.

      (C) leaves open the possibility that the head of the department never, in fact, authorizes any announcements

We don't care if he/she never authorizes any announcements. Rather, we're interested in whether announcements that are not authorized are unimportant. Again, stay close to the conclusion.

      (D) assumes without warrant that just because satisfying a given condition is enough to ensure an announcement's importance, satisfying that condition is necessary for its importance

I don't get it. Let's leave it for now.

      (E) fails to distinguish between the importance of the position someone holds and the importance of what that person may actually be announcing on a particular occasion

The author does not fail to make this distinction. Furthermore, the importance of someone's position is irrelevant to this argument. Eliminate it.

DECISION #6: What is the best available answer?

There's only one answer left, (D). Let's evaluate how (D) actually expresses the flaw that we had anticipated. Let's review the anticipated flaw:

    AHD guarantees I.

    So, –AHD means –I.

The author negates the original conditional in order to draw a faulty conclusion. Now back to (D).

    (D) assumes without warrant that just because satisfying a
    given condition is enough to ensure an announcement's
    importance, satisfying that condition is necessary for its
    importance

Wow! This is tough language! We can see that "assumes without warrant" is a fancy way of saying "assumes." Now let's decode "…satisfying a given condition is enough to ensure an announcement's importance." What given condition could they be talking about? Do we know of any condition that, when satisfied, would be enough to ensure an announcement's importance? Sure we do! We know that if an announcement is authorized by the head of the department, then it must be important! In other words, being authorized by the head is *sufficient,* or *enough,* to guarantee importance. AHD ⟶ I.

So, the "satisfying a given condition" referred to in answer (D) is the *authorization by the head of the department.* Let's just substitute this into the answer choice and read it again:

    (D) assumes without warrant that just because *authorization
    by the head of the department* is sufficient to ensure an
    announcement's importance, *authorization by the head of
    the department* is necessary for its importance

Now let's focus on the second part of the statement, the part after the comma: authorization by the head of the department is *necessary* for its (the announcement's) importance. If you get past the initial shock of the wording, this part is actually not so tough to decode—it clearly tells us which part is necessary!

So, (D) is really just saying this:

    (D) assumes that because authorization by the head is *sufficient*
    for importance (AHD ⟶ I), it must also be true that
    authorization by the head is *necessary* for importance (I
    ⟶ AHD)

Answer (D) describes an illegal reversal of logic! We're almost there. Remember, the flaw that we spotted earlier on was that the argument illegally *negates* the logic:

    AHD guarantees I.
    So, –AHD means –I.

What we have in answer (D) is close:

    AHD guarantees I.
    So, I means AHD.

But once again, we've been provided the contrapositive of what was expected:

    –AHD means –I = I means AHD.

So, to say that just because AHD is *sufficient* for importance means that AHD is *necessary* for importance is the same as saying the author makes an illegal reversal of a conditional statement, which is the same as saying the author makes an illegal negation of a conditional statement!

Phew! Tough problem! There's no way we could've gotten that without recognizing the disguised conditonal in the argument, and without understanding the *sufficient* and *necessary* terminology used in answer choice (D).

Here's a general representation for you to study.

Let's say we have this argument:

> X ——→ Y
> Thus, Y ——→ X. (Which also means –X ——→ –Y, if you take the contrapositive.)

The author of this argument has:

1. Illegally reversed the logic.
2. Illegally negated the logic.
3. Confused a sufficient condition (X) for a necessary condition.
4. Confused a necessary condition (Y) for a sufficient condition.
5. Assumed that because X is sufficient to guarantee Y, it is also necessary for Y.

All five of these statements express the same overarching flaw. They all mean the same thing—the author made an invalid inference from a conditional statement. We tend to think and talk in terms of #1 and #2, but the LSAT will tend to use #3, #4, and #5 when writing answer choices.

Except Perhaps and Unless

Except Perhaps

It's time to discuss two of the most disguised conditional structures you'll see on the LSAT: except perhaps statements and unless statements. Take a look:

> Javier arrives to work on time except perhaps if there is traffic.

We've learned that conditional statements are guarantees. This doesn't look much like a guarantee, does it? Well, think about it again. What do you know if there is NOT traffic? You got it. Javier arrives to work on time… guaranteed! So, if there is no traffic, Javier arrives to work on time.

> NO traffic ——→ Javier arrives on time

This is what we call an "except perhaps" statement. Something, call it the normal state of affairs, always happens *except perhaps* when something else intrudes on the situation (call it the intruder). If the intruder does not occur, then we're guaranteed to have the normal state of affairs. Here's another example:

> Gloria reads before bed except perhaps if there is something good on TV.

Normal state of affairs: Gloria reads before bed.
Intruder: Something good on TV.

If the intruder does not intrude, then we're assured to get the normal state of affairs:

NOT something good on TV ——→ Gloria reads before bed

Now, it's important that you don't fall into the "except perhaps" trap. The trap is to assume that if the intruder *does* intrude, you *won't* get the normal state. Here's how this would be written:

something good on TV ——→ Gloria does NOT read before bed

Note that this is an illegal negation of what we got earlier. It's wrong. Yes, the intruder is the only thing that can disrupt the normal state of affairs, but it doesn't *necessarily* disrupt the normal state. Say there was something good on TV. *Perhaps* Gloria would watch TV instead of reading, but just maybe she'd stick with her book if the book were particularly interesting. The operative word is *perhaps*. When the intruder intrudes, *perhaps* the normal state is affected, but not necessarily. Be careful!

So, here's the general formula for interpreting "except perhaps" statements:

1. Identify the normal state of affairs.
2. Identify the intruder.
3. Think: If the intruder does NOT intrude, we must get the normal state.
4. Write your conditional statement accordingly (NOT intruder ——→ normal state).

Try this one. Make sure you give it your best shot before reading on:

The Patriots will win the Super Bowl except perhaps if Tom Brady gets injured.

Normal state of affairs: Patriots will win the Super Bowl.
Intruder: Brady gets injured.
Think: If Brady does NOT get injured, we must get the normal state of affairs.
Conditional statement: Brady does NOT get injured ——→ Patriots win the Super Bowl

Don't fall for the trap. Note that if Brady *does* get injured, this doesn't necessarily mean the Patriots will lose. Maybe their backup quarterback will lead them to a win.

Unless

"Unless" statements are identical to "except perhaps" statements. They work exactly the same way:

Javier cannot be chosen for the position (guaranteed) unless he prepares for the interview (then *maybe* he can be chosen).

Normal state of affairs: Javier cannot be chosen.
Intruder: Preparation.
Think: If there is NO preparation, we must get the normal state of affairs.
Conditional statement: NO preparation ——→ Javier cannot be chosen.

Time to practice.

DRILL IT: Except Perhaps and Unless Statements

Translate the following statements into conditional notation. Be sure to check your answer after each exercise.

Example: Javier cannot be chosen for the position unless he prepares for the interview.

(–preparation ⟶ –chosen)

1. Tommy cannot win the marathon except perhaps if Eugene drops out.

2. The carnival cannot proceed unless the clown gets better.

3. The car won't start except perhaps if we fill it with gas.

4. Jill does not carry the bucket unless Jack gets tired.

5. Unless the field dries, the game cannot be played.

8

SOLUTIONS: Except Perhaps and Unless Statements

1. Tommy cannot win the marathon except perhaps if Eugene drops out.

   –Eugene drops out (or "Eugene races") ——→ –Tommy wins

2. The carnival cannot proceed unless the clown gets better

   –clown better ——→ –carnival proceed

3. The car won't start except perhaps if we fill it with gas.

   –fill with gas ——→ –car start

4. Jill does not carry the bucket unless Jack gets tired.

   –jack tired ——→ –jill carries bucket

5. Unless the field dries, the game cannot be played.

   –dries ——→ –game played

Applying Conditional Logic 4: Unless Statements

It's time to test your knowledge. Give yourself 1:20, and then we'll discuss.

PT15, S3, Q7

Politician: Unless our nation redistributes wealth, we will be unable to alleviate economic injustice and our current system will lead inevitably to intolerable economic inequities. If the inequities become intolerable, those who suffer from the injustice will resort to violence to coerce social reform. It is our nation's responsibility to do whatever is necessary to alleviate conditions that would otherwise give rise to violent attempts at social reform.

The statements above logically commit the politician to which one of the following conclusions?

(A) The need for political reform never justifies a resort to violent remedies.
(B) It is our nation's responsibility to redistribute wealth.
(C) Politicians must base decisions on political expediency rather than on abstract moral principles.
(D) Economic injustice need not be remedied unless it leads to intolerable social conditions.
(E) All that is required to create conditions of economic justice is the redistribution of wealth.

This is an Inference question. We'll discuss Inference questions in a later chapter, but for now just know that an inference question basically requires us to choose an answer that we can prove from the given information in the passage. Note that this is NOT an Assumption Family question. We do not need to identify gaps or holes in the argument. Rather, we need to consider the information given, synthesize it, and then choose an answer that follows logically.

Many of you likely got this question correct without using any formal conditional logic. If the argument made sense to you, and you were able to anticipate the logical outcome, great! The conditional logic thought process we're about to demonstrate will give you a slightly different perspective on the question. If you weren't able to see the logical outcome, the conditional logic angle should help. Let's give it a shot. We'll start with the first sentence:

Politician: Unless our nation redistributes wealth, we will be unable to alleviate economic injustice and our current system will lead inevitably to intolerable economic inequities.

An "unless" statement! Let's break it down using the steps we outlined above:

Normal state of affairs: We will be unable to alleviate economic injustice and our current system will lead inevitably to intolerable economic injustice.

8

Intruder: Our nation redistributes wealth.

Think: If our nation does NOT redistribute wealth, then the normal state will occur.

Conditional statement: –redistribute ⟶ economic injustice + intolerable economic inequities

> If the inequities become intolerable, those who suffer from the injustice will resort to violence to coerce social reform.

Another conditional statement! This one is in standard "If/Then" form:

> intolerable economic inequities ⟶ violence

Notice that this conditional statement can be "hooked" onto the first one:

> –redistribute ⟶ economic injustice + intolerable economic inequities ⟶ violence

In other words, if we don't redistribute, we'll end up with violence (follow the chain!):

> –redistribute ⟶ violence

> It is our nation's responsibility to do whatever is necessary to alleviate conditions that would otherwise give rise to violent attempts at social reform.

So, we must do whatever we can to avoid violence. Well, if we don't want violence, we need to redistribute wealth. The contrapositive tells us as much:

> –violence ⟶ redistribute

Answer choice (B) is the correct answer that follows logically from the information given:

> (B) It is our nation's responsibility to redistribute wealth.

Again, you may have arrived at (B) without resorting to conditional diagramming. That's okay. In fact, that's good. You should diagram the statements only when you're not able to make sense of the information in your head. It's kind of like asking someone for directions. We all resist writing them down, especially if they're easy to remember (like "drive to the river and make a left"), but as soon as they get complicated, we reach for a pen. That's the way you should think about conditional logic diagramming.

The Conditional Chain: Linking Conditional Statements

This last problem provides a good transition into the next section of the chapter. In our solution to the last question, we linked two conditional statements that shared a common element (intolerable economic inequities). Linking conditionals into a longer chain is crucial to getting the most out of your conditional logic knowledge on the LSAT. There are two basic types of linkages that you'll want to master:

1. The direct link.

> Given: A ⟶ B
> Given: B ⟶ C
> The direct link: A ⟶ B ⟶ C
> We can infer: A ⟶ C

2. The contrapositive link.

> Given: A ⟶ B
> Given: C ⟶ –B
> Take the contrapositive to get a like term: B ⟶ –C
> The link: A ⟶ B ⟶ –C
> We can infer: A ⟶ –C

Now, there's one type of *invalid* link that you will be tempted to make. Let's exercise these temptations right here and now:

> Given: A ⟶ B
> Given: A ⟶ C
> Temptation: B ⟶ C

No, no, no! This is the equivalent of saying:

> All apples are fruits. (A ⟶ F)
> All apples are red. (A ⟶ R)
> So, all fruits are red. (F ⟶ R)

This doesn't work. In fact, there is no way to create a chain from this information, even after we try taking the contrapositives of the statements.

Let's practice making links.

8

DRILL IT: Conditional Chains

For each exercise, connect the pair of conditional statements into a chain. Some won't connect. Don't be tempted to jam them together! Be sure to check your answer after each exercise.

Example: If you invite Aaron, Brian must be invited as well. If Chuck isn't invited, neither is Brian.
               A ⟶ B ⟶ C

1. If Sam eats a piece of cake, he will not be hungry for dinner. If Jeremy bakes a cake, Sam will eat a piece of it.

2. If it's raining out, the picnic will be cancelled. Simone will be sad if the picnic is cancelled.

3. Every pianist knows the music of Bach. No one in my family knows the music of Bach.

4. A good apple is a ripe apple, and an apple will not be picked unless it is ripe.

5. Carrie is anxious when her dog misbehaves, and if Carrie is anxious, then her boyfriend is anxious as well.

6. Only troublemakers stay after school. All students who arrive late will stay after school.

7. Sarah apologizes only when she means it, and she always wears her purple sweater when she apologizes.

8. Being a good parent requires understanding and empathy. Those without experience cannot be empathetic.

9. Almost all flowers are pretty, and anything that is pretty is worth displaying in the home.

10. A wise person is never a talkative person, but every talkative person has something interesting to say.

11. Unless the street is dark, Jeffrey will walk home. The street is dark only on the weekends.

8

12. Tall trees require sunlight to survive. Tall trees get sunlight only when they are not blocked by other trees.

SOLUTIONS: Conditional Chains

1. If Sam eats a piece of cake, he will not be hungry for dinner. If Jeremy bakes a cake, Sam will eat a piece of it.

   Jeremy bakes a cake ⟶ Sam eats a piece of cake ⟶ –Sam hungry for dinner

2. If it's raining out, the picnic will be cancelled. Simone will be sad if the picnic is cancelled.

   raining ⟶ picnic cancelled ⟶ Simone sad

3. Every pianist knows the music of Bach. No one in my family knows the music of Bach.

   in my family ⟶ –know Bach ⟶ –pianist

   Or, perhaps you came up with a chain of contrapositives of the above:

   pianist ⟶ know Bach ⟶ –in my family

   Note that for each of these exercises, the contrapositives of the relationships are also correct.

4. A good apple is a ripe apple, and an apple will not be picked unless it is ripe.

   good ⟶ ripe
   –ripe ⟶ –picked

   These can't be linked!

5. Carrie is anxious when her dog misbehaves, and if Carrie is anxious, then her boyfriend is anxious as well.

   dog misbehaves ⟶ Carrie anxious ⟶ boyfriend anxious

6. Only troublemakers stay after school. All students who arrive late will stay after school.

   arrive late ⟶ stay after school ⟶ troublemaker

7. Sarah apologizes only when she means it, and she always wears her purple sweater when she apologizes.

    sarah apologizes ⟶ sarah means it
    sarah apologizes ⟶ wears purple sweater

    These can't be linked!

8. Being a good parent requires understanding and empathy. Those without experience cannot be empathetic.

    –experience ⟶ –empathy ⟶ –good parent

9. Almost all flowers are pretty, and anything that is pretty is worth displaying in the home.

    "Almost all" is not a guarantee!

    pretty ⟶ worth displaying

    Don't worry, we'll talk about how to handle "almost," "some," and related terms later on.

10. A wise person is never a talkative person, but every talkative person has something interesting to say.

    wise ⟶ –talkative
    talkative ⟶ has something interesting to say

    These cannot be linked!

11. Unless the street is dark, Jeffrey walks home from work. The street is dark only on the weekends.

    –jeffrey walks home ⟶ street dark ⟶ weekend

12. Tall trees require sunlight to survive. Tall trees get sunlight only when they are not blocked by other trees.

    tall trees survive ⟶ sunlight ⟶ –blocked by other trees

8

Applying Conditional Logic 5: Conditional Chains

Let's give it a try on a real one. Take a bit longer for this one, 1:40, so you can try approaching it using formal logic.

PT13, S2, Q10

Every political philosopher of the early twentieth century who was either a socialist or a communist was influenced by Rosa Luxemburg. No one who was influenced by Rosa Luxemburg advocated a totalitarian state.

If the statements above are true, which one of the following must on the basis of them also be true?

(A) No early twentieth century socialist political philosopher advocated a totalitarian state.

(B) Every early twentieth century political philosopher who did not advocate a totalitarian state was influenced by Rosa Luxemburg.

(C) Rosa Luxemburg was the only person to influence every early twentieth century political philosopher who was either socialist or communist.

(D) Every early twentieth century political philosopher who was influenced by Rosa Luxemburg and was not a socialist was a communist.

(E) Every early twentieth century philosopher who did not advocate a totalitarian state was either socialist or communist.

8

Notice that the two statements given in the original "argument" are facts. There is no conclusion. In fact, this is not an argument at all. This question is asking us to choose an answer that must be true based on the information in the text. This is another Inference question (again, we'll cover these in more detail later on).

The first word is "every," a common conditional trigger. The start of the second sentence is "no one," another absolute term that expresses a guarantee. So, both sentences in the passage are conditional statements. Most likely, we're going to need to connect the conditionals in order to draw an inference. Let's take it one step at a time. Take a minute to translate the first sentence into conditional terms:

Every political philosopher of the early twentieth century who was either a socialist or a communist was influenced by Rosa Luxemburg.

How would you convert this into standard "If/Then" form? Well, *every* socialist political philosopher (SPP) and every communist political philosopher (CPP) of the twentieth century was influenced by Rosa Luxemburg (IRL). So, if you were a SPP, then you were IRL. Furthermore, if you were a CPP, then you were IRL. Given the complex nature of this particular statement, it would be a good idea to get this down on paper.

SPP or CPP $\longrightarrow$ IRL

No one who was influenced by Rosa Luxemburg advocated a totalitarian state.

What about this one? Translate before reading on.

If you were IRL, then you did not advocate a totalitarian state (ATS):

IRL $\longrightarrow$ –ATS

Taking both of these together, the link should be clear!

SPP or CPP $\longrightarrow$ IRL $\longrightarrow$ –ATS

By making this connection we can infer a number of things:

SPP $\longrightarrow$ –ATS (and contrapositive: ATS $\longrightarrow$ –SPP)
CPP $\longrightarrow$ –ATS (and contrapositive: ATS $\longrightarrow$ –CPP)

We just need to be sure we can trace our abbreviations back to their actual meanings! Let's look at the answers:

(A) No early twentieth century socialist political philosopher advocated a totalitarian state.

If no SPP advocated a totalitarian state (ATS), then if you were an SPP, you did not ATS.

SPP $\longrightarrow$ –ATS

This is exactly one of the inferences we made by connecting the two conditionals. This is the correct answer.

(B) Every early twentieth century political philosopher who did not advocate a totalitarian state was influenced by Rosa Luxemburg.

We know that IRL $\longrightarrow$ –ATS. This was given to us. Answer (B) says –ATS $\longrightarrow$ IRL. An illegal reversal! While it might *be true, we can't* infer *that it is true for certain. Eliminate it.*

(C) Rosa Luxemburg was the only person to influence every early twentieth century political philosopher who was either socialist or communist.

We can't know if she was the only person. This is way too extreme. Eliminate it.

(D) Every early twentieth century political philosopher who was influenced by Rosa Luxemburg and was not a socialist was a communist.

We don't know this to be true from the information given. There could have been people who were influenced by Rosa but were not socialist OR communist.

(E) Every early twentieth century political philosopher who did not advocate a totalitarian state was either socialist or communist.

Perhaps there were political philosophers that were anarchists and who did not advocate a totalitarian state. From the stimulus, we didn't learn anything we can infer about –ATS.

Let's try another one. Same idea—1:40.

PT22, S4, Q25

Essayist: Every contract negotiator has been lied to by someone or other, and whoever lies to anyone is practicing deception. But, of course, anyone who has been lied to has also lied to someone or other.

If the essayist's statements are true, which one of the following must also be true?

(A) Every contract negotiator has practiced deception.
(B) Not everyone who practices deception is lying to someone.
(C) Not everyone who lies to someone is practicing deception.
(D) Whoever lies to a contract negotiator has been lied to by a contract negotiator.
(E) Whoever lies to anyone is lied to by someone.

This question asks us to find an answer choice that "must be true" based on the information given in the passage. Again, this is what we call an Inference question (to be discussed in greater detail later on).

8

Take a second and read through the paragraph again. Make a list of all the conditional triggers that you encounter. Don't read on until you've given it a shot.

Did you spot the following triggers?

Every
Whoever (meaning every person)
Anyone

Every piece of this paragraph contains conditional logic. Thus, we pretty much know that we can infer the correct answer from a conditional chain. We'll start by translating the conditional statements into arrow diagrams. (Again, if you were able to track the conditionals in your head, that's great. Seeing it written out should strengthen your understanding. If you weren't able to track the pieces mentally, then the diagram will certainly help.)

Every contract negotiator has been lied to by someone or other,

Contract negotiator ⟶ has been lied to

and whoever lies to anyone is practicing deception.

Lie ⟶ deception

But, of course, anyone who has been lied to has also lied to someone or other.

Has been lied to ⟶ lied

Now take a second and see if you can make a chain. Remember, if you're given multiple conditionals, chances are you'll be able to connect them.

Contract negotiator ⟶ has been lied to ⟶ lied ⟶ deception

So, this is saying that every contract negotiator has been lied to, which means every contract negotiator has lied to someone else, which means every contract negotiator has practiced deception!

Contract negotiator ⟶ deception

Let's look at the answer choices:

(A) Every contract negotiator has practiced deception.

This is exactly the inference that we were able to draw above. This must be true, and so this is the correct answer.

(B) Not everyone who practices deception is lying to someone.

We know that if you lie to someone you are practicing deception: lie ⟶ deception. But, we don't know if the reverse is true: deception ⟶ lie. It may or may not be. It's not something we can determine for certain, so this is incorrect.

(C) Not everyone who lies to someone is practicing deception.

We know this is false. We know: lie ⟶ deception. If you lie, you are practicing deception. Every time.

(D) Whoever lies to a contract negotiator has been lied to by a contract negotiator.

There's no way we can know this from our conditional chain.

(E) Whoever lies to anyone is lied to by someone.

We know: have been lied to ⟶ lied, but we don't know the reverse!

Here's another one. This one is a Matching question (to be discussed in greater depth later) that uses conditional logic.

PT15, S2, Q18

Everyone who is a gourmet cook enjoys a wide variety of foods and spices. Since no one who enjoys a wide variety of foods and spices prefers bland foods to all other foods, it follows that anyone who prefers bland foods to all other foods is not a gourmet cook.

The pattern of reasoning displayed in the argument above is most similar to that displayed in which one of the following?

(A) All of the paintings in the Huang Collection will be put up for auction next week. Since the paintings to be auctioned next week are by a wide variety of artists, it follows that the paintings in the Huang Collection are by a wide variety of artists.

(B) All of the paintings in the Huang Collection are abstract. Since no abstract painting will be included in next week's art auction, nothing to be included in next week's art auction is a painting in the Huang Collection.

(C) All of the paintings in the Huang Collection are superb works of art. Since none of the paintings in the Huang Collection is by Roue, it stands to reason that no painting by Roue is a superb work of art.

(D) Every postimpressionist painting from the Huang Collection will be auctioned off next week. No pop art paintings from the Huang Collection will be auctioned off next week. Hence none of the pop art paintings to be auctioned off next week will be from the Huang Collection.

(E) Every painting from the Huang Collection that is to be auctioned off next week is a major work of art. No price can adequately reflect the true value of a major work of art. Hence the prices that will be paid at next week's auction will not adequately reflect the true value of the paintings sold.

Our goal for this question is to choose an answer that uses the same logic structure as the original argument. In this case, the original argument uses conditional logic. Let's translate statement by statement.

Everyone who is a gourmet cook enjoys a wide variety of foods and spices.

gourmet cook ⟶ enjoys wide variety

Since no one who enjoys a wide variety of foods and spices prefers bland foods to all other foods, enjoys wide variety ⟶ −prefers bland foods

it follows that anyone who prefers bland foods to all other foods is not a gourmet cook.

prefers bland foods ⟶ −gourmet cook

The two premises in this argument can be linked to form a three-part chain:

gourmet cook ⟶ enjoys wide variety ⟶ −prefers bland foods

From this, we can infer:

gourmet cook ⟶ −prefers bland foods

Notice that the conclusion is simply the contrapositive of this statement:

it follows that anyone who prefers bland foods to all other foods is not a gourmet cook.

So the argument presents two premises that are linked to form a three-part chain, and the conclusion is simply the contrapositive:

A ⟶ B ⟶ C
So, −C ⟶ −A

That's what we're looking for in our answer choice:

(A) All of the paintings in the Huang Collection will be put up for auction next week. Since the paintings to be auctioned next week are by a wide variety of artists, it follows that the paintings in the Huang Collection are by a wide variety of artists.

Huang paintings ⟶ auction ⟶ wide variety
Thus, Huang paintings ⟶ wide variety

Did you get the relationship above? If so, be careful. This is misleading. Consider the following example:

All of the Dominguez children are at the party. Since the people at the party are of a wide variety of nationalities, the Dominguez children are of a wide variety of nationalities.

Dominguez children ⟶ at party ⟶ wide variety of nationalities

Does this mean: Dominguez children ⟶ wide variety of nationalities? Of course not! The reason is that the conditional logic treats the group as a whole and not the individuals in that group. The same thing is happening with answer (A).

Besides, even if the conclusion were valid, it's not the contrapositive. We want an answer that uses a contrapositive.

(B) All of the paintings in the Huang Collection are abstract. Since no abstract painting will be included in next week's art auction, nothing to be included in next week's art auction is a painting in the Huang Collection.

Huang painting ⟶ abstract ⟶ –auction
So, auction ⟶ –Huang painting

This is the same exact logic! This is the correct answer.

(C) All of the paintings in the Huang Collection are superb works of art. Since none of the paintings in the Huang Collection is by Roue, it stands to reason that no painting by Roue is a superb work of art.

Huang painting ⟶ superb
Huang painting ⟶ –Roue
So, Roue ⟶ –superb

In this case, the two premises cannot be linked, so the conclusion is invalid.

(D) Every postimpressionist painting from the Huang Collection will be auctioned off next week. No pop art paintings from the Huang Collection will be auctioned off next week. Hence none of the pop art paintings to be auctioned off next week will be from the Huang Collection.

Postimpressionist Huang ⟶ auction
Pop art Huang ⟶ –auction
So, auction ⟶ –Huang

We can link the premises to get:

Postimpressionist Huang ⟶ auction ⟶ –pop art Huang
So, pop art auction ⟶ –Huang

This isn't the same structure.

(E) Every painting from the Huang Collection that is to be auctioned off next week is a major work of art. No price can adequately reflect the true value of a major work of art. Hence the prices that will be paid at next week's auction will not adequately reflect the true value of the paintings sold.

Huang auction ⟶ major work ⟶ no price can reflect value

So, prices to be paid at auction will not reflect value.

None of the prices? Not even those paid for works other than Huang paintings? We can't know this. Furthermore, this doesn't use the contrapositive of the chain.

Linking Assumptions

Conditional logic is often used on Assumption questions. Here's a simple example:

> Every child likes ice cream. Everyone who likes ice cream buys ice cream. Thus, every child is rich.

Hmm. Bad argument, right? Where did the "rich" come from? "Rich" seems to be the odd man out—we'll call it the "odd man."

There's obviously a problem here.

Let's translate the conditionals into arrow notation. We'll start with the premises:

> child ⟶ likes ice cream
> likes ice cream ⟶ buys ice cream

And now the conclusion:

> child ⟶ rich

Just as we practiced, we can link the premises together. Look for the shared term and use that as the middle of your link. In this case, the shared term is "likes ice cream."

> child ⟶ likes ice cream ⟶ buys ice cream

Now, think. If the odd man, "rich," were hooked to the end of the chain, we'd be able to go from "child" all the way across to "rich."

> child ⟶ likes ice cream ⟶ buys ice cream ┈┈▸ *rich*

But what did we need to assume in order to connect "rich" to the chain? We needed to assume "buys ice cream ⟶ *rich.*" In other words, we needed to assume:

> Anyone who buys ice cream is rich.

If we put this back into the argument we'll see that this is exactly the missing link that we needed:

> Every child likes ice cream. Everyone who likes ice cream buys ice cream. (Anyone who buys ice cream is rich.) Thus, every child is rich.

Let's review the steps we took:

1. We recognized the conditional triggers. Since there were three conditional statements in the original argument, we knew we could attack this question by linking conditionals.
2. We translated the conditionals into arrow notation.
3. We linked the premises by linking the conditionals. Remember, look for the shared term and make that the middle of the linkage.
4. We hooked the "odd man" to the chain.
5. We identified the assumption by considering what we needed to link the odd man.

Let's try it on a real question. Give yourself 1:20 to answer, and then we'll discuss.

PT35, S1, Q14

Novelists cannot become great as long as they remain in academia. Powers of observation and analysis, which schools successfully hone, are useful to the novelist, but an intuitive grasp of the emotions of everyday life can be obtained only by the kind of immersion in everyday life that is precluded by being an academic.

Which one of the following is an assumption on which the argument depends?

(A) Novelists require some impartiality to get an intuitive grasp of the emotions of everyday life.
(B) No great novelist lacks powers of observation and analysis.
(C) Participation in life, interspersed with impartial observation of life, makes novelists great.
(D) Novelists cannot be great without an intuitive grasp of the emotions of everyday life.
(E) Knowledge of the emotions of everyday life cannot be acquired by merely observing and analyzing life.

Let's look at this question through two lenses. We'll start by approaching this question just as we would any other assumption question. Determine our task, find the core, spot the gap (if we can), eliminate answers not related to the core, and choose between the last men standing. We'll run through a quick, abbreviated version of this now.

Our task is to find a necessary assumption, so we'll need to begin by identifying the argument core:

An intuitive grasp of the emotions of everyday life can be obtained only by the kind of immersion in everyday life that is precluded by being an academic. Academic novelists cannot become great.

In other words:

Academics can't immerse
themselves in daily life, so they
can't get an intuitive grasp of the
emotions of everyday day life.   Academic novelists cannot
                                                                              become great.

Assumption: One who can't get an intuitive grasp of the emotions of everyday life can't be a great novelist.

    (A) Novelists require some impartiality to get an intuitive
          grasp of the emotions of everyday life.

But can they be great without this intuitive grasp? This answer relates to the premise, but fails to connect to the conclusion. Eliminate it.

    (B) No great novelist lacks powers of observation and analysis.

Okay, but what if they lack a grasp of everyday emotions? Can they be great then? This answer relates to the conclusion (being great), but fails to connect to the premise (intuitive grasp of emotions). Eliminate it.

    (C) Participation in life, interspersed with impartial
          observation of life, makes novelists great.

Again, what about lacking an emotional grasp of everyday emotions? Eliminate it.

    (D) Novelists cannot be great without an intuitive grasp of the
          emotions of everyday life.

This one relates the two concepts. Keep it for now.

    (E) Knowledge of the emotions of everyday life cannot be
          acquired by merely observing and analyzing life.

Okay, but what about being great? This one references the premise but fails to tie in the conclusion.

Answer (D) is the correct answer.

How did you do? Did you successfully identify the core? Were you able to spot the gap between not having a grasp of the emotions of everyday life and not being a great writer? Were you able to eliminate at least some of the answer choices quickly? Did you get the right answer? Hopefully this type of question is beginning to feel comfortable for you.

Let's take another look at this question through the conditional logic lens. For those who got this question right the first time, this new perspective will strengthen your understanding of the logic. For those who struggled with this question, the conditional logic approach will allow you to see the inner workings of the logic in a way that perhaps you missed the first time. Here we go.

We'll look at the argument one more time, looking at each sentence in isolation to see if we can express it in conditional terms:

Novelists cannot become great as long as they remain in academia.

Believe it or not, this is a conditional statement. The big clue is the verb of certainty, *cannot*. Think about in terms of guarantees. Does being or doing one thing guarantee another? Indeed. Being an academic novelist guarantees that you will NOT be, or *cannot* be, a great novelist. In other words, if you are an academic novelist, then you are NOT a great novelist.

> academic novelist ⟶ –great novelist

> Powers of observation and analysis, which schools successfully hone, are useful to the novelist,

This statement has no conditional structure, so let's leave it for now.

> but an intuitive grasp of the emotions of everyday life can be obtained only by the kind of immersion in everyday life that is precluded by being an academic.

Did you spot the "only" trigger? An intuitive grasp of the emotions of everyday life can be obtained only by immersion in everyday life. Thus, if you are to have an intuitive grasp of everyday emotions, then you must immerse yourself in everyday life.

> intuitive grasp of emotions ⟶ immerse in everyday life

This sentence also contains a second conditional. Immersion in everyday life is precluded by being an academic. In other words, if you are an academic, you cannot immerse yourself in everyday life.

> academic ⟶ –immerse in everyday life

So, we have the following conditionals:

> intuitive grasp of emotions ⟶ immerse in everyday life
> academic ⟶ –immerse in everyday life

And these premises lead to the following conclusion:

> academic novelist ⟶ –great novelist

Next step, link them up! Notice that the shared term between the premises is "immerse in everyday life." We'll want to use this as the middle of our chain. Also notice, however, that "immerse in everyday life" is positive in the first premise but negative in the second. We can't immediately link them this way. In order to get them both positive or both negative we'll need to take the contrapositive of one of them. Let's do the first one. So we'd get:

> –immerse in everyday life ⟶ –intuitive grasp of emotions
> academic ⟶ –immerse in everyday life

Now we can link them:

> academic ⟶ –immerse in everyday life ⟶ –intuitive grasp of emotions

And these premises are used to support this conclusion:

MANHATTAN
LSAT

academic novelist ———➤ –great novelist

"Great novelist" is the odd man here. It appears only in the conclusion. Let's hook the odd man to the chain:

academic ——➤ –immerse in everyday life ——➤ –intuitive grasp of emotions ·····➤ *–great novelist*

Now we can see that "academic" leads to "*-great novelist,*" and the conclusion is now valid. But what did we need to assume in order to hook the odd man to the chain? We needed to assume:

–intuitive grasp of emotions ———➤ *–great novelist*

In other words, if you don't have an intuitive grasp of emotions, you can't be a great novelist. This is exactly what answer (D) says:

(D) Novelists cannot be great without an intuitive grasp of the
     emotions of everyday life.

So, we looked at two ways to tackle this Assumption question. The first used our standard argument core approach, and the second used a conditional logic diagram approach. Ideally, you should be familiar with each of these methods.

Some and Most

Okay, we've spent the entire chapter harping on the idea that conditional statements express guarantees. We include a discussion of "some" and "most" here because "some" and "most" statements do NOT express guarantees, but they are often confused with conditional statements. Here's an example illustrating the difference:

All movies have a message. (movie ——➤ message)

This means every movie. Every time. Always. No exceptions. Guaranteed.

Most movies have a message.

We might be tempted to write "movie ——➤ message," but "most" means "most," NOT "all!" In other words, for any given movie, there's a good chance (more than half) that it will have a message, but it's NOT guaranteed.

Some movies have a message.

This is even less certain. "Some" simply means more than zero—at least one. "Some" is definitely not a guarantee.

If we can't treat "some" and "most" statements in the same way that we treat conditional statements, what do we do with them?

First, it's important to understand the context of "some" and "most" on the LSAT. Generally speaking, "some" and "most" statements are used most often on Inference questions (to be discussed in a later chapter). So, when learning how to deal with these statements, it's very important to think about these statements in terms of inferences. In other words, given a set of "some" and "most" statements, what can we infer? What can we conclude? What do we know *for sure*? Let's develop a set of rules that will come in handy in drawing valid inferences from "some" and "most" statements.

"Some" and "Most" Equivalents

The first step is to be able to recognize and understand the words and phrases that are synonyms of "some" and "most." Here's a list of the most common:

Words and Phrases	Definition
some	**one or more**
most	**more than half**
a few	= some
majority	= most
nearly all	= most
many	= some

Single Statement Inferences

Next, we need to understand what sorts of inferences we can draw from a single "some" or "most" statement. Look at this:

Some teachers are musicians.

Can we reverse this statement? Indeed we can. If some teachers are musicians, then it must be true that some musicians are teachers (maybe not most or all, but definitely some). So, we have our first inference:

Original Statement	Inference
Some A's are B's.	Some B's are A's.

What about this one?

Most ice cream is delicious.

Can we reverse this one? We've purposely chosen a real-life statement to make it easier to consider. Think about it. Most ice cream is delicious. Are most delicious things ice cream? Of course not. There are zillions of delicious foods that are not ice cream. This statement cannot necessarily be reversed. The only thing we know for sure is that *some* delicious things (even if just a tiny fraction) are ice cream. This leads to our second inference:

Original Statement	Inference
Some A's are B's.	Some B's are A's.
Most A's are B's.	Some B's are A's.

Now let's look at this one:

> All apples are fruits.

This sort of statement should be familiar—it's a conditional statement, a guarantee. All apples, every apple, every single one, is a fruit. We already know that we can NOT reverse this one, but we also know from this statement that some fruits must be apples:

Original Statement	Inference
Some A's are B's.	Some B's are A's.
Most A's are B's.	Some B's are A's.
All A's are B's.	Some B's are A's.

Not too bad, right? Now let's see what happens when we get more than one statement.

Multiple Statement Inferences

Suppose we had the following two statements:

> Some people are happy.
> Some people are old.

What can you infer? Can you infer that some happy people are old? Or that most happy people are old? Or maybe that all happy people are old? Let's use a diagram to figure this out. Assume that the box below represents all people:

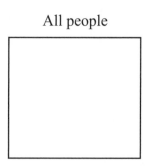

All people

We know that *some* of these people are happy. Remember "some" means one or more. So, if we were going to shade part of the box to represent the happy people, how much would we shade? Well, it's unclear. It could be less than half, but it could also be more than half. We'll start with this—the stars will represent the happy people:

All people

We also know that *some* people are old. "Some" means one or more. Let's use circles to represent the old people:

All people

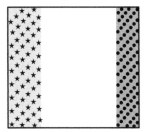

This is a valid representation of our statements, isn't it? Some are happy, and some are old. So what can we conclude? It seems from the picture that we would conclude that no happy people are old. In other words, the patterns don't overlap. Be careful though. Couldn't we have represented our statements like this?

All people

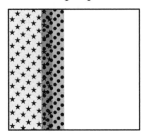

Or maybe even like this?

All people

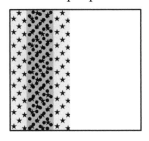

The answer is yes. All three of these representations are accurate. Each one of them *could* be an actual representation of the statements. However, we don't know *for sure* that any of them represent the actual scenario, so we can't really conclude anything. Maybe none of them overlap (no old people are happy), maybe some of them overlap (some old people are happy), or maybe all of them overlap (all old people are happy). Without more information, we can't know for sure. This leads to our first overlap inference:

Original Statement	Overlap Type	Overlap Inference
Some A's are B's. Some A's are C's.	Some + Some	Can't infer anything about overlap between B and C. (They may or may not overlap.)

Let's look at two more statements:

> Most people are happy.
> Some people are old.

We can analyze this using the same thought process. "Most" means more than half, and "some" means one or more. We'll start by filling in "most" of the box with happy people:

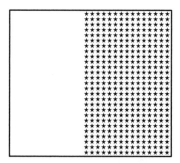

Since we're dealing with a "most" statement, we need to be sure that more than half of the box is filled.

Take a second and think about how you could shade the box with old people. Remember, "some" people are old. There are actually a number of possibilities, aren't there? Here are three such possibilities:

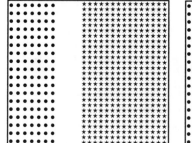 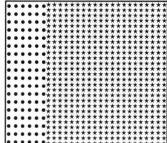 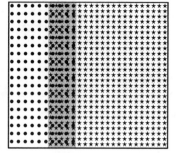

Most people are happy (stars), and some people are old (circles). Do we know if they overlap? Well, they might (the right picture), but they might not (the left picture and the center picture). Perhaps all the old people are happy! We don't know for sure, so we can't infer anything about the overlap.

Original Statement	Overlap Type	Overlap Inference
Some A's are B's. Some A's are C's.	Some + Some	Can't infer anything about overlap between B and C. (They may or may not overlap.)
Most A's are B's. Some A's are C's.	Most + Some	Can't infer anything about overlap between B and C. (They may or may not overlap.)

One more combination:

> Most people are happy.
> Most people are old.

Now, set your watch for 2 minutes. Use this time to really think about what you can or cannot infer about the overlap of happy and old in this case. Use a box diagram if need be, and don't read on until you have an answer.

Again, we'll start by filling "most" of the box with happies:

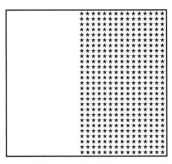

"Most" people are also old. We'll need to fill "most" of the box with old people as well. There are a few ways we can do this:

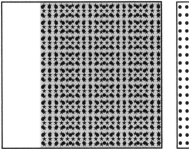  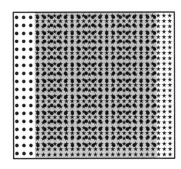

All of these are valid, aren't they? In all three cases, more than half the box are stars, and more than half are circles. And, in every case, there is at least *some* overlap. Try to come up with a shaded scenario for which there is no overlap. You can't do it. (If you're having trouble seeing that, imagine there are only 10 people in the world; you'll need at least 6 happies and 6 oldies. Can you avoid an overlap?) When we combine two "most" statements, at least *some* will always overlap.

Original Statement	Overlap Type	Overlap Inference
Some A's are B's. Some A's are C's.	Some + Some	Can't infer anything about overlap between B and C. (They may or may not overlap.)
Most A's are B's. Some A's are C's.	Most + Some	Can't infer anything about overlap between B and C. (They may or may not overlap.)
Most A's are B's. Most A's are C's.	Most + Most	Some B's are C's.

Got it? Time to practice.

DRILL IT: Some and Most

Choose the answer that must be true from the information given.

1. Some cars are sedans and some cars are red.

    (A) Most cars that are sedans are red.

    (B) Some things that are red are cars.

    (C) None of the above.

2. Most people are patient and most people are sympathetic.

    (A) Some sympathetic people are patient.

    (B) Most patient people are sympathetic.

    (C) None of the above.

3. Most children play sports, and some children play instruments.

    (A) Some children who play instruments play sports.

    (B) Some people who play sports are children.

    (C) None of the above.

4. Many dogs weigh more than 20 pounds, and many dogs are difficult to train.

    (A) Most dogs that weigh more than 20 pounds are difficult to train.

    (B) Some dogs that are difficult to train weigh more than 20 pounds.

    (C) None of the above.

5. The majority of flights arrive late, and few flights have empty seats.

    (A) Some flights with empty seats arrive late.

    (B) Most flights that arrive late have empty seats.

    (C) None of the above.

6. Every ethical person succeeds, and some Americans are ethical.

    (A) Some people who succeed are Americans.

    (B) Most Americans succeed.

    (C) None of the above.

7. Nearly all of Jason's books are fiction books, and all of Jason's books are written in Spanish.

    (A) Most of Jason's books are fiction books written in Spanish.

    (B) Most of Jason's books are not fiction books.

    (C) None of the above.

8. Some children are happy, some children are healthy, and some children are smart.

    (A) Some children are both happy and healthy.

    (B) Some children are at once happy, healthy, and smart.

    (C) None of the above.

> Want more practice? Try playing "Ah-hah" in our LSAT Arcade. (www.manhattanlsat.com/arcade)

8

Solutions: Some and Most

Choose the answer that must be true from the information given.

1. Some cars are sedans and some cars are red.

   (A) Most cars that are sedans are red.

   (B) Some things that are red are cars.

   (C) None of the above.

2. Most people are patient and most people are sympathetic.

   (A) Some sympathetic people are patient.

   (B) Most patient people are sympathetic.

   (C) None of the above.

3. Most children play sports, and some children play instruments.

   (A) Some children who play instruments play sports.

   (B) Some people who play sports are children.

   (C) None of the above.

4. Many dogs weigh more than 20 pounds, and many dogs are difficult to train.

   (A) Most dogs that weigh more than 20 pounds are difficult to train.

   (B) Some dogs that are difficult to train weigh more than 20 pounds.

   (C) None of the above.

5. The majority of flights arrive late, and few flights have empty seats.

   (A) Some flights with empty seats arrive late.

   (B) Most flights that arrive late have empty seats.

   (C) None of the above.

6. Every ethical person succeeds, and some Americans are ethical.

   (A) Some people who succeed are Americans.

   (B) Most Americans succeed.

   (C) None of the above.

7. Nearly all of Jason's books are fiction books, and all of Jason's books are written in Spanish.

   (A) Most of Jason's books are fiction books written in Spanish.

   (B) Most of Jason's books are not fiction books.

   (C) None of the above.

8. Some children are happy, some children are healthy, and some children are smart.

   (A) Some children are both happy and healthy.

   (B) Some children are at once happy, healthy, and smart.

   (C) None of the above.

Conclusion

We've covered a lot of tough material in this chapter. Here's a summary of the main points:

1. A standard conditional statement is expressed in "If/Then" form:

   IF one is happy, THEN one is smiling.

2. The "IF" part of the statement is called the *sufficient* condition because it is *sufficient* on its own to guarantee the "THEN" part of the statement. The "THEN" part of the statement is called the *necessary* condition because it must be true when the sufficient condition is satisfied.

3. We can express conditional statements using arrow notation:

   happy $\longrightarrow$ smiling

4. For any conditional statement, the *contrapositive* can be inferred. The *contrapositive* is found be reversing and negating the original statement:

   –smiling $\longrightarrow$ –happy

5. There are four types of compound conditionals. Some can be split into two separate statements, others cannot:

   AND in the Outcome (split):

   If one is happy, then one is smiling AND cheerful.

   happy $\longrightarrow$ smiling
   happy $\longrightarrow$ cheerful

   OR in the Trigger (split):

   If one is happy OR cheerful, then one is smiling.

   happy $\longrightarrow$ smiling
   cheerful $\longrightarrow$ smiling

   AND in the Trigger (can't split):

   If one is happy AND cheerful, then one is smiling.

   happy + cheerful $\longrightarrow$ smiling

   OR in the Outcome (can't split):

   If one is happy, then one is smiling OR cheerful.

   happy $\longrightarrow$ smiling or cheerful

6. To take the contrapositive of a compound conditional statement, reverse and negate the terms, and swap AND for OR (or vice versa):

   happy + cheerful $\longrightarrow$ smiling
   –smiling $\longrightarrow$ –happy or –cheerful

party $\longrightarrow$ birthday or graduation

–birthday + –graduation $\longrightarrow$ –party

7. "Only" is one of the most important words on the LSAT. Watch out for "only if" and "if and only if" language:

Jenny smiles only if she is happy.

smiles $\longrightarrow$ happy

Jenny smiles if, and only if, she is happy.

smiles $\longleftrightarrow$ happy

8. Be on the lookout for words that express a guarantee. Words like *always, never, every, anyone, everyone, etc.* are generally used on the LSAT to express conditional relationships:

Every child likes chocolate.

child $\longrightarrow$ likes chocolate

9. "Except perhaps" and "unless" are used to express conditional statements:

The picnic will be canceled unless the sun comes out.

–sun comes out $\longrightarrow$ canceled picnic

10. Learn to link conditional statements to form a conditional chain:

A $\longrightarrow$ B

B $\longrightarrow$ C

So, A $\longrightarrow$ B $\longrightarrow$ C

11. "Some" and "most" are not "all!" Don't confuse "some" and "most" with conditional logic. Know your "some" and "most" rules—you'll need them on some Inference questions.

DRILL IT: Conditional Logic Questions

The following eight questions represent a mix of question types, some of which you have not yet studied. The common thread is that each question contains conditional logic. You will be forced to use your understanding of conditional logic in flexible ways, so don't get too mechanical! If you're still feeling shaky, do these untimed on another sheet of paper. Otherwise, give yourself about 11 minutes.

1. PT13, S2, Q9

In a mature tourist market such as Bellaria there are only two ways hotel owners can increase profits: by building more rooms or by improving what is already there. Rigid land-use laws in Bellaria rule out construction of new hotels or, indeed, any expansion of hotel capacity. It follows that hotel owners cannot increase their profits in Bellaria since Bellarian hotels _____.

Which one of the following logically completes the argument?

(A) are already operating at an occupancy rate approaching 100 percent year-round

(B) could not have been sited any more attractively than they are even in the absence of land-use laws

(C) have to contend with upward pressures on the cost of labor which stem from an incipient shortage of trained personnel

(D) already provide a level of luxury that is at the limits of what even wealthy patrons are prepared to pay for

(E) have shifted from serving mainly Bellarian tourists to serving foreign tourists traveling in organized tour groups

2. PT23, S2, Q9

Every action has consequences, and among the consequences of any action are other actions. And knowing whether an action is good requires knowing whether its consequences are good, but we cannot know the future, so good actions are impossible.

Which one of the following is an assumption on which the argument depends?

(A) Some actions have only other actions as consequences.

(B) We can know that past actions were good.

(C) To know that an action is good requires knowing that refraining from performing it is bad.

(D) Only actions can be the consequences of other actions.

(E) For an action to be good we must be able to know that it is good.

3. PT13, S2, Q26

If Blankenship Enterprises has to switch suppliers in the middle of a large production run, the company will not show a profit for the year. Therefore, if Blankenship Enterprises in fact turns out to show no profit for the year, it will also turn out to be true that the company had to switch suppliers during a large production run.

The reasoning in the argument is most vulnerable to criticism on which one of the following grounds?

(A) The argument is a circular argument made up of an opening claim followed by a conclusion that merely paraphrases that claim.

(B) The argument fails to establish that a condition under which a phenomenon is said to occur is the only condition under which that phenomenon occurs.

(C) The argument involves an equivocation, in that the word "profit" is allowed to shift its meaning during the course of the argument.

(D) The argument erroneously uses an exceptional, isolated case to support a universal conclusion.

(E) The argument explains one event as being caused by another event, even though both events must actually have been caused by some third, unidentified event.

8

4. PT23, S3, Q14

If the proposed tax reduction package is adopted this year, the library will be forced to discontinue its daily story hours for children. But if the daily story hours are discontinued, many parents will be greatly inconvenienced. So the proposed tax reduction package will not be adopted this year.

Which one of the following, if assumed, allows the argument's conclusion to be properly drawn?

(A) Any tax reduction package that will not force the library to discontinue daily story hours will be adopted this year.

(B) Every tax reduction package that would force the library to discontinue daily story hours would greatly inconvenience parents.

(C) No tax reduction package that would greatly inconvenience parents would fail to force the library to discontinue daily story hours.

(D) No tax reduction package that would greatly inconvenience parents will be adopted this year.

(E) Any tax reduction package that will not greatly inconvenience parents will be adopted this year.

Challenge Questions

5. PT14, S4, Q9

Since anyone who supports the new tax plan has no chance of being elected, and anyone who truly understands economics would not support the tax plan, only someone who truly understands economics would have any chance of being elected.

The reasoning in the argument is flawed because the argument ignores the possibility that some people who

(A) truly understand economics do not support the tax plan

(B) truly understand economics have no chance of being elected

(C) do not support the tax plan have no chance of being elected

(D) do not support the tax plan do not truly understand economics

(E) have no chance of being elected do not truly understand economics

6. PT24, S2, Q24

No mathematical proposition can be proven true by observation. It follows that it is impossible to know any mathematical proposition to be true.

The conclusion follows logically if which one of the following is assumed?

(A) Only propositions that can be proven true can be known to be true.

(B) Observation alone cannot be used to prove the truth of any proposition.

(C) If a proposition can be proven true by observation, then it can be known to be true.

(D) Knowing a proposition to be true is impossible only if it cannot be proven true by observation.

(E) Knowing a proposition to be true requires proving it true by observation.

7. PT18, S2, Q23

Teachers are effective only when they help their students become independent learners. Yet not until teachers have the power to make decisions in their own classrooms can they enable their students to make their own decisions. Students' capability to make their own decisions is essential to their becoming independent learners. Therefore, if teachers are to be effective, they must have the power to make decisions in their own classrooms.

According to the argument, each of the following could be true of teachers who have enabled their students to make their own decisions EXCEPT:

(A) Their students have not become independent learners.

(B) They are not effective teachers.

(C) They are effective teachers.

(D) They have the power to make decisions in their own classrooms.

(E) They do not have the power to make decisions in their own classrooms.

8. PT24, S3, Q10

All material bodies are divisible into parts, and everything divisible is imperfect. It follows that all material bodies are imperfect. It likewise follows that the spirit is not a material body.

The final conclusion above follows logically if which one of the following is assumed?

    (A) Everything divisible is a material body.
    (B) Nothing imperfect is indivisible.
    (C) The spirit is divisible.
    (D) The spirit is perfect.
    (E) The spirit is either indivisible or imperfect.

8

SOLUTIONS: Conditional Logic Questions

1. PT13, S2, Q9

In a mature tourist market such as Bellaria there are only two ways hotel owners can increase profits: by building more rooms or by improving what is already there. Rigid land-use laws in Bellaria rule out construction of new hotels or, indeed, any expansion of hotel capacity. It follows that hotel owners cannot increase their profits in Bellaria since Bellarian hotels _____.

Which one of the following logically completes the argument?

  (A) are already operating at an occupancy rate approaching 100 percent year-round
  (B) could not have been sited any more attractively than they are even in the absence of land-use laws
  (C) have to contend with upward pressures on the cost of labor which stem from an incipient shortage of trained personnel
  (D) already provide a level of luxury that is at the limits of what even wealthy patrons are prepared to pay for
  (E) have shifted from serving mainly Bellarian tourists to serving foreign tourists traveling in organized tour groups

(D) is the correct answer.

We're facing an Inference question, which is not in the Assumption Family, so there's no core to find. We'll learn more about this question type later. Instead of a core, we're given a rule and asked to apply it. The rule is:

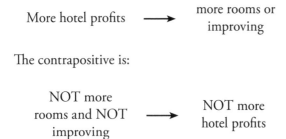

The contrapositive is:

Then we're told that it's impossible to build more rooms, and thus hotel owners cannot increase their profits since _____.

We're looking for something that completes this argument. If the conclusion is NOT more hotel profits, we can arrive at that by "triggering" the sufficient side of the contrapositive shown above. We already know that the hotels cannot build more rooms, so the argument will be valid if improvements to the hotels are also impossible.

(D) provides the other sufficient factor. If hotels are already providing the highest level of luxury possible (or at least what even the wealthy customers are willing to pay for), then the hotels cannot improve upon what already exists. Because of how it's phrased, this isn't an obvious answer, so understanding why the wrong answers are wrong comes in handy.

(A) is irrelevant to the argument. Full occupancy does not lead to "NOT more hotel profits." Perhaps in the real world this would be relevant, but we're asked to complete the argument provided.

(B) is out of scope. Where the hotel is sited is irrelevant as far as the argument is concerned.

(C) is out of scope—the cost of labor is relevant in the real world, but it's not discussed in the argument. Furthermore, how much will the cost of labor rise? Will it become a problem?

(E) is completely irrelevant.

2. PT23, S2, Q9

Every action has consequences, and among the consequences of any action are other actions. And knowing whether an action is good requires knowing whether its consequences are good, but we cannot know the future, so good actions are impossible.

Which one of the following is an assumption on which the argument depends?

(A) Some actions have only other actions as consequences.

(B) We can know that past actions were good.

(C) To know that an action is good requires knowing that refraining from performing it is bad.

(D) Only actions can be the consequences of other actions.

(E) For an action to be good we must be able to know that it is good.

(E) is the correct answer.

Let's look at this question using a formal conditional logic approach and then again using the core approach:

Formal Approach

Let's take this problem phrase by phrase:

Every action has consequences,

$$\text{action} \longrightarrow \text{consequence}$$

and among the consequences of any action are other actions.

$$\text{consequence} \longrightarrow \text{action}$$

So far we have a circular argument!

And knowing whether an action is good requires knowing whether its consequences are good,

$$\text{know if action good} \longrightarrow \text{know if consequences good}$$

but we cannot know the future, so good actions are impossible.

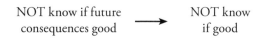

Let's try to chain something to lead towards the conclusion, starting with NOT knowing future consequences are good:

And now we have to attach the conclusion somehow:

$$\text{NOT know if future consequences good} \longrightarrow \text{NOT know if good} \longrightarrow \text{good actions are NOT possible}$$

So what we're missing is

$$\text{NOT know if good} \longrightarrow \text{good actions are NOT possible}$$

Looking for an answer that might be a match, (A) through (D) do not include any reference to being good, but let's check (E):

(E) For an action to be good, we must be able to know that it is good.

$$\text{action is good} \longrightarrow \text{know that the action is good}$$

And the contrapositive:

$$\text{NOT know that the action is good} \longrightarrow \text{action is NOT good}$$

It's a match!

It turns out that the first conditional statement

about every action having a consequence is not part of the chain we used to arrive at the conclusion. (However, it is important background that makes the complete argument valid since if not every action had consequences, then there could be good, though consequenceless actions that could not be evaluated.) This is why it's important to not be overly formal with formal logic! Keep your eye on the linkable premises and the conclusion.

Core Approach

The conclusion of this argument is that good actions are impossible. How sad. Support for this is provided in the beginning of that sentence: "we cannot know the future and thus whether consequences are good." But why is that relevant? The first sentence provides the other premise: knowing whether an action is good requires knowing whether its consequences are good.

The core can be represented like this:

> We have to know if consequences are good to know if an action is good.
>
> +
>
> We cannot know future (consequences) ➡️ Good actions are impossible.

With a bit of thinking, the two premises can be combined into one premise, leaving us with this core:

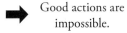

> We cannot know if an ➡️ Good actions are
> action is good.   impossible.

Did you notice the term shift? The premises are focused on whether an action or its consequences can be known to be good, while the conclusion is about whether a good action can be possible.

Scanning the answer choices, only (E) connects knowing whether an action is good and that action being good. If we negate (E)—this is a Necessary Assumption question, so the negation test applies here—we're left with an action can be good even if we don't know that it is good. If that were true, the argument would not make sense since good actions would be possible.

The wrong answers all fail to connect the premises to the conclusion.

(A) does not discuss actions being possible.

(B) similarly fails to connect to the conclusion. Furthermore, we are not concerned with past actions!

(C) is out of scope—the argument is not about whether one refrains from an action or what one knows if one refrains. It is flawed also because it doesn't discuss an action being good.

(D) does not discuss an action being good. Another premise booster (or premise confuser!).

Which approach is easier or faster? It's important to be judicious in using your formal logic notation—sometimes fancier isn't faster.

3. PT13, S2, Q26

If Blankenship Enterprises has to switch suppliers in the middle of a large production run, the company will not show a profit for the year. Therefore, if Blankenship Enterprises in fact turns out to show no profit for the year, it will also turn out to be true that the company had to switch suppliers during a large production run.

The reasoning in the argument is most vulnerable to criticism on which one of the following grounds?

(A) The argument is a circular argument made up of an opening claim followed by a conclusion that merely paraphrases that claim.

(B) The argument fails to establish that a condition under which a phenomenon is said to occur is the only condition under which that phenomenon occurs.

(C) The argument involves an equivocation, in that the word "profit" is allowed to shift its meaning during the course of the argument.

(D) The argument erroneously uses an exceptional, isolated case to support a universal conclusion.

(E) The argument explains one event as being caused by another event, even though both events must actually have been caused by some third, unidentified event.

(B) is the correct answer.

This flaw question hinges on a flaw in conditional logic. The conclusion of this argument is actually a relationship: B.E. not profit → B.E. switch suppliers. The support for this is a different relationship: B.E. switch suppliers → B.E. not profit.

Notice something fishy? To boil it down further: –profit → switch, because switch → –profit. It's reversed logic!

(B) uses tricky language to describe this flaw. One way to unpack (B) is to consider what relationship added to switch → –profit would allow us to conclude that –profit → switch? We would need the reverse of the premise (giving us a bi-conditional): Blankenship Enterprises will not show a profit if, and only if, the company has to switch suppliers during a large production run (–profit ←→ sharing). The argument "acts" as if this added relationship exists—it assumes it.

Since (B) seems rather intimidating, let's decode each part:

The argument fails to establish…

> *The argument doesn't say…*

that a condition under which a phenomenon is said to occur…

> *that not showing a profit because of switching suppliers (switch → –profit)*

is the only condition under which that phenomenon occurs…

> *is the only reason the company wouldn't show a profit (–profit → switch).*

Let's look at the other answer choices:

(A) is tempting because there is something wrong with the argument's logic, and the same elements are used repeatedly, which might feel circular. But this is not a circular argument in which the premise is restated as a conclusion. (Here's an example of a circular argument: Flying on planes is not dangerous, therefore one form of travel, flying, is not dangerous). It should be rather apparent if an argument is circular.

(C) is incorrect because there is no shifting of the meaning of "profit." A shift in word meaning is rare on the LSAT, and is usually pretty noticeable.

(D) is not true; there's no indication that the year that the argument mentions is exceptional or isolated, and the conclusion is not particularly universal.

(E) is a flaw, but not of this argument. The support for the conclusion is a causal relationship, not simply two correlated events.

4. PT23, S3, Q14

If the proposed tax reduction package is adopted this year, the library will be forced to discontinue its daily story hours for children. But if the daily story hours are discontinued, many parents will be greatly inconvenienced. So the proposed tax reduction package will not be adopted this year.

Which one of the following, if assumed, allows the argument's conclusion to be properly drawn?

(A) Any tax reduction package that will not force the library to discontinue daily story hours will be adopted this year.

(B) Every tax reduction package that would force the library to discontinue daily story hours would greatly inconvenience parents.

(C) No tax reduction package that would greatly inconvenience parents would fail to force the library to discontinue daily story hours.

(D) No tax reduction package that would greatly inconvenience parents will be adopted this year.

(E) Any tax reduction package that will not greatly inconvenience parents will be adopted this year.

8

(D) is the correct answer.

This argument can be approached formally:

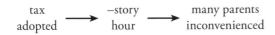

Therefore, tax NOT adopted.

How can this argument chain lead to the tax package NOT being adopted? The contrapositive of the chain leads to that:

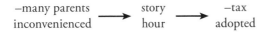

To trigger this chain, we'd need to know that parents will not accept being inconvenienced. More specifically, as (D) states, no legislation that will inconvenience parents will be adopted. In other words, parents will not accept the original chain being triggered as they refuse to endure its final result.

(A) is out of scope since it is about tax reductions that do not discontinue story hours. (A)'s logic, story hour → adopted, is not helpful to the argument.

(B) is an extreme premise booster. We already know that –story hour → inconvenience. It's irrelevant whether this is true for all tax reduction packages.

(C) is a bit confusing. When a statement is filled with negatives, try to restate it in the positive. We can rephrase (C) as, "Every tax reduction package that would inconvenience parents will force the end of story hours." This is similar to (B). We already know what would happen if the proposed tax reduction package were to pass.

(E) is similar to (A). We aren't interested in tax reductions that do not inconvenience parents.

Challenge Problems

5. PT14, S4, Q9

Since anyone who supports the new tax plan has no chance of being elected, and anyone who truly understands economics would not support the tax plan, only someone who truly understands economics would have any chance of being elected.

The reasoning in the argument is flawed because the argument ignores the possibility that some people who

(A) truly understand economics do not support the tax plan
(B) truly understand economics have no chance of being elected
(C) do not support the tax plan have no chance of being elected
(D) do not support the tax plan do not truly understand economics
(E) have no chance of being elected do not truly understand economics

(D) is the correct answer.

This argument is best approached formally since the stimulus contains three conditional logic statements, and each answer choice is a conditional statement as well. Let's dig in:

Since anyone who supports the new tax plan has no chance of being elected,

$$\text{support} \longrightarrow \text{NO chance}$$

and anyone who truly understands economics would not support the tax plan,

$$\text{understand econ.} \longrightarrow \text{NOT support}$$

only someone who truly understands economics would have any chance of being elected.

$$\text{chance} \longrightarrow \text{understand econ.}$$

The last sentence is the conclusion. Let's see if we can link up the premises to make the conclusion correct. We'll start with the sufficient part of the conclusion:

$$chance \longrightarrow understand\ econ.$$

We can link the contrapositive of the first statement to that:

$$chance \longrightarrow \begin{matrix} NOT \\ support \end{matrix} \longrightarrow \begin{matrix} understand \\ econ. \end{matrix}$$

But there's no way to connect anything to NOT support or to understand econ. This is the flaw. It's assuming that NOT support → understand econ., and this is what (D) points out by providing a counterexample (a situation in which there is both NOT support and NOT understand econ.).

Each of the other answer choices is a counterexample to a link that wouldn't complete the argument (and neither would their contrapositives).

(A) understand econ. $\longrightarrow$ support

(B) understand econ. $\longrightarrow$ chance

(C) NOT support $\longrightarrow$ chance

(E) NO chance $\longrightarrow$ understand econ

6. PT24, S2, Q24

No mathematical proposition can be proven true by observation. It follows that it is impossible to know any mathematical proposition to be true.

The conclusion follows logically if which one of the following is assumed?

(A) Only propositions that can be proven true can be known to be true.

(B) Observation alone cannot be used to prove the truth of any proposition.

(C) If a proposition can be proven true by ob-servation, then it can be known to be true.

(D) Knowing a proposition to be true is im-possible only if it cannot be proven true by observation.

(E) Knowing a proposition to be true requires proving it true by observation.

(E) is the correct answer.

Math proposition can't be proven true by observation → Math proposition can't be known to be true

With this problem, the core approach and a more formal approach are one and the same. The key is to notice the term shift. The premise is about proving something true by observation, while the conclusion is about something being known to be true. If you were reading like a debater, you may have thought, "Perhaps some things are known to be true though they cannot be proven true by observation (for example, provable through deduction)."

(E) fills this gap: know that proposition is true → proving true by observation. Its contrapositive is: can't be proven true by observation → can't know proposition to be true.

There are some very tempting wrong answers here:

(A) provides us this: propositions known to be true → propositions proven true. This seems like what we need—it definitely has terms we saw in the argument. However, (A) is not specific about proving true "by observation." (A) may seem like a sufficient assumption since it is broader than what we need. However, the fact that something can't be proven true by observation does not mean that it cannot be proven true by some other means.

Consider this analogous flaw:

If you don't own some sort of vehicle, you can't move heavy furniture. So, since Peter doesn't have an SUV, he can't move the couch.

Perhaps Peter has a truck!

(B) connects observation and proving the truth of something. This is a premise booster. We already know that observation can't prove a mathematical proposition. Where's the connection to knowing something to be true?

(C) tells us that proposition proven true → known to be true. This is the negation of what we need, (and, like (A), is not specific to proving true by observation).

(D) is tempting since it references proving by observation. But the logic is the reverse of what we need. The conditional logic in (D) is NOT knowing a proposition to be true → NOT proven by observation. We need NOT proven true by observation → NOT know proposition to be true.

7. PT18, S2, Q23

Teachers are effective only when they help their students become independent learners. Yet not until teachers have the power to make decisions in their own classrooms can they enable their students to make their own decisions. Students' capability to make their own decisions is essential to their becoming independent learners. Therefore, if teachers are to be effective, they must have the power to make decisions in their own classrooms.

According to the argument, each of the following could be true of teachers who have enabled their students to make their own decisions EXCEPT:

    (A) Their students have not become independent learners.
    (B) They are not effective teachers.
    (C) They are effective teachers.
    (D) They have the power to make decisions in their own classrooms.
    (E) They do not have the power to make decisions in their own classrooms.

(E) is the correct answer.

What a hairy looking question! But, when taken apart carefully, this one actually folds quite easily. First, let's notice that this is not an Assumption Family question. Here we're asked to apply an argument in order to find something that we can infer (prove) to be false. There's no flaw or assumption to uncover in the argument. Thus, we're not reading the argument like a debater; we're reading to grasp the rules. We can translate each sentence as follows:

Sentence 1: t. effective → s. ind. learners

Sentence 2: (t. enables) s. decisions → t. decisions

Sentence 3: s. ind. learning → s. decisions

Conclusion: t. effective → t. decisions

Notice that we've taken some liberty in paraphrasing, and that's both crucial and dangerous. In order to quickly boil down an argument to simple statements, we often have to reduce ideas like "the power to make decisions in their own classrooms" to "t. decisions," but it's important to know that we may have lost some crucial details and that we may need to reconsider those details if we find multiple tempting answer choices.

Let's link up our statements. From the conclusion, we know that we can link all the way from t. effective to t. decisions. Indeed, it is possible:

t. effective → s. ind. learners → s. decisions → t. decisions

The question asks us what cannot be possible if (t. enables) s. decisions. Looking at our chain, that's triggering our third element, requiring (i.e., triggering) all the elements that are down the chain. In this case, all that is required is t. make decisions, and so we know that (E) cannot be true.

All the wrong answers are either "upstream" on the chain, or are not even on it:

(A) offers something not even on the chain: s. NOT ind. learners.

(B) is similar: t. NOT effective.

(C) is tempting, since t. effective is on the chain. However, we cannot infer up a logic chain.

(D) is t. make decisions, something that we can infer! But don't forget your mission—we need to find what CANNOT be true.

8

8. PT24, S3, Q10

All material bodies are divisible into parts, and everything divisible is imperfect. It follows that all material bodies are imperfect. It likewise follows that the spirit is not a material body.

The final conclusion above follows logically if which one of the following is assumed?

(A) Everything divisible is a material body.
(B) Nothing imperfect is indivisible.
(C) The spirit is divisible.
(D) The spirit is perfect.
(E) The spirit is either indivisible or imperfect.

(D) is the correct answer.

Core Approach

material
bodies NOT   ➡   spirit is NOT
perfect   material body

The gap here is that if something is imperfect, it can't be the spirit. Or, as (D) states, the spirit is perfect.

Formal Approach

material bodies → (material bodies) divisible → (material bodies) NOT perfect → (material bodies) NOT spirit

We're asked to find a sufficient assumption. (D) provides us the link between the last two elements of the chain, specifically the contrapositive: spirit → perfect (e.g., NOT imperfect).

Which is easier? It depends on you. The approaches were not very different because, as is often the case, the gap that the answer hinges upon is found in the final connection, which is essentially the core of the argument. In short, if you can get to the core of an argument, it's often faster than a more formal approach.

Looking at the wrong answers, none of them provide the right connection:

(A) provides a reversal of a relationship in the premise: divisible → material.

(B) also provides a reversal of a relationship in the premise: imperfect → divisible.

(C) tells us that spirit → divisible. If that's true, then spirit is imperfect. This doesn't help the argument, it actually negates it!

(E) offers a choice: spirit → NOT divisible or NOT perfect. If we knew that spirit is definitely NOT divisible, then we could conclude that spirit is not material (by applying the contrapositive of "All material bodies are divisible…"). However, we don't know that spirit is definitely NOT divisible, since it might be NOT perfect (it's an either/or statement!). If spirit were NOT perfect, we could not infer that spirit is immaterial; actually, we would be unable to infer anything about that using the given premises.

Chapter *of* 9

Logical Reasoning

Principle Example
Questions

Beyond Assumption Family Questions

Up until now, we've focused almost exclusively on Assumption Family questions. We've looked at Assumption questions, Flaw questions, Strengthen questions, Weaken questions, and Principle Support questions. All of these require that we find the argument core, and then choose an answer to address that core.

Now it's time to move beyond Assumption Family questions. The first NON-Assumption Family question type we'll look at is called Principle Example. This type is not to be confused with Principle Support questions that we studied earlier.

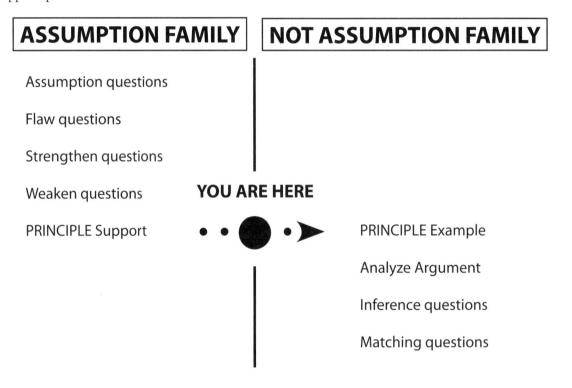

ASSUMPTION FAMILY	NOT ASSUMPTION FAMILY
Assumption questions	
Flaw questions	
Strengthen questions	
Weaken questions	**YOU ARE HERE**
PRINCIPLE Support	PRINCIPLE Example
	Analyze Argument
	Inference questions
	Matching questions

Principle Support Review

Remember that Principle Support questions are Assumption Family questions. They require us to find the core in a given argument, then choose a principle that supports that core by bridging the gap between the premise and the conclusion. Here's a very simple example to jog your memory:

> The bag of cash that Sanjay found was not claimed by anyone. Thus, Sanjay should keep the bag of cash for himself.

This argument has a premise and conclusion, and a pretty significant gap between the two. If this were a Principle Support question, we would want to choose a principle to bridge the gap. Perhaps the correct answer would be something like:

> One should keep for himself anything that he finds that is not claimed by anyone else.

If we insert the principle into the core, we get:

> The bag of cash that Sanjay found was not claimed by anyone. (One should keep for himself anything that he finds that is not claimed by anyone else.) Thus, Sanjay should keep the bag of cash for himself.

In short, we're given an argument and we're asked to choose a principle to support the argument. We know we're dealing with a Principle Support question when we get language such as:

> *Which one of the following PRINCIPLES most helps to JUSTIFY the reasoning above?*

> *Which one of the following PRINCIPLES provides the most SUPPORT for the argument?*

Principle Example questions are different. For Principle Example questions, we're *given* a principle and then asked to choose an example that conforms to that principle.

The Principle Example Mind-set: Conform to the Conditions

Have a look at this. You'll notice that this is the same principle from above:

> One should keep for himself anything that he finds that is not claimed by anyone else.

> *Which one of the following judgments most closely CONFORMS to the PRINCIPLE above?*

This time, the principle is given to us and we're asked to choose an answer that conforms to the principle. Did you notice that the principle can be expressed in conditional terms? The word "anything" should have been a clue.

Here's an answer choice that would work:

> The bag of cash that Sanjay found was not claimed by anyone. Thus, Sanjay should keep the bag of cash for himself.

Notice that the statement above satisfies the criteria in the sufficient condition (found it + no one claimed it), which means the necessary condition is triggered (he should keep it).

Much of the time (not always), this is how these questions work. We're given a general principle that can be expressed in conditional form, and then we're asked to choose an answer that conforms to the conditional statement.

Pretty easy, right? Let's try it on a real LSAT question. Focus on getting a good translation of the principle. Give yourself 1:20 for the following question, and then we'll discuss.

<u>PT23, S3, Q24</u>

A person's failure to keep a promise is wrong only if, first, doing so harms the one to whom the promise is made and, second, all of those who discover the failure to keep the promise lose confidence in the person's ability to keep promises.

Which one of the following judgments most closely conforms to the principle above?

(A) Ann kept her promise to repay Felicia the money she owed her. Further, this convinced everyone who knew Ann that she is trustworthy. Thus, Ann's keeping her promise was not wrong.

(B) Jonathan took an oath of secrecy concerning the corporation's technical secrets, but he sold them to a competitor. His action was wrong even though the corporation intended that he leak these secrets to its competitors.

(C) George promised to repay Reiko the money he owed her. However, George was unable to keep his promise to Reiko and as a result, Reiko suffered a serious financial loss. Thus, George's failure to keep his promise was wrong.

(D) Because he lost his job, Carlo was unable to repay the money he promised to Miriam. However, Miriam did not need this money nor did she lose confidence in Carlo's ability to keep promises. So, Carlo's failure to keep his promise to Miriam was not wrong.

(E) Elizabeth promised to return the book she borrowed from Steven within a week, but she was unable to do so because she became acutely ill. Not knowing this, Steven lost confidence in her ability to keep a promise. So, Elizabeth's failure to return the book to Steven was wrong.

Were you able to translate the original principle into a conditional statement? If you had trouble, go back and start with the "only if" conditional trigger. Try it again before reading on.

Here's how the principle breaks down into conditional form:

$$\text{failure to keep promise is wrong} \longrightarrow \begin{array}{c} \text{harm} \\ + \\ \text{lost confidence} \end{array}$$

We can split this into two conditionals:

failure to keep promise is wrong   ➡   harm

failure to keep promise is wrong   ➡   lost confidence

Now, we're looking for an answer choice that conforms to one of both of these conditional statements. If you had to guess, what do you think the wrong answers will look like? You got it. The wrong answers are likely to reverse the logic or negate the logic. Let's look at the answer choices.

(A) Ann kept her promise to repay Felicia the money she owed her. Further, this convinced everyone who knew Ann that she is trustworthy. Thus, Ann's keeping her promise was not wrong.

We know what happens when failing to keep a promise is wrong (there are two outcomes), but do we know anything about what happens when a promise is kept? *We don't. This answer does not conform to the principle, so we can eliminate it.*

(B) Jonathan took an oath of secrecy concerning the corporation's technical secrets, but he sold them to a competitor. His action was wrong even though the corporation intended that he leak these secrets to its competitors.

Jonathan failed to keep a promise, and this was apparently wrong, but this answer gives no indication of whether this leads to harm or lost confidence. In other words, we get no necessary condition with this answer choice. This does not conform to the principle.

(C) George promised to repay Reiko the money he owed her. However, George was unable to keep his promise to Reiko and as a result, Reiko suffered a serious financial loss. Thus, George's failure to keep his promise was wrong.

Harm was done to Reiko, so George's failure to keep his promise was wrong.

harm   ➡   failure to keep promise is wrong

This is reversed logic! This answer looks attractive because it contains many of the component parts of the conditional statement, but it does not conform.

(D) Because he lost his job, Carlo was unable to repay the money he promised to Miriam. However, Miriam did not need this money nor did she lose confidence in Carlo's ability to keep promises. So, Carlo's failure to keep his promise to Miriam was not wrong.

Miriam was NOT harmed, nor did she lose confidence in Carlo's ability to keep promises. Thus, Carlo's failure to keep his promise was not wrong.

–harm	➡	–failure to keep promise is wrong
–lost confidence	➡	–failure to keep promise is wrong

Does this conform? Indeed it does. This answer choice represents the contrapositive of the original principle. This is the correct answer.

(E) Elizabeth promised to return the book she borrowed from Steven within a week, but she was unable to do so because she became acutely ill. Not knowing this, Steven lost confidence in her ability to keep a promise. So, Elizabeth's failure to return the book to Steven was wrong.

Steven lost confidence in Elizabeth's ability to keep a promise, so Elizabeth's failure to return the book (or, Elizabeth's failure to keep her promise) was wrong.

lost confidence	➡	failure to keep promise is wrong

Another answer choice with reversed logic. This does not conform.

9

Let's try another one. Take 1:20, and then we'll discuss.

PT28, S1, Q10

It is a principle of economics that a nation can experience economic growth only when consumer confidence is balanced with a small amount of consumer skepticism.

Which one of the following is an application of the economic principle above?

(A) Any nation in which consumer confidence is balanced with a small amount of consumer skepticism will experience economic growth.

(B) Any nation in which the prevailing attitude of consumers is not skepticism will experience economic growth.

(C) Any nation in which the prevailing attitude of consumers is either exclusively confidence or exclusively skepticism will experience economic growth.

(D) Any nation in which the prevailing attitude of consumers is exclusively confidence will not experience economic growth.

(E) Any nation in which consumer skepticism is balanced with a small amount of consumer confidence will experience economic growth.

We're looking for an answer choice that is an "application" of the economic principle given. In other words, we're looking for an answer that conforms to the principle (in either its original form or its contrapositive). The "only when" in the principle is a clue that we should translate the principle into a conditional statement. If you didn't do this the first time through, take a second to try it now.

"Only when" functions exactly the same way as "only if." So, we can translate as follows:

economic growth   consumer confidence balanced with small amount of consumer skepticism

Let's evaluate the choices. Watch out for common conditional traps!

(A) Any nation in which consumer confidence is balanced with a small amount of consumer skepticism will experience economic growth.

consumer confidence balanced with small amount of consumer skepticism   economic growth

Reversed logic! This does not conform. Eliminate it.

(B) Any nation in which the prevailing attitude of consumers
is not skepticism will experience economic growth.

This says nothing about having a "balance" of confidence and skepticism. Besides, this logic moves in the wrong direction as well.

(C) Any nation in which the prevailing attitude of consumers
is either exclusively confidence or exclusively skepticism
will experience economic growth.

If the consumer attitude is either exclusively confidence or exclusively skepticism, then there is NO balance. So, this is saying NO balance leads to economic growth.

–consumer confidence balanced with small
amount of consumer skepticism   economic growth

This does not conform to the original principle. Eliminate it.

(D) Any nation in which the prevailing attitude of consumers
is exclusively confidence will not experience economic
growth.

Again, if the attitude is exclusively confidence, then there is NO balance. And notice in this case this leads to NO economic growth. In other words, this is the reverse and negated form of the original:

–consumer confidence balanced with small
amount of consumer skepticism   –economic growth

The contrapositive! This does conform, so this is the correct answer.

(E) Any nation in which consumer skepticism is balanced
with a small amount of consumer confidence will
experience economic growth.

This looks a lot like (A), reversed logic, but it has another problem as well. The modifier "small amount of" is attached to "consumer confidence." In the original, this modifier is attached to "consumer skepticism."

The Implied Principle

In the above questions, the principle was given to us directly. Sometimes, however, the LSAT will give us the principle indirectly by using a scenario to *illustrate* a principle. For example, imagine we had the following:

Professional athletes should donate a portion of their salary to projects that improve the local community, since most professional athletes make more money than they need.

MANHATTAN
LSAT

9

In this case, our job involves an extra dimension: we need to extract the principle from an example before we match it to the answer choices. Remember, principles can be thought of in much the same way as assumptions—they complete the connection between the premises and conclusion. The argument above can be said to be an illustration of the following principle:

> If one makes more money than one needs, then one should donate a portion of that money to the local community.

So, from the scenario we generate a principle, and, in this case, we can think of the principle in conditional terms:

make more money than needed should donate some to community

Then, we would look for an answer choice that conforms.

So, how do you know when to evaluate the argument (as you would for an Assumption Family question) and how do you know when to generate a principle from the argument? It all comes down to the question stem. If the question asks you to choose an answer that conforms to the principle illustrated, you simply want to generate a principle from the given information. Let's see an example:

> *PT29, S4, Q10*
>
> Parents should not necessarily raise their children in the ways experts recommend, even if some of those experts are themselves parents. After all, parents are the ones who directly experience which methods are successful in raising their own children.
>
> Which one of the following most closely conforms to the principle that the passage above illustrates?
>
> (A) Although music theory is intrinsically interesting and may be helpful to certain musicians, it does not distinguish good music from bad: that is a matter of taste and not of theory.
> (B) One need not pay much attention to the advice of automotive experts when buying a car if those experts are not interested in the mundane factors that concern the average consumer.
> (C) In deciding the best way to proceed, a climber familiar with a mountain might do well to ignore the advice of mountain climbing experts unfamiliar with that mountain.
> (D) A typical farmer is less likely to know what types of soil are most productive than is someone with an advanced degree in agricultural science.
> (E) Unlike society, one's own conscience speaks with a single voice; it is better to follow the advice of one's own conscience than the advice of society.

9

The given information is clearly an argument. The premise is that parents directly experience which methods are successful and which ones are not. The conclusion is that parents shouldn't necessarily listen to experts. So, because parents have direct experience, they shouldn't always listen to experts. There are gaps in this argument, but this question asks us to choose an answer that conforms to the principle. We need to use the argument to generate a principle:

If one has direct experience, one should not necessarily act on the advice of experts.

direct experience –act on advice of experts

(A) Although music theory is intrinsically interesting and may be helpful to certain musicians, it does not distinguish good music from bad: that is a matter of taste and not of theory.

This has nothing to do with having experience or listening to experts. Eliminate it.

(B) One need not pay much attention to the advice of automotive experts when buying a car if those experts are not interested in the mundane factors that concern the average consumer.

This does say that the advice of experts need not be heeded, but this answer choice is wrong. The advice of experts should not be heeded when "those experts are not interested...." This has nothing to do with the car buyer having direct experience. Eliminate it.

(C) In deciding the best way to proceed, a climber familiar with a mountain might do well to ignore the advice of mountain climbing experts unfamiliar with that mountain.

Ah, yes. The climber has direct experience, so she should ignore the advice of experts who are less familiar. This conforms to the principle, so this is the correct answer.

(D) A typical farmer is less likely to know what types of soil are most productive than is someone with an advanced degree in agricultural science.

So, should the farmer ignore the advice of experts? This isn't even close.

(E) Unlike society, one's own conscience speaks with a single voice; it is better to follow the advice of one's own conscience than the advice of society.

What about experts? What about experience? Wrong.

9

Conclusion

You're ready to try some on your own. First, let's review:

1. Don't confuse Principle Support with Principle Example! Principle Support questions ask you to support the argument by bridging the gap between the premise and the conclusion. The principle is the answer choice. Principle Example questions ask you to choose an answer that conforms to a *given* principle. No need to evaluate the logic of the argument.

2. Conform to the conditions. Many Principle Example questions will give you a principle that can be translated directly into conditional form. Your job is to choose the answer that conforms to the conditional statement.

3. Generate a principle when the principle is implied. Sometimes a scenario will be presented in argument form (with a premise and conclusion). Use this argument to generate a principle, and then choose an answer that conforms.

Now, let's practice.

DRILL IT: Principle Example Questions

Give yourself no more than 11 minutes to answer the following problems.

1. PT43, S3, Q5

Art critic: The aesthetic value of a work of art lies in its ability to impart a stimulating character to the audience's experience of the work.

Which one of the following judgments most closely conforms with the principle cited above?

(A) This painting is aesthetically deficient because it is an exact copy of a painting done 30 years ago.

(B) This symphony is beautiful because, even though it does not excite the audience, it is competently performed.

(C) This sculpted four-inch cube is beautiful because it is carved from material which, although much like marble, is very rare.

(D) This painting is aesthetically valuable because it was painted by a highly controversial artist.

(E) This poem is aesthetically deficient because it has little impact on its audience.

2. PT35, S1, Q7

Due to wider commercial availability of audio recordings of authors reading their own books, sales of printed books have dropped significantly.

Which one of the following conforms most closely to the principle illustrated above?

(A) Because of the rising cost of farm labor, farmers began to make more extensive use of machines.

(B) Because of the wide variety of new computer games on the market, sales of high-quality computer video screens have improved.

(C) Because a new brand of soft drink entered the market, consumers reduced their consumption of an established brand of soft drink.

(D) Because a child was forbidden to play until homework was completed, that child did much less daydreaming and focused on homework.

(E) Because neither of the two leading word processing programs has all of the features consumers want, neither has been able to dominate the market.

3. PT39, S2, Q11

A gift is not generous unless it is intended to benefit the recipient and is worth more than what is expected or customary in the situation; a gift is selfish if it is given to benefit the giver or is less valuable than is customary.

Which one of the following judgments most closely conforms to the principle above?

(A) Charles, who hates opera, was given two expensive tickets to the opera. He in turn gave them to his cousin, who loves opera, as a birthday gift. Charles's gift was selfish because he paid nothing for the tickets.

(B) Emily gives her brother a year's membership in a health club. She thinks that this will allow her brother to get the exercise he needs. However, the gift is selfish because Emily's brother is hurt and offended by it.

(C) Amanda gives each of her clients an expensive bottle of wine every year. Amanda's gifts are generous, since they cause the clients to continue giving Amanda business.

(D) Olga gives her daughter a computer as a graduation gift. Since this is the gift that all children in Olga's family receive for graduation, it is not generous.

(E) Michael gave his nephew $50 as a birthday gift, more than he had ever given before. Michael's nephew, however, lost the money. Therefore, Michael's gift was not generous because it did not benefit the recipient.

4. PT39, S4, Q24

A park's user fees are employed to maintain the park. When fewer people use the park, it suffers less wear. Thus raising user fees improves park maintenance even if the number of people who stop using the park because of higher fees is great enough to reduce the revenues devoted to maintenance.

Which one of the following conforms most closely to the principle illustrated by the statements above?

(A) To increase its market share, a car company improves the service warranty it provides to those who purchase a new car. Making good on the warranties proves expensive enough that the company's profits decrease even though its market share increases.

(B) A grocery store's overall revenues increase even though it no longer remains open 24 hours daily. The manager theorizes that customers find the store more pleasant because it can be cleaned well during the hours it is closed.

(C) Road taxes are raised to encourage more people to use mass transit. But since the fee paid by each commuter does not equal the cost of providing transit for that commuter, a mass transit service will deteriorate even as it takes in more money.

(D) By spending more on zoo maintenance, a city increases the number of zoo patrons. The extra revenue generated by the sale of memorabilia more than makes up for the extra costs of maintenance.

(E) Library fees have been increased to raise money for book repair. Since the library now has fewer patrons, the books are in better repair even though the number of library patrons has decreased to such an extent that the money available for book repair has decreased.

5. PT52, S1, Q22

Moralist: A statement is wholly truthful only if it is true and made without intended deception. A statement is a lie if it is intended to deceive or its speaker, upon learning that the statement was misinterpreted, refrains from clarifying it.

Which one of the following judgments most closely conforms to the principles stated above by the moralist?

(A) Ted's statement to the investigator that he had been abducted by extraterrestrial beings was wholly truthful even though no one has ever been abducted by extraterrestrial beings. After all, Ted was not trying to deceive the investigator.

(B) Tony was not lying when he told his granddaughter that he did not wear dentures, for even though Tony meant to deceive his granddaughter, she made it clear to Tony that she did not believe him.

(C) Siobhan did not tell a lie when she told her supervisor that she was ill and hence would not be able to come to work for an important presentation. However, even though her statement was true, it was not wholly truthful.

(D) Walter's claim to a potential employer that he had done volunteer work was a lie. Even though Walter had worked without pay in his father's factory, he used the phrase "volunteer work" in an attempt to deceive the interviewer into thinking he had worked for a socially beneficial cause.

(E) The tour guide intended to deceive the tourists when he told them that the cabin they were looking at was centuries old. Still, his statement about the cabin's age was not a lie, for if he thought that this statements had been misinterpreted, he would have tried to clarify it.

6. PT42, S2, Q9

Challenge can be an important source of self-knowledge, since those who pay attention to how they react, both emotionally and physically, to challenge can gain useful insights into their own weaknesses.

Which one of the following most closely conforms to the principle above?

(A) A concert pianist should not have an entirely negative view of a memory lapse during a difficult performance. By understanding why the memory lapse occurred, the pianist can better prepare for future performances.

(B) A salesperson should understand that the commission earned is not the only reward of making a sale. Salespeople should also take satisfaction from the fact that successful sales reflect well on their personalities.

(C) Compassion is valuable not only for the wonderful feelings it brings, but also for the opportunities it affords to enrich the lives of other people.

(D) While some of the value of competition comes from the pleasure of winning, the primary reward of competition is competition itself.

(E) Even people who dread public speaking should accept invitations to speak before large groups. People will admire their courage and they will experience the fulfillment of having attempted something that is difficult for them.

7. PT42, S2, Q21

If one has evidence that an act will benefit other people and performs that act to benefit them, then one will generally succeed in benefiting them.

Which one of the following best illustrates the proposition above?

(A) A country's leaders realized that fostering diplomatic ties with antagonistic nations reduces the chances of war with those nations. Because those leaders worried that war would harm their chances of being reelected, they engaged in diplomatic discussions with a hostile country, and the two countries avoided a confrontation.

(B) A government study concluded that a proposed bureaucratic procedure would allow people to register their cars without waiting in line. The government adopted the procedure for this reason, and, as with most bureaucratic procedures, it was not successful.

(C) Betsy overheard a heating contractor say that regularly changing the filter in a furnace helps to keep the furnace efficient. So Betsy has regularly changed the furnace filter in her daughter's house. As a result, the furnace has never required maintenance due to becoming clogged with dust or dirt.

(D) Sejal learned in a psychology class that the best way to help someone overcome an addiction is to confront that person. So she confronted her friend Bob, who was struggling with a chemical dependency.

(E) Zachary hoped that psychotherapy could help his parents overcome their marital difficulties. He persuaded his parents to call a psychotherapist, and eventually their problems were resolved.

9

8. PT42, S4, Q8

When presented with the evidence against him, Ellison freely admitted to engaging in illegal transactions using company facilities. However, the company obtained the evidence by illegally recording Ellison's conversations. Therefore, although the company may demand that he immediately cease, it cannot justifiably take any punitive measures against him.

Which one of the following judgments best illustrates the principle illustrated by the argument above?

(A) After Price confessed to having stolen money from Long over a period of several years, Long began stealing from Price. Despite Price's guilt, Long was not justified in taking illegal action against him.

(B) Shakila's secretary has admitted that he is illegally receiving cable television without paying for it. Shakila would not be justified in reporting him, though, since she once did the same thing.

(C) After Takashi told Sarah's parents that he had seen her at the movies on Tuesday, Sarah confessed to sneaking out that day. On Monday, however, Takashi had violated the local curfew for minors. Hence Sarah's parents cannot justifiably punish her in this case.

(D) After a conservation officer discovered them, Kuttner admitted that he had set the illegal animal traps on his land. But, because she was trespassing at the time, the conservation officer cannot justifiably punish Kuttner in this case.

(E) Ramirez was forced by the discovery of new evidence to admit that she lied about her role in managing the chief of staff's financial affairs. Nevertheless, the board of directors cannot justifiably take action against Ramirez, because in past instances it has pardoned others guilty of similar improprieties.

9

SOLUTIONS: Principle Example Questions

1. PT43, S3, Q5

Art critic: The aesthetic value of a work of art lies in its ability to impart a stimulating character to the audience's experience of the work.

Which one of the following judgments most closely conforms with the principle cited above?

(A) This painting is aesthetically deficient because it is an exact copy of a painting done 30 years ago.

(B) This symphony is beautiful because, even though it does not excite the audience, it is competently performed.

(C) This sculpted four-inch cube is beautiful because it is carved from material which, although much like marble, is very rare.

(D) This painting is aesthetically valuable because it was painted by a highly controversial artist.

(E) This poem is aesthetically deficient because it has little impact on its audience.

(E) is correct.

We're given a principle that, though not obviously a conditional statement, can be translated into conditional form:

has aesthetic value ➡ imparts a stimulating character to audience's experience

Now we just need to find an example that conforms to this conditional statement.

(A) is out of scope. We need to know whether the work is stimulating. Whether it's a copy doesn't tell us anything with respect to our principle.

(B) clearly violates the principle; if a work does not excite the audience, it doesn't have aesthetic value.

(C) is out of scope. Rareness is irrelevant.

(D) is similarly out of scope. Controversial artist?

That leaves (E).

We can translate this to:

−stimulating ➡ −aesthetic value

That's the contrapositive of our original conditional statement, so it conforms to the principle. Therefore, (E) is correct.

2. PT35, S1, Q7

Due to wider commercial availability of audio recordings of authors reading their own books, sales of printed books have dropped significantly.

Which one of the following conforms most closely to the principle illustrated above?

(A) Because of the rising cost of farm labor, farmers began to make more extensive use of machines.

(B) Because of the wide variety of new computer games on the market, sales of high-quality computer video screens have improved.

(C) Because a new brand of soft drink entered the market, consumers reduced their consumption of an established brand of soft drink.

(D) Because a child was forbidden to play until homework was completed, that child did much less daydreaming and focused on homework.

(E) Because neither of the two leading word processing programs has all of the features consumers want, neither has been able to dominate the market.

(C) is correct.

Here, we're not explicitly given a principle; we need to derive one from the example, something like:

wider availability of newer, competing product ➡ decline in sales of older existing product

MANHATTAN
LSAT

Now let's find an answer choice that conforms to our principle.

(A) is about rising cost, not availability, and it doesn't mention anything declining. Get rid of it.

(B) has wider availability of a new product leading to an increase in sales of a related product, so it's not a match.

(D) is just from outer space. No part of it comes close to our principle.

(E) makes no mention of a more widely available product driving down sales of another, so it's no good.

We're down to (C).

This looks pretty good:

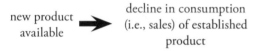

This is definitely the closest fit, so (C) is correct.

3. PT39, S2, Q11

A gift is not generous unless it is intended to benefit the recipient and is worth more than what is expected or customary in the situation; a gift is selfish if it is given to benefit the giver or is less valuable than is customary.

Which one of the following judgments most closely conforms to the principle above?

(A) Charles, who hates opera, was given two expensive tickets to the opera. He in turn gave them to his cousin, who loves opera, as a birthday gift. Charles's gift was selfish because he paid nothing for the tickets.

(B) Emily gives her brother a year's membership in a health club. She thinks that this will allow her brother to get the exercise he needs. However, the gift is selfish because Emily's brother is hurt and offended by it.

(C) Amanda gives each of her clients an expensive bottle of wine every year. Amanda's gifts are generous, since they cause the clients to continue giving Amanda business.

(D) Olga gives her daughter a computer as a graduation gift. Since this is the gift that all children in Olga's family receive for graduation, it is not generous.

(E) Michael gave his nephew $50 as a birthday gift, more than he had ever given before. Michael's nephew, however, lost the money. Therefore, Michael's gift was not generous because it did not benefit the recipient.

(D) is correct.

This principle can be broken down into four conditional statements if we split up the "and" and "or," which can help avoid confusion:

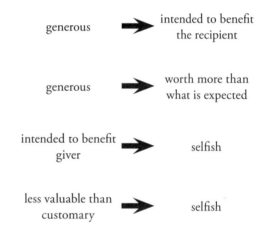

We're looking for an example that conforms to some or all of these rules, and we can expect some of the wrong answers to try to entice us with reversed or negated logic.

(A) concludes that a gift is selfish because it doesn't cost the giver any money. But according to our principle, the cost of the gift doesn't tell us anything; we would need to know the giver's intent or the *value* of the gift, which is different from its cost, to know whether it was selfish.

(B) concludes that a gift is selfish, but like (A), it doesn't base that conclusion on the gift's value or on the giver's intent, so it doesn't conform.

(C) concludes that a gift is generous. But looking back at our conditional statements, "generous" is always the sufficient condition, so we have no way of concluding whether something is generous.

9

(E) is tempting. It concludes that a gift is not generous because it doesn't benefit the recipient. But notice that the first necessary condition of a generous gift is that it is *intended* to benefit the recipient. Whether it *actually* benefits the recipient is irrelevant to the principle.

We're left with one answer: (D).

This one concludes that Olga's gift is not generous. Why? Because it's the gift that all the children in the family receive in that context—in other words, it's worth no more than what's expected. In terms of our principle, that gives us:

$$\text{--worth more than expected} \longrightarrow \text{--generous}$$

That's the contrapositive of the second conditional statement, so it conforms!

Therefore, (D) is correct.

4. PT39, S4, Q24

A park's user fees are employed to maintain the park. When fewer people use the park, it suffers less wear. Thus raising user fees improves park maintenance even if the number of people who stop using the park because of higher fees is great enough to reduce the revenues devoted to maintenance.

Which one of the following conforms most closely to the principle illustrated by the statements above?

(A) To increase its market share, a car company improves the service warranty it provides to those who purchase a new car. Making good on the warranties proves expensive enough that the company's profits decrease even though its market share increases.

(B) A grocery store's overall revenues increase even though it no longer remains open 24 hours daily. The manager theorizes that customers find the store more pleasant because it can be cleaned well during the hours it is closed.

(C) Road taxes are raised to encourage more people to use mass transit. But since the

fee paid by each commuter does not equal the cost of providing transit for that commuter, a mass transit service will deteriorate even as it takes in more money.

(D) By spending more on zoo maintenance, a city increases the number of zoo patrons. The extra revenue generated by the sale of memorabilia more than makes up for the extra costs of maintenance.

(E) Library fees have been increased to raise money for book repair. Since the library now has fewer patrons, the books are in better repair even though the number of library patrons has decreased to such an extent that the money available for book repair has decreased.

(E) is correct.

This one is a little trickier. Again, we need to derive a principle from the given statements. Since the statements are in argument form, isolating the premise and conclusion should allow us to generate the principle we need.

The argument concludes that raising user fees improves park maintenance, even if the higher fees dissuade enough people from coming that the maintenance revenues go down. That *whole thing* is the conclusion. It's based on the premise that when fewer people use the park, the park suffers less wear. So our argument core, abstracted away from the park example, looks like this:

$$\text{fewer users means less wear} \longrightarrow \text{even if they lead to fewer users and lower revenues, raising fees improves maintenance.}$$

So that's our principle, more or less. Now let's see if we can find the example that fits this principle most closely.

(A) talks about market share vs. profits, improving the service warranty, etc., which has nothing to do with fewer users, raising fees, maintenance, or anything we're interested in. It's way out of scope; eliminate it.

(B) is a bit more tempting, but we have no idea whether there are fewer users. Further, our principle is about revenues *decreasing*, not increasing.

(C) concludes that the mass transit service will deteriorate. Our principle is about maintenance being improved. Get rid of it.

(D) is also tempting, but it doesn't mention the zoo raising any fees, and it has the number of patrons *increasing,* when we're looking for a decrease.

So, how about the last answer: (E)?

Let's see: Raising fees has decreased the number of patrons to the extent that there's less book-repair money available, but because there are fewer patrons, the books are in better shape. This is a direct match!

So, (E) is correct.

5. PT52, S1, Q22

Moralist: A statement is wholly truthful only if it is true and made without intended deception. A statement is a lie if it is intended to deceive or its speaker, upon learning that the statement was misinterpreted, refrains from clarifying it.

Which one of the following judgments most closely conforms to the principles stated above by the moralist?

(A) Ted's statement to the investigator that he had been abducted by extraterrestrial beings was wholly truthful even though no one has ever been abducted by extraterrestrial beings. After all, Ted was not trying to deceive the investigator.

(B) Tony was not lying when he told his granddaughter that he did not wear dentures, for even though Tony meant to deceive his granddaughter, she made it clear to Tony that she did not believe him.

(C) Siobhan did not tell a lie when she told her supervisor that she was ill and hence would not be able to come to work for an important presentation. However, even though her statement was true, it was not wholly truthful.

(D) Walter's claim to a potential employer that he had done volunteer work was a lie. Even though Walter had worked without pay in his father's factory, he used the phrase "volunteer work" in an attempt to deceive the interviewer into thinking he had worked for a socially beneficial cause.

(E) The tour guide intended to deceive the tourists when he told them that the cabin they were looking at was centuries old. Still, his statement about the cabin's age was not a lie, for if he thought that this statements had been misinterpreted, he would have tried to clarify it.

(D) is correct.

Here we're given a series of conditional statements. We're told of two necessary conditions for a statement to be wholly truthful (it must be true and made without intended deception) and two sufficient conditions that make a statement a lie (if it's intended to deceive or the speaker doesn't clarify it, it's a lie). We can express the conditionals like this:

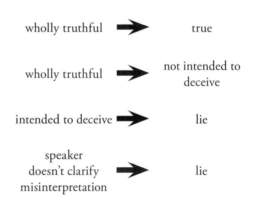

Now we just need to find a statement that conforms with these conditionals, keeping an eye out for illegal negations and reversals.

(A) is reversed. Not intending to deceive is a necessary, not sufficient, condition of a wholly truthful statement.

(B) violates the principle, according to which Tony definitely *was* lying if he intended to deceive his granddaughter. Whether she believed him or not is irrelevant.

(C) says that a statement is not a lie and not wholly truthful, but doesn't base those judgments on any sufficient conditions.

(E) violates the principle in the same way as (B): the tour guide intended to deceive the tourists, so his statement was absolutely a lie—end of story!

That leaves (D).

Walter attempted to deceive the interviewer, so his statement was a lie. This directly conforms to our third conditional statement.

Therefore, (D) is correct.

6. PT42, S2, Q9

Challenge can be an important source of self-knowledge, since those who pay attention to how they react, both emotionally and physically, to challenge can gain useful insights into their own weaknesses.

Which one of the following most closely conforms to the principle above?

(A) A concert pianist should not have an entirely negative view of a memory lapse during a difficult performance. By understanding why the memory lapse occurred, the pianist can better prepare for future performances.

(B) A salesperson should understand that the commission earned is not the only reward of making a sale. Salespeople should also take satisfaction from the fact that successful sales reflect well on their personalities.

(C) Compassion is valuable not only for the wonderful feelings it brings, but also for the opportunities it affords to enrich the lives of other people.

(D) While some of the value of competition comes from the pleasure of winning, the primary reward of competition is competition itself.

(E) Even people who dread public speaking should accept invitations to speak before large groups. People will admire their courage and they will experience the fulfillment of having attempted something that is difficult for them.

(A) is correct.

This principle is stated as an argument. The premise is that those who pay attention to their reactions to challenge can gain useful insights into their weaknesses. The conclusion is that challenge can therefore be an important source of self-knowledge. From this, we generate the principle:

paying attention to reactions to challenge leads to useful insights		challenge can be an important source of self-knowledge.

Now let's compare the answer choices to this principle.

(B) has nothing to do with challenge, insight, or self-knowledge. It's way out of scope; get rid of it.

(C) tells us two ways in which compassion is valuable, neither of which has anything to do with our principle; further, it's stated simply as fact, not as a conclusion supported by a premise.

(D) is incorrect in basically the same way: we get two ways in which competition is valuable, but it's not an argument, and it has nothing to do with challenge as a source of insights or self-knowledge.

(E) is an argument, at least, but our principle is about challenge being useful because it leads to useful insights, not because people admire your courage or because you experience fulfillment. So this doesn't conform.

So we're down to (A).

This looks like an argument: because understanding the cause of a memory lapse during a difficult performance can help the pianist better prepare, he shouldn't have an entirely negative view of it. Does this match? Well, "a difficult performance" is certainly a challenge, and the memory lapse is a reaction to it; understanding that reaction leads to better preparation, which sounds like a useful insight. So far, we've got our premise. Now does the conclusion match? Well, it's not exactly the same, since it doesn't talk about self-knowledge, but it does say that the pianist shouldn't have an entirely negative view, which does jive somewhat:

if it's a source of self-knowledge, we can reasonably say it's not entirely a bad thing. So this is a pretty good match.

Therefore, (A) is correct.

7. PT42, S2, Q21

If one has evidence that an act will benefit other people and performs that act to benefit them, then one will generally succeed in benefiting them.

Which one of the following best illustrates the proposition above?

(A) A country's leaders realized that fostering diplomatic ties with antagonistic nations reduces the chances of war with those nations. Because those leaders worried that war would harm their chances of being reelected, they engaged in diplomatic discussions with a hostile country, and the two countries avoided a confrontation.

(B) A government study concluded that a proposed bureaucratic procedure would allow people to register their cars without waiting in line. The government adopted the procedure for this reason, and, as with most bureaucratic procedures, it was not successful.

(C) Betsy overheard a heating contractor say that regularly changing the filter in a furnace helps to keep the furnace efficient. So Betsy has regularly changed the furnace filter in her daughter's house. As a result, the furnace has never required maintenance due to becoming clogged with dust or dirt.

(D) Sejal learned in a psychology class that the best way to help someone overcome an addiction is to confront that person. So she confronted her friend Bob, who was struggling with a chemical dependency.

(E) Zachary hoped that psychotherapy could help his parents overcome their marital difficulties. He persuaded his parents to call psychotherapist, and eventually their problems were resolved.

(C) is correct.

This principle is given as a straightforward conditional statement:

So we need to find an example that illustrates this conditional relationship.

(A) has people succeeding at something, but if we look closely, we see that the leaders engage in diplomacy in order to protect their own chances of being reelected, so they're performing the act to benefit *themselves.* We have the necessary condition, but not the sufficient. This doesn't conform.

(B) starts strong: the government has evidence (a study) that a procedure will help people and it adopts this procedure in order to help them. But according to our principle, this should generally lead to success; instead we're told that "as with most bureaucratic procedures, it was not successful." This is the opposite of our desired outcome.

(D) gives us the sufficient conditions—Sejal has evidence that confrontation will help, and she confronts Bob with that goal—but we never find out the necessary, that is, whether she's successful.

(E) tells us that Zachary has hope, but not evidence, that psychotherapy will help his parents. Further, if psychotherapy is the act in question, Zachary doesn't actually perform it himself. So we have neither of the sufficient conditions.

That leaves (C).

Betsy overhears a contractor describing the benefit of changing the filter in a furnace. That may not be conclusive proof, but it is a form of evidence. Then she changes the filter in her daughter's house. Although we aren't told explicitly that she takes the action to benefit her daughter, we can reasonably infer that she does. So we have our two sufficient conditions. As a result, we're told, the furnace has never required maintenance—so

9

Betsy is successful in her goal of keeping her daughter's furnace efficient.

Even though this isn't a 100% match—it would be nice to know explicitly Betsy's reason for changing the filter—it comes by far the closest to giving us our sufficient and necessary conditions.

Therefore, (C) is correct.

8. PT42, S4, Q8

When presented with the evidence against him, Ellison freely admitted to engaging in illegal transactions using company facilities. However, the company obtained the evidence by illegally recording Ellison's conversations. Therefore, although the company may demand that he immediately cease, it cannot justifiably take any punitive measures against him.

Which one of the following judgments best illustrates the principle illustrated by the argument above?

(A) After Price confessed to having stolen money from Long over a period of several years, Long began stealing from Price. Despite Price's guilt, Long was not justified in taking illegal action against him.

(B) Shakila's secretary has admitted that he is illegally receiving cable television without paying for it. Shakila would not be justified in reporting him, though, since she once did the same thing.

(C) After Takashi told Sarah's parents that he had seen her at the movies on Tuesday, Sarah confessed to sneaking out that day. On Monday, however, Takashi had violated the local curfew for minors. Hence Sarah's parents cannot justifiably punish her in this case.

(D) After a conservation officer discovered them, Kuttner admitted that he had set the illegal animal traps on his land. But, because she was trespassing at the time, the conservation officer cannot justifiably punish Kuttner in this case.

(E) Ramirez was forced by the discovery of new evidence to admit that she lied about her role in managing the chief of staff's

financial affairs. Nevertheless, the board of directors cannot justifiably take action against Ramirez, because in past instances it has pardoned others guilty of similar improprieties.

(D) is correct.

Here we have to generate a principle from the given argument, which concludes that the company cannot justifiably punish Ellison for his illegal activity. Why? Because although he confessed when presented with the evidence against him, that evidence was obtained illegally. So the argument core, and therefore our principle, looks like this:

evidence obtained illegally illegal activity cannot justifiably be punished (even if confessed)

There are a couple of major assumptions there, but our job here is not to evaluate the argument, it's to find an example that most closely conforms to it. Let's look.

(A) has someone confessing to a crime, but doesn't tell us anything about where the evidence comes from, so it doesn't conform.

(B) concludes that Shakila can't report her secretary, but bases that conclusion not on her obtaining the evidence illegally, but on her having once done the same thing. This has nothing to do with our principle.

(C) is very tempting. The conclusion looks right: Sarah's parents can't justifiably punish her. And we have Sarah confessing to her misdeed after the evidence is presented. There's only one problem: although Takashi violated the curfew, that was on Monday, he saw Sarah on Tuesday. So his violation was not the source of the evidence against Sarah. Since we don't know whether the evidence was obtained illegally, we can't conclude whether Sarah's parents are justified in punishing her.

(E) is also tempting, but as in (B), the conclusion that punishment is unjustified is based on the wrong premise. We care about the source of the evidence, not about past pardons.

We're down to (D).

This core breaks down into:

officer trespassing
at time of
discovery of crime

can't justifiably
punish Kuttner for
illegal traps (even
though he confessed)

That's a match! Because the evidence was obtained illegally, the admitted perpetrator cannot be punished justifiably.

So, (D) is correct.

9

Chapter 10
of

Logical Reasoning

Analyze Argument
Structure Questions

Getting Familiar

To start, go ahead and try these Analyze Argument Structure questions. Give yourself no more than eight minutes total. We'll revisit these questions later on in the chapter.

_PT29, S1, Q11_

It is well known that many species adapt to their environment, but it is usually assumed that only the most highly evolved species alter their environment in ways that aid their own survival. However, this characteristic is actually quite common. Certain species of plankton, for example, generate a gas that is converted in the atmosphere into particles of sulfate. These particles cause water vapor to condense, thus forming clouds. Indeed, the formation of clouds over the ocean largely depends on the presence of these particles. More cloud cover means more sunlight is reflected, and so the Earth absorbs less heat. Thus plankton cause the surface of the Earth to be cooler and this benefits the plankton.

Of the following, which one most accurately expresses the main point of the argument?

(A) The Earth would be far warmer than it is now if certain species of plankton became extinct.

(B) By altering their environment in ways that improve their chances of survival, certain species of plankton benefit the Earth as a whole.

(C) Improving their own chances of survival by altering the environment is not limited to the most highly evolved species.

(D) The extent of the cloud cover over the oceans is largely determined by the quantity of plankton in those oceans.

(E) Species such as plankton alter the environment in ways that are less detrimental to the well-being of other species than are the alterations to the environment made by more highly evolved species.

_PT36, S3, Q6_

Government official: A satisfactory way of eliminating chronic food shortages in our country is not easily achievable. Direct aid from other countries in the form of food shipments tends to undermine our prospects for long-term agricultural self-sufficiency. If external sources of food are delivered effectively by external institutions, local food producers and suppliers are forced out of business. On the other hand, foreign capital funneled to long-term development projects would inject so much cash into our economy that inflation would drive the price of food beyond the reach of most of our citizens.

The claim that foreign capital funneled into the economy would cause inflation plays which one of the following roles in the government official's argument?

(A) It supports the claim that the official's country must someday be agriculturally self-sufficient.

(B) It supports the claim that there is no easy solution to the problem of chronic food shortages in the official's country.

(C) It is supported by the claim that the official's country must someday be agriculturally self-sufficient.

(D) It supports the claim that donations of food from other countries will not end the chronic food shortages in the official's country.

(E) It is supported by the claim that food producers and suppliers in the official's country may be forced out of business by donations of food from other countries.

_PT38, S1, Q5_

Naima: The proposed new computer system, once we fully implemented it, would operate more smoothly and efficiently than the current system. So we should devote the resources necessary to accomplish the conversion as soon as possible.

Nakai: We should keep the current system as long as we can. The cost in time and money of converting to the new system would be greater than any predicted benefits.

Naima and Nakai disagree with each other over whether

(A) the predicted benefits of the new computer system will be realized

(B) it is essential to have the best computer system available

(C) accomplishing the conversion is technically impossible

(D) the current computer system does not work well enough to do what it is supposed to do

(E) the conversion to a new computer system should be delayed

_PT30, S2, Q7_

Opponent of offshore oil drilling: The projected benefits of drilling new oil wells in certain areas in the outer continental shelf are not worth the risk of environmental disaster. The oil already being extracted from these areas currently provides only 4 percent of our country's daily oil requirement, and the new wells would only add one-half of 1 percent.

Proponent of offshore oil drilling: Don't be ridiculous! You might just as well argue that new farms should not be allowed, since no new farm could supply the total food needs of our country for more than a few minutes.

The drilling proponent's reply to the drilling opponent proceeds by

(A) offering evidence in support of drilling that is more decisive than is the evidence offered by the drilling opponent

(B) claiming that the statistics cited as evidence by the drilling opponent are factually inaccurate

(C) pointing out that the drilling opponent's argument is a misapplication of a frequently legitimate way of arguing

(D) citing as parallel to the argument made by the drilling opponent an argument in which the conclusion is strikingly unsupported

(E) proposing a conclusion that is more strongly supported by the drilling opponent's evidence than is the conclusion offered by the drilling opponent

10

PT35, S1, Q11

Linguist: Some people have understood certain studies as showing that bilingual children have a reduced "conceptual map" because bilingualism overstresses the child's linguistic capacities. Vocabulary tests taken by bilingual children appear to show that these children tend to have a smaller vocabulary than do most children of the same age group. But these studies are deeply flawed since the tests were given in only one language. Dual-language tests revealed that the children often expressed a given concept with a word from only one of their two languages.

The linguist's argument proceeds by

(A) offering evidence for the advantages of bilingualism over monolingualism

(B) pointing out an inconsistency in the view that bilingualism overstresses a child's linguistic capacities

(C) offering evidence that undermines the use of any vocabulary test to provide information about a child's conceptual map

(D) providing a different explanation for the apparent advantages of bilingualism from the explanation suggested by the results of certain studies

(E) pointing out a methodological error in the technique used to obtain the purported evidence of a problem with bilingualism

Analyze Argument Structure Questions on the LSAT

The ability to think about an argument in terms of structure is a necessary tool for all test-takers who want to get a top score. Approximately 15 percent of all Logical Reasoning questions will directly test your ability to analyze the structure of an argument.

Fortunately for us, we've been thinking about argument structure from the beginning of the book. Argument structure can simply be thought of as the organization of background information, supporting premises, and opposing points relative to a main conclusion, and we've needed to consider this structure for all Assumption Family questions.

Analyze Argument Structure questions do differ just a bit from Assumption Family questions, and we'll review these differences later. For now, let's use the following example to review the different components that make up the structure of an argument.

> The Law School Admissions Test (LSAT) is an exam that tests certain logical instincts and processing abilities. The LSAT is a useful and necessary tool for the law school admissions process. Some critics disagree with the use of the LSAT in admissions decisions. They argue that the exam is culturally biased, and bears no direct relation to the process of being a lawyer. Though the test is imperfect, as all standardized tests are, it is necessary and useful because, without it, admissions officers would have no objective way to compare applicants from different backgrounds. After all, grading standards vary from university to university, and placing value on life or work experience is a highly subjective enterprise.

The Law School Admissions Test (LSAT) is an exam that tests certain logical instincts and processing abilities.	**BACKGROUND INFORMATION** Background information helps the reader become more familiar with the subject matter of the argument. Background information is often necessary for the reader to understand and contextualize the argument being made.
The LSAT is a useful and necessary tool for the law school admissions process.	**THE CONCLUSION** The conclusion is the main point of an argument. It is always a claim of some sort, and therefore it is always subjective. If there are multiple claims made in an argument, the conclusion is always the ultimate, or final, effect of those claims. Another way to think about the conclusion is that it is always last in the chain of logic. Identifying the correct conclusion is the most important step involved in correctly understanding argument structure.

10

Some critics disagree with the use of the LSAT in admissions decisions. They argue that the exam is culturally biased, and bears no direct relation to the process of being a lawyer. Though the test is imperfect…	**OPPOSING POINT** An opposing point is an opinion, or support for an opinion, that runs counter to the main conclusion of the argument.
…without it, admissions officers would have no objective way to compare applicants from different backgrounds.	**INTERMEDIATE CONCLUSION** Intermediate conclusions are conclusions that are used to support the main conclusion. Note that this conclusion is NOT the main point of the argument.
After all, grading standards vary from university to university, and placing value on life or work experience is a highly subjective enterprise.	**SUPPORTING PREMISE** Supporting premises present information that supports, in a direct or indirect way, the main conclusion of an argument.

Intermediate Conclusions, Supporting Premises, and Main Conclusions

Differentiating between intermediate conclusions and supporting premises can be messy, and it is generally unnecessary. There is great overlap between those two roles—after all, intermediate conclusions always support the main conclusion. One can think of an intermediate conclusion as any supporting premise that has two characteristics—it is a claim of some sort, and it is supported by other premises in the argument.

It *is* imperative that you correctly differentiate between intermediate conclusions and the main conclusion of an argument. Remember, the main conclusion will always be last in the chain of logic.

Let's look at a visual representation of the relationship between the supporting evidence, the intermediate conclusion, and the main conclusion of our argument.

10

Supporting Premises		Intermediate Conclusion		Conclusion
Grading standards vary from university to university	→	Without LSAT, admissions officers would have no objective way to compare applicants from different backgrounds.	→	The LSAT is a useful and necessary part of the admissions process.
Placing value on life or work experience is highly subjective	→			

On your LSAT exam, you'll see four different question types that will require you to understand the structure of an argument: (1) Identify the Conclusion of an argument, (2) Determine the Function of a component of an argument, (3) Identify the Disagreement between two people in a conversation, and (4) summarize the Procedure used by the author of an argument. Let's discuss each in depth.

Identify the Conclusion Questions

Identify the Conclusion questions ask you to identify the main point, or final conclusion, of an argument. These questions can be made easier if you keep a few key points in mind:

1. Always identify the conclusion first! This may seem like an obvious step, but some test-takers might be tempted to read the argument and then jump directly into the answer choices. Remember to take a moment after you finish the argument to make sure that you've correctly identified its conclusion *before* you look at the answer choices.

2. Stuck in the middle. We mentioned earlier in the book that the conclusion of the argument can appear at the start of the argument, in the middle, or at the end. Typically, it's much easier to spot a conclusion when it appears at the beginning or at the end of an argument. For this reason, when the LSAT asks you to identify a conclusion, they usually bury it somewhere in the middle of the argument, just to make things a bit more difficult on you. Let's look at two versions of the same argument to illustrate:

PREMISE – PREMISE – CONCLUSION:
My electricity bill was $45 last month. I will be out of town more this month than I was last month. Thus, my electricity bill will be less than $45 this month.

PREMISE – CONCLUSION – PREMISE:
My electricity bill was $45 last month. My electricity bill will be less than $45 this month since I will be out of town more this month than I was last month.

In each case, we have two premises that support a conclusion: My bill will be less than $45 this month. The *logical* structure is identical, and the conclusion comes last in the *logical* chain each time (each of the premises leads up to, or supports, the conclusion). What is different is the *organizational* structure. In the second case, the conclusion is buried in the middle of the passage. For Identify the Conclusion questions, you can expect the second structure more often than the first.

3. The author's conclusion, NOT yours. In the next chapter, we'll examine other question types (Inference questions) that require you to *infer* from information given in the text—that is, to uncover a truth beyond what is literally stated. When a question asks you to *identify* the main conclusion of an argument, however, you must NOT infer anything at all. Remember, you're looking for the author's conclusion, not yours. Here's an example:

> **Legislator:** We are joining a nationwide campaign to reduce the number of car accidents. In our state, the majority of serious car accidents occur between the hours of 11 p.m. and 4 a.m. Thus, most serious car accidents are the result of drivers being overly tired while they drive.

Imagine you were asked to choose an answer that best represents the conclusion made in the argument. You might be tempted by an answer choice such as: People shouldn't drive if they are overly tired. It makes sense to draw this conclusion based on the argument and based on our outside knowledge, but this is NOT what the legislator has concluded! The legislator's conclusion is: Most serious car accidents are the result of drivers being overly tired. Don't be tempted to draw your own conclusion!

4. Last in the chain of logic. If you have trouble identifying the final conclusion, it's probably because the argument contains an intermediate conclusion that seems like it could be the final conclusion.

Earlier in the book, we learned to use the Therefore Test to help determine which point actually comes last in the chain of logic. Here's the example we used previously:

> A new lemonade stand has just opened for business in the town square. The stand will surely fail. A local juice store already sells lemonade in the town square, and consumers in the town have historically been very loyal to local businesses. The new lemonade stand will not be able to attract customers.

This argument seems to have two possible conclusions: 1) the stand will surely fail, and 2) the new lemonade stand will not be able to attract customers. There can only be one final conclusion. Again, we can use "The Therefore Test" to identify the final conclusion:

Case #1: The stand will surely fail. THEREFORE, the new lemonade stand will not be able to attract customers.

Case #2: The new lemonade stand will not be able to attract customers. THEREFORE, the stand will surely fail.

We've proposed two different logical statements by changing the order of the two possible conclusions. The first case doesn't make a whole lot of sense. In the second case, however, the first part of the statement clearly supports, or leads into, the second part of the statement. Because the stand will not be able to attract customers, it will surely fail. Thus, the final conclusion is that "The stand will surely fail." Don't get fooled by intermediate conclusions!

5. Don't be fooled by rewordings of the conclusion. The LSAT will often attempt to disguise the correct answer by rewording the conclusion in the correct answer choice. You should NOT expect the correct answer to be an exact replica of the conclusion as it is presented in the argument. Consider this example:

> Many people who work for non-profit companies claim that they are not motivated at all by personal gain. This just isn't true. The executive director of Bright Lives, a local non-profit, makes over $100,000 per year.

This argument has the form OPPOSING POINT–CONCLUSION–PREMISE. If we were to identify the conclusion in this argument, we would point to: "This just isn't true." However, we can be sure that the correct answer will be written much differently. After you've identified the conclusion in the argument, you may need to clarify in your own mind what the different pieces actually mean. For example, what does "this" refer to? If you remember back to Chapter 2, we emphasized the importance of unpacking this type of "borrowed language." "This" is obviously borrowing meaning from earlier in the argument. "This" refers to the claim that "the employees are not motivated at all by personal gain." So, the conclusion actually says:

> [The claim made by many non-profit employees that they are not motivated at all by personal gain] just isn't true.

Furthermore, we can probably expect the correct answer choice to be one that rephrases even more. For example:

> Many employees of non-profit companies are motivated by personal gain.

Notice that this rewording takes a double negative ("It ISN'T true that they are NOT motivated by personal gain") and turns it into a positive ("They ARE motivated by personal gain"). Expect that the correct answer will be disguised by a rewording!

Let's apply these concepts to a question that you looked at to begin the chapter:

> *PT29, S1, Q11*
>
> It is well known that many species adapt to their environment, but it is usually assumed that only the most highly evolved species alter their environment in ways that aid their own survival. However, this characteristic is actually quite common. Certain species of plankton, for example, generate a gas that is converted in the atmosphere into particles of sulfate. These particles cause water vapor to condense, thus forming clouds. Indeed, the formation of clouds over the ocean largely depends on the presence of these particles. More cloud cover means more sunlight is reflected, and so the Earth absorbs less heat. Thus plankton cause the surface of the Earth to be cooler and this benefits the plankton.
>
> Of the following, which one most accurately expresses the main point of the argument?
>
> (A) The Earth would be far warmer than it is now if certain species of plankton became extinct.
> (B) By altering their environment in ways that improve their chances of survival, certain species of plankton benefit the Earth as a whole.
> (C) Improving their own chances of survival by altering the environment is not limited to the most highly evolved species.
> (D) The extent of the cloud cover over the oceans is largely determined by the quantity of plankton in those oceans.
> (E) Species such as plankton alter the environment in ways that are less detrimental to the well-being of other species than are the alterations to the environment made by more highly evolved species.

Last in the chain of logic. Did you start by identifying the conclusion in the argument before looking at the answer choices? If so, did you identify the last sentence of the argument as the conclusion? Be careful! This is an understandable choice, since it begins with the word "thus," but what about the statement that "this characteristic is actually quite common"? This statement feels like a claim as well. How do we decide which is the final conclusion? We'll use the Therefore Test:

POSSIBILITY #1: This characteristic [species altering their own environment] is actually quite common. THEREFORE, plankton cause the surface of the earth to be cooler and this benefits the plankton.

POSSIBILITY #2: Plankton cause the surface of the earth to be cooler and this benefits the plankton. THEREFORE, this characteristic [species altering their own environment] is actually quite common.

Possibility #2 gives us the correct ordering. The fact that even lowly life forms such as plankton alter their environment supports the claim that the characteristic (species altering their environment) is actually quite common and not just a characteristic of the most highly evolved species.

So the conclusion of the argument is: However, this characteristic is actually quite common.

Stuck in the middle. Furthermore, notice how the final conclusion is "stuck in the middle" of the argument. This argument has the form: OPPOSING POINT—CONCLUSION—SUPPORTING PREMISES—INTERMEDIATE CONCLUSION, a common argument form for Identify the Conclusion questions. When in doubt, look for the conclusion in the middle of the passage.

The author's conclusion, NOT yours. Now that we've identified our conclusion, we'll search for an answer choice that best expresses this conclusion. Notice that some of the incorrect answer choices are tempting because they seem like reasonable conclusions that a reasonable person might make. Take answer (A) as an example:

> (A) The Earth would be far warmer than it is now if certain
>   species of plankton became extinct.

Given the information in the passage, answer (A) seems right, doesn't it? Remember, though, that we're looking for the conclusion made by the *author,* not a conclusion that we might infer ourselves.

Don't be fooled by rewordings. We want an answer choice that basically rewords the conclusion we've identified. Answer (C) does just that. Let's compare the conclusion as stated in the argument with the language used in the correct answer:

> **CONCLUSION:** However, this characteristic is actually quite common.

> **CORRECT ANSWER (C):** Improving their own chances of survival by altering the environment is not limited to the most highly evolved species.

Notice the difference in wording. In order to see that these actually say the same thing, we need to do some translating.

10

The conclusion contains some tricky language. The "characteristic" referred to is: the tendency for species to alter their environment in order to aid their own survival. Let's rewrite the original conclusion to make this clear:

> **CONCLUSION REWRITTEN:** The tendency for species to alter their environment
> in order to aid their own survival is actually quite common.

The wording of the correct answer (C) presents its own challenges. The answer uses the negatively phrased "not limited to the most highly evolved species" to stand in for "common." If the characteristic is "not limited to" certain species, then this characteristic is "common." Let's rewrite it:

> **CORRECT ANSWER (C) REWRITTEN:** Improving their own chances of survival
> by altering the environment is common.

Now let's compare our rewritten sentences:

CONCLUSION REWRITTEN: The tendency for species to alter their environment in order to aid their own survival is actually quite common.

CORRECT ANSWER (C) REWRITTEN: Improving their own chances of survival by altering the environment is common.

The initial differences boil down to simple rewordings. While the correct answer uses different words from the conclusion, they mean the same thing. (NOTE: You wouldn't want to spend the time on the exam to *write out* these rewordings, but you do want to compare and contrast the phrasing used to see if they say the same things using different words.)

Okay, now let's try it out on another one. Give yourself 1:20.

PT29, S4, Q6

Some judges complain about statutes that specify mandatory minimum sentences for criminal offenses. These legal restrictions, they complain, are too mechanical and prevent judges from deciding when a given individual can or cannot be rehabilitated. But that is precisely why mandatory minimum sentences are necessary. History amply demonstrates that when people are free to use their own judgment they invariably believe themselves to act wisely when in fact they are often arbitrary and irrational. There is no reason to think that judges are an exception to this rule.

Which one of the following sentences most accurately expresses the main point of the passage?

(A) People believe that they have good judgment but never do.
(B) Mandatory minimum sentences are too mechanical and reduce judicial discretion.
(C) Judges should be free to exercise their own judgment.
(D) Judges are often arbitrary and irrational.
(E) Mandatory minimum sentences are needed to help prevent judicial arbitrariness.

10

Once again, we want to remember to identify the conclusion in the argument before we evaluate the answer choices. Once again, we have multiple claims we have to choose between:

Claim 1: Mandatory minimum sentences are necessary to prevent judges from deciding…

Claim 2: When free to use their own judgment, people invariably… act in an arbitrary and irrational manner.

Which of these is a consequence of the other? Are judges acting arbitrarily because mandatory minimum sentences are necessary? No, that doesn't make sense. Are mandatory minimum sentences necessary because judges are acting arbitrarily? That makes a lot more sense, and so we want to take Claim number 1 as our conclusion. Notice, once again, that the conclusion comes in the middle of the argument.

Let's evaluate each of the answer choices relative to our conclusion.

Conclusion: Mandatory minimum sentences are necessary to prevent judges from deciding when a given individual can or cannot be rehabilitated.

    (A) People believe that they have good judgment but never do.

This is not the final conclusion. Furthermore, the "never" is stronger than what the argument presents.

    (B) Mandatory minimum sentences are too mechanical and reduce judicial discretion.

This is given as a potential criticism, but it is not the main point.

    (C) Judges should be free to exercise their own judgment.

This answer is actually the opposite of what the author seems to feel.

    (D) Judges are often arbitrary and irrational.

This is a nice representation of the second claim, and, as such, probably the most attractive wrong answer. However, as we've discussed, this is not the author's main, or final, point.

    (E) Mandatory minimum sentences are needed to help prevent judicial arbitrariness.

This is the correct answer. It's a very close match to the conclusion in the argument.

As we've discussed earlier, it is common that the test writers try to challenge us by using relative pronouns in the actual conclusion. In the above example, we had "that" in the place of judges deciding when a given individual can or cannot be rehabilitated. On the exam, once we've found an answer we like, we want to make sure to check any "this" or "that" from the conclusion of the argument against that answer to make sure there hasn't been any significant change in what the pronoun represents.

Determine the Function Questions

Determine the Function questions require you to correctly identify the role a specific part of the argument plays. Keep the following in mind as you work to determine the function of an argument component.

1. Identify the conclusion first. Without knowing the conclusion, it's virtually impossible to assign a function to any other part of the argument. Thus, always start by identifying the conclusion.

MANHATTAN
LSAT

2. Relate the element in question to the conclusion. Does it support the conclusion, or does it oppose it? Is it the conclusion?

Let's take a look back at a question from the Getting Familiar Section:

> *PT36, S3, Q6*
>
> Government official: A satisfactory way of eliminating chronic food shortages in our country is not easily achievable. Direct aid from other countries in the form of food shipments tends to undermine our prospects for long-term agricultural self-sufficiency. If external sources of food are delivered effectively by external institutions, local food producers and suppliers are forced out of business. On the other hand, foreign capital funneled to long-term development projects would inject so much cash into our economy that inflation would drive the price of food beyond the reach of most of our citizens.
>
> The claim that foreign capital funneled into the economy would cause inflation plays which one of the following roles in the government official's argument?
>
> (A) It supports the claim that the official's country must someday be agriculturally self-sufficient.
>
> (B) It supports the claim that there is no easy solution to the problem of chronic food shortages in the official's country.
>
> (C) It is supported by the claim that the official's country must someday be agriculturally self-sufficient.
>
> (D) It supports the claim that donations of food from other countries will not end the chronic food shortages in the official's country.
>
> (E) It is supported by the claim that food producers and suppliers in the official's country may be forced out of business by donations of food from other countries.

In order to understand the role played by any part of the argument, we must first identify the author's main point, or conclusion. In this argument, there are multiple claims being made. Let's review them here:

1. A satisfactory way of eliminating chronic food shortages in our country is not easily achievable.
2. Direct aid from other countries in the form of food shipments tends to undermine our prospects for long-term agricultural self-sufficiency.
3. If external sources of food are delivered effectively by external institutions, local food producers and suppliers are forced out of business.
4. Foreign capital funneled to long-term development projects would inject so much cash into our economy that inflation would drive the price of food beyond the reach of most of our citizens.

Which one of these is the ultimate conclusion? We are typically looking for something that generalizes, and we are always looking for something that comes last in a chain of reasoning. In this case, the first claim has both of those characteristics.

Let's imagine you saw the above argument on the exam and weren't certain about the conclusion. Perhaps you think another claim could be the final claim in the chain of reasoning. How can you verify? Remember, the Therefore Test can be a great tool. Let's use it to compare the first claim with the one mentioned in the question stem.

Which relationship makes more sense?

Scenario #1: Eliminating chronic food shortages in our country is not easily achievable. THEREFORE, foreign capital would drive the price of food beyond the reach of most of our citizens.

Scenario #2: Foreign capital would drive the price of food beyond the reach of most of our citizens. THEREFORE, eliminating chronic food shortages in our country is not easily achievable.

In terms of an order of reasoning, scenario #2 makes a lot more sense, and we can see, therefore, that the part of the argument that's in question is meant to *support* the conclusion that a satisfactory way of eliminating chronic food shortages in our country is not easily achievable.

Let's evaluate the answer choices:

> (A) It supports the claim that the official's country must someday be agriculturally self-sufficient.

This answer correctly identifies the role—"supports"—but incorrectly identifies the actual conclusion. The conclusion in this answer extrapolates well beyond what the argument discusses.

> (B) It supports the claim that there is no easy solution to the problem of chronic food shortages in the official's country.

This answer choice matches what we predicted and is correct.

> (C) It is supported by the claim that the official's country must someday be agriculturally self-sufficient.

This answer choice brings in an issue—the country must someday be agriculturally self-sufficient—that is not discussed in the argument, and assigns this issue to an incorrect role relative to the part of the argument in question.

> (D) It supports the claim that donations of food from other countries will not end the chronic food shortages in the official's country.

This answer represents a misunderstanding of the author's main conclusion. The claim about the donations of food is not the main conclusion of the argument, and it is not what the element in question is meant to support.

(E) It is supported by the claim that food producers and suppliers in the official's country may be forced out of business by donations of food from other countries.

The claim mentioned in the question plays a parallel role to the claim mentioned in this answer—both support the general conclusion. They do not directly support one another.

Here's one more. Remember your process and take 1:20.

PT29, S4, Q15

Ambiguity inspires interpretation. The saying, "We are the measure of all things," for instance, has been interpreted by some people to imply that humans are centrally important in the universe, while others have interpreted it to mean simply that, since all knowledge is human knowledge, humans must rely on themselves to find the truth.

The claim that ambiguity inspires interpretation figures in the argument in which one of the following ways?

(A) It is used to support the argument's conclusion.
(B) It is an illustration of the claim that we are the measure of all things.
(C) It is compatible with either accepting or rejecting the argument's conclusion.
(D) It is a view that other statements in the argument are intended to support.
(E) It sets out a difficulty the argument is intended to solve.

Once again, our first task is to identify the conclusion. In this case, our job is made a bit easier for us because there is only one opinion, or claim, in the argument: ambiguity inspires interpretation. What follows—information about how different people interpret a particular statement—is fact, and therefore cannot be the author's main point.

Fortunately for us, the conclusion also happens to be the part of the argument that is being asked about. Armed with this understanding, we can evaluate each of the answer choices:

10

(A) It is used to support the argument's conclusion.

We know this answer choice represents an incorrect role.

(B) It is an illustration of the claim that we are the measure of all things.

The statement "We are the measure of all things" is used as part of the support for the conclusion. This answer states a reverse relationship.

(C) It is compatible with either accepting or rejecting the argument's conclusion.

This answer would be tempting if we misunderstood what the conclusion of the argument was. Otherwise, it can be easily eliminated. The part in question is the argument's conclusion.

(D) It is a view that other statements in the argument are intended to support.

This is another way of saying that the part of the argument in the question stem is the conclusion, or main point, of the argument. This is the correct answer.

(E) It sets out a difficulty the argument is intended to solve.

It is not a difficulty, and there is nothing the argument is intended to solve.

Identify the Disagreement Questions

Identify the Disagreement questions present you with two perspectives on an argument (in the form of a conversation between two people), and then ask you to find their specific point of disagreement. The two opinions can be directly opposing sides of one argument, or they can be indirectly related to a common argument.

Success on Identify the Disagreement questions depends on your ability to analyze the relationship between two perspectives. Keep the following in mind:

1. Don't infer. There may be hints that the authors have different opinions, or different definitions of a particular phrase, or different ways of seeing evidence, but an answer choice is unlikely to be correct unless it contains elements that are *specifically*, rather than indirectly, mentioned in the text. This leads to the next point…

2. Identify the overlap! Two people can only disagree about something they each have an opinion about. Most of the time, there is only one point of overlap, and recognizing this overlap will point you towards the right answer.

Take the following simple example to illustrate these two concepts:

Julie: It's really raining hard outside. The school should cancel the football game.

Scott: It's not really raining very much at all. Look! None of the people outside are using umbrellas.

We know that Julie thinks the school should cancel the game because of the rain. It would be very easy to *infer* that Scott thinks the school should go ahead with the game. After all, he doesn't think it's really raining at all! If we were to make this inference, we might choose an answer such as: Julie and Scott disagree over whether the school should cancel the football game. However, this would be a big mistake on our part. Scott mentions nothing about the game at all, which makes it very difficult to *infer* his opinion on canceling the game.

Consider the following diagram that is designed to identify the specific point of disagreement:

	Julie	**Scott**
How much it's raining	Raining hard	Not really raining at all
Cancelling the game	Cancel it!	
People outside		Not using umbrellas

While you wouldn't take the time to draw this out on the test, this diagram does a good job of keeping us honest. Of all the topics discussed (listed along the left side), only one is common between them. The only point of overlap is in regard to the degree to which it is raining. Since this is the only point of overlap, it is the *only* possible point of disagreement. They disagree over how hard it is raining, and our correct answer would represent this.

3. Anticipate the point of disagreement. The two participants in a conversation will likely express their disagreement over 1) the main conclusion, or 2) a supporting premise. In the previous example, Scott takes issue with Julie's *supporting premise* (the degree to which it is raining). He mentions nothing of her conclusion (cancel the game). If you know that disagreements will most often occur 1) over the conclusion, or 2) over a piece of supporting evidence, you'll have a better shot at identifying the correct answer.

Let's look back at a question you completed earlier in the chapter:

> *PT38, S1, Q5*
>
> Naima: The proposed new computer system, once we fully implemented it, would operate more smoothly and efficiently than the current system. So we should devote the resources necessary to accomplish the conversion as soon as possible.
>
> Nakai: We should keep the current system as long as we can. The cost in time and money of converting to the new system would be greater than any predicted benefits.
>
> Naima and Nakai disagree with each other over whether
>
> (A) the predicted benefits of the new computer system will be realized
> (B) it is essential to have the best computer system available
> (C) accomplishing the conversion is technically impossible
> (D) the current computer system does not work well enough to do what it is supposed to do
> (E) the conversion to a new computer system should be delayed

While this question is pretty straightforward, it does illustrate the idea of overlap. The best way to consider the overlapping and non-overlapping parts of Naima and Nakai's arguments is to create a visual representation, as we did before. Again, while you probably wouldn't want to take the time during your actual exam to draw out the following diagram, you would want to keep this representation in your mind's eye:

	Naima	Nakai
Current vs. new system	New will operate more smoothly and efficiently	
When to convert	As soon as possible	Wait as long as we can
Cost of conversion		Would outweigh any predicted benefits

In this diagram, we have represented every point made by either of the two conversation participants. While it may have initially seemed as if their arguments were related in many ways, there is actually only one point of intersection, or overlap, between the two: when to convert to the new system. Both participants support their claims with a supporting premise, but these premises do not overlap. Naima uses a comparison of *system quality* to justify her point, while Nakai cites the *cost* of making the conversion to justify his point. So in the end, they disagree over the main conclusion.

Thus, the only point of overlap, and therefore the only possible point of disagreement, is when to convert to the new system. Answer (E) is the correct answer.

Notice that some of the other answer choices are tempting because they *seem* related, and they *seem* like points of disagreement. Take (B), for example. It seems like Naima would believe that "it is essential to have the best computer system available," and that Nakai wouldn't necessarily agree with this (especially if it's too expensive). But neither of them ever really addresses this point directly. Don't infer!

10

Here's another one. It's tough! Remember to find the overlap and don't infer. Give yourself 1:20.

PT33, S3, Q19

Raphaela: Forcing people to help others is morally wrong. Therefore, no government has the right to redistribute resources via taxation. Anyone who wants can help others voluntarily.

Edward: Governments do have that right, insofar as they give people the freedom to leave and hence not to live under their authority.

Raphaela and Edward disagree about the truth of which one of the following?

(A) Any government that does not permit emigration would be morally wrong to redistribute resources via taxation.
(B) Any government that permits emigration has the right to redistribute resources via taxation.
(C) Every government should allow people to help others voluntarily.
(D) Any government that redistributes resources via taxation forces people to help others.
(E) Any government that forces people to help others should permit emigration.

This question presents us with a higher level of challenge. Each of the five answer choices seems to be related to points made by the conversation participants. We can make our job much easier by identifying the overlap (in our mind if not on paper):

	Raphaela	Edward
Forcing people to help others	Morally wrong; should be done voluntarily	
Government rights	Not right to redistribute resources through taxation	Governments do have this right
Emigration		Governments give people the freedom to leave

Notice that there is just one point of intersection: the main conclusion (governments' rights to redistribute resources through taxation). This shouldn't be surprising. Remember, the overlap will generally occur on 1) the main conclusion, or 2) a supporting premise. Raphaela argues that governments do NOT have this right, while Edward argues that they DO have this right. Each participant uses a supporting premise to support his or her argument, but there is no overlap between these premises.

Thus, there is just one possible point of disagreement.

    (A) Any government that does not permit emigration would be morally wrong to redistribute resources via taxation.

This does not address the issue of government rights. Eliminate it.

    (B) Any government that permits emigration has the right to redistribute resources via taxation.

This addresses a government's right to redistribute resources (the point of overlap), but it also mentions emigration, which is a topic unique to Edward's argument. Let's put this one on hold for now.

    (C) Every government should allow people to help others voluntarily.

Answer (C) discusses the concept of people helping others (unique to Raphaela's argument) and fails to mention anything about the right of governments. Eliminate it.

    (D) Any government that redistributes resources via taxation forces people to help others.

Answer (D) mentions forcing people to help others (unique to Raphaela's argument) and fails to mention anything about the right of governments. Eliminate it.

    (E) Any government that forces people to help others should permit emigration.

This mentions forcing people to help others (unique to Raphaela) and emigration (unique to Edward) and fails to mention anything about the right of governments. Eliminate it.

(B) is the correct answer as it addresses the one point of overlap. It does mention emigration (unique to Edward's argument), but this is appropriate. After all, Raphaela argues that NO government has the right to redistribute resources through taxation. Edward argues that governments do have this right, as long as they allow emigration. In other words, the two disagree only if emigration is allowed. Thus, this qualification must be part of the answer.

10

Procedure Questions

Procedure questions are fairly rare, but they come up frequently enough to warrant a short discussion. Procedure questions ask you to identify the "procedure," or strategy, used in presenting an argument or responding to an argument. Just as all Analyze Argument Structure questions do, these questions require a strong understanding of how arguments are formed.

Let's review a question you tried at the beginning of the chapter:

PT35, S1, Q11

Linguist: Some people have understood certain studies as showing that bilingual children have a reduced "conceptual map" because bilingualism overstresses the child's linguistic capacities. Vocabulary tests taken by bilingual children appear to show that these children tend to have a smaller vocabulary than do most children of the same age group. But these studies are deeply flawed since the tests were given in only one language. Dual-language tests revealed that the children often expressed a given concept with a word from only one of their two languages.

The linguist's argument proceeds by

(A) offering evidence for the advantages of bilingualism over monolingualism

(B) pointing out an inconsistency in the view that bilingualism overstresses a child's linguistic capacities

(C) offering evidence that undermines the use of any vocabulary test to provide information about a child's conceptual map

(D) providing a different explanation for the apparent advantages of bilingualism from the explanation suggested by the results of certain studies

(E) pointing out a methodological error in the technique used to obtain the purported evidence of a problem with bilingualism

For this problem, our job is to understand the author's method of reasoning, or the manner in which he attempts to prove his point. This problem is asking us to describe something we've become very familiar with: the argument core.

What is the author's conclusion? It comes in the middle of the argument:

> But these studies are deeply flawed

Why are these studies deeply flawed?

> ...since the tests were given in only one language.

10

Of course, we need to reference other parts of the argument in order to know what the studies are, and we need to reference other parts of the argument to understand why it might be an issue that the tests were only given in one language, and in real time during the exam we want our understanding to be rounded out in this way, but we can also essentialize the core as follows:

tests were given in only one language → *the studies are deeply flawed*

The question asks us to find an answer that represents how the argument plays out. Let's evaluate the answer choices against our core:

(A) offering evidence for the advantages of bilingualism over monolingualism

Close but no cigar. There is comparison of the two, but the author does not present evidence for the advantages of bilingualism. This answer can be eliminated quickly.

(B) pointing out an inconsistency in the view that bilingualism overstresses a child's linguistic capacities

The author is not pointing out an inconsistency in the view, but rather a flaw in the method of testing.

(C) offering evidence that undermines the use of any vocabulary test to provide information about a child's conceptual map

Sure, these answers can all sound alike, but by this point you should be hyper-sensitive to words like "any"—is the author talking about one specific test, or all vocabulary tests? We can eliminate this answer very quickly.

(D) providing a different explanation for the apparent advantages of bilingualism from the explanation suggested by the results of certain studies

The author does not provide a different explanation.

(E) pointing out a methodological error in the technique used to obtain the purported evidence of a problem with bilingualism

This is what the author does. She points out an error in the methods used to gather evidence—the error being that the children were tested in only one language. This is the correct answer.

With this problem, we can see that questions that ask you for the author's method of reasoning are much easier to solve if you have a strong and simple understanding of the core.

Oftentimes, as evidenced by the question above, these questions come with longer arguments, and the test writer tends to make it tougher than normal to identify the core. If you can't see the core completely, that's fine—make sure you focus in on the conclusion of the argument, and use this as a way to eliminate wrong answers and identify the right one.

In our example above, simply knowing that the author's point was that the study was flawed would have made several answer choices—such as (A), (B), and (D)—seem very unlikely to be correct (and in real time you would check each of these against the rest of the argument to confirm that they are indeed incorrect). Plus, knowing the conclusion would have made (E) the clear favorite because it is the only answer that speaks directly to a flaw in the study. It is often true of Method of Reasoning questions that an understanding of the author's conclusion can, in and of itself, help you eliminate several of the answer choices.

The second type of Procedure question asks that we consider how a certain author proceeds in rebutting another argument. Let's look at an example you tried at the start of the chapter:

PT30, S2, Q7

Opponent of offshore oil drilling: The projected benefits of drilling new oil wells in certain areas in the outer continental shelf are not worth the risk of environmental disaster. The oil already being extracted from these areas currently provides only 4 percent of our country's daily oil requirement, and the new wells would only add one-half of 1 percent.

Proponent of offshore oil drilling: Don't be ridiculous! You might just as well argue that new farms should not be allowed, since no new farm could supply the total food needs of our country for more than a few minutes.

The drilling proponent's reply to the drilling opponent proceeds by

(A) offering evidence in support of drilling that is more decisive than is the evidence offered by the drilling opponent

(B) claiming that the statistics cited as evidence by the drilling opponent are factually inaccurate

(C) pointing out that the drilling opponent's argument is a misapplication of a frequently legitimate way of arguing

(D) citing as parallel to the argument made by the drilling opponent an argument in which the conclusion is strikingly unsupported

(E) proposing a conclusion that is more strongly supported by the drilling opponent's evidence than is the conclusion offered by the drilling opponent

In order to be successful on questions such as the above, it is essential to have a clear and *simple* understanding of an argument's structure. We can organize the Opponent's argument as follows:

Conclusion: The projected benefits of drilling new oil wells in certain areas in the outer continental shelf are not worth the risk of environmental disaster.

Supporting Premises: The oil already being extracted from these areas currently provides only 4 percent of our country's daily oil requirement, and the new wells would only add one-half of 1 percent.

Now let's consider the Proponent's rebuttal relative to the structure of the original argument:

Don't be ridiculous! **This doesn't give us very much that is specific.**

You might just as well argue that new farms should not be allowed. **This is a conclusion that is analogous to the conclusion the opponent reached.**

Since no new farm could supply the total food needs of our country for more than a few minutes. **This part is analogous to the premises in the original argument.**

So, what do we have in the Proponent's response? We have an argument with the same structure as the original—but one that isn't reasonable. Just because one farm can't feed the country doesn't mean, of course, that no new farms should be allowed. The proponent proceeds by presenting an analogous argument that is obviously flawed.

Answer choice (D) represents this, and is therefore the correct answer.

Let's review the other answer choices quickly:

(A) offering evidence in support of drilling that is more decisive than is the evidence offered by the drilling opponent

The proponent could have done this, but did not. In fact, he did not offer any direct evidence, one way or the other, that related to drilling.

(B) claiming that the statistics cited as evidence by the drilling opponent are factually inaccurate

This is incorrect. The proponent is questioning the use *of the stats, not their accuracy.*

(C) pointing out that the drilling opponent's argument is a misapplication of a frequently legitimate way of arguing

The proponent does try to point out flaws in the reasoning structure of the opponent's argument, but we have no direct indication that the drilling opponent's argument method is usually legitimate. Perhaps it's always illegitimate!

(E) proposing a conclusion that is more strongly supported by the drilling opponent's evidence than is the conclusion offered by the drilling opponent

The proponent does not present a conclusion that can be related to the evidence presented by the opponent, and therefore this answer cannot represent the correct procedure.

Conclusion

There are four types of questions that require you to analyze the argument structure in one way or another. Here they are again with a list of takeaways for each.

Identify the Conclusion

1. Always identify the conclusion first! This may seem like an obvious step, but some test-takers might be tempted to read the argument and then jump directly into the answer choices. Remember to take a moment after you finish an argument to make sure that you've correctly identified its conclusion <u>before</u> you look at the answer choices.

2. Stuck in the middle. We mentioned earlier in the book that the conclusion of the argument can appear at the start of the argument, in the middle, or at the end. Typically, it's much easier to spot a conclusion when it appears at the beginning of or at the end of an argument. For this reason, when the LSAT asks you to identify a conclusion, they usually bury it somewhere in the middle of the argument, just to make things a bit more difficult on you.

3. The author's conclusion, NOT yours. When a question asks you to *find* the main conclusion of an argument, you must NOT infer anything at all. Remember, you're looking for the author's conclusion. Don't be tempted to draw your own conclusion.

4. Last in the chain of logic. If you have trouble identifying the final conclusion, it's probably because the argument contains an intermediate conclusion that seems like it could be the final conclusion. Use the Therefore Test to help determine which point actually comes last in the chain of logic.

5. Don't be fooled by rewordings of the conclusion. The LSAT will often attempt to disguise the correct answer by rewording the conclusion in the correct answer choice. You should NOT expect the correct answer to be an exact replica of the conclusion as it is presented in the argument.

Determine the Function

1. Identify the conclusion first. Without knowing the conclusion, it's virtually impossible to assign a function to any other part of the argument. Thus, always start by identifying the conclusion.

2. Keep the sides straight. Your ability to avoid trap answers on Determine the Function questions will often depend on how well you can separate the sides of the argument. Make sure to separate supporting premises from opposing points.

Identify the Disagreement

1. Don't infer. There may be hints that the authors have different opinions, or different definitions of a particular phrase, or different ways of seeing evidence, but an answer choice is unlikely to be correct unless it contains elements that are specifically, rather than indirectly, mentioned in the text. This leads us to...

10

2. Identify the overlap! Two people can only disagree about something they each have an opinion about. Most of the time, there is only one point of overlap, and recognizing this overlap will point you towards the right answer.

3. Anticipate the point of disagreement. Generally speaking, the two participants in a conversation will likely express their disagreement through opposing conclusions. However, the participants will sometimes disagree over a piece of supporting evidence instead. If you know that disagreements will most often occur 1) over the conclusion, or 2) over a piece of supporting evidence, you'll have a better shot at identifying the correct answer.

Procedure

1. Know your argument components and how they work to form an argument!

DRILL IT: Analyze Argument Structure Questions

Give yourself no more than 22 minutes to solve the following problems.

1. PT29, S4, Q2

Economist: To the extent that homelessness arises from a lack of available housing, it should not be assumed that the profit motive is at fault. Private investors will, in general, provide housing if the market allows them to make a profit; it is unrealistic to expect investors to take risks with their property unless they get some benefit in return.

Which one of the following most accurately describes the role played in the economist's argument by the phrase "To the extent that homelessness arises from a lack of available housing"?

(A) It limits the application of the argument to a part of the problem.

(B) It suggests that the primary cause of homelessness is lack of available housing.

(C) It is offered as evidence crucial to the conclusion.

(D) It expresses the conclusion to be argued for.

(E) It suggests a possible solution to the problem of homelessness.

2. PT32, S4, Q1

Yuriko: Our city's campaign to persuade parents to have their children vaccinated ought to be imitated by your city. In the 16 months since the enactment of legislation authorizing the campaign, vaccinations in our city have increased by 30 percent.

Susan: But the major part of that increase occurred in the first 6 months after that legislation was enacted, right after your city's free neighborhood health clinics opened, and before the vaccination campaign really got going.

In responding to Yuriko, Susan does which one of the following?

(A) She denies Yuriko's assumption that Susan's city wants to increase the vaccination rate for children.

(B) She cites facts that tend to weaken the force of the evidence with which Yuriko supports her recommendation.

(C) She introduces evidence to show that the campaign Yuriko advocates is only effective for a short period to time.

(D) She advances the claim that a campaign such as Yuriko recommends is not necessary because most parents already choose to have their children vaccinated.

(E) She presents evidence to suggest that vaccination campaigns are usually ineffective.

3. PT18, S4, Q2

Zoo director: The city is in a financial crisis and must reduce its spending. Nevertheless, at least one reduction measure in next year's budget, cutting City Zoo's funding in half, is false economy. The zoo's current budget equals less than 1 percent of the city's deficit, so withdrawing support from the zoo does little to help the city's financial situation. Furthermore, the zoo, which must close if its budget is cut, attracts tourists and tax dollars to the city. Finally, the zoo adds immeasurably to the city's cultural climate and thus makes the city an attractive place for business to locate.

Which one of the following is the main conclusion of the zoo director's argument?

(A) Reducing spending is the only means the city has of responding to the current financial crisis.

(B) It would be false economy for the city to cut the zoo's budget in half.

(C) City Zoo's budget is only a very small portion of the city's entire budget.

(D) The zoo will be forced to close if its budget is cut.

(E) The city's educational and cultural climate will be irreparably damaged if the zoo is forced to close.

4. PT16, S2, Q13

Alexander: The chemical waste dump outside our town should be cleaned up immediately. Admittedly, it will be very costly to convert that site into woodland, but we have a pressing obligation to redress the harm we have done to local forests and wildlife.

Teresa: But our town's first priority is the health of its people. So even if putting the dump there was environmentally disastrous, we should not spend our resources on correcting it unless it presents a significant health hazard to people. If it does, then we only need to remove that hazard.

Which one of the following is the point at issue between Alexander and Teresa?

(A) whether the maintenance of a chemical waste dump inflicts significant damage on forests and wildlife

(B) whether it is extremely costly to clean up a chemical waste dump in order to replace it by a woodland

(C) whether the public should be consulted in determining the public health risk posed by a chemical waste dump

(D) whether the town has an obligation to redress damage to local forests and wildlife if that damage poses no significant health hazard to people

(E) whether destroying forests and wildlife in order to establish a chemical waste dump amounts to an environmental disaster

10

5. PT33, S1, Q5

A recent national study of the trash discarded in several representative areas confirmed that plastics constitute a smaller proportion of all trash than paper products do, whether the trash is measured by weight or by volume. The damage that a given weight or volume of trash does to the environment is roughly the same whether the trash consists of plastics or paper products. Contrary to popular opinion, therefore, the current use of plastics actually does less harm to the environment nationwide than that of paper products.

The main conclusion of the argument is that

(A) plastics constitute a smaller proportion of the nation's total trash than do paper products

(B) the ratio of weight to volume is the same for plastic trash as it is for paper trash

(C) popular opinion regards the use of paper products as less harmful to the environment than the use of products made from plastic

(D) contrary to popular opinion, a shift away from the use of paper products to the use of plastics would benefit the environment nationwide

(E) at this time more harm is being done to the environment nationwide by the use of paper than by the use of plastics

6. PT16, S3, Q4

Bart: A mathematical problem that defied solution for hundreds of years has finally yielded to a supercomputer. The process by which the supercomputer derived the result is so complex, however, that no one can fully comprehend it. Consequently, the result is unacceptable.

Anne: In scientific research, if the results of a test can be replicated in other tests, the results are acceptable even though the way they were derived might not be fully understood. Therefore, if a mathematical result derived by a supercomputer can be reproduced by other supercomputers following the same procedure, it is acceptable.

The exchange between Bart and Anne most strongly supports the view that they disagree as to

(A) whether a scientific result that has not been replicated can properly be accepted

(B) whether the result that a supercomputer derives for a mathematical problem must be replicated on another supercomputer before it can be accepted

(C) the criterion to be used for accepting a mathematical result derived by a supercomputer

(D) the level of complexity of the process to which Bart refers in his statements

(E) the relative complexity of mathematical problems as compared to scientific problems

10

_7. PT34, S3, Q14_

People's political behavior frequently does not match their rhetoric. Although many complain about government intervention in their lives, they tend not to reelect inactive politicians. But a politician's activity consists largely in the passage of laws whose enforcement affects voters' lives. Thus, voters often reelect politicians whose behavior they resent.

Which one of the following most accurately describes the role played in the argument by the claim that people tend not to reelect inactive politicians?

(A) It describes a phenomenon for which the argument's conclusion is offered as an explanation.

(B) It is a premise offered in support of the conclusion that voters often reelect politicians whose behavior they resent.

(C) It is offered as an example of how a politician's activity consists largely in the passage of laws whose enforcement interferes with voters' lives.

(D) It is a generalization based on the claim that people complain about government intervention in their lives.

(E) It is cited as evidence that people's behavior never matches their political beliefs.

_8. PT32, S4, Q20_

Dana: It is wrong to think that the same educational methods should be used with all children. Many children have been raised in more communal environments than others and would therefore learn better through group, rather than individual, activities. A child's accustomed style of learning should always dictate what method is used.

Pat: No, not always. The flexibility of being able to work either on one's own or in a group is invaluable in a world where both skills are in demand.

The conversation lends the most support to the claim that Dana and Pat disagree on which one of the following?

(A) All children can learn valuable skills from individual activities.

(B) All children should learn to adapt to various educational methods.

(C) Many children would learn better through group, rather than individual, activities.

(D) The main purpose of education is to prepare children to meet the demands of the job market as adults.

(E) It is sometimes desirable to tailor educational methods to the way a child learns best.

10

9. PT33, S1, Q3

Juan: Unlike the ancient Olympic games on which they are based, the modern Olympics include professional as well as amateur athletes. But since amateurs rarely have the financial or material resources available to professionals, it is unlikely that the amateurs will ever offer a serious challenge to professionals in those Olympic events in which amateurs compete against professionals. Hence, the presence of professional athletes violates the spirit of fairness essential to the games.

Michiko: But the idea of the modern Olympics is to showcase the world's finest athletes, regardless of their backgrounds or resources. Hence, professionals should be allowed to compete.

Which one the following most accurately expresses the point at issue between Juan and Michiko?

(A) whether the participation of both amateur and professional athletes is in accord with the ideals of the modern Olympics

(B) whether both amateur and professional athletes competed in the ancient Olympic games upon which the modern Olympics are based

(C) whether the athletes who compete in the modern Olympics are the world's finest

(D) whether any amateur athletes have the financial or material resources that are available to professional athletes

(E) whether governments sponsor professional as well as amateur athletes in the modern Olympics

10. PT37, S2, Q13

Adam: Marking road edges with reflecting posts gives drivers a clear view of the edges, thereby enabling them to drive more safely. Therefore, marking road edges with reflecting posts will decrease the annual number of road accidents.

Aiesha: You seem to forget that drivers exceed the speed limit more frequently and drive close to the road edge more frequently on roads that are marked with reflecting posts than on similar roads without posts, and those are driving behaviors that cause road accidents.

Aiesha responds to Adam's argument by

(A) questioning Adam's assertion that reflecting posts give drivers a clear view of road edges

(B) presenting a possible alternative method for decreasing road accidents

(C) raising a consideration that challenges the argument's assumption that facilitating safe driving will result in safer driving

(D) denying that the drivers' view of the road is relevant to the number of road accidents

(E) providing additional evidence to undermine the claim that safer driving does not necessarily reduce the number of road accidents

10

Challenge Questions

11. PT18, S2, Q10

Most people are indignant at the suggestion that they are not reliable authorities about their real wants. Such self-knowledge, however, is not the easiest kind of knowledge to acquire. Indeed, acquiring it often requires hard and even potentially risky work. To avoid such effort, people unconsciously convince themselves that they want what society says they should want.

The main point of the argument is that

(A) acquiring self-knowledge can be risky

(B) knowledge of what one really wants is not as desirable as it is usually thought to be

(C) people cannot really want what they should want

(D) people usually avoid making difficult decisions

(E) people are not necessarily reliable authorities about what they really want

12. PT32, S4, Q23

Some vegetarians have argued that there are two individually sufficient reasons for not eating meat—one based on health considerations, and the other based on the aversion to living at the expense of other conscious creatures. But suppose that eating meat were essential to good health for humans. Then it would be less clear that an aversion to living at the expense of other conscious creatures is enough of a reason to stop eating meat.

Which one of the following most accurately describes the role played in the argument by the supposition that eating meat is essential to good health?

(A) It is used to disprove the vegetarian position that we should not eat meat.

(B) It is used to show that the two types of reasons cited in favor of vegetarianism are independent.

(C) It is used to disprove the claim that a vegetarian diet is healthy.

(D) It is used to weaken the claim that the consciousness of animals is a sufficient reason for not eating meat.

(E) It is used to show that there is no sufficient reason for not eating meat.

13. PT32, S4, Q12

Surrealist: Many artists mistakenly think that models need be taken only from outside the psyche. Although human sensibility can confer beauty upon even the most vulgar external objects, using the power of artistic representation solely to preserve and reinforce objects that would exist even without artists is an ironic waste.

Which one of the following most accurately expresses the conclusion of the surrealist's argument?

(A) An artist's work should not merely represent objects from outside the psyche.

(B) Artistic representation is used solely to preserve and reinforce objects.

(C) Artists should not base all their work on mere representation.

(D) Great art can confer beauty even upon very vulgar external objects.

(E) True works of art rarely represent objects from outside the psyche.

14. PT34, S2, Q22

Sociologist: Some people argue that capital punishment for theft was an essential part of the labor discipline of British capitalism. Critics of such a view argue that more people were executed for theft in preindustrial England than were executed in England after industrialization. But such a criticism overlooks the fact that industrialization and capitalism are two very different social phenomena, and that the latter predated the former by several centuries.

Which one of the following most accurately describes the role played in the passage by the point that capitalism and industrialization are distinct?

(A) It is cited as some evidence against the claim that capital punishment for theft was an essential part of the labor discipline of British capitalism.

(B) It is cited as a direct contradiction of the claim that capital punishment for theft was an essential part of the labor discipline of British capitalism.

(C) It is an attempt to conclusively prove the claim that capital punishment for theft was an essential part of the labor discipline of British capitalism.

(D) It is cited as a fact supporting the critics of the view that capital punishment for theft was an essential part of the labor discipline of British capitalism.

(E) It is an attempt to undermine the criticism cited against the claim that capital punishment for theft was an essential part of the labor discipline of British capitalism.

10

15. PT36, S1, Q7

It is widely believed that eating chocolate can cause acne. Indeed, many people who are susceptible to acne report that, in their own experience, eating large amounts of chocolate is invariably followed by an outbreak of that skin condition. However, it is likely that common wisdom has mistaken an effect for a cause. Several recent scientific studies indicate that hormonal changes associated with stress can cause acne and there is good evidence that people who are fond of chocolate tend to eat more chocolate when they are under stress.

The argument employs which one of the following argumentative strategies?

(A) It cites counter-evidence that calls into question the accuracy of the evidence advanced in support of the position being challenged.

(B) It provides additional evidence that points to an alternative interpretation of the evidence offered in support of the position being challenged.

(C) It invokes the superior authority of science over common opinion in order to dismiss out of hand the relevance of evidence based on everyday experience.

(D) It demonstrates that the position being challenged is inconsistent with certain well-established facts.

(E) It provides counterexamples to show that, contrary to the assumption on which the commonly held position rests, causes do not always precede their effects.

10

SOLUTIONS: Analyze Argument Structure Questions

1. PT29, S4, Q2

Economist: To the extent that homelessness arises from a lack of available housing, it should not be assumed that the profit motive is at fault. Private investors will, in general, provide housing if the market allows them to make a profit; it is unrealistic to expect investors to take risks with their property unless they get some benefit in return.

Which one of the following most accurately describes the role played in the economist's argument by the phrase "To the extent that homelessness arises from a lack of available housing"?

    (A) It limits the application of the argument to a part of the problem.

    (B) It suggests that the primary cause of homelessness is lack of available housing.

    (C) It is offered as evidence crucial to the conclusion.

    (D) It expresses the conclusion to be argued for.

    (E) It suggests a possible solution to the problem of homelessness.

(A) is correct.

The first sentence is the conclusion of the argument. The following sentences provide support for that conclusion. What's interesting about this particular problem is that we are asked to define the role of *one phrase* within the conclusion. So what does that phrase actually do? By saying "To the extent that," the author is qualifying, or setting boundaries on, the conclusion. Let's look for a choice that reflects this.

(A) is the one! The key word "limits" is another of saying "To a certain extent." To part of which problem? The whole problem of homelessness.

(B) is certainly incorrect—this particular phrase does not say anything about the primacy of the cause.

(C) is not quite right. While the phrase certainly relates to the conclusion in an intimate way, it is not a fact (it's not even a complete grammatical sentence) and thus cannot be called "evidence."

(D) is very close. It is *part* of the conclusion, but certainly does not represent the conclusion itself, for the main conclusion is about private motive not being at fault.

(E) is not even close.

2. PT32, S4, Q1

Yuriko: Our city's campaign to persuade parents to have their children vaccinated ought to be imitated by your city. In the 16 months since the enactment of legislation authorizing the campaign, vaccinations in our city have increased by 30 percent.

Susan: But the major part of that increase occurred in the first 6 months after that legislation was enacted, right after your city's free neighborhood health clinics opened, and before the vaccination campaign really got going.

In responding to Yuriko, Susan does which one of the following?

    (A) She denies Yuriko's assumption that Susan's city wants to increase the vaccination rate for children.

    (B) She cites facts that tend to weaken the force of the evidence with which Yuriko supports her recommendation.

    (C) She introduces evidence to show that the campaign Yuriko advocates is only effective for a short period to time.

    (D) She advances the claim that a campaign such as Yuriko recommends is not necessary because most parents already choose to have their children vaccinated.

    (E) She presents evidence to suggest that vaccination campaigns are usually ineffective.

(B) is correct.

As if we haven't mentioned it enough, focusing on structure is essential to speed, efficiency, and effectiveness on Logical Reasoning problems. First, we must understand Yuriko's argument. If we recognize her argument structure as causal—that she is saying that Susan's city should imitate the campaign because the campaign *caused* the increase in vaccinations—then answering the question becomes easier.

Susan begins "But" and we can anticipate that she is going to disagree either with Yuriko's conclusion itself, or with the *causal* nature (the support) of Yuriko's argument. She attacks the latter by citing a possible alternative cause for the increase in vaccines. This is vintage LSAT. We can think of it this way:

Yuriko: The campaign caused an increase in vaccines, so you should do a campaign.

Susan: But free health clinics opened right before the campaign. (So maybe the campaign was not responsible for the increase.)

(A) is an appealing choice. Yuriko does assume this, but Susan does not deny this assumption.

(B) is a good match. Susan does cite facts, and those facts suggest that Yuriko's evidence is not as strong as she thinks it is.

(C) is a poor match. We do not know whether 6 months is a short time, and furthermore, Susan's evidence does not actually do this—rather, it seems to suggest that the campaign may not have been effective at all.

(D) is interesting because the first half is not such a bad match—Susan does seem to suggest that the campaign is not necessary. However, the second half is not supported by the argument at all, as there is no mention of how many parents already get vaccinations.

(E) goes beyond the proper scope with "usually ineffective." Susan's argument only pertains to this specific campaign.

3. PT18, S4, Q2

Zoo director: The city is in a financial crisis and must reduce its spending. Nevertheless, at least one reduction measure in next year's budget, cutting City Zoo's funding in half, is false economy. The zoo's current budget equals less than 1 percent of the city's deficit, so withdrawing support from the zoo does little to help the city's financial situation. Furthermore, the zoo, which must close if its budget is cut, attracts tourists and tax dollars to the city. Finally, the zoo adds immeasurably to the city's cultural climate and thus makes the city an attractive place for business to locate.

Which one of the following is the main conclusion of the zoo director's argument?

(A) Reducing spending is the only means the city has of responding to the current financial crisis.

(B) It would be false economy for the city to cut the zoo's budget in half.

(C) City Zoo's budget is only a very small portion of the city's entire budget.

(D) The zoo will be forced to close if its budget is cut.

(E) The city's educational and cultural climate will be irreparably damaged if the zoo is forced to close.

(B) is correct.

This argument is a great example of the "conclusion in the middle" structure that we've emphasized. It goes a bit further, in fact, adding premise—premise—premise to the tail end! The key word "nevertheless" is a telltale signal that the argument is turning away from the first statement and into "conclusion" territory.

(A) is the trap answer for folks who believe the first sentence is the conclusion. But notice how the rest of the argument simply takes it as known fact that the city must reduce its budget. In order to be a true conclusion, a claim must have support in the argument. All of the support in this argument, however, is designed to add logical weight to the second sentence, which is the true conclusion.

MANHATTAN
LSAT

10

(B) is definitely the conclusion, supported by the final three sentences of the argument. A quick "therefore" test would settle any lingering doubts about this one.

(C) is true, but is not a claim, so it's not a viable candidate for the conclusion. It is a simple fact.

(D) functions the same as (C).

(E) goes beyond the scope of the argument and therefore cannot be the main conclusion.

4. PT16, S2, Q13

Alexander: The chemical waste dump outside our town should be cleaned up immediately. Admittedly, it will be very costly to convert that site into woodland, but we have a pressing obligation to redress the harm we have done to local forests and wildlife.

Teresa: But our town's first priority is the health of its people. So even if putting the dump there was environmentally disastrous, we should not spend our resources on correcting it unless it presents a significant health hazard to people. If it does, then we only need to remove that hazard.

Which one of the following is the point at issue between Alexander and Teresa?

- (A) whether the maintenance of a chemical waste dump inflicts significant damage on forests and wildlife
- (B) whether it is extremely costly to clean up a chemical waste dump in order to replace it by a woodland
- (C) whether the public should be consulted in determining the public health risk posed by a chemical waste dump
- (D) whether the town has an obligation to redress damage to local forests and wildlife if that damage poses no significant health hazard to people
- (E) whether destroying forests and wildlife in order to establish a chemical waste dump amounts to an environmental disaster

(D) is correct.

Notice that it's left unclear whether Teresa actually agrees or disagrees with cleaning up the waste dump. She only states that if it were to be done, it should be done based on particular reasons, and within certain parameters.

So what is the point of disagreement? Is it Alexander's second sentence, that it would be very costly to convert to woodland? No. Teresa doesn't comment on that.

What about Alexander's final point, that we have a pressing obligation to redress the harm we have done to local forests and wildlife? Yes, Teresa does disagree with this, albeit in a somewhat indirect fashion. She says that the only thing that ought to trigger action is the impact it has on people, and that the only result to be considered is the consequence to people.

Let's evaluate the answers:

(A) is something Alexander would agree with, but Teresa may or may not. We don't actually know.

(B) is something Alexander would agree with, while Teresa may or may not.

(C) is not mentioned by either person.

(D) would be quite acceptable to Alexander—his position is that the town has an obligation to redress the harm done to the environment. Teresa would definitely disagree, so this must be the right answer.

(E) is interesting in that Alexander definitely thinks harm has been done, but he never mentions the word "disaster." Furthermore, Teresa does not reveal her own opinion about this matter, so we can eliminate the choice for that reason. Her argument simply says "even if" it is a disaster—we don't know whether she believes it is.

5. PT33, S1, Q5

A recent national study of the trash discarded in several representative areas confirmed that plastics constitute a smaller proportion of all trash than paper products do, whether the trash is measured

10

by weight or by volume. The damage that a given weight or volume of trash does to the environment is roughly the same whether the trash consists of plastics or paper products. Contrary to popular opinion, therefore, the current use of plastics actually does less harm to the environment nationwide than that of paper products.

The main conclusion of the argument is that

(A) plastics constitute a smaller proportion of the nation's total trash than do paper products

(B) the ratio of weight to volume is the same for plastic trash as it is for paper trash

(C) popular opinion regards the use of paper products as less harmful to the environment than the use of products made from plastic

(D) contrary to popular opinion, a shift away from the use of paper products to the use of plastics would benefit the environment nationwide

(E) at this time more harm is being done to the environment nationwide by the use of paper than by the use of plastics

(E) is correct.

This problem is rather straightforward if you have trained yourself effectively in identifying pivots that lead to conclusions. Remember that "therefore" does not always indicate the main conclusion, but most of the time, as in this case, it does.

The first two sentences are facts that we must take to be true, and the final sentence is a claim that synthesizes these two facts, thus it is last in the chain of logic and must be the conclusion. Though this conclusion may look like another fact, it makes a subtle but important leap in logic. Can you identify a big assumption that the conclusion makes?

(A) is a fact, and therefore not the conclusion.

(B) is unsupported by the argument.

(C) would be a great answer for an Inference question. It is not, however, the author's point.

(D) would be a bad answer for an Inference question, as a "beneficial shift" is not at all supported by the argument.

(E) is the conclusion! It has simply been reworded from "plastics...less" to "paper...more." This kind of rewording is quite common.

6. PT16, S3, Q4

Bart: A mathematical problem that defied solution for hundreds of years has finally yielded to a supercomputer. The process by which the supercomputer derived the result is so complex, however, that no one can fully comprehend it. Consequently, the result is unacceptable.

Anne: In scientific research, if the results of a test can be replicated in other tests, the results are acceptable even though the way they were derived might not be fully understood. Therefore, if a mathematical result derived by a supercomputer can be reproduced by other supercomputers following the same procedure, it is acceptable.

The exchange between Bart and Anne most strongly supports the view that they disagree as to

(A) whether a scientific result that has not been replicated can properly be accepted

(B) whether the result that a supercomputer derives for a mathematical problem must be replicated on another supercomputer before it can be accepted

(C) the criterion to be used for accepting a mathematical result derived by a supercomputer

(D) the level of complexity of the process to which Bart refers in his statements

(E) the relative complexity of mathematical problems as compared to scientific problems

(C) is correct.

Bart says the result is unacceptable because the manner in which it was derived cannot be comprehended by humans. Anne says the result is acceptable if it can be reproduced by other supercomputers, and doesn't require that humans fully understand it.

(A) is a tempting choice. But do we actually know what Bart's opinion is about a process being verified via replication? No. And, while we know Anne believes that replication can make results acceptable, do we know whether she believes that replication is *required* for acceptance? No.

(B) is another tempting choice. Read carefully. Does Anne think that the result *must* be replicated in order to be accepted? Not quite. We simply know that Anne believes replication *allows* results to be accepted. This is a bit of conditional logic. While Anne says that replication would be sufficient for this result to be accepted, she does not say that it is necessary.

(C) is better. Bart believes that, since the *method* used for this result is incomprehensible, the result is unacceptable. Anne, on the other hand, believes that if this result can be *replicated*, it is acceptable. Bart focuses on understanding as his criterion, while Anne focuses on replication.

(D) is out because Anne does not offer an opinion on the complexity.

(E) is out because science vs. math is not mentioned by either Bart or Anne.

7. PT34, S3, Q14

People's political behavior frequently does not match their rhetoric. Although many complain about government intervention in their lives, they tend not to reelect inactive politicians. But a politician's activity consists largely in the passage of laws whose enforcement affects voters' lives. Thus, voters often reelect politicians whose behavior they resent.

Which one of the following most accurately describes the role played in the argument by the claim that people tend not to reelect inactive politicians?

(A) It describes a phenomenon for which the argument's conclusion is offered as an explanation.

(B) It is a premise offered in support of the conclusion that voters often reelect politicians whose behavior they resent.

(C) It is offered as an example of how a politician's activity consists largely in the passage of laws whose enforcement interferes with voters' lives.

(D) It is a generalization based on the claim that people complain about government intervention in their lives.

(E) It is cited as evidence that people's behavior never matches their political beliefs.

(B) is correct.

This problem presents a good lesson in flexibility. Though the LSAT is filled with predictable patterns, it does pitch us a curveball every now and again. The first and last sentences both seem to state the conclusion, and the "But" does not really represent the same kind of logical pivot we've come to expect from it—here it's merely used to define "activity." The sentence could begin with the word "and," a non-pivot word, and retain its meaning.

So let's try assembling the facts to see how they lead to the conclusion.

1. Many people complain about government intervention in their lives.
2. They tend not to reelect inactive politicians.
3. Active politicians pass laws that affect people's lives.

Therefore, voters often reelect politicians whose behavior they resent (political behavior does not match rhetoric). "Often" and "resent" are rather strong, but the flow of logic generally works. If people do not reelect inactive politicians, we might infer that they reelect active ones, and complaining about something is roughly equivalent to resenting it.

So how does the claim in question relate to the conclusion? It supports it! In the end, this argument is actually rather straightforward, though it may not have seemed so at the beginning.

(A) is not quite right. The conclusion does not tell us *why* people do not reelect inactive politicians.

10

(B) is spot on.

(C) is not even close.

(D) is incorrect because the claim in question is not *based* on the claim about peoples' complaints simply because the two follow one another in a sentence—rather, they are both claims upon which the conclusion is based.

(E) is too extreme.

8. PT32, S4, Q20

Dana: It is wrong to think that the same educational methods should be used with all children. Many children have been raised in more communal environments than others and would therefore learn better through group, rather than individual, activities. A child's accustomed style of learning should always dictate what method is used.

Pat: No, not always. The flexibility of being able to work either on one's own or in a group is invaluable in a world where both skills are in demand.

The conversation lends the most support to the claim that Dana and Pat disagree on which one of the following?

(A) All children can learn valuable skills from individual activities.
(B) All children should learn to adapt to various educational methods.
(C) Many children would learn better through group, rather than individual, activities.
(D) The main purpose of education is to prepare children to meet the demands of the job market as adults.
(E) It is sometimes desirable to tailor educational methods to the way a child learns best.

(B) is correct.

Dana makes the point that a child's accustomed style of learning should always dictate the method (of education) used, and Pat responds by saying, "No, not always." Pat does not feel that the child's accustomed style of learning should always dictate the method of education used. Why? Because she

feels that the ability to work in different ways—on one's own or in a group—is an invaluable tool in today's world.

Answer choice (B) is the only one about which we know strong feelings on both sides. We know for sure that Dana disagrees with this statement, because she thinks the child's accustomed style should always dictate the educational method. We have a strong sense Pat agrees with this statement. We know she doesn't think accustomed learned style should always dictate the educational method, and we know she feels this way *because* she thinks it's important for children to learn to work in a variety of ways.

(A) is not directly discussed by either person.

(C) is not discussed by Pat, nor is it insinuated that Pat would disagree with this.

(D) goes well beyond the scope of either statement.

(E) is tempting, but not necessarily something they would disagree about. It is something Dana would likely agree with, but not an answer Pat would definitely disagree with.

9. PT33, S1, Q3

Juan: Unlike the ancient Olympic games on which they are based, the modern Olympics include professional as well as amateur athletes. But since amateurs rarely have the financial or material resources available to professionals, it is unlikely that the amateurs will ever offer a serious challenge to professionals in those Olympic events in which amateurs compete against professionals. Hence, the presence of professional athletes violates the spirit of fairness essential to the games.

Michiko: But the idea of the modern Olympics is to showcase the world's finest athletes, regardless of their backgrounds or resources. Hence, professionals should be allowed to compete.

Which one the following most accurately expresses the point at issue between Juan and Michiko?

(A) whether the participation of both amateur and professional athletes is in accord with the ideals of the modern Olympics

(B) whether both amateur and professional athletes competed in the ancient Olympic games upon which the modern Olympics are based

(C) whether the athletes who compete in the modern Olympics are the world's finest

(D) whether any amateur athletes have the financial or material resources that are available to professional athletes

(E) whether governments sponsor professional as well as amateur athletes in the modern Olympics

(A) is correct.

Juan thinks that the presence of professional athletes violates the spirit of the Olympics, because amateurs do not have the financial resources to compete with them. Michiko thinks professionals should be allowed to compete because the Olympics are supposed to showcase the world's finest athletes.

(A) is the correct answer. Do not be fooled by the presence of "amateur." Juan would say "no" on the basis of fairness, Michiko would say "yes" on the basis of having the finest athletes.

(B) is supported by Juan, but Michiko does not state an opinion.

(C) is not actually supported by either person. Michiko says the games *should* showcase the world's finest, but does not actually state whether they *do*.

Juan might disagree with (D) because he does not say that amateurs *never* have financial resources equal to pros, he just says they *rarely* do.

(E) is not supported by either person.

10. PT37, S2, Q13
Adam: Marking road edges with reflecting posts gives drivers a clear view of the edges, thereby enabling them to drive more safely. Therefore, marking road edges with reflecting posts will decrease the annual number of road accidents.

Aiesha: You seem to forget that drivers exceed the speed limit more frequently and drive close to the road edge more frequently on roads that are marked with reflecting posts than on similar roads without posts, and those are driving behaviors that cause road accidents.

Aiesha responds to Adam's argument by

(A) questioning Adam's assertion that reflecting posts give drivers a clear view of road edges

(B) presenting a possible alternative method for decreasing road accidents

(C) raising a consideration that challenges the argument's assumption that facilitating safe driving will result in safer driving

(D) denying that the drivers' view of the road is relevant to the number of road accidents

(E) providing additional evidence to undermine the claim that safer driving does not necessarily reduce the number of road accidents

(C) is correct.

Notice that Adam's argument is causal! Essentially, Adam says that marking road edges will allow drivers to drive safely and thus decrease accidents (*cause* accidents to decrease). Aiesha says that drivers actually drive *unsafely* on roads with marked edges (ballpark: marked edges *cause* unsafe driving). How does this relate to Adam's argument? We might say that it contradicts Adam's evidence—that marked edges allow drivers to drive safely. With this contradictive aspect in mind, we should go to the choices.

(A) is not quite right. She doesn't argue with the fact that the marked edges give a better view.

(B) is totally incorrect—she does not present an alternative method.

(C) seems good at first glance—"challenge" is a good description. We just have to match the pieces to be sure. Is "Facilitating safety leads to safety" equivalent to "marking edges decreases accidents?" Definitely. This is our answer.

10

(D) is kind of like (A). This is not quite right. In fact, Aiesha seems to believe the opposite—view of the road *is* relevant, it just increases, rather than decreases, accidents in this case.

(E) is a tempting choice. Read it carefully. Is that the claim that Aiesha is undermining? Not quite. First of all, she does not even think that the marked edges will, in fact, result in "safer driving," and we can eliminate the choice for this reason. Secondly, if we did not spot that error, we know that Aiesha's statements *support* rather than undermine the idea that *something* (marking edges) does not necessarily lead to fewer accidents.

Challenge Questions

11. PT18, S2, Q10

Most people are indignant at the suggestion that they are not reliable authorities about their real wants. Such self-knowledge, however, is not the easiest kind of knowledge to acquire. Indeed, acquiring it often requires hard and even potentially risky work. To avoid such effort, people unconsciously convince themselves that they want what society says they should want.

The main point of the argument is that

  (A) acquiring self-knowledge can be risky
  (B) knowledge of what one really wants is not as desirable as it is usually thought to be
  (C) people cannot really want what they should want
  (D) people usually avoid making difficult decisions
  (E) people are not necessarily reliable authorities about what they really want

(E) is correct.

This is a tough problem if we are too entrenched in the details and fail to pay sufficient attention to structure. When an argument begins with "Most people/experts/critics" or "Some critics/scientists/economists," it is often true that we will see a pivot into the main conclusion (but/however, these people are wrong/misguided) and then support for that conclusion; the OPPOSING

POINT – CONCLUSION – PREMISE structure is one that is very common.

Here, then, we may identify the conclusion as "self-knowledge about wants is not the easiest knowledge to acquire." However, this does not appear in any of the choices. Sometimes, on tricky questions like this one, the correct choice is phrased *in reference to* the opposing point: "[the opposing point] is not true" or something similar. For example, here we could also ballpark the conclusion as "people are not reliable authorities about their wants."

(A) is an appealing choice, especially if we are looking for a choice that is a simple rewording of the argument's second sentence. However, the "risky" part of this choice is not a good match. The notion of risk and hard work is brought up to support the idea that acquiring this self-knowledge is not easy. Since the function of "risky work" here is to support, then it cannot be the main conclusion.

(B) is also close, but the desirability of the knowledge is not mentioned.

(C) is merely a play on words utilizing concepts from the argument. Whether people can or cannot want is not mentioned in the argument.

(D) is totally out of scope. "Difficult decisions" do not appear in the argument at all.

(E) is very similar to our second phrasing of the conclusion above, and it is correct.

12. PT32, S4, Q23

Some vegetarians have argued that there are two individually sufficient reasons for not eating meat—one based on health considerations, and the other based on the aversion to living at the expense of other conscious creatures. But suppose that eating meat were essential to good health for humans. Then it would be less clear that an aversion to living at the expense of other conscious creatures is enough of a reason to stop eating meat.

Which one of the following most accurately describes the role played in the argument by the supposition that eating meat is essential to good health?

(A) It is used to disprove the vegetarian position that we should not eat meat.

(B) It is used to show that the two types of reasons cited in favor of vegetarianism are independent.

(C) It is used to disprove the claim that a vegetarian diet is healthy.

(D) It is used to weaken the claim that the consciousness of animals is a sufficient reason for not eating meat.

(E) It is used to show that there is no sufficient reason for not eating meat.

(D) is correct.

This argument follows a recognizable pattern. When we see "Some vegetarians have two ideas," we should anticipate a pivot followed by a counter of some sort to one or both of the vegetarians' ideas. "But" is the pivot, and begins the sentence that the question asks us about. What follows is the conclusion based on that pivot.

It helps if we recognize that a "supposition" is indicated by the word "suppose." Suppose means "if," so the argument basically says, "If it were true that *blablabla*, then it would be less clear that [vegetarian idea #2] is enough to stop eating meat."

So how is that sentence used in the argument? In a nutshell, it supports the final conclusion, which is to say it helps to hurt vegetarian idea #2.

(A) is a tempting answer, but goes too far. Nothing was concretely disproven.

(B) is actually the reverse of what is true. The author uses the phrase to show that #2 is NOT sufficient, or enough by itself.

(C) is too extreme. Again, nothing was concretely disproven, only made "less clear."

(D) is what we said above: "helps to hurt vegetarian idea #2." The wording of this answer is an extremely roundabout way of saying that the example is meant to show that reason #2 is not sufficient by itself.

(E) is too extreme. One sufficient reason is made less clear, and that's all.

13. PT32, S4, Q12

Surrealist: Many artists mistakenly think that models need be taken only from outside the psyche. Although human sensibility can confer beauty upon even the most vulgar external objects, using the power of artistic representation solely to preserve and reinforce objects that would exist even without artists is an ironic waste.

Which one of the following most accurately expresses the conclusion of the surrealist's argument?

(A) An artist's work should not merely represent objects from outside the psyche.

(B) Artistic representation is used solely to preserve and reinforce objects.

(C) Artists should not base all their work on mere representation.

(D) Great art can confer beauty even upon very vulgar external objects.

(E) True works of art rarely represent objects from outside the psyche.

(A) is correct.

The phrase "Many artists" is our signal that the author almost certainly disagrees with whatever these artists believe. A sharp test-taker will recognize and utilize this structure to avoid getting bogged down in the messy details. We might anticipate the conclusion to be "these artists are wrong," or, "models need *not* be taken only from outside the psyche," or even "models should be taken from *inside* the psyche."

In trying to understand the remainder of the argument, one good approach is to ignore for a moment the qualifying phrase "Although…" and focus on the heart of that second sentence: "using… is an ironic waste." The derisive language clearly matches our anticipation that the author would disagree with the artists, and this helps us to understand that when the author says "using artistic representation…," he is referring to what the artists believe. Thus, "taking models from outside the psyche" is equivalent to "representing objects that would exist without artists." Thus, by using our knowledge of structure and actively anticipating that structure, we are able to understand a near-incomprehensible phrase simply by matching the pieces together. As you can see, this is a powerful and effective way of analyzing tough LSAT arguments.

(A) is a great choice, because the author believes that artists are mistaken to think otherwise.

(B) is unsupported. Representation *can* be used to do this, but is not *only* used so.

(C) is an appealing choice. However, it fails to answer the question "representation of what?" The author does not believe that all representation is bad, but that representing only objects outside the psyche is bad.

(D) is out of scope. The argument states that sensibility can do this, but never mentions "great art."

(E) may be an appealing choice for some, but goes astray with "true works" and "rarely"—two concepts that do not appear in the argument.

14. PT34, S2, Q22

Sociologist: Some people argue that capital punishment for theft was an essential part of the labor discipline of British capitalism. Critics of such a view argue that more people were executed for theft in preindustrial England than were executed in England after industrialization. But such a criticism overlooks the fact that industrialization and capitalism are two very different social phenomena, and that the latter predated the former by several centuries.

Which one of the following most accurately describes the role played in the passage by the point that capitalism and industrialization are distinct?

(A) It is cited as some evidence against the claim that capital punishment for theft was an essential part of the labor discipline of British capitalism.

(B) It is cited as a direct contradiction of the claim that capital punishment for theft was an essential part of the labor discipline of British capitalism.

(C) It is an attempt to conclusively prove the claim that capital punishment for theft was an essential part of the labor discipline of British capitalism.

(D) It is cited as a fact supporting the critics of the view that capital punishment for theft was an essential part of the labor discipline of British capitalism.

(E) It is an attempt to undermine the criticism cited against the claim that capital punishment for theft was an essential part of the labor discipline of British capitalism.

(E) is correct.

This is a fun problem because the argument (finally!) sets up a common pattern and throws in a little twist. The argument begins with "Some people," so we anticipate that the author will pivot the argument and disagree with those people. Things take an unexpected turn, however, when we run into "Critics." At this point, we must be curious as to which side the author will finally settle on. We find out at the very beginning of the next sentence, which begins with that all-important pivot word "But," leading into a criticism of the criticism! What we are left with is nothing more than the *implied* conclusion that the author disagrees with the critics.

Notice how the structure of this tricky argument can be easily seen by focusing on three tiny but important pieces: some people, critics, but.

Now, what is the role of the point mentioned in the question? It's the criticism of the critics!

(A) is incorrect. If anything, the point in question *supports* that claim by criticizing the critics of that claim.

(B) is wrong for the same reasons. When we know the sides of the argument (structure), we can eliminate choices like this without getting tangled up in heady interpretations.

(C) is on the right side of the argument, but goes too far. The point is designed merely to weaken the criticism of that claim—a far cry from *proving* that claim.

(D) is tempting, but it too is on the opposite side of the argument. It is not meant to be support for the *critics*, but rather a counter to the critics.

(E) is the answer. It is the only one that accurately represents the role—the point in question is meant to counter the critics.

15. PT36, S1, Q7

It is widely believed that eating chocolate can cause acne. Indeed, many people who are susceptible to acne report that, in their own experience, eating large amounts of chocolate is invariably followed by an outbreak of that skin condition. However, it is likely that common wisdom has mistaken an effect for a cause. Several recent scientific studies indicate that hormonal changes associated with stress can cause acne and there is good evidence that people who are fond of chocolate tend to eat more chocolate when they are under stress.

The argument employs which one of the following argumentative strategies?

(A) It cites counter-evidence that calls into question the accuracy of the evidence advanced in support of the position being challenged.

(B) It provides additional evidence that points to an alternative interpretation of the evidence offered in support of the position being challenged.

(C) It invokes the superior authority of science over common opinion in order to dismiss out of hand the relevance of evidence based on everyday experience.

(D) It demonstrates that the position being challenged is inconsistent with certain well-established facts.

(E) It provides counterexamples to show that, contrary to the assumption on which the commonly held position rests, causes do not always precede their effects.

(B) is correct.

This is clearly a very challenging question, and we want to begin by understanding the core as carefully as we can.

The author's main point, "it is likely that common wisdom has mistaken an effect for a cause," is not terribly difficult to find, but it takes some diligence to understand what it means specifically. The cause in question is discussed in the first sentence: eating chocolate can cause acne (notice the close relationship between "common wisdom" and "widely believed"). The author is stating that eating chocolate is an *effect* that has been mistaken for a *cause*.

How does the author try to prove this? By saying that studies show both eating chocolate and getting acne may be caused by something else: stress. We can think of the reasoning in the core as follows:

Studies show that stress can cause chocolate eating and acne Likely that common wisdom has mistaken chocolate to be a cause of acne when it is actually an effect of something else.

This type of issue should be very familiar to you by this point! Many LSAT arguments include mistaken causal claims. However, it's important to note here that our job is NOT to evaluate the *validity* of this particular argument's reasoning. Rather, it's simply to understand the argument's structure. We want to spend time being careful thinking about the structure laid out above, and we don't want to distract ourselves by worrying about whether the author's argument is a valid one.

We need to keep our focus in order to successfully evaluate what turn out to be some very challenging answer choices:

10

(A) It cites counter-evidence that calls into question the accuracy of the evidence advanced in support of the position being challenged.

This answer is certainly tempting, but the counter-evidence presented does not call into question the *accuracy* of the other evidence—more specifically, it does not call into question whether people actually get acne after eating chocolate, nor does it call into question the fact that they report this to be the case. Rather, the counter-evidence is used to call into question the causal connection between chocolate and acne—that is, it calls into the question the *interpretation* of that evidence.

(B) It provides additional evidence that points to an alternative interpretation of the evidence offered in support of the position being challenged.

Though it is worded in a somewhat challenging fashion, this is the answer we ought to expect, and this is the correct answer. The additional evidence gives us another reason, or *an alternative interpretation*, for the fact that eating chocolate and getting acne are correlated—they have a common cause: stress. Thus, the argument does exactly what this answer choice claims.

(C) It invokes the superior authority of science over common opinion in order to dismiss out of hand the relevance of evidence based on everyday experience.

This could be a tempting answer, but in order for an answer like this to be correct on the LSAT, the argument would have to literally state something that is very close to "scientific authority is superior to common opinion." Without a statement like that actually in the argument, this answer requires too much speculation on our part. Furthermore, the author does not dismiss the *relevance* of the other evidence. Rather, she gives an alternative explanation for it.

(D) It demonstrates that the position being challenged is inconsistent with certain well-established facts.

Another very attractive answer! However, the very big shift from "well-established facts" in the answer choice to "recent scientific studies" (i.e., not well-established) and "good evidence" (i.e., not facts) in the argument should make it clear that this answer is not representative of the given argument.

(E) It provides counterexamples to show that, contrary to the assumption on which the commonly held position rests, causes do not always precede their effects.

This answer choice is about a general idea that causes always come before their effects. The original argument did not depend on the idea that causes always happen before their effects, and the counterexample was not given to show that causes don't always happen before their effects.

Chapter 11

of

11

Logical Reasoning

Inference Questions

Getting Familiar

To start, go ahead and try these four Inference questions. Give yourself no more than six minutes total. We'll revisit these questions later on in the chapter.

PT31, S2, Q20

One of the most vexing problems in historiography is dating an event when the usual sources offer conflicting chronologies of the event. Historians should attempt to minimize the number of competing sources, perhaps by eliminating the less credible ones. Once this is achieved and several sources are left, as often happens, historians may try, though on occasion unsuccessfully, to determine independently of the usual sources which date is more likely to be right.

Which one of the following inferences is most strongly supported by the information above?

(A) We have no plausible chronology of most of the events for which attempts have been made by historians to determine the right date.

(B) Some of the events for which there are conflicting chronologies and for which attempts have been made by historians to determine the right date cannot be dated reliably by historians.

(C) Attaching a reliable date to any event requires determining which of several conflicting chronologies is most likely to be true.

(D) Determining independently of the usual sources which of several conflicting chronologies is more likely to be right is an ineffective way of dating events.

(E) The soundest approach to dating an event for which the usual sources give conflicting chronologies is to undermine the credibility of as many of these sources as possible.

PT25, S2, Q21

If this parking policy is unpopular with the faculty, then we should modify it. If it is unpopular among students, we should adopt a new policy. And, it is bound to be unpopular either with the faculty or among students.

If the statements above are true, which one of the following must also be true?

(A) We should attempt to popularize this parking policy among either the faculty or students.

(B) We should modify this parking policy only if this will not reduce its popularity among students.

(C) We should modify this parking policy if modification will not reduce its popularity with the faculty.

(D) If the parking policy is popular among students, then we should adopt a new policy.

(E) If this parking policy is popular with the faculty, then we should adopt a new policy.

11

PT36, S1, Q4

Most antidepressant drugs cause weight gain. While dieting can help reduce the amount of weight gained while taking such antidepressants, some weight gain is unlikely to be preventable.

The information above most strongly supports which one of the following?

(A) A physician should not prescribe any antidepressant drug for a patient if that patient is overweight.

(B) People who are trying to lose weight should not ask their doctors for an antidepressant drug.

(C) At least some patients taking antidepressant drugs gain weight as a result of taking them.

(D) The weight gain experienced by patients taking antidepressant drugs should be attributed to lack of dieting.

(E) All patients taking antidepressant drugs should diet to maintain their weight.

PT30, S4, Q22

In a recent study, a group of subjects had their normal daily caloric intake increased by 25 percent. This increase was entirely in the form of alcohol. Another group of similar subjects had alcohol replace nonalcoholic sources of 25 percent of their normal daily caloric intake. All subjects gained body fat over the course of the study, and the amount of body fat gained was the same for both groups.

Which one of the following is most strongly supported by the information above?

(A) Alcohol is metabolized more quickly by the body than are other foods or drinks.

(B) In the general population, alcohol is the primary cause of gains in body fat.

(C) An increased amount of body fat does not necessarily imply a weight gain.

(D) Body fat gain is not dependent solely on the number of calories one consumes.

(E) The proportion of calories from alcohol in a diet is more significant for body fat gain than are the total calories from alcohol.

Introduction

About one in every eight Logical Reasoning questions can be categorized as "Inference" questions. These questions require you to *derive* a conclusion (not to be confused with *identifying* a conclusion) based on information given.

Inference questions can be asked in a variety of ways:

1. Support (the most common)

> *Example:* The statements above, if true, most strongly *support* which one of the following?

2. Must be true (occasionally "must be false")

> *Example:* If the statements above are true, which one of the following *must be true*?

3. Infer

> *Example:* Which one of the following can be properly *inferred* from the statements above?

4. Completes the argument (fill in the blank)

> *Example:* Which one of the following most logically *completes the argument*?

5. "Follows logically

> *Example:* Which one of the following claims *follows logically* from the statements?

There are some subtle differences in what these question stems are asking of us, but there is also great commonality. For Inference questions, our main task is to identify the most provable answer of the five available.

Let's start our discussion of Inference questions by first contrasting them with some of the other question types we've already reviewed.

What Inference Questions Are NOT

1. Inference questions are NOT in the Assumption Family. To be effective and efficient on the Logical Reasoning section, it is critical that you have a clear understanding of the unique processes required by the various question types.

For questions in the Assumption Family, we want to identify a main point and the supporting premises, and we want to evaluate the relationship between them. Our success on Assumption Family questions hinges on our ability to evaluate the reasoning within the argument core, and when we are working on an Assumption Family question, that ought to be our focus.

Inference questions do not require us to evaluate reasoning in the same way. Though some right answers for Inference questions will require that we connect two or more statements from the argument together, these questions, in general, are not testing our ability to evaluate how premises lead to a conclusion. In fact, many Inference questions will involve a series of statements that are not meant to fit into an "argument core" sort of mold, so don't force it.

Why is this important? At the least, evaluating the reasoning in an argument for an Inference question can be a waste of your precious time. At the worst, it can distract you from the correct answer and make incorrect answers more tempting.

2. Inference questions are NOT Strengthen questions. The danger comes from how similar the question stems for the two can look.

Take a look at the following:

> The statements above, if true, most strongly support which one of the following?

> Which of the following, if true, most strongly supports the argument above?

The first is an example of an Inference question—we're asked to identify an answer that is most provable based on the information given.

The second is an example of a Strengthen question—we're asked to identify an answer that helps support the given argument.

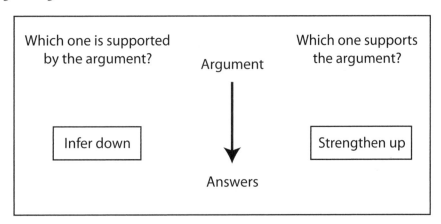

Again, be careful not to confuse one question type for the other.

3. Inference questions are NOT Identify the Conclusion questions. This is a misunderstanding that is far more common, understandable, and dangerous. Perhaps part of the reason that this is such an issue is that many of us, when asked to identify an inference or a conclusion, instinctually look for the *main* inference or conclusion.

Sometimes, right answers will match up with what seems to be the logical *main* inference or conclusion the argument seems designed to reach, but other times they won't. That is, whether an answer represents the main conclusion is NOT the determining factor in whether an Inference answer is correct.

11

It's important you keep Identify the Conclusion and Inference questions distinct in your head. Remember, Conclusion questions require little extrapolation, or "inferring," from us, and for those questions our job is to find the answer that most closely matches the conclusion given in the text. Your job for Inference questions is quite different, and, in fact, the right answer for an Inference question will *never* match up with what is given directly in the text (because it will be something to *infer*!).

Again, it is critical that you understand the specific task that each question presents. Now that we've discussed what Inference questions are not, let's talk about the characteristics that *do* define Inference questions.

Inference Questions Have Unpredictable Answers

To begin this discussion, take a look at the following argument. Take as much time as you'd like to take notes, underline, diagram, infer, and do whatever else you would like before moving further.

> *Most voters prefer Candidate A to Candidate B. Of those who prefer Candidate A, some feel that budgeting for schools is the most important issue. All voters who prefer Candidate B feel that budgeting for schools is the most important issue.*

Here are three potential answer choices. Do your best to identify which of these answer choices, if any, can be logically concluded, and which, if any, cannot. Cover up the explanations that follow if you are tempted to peek!

(A) Some voters who feel budgeting for schools is the most important issue prefer Candidate B.

(B) Budgeting for schools is the most important issue for at least some of the voters.

(C) Some voters who prefer Candidate A are concerned about at least one issue about which voters who prefer Candidate B are concerned.

Now let's evaluate the answer choices.

(A) is inferable. We know that all voters who prefer Candidate B feel that budgeting for schools is the most important issue, so that must mean that at least some of the people who find budgeting for schools to be the most important issue prefer Candidate B.

(B) is inferable. We're given ample evidence that budgeting for schools is the most important issue for at least some people. In fact, we know that at least some people who prefer Candidate A find it most important, and all people who prefer Candidate B do so.

(C) is inferable. We know that *some* people who prefer Candidate A are concerned about budgeting for schools. Since we also know that *all* people who prefer Candidate B have *the same concern*, we can say that some people who prefer Candidate A share a concern in common with those who prefer Candidate B.

MANHATTAN
LSAT

11

If you were correct in assessing all of these answers, fantastic. You have a great knack for this! If you weren't, that's fine too. We'll all get better and better as we go. For now, consider two issues for your own assessment:

1.   Did you find yourself predicting certain answers, and, as a consequence, being dissuaded from any of the choices that were provided?

2.   Did you diagram or draw out this information, and, if so, was it helpful in evaluating all, or some, of the answers?

We anticipate many of you may answer the above questions differently—that's understandable. In particular, some of you will find diagramming to be more useful than others will. However, one point we do want to make clear is that correct answers to Inference questions are generally not predictable. Many scenarios that are given can yield multiple, equally valid answers.

Here are three more answer choices for you to evaluate. We've transferred the argument for your convenience—please transfer any notation you had made previously. Once again, cover up the explanations if you'd like.

> *Most voters prefer Candidate A to Candidate B. Of those who prefer Candidate A, some feel that budgeting for schools is the most important issue. All voters who prefer Candidate B feel that budgeting for schools is the most important issue.*

(A)   A majority of voters feel that budgeting for schools is the most important issue.

(B)   At least some voters who prefer Candidate B do not share at least one common concern with at least one voter who prefers Candidate A.

(C)   Most voters in our district who find budgeting for schools to be the most important issue prefer Candidate B.

(A) is *not* inferable. Like many other tempting wrong answers, this is a statement that could either be true or false based on the given information:

Imagine that there are five voters.

Imagine three prefer A, and two prefer B.

Of those who prefer A, one finds school budgeting to be the most important issue.

We already know that the two who prefer B find school budgeting to be most important.

Therefore, we would have three out of five people, a *majority*, who find school budgeting to be the most important issue. So we know that (A) is *possible*. But let's look at a counterexample:

Now let's imagine four voters prefer A, and one prefers B.

Of those who prefer A, one finds school budgeting to be the most important issue.

We already know that the one who prefers B finds school budgeting to be most important.

In this case, only 2/5, a *minority*, would find school budgeting to be the most important issue.

Therefore, based on the information given, this statement can be true or false, and so it is not inferable.

(B) is *not* inferable. In fact, it is false. All voters who prefer Candidate B are concerned with school budgeting, and some voters who prefer Candidate A are as well, so it must be true that at least one voter who prefers Candidate A shares a concern in common with *all* of the voters who prefer Candidate B.

(C) is *not* inferable. This is another statement that could either be true or false based on the given information:

Once again, imagine five voters.

And let's imagine three prefer A, and two prefer B.

Of those who prefer A, one finds school budgeting most important.

We already know that the two who prefer B find school budgeting to be most important.

In this case, a majority of voters who felt school budgeting was the most important issue could be said to prefer B.

However, if four prefer A, and one prefers B…

And of those who prefer A, three find school budgeting to be the most important issue, this answer would be false. Keep in mind that the word "some," at least for the purposes of the LSAT, does NOT mean "less than half." (Please refer to the Conditional Logic chapter for more discussion on "some" issues.)

If you were drawn to any of those three answers, chances are you were tempted into making false inferences, perhaps linking information in an incorrect way. It's understandable. Consistently, we've found that some of the most tempting incorrect choices for challenging Inference questions involve such false connections.

Here's a question from the Getting Familiar section. Solve it again if you'd like. Focus on identifying the most provable answer.

PT31, S2, Q20

One of the most vexing problems in historiography is dating an event when the usual sources offer conflicting chronologies of the event. Historians should attempt to minimize the number of competing sources, perhaps by eliminating the less credible ones. Once this is achieved and several sources are left, as often happens, historians may try, though on occasion unsuccessfully, to determine independently of the usual sources which date is more likely to be right.

Which one of the following inferences is most strongly supported by the information above?

(A) We have no plausible chronology of most of the events for which attempts have been made by historians to determine the right date.

(B) Some of the events for which there are conflicting chronologies and for which attempts have been made by historians to determine the right date cannot be dated reliably by historians.

(C) Attaching a reliable date to any event requires determining which of several conflicting chronologies is most likely to be true.

(D) Determining independently of the usual sources which of several conflicting chronologies is more likely to be right is an ineffective way of dating events.

(E) The soundest approach to dating an event for which the usual sources give conflicting chronologies is to undermine the credibility of as many of these sources as possible.

Again, for this type of argument, searching for a conclusion or a core is likely going to be an ineffective use of your time. We simply want to have a general sense of the discussion, and we want to move on quickly to the answer choices.

In this case, the argument begins by describing a problem in dating certain events in history, and describes one method of trying to solve this problem.

(A) We have no plausible chronology of most of the events for which attempts have been made by historians to determine the right date.

Is (A) provable?

No. The word that should jump out is "most"—we don't have nearly enough evidence to prove the information is missing most of the time.

11

(B) Some of the events for which there are conflicting chronologies and for which attempts have been made by historians to determine the right date cannot be dated reliably by historians.

Is (B) provable?

It seems so. We are told specifically that historians are sometimes unsuccessful in their attempts to date (no pun intended). Let's keep this for now.

(C) Attaching a reliable date to any event requires determining which of several conflicting chronologies is most likely to be true.

Is (C) provable?

No. The word that perhaps tips us off right away is "any"—there are many events (what time you woke up this morning, for example) for which a time can be determined without examining conflicting chronologies.

(D) Determining independently of the usual sources which of several conflicting chronologies is more likely to be right is an ineffective way of dating events.

Is (D) provable?

No. It might be tempting if we are looking for some bigger point to be extracted from this argument, but it is not a statement that we can say can be "proven" based on this argument. It hasn't discussed "effectiveness" directly, and it hasn't given us a way to gauge whether the success rate determined in the argument can be considered effective.

(E) The soundest approach to dating an event for which the usual sources give conflicting chronologies is to undermine the credibility of as many of these sources as possible.

Is (E) provable?

Absolutely not! To eliminate less credible sources is not the same thing as undermining credibility. The author is not suggesting that undermining credibility is a sound approach.

Let's return to (B), the correct answer.

(B) Some of the events for which there are conflicting chronologies and for which attempts have been made by historians to determine the right date cannot be dated reliably by historians.

Down to one answer, you want to check each part of the argument. We know for sure that there are some events for which there are conflicting chronologies, and we know for sure that historians have made attempts to date these events. We're told they are sometimes unsuccessful. Nothing in this answer requires too great a leap from what we've been given.

Was this answer the author's main point? No, and, in fact, the information that most supports this answer—
"though on occasion unsuccessfully"—could be thought of as playing a secondary role in the argument.

Is this answer 100% provable? The truth is, no. There are many reasons why this does not have to be 100%
true. For one, perhaps at some point in the future a more accurate dating system for historians will emerge.

This leads us to the next part of our discussion…

Right Answers Will Have a Range of Provability

For some Inference questions, we are asked to identify one answer that MUST be true based on the information given. For these questions, the right answer is designed to be *perfectly provable*. For other Inference questions, we are asked to identify the MOST provable answer based on the information given. In these latter cases, right answers are typically not designed to be perfectly provable.

Let's take a look at an example of one of each. Both of these questions are from the Getting Familiar section.

Here's a MUST be true:

> *PT25, S2, Q21*
>
> If this parking policy is unpopular with the faculty, then we should modify it. If it is unpopular among students, we should adopt a new policy. And, it is bound to be unpopular either with the faculty or among students.
>
> If the statements above are true, which one of the following must also be true?
>
> (A) We should attempt to popularize this parking policy among either the faculty or students.
> (B) We should modify this parking policy only if this will not reduce its popularity among students.
> (C) We should modify this parking policy if modification will not reduce its popularity with the faculty.
> (D) If the parking policy is popular among students, then we should adopt a new policy.
> (E) If this parking policy is popular with the faculty, then we should adopt a new policy.

We're told to assume that the statements in the argument are true, so we need not doubt, for example, whether the policy will indeed be unpopular either with the faculty or among students.

From our initial read, what we know is that the stimulus contains some suggestions of what to do if a parking policy is unpopular with either the faculty or the students, then states that the policy will indeed be unpopular with either the faculty or the students.

The correct answer is (E), and it is provable based on the text.

We are told that the policy is unpopular either with the faculty or the students. If it is popular with the faculty, therefore, it MUST BE TRUE that it is unpopular with the students. If it is unpopular with the students, we are told, we should adopt a new policy. Therefore, if it is popular with faculty, it must be true that we should adopt a new policy.

Let's take a look at the other answer choices:

(A) We should attempt to popularize this parking policy among either the faculty or students.

This is not provable. The author gives no indication that an attempt should be made to popularize *the policy with one group or another.*

(B) We should modify this parking policy only if this will not reduce its popularity among students.

This is not provable. It links elements of the argument together in incorrect ways. Reducing popularity with students has no direct relation to when the policy should be modified.

(C) We should modify this parking policy if modification will not reduce its popularity with the faculty.

This is not provable. We haven't been given information that can help us evaluate whether modifications will or won't result in reducing popularity with faculty.

(D) If the parking policy is popular among students, then we should adopt a new policy.

This is not provable. In fact, we're told we should adopt a new policy if it is unpopular *with students.*

Notice the "If" and the "then" in the original sentence. This argument can also be more formally considered in terms of conditional logic, and it can be helpful to do so. To illustrate, let's break this argument down into a simpler form:

If this parking policy is unpopular with the faculty, then we should modify it.

We can notate this as follows: –PF → M

If it is unpopular among students, we should adopt a new policy.

–PS → N

And, it is bound to be unpopular either with the faculty or among students.

If this statement is true, we know that if it is popular with the faculty, it must be unpopular with the students, and if it is popular with students, it must be unpopular with the faculty.

We can represent these two relationships in this way:

PF → –PS
PS → –PF

Note that this statement does NOT mean that if it is unpopular with either group, it must be popular with the other. This would be an illegal reversal of the terms (For more on this, please refer to the Conditional Logic chapter.)

The four relationships we know are as follows:

–PF → M
–PS → N
PF → –PS
PS → –PF

If you can see the links easily, go ahead and write them out quickly:

PS → –PF → M (If it's popular with students, we should modify it.)
PF → –PS → N (If it's popular with faculty, we should adopt a new policy.)

Now, let's see if any of our answers match one of the two chains above.

(A) We should attempt to popularize this parking policy
        among either the faculty or students.

It's tough to match this answer up with the conditionals above, and that's with good reason—who we ought to popularize this policy with is not discussed.

(B) We should modify this parking policy only if this will not
        reduce its popularity among students.

M → reduce PS.

Reducing popularity is also not discussed. Notice in no way can we manipulate any of the known conditionals so that M acts as a trigger that results in this particular consequence.

(C) We should modify this parking policy if modification will
        not reduce its popularity with the faculty.

We can try to warp this into a conditional:

(M → –PF) → M

But that's a bit of a stretch and, in any case, clearly not something provable based on the text.

(D) If the parking policy is popular among students, then we
        should adopt a new policy.

PS → N

This answer translates more cleanly, but it is not something provable from the conditionals we laid out above.

11

(E) If this parking policy is popular with the faculty, then we
should adopt a new policy.

PF → N

This is indeed provable. It's the second of our two chains.

That is, if the policy is popular with the faculty, we should adopt a new policy.

As you can see, being able to notate arguments in a formal fashion can be very helpful, especially for verifying the correct answer, or choosing between two attractive answers to a MUST BE TRUE Inference question.

Do always keep in mind that these notations are one tool, but not your only tool. When transferring from English to conditional notation, be careful that you don't forget about the nuances of the argument.

In the above example, it is critical to recognize the fact that the argument is about the consequences of *being* popular or unpopular, whereas several of the answer choices are about *becoming* more or less popular. This is the type of difference that can be obscured by notation.

Now let's take a look at a question that asks us to find the MOST provable answer:

_PT36, S1, Q4_

Most antidepressant drugs cause weight gain. While dieting can help reduce the amount of weight gained while taking such antidepressants, some weight gain is unlikely to be preventable.

The information above most strongly supports which one of the following?

(A) A physician should not prescribe any antidepressant drug for a patient if that patient is overweight.
(B) People who are trying to lose weight should not ask their doctors for an antidepressant drug.
(C) At least some patients taking antidepressant drugs gain weight as a result of taking them.
(D) The weight gain experienced by patients taking antidepressant drugs should be attributed to lack of dieting.
(E) All patients taking antidepressant drugs should diet to maintain their weight.

The correct answer for this problem was (C).

What we know from the argument is that most antidepressant drugs cause weight gain, and that some weight gain from such antidepressants is unlikely to be preventable.

Taken together, it's reasonable to conclude that at least some patients taking antidepressant drugs gain weight as a result of taking them.

Is this answer 100% provable? Far from it. For one, "unlikely to be preventable" does not mean it won't be preventable. Furthermore, imagine a scenario where most antidepressant drugs cause weight gain, but everyone happens to take the one antidepressant drug that doesn't cause weight gain. In this case, (C) would not be true.

So, (C) is far from totally provable, but it is clearly the best available answer.

Let's discuss the other answer choices:

(A) A physician should not prescribe any antidepressant drug for a patient if that patient is overweight.

This is an answer that might be tempting if you oversimplify the argument, but it makes little sense otherwise. There could be other reasons, far more important than weight, that would cause a physician to prescribe such antidepressants anyway. The argument hasn't given us proof otherwise.

(B) People who are trying to lose weight should not ask their doctors for an antidepressant drug.

This is similar to (A). Perhaps there are people for whom the benefits of antidepressants outweigh the negative consequences of weight gain.

(D) The weight gain experienced by patients taking antidepressant drugs should be attributed to lack of dieting.

This answer is clearly not provable based on the statements in the argument. While dieting is mentioned as something that can sometimes alleviate the weight gain, lack of dieting is not mentioned as the cause of weight gain.

(E) All patients taking antidepressant drugs should diet to maintain their weight.

This answer extrapolates too far from the argument. Perhaps there are patients for whom dieting has negative consequences more significant than gaining weight.

Note that there will be right answers to "Must be true" questions that seem less than perfect, and answers to "Support" questions that seem 100 percent provable. However, in general, it is helpful to look out for absolute terms, such as "must," versus relative terms, such as "most," to help get a sense of how strongly the right answer needs to be supported.

Note that there are many other questions that fall into a gray area between the two. Here is one more problem. Take 1:30 to solve before reading the explanation.

PT27, S4, Q5

Ticks attach themselves to host animals to feed. Having fed to capacity, and not before then, the ticks drop off their host. Deer ticks feeding off white-footed mice invariably drop off their hosts between noon and sunset, regardless of time of attachment. White-footed mice are strictly nocturnal animals that spend all daytime hours in their underground nests.

Which one of the following conclusions can be properly drawn from the statements above?

(A) Deer ticks all attach themselves to white-footed mice during the same part of the day, regardless of day of attachment.
(B) Deer ticks sometimes drop off their hosts without having fed at all.
(C) Deer ticks that feed off white-footed mice drop off their hosts in the hosts' nests.
(D) White-footed mice to which deer ticks have attached themselves are not aware of the ticks.
(E) White-footed mice are hosts to stable numbers of deer ticks, regardless of season of the year.

Notice that in this stimulus we are given many absolute statements:

1. Ticks drop off host when fed to capacity, and not before.
2. Deer ticks feeding off white-footed mice must drop off between noon and sunset.
3. White-footed mice are strictly nocturnal.
4. White-footed mice spend all daytime hours in underground nests.

Armed with all these truths, let's see which answer can be properly drawn:

> (A) Deer ticks all attach themselves to white-footed mice during the same part of the day, regardless of day of attachment.

We don't know what time of day ticks attach to the mice, and we don't have a clear way to define "same part" of day.

> (B) Deer ticks sometimes drop off their hosts without having fed at all.

This is not inferable. In fact, it's false. We know they don't fall off until fed to capacity.

> (C) Deer ticks that feed off white-footed mice drop off their hosts in the hosts' nests.

The deer ticks fall off during the day, and the mice are in underground nests during the day. Let's keep it.

> (D) White-footed mice to which deer ticks have attached themselves are not aware of the ticks.

We don't know anything about what the mice are aware of!

> (E) White-footed mice are hosts to stable numbers of deer ticks, regardless of season of the year.

The number of ticks on any mouse, and the consistency of that number, is not discussed in the argument. (E) is not inferable.

(C) is the only viable answer, and (C) is the correct answer.

One might think, based on the stringency of the LSAT in general, that a conclusion that is *properly drawn* must be 100 percent provable.

Is (C) 100 percent provable? That's a matter of debate perhaps, but people who live at the higher latitudes, at which night can sometimes take up 23 hours of the day, might feel it's not.

Again, one point we strongly want to emphasize is that while it might be helpful during your studies to develop a good sense of what is 90 percent provable versus 100 percent provable, this type of thinking can be a distraction during the exam.

11

It is important for you to know that these questions are not designed for you to differentiate between that which is almost provable and that which is absolutely provable—almost all of these problems are designed for you to separate out one answer that could fall into *either* of those categories from the four that, upon careful review, clearly cannot.

Therefore, your ability to see that four answers are indeed *not* provable is what is most crucial to your success.

Get to the Right Answer by Eliminating Wrong Answers

Because there are so many potentially correct answers, and because the paths to these potential answers are fraught with danger, the best approach for Inference questions is to focus on knocking off those answers that are most certainly *not* provable based on the information given.

Here are some guiding principles to help you in your process:

1. Look for term shifts between argument and answer choice. Many answer choices to Inference questions are designed to test your ability to accurately discern differences in the meaning of words and phrases. A great way to spot these differences is to actively look for "mismatches" in subject matter or attribute between the answer choice and the stimulus. Once you get in this habit, you will see that these differences jump out at you more and more.

Let's use the following stimulus to discuss some significant term shifts that you are likely to see in incorrect answers to Inference questions.

Most people with significant credit card debt will benefit from this bill. Many of these people may be able to eliminate interest payments altogether.

Invalid Inference	Why the Answer Would Be Incorrect
This bill will benefit **all** people with significant credit card debt.	This answer has a **degree** issue. We're told the bill can benefit "most" of these people, not all.
Very few people with significant credit card debt will benefit from this bill.	This answer has the **opposite meaning**. This is more common than you might think.
Most people who **pay large credit card bills** monthly will benefit from this bill.	This answer has a **detail creep**, or a subtle change in detail. Paying a large credit card bill is not the same as having a large credit card debt. For example, the person can pay the complete bill each month and have no debt.
This new bill is **popular** with most people with significant credit card debt.	This answer has **scope** issues. We have not been given any evidence to show that the bill is *popular* with one group or another.

11

MANHATTAN
LSAT

2. Be suspicious of answers with faulty reasoning. Many answers are incorrect because they require inferences that go beyond what the given stimulus can reasonably support. Here are some examples that are representative of common reasoning issues:

Most people with significant credit card debt will benefit from this bill. Many of these people may be able to eliminate interest payments altogether.

Invalid Inference	Why the Answer Would Be Incorrect
If someone with significant credit card debt benefited, it was due to this bill.	This answer **reverses the logic** of the argument. We're told the bill will benefit the people, but that does not mean that if people benefit, it was due to the bill. They can benefit through other means.
This bill will benefit the debt situation of the country as a whole.	This answer incorrectly **generalizes** from the text. We don't have nearly enough evidence to show that the bill will impact the country as a whole.
All people with interest payments have significant credit card debt.	This answer hinges on **unjustified connections**. The argument discusses interest payments, and it discusses those with significant credit card debt, but this answer choice falsely connects those ideas.

As we've stated in other chapters, there is great overlap in incorrect answer characteristics, and many answers are incorrect for multiple reasons. However, it's to your benefit to develop as specific a sense as you can of incorrect answer characteristics. This will help in both your timing and your accuracy.

Let's finish this lesson by taking a look at four final sample problems. We will use these to get a more complete understanding of incorrect answer characteristics.

The first is from the "Getting Familiar" section. Consider carefully why you eliminated each incorrect choice before moving on to the explanation.

11

PT30, S4, Q22

In a recent study, a group of subjects had their normal daily caloric intake increased by 25 percent. This increase was entirely in the form of alcohol. Another group of similar subjects had alcohol replace nonalcoholic sources of 25 percent of their normal daily caloric intake. All subjects gained body fat over the course of the study, and the amount of body fat gained was the same for both groups.

Which one of the following is most strongly supported by the information above?

(A) Alcohol is metabolized more quickly by the body than are other foods or drinks.
(B) In the general population, alcohol is the primary cause of gains in body fat.
(C) An increased amount of body fat does not necessarily imply a weight gain.
(D) Body fat gain is not dependent solely on the number of calories one consumes.
(E) The proportion of calories from alcohol in a diet is more significant for body fat gain than are the total calories from alcohol.

As you evaluate the answers, you should be focused on trying to identify the characteristics that indicate that a particular answer is *not* provable based on the text. We've highlighted some of them here.

(A) Alcohol is **metabolized more quickly** by the body than are other foods or drinks.

How fast alcohol and other food or drinks are metabolized is not discussed, and we can consider this answer out of scope.

(B) In the **general population**, alcohol is the **primary** cause of gains in body fat.

This answer generalizes and has degree issues. We know nothing of the general population; this stimulus presents no evidence that proves that alcohol is a primary cause, let alone the primary cause, of gains in body fat for this population.

(C) An increased amount of body fat **does not necessarily imply a weight gain**.

We don't have enough information to infer any relationship between body fat and weight gain, and in fact, weight gain is never discussed.

(D) Body fat gain is not dependent solely on the number of calories one consumes.

(D) is the correct answer. Notice that one group changed the total amount of calories it consumed, while the other group did not. Both groups gained the same amount of body fat. Since both groups attained the same result even though they consumed a different number of calories, it's reasonable to conclude there must be factors other than calories that are involved.

(E) The proportion of calories from alcohol in a diet is more significant for body fat gain than are the total calories from alcohol.

(E) is a tempting answer that brings together various elements of the argument, but it is not provable. In fact, the evidence seems to suggest that since the results were the same for both groups, calories from alcohol may play a bigger role than proportion. Even if it wasn't a reversal of what the text implies, there would not be enough evidence from this argument to support a claim such as this one. This is an answer that relies on an incorrect linking of elements of the stimulus.

Here's another example. Again, be specific about why you feel the wrong answers are wrong before moving on to the explanation.

PT37, S4, Q8

Commentator: In the new century, only nations with all the latest electronic technology will experience great economic prosperity. The people in these nations will be constantly bombarded with images of how people in other countries live. This will increase their tendency to question their own customs and traditions, leading to a dissolution of those customs and traditions. Hence, in the new century, the stability of a nation's cultural identity will likely _____.

Which one of the following most logically completes the commentator's argument?

(A) depend on a just distribution of electronic technology among all nations

(B) decrease if that nation comes to have a high level of economic wealth

(C) be ensured by laws that protect the customs and traditions of that culture

(D) be threatened only if the people of that culture fail to acquire the latest technical skills

(E) be best maintained by ensuring gradual assimilation of new technical knowledge and skills

Of all questions that are categorized as Inference, Completes the Argument are perhaps the questions that have the *most* predictable correct answers. This is due to a few reasons. One reason is that these questions tend to be associated with arguments that have clean, almost mathematical, structures to their logic.

In this problem, the first sentence gives us our first absolute statement: *"only* nations with…." From there, there is a simple order to the new ideas that are introduced, and we can see that these ideas are meant to link together:

only nations with all the latest electronic technology will experience great economic prosperity → the people in these nations will be constantly bombarded with images of how people in other countries live → this will increase their tendency to question their own customs and traditions → leading to a dissolution of those customs and traditions

Remember, our job in an Inference question is NOT to question the validity of the reasoning, but rather just to see it clearly.

A second reason why answers to Completes the Argument are a bit more predictable has to do with the structure of stimulus: we are given a portion of that which we are meant to infer. This narrows the scope of what could be the right answer.

In this case, we are given the phrase, "Hence, in the new century, the stability of a nation's cultural identity will likely _____ ." In terms of the information we've already been presented with in the argument, "stability of a nation's cultural identity" is most directly related to the statement that immediately precedes the sentence: "a dissolution of those customs and traditions."

Let's discuss the exact wording of the question: "completes the commentator's argument." We are not looking for something that we ourselves *can* conclude from the given information, but rather what we expect that the commentator is *likely* to conclude—what is most reasonable for this commentator to conclude.

We know that those with the latest technology—the only ones who will experience economic prosperity—will have a dissolution of customs and traditions. A dissolution of customs and traditions is something that typically goes very much against the idea of having stability in cultural identity—if customs and traditions are being dissolved, cultural identity is losing stability. If we know that he believes those with the latest technology—the only ones who will experience economic prosperity— will have a decrease in the stability of their cultural identity, we can predict that the author would conclude…

> *"Hence, in the new century, the stability of a nation's cultural identity will likely decrease if that nation comes to have a high level of economic wealth."*

This is what answer choice (B) states, and (B) is the correct answer.

If you were able to predict that answer, great. However, we want to stress that even if you know that you are amazing at predicting the right answer, we strongly recommend that you arrive at that right answer by eliminating wrong ones. There will be Completes the Argument questions where the answer is not what you would predict, and there will be ones where the right answer is written in such a convoluted way that you can't tell that it's what you predicted. Eliminating wrong choices first gives you the best chance at consistent success.

Whether you predicted (B) or not, you can get there by eliminating the other answers:

11

(A) depend on a just distribution of electronic technology
       among all nations

This answer is tempting, because a just distribution seems like it could pass for being the opposite of only wealthy nations having the latest technology, but we have no evidence at all that just distribution would lead in any way to stability. There is also a detail creep—distribution of technology is different from the distribution of the latest *technology. By this point, we can see that this answer is clearly not inferable based on the text.*

(C) be ensured by laws that protect the customs and traditions
       of that culture

We are given no information about such laws, and this answer can be eliminated very quickly because it is out of scope.

(D) be threatened only if the people of that culture fail to
       acquire the latest technical skills

This is an answer that conflicts with the information we are given. Per the given argument, those who acquire the latest technology will feel a threat to their stability. There is also an unjustified shift from technology to technical skills.

(E) be best maintained by ensuring gradual assimilation of
       new technical knowledge and skills

Like (A), (E) poses as some sort of opposite or remedy of the situation the author describes. However, the author's argument is only about nations with the latest technology, and it's unlikely that those nations who "ensure" gradual assimilation will be relevant to this discussion. Furthermore, as mentioned before, technical knowledge and skills are not the same as technology itself. Finally, and perhaps most importantly, we have not nearly enough information to conclude anything about what would be "best" for maintaining a stable social identity.

The four wrong choices have clearly defining characteristics. Once we eliminate these choices, we are left with (B), the correct choice.

Here's another one. Again, focus your attention on eliminating answers that are not provable.

11

PT27, S4, Q23

Much of today's literature is inferior: most of our authors are intellectually and emotionally inexperienced, and their works lack both the intricacy and the focus on the significant that characterize good literature. However, Hypatia's latest novel is promising; it shows a maturity, complexity, and grace that far exceeds that of her earlier works.

Which one of the following statements is most strongly supported by the information in the passage?

(A) Much of today's literature focuses less on the significant than Hypatia's latest novel focuses on the significant.

(B) Much of today's literature at least lacks the property of grace.

(C) Hypatia's latest novel is good literature when judged by today's standards.

(D) Hypatia's latest novel is clearly better than the majority of today's literature.

(E) Hypatia's latest novel has at least one property of good literature to a greater degree than her earlier works.

In this argument there is discussion of two distinct subjects—"Much of today's literature," and the work of Hypatia. There is a temptation, built into the structure of the argument itself, to compare Hypatia's work to today's literature, but read though the argument again carefully and you should realize that there is very little overlap between these two subjects.

(A) Much of today's literature **focuses less** on the significant **than** Hypatia's latest novel focuses on the significant.

(A) links elements from the text together incorrectly. We have no idea how much Hypatia's latest novel focuses on the significant, and, in this regard, we have no idea how it relates to much of today's literature.

(B) Much of **today's literature** at least lacks the property of **grace**.

(B) links elements from the text together incorrectly. We're told Hypatia's latest novel has a grace that was lacking from her earlier work, but, again, we have no idea how this relates to today's literature. The author does not connect the concept of grace together with much of today's literature.

(C) **Hypatia's latest novel** is **good literature** when judged by today's standards.

(C) links elements from the text together incorrectly. Again, we have no idea how Hypatia's novel compares to much of today's literature, and we have no idea if it is good enough to fall into the category of good literature—we only know that her novel is stronger, in certain ways, than her own previous work.

(D) Hypatia's latest novel is clearly **better than** the majority of today's literature.

(D) links elements from the text together incorrectly. Again, we have no idea how Hypatia's novel compares to much of today's literature.

(E) Hypatia's latest novel has at least one property of good literature to a greater degree than her earlier works.

(E) is the correct answer. We know that intricacy is a characteristic of good literature. Intricacy and complexity are very similar concepts, and we know that her current novel has more complexity than her previous work. Therefore, it's reasonable to conclude that Hypatia's latest novel has at least one property of good literature to a greater degree than her earlier works.

Here is one final challenging example for which it can be tempting to make false links. Remember to eliminate incorrect answers before verifying the correct one.

PT29, S1, Q18

Some planning committee members—those representing the construction industry—have significant financial interests in the committee's decisions. No one who is on the planning committee lives in the suburbs, although many of them work there.

If the statements above are true, which one of the following must also be true?

(A) No persons with significant financial interests in the planning committee's decisions are not in the construction industry.

(B) No person who has significant financial interest in the planning committee's decisions lives in the suburbs.

(C) Some persons with significant financial interests in the planning committee's decisions work in the suburbs.

(D) Some planning committee members who represent the construction industry do not work in the suburbs.

(E) Some persons with significant financial interests in the planning committee's decisions do not live in the suburbs.

Each part of the argument taken by itself is simple enough. However, for those who are familiar with the LSAT, this is the type of argument that SCREAMS danger. There is various information that can be connected in a variety of ways, and there is also a great risk of combining information in an incorrect way—in fact, the four wrong answers will try to tempt you to do just that.

One way we can organize this information is to consider it in terms of larger groups and subgroups. Let's think about each sentence in those terms:

11

"Some planning committee members—those representing the construction industry—have significant financial interests in the committee's decisions."

The larger group, in this case, are the members of the planning committee. Out of this larger group, a subgroup—those members representing the construction industry—have a significant financial interest in the committee's decisions. We can visualize this in the following manner:

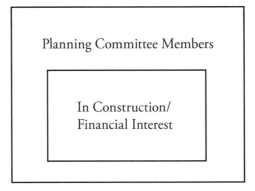

Now let's take a look at the second statement:

"No one who is on the planning committee lives in the suburbs, although many of them work there."

Notice the larger group in this case is also the planning committee—of this group, we know none live in the suburbs, and many work there. We can represent that as follows:

```
┌─────────────────────────────────────────┐
│  Planning Committee Members              │
│  (No one lives in suburbs)               │
│        ┌─────────────────────┐           │
│        │                     │           │
│        │   Work in Suburbs   │           │
│        │                     │           │
│        └─────────────────────┘           │
└─────────────────────────────────────────┘
```

These diagrams are just meant to be learning tools, and in general we do not feel it is necessary to draw the arguments out in this manner in order to get the questions correct. However, if you find these types of visual systems helpful, you may want to practice such drawing tools to be used for test day. Let's put the images up one more time, side by side, and use them to knock off the four wrong choices.

11

(A) No persons with significant financial interests in the
      planning committee's decisions are not in the construction
      industry.

Notice that we only know about people who are on the planning committee—we know nothing about people in general with financial interests. Some people with a financial interest in the committee's decisions may not be on the committee! Therefore, we don't have the information to evaluate this conclusion, and it cannot be proven.

(B) No person who has significant financial interest in the
      planning committee's decisions lives in the suburbs.

For the same reason, (B) can't be proven. We have some information about people with a financial interest who happen to be on the committee, but without knowing more about others who have financial interests, we can't prove that this answer is true.

(C) Some persons with significant financial interests in the
      planning committee's decisions work in the suburbs.

Again, since we don't know about all the people with financial interests, this answer could be true. We also know many committee members work in the suburbs, and that makes this answer tempting. However, we have no direct proof that those with financial interests are the ones working in the suburbs (perhaps the "many" committee members who work in the suburbs don't have a financial interest).

(D) Some planning committee members who represent the
      construction industry do not work in the suburbs.

This answer is similar to (C)—we know many members work in the suburbs, but we don't know which ones. It could be those in the construction industry, or it could not.

(E) Some persons with significant financial interests in the
      planning committee's decisions do not live in the suburbs.

We know that those on the committee who are in the construction industry have a significant financial interest, and we know they do not live in the suburbs. Therefore, we can prove that at least some people who have a financial interest do not live in the suburbs.

Answer choice (E) is correct.

Conclusion

1. Understand what inference questions are NOT. It is critical that you develop processes that are specific to each question type. Be careful not to let your understanding of Assumption Family questions hinder your process on Inference questions.

2. Right answers are not predictable. Again, some right answers will match up with your expectations, and others will not. Therefore, in general, you should not expect to predict the right answer.

3. Right answers have a range of provability. Some questions require us to find the answer that must be true, others ask for something that is most provable, and finally others fall somewhere in between. It's dangerous to think every answer must be 100 percent provable. No matter the question stem, you can never go wrong by trying to find the *most* provable of the five choices.

4. Get to the right answer by eliminating wrong answers. Incorrect answers for Inference questions are generally easier to identify than correct answers are. Many don't match up with the stimulus in terms of what is being discussed. Many contain reasoning that is faulty. Your success on Inference questions hinges on your ability to see what is not provable.

11

DRILL IT: Inference Questions

Give yourself no more than 20 minutes to complete the following problems.

1. PT39, S2, Q6

Poor writers often express mundane ideas with elaborate syntax and esoteric vocabulary. Inattentive readers may be impressed but may well misunderstand the writing, while alert readers will easily see through the pretentiousness. Thus, a good principle for writers is: _____.

Which one of the following completes the passage most logically?

(A) the simpler the style, the better the writing

(B) inattentive readers are not worth writing for

(C) only the most talented writers can successfully adopt a complex style

(D) a writing style should not be more complex than the ideas expressed

(E) alert readers are the only readers who are sensitive to writing style

2. PT30, S4, Q4

A certain gene can be stimulated by chemicals in cigarette smoke, causing lung cells to metabolize the chemicals in a way that makes the cells cancerous. Yet smokers in whom this gene is not stimulated have as high a risk of developing lung cancer from smoking as other smokers do.

If the statements above are true, it can be concluded on the basis of them that

(A) stimulation of the gene by chemicals in cigarette smoke is not the only factor affecting the risk for smokers of developing lung cancer

(B) nonsmokers have as high a risk of developing lung cancer as do smokers in whom the gene has not been stimulated

(C) smokers in whom the gene has been stimulated are more likely to develop lung cancer than are other smokers

(D) the gene is more likely to be stimulated by chemicals in cigarette smoke than by other chemicals

(E) smokers are less likely to develop lung cancer if they do not have the gene

3. PT37, S2, Q2

The solidity of bridge piers built on pilings depends largely on how deep the pilings are driven. Prior to 1700, pilings were driven to "refusal," that is, to the point at which they refused to go any deeper. In a 1588 inquiry into the solidity of piers for Venice's Rialto Bridge, it was determined that the bridge's builder, Antonio Da Ponte, had met the contemporary standard for refusal: he had caused the pilings to be driven until additional penetration into the ground was no greater than two inches after twenty-four hammer blows.

Which one of the following can properly be inferred from the passage?

(A) The Rialto Bridge was built on unsafe pilings.

(B) The standard of refusal was not sufficient to ensure the safety of a bridge.

(C) Da Ponte's standard of refusal was less strict than that of other bridge builders of his day.

(D) After 1588, no bridges were built on pilings that were driven to the point of refusal.

(E) It is possible that the pilings of the Rialto Bridge could have been driven deeper even after the standard of refusal had been met.

11

4. PT37, S4, Q3

An instructor presented two paintings to a class. She said that the first had hung in prestigious museums but the second was produced by an unknown amateur. Each student was asked which painting was better. Everyone selected the first. The instructor later presented the same two paintings in the same order to a different class. This time she said that the first was produced by an unknown amateur but the second had hung in prestigious museums. In this class, everyone said that the second painting was better.

The statements above, if true, most strongly support which one of the following?

(A) Most of the students would not like any work of art that they believed to have been produced by an unknown amateur.

(B) None of the claims that the instructor made about the paintings was true.

(C) Each of the students would like most of the paintings hanging in any prestigious museum.

(D) In judging the paintings, some of the students were affected by what they had been told about the history of the paintings.

(E) Had the instructor presented the paintings without telling the students anything about them, almost all of the students would have judged them to be roughly equal in artistic worth.

5. PT37, S4, Q1

Criminals often have an unusual self-image. Embezzlers often think of their actions as "only borrowing money." Many people convicted of violent crimes rationalize their actions by some sort of denial; either the victim "deserved it" and so the action was justified, or "it simply wasn't my fault." Thus, in many cases, by criminals' characterization of their situations, .

Which one of the following most logically completes the passage?

(A) they ought to be rewarded for their actions

(B) they are perceived to be the victim of some other criminal

(C) their actions are not truly criminal

(D) the criminal justice system is inherently unfair

(E) they deserve only a light sentence for their crimes

6. PT37, S4, Q6

In a study, infant monkeys given a choice between two surrogate mothers—a bare wire structure equipped with a milk bottle, or a soft, suede-covered wire structure equipped with a milk bottle—unhesitatingly chose the later. When given a choice between a bare wire structure equipped with a milk bottle and a soft, suede-covered wire structure lacking a milk bottle, they unhesitatingly chose the former.

Which one of the following is most supported by the information above?

(A) Infant monkeys' desire for warmth and comfort is nearly as strong as their desire for food.

(B) For infant monkeys, suede is a less convincing substitute for their mother's touch than animal fur would be.

(C) For infant monkeys, a milk bottle is a less convincing substitute for their mother's teat than suede is for their mother's touch.

(D) For infant monkeys, a milk bottle is an equally convincing substitute for their mother's teat as suede is for their mother's touch.

(E) Infant monkeys' desire for food is stronger than their desire for warmth and comfort.

7. PT39, S4 , Q6

A politician can neither be reelected nor avoid censure by his or her colleagues if that politician is known to be involved in any serious scandals. Several prominent politicians have just now been shown to be involved in a conspiracy that turned into a serious scandal. These politicians will therefore not be reelected.

If the statements above are all true, which one of the following statements must also be true?

(A) The prominent politicians cannot escape censure by their colleagues.

(B) If there had been no scandal, the prominent politicians would be reelected.

(C) No politician is censured unless he or she is known to be involved in a serious scandal.

(D) The prominent politicians initially benefited from the conspiracy that caused the scandal.

(E) Some politicians who are involved in scandalous conspiracies avoid detection and censure.

8. PT33, S3, Q13

Editorialist: Some people argue that ramps and other accommodations for people using wheelchairs are unnecessary in certain business areas because those areas are not frequented by wheelchair users. What happens, however, is that once ramps and other accommodations are installed in these business areas, people who use wheelchairs come there to shop and work.

Which one of the following is most strongly supported by the editorialist's statements?

(A) Owners of business areas not frequented by wheelchair users generally are reluctant to make modifications.

(B) Businesses that install proper accommodations for wheelchair users have greater profits than those that do not.

(C) Many businesses fail to make a profit because they do not accommodate wheelchair users.

(D) Most businesses are not modified to accommodate wheelchair users.

(E) Some business areas are not frequented by wheelchair users because the areas lack proper accommodations.

9. PT30, S4, Q10

Twelve healthy volunteers with the Apo-A-IV-1 gene and twelve healthy volunteers who instead have the Apo-A-IV-2 gene each consumed a standard diet supplemented daily by a high-cholesterol food. A high level of cholesterol in the blood is associated with an increased risk of heart disease. After three weeks, the blood cholesterol levels of the subjects in the second group were unchanged, whereas the blood cholesterol levels of those with the Apo-A-IV-1 gene rose 20 percent.

Which one of the following is most strongly supported by the information above?

(A) Approximately half the population carries a gene that lowers cholesterol levels.

(B) Most of those at risk of heart disease may be able to reduce their risk by adopting a low-cholesterol diet.

(C) The bodies of those who have the Apo-A-IV-2 gene excrete cholesterol when blood cholesterol reaches a certain level.

(D) The presence of the Apo-A-IV-1 gene seems to indicate that a person has a lower risk of heart disease.

(E) The presence of the Apo-A-IV-2 gene may inhibit the elevation of blood cholesterol.

10. PT37, S2, Q7

Newtonian physics dominated science for over two centuries. It found consistently successful application, becoming one of the most highly substantiated and accepted theories in the history of science. Nevertheless, Einstein's theories came to show the fundamental limits of Newtonian physics and to surpass the Newtonian view in the early 1900s, giving rise once again to a physics that has so far enjoyed wide success.

Which one of the following logically follows from the statements above?

(A) The history of physics is characterized by a pattern of one successful theory subsequently surpassed by another.

(B) Long-standing success of substantiation of a theory of physics is no guarantee that the theory will continue to be dominant indefinitely.

(C) Every theory of physics, no matter how successful, is eventually surpassed by one that is more successful.

(D) Once a theory of physics is accepted, it will remain dominant for centuries.

(E) If a long-accepted theory of physics is surpassed, it must be surpassed by a theory that is equally successful.

Challenge Questions

11. PT36, S3, Q17

The purpose of a general theory of art is to explain every aesthetic feature that is found in any of the arts. Premodern general theories of art, however, focused primarily on painting and sculpture. Every premodern general theory of art, even those that succeed as theories of painting and sculpture, fails to explain some aesthetic feature of music.

The statements above, if true, most strongly support which one of the following?

(A) Any general theory of art that explains the aesthetic features of painting also explains those of sculpture.

(B) A general theory of art that explains every aesthetic feature of music will achieve its purpose.

(C) Any theory of art that focuses primarily on sculpture and painting cannot explain every aesthetic feature of music.

(D) No premodern general theory of art achieves its purpose unless music is not art.

(E) No premodern general theory of art explains any aesthetic features of music that are not shared with painting and sculpture.

12. PT37, S2, Q12

Rosen: One cannot prepare a good meal from bad food, produce good food from bad soil, maintain good soil without good farming, or have good farming without a culture that places value on the proper maintenance of all its natural resources so that needed supplies are always available.

Which one of the following can be properly inferred from Rosen's statement?

(A) The creation of good meals depends on both natural and cultural conditions.

(B) Natural resources cannot be maintained properly without good farming practices.

(C) Good soil is a prerequisite of good farming.

(D) Any society with good cultural values will have a good cuisine.

(E) When food is bad, it is because of poor soil and, ultimately, bad farming practices.

13. PT38, S4, Q24

Most land-dwelling vertebrates have rotating limbs terminating in digits, a characteristic useful for land movement. Biologists who assume that this characteristic evolved only after animals abandoned aquatic environments must consider the Acanthostega, a newly discovered ancestor of all land vertebrates. It possessed rotating limbs terminating in digits, but its skeleton was too feeble for land movement. It also breathed using only internal gills, indicating that it and its predecessors were exclusively aquatic.

The statements above, if true, most strongly support which one of the following?

(A) Many anatomical characteristics common to most land animals represent a disadvantage for survival underwater.

(B) None of the anatomical characteristics common to most aquatic animals represent an advantage for survival on land.

(C) Acanthostega originated as a land-dwelling species, but evolved gills only after moving to an underwater environment.

(D) All anatomical characteristics not useful for land movement but common to most land animals represent an advantage for survival underwater.

(E) Certain anatomical characteristics common to some aquatic animals represent an advantage for survival on land.

14. PT33, S3, Q8

Most people invest in the stock market without doing any research of their own. Some of these people rely solely on their broker's advice, whereas some others make decisions based merely on hunches. Other people do some research of their own, but just as often rely only on their broker or on hunches. Only a few always do their own research before investing. Nonetheless, a majority of investors in the stock market make a profit.

If the statements in the passage are true, which one of the following must also be true?

(A) Some people who make a profit on their investments in the stock market do so without doing any research of their own.

(B) Most people who invest in the stock market either rely solely on their broker or make decisions based merely on hunches.

(C) Some people who do investment research on their own, while just as often relying on their broker or on hunches, make a profit in the stock market.

(D) Most people who invest in the stock market without doing any research of their own make a profit.

(E) Most people who rely solely on their broker rather than on hunches make a profit in the stock market.

15. PT30, S4, Q7

Critic: Emily Dickinson's poetry demonstrates that meaning cannot reside entirely within a poem itself, but is always the unique result of an interaction between a reader's system of beliefs and the poem; and, of course, any two readers from different cultures or eras have radically different systems of beliefs.

If the critic's statements are true, each of the following could be true EXCEPT:

(A) A reader's interpretation of a poem by Dickinson is affected by someone else's interpretation of it.

(B) A modern reader and a nineteenth-century reader interpret one of Shakespeare's sonnets in the same way.

(C) A reader's interpretation of a poem evolves over time.

(D) Two readers from the same era arrive at different interpretations of the same poem.

(E) A reader's enjoyment of a poem is enhanced by knowing the poet's interpretation of it.

11

SOLUTIONS: Inference Questions

Poor writers often express mundane ideas with elaborate syntax and esoteric vocabulary. Inattentive readers may be impressed but may well misunderstand the writing, while alert readers will easily see through the pretentiousness. Thus, a good principle for writers is: _____.

Which one of the following completes the passage most logically?

   (A) the simpler the style, the better the writing
   (B) inattentive readers are not worth writing for
   (C) only the most talented writers can successfully adopt a complex style
   (D) a writing style should not be more complex than the ideas expressed
   (E) alert readers are the only readers who are sensitive to writing style

The correct answer is (D).

In the stimulus we are told that poor writers often represent simple ideas in overly complex ways. Then we are told of two negative consequences of this—poor readers, who may be falsely impressed, may misunderstand the writing, and alert readers will see easily see through the pretentiousness.

Let's consider what could follow logically:

(A) is very attractive. The author seems to be advocating for a simpler style. However, on closer inspection, (A) is not supportable based on the text. The stimulus is about a mismatch in the complexity levels of the subject matter and style of writing—not about simple writing in general.

(B) is not supported by the statements. We are given no indication of who is or is not worth writing for.

(C) is not supported by the statements. We have almost no information about who can or cannot successfully adopt a complex style.

(E) is not supported by the statements. In fact, we know that inattentive readers are sensitive to writing style too—here we are told they may be impressed by poor writing style.

(D) is the answer most supported and it is therefore correct. In the first sentence we are told that a writing style that *is* more complex than the ideas expressed is representative of poor writing, and in the second sentence we are given two negative consequences of a writing style more complex than the ideas expressed. Therefore, it is logical to conclude that a writing style should not have this characteristic.

A certain gene can be stimulated by chemicals in cigarette smoke, causing lung cells to metabolize the chemicals in a way that makes the cells cancerous. Yet smokers in whom this gene is not stimulated have as high a risk of developing lung cancer from smoking as other smokers do.

If the statements above are true, it can be concluded on the basis of them that

   (A) stimulation of the gene by chemicals in cigarette smoke is not the only factor affecting the risk for smokers of developing lung cancer
   (B) nonsmokers have as high a risk of developing lung cancer as do smokers in whom the gene has not been stimulated
   (C) smokers in whom the gene has been stimulated are more likely to develop lung cancer than are other smokers
   (D) the gene is more likely to be stimulated by chemicals in cigarette smoke than by other chemicals
   (E) smokers are less likely to develop lung cancer if they do not have the gene

The correct answer is (A).

The passage states that stimulating a certain gene via smoke can cause cancer, but that smokers

11

without a stimulated gene have as high a risk as developing smoking-related lung cancer as other smokers (who do not have the stimulated gene) do. The words "it can be concluded" signal that we are dealing with an Inference question—there might be an inference that quickly comes to mind (for example, if people with the nonstimulated gene still have a high risk of developing smoking-related lung cancer, then there may be other factors at play)—but remember that what you are expecting may not be what they give you.

(B) is tempting if you misread "nonsmokers" as "smokers"—we are not given any information comparing nonsmokers and smokers at all! The passage only compares smokers with the stimulated gene and those without; this choice is out of scope.

(C) is not supported by the statements. The exact wording of the statements is that smokers with the nonstimulated gene "have as high a risk"—this does not necessarily mean they are *more likely* to develop cancer. Eliminate.

(D) is not supported by the statements. There is no comparison of different chemicals—only the chemicals in cigarette smoke are mentioned.

(E) is not supported by the statements. The passage never distinguishes between those who *have* the gene and those who don't have the gene—it only distinguishes between groups that have the gene *stimulated* and those who do not. Additionally, having the gene (and having it stimulated) does not necessarily mean a lower risk of lung cancer, since those without the stimulated gene had "as high a risk" as other smokers.

Choice (A), in this case, was exactly what we predicted: even though the stimulated gene is cancerous, people without the gene still have as high a risk of developing lung cancer as those with the gene, so something else must affect risk! If it were the *only* factor, then we would see a higher risk for those with the stimulated gene. This is our answer.

3. PT37, S2, Q2

The solidity of bridge piers built on pilings depends largely on how deep the pilings are driven. Prior to 1700, pilings were driven to "refusal," that is, to the point at which they refused to go any deeper. In a 1588 inquiry into the solidity of piers for Venice's Rialto Bridge, it was determined that the bridge's builder, Antonio Da Ponte, had met the contemporary standard for refusal: he had caused the pilings to be driven until additional penetration into the ground was no greater than two inches after twenty-four hammer blows.

Which one of the following can properly be inferred from the passage?

(A) The Rialto Bridge was built on unsafe pilings.
(B) The standard of refusal was not sufficient to ensure the safety of a bridge.
(C) Da Ponte's standard of refusal was less strict than that of other bridge builders of his day.
(D) After 1588, no bridges were built on pilings that were driven to the point of refusal.
(E) It is possible that the pilings of the Rialto Bridge could have been driven deeper even after the standard of refusal had been met.

The correct answer is (E).

When an Inference question contains this much information, the test writers hope that you will forget or confuse details due to the length of the statements. Be vigilant!

(A) is not supported by the passage. What would constitute "unsafe" bridges is never discussed.

(B) is not supported by the passage. What would constitute "the safety" of bridges is never discussed.

(C) is not supported by the passage. Da Ponte "met the contemporary standard for refusal," and we have no other information about others' standards.

(D) is not supported by the passage. The statements only say that building pilings were driven to refusal prior to 1700; we do not have information about any other bridges built between 1588 and 1700.

Choice (E) uses the vague wording "it is possible." Could the pilings of the Rialto have been driven deeper? Da Ponte met the standard and drove the pilings "until additional penetration into the ground was not greater than 2 inches after twenty-four hammer blows"—within 24 hammer blows, the pilings could have gone anywhere from 0 to 2 inches deeper. That is quite different from refusing to go any deeper at all. The standard could be met and exceeded—as long as the additional possible depth was less than 2 inches after 24 hammer blows.

4. PT37, S4, Q3

An instructor presented two paintings to a class. She said that the first had hung in prestigious museums but the second was produced by an unknown amateur. Each student was asked which painting was better. Everyone selected the first. The instructor later presented the same two paintings in the same order to a different class. This time she said that the first was produced by an unknown amateur but the second had hung in prestigious museums. In this class, everyone said that the second painting was better.

The statements above, if true, most strongly support which one of the following?

(A) Most of the students would not like any work of art that they believed to have been produced by an unknown amateur.

(B) None of the claims that the instructor made about the paintings was true.

(C) Each of the students would like most of the paintings hanging in any prestigious museum.

(D) In judging the paintings, some of the students were affected by what they had been told about the history of the paintings.

(E) Had the instructor presented the paintings without telling the students anything about them, almost all of the students would have judged them to be roughly equal in artistic worth.

The correct answer is (D).

All we know is that every single one of the students in each class preferred the museum painting (even though that painting was not preferred when presented as an unknown artist's painting). If we had heard this story in real life, we might jump to all kinds of conclusions about the reason for the discrepancy in the two different classes. However, be extra suspicious of what a "normal" person might think when confronted with LSAT information—the test-writers will try to trip us up with those expectations!

(A) is not supported by the statements. The extreme wording "any" demands an extreme justification, as does "most." If choice (A) were true, then the situation we described might result—but we want to know what is most likely to be true given the situation, not the other way around. Technically, we don't know anything about *why* students said one painting was better than the other; we just know that under these two different circumstances, two different classes said they preferred different paintings. Eliminate it.

(B) is tempting, because the instructor switches the description of the paintings to the different classes, and these descriptions may at first seem to be mutually exclusive. However, the statements don't tell us anything about the accuracy of the claims. In fact, either set of claims (or both!) could be true. A painting produced by an unknown amateur could be sold and find its way into a prestigious museum. Eliminate it.

(C) is not supported by the statements. Notice the extreme wording here: "any" prestigious museum? "Each" (meaning every single one) of the students? Eliminate it.

(E) is not supported by the statements. This is an extreme claim in disguise. "Equal" artistic worth? That is a very specific claim to make about a hypothetical situation, and nothing in the statements is strong enough to give us that degree of specificity. Eliminate it.

Choice (D) is not something that *must* be true. It is possible that the students were not swayed by what they had been told. But the fact that everyone in each class preferred the "museum"

11

painting (even when those paintings were different pieces) does imply there was something related to that information involved in the decision, even if we can't be certain about to what degree.

Notice the word "some" is used here—a nice, vague term that could mean as few as one. Choice (D) is by no means provably true—in fact, there are many other possibilities that could have caused the discrepancy (the differences in students themselves, the instructor's nonverbal cues, etc.). But out of the five choices, this is the one that requires the smallest jump in logic to justify, because so many of the other answers make specific and more extreme claims. This is our answer.

5. PT37, S4, Q1

Criminals often have an unusual self-image. Embezzlers often think of their actions as "only borrowing money." Many people convicted of violent crimes rationalize their actions by some sort of denial; either the victim "deserved it" and so the action was justified, or "it simply wasn't my fault." Thus, in many cases, by criminals' characterization of their situations, _____.

Which one of the following most logically completes the passage?

(A) they ought to be rewarded for their actions

(B) they are perceived to be the victim of some other criminal

(C) their actions are not truly criminal

(D) the criminal justice system is inherently unfair

(E) they deserve only a light sentence for their crimes

The correct answer is (C).

The information in this paragraph can be boiled down to the following:

- Criminals have unusual self-image.
- Embezzlers often think they are "only borrowing money."
- Many violent criminals rationalize or deny their crimes.

(A) is not supported by the statements. While the criminals may not accept blame for their actions, nowhere is it said that these people actually expect a reward. This generalization goes too far.

(B) is not supported by the statements. Nowhere are "other criminals" mentioned.

(D) is not supported by the statements. There is nothing mentioned about the criminal justice system; the passage only discusses how criminals perceive their own actions.

(E) is not supported by the statements. Someone in the "real world" might infer that these criminals (who take their own actions lightly) would think they deserved only a light sentence, but this is the LSAT! There is nothing mentioned about what types of sentences are deserved. Since none of the criminals seem to think their actions were that bad, it's quite possible that they might think they don't deserve sentences at all.

Choice (C) does require a small jump—what would it mean for an action to be "truly criminal?" We're never told, but if the criminals are rationalizing or denying their crimes, it's likely that their perceptions fall short of their own standard for being "truly criminal." The question asks for which choice "most logically completes the passage," and the other choices contain more concrete and severe flaws, so (C) is our answer.

6. PT37, S4, Q6

In a study, infant monkeys given a choice between two surrogate mothers—a bare wire structure equipped with a milk bottle, or a soft, suede-covered wire structure equipped with a milk bottle—unhesitatingly chose the latter. When given a choice between a bare wire structure equipped with a milk bottle and a soft, suede-covered wire structure lacking a milk bottle, they unhesitatingly chose the former.

Which one of the following is most supported by the information above?

(A) Infant monkeys' desire for warmth and comfort is nearly as strong as their desire for food.

11

(B) For infant monkeys, suede is a less convincing substitute for their mother's touch than animal fur would be.

(C) For infant monkeys, a milk bottle is a less convincing substitute for their mother's teat than suede is for their mother's touch.

(D) For infant monkeys, a milk bottle is an equally convincing substitute for their mother's teat as suede is for their mother's touch.

(E) Infant monkeys' desire for food is stronger than their desire for warmth and comfort.

The correct answer is (E).

We know the following facts:

1. baby monkeys preferred the soft/milk mother to the wire/milk mother.
2. baby monkeys preferred the wire/milk mother to the soft/no-milk mother.

What is the difference between these two sets of circumstances? In the second, the softer suede mother no longer had milk—and the babies switched their previous preference. This suggests that this variable (milk/no milk) is somehow important.

(A) is tempting because it seems to address the underlying decision between warmth/food, but this choice is ultimately not supported by the statements. We know that the babies chose milk over no-milk in the second experiment (and can infer that this is a choice of food over warmth), but we have no way to compare that desire with the *level* of preference for the soft mother in the first experiment. What if they strongly preferred food, but only marginally cared about warmth/comfort? We have no way of knowing.

(B) is not supported by the statements. We cannot make a comparison to fur when this experiment only involves a distinction between suede and wire.

(C) is not supported by the statements. The only comparisons in this experiment are between soft/wire and milk/no milk—we cannot make

any inferences about how comparable the experimental conditions were to "real" mother conditions.

(D) is not supported by the statements. We cannot make a comparison to the features of a real monkey mother when this experiment only involves a distinction between suede and wire.

Choice (E) contains many of the same words as choice (A), but with an important difference: choice (E) only makes a statement about which of the two types of desire (for food/for warmth)—when in conflict with each other—wins out. If the monkeys preferred the soft mother all other things being equal, but when confronted with a choice between soft/no food and wire/food went with the wire/food mother, this indicates that their previous preference was overpowered by the food/no food distinction. This is our answer.

7. PT39, S4 , Q6

A politician can neither be reelected nor avoid censure by his or her colleagues if that politician is known to be involved in any serious scandals. Several prominent politicians have just now been shown to be involved in a conspiracy that turned into a serious scandal. These politicians will therefore not be reelected.

If the statements above are all true, which one of the following statements must also be true?

(A) The prominent politicians cannot escape censure by their colleagues.

(B) If there had been no scandal, the prominent politicians would be reelected.

(C) No politician is censured unless he or she is known to be involved in a serious scandal.

(D) The prominent politicians initially benefited from the conspiracy that caused the scandal.

(E) Some politicians who are involved in scandalous conspiracies avoid detection and censure.

The correct answer is (A).

From the statement we know the following truths:

- If politician is known to be involved in serious scandals, politician can't be reelected.
- If politician is known to be involved in serious scandals, politician can't avoid censure.
- Several prominent politicians now known to be involved in conspiracy that is now serious scandal.
- These politicians will not be reelected.

(A) must be true. We are told these politicians are known to be involved in a serious scandal, and we know that an absolute consequence is that they cannot avoid censure.

(B) is not supported. The statement gives us no evidence that the politicians would be reelected otherwise. They could not get reelected for other reasons.

(C) is not supported. Just because being involved in scandal results in censure does not meant it is the only action that results in censure. Perhaps a politician can be censured for another reason.

(D) is not supported by any part of the text.

(E) is not supported by any part of the text.

8. PT33, S3, Q13

Editorialist: Some people argue that ramps and other accommodations for people using wheelchairs are unnecessary in certain business areas because those areas are not frequented by wheelchair users. What happens, however, is that once ramps and other accommodations are installed in these business areas, people who use wheelchairs come there to shop and work.

Which one of the following is most strongly supported by the editorialist's statements?

(A) Owners of business areas not frequented by wheelchair users generally are reluctant to make modifications.

(B) Businesses that install proper accommodations for wheelchair users have greater profits than those that do not.

(C) Many businesses fail to make a profit because they do not accommodate wheelchair users.

(D) Most businesses are not modified to accommodate wheelchair users.

(E) Some business areas are not frequented by wheelchair users because the areas lack proper accommodations.

The correct answer is (E).

This passage is fairly brief and straightforward, but be just as vigilant about sticking to the details.

(A) is not supported by the statements. We do not have enough information about what owners of these types of businesses "generally" are or are not reluctant to do. The statements only mention that "some people" argue that ramps/accommodations are unnecessary. Watch out for detail creep— these two groups are not interchangeable!

(B) is not supported by the statements. Profitability is not mentioned for either type of business.

(C) is not supported by the statements. Profitability is not mentioned for either type of business.

(D) is not supported by the statements. There is no information about what "most businesses" do— only what "some people" argue and what happens when "certain" businesses adopt accommodations.

Notice the vague wording of (E)—"some business areas." Is there at least one instance in which a business area may not be frequented by wheelchair users due to a lack of accommodations? If a certain area without accommodations was not frequented by wheelchair users, then accommodations are installed and wheelchair users begin to frequent that business area, then that does imply that the lack of accommodations may have kept them away in the first place. Is this *necessarily* true? No. But it is likely, since wheelchair users would not have been able to easily access the businesses before, and once that variable shifts the wheelchair users' behavior also shifts.

11

9. PT30, S4, Q10

Twelve healthy volunteers with the Apo-A-IV-1 gene and twelve healthy volunteers who instead have the Apo-A-IV-2 gene each consumed a standard diet supplemented daily by a high-cholesterol food. A high level of cholesterol in the blood is associated with an increased risk of heart disease. After three weeks, the blood cholesterol levels of the subjects in the second group were unchanged, whereas the blood cholesterol levels of those with the Apo-A-IV-1 gene rose 20 percent.

Which one of the following is most strongly supported by the information above?

(A) Approximately half the population carries a gene that lowers cholesterol levels.

(B) Most of those at risk of heart disease may be able to reduce their risk by adopting a low-cholesterol diet.

(C) The bodies of those who have the Apo-A-IV-2 gene excrete cholesterol when blood cholesterol reaches a certain level.

(D) The presence of the Apo-A-IV-1 gene seems to indicate that a person has a lower risk of heart disease.

(E) The presence of the Apo-A-IV-2 gene may inhibit the elevation of blood cholesterol.

The correct answer is (E).

Two healthy groups with two different genes consumed standard diets plus a high-cholesterol food, but only one group had a 20% increase in blood cholesterol. We are also told that high blood cholesterol is associated with increased heart disease risk. What is most likely to be true given these facts?

(A) is not supported by the statements. We are not given any information about the relative frequency of Apo-A-IV-1 and –2 in the general population. Also, does the gene "lower" cholesterol levels? The statements say that the type 2 group was stable, while the type 1 group's levels increased—there is no lowering mentioned.

(B) is not supported by the statements. A low-cholesterol diet is never mentioned, so this answer choice is out of scope.

(C) is tempting because it may be a plausible explanation for the results, but the question does not ask for an explanation, it merely asks what is most strongly supported. Eliminate it.

(D) is tempting because there is a link between the two types of genes and high blood cholesterol, which in turn is linked to risk of heart disease. But be very careful! There is an important detail creep here—the type 1 gene group had *higher* blood cholesterol levels after the diet, and this choice implies the opposite. Eliminate it.

Choice (E) is not necessarily true—there could be other explanations for the results of this experiment. But the test writers use the vague word "may," and since the type 1 group had levels of cholesterol that rose, while the type 2 group had stable levels, this statement expresses a very strong possibility (and is certainly more strongly supported than (A) through (D), which have fatal flaws).

10. PT37, S2, Q7

Newtonian physics dominated science for over two centuries. It found consistently successful application, becoming one of the most highly substantiated and accepted theories in the history of science. Nevertheless, Einstein's theories came to show the fundamental limits of Newtonian physics and to surpass the Newtonian view in the early 1900s, giving rise once again to a physics that has so far enjoyed wide success.

Which one of the following logically follows from the statements above?

(A) The history of physics is characterized by a pattern of one successful theory subsequently surpassed by another.

(B) Long-standing success of substantiation of a theory of physics is no guarantee that the theory will continue to be dominant indefinitely.

(C) Every theory of physics, no matter how successful, is eventually surpassed by one that is more successful.

(D) Once a theory of physics is accepted, it will remain dominant for centuries.

(E) If a long-accepted theory of physics is surpassed, it must be surpassed by a theory that is equally successful.

The correct answer is (B).

(A) is not supported by the statements. Only two theories are mentioned in the statements, and we cannot generalize a pattern about the history of physics from these two theories.

(C) is not supported by the statements. Notice the extreme wording here—"every" theory is surpassed by a more successful theory? Only two theories are mentioned.

(D) is not supported by the statements. Once *any* theory of physics is accepted it will remain dominant? Only two theories are mentioned in the statements, so we cannot make such a broad generalization.

(E) is tempting because it seems like "real-world" logic—if a theory is surpassed, the newer theory must be just as successful, right? However, we are looking for what follows logically from the exact information given, and there is no explicit comparison of the success of the two theories.

Choice (B) is demonstrably true. Newtonian physics had long-standing successful applications and was highly substantiated, but was surpassed by Einstein's theories (i.e., lost its dominance). This is our answer.

Notice how many of the distracters contained generalizations that were too broad given the exact statements. Stick closely to what you're given!

Challenge Question

11. PT36, S3, Q17

The purpose of a general theory of art is to explain every aesthetic feature that is found in any of the arts. Premodern general theories of art, however, focused primarily on painting and sculpture. Every premodern general theory of art, even those that succeed as theories of painting and sculpture, fails to explain some aesthetic feature of music.

The statements above, if true, most strongly support which one of the following?

(A) Any general theory of art that explains the aesthetic features of painting also explains those of sculpture.

(B) A general theory of art that explains every aesthetic feature of music will achieve its purpose.

(C) Any theory of art that focuses primarily on sculpture and painting cannot explain every aesthetic feature of music.

(D) No premodern general theory of art achieves its purpose unless music is not art.

(E) No premodern general theory of art explains any aesthetic features of music that are not shared with painting and sculpture.

The correct answer is (D).

We know from the argument the following:

- The purpose of general theories of art (GTA) is to explain EVERY aesthetic feature of ANY art (notice the extreme wording)
- Premodern GTA focused on painting and sculpture
- EVERY premodern GTA failed to explain SOME aesthetic feature of music

(A) is not supported by the statements. We do not have enough information to make this claim about *any* GTA. Would it be possible, given these statements, for GTA to explain painting but NOT explain sculpture (or vice versa)? Absolutely—the statements say only that premodern theories focused "primarily" on painting and sculpture, and that "some" premodern theories succeeded for painting and sculpture. Eliminate it.

(B) is not supported by the statements. What if the theory explained every feature of music but did *not* explain every feature of painting and sculpture (or other arts)? Eliminate it.

(C) is not supported by the statements. If the word "any" were replaced with "some," we would have our answer, but we do not have enough information to make this claim about "any" GTA. What about non-premodern GTA that focused on painting and sculpture? We don't know anything about them, and there's nothing that says *they* couldn't fully explain music's aesthetic features. Eliminate it.

(E) is tempting because it combines many of the words from the passage, throwing in a "no" and a "not" to confuse us more. But look at exactly what this choice says. All we know about music/premodern GTA is that premodern GTA did not fully explain music—meaning there was at least one feature of music that couldn't be explained by those theories. Does that mean those theories did not explain *any* parts of music that didn't overlap with painting and sculpture? Absolutely not.

Choice (D) combines what we know about premodern GTA (that they failed to fully explain some aesthetic feature of music) and the purpose of GTA—to explain fully all aesthetic features of the arts. If music is an art, then a premodern GTA cannot fulfill its purpose, so a premodern GTA cannot achieve its purpose unless we exclude music as a category. This is our answer.

12. PT37, S2, Q12

Rosen: One cannot prepare a good meal from bad food, produce good food from bad soil, maintain good soil without good farming, or have good farming without a culture that places value on the proper maintenance of all its natural resources so that needed supplies are always available.

Which one of the following can be properly inferred from Rosen's statement?

(A) The creation of good meals depends on both natural and cultural conditions.
(B) Natural resources cannot be maintained properly without good farming practices.
(C) Good soil is a prerequisite of good farming.
(D) Any society with good cultural values will have a good cuisine.
(E) When food is bad, it is because of poor soil and, ultimately, bad farming practices.

The correct answer is (A).

This paragraph contains a string of prerequisites. Good meals require nonbad food; good (nonbad) food requires good (nonbad) soil; maintaining good (nonbad) soil requires good farming; and good farming requires a certain type of culture.

If you prefer, you can also understand prerequisites as if/then statements (A *cannot* lead to B, so if A, there was *not* B). It might be helpful to list them out:

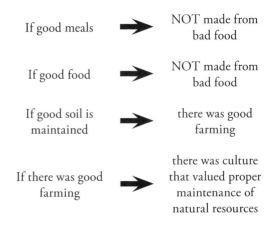

These last two statements can be combined:

Let's keep the links in mind when looking at the answers.

(B) is not supported by the statements. Maintenance of natural resources (or rather a culture that places value on such maintenance) is a prerequisite for (meaning the thing needed *before*) good farming, not the other way around. Eliminate it.

(C) is tempting if you wrote "good soil → good farming" rather than "If good soil is maintained → there *was* good farming"—these two statements are NOT the same. The first statement does not contain the element of time, which is necessary because one element of each if/then statement concerns what had to be in place *before* the other element. Good farming is the prerequisite for good soil, not the other way around. Eliminate it.

(D) is not supported by the statements. What exactly are "good cultural values" or "good cuisine?" This choice is out of scope.

(E) is tempting but goes too far. We know that good (nonbad) soil is a prerequisite for good food, but we are never told that good soil is sufficient in and of itself to make food good. What if the soil was good, but the food was left out for weeks and spoiled? Likewise, you could argue that bad soil could have been the result of good farming practices (for example, if a natural disaster wrecked a good farmer's work). Eliminate it.

If you understood that all the things mentioned were prerequisites for good meals, you may have arrived at choice (A) quickly—good meals depend on good food, which depends on good soil/farming (natural conditions) and cultural conditions (valuing maintenance of natural resources).

If you chose instead to use a more formal approach and write these prerequisites as if/then statements, we could say the following:

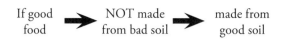

String these together to get the following:

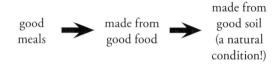

We also know that

Therefore, (A) is our answer.

Note: you could make the very real criticism that soil doesn't have to be "good" or "bad"—it could also be "neutral," but it's unclear what "neutral" would mean in this context. And doing so would leave us without a correct answer, since all the other choices have more severe flaws. In this case, as in many others, you must go with what is the smallest possible jump in logic.

13. PT38, S4, Q24

Most land-dwelling vertebrates have rotating limbs terminating in digits, a characteristic useful for land movement. Biologists who assume that this characteristic evolved only after animals abandoned aquatic environments must consider the Acanthostega, a newly discovered ancestor of all land vertebrates. It possessed rotating limbs terminating in digits, but its skeleton was too feeble for land movement. It also breathed using only internal gills, indicating that it and its predecessors were exclusively aquatic.

The statements above, if true, most strongly support which one of the following?

(A) Many anatomical characteristics common to most land animals represent a disadvantage for survival underwater.

(B) None of the anatomical characteristics common to most aquatic animals represent an advantage for survival on land.

(C) Acanthostega originated as a land-dwelling species, but evolved gills only after moving to an underwater environment.

(D) All anatomical characteristics not useful for land movement but common to most land animals represent an advantage for survival underwater.

(E) Certain anatomical characteristics common to some aquatic animals represent an advantage for survival on land.

The correct answer is (E).

Remember that for an Inference question, the right answer does not need to represent the author's conclusion. Here, the argument seems to imply that certain biologists (who assume that rotating limbs ending in digits evolved in land, not aquatic, animals) are wrong. However, none of the choices directly address this implication—our job in an Inference question is merely to identify what is most likely to be true given the statements. What have we been told explicitly?

• Most land-dwelling vertibrates have rotating limbs w/digits.

• *Acanthostega* had rotating limbs w/ digits but was too feeble for land movement.

• *Acanthostega* breathed with gills, so it must have been aquatic.

Acanthostega seems to refute certain biologists' expectations, but we can't necessarily predict what else will follow, so stick closely to the exactly wording of the statements when approaching the answers.

(A) is not supported by the statements, which do not discuss "many anatomical characteristics common to most land animals." Only one characteristic related to land animals (rotating limbs with digits) is discussed. Eliminate.

(B) is not supported by the statements. Only two characteristics of aquatic animals are discussed—gills and the rotating limbs of *Acanthostega*. This is not enough information to make an extreme claim about all possible anatomical characteristics' usefulness.

(C) is tempting because it would explain the discrepancy, but this is not an "explain the discrepancy" question! We want to know what is *most likely* to be true given the statements, not just something that *could* be true.

(D) is not supported by the statements. Characteristics that represent an advantage for survival underwater are never mentioned (unless you count gills), and there is not enough information to make an extreme claim about all possible characteristics not useful for land movement.

Choice (E) contains many of the same words as choices (A), (B), and (D), but notice that (E) makes a far weaker claim ("certain" characteristics and "some" animals). Weaker claims are often easier to support—an extreme claim may be disproved by one exception, but a vague claim may not be. The "anatomical characteristics common to some aquatic animals" mentioned in the statements are *Acanthostega*'s gills and rotating limbs—does one of these "represent an advantage for survival on land?" Absolutely—the first statement says that rotating limbs with digits is useful for land movement. This is our answer.

14. PT33, S3, Q8

Most people invest in the stock market without doing any research of their own. Some of these people rely solely on their broker's advice, whereas some others make decisions based merely on hunches. Other people do some research of their own, but just as often rely only on their broker or on hunches. Only a few always do their own research before investing. Nonetheless, a majority of investors in the stock market make a profit.

If the statements in the passage are true, which one of the following must also be true?

(A) Some people who make a profit on their investments in the stock market do so without doing any research of their own.

(B) Most people who invest in the stock market either rely solely on their broker or make decisions based merely on hunches.

(C) Some people who do investment research on their own, while just as often relying on their broker or on hunches, make a profit in the stock market.

(D) Most people who invest in the stock market without doing any research of their own make a profit.

(E) Most people who rely solely on their broker rather than on hunches make a profit in the stock market.

The correct answer is (A).

This paragraph contains the same few terms—"invest," "research," "broker," and "hunches"—over and over again, so it may help to rewrite the claims in simpler terms:

• Most people invest w/o research (some rely only on brokers, some only on hunches).

• Others do research sometimes (but sometimes rely only on brokers or hunches).

• A few always do research.

• BUT a majority make a profit.

What "must also be true" given these facts? Be vigilant about the specific small words in each answer, and don't let the repetitive nature of the choices confuse you.

(B) is not supported by the statements. What does the passage tell us about those who rely solely on their brokers or solely on hunches? Out of the group of people who invest without research, "some" rely only on brokers, and "some others" on hunches. Are these the only possible groups? No, they could be just "some" of the people. What if the rest of the people (a potentially large proportion) rely both on their broker's advice AND hunches, or neither? Eliminate it.

(C) is tempting because if most investors make a profit, it may be possible that members of the group of "other people" who do research AND rely on their broker AND rely on hunches make a profit. But is this *necessarily* true? Is it possible that this could be the one subgroup that *fails* to make a profit? Yes, so eliminate it.

(D) is tempting because most people invest in the stock market without research, and a majority of investors make a profit. But what exactly constitutes a majority? Anything over 50 percent. Try testing the smallest possible majorities: if 51 out of 100 people make a profit, and 51 out of 100 people invest without doing research, does that mean that most of the 51 who invested without research made a profit? Is there a way this could be false? Absolutely—check out the Venn diagram below:

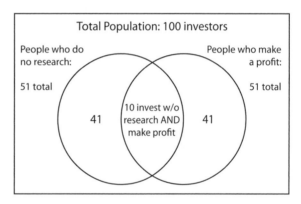

In this scenario, only 10 out of the 41 people who invested without research made a profit. Testing the "extremes" of the words "some," "most," etc. can often be a useful tactic. Eliminate it.

(E) is not supported by the statements. We don't know anything about the number of people who rely solely on their brokers rather than on hunches (except that it is "some" of the population), so we can't make a claim about what "most" of this group does.

The meaning of choice (A) is very similar to that of (D), but with the substitution of "some" for "most" to describe the overlap between these two groups. Does choice (A) *have* to be true? Is there any way it could *not* be? Imagine if none of the people who make a profit on their investments in

11

the stock market do so without doing research, then the overlap of the two circles would be empty—0 people. This would leave 51 investors who make a profit (w/o research) and 51 people who do no research (w/o profit). That would mean we would have a minimum of 51 + 51 = 102 people—more people than our total population of 100!

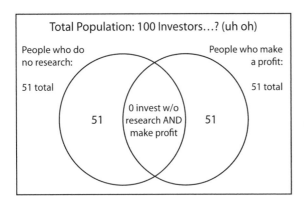

Of course, that's not possible. In order for our numbers to work out, we must have *some* overlap, so choice (A) is our answer.

By the way, we're not suggesting you draw Venn diagrams—there are plenty of times when they will not work (e.g., when there are five categories).

15. PT30, S4, Q7

Critic: Emily Dickinson's poetry demonstrates that meaning cannot reside entirely within a poem itself, but is always the unique result of an interaction between a reader's system of beliefs and the poem; and, of course, any two readers from different cultures or eras have radically different systems of beliefs.

If the critic's statements are true, each of the following could be true EXCEPT:

(A) A reader's interpretation of a poem by Dickinson is affected by someone else's interpretation of it.

(B) A modern reader and a nineteenth-century reader interpret one of Shakespeare's sonnets in the same way.

(C) A reader's interpretation of a poem evolves over time.

(D) Two readers from the same era arrive at different interpretations of the same poem.

(E) A reader's enjoyment of a poem is enhanced by knowing the poet's interpretation of it.

The correct answer is (B).

This question is tricky not only because it asks us to distinguish what *could* be true (whereas we're more often asked what *must be* or is *most likely to be* true), but also because it is an EXCEPT question. That means we should expect four answers that could be true and one that *must be false*.

(A) could be true. There is nothing in the passage that makes it impossible for one reader's interpretation to affect another's—in fact, the interplay between two readers' interpretations is never mentioned, so this answer choice is fair game.

(C) could be true. There is nothing in the passage that says one person's interpretation can't change over time.

(D) is tempting because the critic distinguishes between readers of different time periods, saying these readers will have radically different systems of belief. Does that mean, however, that readers from the same period must have the same systems of belief? No. In fact, the critic states that meaning is "always the unique result" of the poem colliding with the reader's system of beliefs—if meaning is always unique, then interpretations cannot be identical.

(E) could be true. There is nothing in the passage that makes it impossible for the poet's interpretation to affect the reader's—this type of interplay is never mentioned, so choice (E) is fair game.

As mentioned in our discussion of choice (D), the passage implies that meaning is unique to every reader. Furthermore, the critic states that two readers from different eras have *radically* different systems of belief. If each of the two meanings/

interpretations of the readers in (B) are unique
results of the poem colliding with their radically
different systems of belief, then these meanings/
interpretations cannot be identical.

Chapter 12

of

Logical Reasoning

Matching Questions

Getting Familiar

Give yourself about seven minutes to answer the following four questions (we're giving you a bit more time for these because they tend to be longer—in general, don't be afraid to take up to two minutes for a Matching question). Later in the chapter, we'll use these questions to illustrate the important concepts related to Matching questions.

PT30, S2, Q14

It is inaccurate to say that a diet high in refined sugar cannot cause adult-onset diabetes, since a diet high in refined sugar can make a person overweight, and being overweight can predispose a person to adult-onset diabetes.

The argument is most parallel, in its logical structure, to which one of the following?

(A) It is inaccurate to say that being in cold air can cause a person to catch a cold, since colds are caused by viruses, and viruses flourish in warm, crowded places.

(B) It is accurate to say that no airline flies from Halifax to Washington. No airline offers a direct flight, although some airlines have flights from Halifax to Boston and others have flights from Boston to Washington.

(C) It is correct to say that overfertilization is the primary cause of lawn disease, since fertilizer causes lawn grass to grow rapidly and rapidly growing grass has little resistance to disease.

(D) It is incorrect to say that inferior motor oil cannot cause a car to get poorer gasoline mileage, since inferior motor oil can cause engine valve deterioration, and engine valve deterioration can lead to poorer gasoline mileage.

(E) It is inaccurate to say that Alexander the Great was a student of Plato; Alexander was a student of Aristotle and Aristotle was a student of Plato.

PT34, S3, Q23

Societies in which value is measured primarily in financial terms invariably fragment into isolated social units. But since money is not the main measure of value in nonindustrial societies, they must tend in contrast to be socially unified.

The flawed reasoning in which one of the following is most similar to that in the argument above?

(A) Animals of different genera cannot interbreed. But that does not prove that jackals and wolves cannot interbreed, for they belong to the same genus.

(B) Ecosystems close to the equator usually have more species than those closer to the poles. Thus, the Sahara Desert must contain more species than Siberia does, since the latter is farther from the equator.

(C) Insects pass through several stages of maturation: egg, larva, pupa, and adult. Since insects are arthropods, all arthropods probably undergo similar maturation processes.

(D) Poets frequently convey their thoughts via nonliteral uses of language such as metaphors and analogies. But journalists are not poets, so surely journalists always use language literally.

(E) Technologically sophisticated machines often cause us more trouble than simpler devices serving the same function. Since computers are more technologically sophisticated than pencils, they must tend to be more troublesome.

12

PT31, S2, Q23

Town councilor: The only reason for the town to have ordinances restricting where skateboarding can be done would be to protect children from danger. Skateboarding in the town's River Park is undoubtedly dangerous, but we should not pass an ordinance prohibiting it. If children cannot skateboard in the park, they will most certainly skateboard in the streets. And skateboarding in the streets is more dangerous than skateboarding in the park.

The pattern of reasoning in which one of the following is most similar to that in the town councilor's argument?

(A) The reason for requiring environmental reviews is to ensure that projected developments do not harm the natural environment. Currently, environmental concerns are less compelling than economic concerns, but in the long run, the environment must be protected. Therefore, the requirement for environmental reviews should not be waived.

(B) Insecticides are designed to protect crops against insect damage. Aphids damage tomato crops, but using insecticides against aphids kills wasps that prey on insecticide-resistant pests. Since aphids damage tomato crops less than the insecticide-resistant pests do, insecticides should not be used against aphids on tomato crops.

(C) The purpose of compulsory vaccination for schoolchildren was to protect both the children themselves and others in the community against smallpox. Smallpox was indeed a dreadful disease, but it has now been eliminated from the world's population. So children should not be vaccinated against it.

(D) The function of a sealer on wood siding is to retard deterioration caused by weather. However, cedar is a wood that is naturally resistant to weather-related damage and thus does not need additional protection. Sealers, therefore, should not be applied to cedar siding.

(E) Traffic patterns that involve one-way streets are meant to accelerate the flow of traffic in otherwise congested areas. However, it would be detrimental to the South Main Street area to have traffic move faster. So traffic patterns involving one-way streets should not be implemented there.

PT30, S2, Q6

The student body at this university takes courses in a wide range of disciplines. Miriam is a student at this university, so she takes courses in a wide range of disciplines.

Which one of the following arguments exhibits flawed reasoning most similar to that exhibited by the argument above?

(A) The students at this school take mathematics. Miguel is a student at this school, so he takes mathematics.

(B) The editorial board of this law journal has written on many legal issues. Louise is on the editorial board, so she has written on many legal issues.

(C) The component parts of bulldozers are heavy. This machine is a bulldozer, so it is heavy.

(D) All older automobiles need frequent oil changes. This car is new, so its oil need not be changed as frequently.

(E) The individual cells of the brain are incapable of thinking. Therefore, the brain as a whole is incapable of thinking.

12

Recognizing the Two Types of Matching Questions

These are the LSAT Logical Reasoning questions we love to hate. They are long (each answer choice is an entire argument in and of itself), they are complex, and they generally show up right when we realize we're running out of time. All that said, you can learn to handle these questions quickly (or at least *more* quickly) if you know what you're looking for.

As always, the first step in tackling a particular question is recognizing what your task is. Here's an outline of the two Matching question types with some simple examples to illustrate:

1. Match the Reasoning. Your job is to choose the answer that best matches the logic used in the original argument.

> **ORIGINAL:** All of the songs on The Duster's new album are ballads. The song "Rain" is on the The Duster's new album. Thus, the song "Rain" is a ballad.

> **CORRECT ANSWER:** All of the children on the playground are in the fifth grade. Lisa is a child on the playground. Therefore, Lisa is in the fifth grade.

Notice that the subject matter of the original (songs on an album) has nothing to do with the subject matter of the correct answer (children on a playground). We don't need to match the subject matter. We want to match the *logic*. In this case, the common logical structure is:

> All X are Y. Z is an X. Therefore, Z is a Y.

2. Match the Flaw. Your job is to choose the answer that contains a flaw similar to the flaw present in the original argument.

> **ORIGINAL:** John is a member of the steering committee, and John is a manager. Since Julie is also a member of the steering committee, she must be a manager.

> **CORRECT ANSWER:** The oak tree in the park is over 15 feet tall. Since the dogwood tree is also in the park, it must be over 15 feet tall.

Again, the subject matter is irrelevant. The important thing is that the correct answer matches the *logical flaw* of the original. In this case, the flawed argument is:

> A is B and A is C. Since D is B, D must also be C.

Match the Reasoning

Let's revisit one of the questions from earlier on:

> *PT30, S2, Q14*
>
> It is inaccurate to say that a diet high in refined sugar cannot cause adult-onset diabetes, since a diet high in refined sugar can make a person overweight, and being overweight can predispose a person to adult-onset diabetes.
>
> The argument is most parallel, in its logical structure, to which one of the following?
>
> (A) It is inaccurate to say that being in cold air can cause a person to catch a cold, since colds are caused by viruses, and viruses flourish in warm, crowded places.
>
> (B) It is accurate to say that no airline flies from Halifax to Washington. No airline offers a direct flight, although some airlines have flights from Halifax to Boston and others have flights from Boston to Washington.
>
> (C) It is correct to say that overfertilization is the primary cause of lawn disease, since fertilizer causes lawn grass to grow rapidly and rapidly growing grass has little resistance to disease.
>
> (D) It is incorrect to say that inferior motor oil cannot cause a car to get poorer gasoline mileage, since inferior motor oil can cause engine valve deterioration, and engine valve deterioration can lead to poorer gasoline mileage.
>
> (E) It is inaccurate to say that Alexander the Great was a student of Plato; Alexander was a student of Aristotle and Aristotle was a student of Plato.

The key to Match the Reasoning questions is to match up the individual components of the original argument with the individual components of each of the five answer choices. Your job is NOT to look for *subject matter* connections. Rather, you are looking to match up the corresponding components of the *logical structure*; that is, you are looking for an answer that reaches the same type of conclusion as the original argument, and uses evidence in the same manner to arrive at that conclusion. The corresponding components of the right answer will be a virtual dead match for those in the original argument.

Let's start by breaking down the original argument:

CONCLUSION: It is inaccurate to say that a diet high in refined sugar cannot cause adult-onset diabetes,

SUPPORTING PREMISE: since a diet high in refined sugar can make a person overweight,

SUPPORTING PREMISE: and being overweight can predispose a person to adult-onset diabetes.

If we were to think of this in argument core form, we'd have:

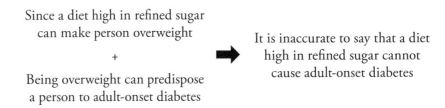

Since a diet high in refined sugar
can make person overweight

+

Being overweight can predispose
a person to adult-onset diabetes

→

It is inaccurate to say that a diet
high in refined sugar cannot
cause adult-onset diabetes

If we strip away the context, we'd have:

Since X can cause Y

+

Y can predispose to Z

→

**Inaccurate to say that X cannot
cause Z**

That's it! That's what this whole mess boils down to. Notice that the bolded version strips away the subject matter of the argument. The subject matter is unimportant. That said, we want to be sure that we maintain the logical structure of the argument, since this is ultimately what we are trying to match. The bold version does this. So, to summarize what we've done so far:

1. Break the argument down into its component parts (e.g., premise + premise ⟶ conclusion).
2. Strip the subject matter. If you need to, write the argument on paper in generic form. (Ideally, you would be able to do this your head, but for some difficult arguments it may be helpful to jot things down.)

Now that you've got the logical structure nailed down, go back and try this question again. Attempt to distill each answer choice down to a simple logical form, and see if you can find the one that matches the original. Don't read on until you've given it a fair shot.

Okay, here's our analysis of the choices. The expression inside the box represents our breakdown of the original argument.

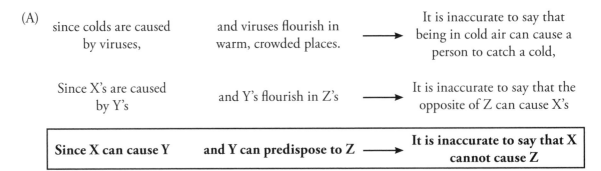

(A)   since colds are caused
by viruses,

and viruses flourish in
warm, crowded places.

⟶

It is inaccurate to say that
being in cold air can cause a
person to catch a cold,

Since X's are caused
by Y's

and Y's flourish in Z's

⟶

It is inaccurate to say that the
opposite of Z can cause X's

| **Since X can cause Y** | **and Y can predispose to Z** ⟶ | **It is inaccurate to say that X cannot cause Z** |

| CLOSE, NOT PERFECT "can cause" vs. "are caused" (believe it or not, this subtle difference can matter) | BAD MATCH "can predispose to" (lead to) vs. "flourish in" (two very different things) | BAD MATCH "X cannot cause Z" vs. "opposite of Z can cause X's" |

(B)

| No airline offers a direct flight, | although some airlines have flights from Halifax to Boston and others have flights from Boston to Washington. | → | It is accurate to say that no airline flies from Halifax to Washington. |

| TERRIBLE MATCH |
| None of this is even close! There is no causal relationship between any of these statements. |

(C)

| since fertilizer causes lawn grass to grow rapidly | and rapidly growing grass has little resistance to disease. | → | It is correct to say that overfertilization is the primary cause of lawn disease, |
| Since X causes Y | and Y has little resistance to Z | → | It is correct to say that too much of X is the primary cause of Z |

| **Since X can cause Y** | **and Y can predispose to Z** → | **It is inaccurate to say that X cannot cause Z** |

| CLOSE, NOT PERFECT "can cause" vs. "causes" (believe it or not, this subtle difference can matter) | BAD MATCH "can predispose to" vs. "has little resistance to" | BAD MATCH "inaccurate" vs. "correct" "X" vs. "too much of X" "cannot cause" vs. "is the primary cause of" |

(D)

| since inferior motor oil can cause engine valve deterioration, | and engine valve deterioration can lead to poorer gasoline mileage. | → | It is incorrect to say that inferior motor oil cannot cause a car to get poorer gasoline mileage, |
| Since X can cause Y | and Y can lead to Z | → | It is incorrect to say that X cannot cause Z |

| **Since X can cause Y** | **and Y can predispose to Z** → | **It is inaccurate to say that X cannot cause Z** |

12

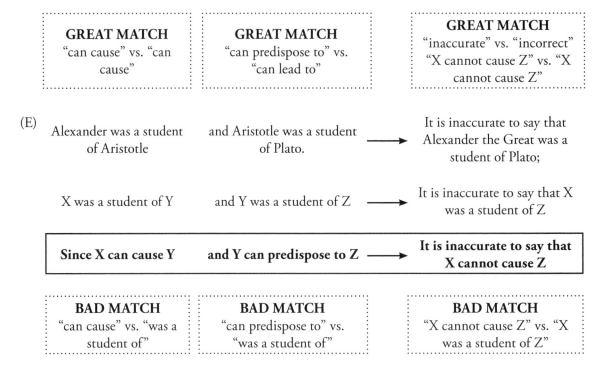

Answer choice (D) clear and away provides the best match with the original argument.

Notice that the key differentiators turned out NOT to be the subject matter (refined sugar, fertilizer, inferior motor oil, etc.). These are placeholders that are completely irrelevant. Thus, we can strip away this content. What DID turn out to be important were the subtle differences in the words and phrases *between* the subject matter elements (inaccurate vs. accurate, can cause vs. cause, cannot cause vs. primary cause of, etc.). We'll talk more about these important details later.

Obviously, creating the complete diagrams we created on the previous pages will not be possible under the time constraints of the exam. You should, however, be able to work through this process mentally as you become more accustomed to searching for the subtle differences in phrasing between the argument and the answer choices.

Order Doesn't Matter

In the previous question, we saw that the correct answer was just about a perfect match with the original argument in its physical structure, even down to the order in which the different argument components were presented. However, this is not a requirement for a correct match. The right answer must match the original argument in terms of logical structure (how they make a point), but logical structure isn't impacted by the order in which information is given. *Logical* structure is important; *organizational* structure is not. Consider the following simple example:

ARGUMENT #1: All of the songs on The Duster's new album are ballads. The song "Rain" is on the The Duster's new album. Thus, the song "Rain" is a ballad.

ARGUMENT #2: The song "Rain" is a ballad since it is on The Duster's new album and all the songs on The Duster's new album are ballads.

Take a second to ask yourself the following questions: Do these two arguments have the same *logical* structure? Do they have the same *organizational* structure?

The *organizational* structure of Argument #1 is: PREMISE–PREMISE–CONCLUSION. The order of Argument #2 is: CONCLUSION–PREMISE–PREMISE. They have different organizational structures.

The *logical* structure of both arguments is: All X are Y. Z is X. Thus, Z is Y. These arguments are logically identical.

When asking you to match an answer choice with the original argument, the LSAT will try to confuse you by shuffling the order of the components. Let's take another look at one of the questions from the start of the chapter to see this in action:

> *PT31, S2, Q23*
>
> Town councilor: The only reason for the town to have ordinances restricting where skateboarding can be done would be to protect children from danger. Skateboarding in the town's River Park is undoubtedly dangerous, but we should not pass an ordinance prohibiting it. If children cannot skateboard in the park, they will most certainly skateboard in the streets. And skateboarding in the streets is more dangerous than skateboarding in the park.
>
> The pattern of reasoning in which one of the following is most similar to that in the town councilor's argument?

(A) The reason for requiring environmental reviews is to ensure that projected developments do not harm the natural environment. Currently, environmental concerns are less compelling than economic concerns, but in the long run, the environment must be protected. Therefore, the requirement for environmental reviews should not be waived.

(B) Insecticides are designed to protect crops against insect damage. Aphids damage tomato crops, but using insecticides against aphids kills wasps that prey on insecticide-resistant pests. Since aphids damage tomato crops less than the insecticide-resistant pests do, insecticides should not be used against aphids on tomato crops.

(C) The purpose of compulsory vaccination for schoolchildren was to protect both the children themselves and others in the community against smallpox. Smallpox was indeed a dreadful disease, but it has now been eliminated from the world's population. So children should not be vaccinated against it.

(D) The function of a sealer on wood siding is to retard deterioration caused by weather. However, cedar is a wood that is naturally resistant to weather-related damage and thus does not need additional protection. Sealers, therefore, should not be applied to cedar siding.

(E) Traffic patterns that involve one-way streets are meant to accelerate the flow of traffic in otherwise congested areas. However, it would be detrimental to the South Main Street area to have traffic move faster. So traffic patterns involving one-way streets should not be implemented there.

12

This is a tough, complicated argument. All the more reason to break it down into its component parts and strip the subject matter. We can start by deconstructing the original argument. Notice the bold statements to the right summarize the argument's components by stripping away the subject matter:

BACKGROUND INFO: The only reason for the town to have ordinances restricting where skateboarding can be done would be to protect children from danger.	**Describes the general function of an action**
	↓
OPPOSING POINT: Skateboarding in the town's River Park is undoubtedly dangerous,	**Specific reason to implement the action**
	↓
CONCLUSION: but we should not pass an ordinance prohibiting it.	**Claim that the action should not be taken in this case**
	↓
SUPPORTING PREMISE: If children cannot skateboard in the park, they will most certainly skateboard in the streets.	**Result if the action were taken**
	↓
SUPPORTING PREMISE: And skateboarding in the streets is more dangerous than skateboarding in the park.	**How the result would end up being worse than what we started with**

Again, we wouldn't necessarily write any of this down, but the representation on the right side of the page is what we want to be *thinking* about as we read.

Have another look at answer choice (B):

> (B) Insecticides are designed to protect crops against insect damage. Aphids damage tomato crops, but using insecticides against aphids kills wasps that prey on insecticide-resistant pests. Since aphids damage tomato crops less than the insecticide-resistant pests do, insecticides should not be used against aphids on tomato crops.

The subject matter in (B) has nothing to do with the original, but we're not interested in matching subject matter. Let's see if the logical structure of (B) gives us a match. Here's (B) broken down:

BACKGROUND INFO: Insecticides are designed to protect crops against insect damage.	Describes the general function of an action
	↓
OPPOSING POINT: Aphids damage tomato crops,	Specific reason to implement the action
	↓
SUPPORTING PREMISE: but using insecticides against aphids kills wasps that prey on insecticide-resistant pests.	Result if the action were taken
	↓
SUPPORTING PREMISE: Since aphids damage tomato crops less than the insecticide-resistant pests do,	How the result would end up being worse than what we started with
	↓
CONCLUSION: insecticides should not be used against aphids on tomato crops.	Claim that the action should not be taken in this case

We can compare the original argument with answer choice (B):

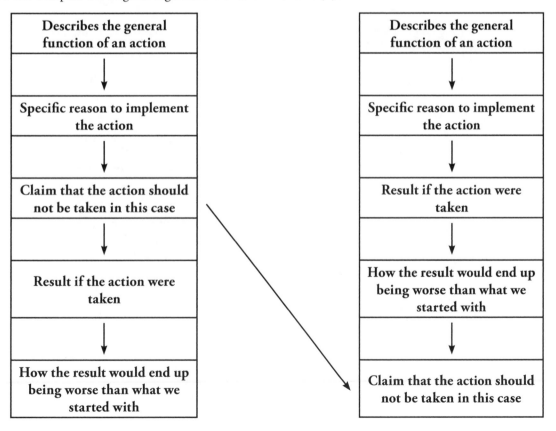

12

Answer (B) is the correct answer. Notice that the *components* of the two arguments match exactly. The only difference is that the conclusion appears in the middle of the original argument whereas the conclusion appears at the end of the argument in answer (B). The components may not be presented in exactly the same order, but remember that order doesn't matter.

Did you eliminate (B) because you were thrown off by the difference in order? If so, adjust your approach; concentrate on matching the components, regardless of where they appear physically within the text.

Watch Out for Modifiers

Throughout this book, we have discussed the importance of paying attention to the details. We saw an example of this earlier in the adult-onset diabetes question when we noted the important differences between "can cause" and "cause," "inaccurate" and "accurate," etc.

Often on Match the Reasoning questions, the LSAT will alter key details in very subtle ways. These details are often modifiers (words that qualify or describe other parts of the argument).

Here's a new problem. Take 2:00 minutes to select an answer and then we'll discuss.

PT22, S2, Q16

Allowing more steel imports would depress domestic steel prices and harm domestic steel manufacturers. Since the present government will not do anything that would harm the domestic steel industry, it will not lift restrictions on steel imports.

The pattern of reasoning in the argument above is most similar to that in which one of the following?

(A) Building construction increases only when people are confident that the economy is doing well. Therefore, since people are now confident in the economy we can expect building construction to increase.

(B) Since workers are already guaranteed the right to a safe and healthful workplace by law, there is no need for the government to establish further costly health regulations for people who work all day at computer terminals.

(C) In countries that have deregulated their airline industry, many airlines have gone bankrupt. Since many companies in other transportation industries are in weaker economic condition than were those airlines, deregulating other transportation industries will probably result in bankruptcies as well.

(D) The chief executive officer of Silicon, Inc., will probably not accept stock in the company as a bonus next year, since next year's tax laws will require companies to pay a new tax on stock given to executives.

(E) The installation of bright floodlights on campus would render the astronomy department's telescope useless. The astronomy department will not support any proposal that would render its telescope useless; it will therefore not support proposals to install bright floodlights on campus.

For this explanation, we'll present the thoughts that a 170+ test-taker might have while answering the question. Everything in italics will represent the test-taker's real-time thoughts.

I'll read the question stem first so that I know what my task is.

> The pattern of reasoning in the argument above is most similar to that in which one of the following?

Matching! This means I need to search for the underlying logical structure in the argument. As much as I can, I'll strip the argument down to its most basic pieces.

> Allowing more steel imports would depress domestic steel prices and harm domestic steel manufacturers. Since the present government will not do anything that would harm the domestic steel industry, it will not lift restrictions on steel imports.

This seems like a good argument. Let me get the logical structure down before moving to the answer choices.

Okay, so "allowing more steel imports" is the same as "lifting restrictions on steel imports." Doing this would "depress steel prices," which in turn would "harm domestic steel manufacturers." So it's like this:

> *Allow more imports* —————▶ *depress steel prices* —————▶ *hurt domestic steel manufacturers*

And we know that the government wouldn't do anything to hurt domestic steel manufacturers, so we can conclude that it won't allow more imports (it won't lift restrictions).

> *Allow more imports* —————▶ *hurt domestic steel manufacturers*

Government won't do anything to hurt domestic steel manufacturers

Thus, government won't allow more imports.

So, it's kind of like a conditional statement that the government does not want to trigger.

$X \longrightarrow Y$
Don't want Y.
So, won't do X.

Got it. Time for the answers.

> (A) Building construction increases only when people are confident that the economy is doing well. Therefore, since people are now confident in the economy, we can expect building construction to increase.

The word "only" is a clue that there may be some conditional logic here. That's a good start.

> *Building construction increase* —————▶ *people are confident that economy is doing well*

And then the conclusion is:

People are now confident → building construction increase
in the economy

This is the reverse of the first statement! This logic is flawed. The original was not flawed. I can eliminate this.

(B) Since workers are already guaranteed the right to a safe
and healthful workplace by law, there is no need for the
government to establish further costly health regulations
for people who work all day at computer terminals.

Where's the conditional logic? We need a conditional relationship followed by a statement that says the conditional statement won't be triggered. No such statement here. Get rid of it.

(C) In countries that have deregulated their airline industry,
many airlines have gone bankrupt. Since many companies
in other transportation industries are in weaker economic
condition than were those airlines, deregulating
other transportation industries will probably result in
bankruptcies as well.

*Look at the conclusion! "Probably?" I know already that this won't be a match. The original doesn't conclude
that the government "probably will not" allow more imports. It says the government "will not" allow imports.
This is a very different kind of conclusion. Get rid of it.*

(D) The chief executive officer of Silicon, Inc., will probably
not accept stock in the company as a bonus next year,
since next year's tax laws will require companies to pay a
new tax on stock given to executives.

*The first sentence is the conclusion, and the second sentence is the supporting premise. Again, the conclusion is
that the chief executive officer "will probably not...." Get rid of it.*

(E) The installation of bright floodlights on campus would
render the astronomy department's telescope useless. The
astronomy department will not support any proposal that
would render its telescope useless; it will therefore not
support proposals to install bright floodlights on campus.

This is the only one left—it better be right! It looks good, but let me break it down.

Installation of bright → render telescope useless
lights

*Astronomy dept. won't support any proposal that would render telescope useless. Thus, astronomy dept. won't
support proposal to install bright lights.*

12

$X \longrightarrow Y$
Don't want Y.
So, won't do X.

This is it! Choose it and move on.

This test-taker was able to move through this question quickly by paying close attention to modifiers. Answer choices (C) and (D) were eliminated immediately because of the word "probably." Saying that someone or something *probably* will or will not do something is NOT the same as saying that someone or something *will* or *will not* do something.

Be on the lookout for modifiers that change the meaning.

Match the Flaw

Find the Flaw First

Your success on Match the Flaw questions will be driven in large part by your ability to identify the flaw in the original argument *before* you begin to analyze the answer choices. This requires that you read the original argument critically. Let's revisit another one of our earlier questions to illustrate:

> *PT30, S2, Q6*
>
> The student body at this university takes courses in a wide range of disciplines. Miriam is a student at this university, so she takes courses in a wide range of disciplines.
>
> Which one of the following arguments exhibits flawed reasoning most similar to that exhibited by the argument above?
>
> (A) The students at this school take mathematics. Miguel is a student at this school, so he takes mathematics.
> (B) The editorial board of this law journal has written on many legal issues. Louise is on the editorial board, so she has written on many legal issues.
> (C) The component parts of bulldozers are heavy. This machine is a bulldozer, so it is heavy.
> (D) All older automobiles need frequent oil changes. This car is new, so its oil need not be changed as frequently.
> (E) The individual cells of the brain are incapable of thinking. Therefore, the brain as a whole is incapable of thinking.

Okay, so let's find the flaw in the original argument first. In this case, the original argument is flawed in that it assigns an attribute belonging to the whole (the student body) to one of the component parts of the whole (Miriam). In other words, just because the entire student body *as a whole* takes courses in a wide range of disciplines does not necessarily mean that Miriam *herself* takes courses in a wide range of disciplines. To put it into concrete terms, assume that the student body is comprised of five students, and that each of these students takes courses in a certain discipline:

Roger: Engineering
Taniya: Mathematics
Abinash: Literature

12

Stan: Spanish
Miriam: Political Science

We can say that the student body as a whole takes courses in a wide range of disciplines, but not that Miriam herself does. She takes courses only in political science. It is therefore flawed reasoning to conclude that the generality necessarily implies something about her specifically.

Now that we have identified the flaw, we can start in on the answer choices. The correct answer will likely have different subject matter, but we know it will contain the same flawed reasoning.

(A) The students at this school take mathematics. Miguel is a
    student at this school, so he takes mathematics.

This is tricky. At first glance it may seem that this argument contains the same flaw: it assigns an attribute belonging to a larger group (the students) to one of the component parts of that group (Miguel). Be careful. In this context, "The students at this school" means each *individual* student. If each individual student at the school takes mathematics, and Miguel is a student at the school, he must take mathematics. This argument is rock solid.

Notice that the LSAT attempts to make this answer more appealing by making the subject matter similar to that of the original argument—both relate to courses at school. Remember that the subject matter is irrelevant.

(B) The editorial board of this law journal has written on
    many legal issues. Louise is on the editorial board, so she
    has written on many legal issues.

This is the correct answer. An attribute belonging to the whole (the editorial board) is assigned to a component part of that whole (Louise). Just because the board as a whole has written on many legal issues doesn't mean that Louise herself has written on many legal issues. This flaw is an identical match with the original.

(C) The component parts of bulldozers are heavy. This
    machine is a bulldozer, so it is heavy.

This argument works in the reverse direction. Instead of assigning an attribute of the whole to a component part, it assigns an attribute of a part to the entire whole. This type of reasoning is usually flawed. Take the following argument as an example:

"The aqueduct was constructed using only rectangular granite blocks. Thus, the aqueduct must have a rectangular shape."

This particular argument would obviously be flawed. Of course, the aqueduct as a whole need not have a rectangular shape just because the blocks do. We can't automatically assign a component part's attribute to the entire whole.

Now, after all that, think about the bulldozer again. In the case of answer choice (C), the logic works! If each component part of a bulldozer is heavy, and the entire bulldozer consists of these component parts, then the entire bulldozer must be heavy as well! This argument contains no flaw. Tricky.

12

(D) All older automobiles need frequent oil changes. This car
    is new, so its oil need not be changed as frequently.

This argument has nothing to do with the relationship between the whole and its component parts. It does, however, contain a conditional logic flaw. Quick quiz—take a second and see if you can identify the flaw before reading on.

(D) tells us that if a car is old, it needs frequent oil changes:

older auto   →   frequent oil changes

Then (D) concludes that a new car (the opposite, or negative, of "older auto") does not need frequent oil changes:

−older auto   →   −frequent oil changes

You CANNOT simply negate the two components of a conditional statement. While this is a classic flaw, it does not match the flaw present in the original argument.

(E) The individual cells of the brain are incapable of thinking.
    Therefore, the brain as a whole is incapable of thinking.

Like answer (C), this argument functions in the reverse direction. Instead of taking an attribute belonging to the whole and giving it to a component part, it takes an attribute belonging to a component part and gives it to the whole. But while (C) was a valid argument, this one is not. Of course the brain is capable of thinking even if the individual components of the brain are not capable of thinking. This argument is flawed, but not in the same "direction" as the original.

This question wasn't too bad, but notice how much there was to learn from the incorrect choices. For Match the Flaw questions in particular, it's crucial that you spend the time during your studies to review the wrong answers. Ask yourself a series of questions:

1. Does this answer choice even contain a flaw?
2. If so, and if it's not the same type of flaw as the original, what kind of flaw is it?
3. How would this answer choice need to be reworded in order to be a correct answer?

For example, let's take answer choice (E):

(E) The individual cells of the brain are incapable of thinking.
    Therefore, the brain as a whole is incapable of thinking.

How could we rewrite this to make it "correct"? Well, remember that we're trying to match the original flaw, which assigned a characteristic of the whole to one of the members of the whole. We could change (E) as follows:

(E) The brain as a whole is capable of thinking. Therefore, the
    individual cells of the brain are also capable of thinking.

This would be a much better match with the original.

12

Forcing yourself through this sort of process is a great way to test the depth of your understanding. In the end, your success on the LSAT won't be determined by how many practice questions you do, but rather by how well you understand the ones you've done.

Let's try another one that's a bit more difficult. Take a few seconds to review the following question from earlier:

> ### PT34, S3, Q23
>
> Societies in which value is measured primarily in financial terms invariably fragment into isolated social units. But since money is not the main measure of value in nonindustrial societies, they must tend in contrast to be socially unified.
>
> The flawed reasoning in which one of the following is most similar to that in the argument above?
>
> (A) Animals of different genera cannot interbreed. But that does not prove that jackals and wolves cannot interbreed, for they belong to the same genus.
>
> (B) Ecosystems close to the equator usually have more species than those closer to the poles. Thus, the Sahara Desert must contain more species than Siberia does, since the latter is farther from the equator.
>
> (C) Insects pass through several stages of maturation: egg, larva, pupa, and adult. Since insects are arthropods, all arthropods probably undergo similar maturation processes.
>
> (D) Poets frequently convey their thoughts via nonliteral uses of language such as metaphors and analogies. But journalists are not poets, so surely journalists always use language literally.
>
> (E) Technologically sophisticated machines often cause us more trouble than simpler devices serving the same function. Since computers are more technologically sophisticated than pencils, they must tend to be more troublesome.

Did you notice the conditional logic cues? If not, go back and look again—they are subtle. Let's start by breaking down the original argument so that we can identify the flaw.

> Societies in which value is measured primarily in financial terms invariably fragment into isolated social units.

The word "invariably" (meaning always) is a conditional trigger! Remember, conditional statements express guarantees. "Invariably" is nothing short of a guarantee. We can express this conditional statement as follows:

$$\text{societies that measure value in financial terms} \longrightarrow \text{fragment into isolated units}$$

MANHATTAN
LSAT

But since money is not the main measure of value in nonindustrial societies, they must tend in contrast to be socially unified.

Now, since the argument started with a conditional statement, there's a good chance that the second statement can be tied to the first in some way. We want to consider the wording carefully to see if we can find a common term. What do we know about nonindustrial societies? For these societies, value is *not* measured primarily in financial terms. The argument uses this piece of information to conclude that these societies tend to be socially unified (the *opposite* of fragmented).

$$\text{–measure value in financial terms} \longrightarrow \text{–fragmented into isolated units}$$

In short, the argument illegally negates the logic given in the first sentence. Flaw! This is the equivalent of saying: "IF something is an apple, THEN it is a fruit. Therefore, IF something is NOT an apple, then it must NOT be a fruit." What about oranges, strawberries, or bananas? At this point in your studies, this flaw should be obvious to you. If it's not, you need to take some time to review the chapter on conditional logic.

Okay, so we're looking for an answer choice with negated logic. If you think you've got it now, try this question again before reading on.

> (A) Animals of different genera cannot interbreed. But that does not prove that jackals and wolves cannot interbreed, for they belong to the same genus.

Wow—complicated argument. The double negatives make it difficult to follow. This is actually a valid argument. Knowing that animals of different genera cannot interbreed tells us nothing about whether animals of the *same* genus can interbreed. If it helps, you can think about this in terms of conditional logic. The first statement is:

$$\text{different genera} \longrightarrow \text{–interbreed}$$

The conclusion states that this does NOT prove that animals of the same genus (the negation of different genera) cannot interbreed. In other words, the conditional statement above does NOT imply:

$$\text{–different genera} \longrightarrow \text{–interbreed}$$

The argument is correct in saying that the second statement CANNOT be inferred from the first. Since there is no flaw, this can't be the answer. Eliminate (A).

> (B) Ecosystems close to the equator usually have more species than those closer to the poles. Thus, the Sahara Desert must contain more species than Siberia does, since the latter is farther from the equator.

This argument is flawed in that it uses a generalization to make a conclusion about a specific case. Ecosystems closer to the equator "*usually*" have more species, but that doesn't mean they "*always*" have more species. Thus, we cannot automatically conclude that the Sahara Desert has more species than Siberia does. The Sahara Desert could be an outlier case that does not conform to the generalization. If the word "*usually*" were replaced with "*always*," this argument would be fine.

12

While this argument is flawed, the flaw is not similar to the conditional flaw present in the original argument. Eliminate (B).

> (C) Insects pass through several stages of maturation: egg, larva, pupa, and adult. Since insects are arthropods, all arthropods probably undergo similar maturation processes.

This argument contains another classic flaw similar to a flaw we saw earlier in the chapter. It takes an attribute of a component part (insects) and assigns it to the entire group (arthropods). This is the equivalent of saying: "Humans can walk on two legs. Since humans are living beings, all living beings probably can walk on two legs." No!

While this argument is flawed, the flaw is not similar to the conditional flaw present in the original argument. Eliminate (C).

> (D) Poets frequently convey their thoughts via nonliteral uses of language such as metaphors and analogies. But journalists are not poets, so surely journalists always use language literally.

This first statement can be written in conditional form:

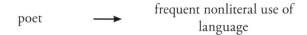

$$\text{poet} \longrightarrow \text{frequent nonliteral use of language}$$

The conclusion attempts to negate both components of the original statement. "Not poet" is the negative of "poet," and note that "always use language literally" can be considered an opposite, or negative of, "frequent nonliteral use of language."

$$-\text{poet} \longrightarrow -\text{frequent nonliteral use of language}$$

Thus, this argument is flawed in exactly the same way as the original argument. This is the correct answer.

> (E) Technologically sophisticated machines often cause us more trouble than simpler devices serving the same function. Since computers are more technologically sophisticated than pencils, they must tend to be more troublesome.

This answer choice is very similar to answer choice (B) in that it uses a generalization to reach a conclusion about a specific case. Technologically sophisticated machines "*often* cause us more trouble" than simpler machines, but not always. Thus, we cannot automatically conclude that computers cause us more trouble than pencils.

While this argument is flawed, the flaw is not similar to the conditional logic flaw present in the original argument. Eliminate (E).

12

Conclusion

Match the Reasoning

1. Strip away the subject matter and match the components. As you read the original argument, see if you can make things simpler for yourself by thinking of the logical structure in generic terms. The correct answer will rarely, if ever, contain a subject matter match, but it will always contain a structural match, component for component.

2. Order doesn't matter. Don't let the LSAT fool you! LSAT test writers will attempt to throw you off track by shuffling the order of the argument components. Remember that two arguments can be logically and structurally identical even when the order of presentation differs.

3. Watch out for modifiers. Keep a close eye on the words and phrases that come *between* the content elements. Must vs. can, most vs. all, sometimes vs. always, probably vs. will, etc. You can often spot incorrect answers by quickly recognizing subtle differences in these modifiers.

Match the Flaw

4. Find the flaw first. Once you know you're dealing with a Match the Flaw question, make it your job to identify the flaw type in the original argument as you read.

5. Learn from the wrong answers. One way to make quick progress on Match the Flaw questions is to make incorrect answer evaluation part of your practice. Analyze each answer choice and try to name the flaw, if one exists. Try to rewrite the answer choice to make it correct. If you can do this consistently, you'll be more likely to see the traps on the real exam.

Time to practice.

DRILL IT: Matching Questions

Give yourself no more than 25 minutes to solve the following problems.

1. PT25, S2, Q2

No one wants this job as much as Joshua does, but he is not applying for it. It follows that there will not be any applicants, no matter how high the salary that is being offered.

The flawed reasoning in the argument above most closely parallels that in which one of the following?

(A) Beth knows better than anyone else how to spot errors in a computer program, yet even she has not found any in this program so far. So it is clear that the errors must all be in the rest of the program.

(B) If anyone can decipher this inscription, it is Professor Alvarez, but she is so involved with her new research that it will be impossible to interest her in this sort of task. Therefore, all we can do now is hope to find someone else.

(C) Although he has the strongest motive of anyone for buying Anna's plot of land, Manfred is not pursuing the matter. Therefore, regardless of how low a price Anna is prepared to accept, she will be looking for a buyer in vain.

(D) The person initially most interested in obtaining the contract was Mr. Moore, but he of all people suddenly withdrew his bid. This means that, no matter how discouraged the other bidders had been, they will now redouble their efforts.

(E) Three times Paul would have liked to take advantage of a special vacation package for himself and his family, but each time he was indispensable at the factory just then. So the more seniority Paul acquires, the greater are the constraints on his personal life.

2. PT24, S2, Q5

Altogether, the students in Ms. Tarnowski's Milton Elementary School class collected more aluminum cans than did the students in any of the school's other classes. Therefore, the Milton student who collected the most aluminum cans was in Ms. Tarnowski's class.

Which one of the following arguments contains flawed reasoning that is most parallel to that in the argument above?

(A) Altogether, more trees were planted by the students in Mr. Kelly's class than were planted by those in Mr. Liang's class and Ms. Jackson's class combined. Therefore, Mr. Kelly's students planted more trees than Ms. Jackson's students planted.

(B) More than half of Milton Elementary School's students play in the band and more than half of the school's students sing in the choir. Therefore, every student at Milton Elementary School either plays in the band or sings in the choir.

(C) Mr. Rowe's Milton Elementary School class raised more money by selling candy bars than Ms. Hunt's class raised by holding a raffle. Therefore, the number of candy bars sold by Mr. Rowe's class was greater than the number of raffle tickets sold by Ms. Hunt's class.

(D) The total number of tickets to the school fair sold by the students in Ms. Ramirez's Milton Elementary School class was greater than the number sold by Milton students from any other class. Therefore, the Milton student who sold the most tickets to the school fair was a student in Ms. Ramirez's class.

(E) Ms. Ventura's Milton Elementary School class assembled more birdhouses than did any of the school's other classes. Since Ms. Ventura's class had fewer students than any other Milton class, her students assembled more birdhouses, on average, than did the students in any other Milton class.

12

<u>3. PT25, S4, Q20</u>

In some ill-considered popularizations of interesting current research, it is argued that higher apes have the capacity for language but have never put it to use—a remarkable biological miracle, given the enormous selectional advantage of even minimal linguistic skills. It is rather like claiming that some animal has wings adequate for flight but has never thought to fly.

Which one of the following is most similar in its reasoning to the argument above?

(A) Arguing that there are some humans who never sleep is rather like discovering a species of lion that does not eat meat.

(B) Arguing that Earth has been visited by aliens from outer space is rather like claiming that early explorers had visited North America but never founded cities.

(C) Arguing that the human brain has telekinetic powers that no humans have ever exercised is rather like arguing that some insect has legs but never uses them to walk.

(D) Claiming that some people raised tobacco but did not smoke it is rather like claiming that a society that knew how to brew alcohol never drank it.

(E) Arguing that not all people with cars will drive them is rather like claiming that humans invented gasoline long before they used it as fuel for transportation.

<u>4. PT22, S4, Q6</u>

A worker for a power company trims the branches of trees that overhang power lines as a prevention against damage to the lines anticipated because of impending stormy season. The worker reasons that there will be no need for her to trim the overhanging branches of a certain tree because the owners of the tree have indicated that they might cut it down anyway.

Which one of the following decisions is based on flawed reasoning that is most similar to the worker's flawed reasoning?

(A) A well inspector has a limited amount of time to inspect the wells of a town. The inspector reasons that the wells should be inspected in the order of most used to least used, because there might not be enough time to inspect them all.

(B) All sewage and incoming water pipes in a house must be replaced. The plumber reasons that the cheaper polyvinyl chloride pipes should be used for sewage rather than copper pipes, since the money saved might be used to replace worn fixtures.

(C) A mechanic must replace the worn brakes on a company's vans that are used each weekday. The mechanic reasons that since one of the vans is tentatively scheduled to be junked, he will not have to replace its brakes.

(D) A candidate decides to campaign in the areas of the city where the most new votes are concentrated. The candidate reasons that campaigning in other areas is unnecessary because in those areas the candidate's message is actually liable to alienate voters.

(E) None of the children in a certain kindergarten class will take responsibility for the crayon drawing on the classroom wall. The teacher reasons that it is best to keep all the kindergarten children in during recess in order to be certain to punish the one who did the drawing on the wall.

12

5. PT23, S2, Q23

An independent audit found no indication of tax avoidance on the part of the firm in the firm's accounts; therefore, no such problem exists.

The questionable reasoning in the argument above is most closely paralleled by that in which one of the following?

(A) The plan for the introduction of the new project has been unmodified so far; therefore, it will not be modified in the future.

(B) The overall budget for the projects has been exceeded by a large amount; therefore, at least one of the projects has exceeded its budget by a large amount.

(C) A compilation of the best student essays of the year includes no essays on current events; therefore, students have become apathetic toward current events.

(D) A survey of schools in the district found no school without a need for building repair; therefore, the education provided to students in the district is substandard.

(E) An examination of the index of the book found no listing for the most prominent critic of the theory the book advocates; therefore, the book fails to refer to that critic.

6. PT20, S4, Q15

Rhonda will see the movie tomorrow afternoon only if Paul goes to the concert in the afternoon. Paul will not go to the concert unless Ted agrees to go to the concert. However, Ted refuses to go to the concert. So Rhonda will not see the movie tomorrow afternoon.

The pattern of reasoning displayed above is most closely paralleled in which one of the following?

(A) If Janice comes to visit, Mary will not pay the bills tomorrow. Janice will not come to visit unless she locates a babysitter. However, Janice has located a babysitter, so she will visit Mary.

(B) Gary will do his laundry tomorrow only if Peter has to go to work. Unless Cathy is ill, Peter will not have to go to work. Since Cathy is not ill, Gary will not do his laundry tomorrow.

(C) Kelly will barbecue fish tonight if it does not rain and the market has fresh trout. Although the forecast does not call for rain, the market does not have fresh trout. So Kelly will not barbecue fish tonight.

(D) Lisa will attend the family reunion next week only if one of her brothers, Jared or Karl, also attends. Karl will not attend the reunion, but Jared will. So Lisa will attend the reunion.

(E) George will not go to the museum tomorrow unless Mark agrees to go. Mark will go to the museum only if he can postpone most of his appointments. Mark has postponed some of his appointments, so he will go to the museum.

7. PT24, S2, Q13

Carl's Coffee Emporium stocks only two decaffeinated coffees: French Roast and Mocha Java. Yusef only serves decaffeinated coffee, and the coffee he served after dinner last night was far too smooth and mellow to have been French Roast. So, if Yusef still gets all his coffee from Carl's, what he served last night was Mocha Java.

The argument above is most similar in its logical structure to which one of the following?

(A) Samuel wants to take three friends to the beach. His mother owns both a sedan and a convertible. The convertible holds four people so, although the sedan has a more powerful engine, if Samuel borrows a vehicle from his mother, he will borrow the convertible.

(B) If Anna wants to walk from her house to the office where she works, she must either go through the park or take the overpass across the railroad tracks. The park paths are muddy, and Anna does not like using the overpass, so she never walks to work.

(C) Rose can either take a two-week vacation in July or wait until October and take a three-week vacation. The trail she had planned to hike requires three weeks to complete but is closed by October, so if Rose takes a vacation, it will not be the one she had planned.

(D) Werdix, Inc., has offered Arno a choice between a job in sales and a job in research. Arno would like to work at Werdix but he would never take a job in sales when another job is available, so if he accepts one of these jobs, it will be the one in research.

(E) If Teresa does not fire her assistant, her staff will rebel and her department's efficiency will decline. Losing her assistant would also reduce its efficiency, so, if no alternative solution can be found, Teresa's department will become less efficient.

Challenge Questions

8. PT21, S2, Q21

If a mechanical aerator is installed in a fish pool, the water in the pool can be properly aerated. So, since John's fish pool does not have a mechanical aerator, it must be that his pool is not properly aerated. Without properly aerated water, fish cannot thrive. Therefore, any fish in John's fish pool will not thrive.

Which one of the following arguments contains an error of reasoning that is also contained in the argument above?

(A) If alum is added to pickle brine, brine can replace the water in the pickles. Therefore, since Paula does not add alum to her pickle brine, the water in the pickles cannot be replaced by brine. Unless their water is replaced with brine, pickles will not stay crisp. Thus, Paula's pickles will not stay crisp.

(B) If pectin is added to jam, the jam will gel. Without a setting agent such as pectin, jam will not gel. So in order to make his jam gel, Harry should add a setting agent such as pectin to the jam.

(C) If stored potatoes are not exposed to ethylene, the potatoes will not sprout. Beets do not release ethylene. Therefore, if Sara stores her potatoes together with beets, the potatoes will not sprout.

(D) If a carrot patch is covered with mulch in the fall, the carrots can be left in the ground until spring. Without a mulch cover, carrots stored in the ground can suffer frost damage. Thus, since Kevin covers his carrot patch with mulch in the fall, the carrots can safely be left in the ground.

(E) If tomatoes are not stored in a dark place, their seeds sometimes sprout. Sprouted seeds can make tomatoes inedible. Therefore, since Maria does not store her tomatoes in a dark place, some of Maria's tomatoes could be inedible.

12

9. PT21, S3, Q22

Anatomical bilateral symmetry is a common trait. It follows, therefore, that it confers survival advantages on organisms. After all, if bilateral symmetry did not confer such advantages, it would not be common.

The pattern of reasoning in which one of the following arguments is most similar to that in the argument above?

(A) Since it is Sawyer who is negotiating for the city government, it must be true that the city takes the matter seriously. After all, if Sawyer had not been available, the city would have insisted that the negotiations be deferred.

(B) Clearly, no candidate is better qualified for the job than Trumbull. In fact, even to suggest that there might be a more highly qualified candidate seems absurd to those who have seen Trumbull at work.

(C) If Powell lacked superior negotiating skills, she would not have been appointed arbitrator in this case. As everyone knows, she is the appointed arbitrator, so her negotiating skills are, detractors notwithstanding, bound to be superior.

(D) Since Varga was away on vacation at the time, it must have been Rivers who conducted the secret negotiations. Any other scenario makes little sense, for Rivers never does the negotiating unless Varga is unavailable.

(E) If Wong is appointed arbitrator, a decision will be reached promptly. Since it would be absurd to appoint anyone other than Wong as arbitrator, a prompt decision can reasonably be expected.

10. PT22, S2, Q23

Several carefully conducted studies showed that 75 percent of strict vegetarians reached age 50 without developing serious heart disease. We can conclude from this that avoiding meat increases one's chances of avoiding serious heart disease. Therefore, people who want to reduce the risk of serious heart disease should not eat meat.

The flawed pattern of reasoning exhibited by which one of the following is most similar to that exhibited by the argument above?

(A) The majority of people who regularly drive over the speed limit will become involved in traffic accidents. To avoid harm to people who do not drive over the speed limit, we should hire more police officers to enforce the speed laws.

(B) Studies have shown that cigarette smokers have a greater chance of incurring heart disease than people who do not smoke. Since cigarette smoking increases one's chances of incurring heart disease, people who want to try to avoid heart disease should give up cigarette smoking.

(C) The majority of people who regularly drink coffee experience dental problems in the latter part of their lives. Since there is this correlation between drinking coffee and incurring dental problems, the government should make coffee less accessible to the general public.

(D) Studies show that people who do not exercise regularly have a shorter life expectancy than those who exercise regularly. To help increase their patients' life expectancy, doctors should recommend regular exercise to their patients.

(E) Most people who exercise regularly are able to handle stress. This shows that exercising regularly decreases one's chances of being overwhelmed by stress. So people who want to be able to handle stress should regularly engage in exercise.

12

11. PT23, S3, Q18

If the recording now playing on the jazz program is really "Louis Armstrong recorded in concert in 1989," as the announcer said, then Louis Armstrong was playing some of the best jazz of his career years after his death. Since the trumpeter was definitely Louis Armstrong, somehow the announcer must have gotten the date of the recording wrong.

The pattern of reasoning in the argument above is most similar to that in which one of the following arguments?

(A) The museum is reported as having acquired a painting "by Malvina Hoffman, an artist who died in 1966." But Hoffman was a sculptor, not a painter, so the report must be wrong about the acquisition being a painting.

(B) This painting titled La Toilette is Berthe Morisot's La Toilette only if a painting can be in two museums at the same time. Since nothing can be in two places at once, this painting must some how have been mistitled.

(C) Only if a twentieth-century Mexican artist painted in Japan during the seventeenth century can this work both be "by Frida Kahlo" as labeled and the seventeenth-century Japanese landscape it appears to be. Since it is what it appears to be, the label is wrong.

(D) Unless Käthe Kollwitz was both a sculptor and a printmaker, the volunteer museum guide is wrong in his attribution of this sculpture. Since what Kollwitz is known for is her prints, the guide must be wrong.

(E) If this painting is a portrait done in acrylic, it cannot be by Elisabeth Vigée-Lebrun, since acrylic paint was developed only after her death. Thus, since it is definitely a portrait, the paint must not be acrylic.

12. PT23, S3, Q23

Candidate: The government spends $500 million more each year promoting highway safety than it spends combating cigarette smoking. But each year many more people die from smoking-related diseases than die in highway accidents. So the government would save lives by shifting funds from highway safety programs to antismoking programs.

The flawed reasoning in which one of the following arguments most closely parallels the flawed reasoning in the candidate's argument?

(A) The government enforces the speed limit on freeways much more closely than on tollways. But many more people die each year in auto accidents on freeways than die in auto accidents on tollway. So the government would save lives by shifting funds from enforcement of speed limits on freeways to enforcement of speed limits on tollways.

(B) A certain professional musician spends several times as many hours practicing guitar as she spends practicing saxophone. But she is hired much more often to play saxophone than to play guitar, so she would increase her number of playing engagements by spending less time practicing guitar and more time practicing saxophone.

(C) Automobiles burn more gas per minute on highways than on residential streets. But they get fewer miles per gallon on residential streets. Therefore, gas would be saved by driving less on residential streets and more on highways.

(D) The local swim team spends many more hours practicing the backstroke than it spends practicing the breaststroke. But the team's lap times for the breaststroke are much better than its times for the backstroke, so the team would win more swim meets if it spent less time practicing the backstroke and more time practicing the breaststroke.

(E) Banks have a higher profit margin on loans that have a high interest rate than on loans that have a low interest rate. But borrowers are willing to borrow larger sums at low rates than at high rates. Therefore, banks would be more profitable if they gave more loans at low rates and fewer loans at high rates.

12

13. PT24, S3, Q16

K, a research scientist, was accused of having falsified laboratory data. Although the original data in question have disappeared, data from K's more recent experiments have been examined and clearly none of them were falsified. Therefore, the accusation should be dismissed.

Which one of the following contains questionable reasoning that is most similar to that in the argument above?

(A) L, an accountant, was charged with having embezzled funds from a client. The charge should be ignored, however, because although the records that might reveal this embezzlement have been destroyed, records of L's current clients show clearly that there has never been any embezzlement from them.

(B) M, a factory supervisor, was accused of failing to enforce safety standards. This accusation should be discussed, because although the identity of the accuser was not revealed, a survey of factory personnel revealed that some violations of the standards have occurred.

(C) N, a social scientist, was charged with plagiarism. The charge is without foundation because although strong similarities between N's book and the work of another scholar have been discovered, the other scholar's work was written after N's work was published.

(D) O, an auto mechanic, has been accused of selling stolen auto parts. The accusation seems to be justified since although no evidence links O directly to these sales, the pattern of distribution of the auto parts points to O as the source.

(E) P, a politician, has been accused of failing to protect the public interest. From at least some points of view, however, the accusation will undoubtedly be considered false, because there is clearly disagreement about where the public interest lies.

14. PT24, S3, Q21

The amount of electricity consumed in Millville on any day in August is directly proportional to peak humidity on that day. Since the average peak humidity this August was three points higher than the average peak humidity last August, it follows that more energy was consumed in Millville this August than last August.

Which one of the following arguments has a pattern of reasoning most similar to the one in the argument above?

(A) The amount of art supplies used in any of the Aesthetic Institute's 25 classes is directly proportional to the number of students in that class. Since in these classes the institute enrolled 20 percent more students overall last year than in the previous year, more art supplies were used in the institute's classes last year than in the previous year.

(B) The number of courses in painting offered by the Aesthetic Institute in any term is directly proportional to the number of students enrolled in the institute in that term. But the institute offers the same number of courses in sculpture each term. Hence, the institute usually offers more courses in painting than in sculpture.

(C) The number of new students enrolled at the Aesthetic Institute in any given year is directly proportional to the amount of advertising the institute has done in the previous year. Hence, if the institute seeks to increase its student body it must increase the amount it spends on advertising.

(D) The fees paid by a student at the Aesthetic Institute are directly proportional to the number of classes in which that student enrolls. Since the number of students at the Aesthetic Institute is increasing, it follows that the institute is collecting a greater amount of fees paid by students than it used to.

(E) The number of instructors employed by the Aesthetic Institute in any term is directly proportional to the number of classes offered in that term and also directly proportional to the number of students enrolled at the institute. Thus, the number of classes offered by the institute in any term is directly proportional to the number of students enrolled in that term.

12

15. PT25, S2, Q22

It is an absurd idea that whatever artistic endeavor the government refuses to support it does not allow, as one can see by rephrasing the statement to read: No one is allowed to create art without a government subsidy.

The pattern of reasoning in which one of the following is most similar to that in the argument above?

(A) The claim that any driver who is not arrested does not break the law is absurd, as one can see by rewording it: Every driver who breaks the law gets arrested.

(B) The claim that any driver who is not arrested does not break the law is absurd, as one can see by rewording it: Every driver who gets arrested has broken the law.

(C) The notion that every scientist who is supported by a government grant will be successful is absurd, as one can see by rewording it: No scientist who is successful is so without a government grant.

(D) The notion that every scientist who is supported by a government grant will be successful is absurd, as one can see by rewording it: No scientist lacking governmental support will be successful.

(E) The notion that every scientist who has been supported by a government grant will be successful is absurd, as one can see by rewording it: No scientist is allowed to do research without a government grant.

SOLUTIONS: Matching Questions

1. PT25, S2, Q2

No one wants this job as much as Joshua does, but he is not applying for it. It follows that there will not be any applicants, no matter how high the salary that is being offered.

The flawed reasoning in the argument above most closely parallels that in which one of the following?

    (A) Beth knows better than anyone else how to spot errors in a computer program, yet even she has not found any in this program so far. So it is clear that the errors must all be in the rest of the program.

    (B) If anyone can decipher this inscription, it is Professor Alvarez, but she is so involved with her new research that it will be impossible to interest her in this sort of task. Therefore, all we can do now is hope to find someone else.

    (C) Although he has the strongest motive of anyone for buying Anna's plot of land, Manfred is not pursuing the matter. Therefore, regardless of how low a price Anna is prepared to accept, she will be looking for a buyer in vain.

    (D) The person initially most interested in obtaining the contract was Mr. Moore, but he of all people suddenly withdrew his bid. This means that, no matter how discouraged the other bidders had been, they will now redouble their efforts.

    (E) Three times Paul would have liked to take advantage of a special vacation package for himself and his family, but each time he was indispensable at the factory just then. So the more seniority Paul acquires, the greater are the constraints on his personal life.

(C) is the correct answer.

If you had to debate this argument, you might say, "People who want the job less than Joshua does might still apply! Especially if the salary is quite high." So, the argument is assuming that those who want the job less would not want the job if Joshua doesn't.

(C) contains a similar assumption. Those who want the land less than Manfred will not want it since he does not. (C) is the only answer that contains this assumption.

We could also arrive at the answer by a more formal process of matching the original argument's structure:

1. Person Y wants X more than anyone. BUT, Person Y isn't trying to obtain X now.
2. Thus, nobody will try to obtain X, even if the offer is made tempting.

The incorrect answers are all mismatches, of course:

(A) somewhat matches the first part; Beth is established as the strongest candidate (a potential match with Joshua's unsurpassed desire), but then the match ends. The original has the strongest candidate not *participating*, while in (A) she is not *succeeding*. Finally, the second part has no match for the original idea of making an offer tempting.

(B) looks attractive at first. Professor Alvarez is the most qualified but is unable to participate. What follows should be that there's no hope of anyone completing the task, but instead we learn about a hope for completing it. We want a more pessimistic conclusion!

(D) starts out seeming like a match. Mr. Moore is the most interested candidate (note that this is a bit stronger than the original), and he is apparently uninterested in participating. Like (B), however, (D) ends with a description of how the venture will proceed. This is not a match since the argument should conclude that the venture (the sale) is *not* going to happen.

(E) can be eliminated based on the first sentence. Paul is not established as being the person whose interest is unrivaled. Furthermore, the conclusion—a proportional relationship—is completely different than the original.

2. PT24, S2, Q5

Altogether, the students in Ms. Tarnowski's Milton Elementary School class collected more aluminum cans than did the students in any of the school's other classes. Therefore, the Milton student who collected the most aluminum cans was in Ms. Tarnowski's class.

Which one of the following arguments contains flawed reasoning that is most parallel to that in the argument above?

(A) Altogether, more trees were planted by the students in Mr. Kelly's class than were planted by those in Mr. Liang's class and Ms. Jackson's class combined. Therefore, Mr. Kelly's students planted more trees than Ms. Jackson's students planted.

(B) More than half of Milton Elementary School's students play in the band and more than half of the school's students sing in the choir. Therefore, every student at Milton Elementary School either plays in the band or sings in the choir.

(C) Mr. Rowe's Milton Elementary School class raised more money by selling candy bars than Ms. Hunt's class raised by holding a raffle. Therefore, the number of candy bars sold by Mr. Rowe's class was greater than the number of raffle tickets sold by Ms. Hunt's class.

(D) The total number of tickets to the school fair sold by the students in Ms. Ramirez's Milton Elementary School class was greater than the number sold by Milton students from any other class. Therefore, the Milton student who sold the most tickets to the school fair was a student in Ms. Ramirez's class.

(E) Ms. Ventura's Milton Elementary School class assembled more birdhouses than did any of the school's other classes. Since Ms. Ventura's class had fewer students than any other Milton class, her students assembled more birdhouses, on average, than did the students in any other Milton class.

(D) is the correct answer.

Since we're reading a flawed argument, you should have read like a debater and thought of a counterexample such as this: "It's possible that the kid who collected the most cans was in another class, but nobody else in his class collected a lot of cans, so his class did not collect the most overall." Debating this argument reveals its flaw: the general characteristics of a group don't necessarily apply to each member of that group. And in this argument, we're specifically looking for an argument that refers to a group having more than any other, and for that fact being (mis)applied to an individual in that group.

(D) has the same flaw. Even though Ms. Ramirez's class sold the most tickets, the student who sold the most might be in a different class.

Let's knock out the incorrect answers:

(A) is not flawed. If you were tempted by (A), play with possible number combinations and you'll see that (A) is true.

(B) is indeed flawed—perhaps many of the same kids play in the band and sing in the choir. We can't assume, as (B) does, that the two groups do not overlap. However, that's a different flaw than the one we're looking to match. You can quickly eliminate (B) since there is no mention of a group or an individual having more of something than any other.

(C) can be eliminated because it introduces two items, candy and tickets, while the original only discusses one. The argument in (C) is flawed; the difference in how much money each class raised can't be used to draw a conclusion about the relative number of items sold since there are two types of items and perhaps one was more expensive. But as with (B), this is not the flaw we're looking to match.

12

(E) can be eliminated because it introduces the element of how many members were in the group.

3. PT25, S4, Q20

In some ill-considered popularizations of interesting current research, it is argued that higher apes have the capacity for language but have never put it to use—a remarkable biological miracle, given the enormous selectional advantage of even minimal linguistic skills. It is rather like claiming that some animal has wings adequate for flight but has never thought to fly.

Which one of the following is most similar in its reasoning to the argument above?

(A) Arguing that there are some humans who never sleep is rather like discovering a species of lion that does not eat meat.

(B) Arguing that Earth has been visited by aliens from outer space is rather like claiming that early explorers had visited North America but never founded cities.

(C) Arguing that the human brain has telekinetic powers that no humans have ever exercised is rather like arguing that some insect has legs but never uses them to walk.

(D) Claiming that some people raised tobacco but did not smoke it is rather like claiming that a society that knew how to brew alcohol never drank it.

(E) Arguing that not all people with cars will drive them is rather like claiming that humans invented gasoline long before they used it as fuel for transportation.

(C) is the correct answer.

For this question we're on the hunt for an answer with a similarly constructed analogy used to draw a similar conclusion. The original uses an analogy to cast doubt on the idea that apes have the capacity for language but haven't used it. The analogy is a hypothetical (and apparently ridiculous) example of an animal having wings for flight but never using them. Note the switch from discussing an unused mental capacity to an unused part of the physical body.

(C) is a strong match. The argument is casting doubt on the idea that we have telekinetic powers, a mental ability, but we choose not to use them. In support, a matching analogy is given: a hypothetical example of an animal having legs but not using them to walk.

Let's look at the incorrect answers:

(A) is a mismatch because it is about "some" humans. The original is about apes in general.

(B) is a mismatch in that it is not about having an ability (and not using it). You might have been tempted by (B) if you thought that the argument implies that aliens have the ability to found a city on whichever planet they visit (and did not choose to do so on Earth). This is a large assumption to make. And, surely aliens might choose not to settle on our planet for legitimate reasons!

(D) is not well-matched to the original because it's about using or not using something that can be *created* by the animal/human, not about a species not using a part of its anatomy or a mental capacity.

(E) is not even close. This is about not using a product. Furthermore, it seems plausible that we invented gasoline before we started using it as fuel for transportation.

4. PT22, S4, Q6

A worker for a power company trims the branches of trees that overhang power lines as a prevention against damage to the lines anticipated because of the impending stormy season. The worker reasons that there will be no need for her to trim the overhanging branches of a certain tree because the owners of the tree have indicated that they might cut it down anyway.

Which one of the following decisions is based on flawed reasoning that is most similar to the worker's flawed reasoning?

(A) A well inspector has a limited amount of time to inspect the wells of a town. The inspector reasons that the wells should be inspected in the order of most used to least used, because there might not be enough time to inspect them all.

(B) All sewage and incoming water pipes in a house must be replaced. The plumber reasons that the cheaper polyvinyl chloride pipes should be used for sewage rather than copper pipes, since the money saved might be used to replace worn fixtures.

(C) A mechanic must replace the worn brakes on a company's vans that are used each weekday. The mechanic reasons that since one of the vans is tentatively scheduled to be junked, he will not have to replace its brakes.

(D) A candidate decides to campaign in the areas of the city where the most new votes are concentrated. The candidate reasons that campaigning in other areas is unnecessary because in those areas the candidate's message is actually liable to alienate voters.

(E) None of the children in a certain kindergarten class will take responsibility for the crayon drawing on the classroom wall. The teacher reasons that it is best to keep all the kindergarten children in during recess in order to be certain to punish the one who did the drawing on the wall.

(C) is the correct answer.

The first hint of the flaw that we have to match in the question is found in the conclusion's strong language: "…there will be **no** need for her to trim the overhanging branches…." That's a strong conclusion to reach simply because the tree's owners *indicated* they *might* cut it down. Will the owners cut it? When? Before the storm?

(C) demonstrates the same flaw. The mechanic concludes he will not have to replace the brakes since the van is *tentatively* scheduled to be junked. Will it be? When? Won't the worn brakes be a danger until then?

(A) does not include a conclusion about not doing something because of a chance it's unnecessary. In (A), a limited amount of time is the consideration.

(B) is an argument about a choice, not about not doing something.

(D) does not include a conclusion about not doing something because it's perhaps unnecessary. In (D), the reasoning is that the plan would backfire.

(E) is hard to match to the original. Where's the tentative evidence? Where's the not doing something? It's clear this answer is not a correct match.

5. PT23, S2, Q23

An independent audit found no indication of tax avoidance on the part of the firm in the firm's accounts; therefore, no such problem exists.

The questionable reasoning in the argument above is most closely paralleled by that in which one of the following?

(A) The plan for the introduction of the new project has been unmodified so far; therefore, it will not be modified in the future.

(B) The overall budget for the projects has been exceeded by a large amount; therefore, at least one of the projects has exceeded its budget by a large amount.

(C) A compilation of the best student essays of the year includes no essays on current events; therefore, students have become apathetic toward current events.

(D) A survey of schools in the district found no school without a need for building repair; therefore, the education provided to students in the district is substandard.

(E) An examination of the index of the book found no listing for the most prominent critic of the theory the book advocates; therefore, the book fails to refer to that critic.

(E) is the correct answer.

The flaw in the original argument probably jumped out at you: just because an independent audit did not find any traces of a problem doesn't mean that there is no such problem! Even though an independent audit is a reasonable way to check for accounting irregularities, the audit's efficacy is not guaranteed since audits are not foolproof. Furthermore, it could be true that there is a problem, but it just doesn't show up in the accounts (maybe the firm's accounts are wrong or incomplete).

(E) contains the same flaw: just because a book's index doesn't list X does not mean that the book definitely does not contain any reference to X. Maybe the indexer made a mistake.

There are several tempting wrong answers:

(A) has a somewhat similar structure in that a strong conclusion is drawn using information that is relevant but not strong enough. However, unlike the argument in the stimulus, the conclusion in (A) hinges on extending a pattern, not on trusting a supposedly reliable authority.

(B) has a similar flaw to the original in that a conclusion is drawn based on potentially misleading evidence. However, this argument does not have an apparent (though not foolproof) authority. Instead, this argument is flawed because it uses the characteristics of the whole to draw a conclusion about a part.

(C) is clearly wrong because the conclusion makes a dramatic shift to discussing apathy while the premise is about the type of essays included in a publication. The original argument has flaws, but it doesn't have a shift like that.

(D) is similar to (C) in that it includes a dramatic term shift, from *schools needing repairs* to the *education provided being substandard*. Again, there's no such shift in the original.

6. PT20, S4, Q15
Rhonda will see the movie tomorrow afternoon only if Paul goes to the concert in the afternoon. Paul will not go to the concert unless Ted agrees to go to the concert. However, Ted refuses to go to the concert. So Rhonda will not see the movie tomorrow afternoon.

The pattern of reasoning displayed above is most closely paralleled in which one of the following?

(A) If Janice comes to visit, Mary will not pay the bills tomorrow. Janice will not come to visit unless she locates a babysitter. However, Janice has located a babysitter, so she will visit Mary.

(B) Gary will do his laundry tomorrow only if Peter has to go to work. Unless Cathy is ill, Peter will not have to go to work. Since Cathy is not ill, Gary will not do his laundry tomorrow.

(C) Kelly will barbecue fish tonight if it does not rain and the market has fresh trout. Although the forecast does not call for rain, the market does not have fresh trout. So Kelly will not barbecue fish tonight.

(D) Lisa will attend the family reunion next week only if one of her brothers, Jared or Karl, also attends. Karl will not attend the reunion, but Jared will. So Lisa will attend the reunion.

(E) George will not go to the museum tomorrow unless Mark agrees to go. Mark will go to the museum only if he can postpone most of his appointments. Mark has postponed some of his appointments, so he will go to the museum.

(B) is the correct answer.

This is a great example of where using formally notated logic can be very helpful. Let's start by uncovering the logical structure of the stimulus. We'll use shorthand to keep a brisk pace.

Rhonda will see the movie tomorrow afternoon only if Paul goes to the concert in the afternoon.

$$R. @ \text{movie} \rightarrow P. @ \text{concert}$$

Paul will not go to the concert unless Ted agrees to go to the concert.

We can link this to the first statement. To save time, we'll do that immediately instead of writing it separately:

$$R. @ \text{movie} \rightarrow P. @ \text{concert} \rightarrow T. \smiley \text{ to concert}$$

However, Ted refuses to go to the concert:

–T. ☺ to concert

So, Rhonda will not see the movie tomorrow afternoon.

–R. @ movie

The conclusion is based on triggering the contrapositive of the three-part chain we formed above:

–T. ☺ to concert → –P. @ concert → –R. @ movie

Let's look for a match!

(A) looks good at first glance, so let's look more closely.

J. visits → –M. pay bills
J. visits → J. locates babysitter
J. locates babysitter

Therefore, J. visits.

Where's the chain? Where's the triggering of the contrapositive? Eliminate (A).

(B) also looks good. Let's translate it into formal notation:

G. laundry → P. work → C. ill
–C. ill
–G. laundry

It's a match!

Here's how one could quickly eliminate (C) through (E):

(C) begins like this:

–Rain + Fresh trout → K. barbecues

We can stop right there! The stimulus is not a compound conditional statement.

(D) begins like this:

L. attend → J. or K. attends

Stop. Déjà vu! The stimulus is not a compound conditional statement.

(E) looks good at first glance, so let's look under the hood:

G. @ museum → M. agrees to go.
M. @ museum → M. postpones most appts.
M. postpones some appts.
Therefore, M. @ museum

This is close, but there's no triggering of the contrapositive. Furthermore, if we read with a lawyer's eye, we might notice that there isn't a chain. Mark agreeing to go to the museum is not the same as Mark going to the museum. Note that "some" is not a negation of "most." On the LSAT, "some" means "one or more," which could include "most."

7. PT24, S2, Q13

Carl's Coffee Emporium stocks only two decaffeinated coffees: French Roast and Mocha Java. Yusef only serves decaffeinated coffee, and the coffee he served after dinner last night was far too smooth and mellow to have been French Roast. So, if Yusef still gets all his coffee from Carl's, what he served last night was Mocha Java.

The argument above is most similar in its logical structure to which one of the following?

(A) Samuel wants to take three friends to the beach. His mother owns both a sedan and a convertible. The convertible holds four people so, although the sedan has a more powerful engine, if Samuel borrows a vehicle from his mother, he will borrow the convertible.

(B) If Anna wants to walk from her house to the office where she works, she must either go through the park or take the overpass across the railroad tracks. The park paths are muddy, and Anna does not like using the overpass, so she never walks to work.

(C) Rose can either take a two-week vacation in July or wait until October and take a three-week vacation. The trail she had planned to hike requires three weeks to complete but is closed by October, so if Rose takes a vacation, it will not be the one she had planned.

(D) Werdix, Inc., has offered Arno a choice between a job in sales and a job in research. Arno would like to work at Werdix but he would never take a job in sales when another job is available, so if he accepts one of these jobs, it will be the one in research.

(E) If Teresa does not fire her assistant, her staff will rebel and her department's efficiency will decline. Losing her assistant would also reduce its efficiency, so, if no alternative solution can be found, Teresa's department will become less efficient.

(D) is the correct answer.

Let's use this problem to practice some informal notation:

The original argument:

> C offers only 2 choices: F or M.
> Y did not use F.
> So, if Y used C's choices,
> Y must have used M.

Answer choice (D):

> W offered A only 2 choices: S or R.
> If possible, A would not choose S.
> So, if A uses W's choices,
> Must be R.

There are some slight mismatches ("Y did not use F" is not a perfect match to "if possible, A would not choose S"), but (D) is definitely the best of the bunch:

(A) discusses a choice between two options; however, it lacks a statement that definitively establishes why one option is not, or will not be, selected.

(B) is lacking a definitive statement about which choice Anna will not select. Another mismatch is that the conclusion is a rejection of both choices, not the selection of one, as is found in the original argument.

(C) is similar to the original argument in that it begins with two options: a July or an October

vacation. However, from there, the structure is quite different. We can think of it as follows:

R has two choices: 2-week vacation in July or 3-week vacation in October.

Plans to hike a trail.

Can't hike trail in October.

If Rose vacations, it won't be what she planned.

The original argument set up two possibilities (French Roast or Mocha), eliminated one possibility, then concluded the other must be true. We don't have that same structure here. If (C) had concluded, "Therefore, Rose will vacation in July," it would have been a much better match, but, as is, this answer brings up complications the original argument did not, and it reaches a conclusion that is quite different from the type of conclusion the original argument reached. Therefore, (C) is not a good match.

(E) is mismatched in several ways. A glaring problem is that there is no explicit discussion of a choice.

Challenge Questions

8. PT21, S2, Q21

If a mechanical aerator is installed in a fish pool, the water in the pool can be properly aerated. So, since John's fish pool does not have a mechanical aerator, it must be that his pool is not properly aerated. Without properly aerated water, fish cannot thrive. Therefore, any fish in John's fish pool will not thrive.

Which one of the following arguments contains an error of reasoning that is also contained in the argument above?

(A) If alum is added to pickle brine, brine can replace the water in the pickles. Therefore, since Paula does not add alum to her pickle brine, the water in the pickles cannot be replaced by brine. Unless their water is replaced with brine, pickles will not stay crisp. Thus, Paula's pickles will not stay crisp.

(B) If pectin is added to jam, the jam will gel. Without a setting agent such as pectin, jam will not gel. So in order to make his jam gel, Harry should add a setting agent such as pectin to the jam.

(C) If stored potatoes are not exposed to ethylene, the potatoes will not sprout. Beets do not release ethylene. Therefore, if Sara stores her potatoes together with beets, the potatoes will not sprout.

(D) If a carrot patch is covered with mulch in the fall, the carrots can be left in the ground until spring. Without a mulch cover, carrots stored in the ground can suffer frost damage. Thus, since Kevin covers his carrot patch with mulch in the fall, the carrots can safely be left in the ground.

(E) If tomatoes are not stored in a dark place, their seeds sometimes sprout. Sprouted seeds can make tomatoes inedible. Therefore, since Maria does not store her tomatoes in a dark place, some of Maria's tomatoes could be inedible.

(A) is the correct answer.

Let's start by finding the flaw in the stimulus. The first sentence starts with "If" and a quick scan of the argument reveals several conditional logic trigger words, so we'll translate this into formal logic as we read. If your ability to grasp a conditional logic flaw is strong enough that you don't have to write down the formal logic, great. But it's good to know how to do this in case the relationships start spinning in your head.

The first sentence is straightforward to translate: m.a. → water aerated.

The second sentence: Thus, since –m.a.→ –water aerated.

The third sentence: –water aerated → –fish.

You can immediately attach that to the second sentence: –m.a.→ –water aerated → –fish

The final sentence gives us the conclusion: –fish. This is basically stating the end of the chain that was triggered by –m.a.

That seems fine, so what's the flaw? Notice that the second sentence is framed as a conclusion (an intermediate one) that is based on the first sentence. If we just look at that part of the argument, we see a problem:

$$\text{m.a.} \rightarrow \text{water aerated, thus,}$$
$$\text{--m.e. in pool} \rightarrow \text{--water aerated.}$$

That's negated logic. Bad logic, bad!

(A) matches perfectly. Let's take it sentence by sentence.

1. alum → brine rep. wat.
2. Thus, –alum → –brine rep. wat.
3. –brine rep. wat. → –crisp
4. Therefore, –crisp

We can link up some of these: –alum → –brine rep. wat. → –crisp. But, once again, the second sentence is an illegal negation of the first.

Let's look at the four wrong answers to see how we could eliminate them.

(B) is suspicious because the conclusion is a suggestion about how to obtain a certain result ("In order to…Harry should…"), not a statement of what *will* occur. Furthermore, the stimulus's conclusion is a negative statement ("not thrive" and "not stay crisp"), not a positive suggestion about how to achieve something.

Formally, (B) is incorrect because its structure is this:

$$\text{pec.} \rightarrow \text{gel}$$
$$\text{--setting agent (pec)} \rightarrow \text{--gel}$$
$$\text{Thus, gel} \rightarrow \text{setting agent (pec)}$$

We don't really see the same illegal negation in the second statement, and the conclusion is not simply declaring the end of a chain of logic. In fact, there are no premises to link.

(C) can be eliminated for a similar reason as (B). The conclusion in (C) is a relationship, not a statement of what will occur. Formally, (C) can be represented as:

12

−ethylene exposure → −potatoes sprout
Beets → −ethylene released
Thus, potatoes w/beets → −potatoes
sprout

Again, where is the possibility of linked premises? Where is the illegal negation of a statement?

(D) has a closely matching conclusion since it states what is true, not what would be true if something were done. However, it's suspicious that the conclusion is a positive prediction, "can safely," instead of a conclusion about how something will *not* occur.

Looking a bit further into (D), we'll see that the structure does not match up. Notice that the second statement is an independent premise, not an intermediate conclusion:

mulch → carrots safe
−mulch → carrots can be damaged
mulch
Thus, carrots safe

This argument is actually valid! If mulch → safe, mulch → safe! No flaw, no match!

(E) has the right sort of conclusion in that it is negative. However, it's not a great match since it discusses what "could" occur, not what will occur. Furthermore, the first two sentences are about what "can" occur and what happens "sometimes." These do not match the original.

Formally, the argument is structured as follows:

−tom. in dark → some sprout
sprout → can be inedible
Maria −tom. in dark
Thus, some can be inedible

This argument is valid. Note that the second sentence is a stand-alone premise, not one that is supported (illegally, and through negation) by the first one.

9. PT21, S3, Q22

Anatomical bilateral symmetry is a common trait. It follows, therefore, that it confers survival advantages on organisms. After all, if bilateral symmetry did not confer such advantages, it would not be common.

The pattern of reasoning in which one of the following arguments is most similar to that in the argument above?

(A) Since it is Sawyer who is negotiating for the city government, it must be true that the city takes the matter seriously. After all, if Sawyer had not been available, the city would have insisted that the negotiations be deferred.

(B) Clearly, no candidate is better qualified for the job than Trumbull. In fact, even to suggest that there might be a more highly qualified candidate seems absurd to those who have seen Trumbull at work.

(C) If Powell lacked superior negotiating skills, she would not have been appointed arbitrator in this case. As everyone knows, she is the appointed arbitrator, so her negotiating skills are, detractors notwithstanding, bound to be superior.

(D) Since Varga was away on vacation at the time, it must have been Rivers who conducted the secret negotiations. Any other scenario makes little sense, for Rivers never does the negotiating unless Varga is unavailable.

(E) If Wong is appointed arbitrator, a decision will be reached promptly. Since it would be absurd to appoint anyone other than Wong as arbitrator, a prompt decision can reasonably be expected.

(C) is the correct answer.

There are a lot of conditional logic triggers and the argument is rather confusing, so we'll use a formal approach.

Anatomical bilateral symmetry is a common trait.

Perhaps the "is" is a conditional logic trigger, but let's keep looking.

It follows, therefore, that it confers survival advantages on organisms.

Ah! This gives us: A.B.S. is common → A.B.S. confers surv. adv.

After all, if bilateral symmetry did not confer such advantages, it would not be common.

This is clearly the support. It translates to: A.B.S. NOT confers surv. adv. → A.B.S. NOT common

This argument is providing the contrapositive of a statement as its support. Strange seeming, but valid!

(C) has the same structure, though it's delivered in reverse:

> Powell –S.N.S. → –appointed arbitrator
> appointed arbitrator → Powell S.N.S.

Remember, for matching questions, the order of the argument is not important as long as the underlying pieces fit together logically in the same manner.

Let's look at the wrong answers, and we'll try comparing what we would "want" each answer to say (to make it a match) to what it actually says:

(A) starts off like this: Sawyer negotiating → city takes matter seriously. To complete the structure, we'd want –city takes matter seriously → –Sawyer negotiating.

Instead, we find a statement about Sawyer's availability.

(B) is clearly wrong because there are not two conditional statements. Furthermore, "seems absurd," seems absurd!

(D) begins as follows: Varga away → Rivera conduct negotiation. To complete this, we'd want –Rivera conduct negotiation → –Varga away.

Instead, we find Rivera conduct negotiation → Varga unavailable. This is the negation of what we need.

(E) starts off with this statement: Wong appointed → prompt decision. To complete the match, we'd want –prompt decision → –Wong appointed.

Instead, the second sentence is quite different: unreasonable to NOT appoint Wong → prompt decision expected.

10. PT22, S2, Q23

Several carefully conducted studies showed that 75 percent of strict vegetarians reached age 50 without developing serious heart disease. We can conclude from this that avoiding meat increases one's chances of avoiding serious heart disease. Therefore, people who want to reduce the risk of serious heart disease should not eat meat.

The flawed pattern of reasoning exhibited by which one of the following is most similar to that exhibited by the argument above?

(A) The majority of people who regularly drive over the speed limit will become involved in traffic accidents. To avoid harm to people who do not drive over the speed limit, we should hire more police officers to enforce the speed laws.

(B) Studies have shown that cigarette smokers have a greater chance of incurring heart disease than people who do not smoke. Since cigarette smoking increases one's chances of incurring heart disease, people who want to try to avoid heart disease should give up cigarette smoking.

(C) The majority of people who regularly drink coffee experience dental problems in the latter part of their lives. Since there is this correlation between drinking coffee and incurring dental problems, the government should make coffee less accessible to the general public.

(D) Studies show that people who do not exercise regularly have a shorter life expectancy than those who exercise regularly. To help increase their patients' life expectancy, doctors should recommend regular exercise to their patients.

(E) Most people who exercise regularly are able to handle stress. This shows that

12

exercising regularly decreases one's chances of being overwhelmed by stress. So people who want to be able to handle stress should regularly engage in exercise.

(E) is the correct answer.

We're asked to match the flaw of this question, so let's find it! The conclusion is that people who want to reduce their risk of serious heart disease shouldn't eat meat. Why? Because avoiding meat increases one's chances of avoiding that serious heart disease. That seems like a reasonable argument. However, that premise is actually an intermediate conclusion based on the premise that 75 percent of vegetarians reached 50 without developing heart disease. Since the problem uses numbers to draw a conclusion, we can expect the gap to involve the numbers.

In this case, the health of the vegetarians doesn't tell us much without a control group. There are a couple of problems with using this data to draw that conclusion, but the most glaring is that we don't know if the vegetarians are healthier than meat eaters. Perhaps far more meat eaters reached 50 without heart disease. To summarize, we're looking for an argument that uses a statistic about one group to draw an intermediate conclusion that involves a comparison between groups. It then should go on to use the intermediate conclusion to proscribe something.

(E) has the same flaw and structure. The conclusion suggests exercise to help people handle stress. And, like the original, this is based on an invalidly-drawn intermediate conclusion; we don't know how well people who don't exercise are able to handle stress.

Let's look at the wrong answers:

(A) is missing an intermediate conclusion. Also, the conclusion introduces a new element, police officers, an addition that doesn't match the original.

(B) The premise compares two groups, and so the intermediate conclusion can be drawn.

(C) starts out promisingly: the premise is about only one group. However, the intermediate conclusion is much weaker than the original. "Correlation" is a far cry from causation. Similar to (A), there is also the suspicious introduction in the last sentence of "the government," a new element.

(D) is similar to (B) in that it avoids the flaw we're trying to match. Similar to (A) and (C), the conclusion adds a new element at the end, doctors.

_11. PT23, S3, Q18_

If the recording now playing on the jazz program is really "Louis Armstrong recorded in concert in 1989," as the announcer said, then Louis Armstrong was playing some of the best jazz of his career years after his death. Since the trumpeter was definitely Louis Armstrong, somehow the announcer must have gotten the date of the recording wrong.

The pattern of reasoning in the argument above is most similar to that in which one of the following arguments?

(A) The museum is reported as having acquired a painting "by Malvina Hoffman, an artist who died in 1966." But Hoffman was a sculptor, not a painter, so the report must be wrong about the acquisition being a painting.

(B) This painting titled La Toilette is Berthe Morisot's La Toilette only if a painting can be in two museums at the same time. Since nothing can be in two places at once, this painting must some how have been mistitled.

(C) Only if a twentieth-century Mexican artist painted in Japan during the seventeenth century can this work both be "by Frida Kahlo" as labeled and the seventeenth-century Japanese landscape it appears to be. Since it is what it appears to be, the label is wrong.

(D) Unless Käthe Kollwitz was both a sculptor and a printmaker, the volunteer museum guide is wrong in his attribution of this sculpture. Since what Kollwitz is known for is her prints, the guide must be wrong.

12

(E) If this painting is a portrait done in acrylic, it cannot be by Élisabeth Vigée-Lebrun, since acrylic paint was developed only after her death. Thus, since it is definitely a portrait, the paint must not be acrylic.

(C) is the correct answer.

In this argument, the author evaluates a claim: "Louis Armstrong recorded in concert in 1989." He supports one part of the claim (that Louis Armstrong *did* record the particular work) but provides evidence (when Louis Armstrong was alive) that definitively proves that another part of the claim ("in 1989") is incorrect.

We need an answer that matches this reasoning structure:

In (C), we have a painting that is supposed to be both from the seventeenth century and painted by Frida Kahlo. We're told that the painting is indeed from the seventeenth century, but we are provided evidence (Frida Kahlo is a twentieth century artist) that definitely proves that she couldn't have painted it.

Though not all parts of (C) match up perfectly with the original argument, when it comes to the key reasoning issues (evidence that proves a claim to be definitively incorrect), (C) matches up far better with the original argument than the remaining choices do.

(A) is tempting. It begins with a similar type of claim, involving someone who created a certain piece of artwork and involving timing. However, unlike the original argument, it fails to provide sufficient evidence to show that a part of the claim is incorrect. The museum simply stated that Malvina Hoffman was an artist who died in 1966. No part of that can be refuted with the evidence provided. Furthermore, the fact that she was a sculptor, and not a painter, does not mean the museum can't have work that she painted. Many museums have paintings and drawings and such created by people who were not considered painters.

(B) does not present a claim to be proven false. The painting simply has the title "La Toilette" and there is no disputing that title. The author goes on to discuss how the painting can't be a *particular* painting called "La Toilette," but this, if anything, only eliminates a possibility about what the painting *can be*—it does not refute any claim about what the painting actually is.

(D) is similar to (A). Even though Käthe Kollwitz is *known* for her prints, we have no definitive evidence that she doesn't sculpt, and so we can't say that the claim about the sculpture is wrong.

(E) does not involve the refutation of a claim. It presents clues that help shed light on characteristics that can or can't go together in a portrait (for example, a portrait cannot, at the same time, be created by Élisabeth Vigée-Lebrun and have acrylic), but it does not present this information in order to show that a claim is incorrect. The reasoning in answer (E) is also heavily flawed. We don't have nearly enough evidence to say that if something is a portrait, it can't be done in acrylic. Since the reasoning in the original argument was not flawed, this is a clear sign (E) can't be correct.

12. PT23, S3, Q23

Candidate: The government spends $500 million more each year promoting highway safety than it spends combating cigarette smoking. But each year many more people die from smoking-related diseases than die in highway accidents. So the government would save lives by shifting funds from highway safety programs to antismoking programs.

The flawed reasoning in which one of the following arguments most closely parallels the flawed reasoning in the candidate's argument?

(A) The government enforces the speed limit on freeways much more closely than on tollways. But many more people die each year in auto accidents on freeways than die in auto accidents on tollway. So the government would save lives by shifting funds from enforcement of speed limits on freeways to enforcement of speed limits on tollways.

(B) A certain professional musician spends several times as many hours practicing guitar as she spends practicing saxophone. But she is hired much more often to play saxophone than to play guitar, so she would increase her number of playing engagements by spending less time practicing guitar and more time practicing saxophone.

(C) Automobiles burn more gas per minute on highways than on residential streets. But they get fewer miles per gallon on residential streets. Therefore, gas would be saved by driving less on residential streets and more on highways.

(D) The local swim team spends many more hours practicing the backstroke than it spends practicing the breaststroke. But the team's lap times for the breaststroke are much better than its times for the backstroke, so the team would win more swim meets if it spent less time practicing the backstroke and more time practicing the breaststroke.

(E) Banks have a higher profit margin on loans that have a high interest rate than on loans that have a low interest rate. But borrowers are willing to borrow larger sums at low rates than at high rates. Therefore, banks would be more profitable if they gave more loans at low rates and fewer loans at high rates.

(B) is the correct answer.

Since we're matching a flawed argument, let's identify the flaws. Reading like a debater, one might counter with the following:

1. It's possible that shifting funds away from highway safety will lead to many more car accidents, endangering more lives instead of saving them, regardless of the increased focus on cigarette smoking. Perhaps the reason the number of highway accidents is so low is because of the well-funded highway safety program.

2. Will the increased investment in preventing smoking actually result in lives saved? Will the

government-sponsored anti-smoking campaigns be effective?

More formally, increasing an investment in X at Y's expense does not necessarily result in Y becoming more effective.

Looking at the structure, notice the similarity between the original and (B):

The original argument:

> Gov't invests more into HS than into CS.
> But, CS is more of a problem in terms of Death,
> So, Gov't would improve situation with Death if it shifts investment from HS to CS.

Answer choice (B):

> Musician invests more into G than into S.
> But, S is more crucial than G in terms of $.
> So, musician would improve situation with $ if she shifts investment from G to S.

This isn't a perfect match (for example, the original discusses investing in reducing a problem, while the answer discusses investing in what is more important), but it is the closest when compared to the other answer choices.

(A) does not match the original's structure. It begins by discussing the comparative investment in tollway and freeway safety in terms of how closely the speed limit is *enforced* in each place. However, (A)'s conclusion is about the amount of *money spent*. To match the original, it should draw a conclusion about shifting enforcement of speed limits. Furthermore, the argument actually reverses the argument's conclusion. If it were to match the original, the fact that more people die on the freeways should support the idea that there be more focus on *freeways*. Instead, the argument suggests increasing enforcement (or funds for enforcement) for *tollways*.

(C) can be eliminated because there is no discussion of the current level of comparative investment in two related options.

(D) is extremely tempting:

> Swim team invests more in Back than
> Breast.
> But, Breast is better in terms of time.
> So, team would win more meets
> if it shifts time from Back to Breast.

Notice that line three does not reference "time," and instead switches to "meets." The original continues to argue its point in terms of Death. Furthermore, in the original, the situation with the choice that's receiving less investment is supposed to be worse (more smoking deaths), but in (D), the situation with the under supported choice is already *better*.

(E) can be eliminated because it is missing a comparison of how much is invested in each of two choices. Profit margin is not a match with this.

13. PT24, S3, Q16

K, a research scientist, was accused of having falsified laboratory data. Although the original data in question have disappeared, data from K's more recent experiments have been examined and clearly none of them were falsified. Therefore, the accusation should be dismissed.

Which one of the following contains questionable reasoning that is most similar to that in the argument above?

(A) L, an accountant, was charged with having embezzled funds from a client. The charge should be ignored, however, because although the records that might reveal this embezzlement have been destroyed, records of L's current clients show clearly that there has never been any embezzlement from them.

(B) M, a factory supervisor, was accused of failing to enforce safety standards. This accusation should be discussed, because although the identity of the accuser was not revealed, a survey of factory personnel revealed that some violations of the standards have occurred.

(C) N, a social scientist, was charged with plagiarism. The charge is without founda-

tion because although strong similarities between N's book and the work of another scholar have been discovered, the other scholar's work was written after N's work was published.

(D) O, an auto mechanic, has been accused of selling stolen auto parts. The accusation seems to be justified since although no evidence links O directly to these sales, the pattern of distribution of the auto parts points to O as the source.

(E) P, a politician, has been accused of failing to protect the public interest. From at least some points of view, however, the accusation will undoubtedly be considered false, because there is clearly disagreement about where the public interest lies.

(A) is the correct answer.

The flaw here is apparent if you are reading like a debater. The fact that recent evidence does not show any mischief doesn't mean that the accusation of falsification based on now-missing data should be dismissed. K may have falsified the data that has disappeared!

(A) has the same flaw. Just because the current records don't show any embezzlement does not mean that the charge of embezzlement should be ignored. Just like with the original, the missing records might indicate embezzlement.

The wrong answers can all be quickly eliminated because of specific phrases:

(B) is clearly a mismatch since it states the accusation "should be discussed." The original is about *dismissing* accusations.

(C) has no loss of evidence. Also, the discussion of work being done *after* something else does not correspond to anything in the original argument.

(D) should be quickly eliminated upon seeing "justified." The argument is supposed to conclude by suggesting that the charges be dismissed.

(E) can be eliminated because it discusses "some points of view." There's no match for that in the original.

14. PT24, S3, Q21

The amount of electricity consumed in Millville on any day in August is directly proportional to peak humidity on that day. Since the average peak humidity this August was three points higher than the average peak humidity last August, it follows that more energy was consumed in Millville this August than last August.

Which one of the following arguments has a pattern of reasoning most similar to the one in the argument above?

(A) The amount of art supplies used in any of the Aesthetic Institute's 25 classes is directly proportional to the number of students in that class. Since in these classes the institute enrolled 20 percent more students overall last year than in the previous year, more art supplies were used in the institute's classes last year than in the previous year.

(B) The number of courses in painting offered by the Aesthetic Institute in any term is directly proportional to the number of students enrolled in the institute in that term. But the institute offers the same number of courses in sculpture each term. Hence, the institute usually offers more courses in painting than in sculpture.

(C) The number of new students enrolled at the Aesthetic Institute in any given year is directly proportional to the amount of advertising the institute has done in the previous year. Hence, if the institute seeks to increase its student body it must increase the amount it spends on advertising.

(D) The fees paid by a student at the Aesthetic Institute are directly proportional to the number of classes in which that student enrolls. Since the number of students at the Aesthetic Institute is increasing, it follows that the institute is collecting a greater amount of fees paid by students than it used to.

(E) The number of instructors employed by the Aesthetic Institute in any term is directly proportional to the number of classes offered in that term and also directly proportional to the number of students enrolled at the institute. Thus, the number of classes offered by the institute in any term is directly proportional to the number of students enrolled in that term.

(A) is the correct answer.

The argument we're to match is pretty straightforward:

> P: E is directly proportional to H.
> P: H was higher in August this year than in previous year.
> C: E was higher this year.

(A) has the same structure:

> P: Art supplies is directly proportional to # of students.
> P: # of students 20% higher last year than previous year.
> C: More art supplies were used last year.

(B) can be eliminated because of the mismatched modifier "usually." Furthermore, (B) is missing a premise about one time period having more of something; instead it states that the number of courses remained constant.

(C) is easily eliminated because it ends with a suggestion. If an original argument doesn't include a suggestion, the match can't either. (C) is also missing a match with the second premise, similar to (B).

(D) first discusses the number of *classes* an individual student enrolls in, and then switches to discussing the number of *students*. This shift is not found in the original.

(E) is a clear mismatch because it includes a second factor that affects the proportional relationship (it's both the number of classes and the number of students). Furthermore, the argument's conclusion is a relationship ("Thus, the number of classes…is proportional…"), instead of a simple statement about number ("…more energy was consumed…").

12

15. PT25, S2, Q22

It is an absurd idea that whatever artistic endeavor the government refuses to support it does not allow, as one can see by rephrasing the statement to read: No one is allowed to create art without a government subsidy.

The pattern of reasoning in which one of the following is most similar to that in the argument above?

(A) The claim that any driver who is not arrested does not break the law is absurd, as one can see by rewording it: Every driver who breaks the law gets arrested.

(B) The claim that any driver who is not arrested does not break the law is absurd, as one can see by rewording it: Every driver who gets arrested has broken the law.

(C) The notion that every scientist who is supported by a government grant will be successful is absurd, as one can see by rewording it: No scientist who is successful is so without a government grant.

(D) The notion that every scientist who is supported by a government grant will be successful is absurd, as one can see by rewording it: No scientist lacking governmental support will be successful.

(E) The notion that every scientist who has been supported by a government grant will be successful is absurd, as one can see by rewording it: No scientist is allowed to do research without a government grant.

(A) is the correct answer.

Bring out the formal logic notation!

It is an absurd idea that whatever artistic endeavor the government refuses to support it does not allow,

Absurd: –gov. support → –gov. allow

as one can see by rephrasing the statement to read: No one is allowed to create art without a government subsidy.

gov. allow → gov. support

For either sentence you may have first derived the contrapositive of what is written above. That's fine, as long as the argument's structure became apparent to you:

It's absurd to say –X → –Y, and this is clear if you reword that as Y → X.

This matches (A).

It's absurd to say –arrested → –break law, and this is clear from break law → arrested.

Most of the incorrect answers are quite tempting until you uncover each one's logic:

(B) has an illegal negation: It's absurd to say that –arrested → –break law, and this is clear from arrested → break law.

(C) has an illegal reversal: It's absurd to say that supp. → succ., and this is clear from succ. → supp.

(D) has an illegal negation: It's absurd to say that supp. → succ., and this is clear from –supp. → –succ.

(E) shifts terms. The first statement is about support and success, while the second is about support and being allowed to do research.

Chapter 13 *of*

Logical Reasoning

Explain a Result
Questions

13

Getting Familiar

Give yourself about four and a half minutes to answer the following three questions. Later in the chapter, we'll use these questions to illustrate the important concepts related to Explain a Result questions.

_PT37, S4, Q5_

After 1950, in response to record growth in worldwide food demand, farmers worldwide sharply increased fertilizer use. As a result, the productivity of farmland more than doubled by 1985. Since 1985, farmers have sought to increase farmland productivity even further. Nevertheless, worldwide fertilizer use has declined by 6 percent between 1985 and the present.

Which one of the following, if true, most helps to resolve the apparent discrepancy in the information above?

(A) Since 1985 the rate at which the world's population has increased has exceeded the rate at which new arable land has been created through irrigation and other methods.

(B) Several varieties of crop plants that have become popular recently, such as soybeans, are as responsive to fertilizer as are traditional grain crops.

(C) Between 1950 and 1985 farmers were able to increase the yield of many varieties of crop plants.

(D) After fertilizer has been added to soil for several years, adding fertilizer to the soil in subsequent years does not significantly improve crop production.

(E) Between 1975 and 1980 fertilizer prices temporarily increased because of labor disputes in several fertilizer-exporting nations, and these disputes disrupted worldwide fertilizer production.

_PT29, S1, Q4_

Cats spend much of their time sleeping; they seem to awaken only to stretch and yawn. Yet they have a strong, agile musculature that most animals would have to exercise strenuously to acquire.

Which one of the following, if true, most helps to resolve the apparent paradox described above?

(A) Cats have a greater physiological need for sleep than other animals.

(B) Many other animals also spend much of their time sleeping yet have a strong, agile musculature.

(C) Cats are able to sleep in apparently uncomfortable positions.

(D) Cats derive ample exercise from frequent stretching.

(E) Cats require strength and agility in order to be effective predators.

PT29, S1, Q25

The indigenous people of Tasmania are clearly related to the indigenous people of Australia, but were separated from them when the land bridge between Australia and Tasmania disappeared approximately 10,000 years ago. Two thousand years after the disappearance of the land bridge, however, there were major differences between the culture and technology of the indigenous Tasmanians and those of the indigenous Australians. The indigenous Tasmanians, unlike their Australian relatives, had no domesticated dogs, fishing nets, polished stone tools, or hunting implements like the boomerang and the spear-thrower.

Each of the following, if true, would contribute to an explanation of differences described above EXCEPT:

(A) After the disappearance of the land bridge the indigenous Tasmanians simply abandoned certain practices and technologies that they had originally shared with their Australian relatives.

(B) Devices such as the spear-thrower and the boomerang were developed by the indigenous Tasmanians more than 10,000 years ago.

(C) Technological innovations such as fishing nets, polished stone tools, and so on, were imported to Australia by Polynesian explorers more recently than 10,000 years ago.

(D) Indigenous people of Australia developed hunting implements like the boomerang and the spear-thrower after the disappearance of the land bridge.

(E) Although the technological and cultural innovations were developed in Australia more than 10,000 years ago, they were developed by groups in northern Australia with whom the indigenous Tasmanians had no contact prior to the disappearance of the land bridge.

13

Explain a Result Questions on the LSAT

Questions that ask you to explain a result make up about 6 percent of all Logical Reasoning questions on the LSAT. While these questions tend to fall on the lower end of the difficulty spectrum, certain ones can be tricky.

Recognizing Explain a Result Questions

An Explain a Result question typically presents a scenario that ends in some unexpected result. Here's a very basic example:

> *The Crab Leg,* a local seafood restaurant on Main Street, expected to see a decrease in sales after a popular seafood restaurant chain opened a new restaurant just two blocks away. However, *The Crab Leg* has actually experienced a 50 percent increase in business since the opening of the new restaurant.

You will be asked to choose an explanation for this unexpected result. The LSAT phrases these questions in a few different ways. Here are the most common phrasings:

"Which one of the following, if true, most effectively resolves the paradox presented above?"

"Which one of the following, if true, most helps to reconcile the apparent discrepancy presented above?"

"Which one of the following, if true, most helps to explain the apparent paradox presented above?"

As you work to recognize these questions, also note that the "argument" is not really an argument at all. There is no conclusion or opinion stated. For Explain a Result questions, the text will be a list of objective facts. It's your job to choose an answer that reconciles these facts.

Let's discuss this task in more detail.

How to Explain a Result

Expected vs. Unexpected

The first step in explaining a result is to identify, and make explicit in your mind, the "paradox" or "discrepancy" presented in the text. Thus, you will start by identifying (1) that which might be EXPECTED given the scenario at hand, and (2) that which is presented as the UNEXPECTED result. Let's look back at the seafood restaurant example:

> *The Crab Leg,* a local seafood restaurant on Main Street, expected to see a decrease in sales after a popular seafood restaurant chain opened a new restaurant just two blocks away. However, *The Crab Leg* has actually experienced a 50 percent increase in business since the opening of the new restaurant.

13

WHAT WOULD BE EXPECTED: *The Crab Leg* loses business after the other restaurant opens.

THE UNEXPECTED RESULT: *The Crab Leg* actually increases its business by 50 percent after the other restaurant opens.

In this case, the expected and the unexpected results are fairly easy to identify. Keep in mind that this won't always be the case. Sometimes you'll have to think a bit harder to separate the two. Regardless, it's always the place to start, since your job will be to explain the UNEXPECTED result.

Should You Anticipate the Explanation?

Sometimes you'll be able to see the explanation coming. In this case, for example, we can perhaps already imagine at least one scenario that would help explain why *The Crab Leg* has experienced growth: maybe the new restaurant is so popular that it continuously has an overflow crowd that dines at *The Crab Leg* when tables aren't available at the new restaurant.

Who knows? Maybe this explanation will show up among the answer choices, maybe not. It's certainly okay to anticipate the answer, but remember that you need to be flexible. Often, the correct answer will be an explanation that you haven't thought of.

The Three Answer Buckets

It's helpful to think about the answers to these questions as falling into one of three buckets:

BUCKET #1	BUCKET #2	BUCKET #3
further evidence for the EXPECTED result	explains the UNEXPECTED result	irrelevant to the discrepancy presented

Of course, you want to choose the one answer that falls into Bucket #2: Explains the UNEXPECTED Result. The LSAT will try to tempt you with answers that provide further evidence for the EXPECTED result (Bucket #1) and with answers that seem related to the subject matter but are actually irrelevant in terms of explaining the paradox or discrepancy. Knowing this ahead of time will help you to avoid the traps. Let's examine some answer choices for the seafood example.

BUCKET #1	BUCKET #2	BUCKET #3
further evidence for the EXPECTED result	explains the UNEXPECTED result	irrelevant to the discrepancy presented
WRONG!	**RIGHT!**	**WRONG!**

The Crab Leg, a local seafood restaurant on Main Street, expected to see a decrease in sales after a popular seafood restaurant chain opened a new restaurant just two blocks away. However, *The Crab Leg* has actually experienced a 50 percent increase in business since the opening of the new restaurant.

Which one of the following, if true, most helps to explain the result above?

(A) Some of *The Crab Leg's* previous patrons have begun dining regularly at the new restaurant.

(B) In anticipation of the opening of the new restaurant, the owner of *The Crab Leg* significantly increased spending on advertising and marketing.

(C) The food at the new restaurant is better and cheaper than the food at *The Crab Leg.*

(D) Some of the servers hired to work at the new restaurant had previously worked at *The Crab Leg.*

(E) Other than *The Crab Leg* and the new restaurant, there are no other seafood restaurants in town.

EXPECTED: *The Crab Leg* experiences a decrease in sales after the new restaurant opens.

UNEXPECTED: *The Crab Leg* actually increases business by 50 percent.

Our job is to choose an answer that explains this UNEXPECTED result.

(A) BUCKET #1: This provides further support for the expected result—decreased sales.

(B) BUCKET #2: Correct answer! This provides an explanation for the unexpected result. If the owners spend more on advertising and marketing, they're likely to increase business.

(C) BUCKET #1: This would seem to pull people away from *The Crab Leg.* This provides further support for the expected result—decreased sales.

(D) BUCKET #3: This neither supports the expected result nor explains the unexpected result. It's irrelevant!

(E) BUCKET #3: Again, irrelevant!

Let's revisit two of the questions from the start of the chapter. We'll again consider the answer choices through the three-bucket lens:

13

BUCKET #1	BUCKET #2	BUCKET #3
further evidence for the **EXPECTED** result **WRONG!**	explains the **UNEXPECTED** result **RIGHT!**	irrelevant to the discrepancy presented **WRONG!**

PT37, S4, Q5

After 1950, in response to record growth in worldwide food demand, farmers worldwide sharply increased fertilizer use. As a result, the productivity of farmland more than doubled by 1985. Since 1985, farmers have sought to increase farmland productivity even further. Nevertheless, worldwide fertilizer use has declined by 6 percent between 1985 and the present.

Which one of the following, if true, most helps to resolve the apparent discrepancy in the information above?

(A) Since 1985 the rate at which the world's population has increased has exceeded the rate at which new arable land has been created through irrigation and other methods.

(B) Several varieties of crop plants that have become popular recently, such as soybeans, are as responsive to fertilizer as are traditional grain crops.

(C) Between 1950 and 1985 farmers were able to increase the yield of many varieties of crop plants.

(D) After fertilizer has been added to soil for several years, adding fertilizer to the soil in subsequent years does not significantly improve crop production.

(E) Between 1975 and 1980 fertilizer prices temporarily increased because of labor disputes in several fertilizer-exporting nations, and these disputes disrupted worldwide fertilizer production.

EXPECTED: To further increase productivity, farmers would use even more fertilizer.

UNEXPECTED: Fertilizer use has declined by 6 percent since 1985.

Our job is to choose an answer that explains this UNEXPECTED result.

(A) BUCKET #1: This gives us even more reason to expect that farmers would want to use more fertilizer (as they did last time in response to similar demand). Don't be fooled!

(B) BUCKET #1: This would seem to support the expected result. If soybeans respond to fertilizer, use more fertilizer!

(C) BUCKET #1: Perhaps they increased the yield through the use of fertilizer; it'd be natural to expect them to use more of it now.

(D) BUCKET #2: Aha! This explains why they would STOP using as much fertilizer. This is the correct answer.

(E) BUCKET #3: A temporary increase in prices between 1975 and 1980 is irrelevant to fertilizer use after 1985. Don't be tempted by this!

13

BUCKET #1	BUCKET #2	BUCKET #3
further evidence for the EXPECTED result **WRONG!**	explains the UNEXPECTED result **RIGHT!**	irrelevant to the discrepancy presented **WRONG!**

PT29, S1, Q4

Cats spend much of their time sleeping; they seem to awaken only to stretch and yawn. Yet they have a strong, agile musculature that most animals would have to exercise strenuously to acquire.

Which one of the following, if true, most helps to resolve the apparent paradox described above?

(A) Cats have a greater physiological need for sleep than other animals.

(B) Many other animals also spend much of their time sleeping yet have a strong, agile musculature.

(C) Cats are able to sleep in apparently uncomfortable positions.

(D) Cats derive ample exercise from frequent stretching.

(E) Cats require strength and agility in order to be effective predators.

EXPECTED: Cats should be out of shape.

UNEXPECTED: Cats have strong, agile musculature.

Our job is to choose an answer that explains this UNEXPECTED result.

(A) BUCKET #1: This gives an explanation for why cats are more inactive and provides further support for the expected result.

(B) BUCKET #3: This answer is tempting, but it doesn't explain why this discrepancy exists specifically for cats.

(C) BUCKET #3: What does this have to do with the argument?

(D) BUCKET #2: This explains it! Now we understand how cats can sleep so much yet stay so muscular. This is the correct answer.

(E) BUCKET #3: Tempting, but irrelevant. This may explain why they need the muscles, but not how they become muscular.

EXCEPT Questions

EXCEPT questions are a common subcategory of Explain a Result questions. While the orientation is slightly different, the process should be the same. Let's look at the EXCEPT question you tried at the start of the chapter. In this case, four of the five answer choices will be explanations for the UNEXPECTED result (Bucket #2), and one will not. We're looking for this outlier.

PT29, S1, Q25

The indigenous people of Tasmania are clearly related to the indigenous people of Australia, but were separated from them when the land bridge between Australia and Tasmania disappeared approximately 10,000 years ago. Two thousand years after the disappearance of the land bridge, however, there were major differences between the culture and technology of the indigenous Tasmanians and those of the indigenous Australians. The indigenous Tasmanians, unlike their Australian relatives, had no domesticated dogs, fishing nets, polished stone tools, or hunting implements like the boomerang and the spear-thrower.

Each of the following, if true, would contribute to an explanation of differences described above EXCEPT:

(A) After the disappearance of the land bridge the indigenous Tasmanians simply abandoned certain practices and technologies that they had originally shared with their Australian relatives.

(B) Devices such as the spear-thrower and the boomerang were developed by the indigenous Tasmanians more than 10,000 years ago.

(C) Technological innovations such as fishing nets, polished stone tools, and so on, were imported to Australia by Polynesian explorers more recently than 10,000 years ago.

(D) Indigenous people of Australia developed hunting implements like the boomerang and the spear-thrower after the disappearance of the land bridge.

(E) Although the technological and cultural innovations were developed in Australia more than 10,000 years ago, they were developed by groups in northern Australia with whom the indigenous Tasmanians had no contact prior to the disappearance of the land bridge.

EXPECTED: Indigenous Australians and Tasmanians ought to be similar 2000 years after the land bridge disappeared.

UNEXPECTED: Tasmanians lacked many of the advances that Australians had.

Our job is to choose an answer that *fails* to explain this UNEXPECTED result.

(A) BUCKET #2: This is a reasonable explanation for the unexpected result, so it's NOT the answer.

(B) BUCKET #3: Hmmm. This answer seems to open up more questions. If these things were developed by the Tasmanians, why did they stop using them? This answer doesn't help explain our discrepancy, and it is therefore correct.

(C) BUCKET #2: This provides a potential explanation for the unexpected result.

(D) BUCKET #2: This also provides a potential explanation for the unexpected result.

(E) BUCKET #2: Again, another reason why the Tasmanians didn't have particular advancements that Australians had.

13

Conclusion

Before you try some of these questions on your own, reconsider the following:

1. Expected result vs. unexpected result. The discrepancy, or paradox, presented in these questions lies in the space between what we might EXPECT from a given scenario and what is actually presented as the UNEXPECTED result. To effectively consider an explanation for the discrepancy, you must start by explicitly identifying and separating what is the EXPECTED vs. the UNEXPECTED result.

2. Three answer buckets. The LSAT will try to get you to confuse the world of expected things with the world of unexpected things. Wrong answers will often provide further evidence for the EXPECTED outcome. Don't be tempted by these. Additionally, some wrong answers will be irrelevant with regard to explaining the discrepancy.

BUCKET #1	BUCKET #2	BUCKET #3
further evidence for the EXPECTED result **WRONG!**	explains the UNEXPECTED result **RIGHT!**	irrelevant to the discrepancy presented **WRONG!**

3. EXCEPT questions. Slightly different orientation, same approach! Four of the answers will be Bucket #2 answers; they'll effectively provide an explanation for the UNEXPECTED result. Your job is to find the one answer that falls outside of Bucket #2.

DRILL IT: Explain a Result Questions

Give yourself no more than six minutes to complete the following problems.

1. PT30, S4, Q5

In a poll of eligible voters conducted on the eve of a mayoral election, more of those polled stated that they favored Panitch than stated that they favored any other candidate. Despite this result, another candidate, Yeung, defeated Panitch by a comfortable margin.

Each of the following, if true, contributes to a resolution of the discrepancy described above EXCEPT:

(A) Of Yeung's supporters, a smaller percentage were eligible to vote than the percentage of Panitch's supporters who were eligible to vote.

(B) A third candidate, Mulhern, conducted a press conference on the morning of the election and withdrew from the race.

(C) The poll's questions were designed by staff members of Panitch's campaign.

(D) Of the poll respondents supporting Yeung, 70 percent described the election as "important" or "very important," while 30 percent of respondents supporting Panitch did the same.

(E) The poll, conducted on a Monday, surveyed persons in the downtown area, and the percentage of Yeung's supporters who work downtown is lower than that of Panitch's supporters.

2. PT31, S2, Q11

Several thousand years ago, people in what is now North America began to grow corn, which grows faster and produces more food per unit of land than do the grains these people had grown previously. Corn is less nutritious than those other grains, however, and soon after these people established corn as their staple grain crop, they began having nutrition-related health problems. Yet the people continued to grow corn as their staple grain, although they could have returned to growing the more nutritious grains.

Which one of the following, if true, most helps to explain why the people mentioned continued to grow corn as their staple grain crop?

(A) The variety of corn that the people relied on as their staple grain produced more food than did the ancestors of that variety.

(B) Modern varieties of corn are more nutritious than were the varieties grown by people in North America several thousand years ago.

(C) The people did not domesticate large animals for meat or milk, either of which could supply nutrients not provided by corn.

(D) Some grain crops that could have been planted instead of corn required less fertile soil in order to flourish than corn required.

(E) The people discovered some years after adopting corn as their staple grain that a diet that supplemented corn with certain readily available nongrain foods significantly improved their health.

13

3. PT31, S3, Q2

One way kidney stones can form is when urine produced in the kidneys is overly concentrated with calcium or oxalate. Reducing dietary calcium has been thought, therefore, to decrease the likelihood that calcium will concentrate and form additional stones. Oddly enough, for many people the chances of recurrence are decreased by increasing calcium intake.

Which one of the following, if true, most helps to resolve the apparent discrepancy described above?

   (A) Laboratory studies on animals with kidney stones reveal that they rarely get additional stones once calcium supplements are added to the diet.

   (B) Increasing dietary oxalate while reducing dietary calcium does not reduce the chances of kidney stone recurrence.

   (C) Kidney stone development is sometimes the result of an inherited disorder that can result in excessive production of calcium and oxalate.

   (D) Increasing calcium intake increases the amount of calcium eliminated through the intestines, which decreases the amount to be filtered by the kidneys.

   (E) Some kidney stones are composed of uric acid rather than a combination of calcium and oxalate.

Challenge Question

4. PT29, S4, Q19

In the decade from the mid-1980s to the mid-1990s, large corporations were rocked by mergers, reengineering, and downsizing. These events significantly undermined employees' job security. Surprisingly, however, employees' perception of their own job security hardly changed over that period. Fifty-eight percent of employees surveyed in 1984 and 55 percent surveyed in 1994 stated that their own jobs were very secure.

Each of the following contributes to an explanation of the surprising survey results described above EXCEPT:

   (A) A large number of the people in both surveys work in small companies that were not affected by mergers, reengineering, and downsizing.

   (B) Employees who feel secure in their jobs tend to think that the jobs of others are secure.

   (C) The corporate downsizing that took place during this period had been widely anticipated for several years before the mid-1980s.

   (D) Most of the major downsizing during this period was completed within a year after the first survey.

   (E) In the mid-1990s, people were generally more optimistic about their lives, even in the face of hardship, than they were a decade before.

SOLUTIONS: Explain a Result Questions

1. PT30, S4, Q5

In a poll of eligible voters conducted on the eve of a mayoral election, more of those polled stated that they favored Panitch than stated that they favored any other candidate. Despite this result, another candidate, Yeung, defeated Panitch by a comfortable margin.

Each of the following, if true, contributes to a resolution of the discrepancy described above EXCEPT:

(A) Of Yeung's supporters, a smaller percentage were eligible to vote than the percentage of Panitch's supporters who were eligible to vote.

(B) A third candidate, Mulhern, conducted a press conference on the morning of the election and withdrew from the race.

(C) The poll's questions were designed by staff members of Panitch's campaign.

(D) Of the poll respondents supporting Yeung, 70 percent described the election as "important" or "very important," while 30 percent of respondents supporting Panitch did the same.

(E) The poll, conducted on a Monday, surveyed persons in the downtown area, and the percentage of Yeung's supporters who work downtown is lower than that of Panitch's supporters.

(A) is correct.

WHAT WOULD BE EXPECTED:
Panitch wins the election. (Because the polls showed him in the lead.)

THE UNEXPECTED RESULT:
Yeung defeats Panitch by a comfortable margin.

Remember our buckets: (1) further evidence for the EXPECTED, (2) evidence for the UNEXPECTED, and (3) irrelevant. For this EXCEPT question, we'll have four answers that explain the unexpected result and one that either provides further evidence for the expected result or is irrelevant.

(B) explains the unexpected result. If a third candidate dropped out, and his supporters went to Yeung, those two blocs combined could have added up to more votes than Panitch's supporters.

(C) explains the unexpected result. Panitch's staff would have a clear motive for designing a skewed poll that would show Panitch in the lead, and this design could explain the poll results.

(D) explains the unexpected result. If a large percentage of Yeung's supporters consider the election "very important" or "important," then those people may have been more likely to cast votes. If only 30 percent of Panitch's supporters felt the same way about the election, only a small portion of the people who supported Panitch in the polls may have cast votes.

(E) explains the unexpected result. This choice provides another explanation for the poll's results—an unrepresentative sample of people were polled. The actual number of Yeung's supporters in the general population may have been higher, but these people could have been underrepresented if this choice were true.

If choice (A) had said "eligible to participate in the poll" rather than "eligible to vote," this answer would have been incorrect. As it stands, however, this answer choice provides further evidence for the *expected* result—that Panitch would win. If a smaller percentage of Yeung's supporters were able to cast a vote than the percentage of Panitch's supporters who were able to vote, then we would expect Yeung to have a smaller number of votes than Panitch.

2. PT31, S2, Q11

Several thousand years ago, people in what is now North America began to grow corn, which grows faster and produces more food per unit of land than do the grains these people had grown previously. Corn is less nutritious than those other grains, however, and soon after these people established corn as their staple grain crop, they began having nutrition-related health problems. Yet the people continued to grow corn as their staple grain, although they could have returned to growing the more nutritious grains.

Which one of the following, if true, most helps to explain why the people mentioned continued to grow corn as their staple grain crop?

(A) The variety of corn that the people relied on as their staple grain produced more food than did the ancestors of that variety.

(B) Modern varieties of corn are more nutritious than were the varieties grown by people in North America several thousand years ago.

(C) The people did not domesticate large animals for meat or milk, either of which could supply nutrients not provided by corn.

(D) Some grain crops that could have been planted instead of corn required less fertile soil in order to flourish than corn required.

(E) The people discovered some years after adopting corn as their staple grain that a diet that supplemented corn with certain readily available nongrain foods significantly improved their health.

(E) is correct.

The wording of this question explicitly gives us our paradox—why did people continue to grow corn as their staple crop even after they started having nutrition-related health problems?

Here are our buckets again: (1) further evidence for the EXPECTED, (2) evidence for the UNEXPECTED, and (3) irrelevant.

(A) is tempting because a higher yield might seem to be a good thing, but look closely—this answer is irrelevant to the unexpected result. The ability to produce more corn relative to ancestral times does not give us any reason why these people would continue to grow corn, since the nutritional problems occurred "soon after these people established corn as their staple grain crop." A comparison to ancestral times is out of scope. This

answer also does not address the main reason for the paradox—the weaker nutrition of corn relative to other grains.

(B) is irrelevant to the unexpected result. The nutrition of "modern" corn would not have affected the decisions of people thousands of years ago.

(C) provides further evidence for the expected result by removing an alternate source of nutrients not provided by corn.

(D) provides further evidence for the expected result. If corn required more fertile soil than some of the other grain crops, then we would expect that growing these other crops would be easier.

(E) explains the unexpected result. The major problem with corn was that it led to nutrition-related health problems—if nongrain foods could be used to supplement nutrition and improve health, then there would be less of a need to switch from corn as the staple grain crop. This is our answer.

3. PT31, S3, Q2

One way kidney stones can form is when urine produced in the kidneys is overly concentrated with calcium or oxalate. Reducing dietary calcium has been thought, therefore, to decrease the likelihood that calcium will concentrate and form additional stones. Oddly enough, for many people the chances of recurrence are decreased by increasing calcium intake.

Which one of the following, if true, most helps to resolve the apparent discrepancy described above?

(A) Laboratory studies on animals with kidney stones reveal that they rarely get additional stones once calcium supplements are added to the diet.

(B) Increasing dietary oxalate while reducing dietary calcium does not reduce the chances of kidney stone recurrence.

(C) Kidney stone development is sometimes the result of an inherited disorder that can result in excessive production of calcium and oxalate.

(D) Increasing calcium intake increases the amount of calcium eliminated through the intestines, which decreases the amount to be filtered by the kidneys.

(E) Some kidney stones are composed of uric acid rather than a combination of calcium and oxalate.

(D) is correct.

WHAT WOULD BE EXPECTED:
Increasing calcium intake shouldn't decrease chance of stones recurring (because decreasing calcium intake is thought to decrease chances for stones, and stones can be formed from calcium).

THE UNEXPECTED RESULT:
For many people, increasing calcium intake decreases chance of recurring stones.

Let's think of our buckets: 1) further evidence for the EXPECTED, 2) evidence for the UNEXPECTED, and 3) irrelevant.

(A) seems like evidence for the unexpected result. It shows that what's true with humans seems to be similarly true in experiments with animals. Let's keep it for now.

(B) is related to the conclusion in a very confusing and ultimately unhelpful way. We'd need more information to see how this relates to the unexpected result.

(C) is irrelevant to the conclusion. It does not have any direct relation to the impact of calcium intake.

(D) is clearly evidence for the unexpected result. It explains why increased calcium intake can decrease the likelihood of recurring stones—because it decreases the amount of calcium the kidneys are required to filter.

(E) is irrelevant to the conclusion. The fact that some kidney stones are composed of something else does not impact our discussion.

Both (A) and (D) seem to be evidence for the

unexpected result. However, (D) is clearly reasoning why the unexpected may occur, whereas (A) is not. (A) does not help to resolve the discrepancy. If anything, it only helps to confirm that the discrepancy exists. Therefore, (D) is the correct answer.

Challenge Question

4. PT29, S4, Q19
In the decade from the mid-1980s to the mid-1990s, large corporations were rocked by mergers, reengineering, and downsizing. These events significantly undermined employees' job security. Surprisingly, however, employees' perception of their own job security hardly changed over that period. Fifty-eight percent of employees surveyed in 1984 and 55 percent surveyed in 1994 stated that their own jobs were very secure.

Each of the following contributes to an explanation of the surprising survey results described above EXCEPT:

(A) A large number of the people in both surveys work in small companies that were not affected by mergers, reengineering, and downsizing.

(B) Employees who feel secure in their jobs tend to think that the jobs of others are secure.

(C) The corporate downsizing that took place during this period had been widely anticipated for several years before the mid-1980s.

(D) Most of the major downsizing during this period was completed within a year after the first survey.

(E) In the mid-1990s, people were generally more optimistic about their lives, even in the face of hardship, than they were a decade before.

(B) is correct.

For Explain a Result questions, first identify the paradox by figuring out the expected and the unexpected results. Given the fact that employees' job security was significantly undermined from the mid-80s to mid-90s, we can say the following:

WHAT WOULD BE EXPECTED:
The survey would show that fewer employees thought their jobs were "very secure" in 1994 than in 1984.

THE UNEXPECTED RESULT:
Employees' perception hardly changed.

Remember our three buckets? Categorize each choice as 1) further evidence for the EXPECTED, 2) evidence for the UNEXPECTED, or 3) irrelevant.

In this case—an EXCEPT question, we'll have four answers that explain the unexpected result and one that either provides further evidence for the expected result or is irrelevant.

(A) explains the unexpected result. If the survey sample contained a disproportionate number of employees whose jobs were not "rocked by mergers, reengineering, and downsizing," these employees' perceptions may not have been affected and the survey results make sense.

(C) explains the unexpected result. If the downsizing were anticipated, then perceptions may have shifted before the survey period rather than during it.

(D) explains the unexpected result. If most of the major downsizing happened immediately after the first survey (at the beginning of the period we're concerned with), then perceptions of job security may have fallen quickly, then had years to recover in time for the next survey in 1994.

(E) explains the unexpected result. If people were generally more optimistic in 1994 than in 1984, then even though their job security may have changed, their perception of that security may have been buoyed by this new optimism.

Choice (B) contains a small but critical shift in language—"the jobs of others." The passage only discusses employees' feelings about their own jobs, so this choice is irrelevant. This is our answer.

Chapter 14

of

Logical Reasoning

Conclusion

Conclusion

Congratulations on making it to the end of this book! We know it's been a challenge, but we expect that you'll be far better off for it on test day. In terms of your study timeline, we expect that most of you are about here:

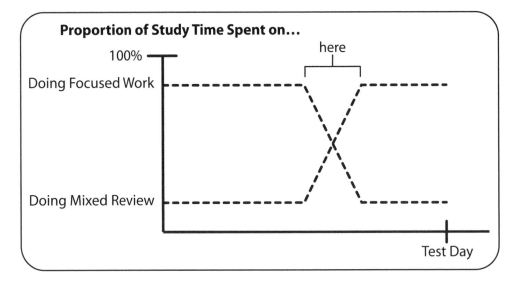

At this point, we have three primary suggestions:

1. Prioritize mixed review
2. Wrap up your focused work
3. Finalize your timing strategy

Let's discuss these three areas in depth.

Prioritize Mixed Review

As we've discussed elsewhere, preparing for the exam by doing only mixed review is not recommended. It is an inefficient way to improve your skills and get better at solving problems. However, it's also a mistake to focus only on content-specific work.

In large part, this is because your LSAT score is based not only on your understanding or your abilities, but also on your *performance*. That is, your score is based on how well you represent your understanding and your talents in a specific context and in one moment in time. As we know from real life, when confronted with pressure situations, two people with the same abilities can have drastically different experiences.

Often, the difference in the performances can be attributed to mind-set and preparation. Consider the mixed review in the final part of your training as preparation for performing at your best on test day.

14

The More Like Test Day, the Better

Thinking about your review in those terms, it makes sense that as you get closer and closer to the exam, you ought to try and make your practice as representative of the real thing as you can.

In general, we recommend that the majority of your mixed review come in the form of full practice exams. Again, the more realistic the better. If you have gotten accustomed to giving yourself "extra" breaks during your practice tests, or if you've allowed yourself to spread a single test out over multiple days, chances are that the real thing is going to feel much tougher, and much more exhausting, than you anticipate. Your final practice exams should take place in test-like conditions. There are many resources, such as the virtual proctor tool on our website and in-person proctored practice exams at our course locations, that are available to help you get practice that is as close to the real thing as possible.

You may also want to supplement your full exams with individual Logical Reasoning sections. This is especially true if you are finding that you perform worse on Logical Reasoning than you do on Logic Games or Reading Comprehension.

Finally, you may want to do some mixed review that specifically targets certain subgroups of question types. These subsets can group questions that have great commonality, such as those belonging to the Assumption Family, or those that are easily mistaken for one another, such as Identify the Conclusion and Inference. Doing mixed review of these subgroups can be very beneficial.

Use your Practice Tests to... Practice

We know that when you take your practice exams, especially right before the actual exam, what's probably going to be most important to you is the overall scaled score. That's natural, and pretty much everyone feels the same way. You want to know how you are doing!

However, keep in mind that the benefit of these exams is supposed to be that of *practicing*. Make sure to use these exams to practice your test-day strategy. Here are two specific areas where practice can have a significant impact on your performance:

1. Timing Strategy. In just a bit, we'll talk in detail about designing a personalized and optimal timing strategy. One of the most important things for you to do is to practice implementing this strategy so that you are *completely* comfortable with it before the exam. That means two things specifically: you are confident that you can and will stay balanced and finish on schedule, and you also know how to adjust as need be in case things happen to go awry.

2. Your Ability to Smoothly Shift Gears. If you've been following our recommendations up to this point, most of your work has been focused on one question type at a time. We feel this is the best way initially to improve your understanding and skill level. However, on the exam, you will have to be comfortable switching from one problem type to another, over and over again. This is a significant challenge, but one that you ought to prepare for.

The most essential key to success is that you have a clear plan for how to attack each type of problem. Here is a quick list of the major question types that you have just studied in depth:

14

Assumptions	Analyze Argument Structure
Identify a Flaw	Identify the Conclusion
Strengthen the Argument	Inference
Weaken the Argument	Match the Reasoning
Principle (support)	Match the Flaw
Principle (example)	Explain a Result

Take a moment to reflect on each question type on the list. Does a clear process quickly come to mind? Do you have a clear sense of the most important issues to consider? If not, and if you don't, you will definitely want to revisit those particular chapters to reinforce their primary takeaways.

The other key, which many test-takers fail to consider, is to be *active* about shifting gears from problem to problem. Force yourself to think about it! Use the question stem to categorize the problem, and use the category to remind yourself of your process. Use your practice exams to build this into your mental routine.

The reason we stress the above is that we know it's very easy, once you get into the rhythm of the exam, to lose sight of the unique task that each question presents. All these questions look alike! An obvious and dangerous consequence can be that you pick the right answer for the wrong question—for example, you pick a weaken answer for a strengthen question. A more subtle, but perhaps more pervasive, consequence of losing sight of your task is that it causes you to waste time. Without a clear sense of what you need to do, you will find yourself thinking about things that do not lead to the right answer. Actively concentrate on shifting gears during your practice exams so that it is second nature by test day.

Use Your Practice Exams to Evaluate and Fine-Tune

Again, we know that the BIG thing that you will be evaluating is your scaled score, but we want to make sure that you also use your exams to get a better sense of more specific strengths and weaknesses. Take notice of one or two question types, or subsets of question types, that seem to cause you the most trouble, and make sure to emphasize these in the focused work that you do. Also try to notice any general skills, such as being able to identify the correct conclusion to any argument, that might need fine-tuning before test day. Isolate these issues and do some focused work on them, then apply this work to your other practice exams.

When you're reviewing your practice test, it's dangerously easy to review only the questions you got wrong. But shouldn't you review the ones you guessed randomly on? And what about the questions where you picked correctly between two attractive choices but lacked confidence in your decision? These need to be reviewed as well. To make it easier to review these questions, develop a system for marking problems to return to. For example, circle the questions that you don't feel 100 percent about, and make it clear which answers were easy eliminations and which were part of your final, agonizing, they-both-look-great moments. Also—and this will take some willpower—we recommend that you try to review these questions and answer choices *before* you score your test, so that you can continue to struggle with them.

Wrap Up Your Focused Work

Though you will want to spend a majority of your remaining study hours on mixed review, it will also be extremely beneficial to do some more focused work. Here are two general suggestions:

Review Individual Question Types

For most of you, it's probably been at least a few weeks since you last spent a significant amount of time focused on, say, Identify a Flaw questions, and perhaps you don't feel as automatic in thinking about them as you did back then. If that's the case, it's okay! That mastery is still in you. It's just time to review.

One suggestion we have is to try to resist the temptation to try and review every single unusual and super difficult challenge that the LSAT might throw your way. The temptation is understandable. Let's call it "Noah's Arc Syndrome": just before the moment of truth, you try to get your hands, or minds, on everything you think could possibly be of use. This type of studying rarely has much positive benefit.

Instead, we encourage you to try to simplify your understanding. Consider carefully what it is that is most important to know about each problem type, and consider carefully what is most important to remember about the process you need to use to get to the right answer. For each question type, make sure you have a clear understanding of the key decisions that will need to be made, and that you have confidence in your ability to make them.

For question types in which you are strong, we imagine the above review can be fairly quick and automatic—it will just be reinforcement of what you already know, and what you already do in solving problems. You will want to spend more time on the areas where you felt weakest. Often, there is great value in revisiting and studying again a lesson that you originally found challenging. This can be especially true now that you have more experience with the questions as a whole.

Firm Up Sagging Skills

It's very common for students to end up being very strong in a variety of areas, but somehow markedly weaker in one particular and fundamental area, such as being able to separate supporting and opposing evidence in an argument. If you have a general area like that that you don't have confidence in, make sure to address it quickly. Don't let it prevent you from making the best of the rest of your abilities.

You probably already know if you have a weakness in one or two of these areas, and if you do, chances are it impacts your performance on a variety of questions. Make sure to do whatever you can to shore up these issues. Practice just identifying conclusions or cores, or review wrong answers to Inference questions to sharpen your sense of faulty reasoning. Utilize the study tools that are available on our website, and if it's a possibility for you and you think it will be of value to you, reach out for one-on-one help.

14

Your Optimal Timing Strategy

It's an unfortunate truth that the test is *designed* to not give you enough time. The vast majority of us would perform better if we had unlimited time, but the exam is meant to test our ability to evaluate arguments *efficiently*, and it wouldn't be able to test that if there wasn't time pressure.

What this means is that how you utilize your time is an important component of your overall score. We've actually been talking about this on a micro-level for the entire book—much of what we discuss in terms of *process* can be thought of in terms of *how you should use your time during a problem*. Now let's talk about it in greater detail.

Your timing strategy should be based on the optimal organization of two factors: 1) your goal score, and 2) the typical, natural construction of each Logical Reasoning section.

Assuming that your strengths and weaknesses are balanced across the three types of sections—Logical Reasoning, Logic Games, and Reading Comprehension, and we understand that this is a huge assumption—here are the approximate number of "misses" you can afford per section to get to your goal score:

If your goal score is...	You can afford to miss...
150	10 questions per section
155	8 questions per section
160	6 questions per section
165	4 questions per section
170	2 or 3 questions per section
175	1 question per section
177+	0 or 1 question per section

Again, these are just approximations, and the scoring scale for every exam will be slightly different. But at this point, it's helpful to think about the number of misses you can live with, and, ideally, you want to make sure that these misses coincide with questions you expect to find most difficult—you don't want to miss problems you can and should get right, and, in terms of your timing, you want to make sure that you don't waste time on the problems that are least likely to reward you with a point.

So think now, if you haven't already, about the types of questions that cause you the most difficulty. If you find Match the Reasoning problems to be the most difficult, and you know that you can afford a few misses in a section, then you should know, going into the exam, that that's a question type you won't spend extra time on. That doesn't mean you won't try your best to get the question correct—it simply means you will go in knowing that you will not spin your wheels on a Match the Reasoning question.

It's also helpful to be mindful of the natural progression of a typical section. The Logical Reasoning section has a tendency to go through certain "zones" of difficulty, and these tendencies are fairly consistent from exam to exam. Here is a rough diagram of these tendencies:

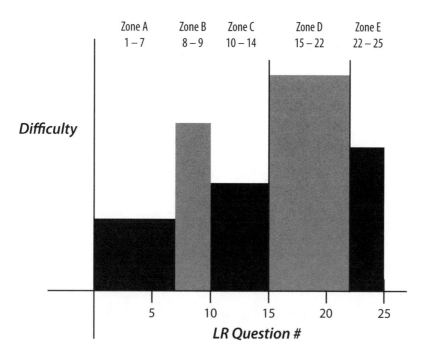

It's important to note, once again, that these are tendencies and not absolutes. Please do not contact us irate if you happen to run into a fourth problem in a section that happens to be particularly difficult—we know that can happen. However, these tendencies are consistent enough that it's helpful to know about them and use them in your planning.

Per the natural ebb and flow of the section, here are some very general timing recommendations that are meant to keep you balanced throughout:

After question...	You should be at about...
5	5 minutes
10	11 minutes
15	18 minutes
20	26 minutes

Again, keep in mind that the above recommendations are meant to be as general as possible, and that, ideally, we are hoping that you will adjust these recommendations to fit your toolset and goals.

If you feel that you miss a lot of questions because you rush, and if you know you can afford, say, five misses in a section, you may want to devote more time to the earlier problems, so that you can make sure you get them correct, knowing that you may have to cut bait on some more difficult problems that may show up later.

If you are aiming for a 180 sort of score, and are concerned about the idea of getting stuck and having to rush on one or two particularly challenging problems, we recommend that you build in an extra "bank" of time. Design your timing strategy so that it adds up to, say, 30 minutes, instead of 35. That way, you know that you have five extra minutes in the "bank" that you can feel free to spend whenever certain problems happen to come up and bite you in ways you didn't expect.

14

Another simple way to gauge timing for those who are seeking an extremely high-level score (and aren't prone to reading or reasoning errors) is to try and solve the first 15 questions in 15 minutes. That should leave plenty of time to carefully reason through the remaining problems.

Make sure to practice these strategies as you take your practice exams, so that you can adjust them as need be, and so that you can implement them automatically on test day. Get comfortable with the pace that is required to stay on schedule, and consider carefully what your plan will be if you get slightly behind on time. Ideally, once you've gotten into the exam, timing is something that you monitor, but not something that takes away from your focus and energy.

Final Thoughts and the NFL

Let's finish by talking about a real-life situation that requires quick and accurate decision making in a stressful situation.

Let's consider the position of NFL quarterback. The position of quarterback has evolved, in our modern age, to be something akin to that of rocket scientist. Every play has dozens upon dozens of variables that need to be considered, and decisions that need to be made in split seconds, with the added pressure of 300-pound super-athletes running towards you with the goal of hitting you as hard as possible. Are the best quarterbacks the ones who try to think about every possible variable all at once? No. We've seen those quarterbacks, and they are typically the ones who trip over their own feet. The best ones see and understand what is most important to consider in any situation, and they have a system for thinking about these things in an organized manner. They've prepared enough to be confident in making the right decisions.

It's easy to get overwhelmed by the intricacies of the exam, and it's easy to fall into trying to think about too much at once. Try to use all of your experience and understanding to focus on what each problem is really about, and what the ideal process is for arriving at the right answer. This simple and strong compass will be your most important tool for success on test day. With it, we are confident that you will represent your abilities at their best.

ALL TEST PREP IS NOT THE SAME

MANHATTAN
GMAT

MANHATTAN
GRE®

MANHATTAN
LSAT

Elite test preparation from 99th percentile instructors.
Find out how we're different.

www.manhattanprep.com